# *Discovering*
# *AutoCAD® 2014*

**Mark Dix**
*CAD Support Associates*

**Paul Riley**
*CAD Support Associates*

**PEARSON**

Boston   Columbus   Indianapolis   New York   San Francisco   Upper Saddle River
Amsterdam   Cape Town   Dubai   London   Madrid   Milan   Munich   Paris   Montreal   Toronto   Delhi
Mexico City   São Paulo   Sydney   Hong Kong   Seoul   Singapore   Taipei   Tokyo

**Executive Editor:** Lisa McClain
**Production Editor:** Katerina Malone
**Cover Designer:** Charlene Will
**Cover Art:** GettyOne/xiaoke ma
**Full-Service Project Management:**
  Mohinder Singh/Aptara®, Inc.

**Composition:** Aptara®, Inc.
**Printer/Binder:** Edwards Brothers Malloy
**Cover Printer:** Edwards Brothers Malloy
**Text Font:** Bookman

Certain images and materials contained in this publication were reproduced with the permission of Autodesk, Inc. © 2014. All rights reserved. Autodesk, AutoCAD, Revit, DWG, and the DWG logo are registered trademarks of Autodesk, Inc., in the U.S.A. and certain other countries.

---

**Disclaimer**

The publication is designed to provide tutorial information about AutoCAD® and/or other Autodesk computer programs. Every effort has been made to make this publication complete and as accurate as possible. The reader is expressly cautioned to use any and all precautions necessary, and to take appropriate steps to avoid hazards, when engaging in the activities described herein.

Neither the author nor the publisher makes any representations or warranties of any kind, with respect to the materials set forth in this publication, express or implied, including without limitation any warranties of fitness for a particular purpose or merchantability. Nor shall the author or the publisher be liable for any special, consequential or exemplary damages resulting, in whole or in part, directly or indirectly, from the reader's use of, or reliance upon, this material or subsequent revisions of this material.

Credits and acknowledgments borrowed from other sources and reproduced, with permission, in this textbook appear on appropriate page within text.

---

Many of the designations by manufacturers and sellers to distinguish their products are claimed as trademarks. Where those designations appear in this book, and the publisher was aware of a trademark claim, the designations have been printed in initial caps or all caps.

**Library of Congress Control Number: 2013946440**

10 9 8 7 6 5 4 3 2 1

ISBN 10:     0-13-337856-X
ISBN 13: 978-0-13-337856-6

# Preface

## Get Active with *Discovering AutoCAD® 2014*

Designed for introductory AutoCAD users, *Discovering AutoCAD® 2014* offers a hands-on, activity-based approach to the use of AutoCAD as a drafting tool—complete with techniques, tips, shortcuts, and insights designed to increase efficiency. Topics and tasks are carefully grouped to lead students logically through the AutoCAD command set, with the level of difficulty increasing steadily as skills are acquired through experience and practice. Straightforward explanations focus on what is relevant to actual drawing procedures, and illustrations show exactly what to expect on the computer screen when steps are correctly completed. This edition features Web-based exercises and projects included in each chapter. These optional exercises both assess and reinforce a student's understanding of the material.

## Features

The book uses a consistent format for each chapter that includes:

- Chapter Objectives and Introduction
- Exercises that introduce new commands and techniques
- Exercise instructions clearly set off from the text discussion
- Lots of illustrations with AutoCAD drawings and screen shots
- Twenty end-of-chapter Review Questions
- Four to eight realistic engineering drawing problems—fully dimensioned working drawings
- Optional Internet Projects at the end of each chapter
- Optional **Autodesk 360** explorations at the end of Chapters 3 through 6

High-quality working drawings include a wide range of applications that focus on mechanical drawings but also include architectural, civil, plumbing, general, and electrical drawings. Appendix A contains 21 drawing projects for additional review and practice.

## Acknowledgments

The authors thank the following reviewers for their feedback: John Irwin, Michigan Technological University; Tony Graham, North Carolina A&T State University; Beverly Jaeger, Northeastern University; Daniel McCall, Amarillo College; and Susan Freeman, Northeastern University.

## Features New to This Edition

1. Updated to reflect changes to the 2014 AutoCAD release
2. New command line features
3. New drawing file tabs
4. New **ARC** command procedures
5. **Autodesk 360** cloud-based collaboration techniques
6. **AutoCAD WS** online editing features

## Style Conventions in *Discovering AutoCAD® 2014*

| Text Element | Example |
|---|---|
| **Key Terms**—Boldface and italic on first mention (first letter lowercase, as it appears in the body of the text). Brief definition in margin alongside first mention. Full definition in Glossary at back of book. | Views are created by placing ***viewport*** objects in the paper space layout. |
| **AutoCAD commands**—Bold and uppercase. | Start the **LINE** command. |
| **Ribbon and panel names, palette names, toolbar names, menu items, and dialog box names**—Bold and follow capitalization convention in AutoCAD toolbar or pull-down menu (generally first letter cap). | The **Layer Properties Manager** palette<br>The **File** menu |
| **Panel tools, toolbar buttons, and dialog box controls/buttons/input items**—Bold and follow the name of the item or the name shown in the AutoCAD tooltip. | Choose the **Line** tool from the **Draw** panel.<br>Choose the **Symbols and Arrows** tab in the **Modify Dimension Style** dialog box.<br>Choose the **New Layer** button in the **Layer Properties Manager** palette.<br>In the **Lines and Arrows** tab, set the **Arrow size:** to **.125**. |
| **AutoCAD prompts**—Dynamic input prompts are set in a different font to distinguish them from the text. Command line prompts are set to look like the text in the command line, including capitalization, brackets, and punctuation. Text following the colon of the prompts specifies user input in bold. | AutoCAD prompts you to *Specify first point:*<br>Specify center point for circle or [3P 2P Ttr (tan tan radius)]: **3.5** |
| **Keyboard Input**—Bold with special keys in brackets. | Type **3.5 <Enter>**. |

# Download Instructor Resources from the Instructor Resource Center

To access supplementary materials online, instructors need to request an instructor access code. Go to **www.pearsonhighered.com/irc** to register for an instructor access code. Within 48 hours of registering, you will receive a confirming e-mail including an instructor access code. Once you have received your code, locate your text in the online catalog and click on the Instructor Resources button on the left side of the catalog product page. Select a supplement, and a login page will appear. Once you have logged in, you can access instructor material for all Prentice Hall textbooks. If you have any difficulties accessing the site or downloading a supplement, please contact Customer Service at **http://247pearsoned. custhelp.com/**.

# Contents

**Part One   Basic Two-Dimensional Entities**

**Chapter 1**   Lines and Essential Tools                                   1
Chapter Objectives                                                          1
Introduction                                                                1
Creating a New Drawing                                                      1
Exploring the Drawing Window                                               4
Interacting with the Drawing Window                                        6
Exploring Command Entry Methods                                            12
Drawing, Undoing, and Erasing Lines                                        17
Saving and Opening Your Drawings                                           28
Getting Started                                                            30
Chapter Summary                                                            34
Chapter Test Questions                                                     34
Chapter Drawing Projects                                                   38

**Chapter 2**   Circles and Drawing Aids                                   51
Chapter Objectives                                                         51
Introduction                                                               51
Changing the Grid Setting                                                  52
Changing the Snap Setting                                                  53
Changing Units                                                             55
Drawing Circles by Specifying a Center Point
    and a Radius                                                           58
Drawing Circles by Specifying a Center Point
    and a Diameter                                                         59
Accessing AutoCAD Online Help Features                                     62
Using the ERASE Command                                                    64
Using Single-Point Object Snap                                             70
Using the RECTANG Command                                                  72
Customizing Your Workspace                                                 73
Plotting or Printing a Drawing                                             75
Chapter Summary                                                            79
Chapter Test Questions                                                     79
Chapter Drawing Projects                                                   82

**Chapter 3**   Layers, Colors, and Linetypes                              95
Chapter Objectives                                                         95
Introduction                                                               95
Creating New Layers                                                        96

Assigning Colors to Layers                                                 98
Assigning Linetypes                                                        100
Assigning Lineweights                                                      101
Changing the Current Layer                                                 102
Changing Linetype Scale                                                    105
Editing Corners Using FILLET                                               106
Editing Corners Using CHAMFER                                              108
Zooming and Panning with the Scroll Wheel                                  110
Using the ZOOM Command                                                     110
Entering Single-Line Text                                                  113
Chapter Summary                                                            115
Chapter Test Questions                                                     115
Chapter Drawing Projects                                                   120

**Chapter 4**   Templates, Copies, and Arrays                              133
Chapter Objectives                                                         133
Introduction                                                               133
Setting Limits                                                             134
Creating a Template                                                        137
Saving a Template Drawing                                                  138
Using the MOVE Command                                                     141
Using the COPY Command                                                     144
Using the ARRAY Command—Rectangular Arrays                                 147
Creating Center Marks                                                      152
Creating Macros with the Action Recorder                                   154
Changing Plot Settings                                                     157
Chapter Summary                                                            161
Chapter Test Questions                                                     161
Chapter Drawing Projects                                                   168

**Chapter 5**   Arcs and Polar Arrays                                      183
Chapter Objectives                                                         183
Introduction                                                               183
Creating Polar Arrays                                                      183
Drawing Arcs                                                               187
Using the ROTATE Command                                                   191
Using Polar Tracking at Any Angle                                          194
Creating Mirror Images of Objects
    on the Screen                                                          196
Creating Page Setups                                                       198

Chapter Summary 202
Chapter Test Questions 202
Chapter Drawing Projects 208

**Chapter 6** Object Snap 221

**Chapter Objectives** 221

**Introduction** 221

**Selecting Points with Object Snap (Single-Point Override)** 222

**Selecting Points with Running Object Snap** 223

**Object Snap Tracking** 227

**Using the OFFSET Command (Creating Parallel Objects with OFFSET)** 230

**Shortening Objects with the TRIM Command** 231

**Extending Objects with the EXTEND Command** 233

**Using STRETCH to Alter Objects Connected to Other Objects** 235

**Creating Plot Layouts** 238

Chapter Summary 249
Chapter Test Questions 249
Chapter Drawing Projects 254

**Part Two** Text, Dimensions, and Other Complex Entities

**Chapter 7** Text 269

**Chapter Objectives** 269

**Introduction** 269

**Entering Single-Line Text with Justification Options** 269

**Entering Text on an Angle and Text Using Character Codes** 274

**Entering Multiline Text Using MTEXT** 275

**Editing Text in Place with DDEDIT and MTEDIT** 278

**Modifying Text with the Quick Properties Panel** 279

**Using the SPELL Command** 282

**Changing Fonts and Styles** 283

**Changing Properties with MATCHPROP** 287

**Scaling Previously Drawn Entities** 289

**Creating Tables and Fields** 291

**Using AutoCAD Templates, Borders, and Title Blocks** 297

Chapter Summary 300
Chapter Test Questions 300
Chapter Drawing Projects 302

**Chapter 8** Dimensions 315

**Chapter Objectives** 315

**Introduction** 315

**Creating and Saving a Dimension Style** 315

**Drawing Linear Dimensions** 320

**Drawing Multiple Linear Dimensions Using QDIM** 324

**Drawing Ordinate Dimensions** 327

**Drawing Angular Dimensions** 331

**Dimensioning Arcs and Circles** 334

**Dimensioning with Multileaders** 336

**Changing Dimension Text** 343

**Using Associative Dimensions** 344

**Using the HATCH Command** 347

**Scaling Dimensions Between Paper Space and Model Space** 352

Chapter Summary 361
Chapter Test Questions 361
Chapter Drawing Projects 364

**Chapter 9** Polylines 381

**Chapter Objectives** 381

**Introduction** 381

**Drawing Polygons** 382

**Drawing Donuts** 384

**Using the FILL Command** 385

**Drawing Straight Polyline Segments** 386

**Drawing Polyline Arc Segments** 389

**Editing Polylines with PEDIT** 390

**Drawing Splines** 393

**Creating Path Arrays** 394

**Drawing Revision Clouds** 396

**Drawing Points** 398

**Using Constraint Parameters** 399

**Using AutoConstrain and Inferred Constraints** 406

Chapter Summary 409
Chapter Test Questions 409
Chapter Drawing Projects 412

**Chapter 10** Blocks, Attributes, and External References 427

**Chapter Objectives** 427

**Introduction** 427

**Creating Groups** 428

**Creating Blocks** 430

Inserting Blocks into the Current Drawing 433

Creating Dynamic Blocks 436

Adding Constraints to Dynamic Blocks 443

Accessing Data in a Block Table 446

Using the Windows Clipboard 450

Inserting Blocks and External References
into Other Drawings 452

Using the AutoCAD DesignCenter 456

Defining Attributes 463

Working with External References 469

Extracting Data from Attributes 471

Creating Tool Palettes 475

Exploding Blocks 476

Chapter Summary 477

Chapter Test Questions 477

Chapter Drawing Projects 482

## Part Three Isometric Drawing and Three-Dimensional Modeling

Chapter 11    Isometric Drawing 493

Chapter Objectives 493

Introduction 493

Using Isometric Snap 493

Switching Isometric Planes 495

Using COPY and Other Edit Commands 496

Drawing Isometric Circles with ELLIPSE 498

Drawing Text Aligned with Isometric Planes 500

Drawing Ellipses in Orthographic Views 502

Saving and Restoring Displays with VIEW 505

Chapter Summary 509

Chapter Test Questions 509

Chapter Drawing Projects 512

Chapter 12    3D Modeling 527

Chapter Objectives 527

Introduction 527

Creating and Viewing a 3D Wireframe Box 528

Defining User Coordinate Systems 533

Exploring the 3D Basics Workspace 538

Creating Solid Boxes and Wedges 540

Accessing Different Visual Styles 543

Creating the Union of Two Solids 544

Working with DUCS 545

Creating Composite Solids with SUBTRACT 547

Creating Chamfers and Fillets on Solid Objects 551

Practicing 3D Gizmo Editing 554

Rendering Solid Models 556

Changing Viewpoints with the ViewCube 567

Creating Layouts with Multiple Views 568

Chapter Summary 573

Chapter Test Questions 573

Chapter Drawing Projects 576

Chapter 13    More Modeling Techniques
and Commands 585

Chapter Objectives 585

Introduction 585

Drawing Polysolids 585

Drawing Cones 589

Drawing Pyramids 591

Drawing Torus 592

Slicing and Sectioning Solids 593

Mesh Modeling 596

Adjusting Viewpoints with 3DORBIT 605

Creating 3D Solids from 2D Outlines 612

Walking Through a 3D Landscape 618

Creating an Animated Walk-Through 621

Chapter Summary 624

Chapter Test Questions 624

Chapter Drawing Projects 626

## Appendix A
Drawing Projects 643

## Appendix B
Creating Customized Panels 665

## Appendix C
Menus, Macros, and the CUI Dialog Box 675

## Appendix D
Additional Tools for Collaboration 679

## Index 683

# NEW to AutoCAD 2014

**Chapter 1**
New Drawing File Tabs   5
New Command Line Features   14

**Chapter 3**
Accessing **Autodesk 360**   117

**Chapter 4**
Uploading Drawing Files to **Autodesk 360**   163

**Chapter 5**
New **ARC** Command Procedures   190
Sharing Drawings in **Autodesk 360**   204

**Chapter 6**
Editing Drawings Online with **AutoCAD WS**   251

# NEW to AutoCAD 2013

**Chapter 1**
New Command Line Format   13

**Chapter 2**
Picking Options from the Command Line   52

**Chapter 4**
New Rectangular Array Procedures   147

**Chapter 5**
New Polar Array Procedures   184

**Chapter 7**
In-Canvas Property Preview   281

**Chapter 9**
New Path Array Procedures   395

**Chapter 12**
Creating Multiple View Layouts   568
Creating Detail Views   571

# chapter**one**

# Lines and Essential Tools

# CHAPTER OBJECTIVES

- Create a new drawing
- Explore the drawing window
- Interact with the drawing window
- Explore command entry methods

- Draw, undo, and erase lines
- Save and open drawings
- Get started

## Introduction

Drawing in AutoCAD can be a fascinating and highly productive activity. AutoCAD 2014 is full of features you can use to become a very proficient design professional. Our goal here is to get you drawing as quickly and efficiently as possible. Discussion and explanation are limited to what is most useful and relevant at the moment but should also give you an understanding of the program to make you a more powerful user.

This chapter introduces some of the basic tools you will use whenever you draw in AutoCAD. You will begin to find your way around the AutoCAD 2014 interface as you learn to control basic elements of the drawing window. You will produce drawings involving straight lines. You will learn to undo your last command with the **U** command and to erase individual lines with the **ERASE** command. Your drawings will be saved, if you wish, using the **SAVE** and **SAVEAS** commands.

# Creating a New Drawing

> **TIP**
>
> A general procedure for creating a new drawing is:
>
> 1. Type <Ctrl>+N or select the **New** tool from the **Quick Access** toolbar.
> 2. Ensure that **acad** is entered in the **File name:** box.
> 3. Press <**Enter**>.

AutoCAD can be customized in many ways, so the exact look and sequence of what you see may be slightly different from what we show you here. We assume that you are working with out-of-the-box settings, but take steps to ensure that your screens resemble ours and that you have no trouble following the sequences presented here. First, however, we have to load AutoCAD.

> **NOTE**
>
> If you see the **AutoCAD 2014 Welcome** window in front of the drawing screen, click the **X** in the upper right corner to close it.

✔ From the Windows desktop, double-click the AutoCAD 2014 icon to start AutoCAD.

✔ Wait . . .
  *When you see the AutoCAD 2014 screen, as shown in Figure 1-1, you are ready to begin.*

**Figure 1-1**
AutoCAD 2014 screen

## Workspaces

AutoCAD may open with a variety of different appearances, including some settings that can be customized and defined as **workspaces**. With typical settings, you open with the **Drafting & Annotation** workspace in a drawing with a generic name such as *Drawing1*, shown in Figure 1-1.

This is one of four standard predefined workspaces. The other three are called **3D Basics, 3D Modeling,** and **AutoCAD Classic.** We focus here on the **Drafting & Annotation** workspace. The **Classic** workspace can also be used in 2D drafting, but it is less efficient and is available primarily for those who have used classic AutoCAD features in previous releases. We do not recommend changing workspaces now, but if for any reason your copy of AutoCAD does not open in the **Drafting & Annotation** workspace, you can switch to it as follows:

- Left-click the **Workspace** drop-down list on the title bar at the top of the screen, as shown in Figure 1-2.

- Highlight **Drafting & Annotation** and left-click to select this workspace.

- If there are elements (toolbars, windows, etc.) on your screen other than those shown in Figure 1-1, close them by clicking the **Close** button (**X**) in the upper right corner of each unwanted element.

## Selecting a Template

In AutoCAD, new drawings are typically created with some form of template. A **template** is a drawing that contains previously defined settings. Simple drawings can be created with the acad.dwt template.

✔ Type <**Ctrl**>+**N**.

*This opens the **Select template** dialog box shown in Figure 1-3. For now, all you need to do is look at the **File name:** box near the bottom of the dialog box. It should read acad or acad.dwt; **dwt** is*

**workspace:** An initial drawing setup with a set of menus, toolbars, palettes, and ribbon panels grouped together to facilitate work on a particular type of drawing. Customized workspaces can be created.

**template:** A drawing that contains previously defined settings.

**dwt:** The file extension given to AutoCAD drawing template files.

**Figure 1-2**
**Workspace** drop-down list

**Figure 1-3**
**Select template** dialog box

*the file extension given to AutoCAD drawing template files. If your* **File name:** *box has a different template, double-click in the box and type* **acad***.*

✔ Assuming the **File name:** box is now showing acad or acad.dwt, press <**Enter**> to complete the dialog.

## Exploring the Drawing Window

You are looking at the AutoCAD 2014 drawing window with the **Drafting & Annotation** workspace and the acad.dwt template. Elements of this workspace are labeled in Figure 1-4. In this section we examine some of the essential features of this interface. If you have worked with other Windows applications, such as any of the Microsoft Office programs, you will find the interface quite familiar.

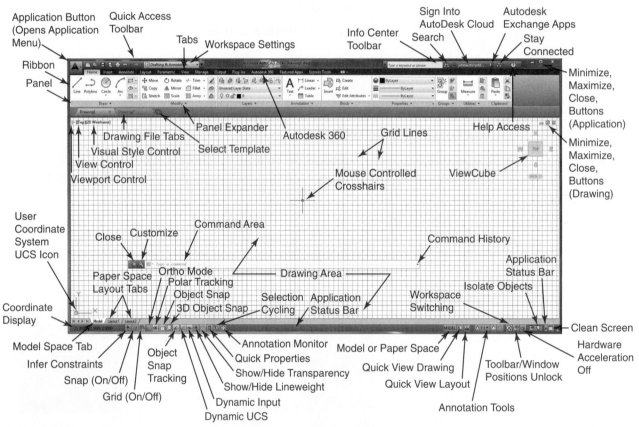

**Figure 1-4**
Elements of **Drafting & Annotation** workspace

At the bottom of your screen you see the Windows taskbar, with the **Start** button on the left and buttons for any open applications to the right of that. You should see a button with the AutoCAD icon here, indicating that you have an AutoCAD window open.

Everything above the taskbar is the AutoCAD application window. At the top left of the screen, the large letter **A** is an AutoCAD icon. Left-clicking on this icon opens a window called the ***application menu***, illustrated later in Figure 1-15. To the right of this is the ***Quick Access toolbar***. By default, it includes the **Workspace** drop-down list and seven tool buttons. These access the **QNEW, OPEN, QSAVE, SAVEAS, PLOT, UNDO,** and **REDO** commands.

**application menu:** The set of menus that opens in a window by clicking the **A** at the left of the application title bar.

**Quick Access toolbar:** A standard set of seven or more tool buttons located on the title bar at the top of the application window, to the right of the application menu button.

It is easy to add frequently used tools to this toolbar, so there may be additional tools added on your system. To the right of the **Quick Access** toolbar is the title bar, with the name of the current drawing. Farther to the right is an area called the **InfoCenter.** Here you find a search box, an online services sign-in box, an X button that opens the **Autodesk Exchange Apps** website, and a ? button that provides access to AutoCAD's Help features. Finally, at the right are the standard **Minimize, Maximize,** and **Close** buttons.

Moving down, we find the AutoCAD *ribbon*. The ribbon comprises tabs and panels. The 12 tabs are labeled with the words across the top of the ribbon: **Home, Insert, Annotate, Layout, Parametric, View, Manage, Output, Plug-ins, Autodesk 360, Featured Apps,** and **Express Tools.** The **Home** tab, shown in Figure 1-4, has nine panels. Each panel has a title at the bottom, and most panels have sets of tool buttons. On the **Home** tab the panels are labeled **Draw, Modify, Layers, Annotation, Block, Properties, Groups, Utilities,** and **Clipboard.**

Immediately below the ribbon are the *drawing file tabs*, as shown in the figure. By default, drawing tabs are created automatically when you create a new drawing. In the figure *Drawing1* was created when you opened the AutoCAD software, and *Drawing2* was created when you created a new drawing by typing **<Ctrl>+N.** These tabs make it easy to switch among open drawings. If you do not see file tabs at the top of your drawing area, it is likely that the file tab feature has been turned off. To turn it on, type **filetab <Enter>.**

Below the ribbon is a large open area with lines like those on a sheet of graph paper. This is called the *drawing window.* This is where you will do most of your work and where your drawing will appear. Notice the X-Y coordinate system icon at the lower left of the drawing window. This is called the *UCS icon.* At the upper right of the window is a compass-like image called the *ViewCube*, and below this is a vertical strip of tools called the *navigation bar.* At the bottom of the drawing area are the **Model** and **Layout** tabs. These are used to move between modeling procedures and presentation procedures. Using layouts you can create many different presentations of the same drawing.

In AutoCAD 2014 you will also see the transparent command line sitting above the line holding the **Model** and **Layout** tabs. Typed commands and options appear here. Typed commands, introduced in the next section, are one of the basic ways of working in AutoCAD. Some functions of the command line are new in 2014, and we will explore this later.

Below the command line is the ***status bar,*** with the coordinate display on the left, currently showing three four-place decimal numbers separated by commas. To the right of the coordinate display are 15 mode buttons. These are switches for turning on and off some extremely important features of the drawing window (**Infer Constraints, Snap Mode, Grid Display, Ortho Mode, Polar Tracking, Object Snap, 3D Object Snap, Object Snap Tracking, Dynamic UCS, Dynamic Input, Lineweight, Transparency, Quick Properties, Selection Cycling,** and **Annotation Monitor).** At the right side of the status bar are 11 more tool buttons, starting with **Model** on the left and ending with **Clean Screen** on the right.

**ribbon:** A set of tabs, panels, and tool buttons located below the title bar and above the drawing area. The ribbon gives access to many commands and features. Panels and tabs change depending on the workspace.

NEW to AutoCAD 2014

**status bar:** A set of tool buttons located below the command window and above the Windows taskbar, beginning with the coordinate display on the left and ending with the **Clean Screen** button on the right.

> **NOTE**
>
> You may also see other windows or toolbars on your screen. If so, close each of these by clicking the **X** in its upper right or left corner.

## Interacting with the Drawing Window

There are many ways to communicate with the drawing window. In this section, we explore the mouse, crosshairs, arrow, and other simple features so that we can begin to use drawing commands.

### The Mouse

Most of your interaction with the drawing window will be communicated through your mouse. Given the graphic interfaces of AutoCAD, a typical two-button mouse is sufficient for most tasks. For our work here, we assume two buttons. If you have a digitizer or a more complex pointing device, the two-button functions will be present, along with other functions that we do not address.

On a common two-button mouse the left button is called the *pick button,* and it is used for point selection, object selection, and menu or tool selection. All mouse instructions in this chapter refer to the left button, unless specifically stated otherwise. The right button most often calls up shortcut menus, as in other Windows applications. These are also called *context menus* because the menu that is called depends on what is happening when the right button is pushed. Learning how and when to use these menus can increase your efficiency. We show you how to use many shortcut menus as we go along. If you click the right button accidentally and open an unwanted shortcut menu, close it by left-clicking anywhere outside the menu.

Your mouse may also have a scroll wheel between the left and right buttons. This wheel has a useful zooming function in AutoCAD. For now, if you happen to click the mouse wheel forward or backward, just click it in the opposite direction to reverse the zooming action.

### Crosshairs

The focus of action in AutoCAD is the crosshairs. This is the cross with a box at its intersection somewhere in the display area of your screen. If you do not see it, move your pointing device until it appears. At any time, the point where the two lines of the crosshairs intersect is the point that will be specified by pressing the left button. Try it, as follows.

✔ Move the mouse and see how the crosshairs move in coordination with your hand movements.

✔ Move the mouse so that the crosshairs move to the top of the screen.
   *When you leave the drawing area, your crosshairs are left behind and you see a standard selection arrow pointing up and to the left. As in other Windows applications, the arrow is used to select tools, tabs, and menu items.*

✔ Move the cursor back into the drawing area.

The selection arrow disappears, and the crosshairs move across the drawing area again.

### The Coordinate Display and Dynamic Input

**Cartesian coordinate system:** Based on the concept first described by Rene Descartes in 1637, a geometric system in which any point on a plane can be identified by values representing its distance from two mutually perpendicular axes.

The coordinate display at the left of the status bar keeps track of screen coordinates as you move the mouse. AutoCAD uses a **Cartesian coordinate system** to identify points in the drawing area. In this system, points are identified by an *x* value, indicating a horizontal position from left to right across the screen, and a *y* value, indicating a vertical position from bottom to top on the screen. Notice the icon at the lower left of the drawing area. This is the *user coordinate system icon,* showing the alignment of the X- and Y-axes. Typically, a point near the lower left of the screen is chosen as the origin, or 0 point, of the coordinate system. Its coordinates are (0,0). Points are specified by pairs of numbers, called *ordered pairs,* in which the horizontal *x* value is first, followed by the vertical *y* value. For example, the point (3,2) identifies a point 3 units over and 2 units up from the origin at the lower left corner of the screen. You will see many ordered pairs as you work in AutoCAD. There is also a *z* value in 3D Cartesian coordinates, which measures an imagined distance in front of or behind the screen, but we do not use this here. For now the *z* value will always be 0, and we can ignore it.

With this in mind, observe the coordinate display as you move the crosshairs.

✔ Move the crosshairs around slowly and keep your eye on the three numbers at the bottom left of the screen.

*The first two should be moving very rapidly through four-place decimal numbers. When you stop moving, the numbers show coordinates for the location of the crosshairs. Notice the four-place x and y values, which change rapidly, and the z value, which is always 0.0000. Coordinates shown in this form, relative to a fixed coordinate grid, are called* **absolute coordinates**. *As we shall see shortly, the coordinate display can also show* **polar coordinates**, *which are given as a length and an angle relative to a given point.*

✔ Carefully move the crosshairs horizontally and watch how the first value (*x*) changes and the second value (*y*) stays more or less the same.

✔ Move the crosshairs vertically and watch how the second value (*y*) changes and the first value (*x*) stays more or less the same.

*The coordinate display has three different modes. You switch among them by left-clicking directly on the coordinate display.*

✔ Move the crosshairs off the drawing area and down to the coordinate display.

*The crosshairs will be replaced by the selection arrow.*

✔ With the arrow on the coordinate display numbers, press the pick button.

*The numbers freeze, and the coordinate display turns gray.*

✔ Move the arrow back into the drawing area and continue to move the crosshairs slowly.

*Now, when you move the crosshairs you see that the coordinate display does not change. You also notice that it is still grayed out.*

✔ Pick any point near the middle of your drawing area.

*Notice that the coordinate display updates to the selected point even though the numbers are grayed out. This is called static mode. In this mode, the coordinate display will change only when you pick a point. Previously the coordinate display was in dynamic mode, in which the numbers update constantly with the movement of the crosshairs.*

**absolute coordinates:** Coordinate values given relative to the origin of a coordinate system, so that a point in two dimensions is identified by an *x* value, giving the horizontal distance from the point of origin of the coordinate system, and a *y* value, giving the vertical distance from the same point of origin.

**polar coordinates:** Coordinates that identify a point by giving a distance and an angle from a previous point.

**Figure 1-5**
Dynamic input display

**Figure 1-6**
**Dynamic Input** button

*You probably will see something else on your screen, as shown in Figure 1-5, called the **dynamic input display**. It is a very powerful feature that in many ways duplicates the function of the coordinate display. However, this display is easier to track because it follows your cursor. Also, there are times when it can be used effectively in conjunction with the coordinate display. Dynamic input can be turned on and off using the **Dynamic Input** button on the status bar.*

✔ Pick the **Dynamic Input** button shown in Figure 1-6.

✔ Move your cursor back into the drawing area.
   *When dynamic input is off, the button will appear in gray instead of blue. With the display off, the dynamic input numbers on your screen disappear.*

✔ Pick the **Dynamic Input** button again.

✔ Move the cursor back into the drawing area.
   *The button appears blue, and the dynamic input display reappears.*
   *Currently, the numbers in the dynamic display are x and y coordinates, just as in the coordinate display. The coordinate display on the status bar is static, whereas the dynamic display still moves through values when you move your crosshairs. In other words, the coordinate display indicates the coordinates of the last point you picked, and the dynamic input display shows the value of any new point you may pick.*

✔ Move the crosshairs to another point on the screen.
   *Something else is happening here that we must address. AutoCAD opens a box on the screen, as shown in Figure 1-7. You are not drawing anything with this box. This is the **object selection window**, used to select objects for editing. It has no effect now*

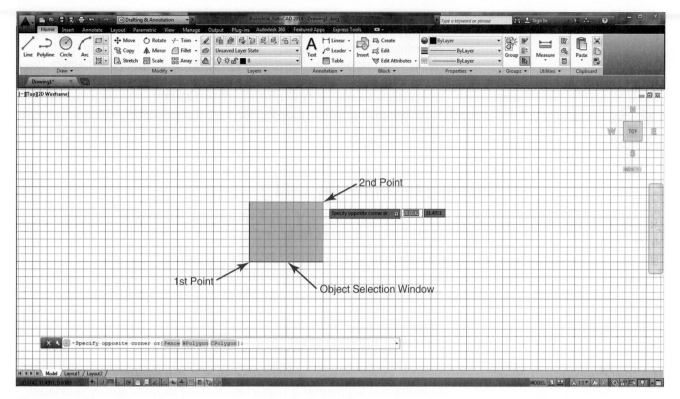

**Figure 1-7**
Object selection window

because there are no objects on your screen. You can give two points to define the window and then it vanishes because there is nothing there to select. Object selection is discussed briefly in the "Drawing, Undoing, and Erasing Lines" section.

AutoCAD prompts for the other corner of the selection window. You see the following in the command line and on the dynamic input display:

Specify opposite corner:

✔ Pick a second point.
This completes the object selection window and the window vanishes. Notice the change in the static coordinate display numbers.

## The Grid

AutoCAD uses a grid of lines like a piece of graph paper as a visual aid. The grid shows a matrix of points in its Cartesian coordinate system.

✔ Pick the **Grid Display** button on the status bar, the third button to the right of the coordinate display, as shown in Figure 1-8, or press **<F7>**.
This turns off the grid. The grid helps you find your way around on the screen. It does not appear on your drawing when it is plotted, and it can be turned on and off at will. You can also change the spacing between lines using the **GRID** command. For now we will make one simple adjustment to center the grid in the drawing area.

**Figure 1-8**
**Grid Display** button

✔ Pick the **Grid Display** button again, or press **<F7>**.

*The grid reappears. With the acad.dwt template, the grid is set up to emulate the shape of an Architectural A-size (12 × 9-inch) sheet of drawing paper, with grid lines at 0.5000 increments. Darker lines are shown at 2.50000 units. The AutoCAD command that controls the outer size and shape of the grid is **LIMITS.** However, by default the grid is set to display beyond the defined limits, so the grid covers the whole drawing area. For now we continue to use the current limits setting.*

## Zooming to Center the Grid

Before going on, we use a simple procedure with the **ZOOM** command to center the grid in your drawing area.

✔ Type **z <Enter>** to execute the **ZOOM** command.

*Z is a shortcut for typing **zoom**. Such keyboard shortcuts, called aliases, are discussed in the "Exploring Command Entry Methods" section. When you type a command, AutoCAD responds with a list of options at the command line prompt. In this case, you see the following in the command line:*

[All Center Dynamic Extents Previous Scale Window Object]<real time>:

*Options are separated by spaces, and the default option is shown at the end between angle brackets. If you press **<Enter>** in response to the prompt, you will execute the default option. Other options can be executed by typing a letter, indicated by the upper-case blue letter in the option. This is usually the first letter, but not always. For our purposes we want the **All** option, so we type **a**. In AutoCAD 2013 and 2014, you can also execute an option by picking the option directly from the command line.*

✔ Type **a <Enter>** to zoom out and show the complete grid.

*Your grid should now be enlarged and centered in your drawing area, as illustrated in Figure 1-9. The grid is positioned so that the area within the drawing limits, between (0,0) and (12,9), is centered in the drawing area. The X-axis is aligned with the bottom of the drawing area, and the origin of the coordinate system (0,0) is at the bottom of the screen. The upper limits of the drawing are at the point (12,9), so the top of the grid (where y = 12) is aligned with the top of the drawing area.*

## Model Space

As you look at the grid and consider its relation to an A-size drawing sheet, you should be aware that there is no need to scale AutoCAD drawings until you are ready to print or plot and that the size and shape of your grid will be determined by what you are drawing, not by the size of your drawing sheet. You will always draw at full scale, where one unit of length on the screen represents one unit of length in real space. This full-scale drawing space is called ***model space***. At the time of plotting, the drawing will be scaled to fit the paper. This process is handled through the creation of a drawing layout in what is called ***paper space***. For now, all your work will be done in model space.

**model space:** The full-scale drawing space on the screen, where one unit of length represents one unit of length in real space.

**paper space:** Use of the computer screen to represent objects in a drawing layout at the scale of the intended drawing sheet.

**Figure 1-9**
Grid enlarged and centered

## Other Buttons on the Status Bar

The mode buttons (the 15 small images on the left side of the status bar) are used to turn powerful features on and off. However, some of the features can interfere with your learning and ability to control the cursor when turned on at the wrong time. For this reason, we encourage you to keep some features off until you need them. In this chapter, generally, the **Snap Mode, Grid Display,** and **Dynamic Input** buttons should be on, and other buttons should be off. **Infer Constraints** controls the powerful constraint feature. **Ortho Mode** and **Polar Tracking** are discussed later in this chapter, and you can use them at your discretion. **Object Snap** and **3D Object Snap** are very important features that force the selection of a geometrically definable point on an object, such as the endpoint or midpoint of a line in 2D or the corner of a box in 3D. We leave object snap alone in this chapter so that you have the freedom to select points without the interference of an object snap selection. **Object Snap Tracking** is an outgrowth of object snap. **Dynamic User Coordinate System** is used only in 3D modeling. **Dynamic Input** controls the dynamic input display. **Lineweight** is not used in this chapter. *Transparency* is an effect that is applied to individual objects, but it will be shown only when the **Transparency** button is on. The **Quick Properties** panel is not treated in this chapter. **Selection Cycling** becomes useful in complex drawings with many overlapping objects, and **Annotation Monitor** comes into play when you begin dimensioning and annotating drawings.

transparency: Objects in AutoCAD have a property called transparency that can be adjusted on a scale from 0 to 90, where 0 is solid and 90 is extremely faint. Display of transparency can be turned on or off for a whole drawing.

## Exploring Command Entry Methods

It is characteristic of AutoCAD that most tasks can be accomplished in a variety of ways. For example, you can enter commands by typing or by selecting an item from the ribbon, a menu, a shortcut menu, or a dialog box. Each method has its advantages and disadvantages, depending on the situation. Often, a combination of two or more methods is the most efficient way to carry out a complete command sequence. Once you get used to the range of options, you will develop your own preferences.

## Heads-Up Design

**heads-up design:** Software designed to allow the user to remain focused on the computer screen.

An important concept in the creation of AutoCAD command procedures is termed *heads-up design*. What this means is that optimal efficiency is achieved when the CAD operator can keep his or her hand on the mouse and eyes focused on the screen. The less time spent looking away from the screen, the better. A major innovation supporting heads-up technique is the dynamic input display. Because this display moves with the cursor, it allows you to stay focused on your drawing area.

We describe each of the basic command and point entry methods in this section. You do not have to try them all out at this time. Read them over to get a feel for the possibilities, and then proceed to exploring the **LINE** command in the "Drawing, Undoing, and Erasing Lines" section.

## Keyboard and Command Line

The keyboard is the oldest and most fundamental method of interacting with AutoCAD, and it is still of great importance for all operators. Toolbars, menus, and dialog boxes all function by automating basic command sequences as they would be typed on the keyboard. Although other methods are often faster, being familiar with keyboard procedures increases your understanding of AutoCAD. Further, in AutoCAD 2014 the command line has been enhanced with a new set of responses to your typing. These add considerably to the functionality of the command line. The keyboard is literally at your fingertips, and if you know the command you want to use, or even a synonym or part of the command name, the command line will help you access it.

It is also worthwhile to point out that some excellent CAD operators may rely too heavily on the keyboard. Do not limit yourself by typing everything. If you know the keyboard sequence, try the other methods to see how they vary and how you can use them to save time and stay screen-focused. Ultimately, you want to keep your hand on the mouse, type as little as possible, and use the various command entry methods to your advantage.

As you type commands and responses to prompts, the characters you are typing appear on the command line after the colon. If dynamic input is on, they may appear in the drawing area next to the crosshairs instead. Remember that you must press **\<Enter\>** to complete your commands and responses.

---

**TIP**

By pressing \<F2\> you can access a text window that gives access to all entries made in the current drawing session. Press \<F2\> again to close the text window and return to the drawing area.

---

Many of the most often used commands, such as **LINE, ERASE,** and **CIRCLE,** have aliases. These one- or two-letter abbreviations are very handy. A few of the most commonly used aliases are shown in Figure 1-10.

There are also a large number of two- and three-letter aliases that you will encounter in your AutoCAD work.

**Figure 1-10**
Commonly used aliases

| COMMAND ALIAS CHART | | |
|---|---|---|
| LETTER + ENTER | | = COMMAND |
| A | ↵ | ARC |
| C | ↵ | CIRCLE |
| E | ↵ | ERASE |
| F | ↵ | FILLET |
| L | ↵ | LINE |
| M | ↵ | MOVE |
| O | ↵ | OFFSET |
| P | ↵ | PAN |
| R | ↵ | REDRAW |
| S | ↵ | STRETCH |
| Z | ↵ | ZOOM |

## Command Line

In AutoCAD 2013 and 2014, the command line sits above the Model and Layout line, but can be moved anywhere in the drawing area. The enhanced command line has the quality of transparency, most noticeable when it is moved into the drawing area. Because it is transparent, it interferes only minimally with objects behind it.

You will also notice that as commands are typed, the last few command line prompts and responses (by default, the last three) are displayed above the line, as shown in Figure 1-11. These lines will disappear after a few seconds if no new action is taken. Later, you will also see that command options can be selected directly from the command line.

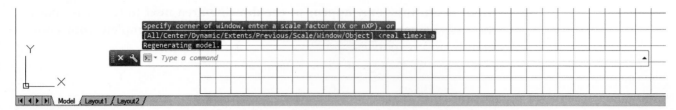

**Figure 1-11**
Transparent command line

NEW to AutoCAD 2014

**AutoComplete:** The process by which AutoCAD displays a list of possible commands after the user has entered only the first few letters. This allows the user to select from the list without typing in the remaining letters.

**AutoCorrect:** The process by which AutoCAD displays a list of possible commands based on the characters entered at the command line, even though there may be no command with the sequence of characters typed, after the user has entered only the first few letters. This may allow the user to select the correct command from the list without retyping the entry.

**Figure 1-12**
**AutoComplete**

**Figure 1-13**
**AutoCorrect**

**Midstring AutoComplete:** The process by which AutoCAD displays a list of possible commands containing the characters entered at the command line, including options where the characters do not appear at the beginning of the option.

> **TIP**
> If you want to see more than the last three lines of command prompts and responses, press <F2> or the up arrow at the right end of the command line. AutoCAD will then display your last 20 lines.

## AutoComplete and AutoCorrect

In AutoCAD 2014, the command line also has **AutoComplete** and **AutoCorrect** features. When these features are turned on, as they are by default, a box with a list of command and system variable choices will appear next to the command line prompt or the dynamic input display as you type commands. Try this:

✔ Type the letter **L,** but do not press **<Enter>.**

*You will see a list of possibilities that begin with the letter L, as shown in Figure 1-12.*

When AutoCAD presents such a list, you may continue typing to narrow down the list of options, or scroll down the list and select a command. The suggestions are most useful when you are searching for an obscure command, when you are uncertain of the name or spelling, or when the command has a very long name and it is inefficient to type it. (Consider, for example, the system variable **LAYOUTLINE,** which is sixth on the list in Figure 1-12, or scroll down the list for even more cumbersome examples, such as **LARGEOBJECTSUPPORT.**)

✔ Now type the letter **N,** but do not press **<Enter>.**

*Your command line or dynamic input prompt should now read **LN,** and the suggestion box will appear similar to Figure 1-13. This demonstrates the **AutoCorrect** feature. There is no AutoCAD command that begins with LN, but instead of replying with "Unknown Command", AutoCAD returns a list of possibilities containing these letters. This list is initially based on the profile of an average user, but over time would remember your most frequently executed commands and put these at the top of your list.*

✔ Press the backspace button to remove the letter N.

✔ Now add the letters **I** and **N,** so that your command line or dynamic input prompt reads **LIN.**

*AutoCAD will return a suggestion list similar to the one in Figure 1-14. Notice that AutoCAD adds the E automatically. This is an example of the **AutoComplete** feature. Looking at the suggestion list you will also see suggestions such as DIMLIN and COMBINEPOLYLINES. These are examples of **Midstring AutoComplete,** also new in 2014. Through this feature, AutoCAD returns not only commands in which the letters being typed appear at the beginning of the command name, but also those in which the letters may occur in the middle or at the end.*

The enhanced command line has other features as well that we will demonstrate as we go along.

**Figure 1-14**
**Midstring AutoComplete**

**Figure 1-15**
Application menu

## The Application Menu

Menus, toolbars, and the ribbon offer the great advantage that instead of typing a complete command, you can simply point and click to select an item without looking away from the screen. The application menu provides access to commands for opening, saving, and preparing drawings for printing and publishing, along with the capability of searching for commands and browsing saved drawings:

✔ To open the application menu, left-click the **A** in the upper left corner of the screen.

> *The menu opens, as shown in Figure 1-15. At the left is a list of commands related to drawing preparation. When you highlight any of these, a submenu of related commands appears to the right. The application menu also has a search box at the top, for locating commands, and a menu of* **Recent Documents** *or* **Open Documents** *at the right.*

**NOTE**
When entering commands, command aliases, keyboard shortcuts, or command options, uppercase and lowercase letters are equivalent.

## The Ribbon

A large number of command tools found on separate toolbars in older versions of AutoCAD are collapsed into a single interface called a ribbon. This combination of tabs and panels gives quick access to a large number of commands without cluttering the screen and obstructing the drawing area. The many drop-down lists on the ribbon allow access to even more tools. The icons on the ribbon are the same as those used in toolbars, but there are more of them available in a single location. The **Home** tab of the ribbon, which is open by default, contains most of the command tools you will need in the beginning.

**The Minimize to Panel Buttons Button.**   In AutoCAD there is a convenient **Minimize** button to the right of the list of ribbon tabs. Click the up arrow on the left once, and the ribbon will contract to show just the icon for the set of panels on the current tab. When you position your cursor on the icon, the tools for that panel will appear. Press the up arrow again, and the icons will contract again to show just the panel label. Press it a third time, and the panel labels will disappear, leaving only the names of the tabs. On the fourth press, the ribbon will return to normal. The advantage of this feature is that it allows you to gain space in the drawing area.

## Tooltips

The icons called *tools,* which are used to represent commands, are a mixed blessing. One picture may be worth a thousand words, but with so many pictures, you may find that a few words can be very helpful as well. As in other Windows applications, you can get information about a tool or a command by allowing the selection arrow to hover over the item for a moment without selecting it. These labels are called ***tooltips****.* There are two levels of information provided by tooltips. Basic tooltips provide the name of the command with a general description. Extended tooltips provide additional information and often include a graphic illustration. Some items have only basic tooltips.

Try the following:

**tooltip:** A window that opens automatically when the cursor rests on a tool button. Basic tooltips provide a label and a general description. Extended tooltips provide more information and an illustration.

✔ Position the selection arrow on the **Line** tool at the left end of the ribbon, as shown in Figure 1-16, but do not press the pick button.
  *First, you see a small information window, as shown in Figure 1-17. This is the basic tooltip for the **LINE** command. If you let your cursor hover over the tool longer, you see the extended tooltip shown in Figure 1-18. Access basic or extended tooltips as you like. Now let us get started drawing.*

**Figure 1-16**
**Line** tool

**Figure 1-17**
Basic tooltip

**Figure 1-18**
Extended tooltip

# Drawing, Undoing, and Erasing Lines

| LINE | |
|---|---|
| Command | Line |
| Alias | L |
| Panel | Draw |
| Tool |  |

> **TIP**
> A general procedure for using the **LINE** command is as follows:
>
> 1. Type **l** or select the **Line** tool from the ribbon.
> 2. Pick a start point.
> 3. Pick an endpoint.
> 4. Pick another endpoint to continue in the **LINE** command, or press **<Enter>** to exit the command.

Drawing lines is a simple matter of entering the **LINE** command and then picking 2 or more endpoints. In order to pick points precisely, however, we need to introduce **Snap** mode, one of CAD's essential tools.

## Snap

**snap:** One of a number of CAD features that facilitate accurate drawing technique by allowing the software to extrapolate a precise geometric point from an approximate screen cursor location.

**Snap** is an important concept in all CAD programs. There are several AutoCAD features through which an approximate screen cursor location locks onto a precise numerical point, a point on an object, or the extension of an object. All these features enhance productivity in that the operator does not have to hunt for or visually guess at precise point locations. In this chapter, we show examples of several of these related techniques. The simplest form of snap is called *incremental snap* or *grid snap*. In AutoCAD 2014, **Snap** mode will be active only when you have entered a command that asks you to pick a point. Here, we enter the **LINE** command.

✔ Select the **Line** tool from the ribbon, as shown previously in Figure 1-16.
  *As soon as you enter the command, the dynamic input prompt appears next to the crosshairs. You should see the following in the command line and the dynamic input prompt:*

    Specify first point:

  *In order to specify a point precisely, we use **Snap** mode.*

✔ Pick the **Snap Mode** button on the status bar, the second button to the right of the coordinate display, as shown in Figure 1-19.

**Figure 1-19**
**Snap Mode** button on status bar

✔ Move the crosshairs slowly around the grid.
  *Watch closely, and you will see that the crosshairs jump from line to line. With your grid on, notice that is impossible to make the crosshairs touch a point that is not on the grid. Try it.*

✔ If your coordinate display is in the static mode, left-click it to switch to dynamic mode. Move the cursor and watch the coordinate display.
  *Notice that the coordinate display shows only values ending in .0000 or .5000.*

✔ Pick the **Snap Mode** button again to turn snap off.
  *Snap should now be off and the **Snap Mode** button is gray.*

*If you move the cursor in a circle now, the crosshairs move smoothly, without jumping. You also observe that the coordinate display moves rapidly through a full range of four-place decimal values again.*

*With snap off, you can move freely on the screen. With snap on you can move only in predetermined increments. With the acad.dwt template default settings, snap is set to a value of .5000 so that you can move only in half-unit increments. Later we will change this setting using the **SNAP** command. For now, we leave the snap settings alone.*

*Using an appropriate snap increment is a tremendous time-saver. It also allows for a degree of accuracy that is not possible otherwise. If all the dimensions in a drawing fall into 1-inch increments, for example, there is no reason to deal with points that are not on a 1-inch grid. You can find the points you want much more quickly and accurately if all those in between are temporarily eliminated. The snap setting allows you to do that.*

> **TIP**
>
> Incremental snap is more than a convenience. In many cases, it is a necessity. With snap off, it is virtually impossible to locate any point precisely with the mouse. If you try to locate the point (6.5000,6.5000,0.0000) with snap off, for example, you may get close, but the probability is very small that you will actually be able to select that exact point. Try it.

✔ Pick the **Snap Mode** button again to turn it on.

> **NOTE**
>
> Make sure that the mode buttons on your status bar resemble those shown in Figure 1-20.

**Figure 1-20**
Blue status bar buttons are on

In particular, note that the **Snap Mode, Grid Display,** and **Dynamic Input** buttons are switched on (blue) and that the **Infer Constraints, Ortho Mode, Polar Tracking, Object Snap, 3D Object Snap,** and **Object Snap Tracking** buttons are all switched off (gray). This keeps things simple and uncluttered for now, which is very important. The other buttons, **Dynamic UCS, Lineweight, Transparency, Quick Properties, Selection Cycling,** and **Annotation Monitor,** will not affect you at this point and may be on or off.

✔ Move your crosshairs to the point (1.0000,1.0000) and press the pick button.

*AutoCAD registers your point selection and responds with another prompt:*

Specify next point or [Undo]:

*This prompts you to pick a second point. The **Undo** option is discussed shortly.*

## Rubber Band

✔ Move your cursor up toward the center of your drawing area and let it rest, but do not press the pick button.

> *There are several other new things to be aware of here. The dynamic input display has become much more complex. With typical settings, there will be three new features on the screen. There is a solid line called the rubber band, stretching from the first point to the new point. There is a linear dimension with a dotted line parallel to and above the rubber band. And there is an angular dimension between the line and the horizon, as illustrated in Figure 1-21. If you move the cursor, you notice that the rubber band stretches, shrinks, or rotates like a tether, keeping you connected to the starting point of the line. Rubber bands have various functions in AutoCAD commands. In this case, the rubber band represents the line you are about to draw.*

**Figure 1-21**
Rubber band

## Polar Coordinates

The two dimensions in the dynamic input display show a visual display of polar coordinates. Polar coordinates are given as a length and an angle relative to a starting point. In this case, you see the length of the line you are drawing and the angle it forms from the horizon, straight out to the right. Typically, the coordinate display will also show polar coordinates. If not, you need to change the coordinate display mode.

✔ If necessary, click on the coordinate display once or twice until it shows something like 6.7268<42,0.0000.

> *There are three values in the polar coordinate display. The first number (6.7268 in our example) is the distance from the starting point of the line to the crosshairs, the same as that shown by the*

*linear dimension in the dynamic display. The second number (42)
is an angle of rotation, measured counterclockwise, with 0 degrees
being straight out to the right. The third number (0.0000) is the z coordinate, which remains at 0 in 2D drawings.*

## Working with Absolute and Polar Coordinates

The presence of the coordinate display with the dynamic display allows you
to use absolute (*x, y, z*) coordinates and polar coordinates simultaneously.
Try this:

✔ Pick the coordinate display several times and watch what it displays.
*As you do this you will notice that there are three coordinate dis-
play modes: static (values grayed out, with no change until you
select a point), absolute xyz (x, y, and z values separated by a
comma), and polar (length < angle, z).*

✔ Pick the coordinate display until you see absolute (*x, y, z*) coordinates
in black.
*With absolute coordinates showing, you can use the coordinate dis-
play to pick a point in your drawing while the dynamic display continues to show the polar coordinates of the line you are drawing.*

✔ Move the cursor to the point with absolute coordinates
(8.0000,8.0000,0.0000).
*Notice that the dynamic input display shows that this line is 9.8995
units long and makes a 45° angle with the horizon.*

✔ Pick the point (8.0000,8.0000,0.0000).
*Your screen should now resemble Figure 1-22. AutoCAD has drawn
a line between (1,1) and (8,8) and is asking for another point:*

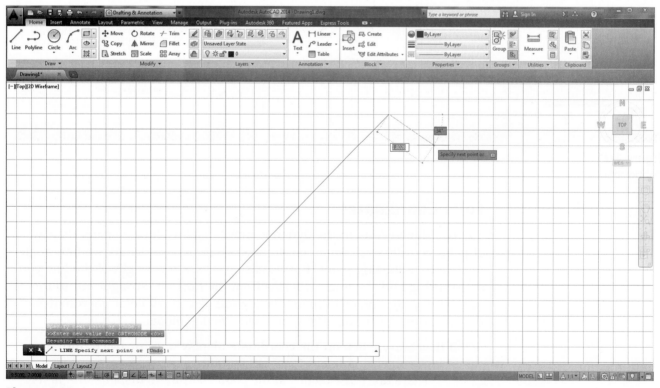

**Figure 1-22**
Absolute and polar coordinates

Specify next point or [Undo]:

*The repetition of this prompt allows you to stay in the **LINE** command to draw a whole series of connected lines if you wish. You can draw a single line from point to point, or a series of lines from point to point to point to point. In either case, you must end the command by pressing <**Enter**> or the spacebar.*

> **NOTE**
>
> When you are drawing a continuous series of lines, the polar coordinates on either display are given relative to the most recent point, not the original starting point.

✔ Press <**Enter**> or the spacebar to end the **LINE** command.
   *You should be back to the command prompt again, and the dynamic input display disappears from the screen.*

## Spacebar and <Enter> Key

In most cases, AutoCAD allows you to use the spacebar as a substitute for the <**Enter**> key. Although this is one of the oldest AutoCAD features, it is a major contributor to the goal of heads-up drawing. It is a great convenience, because the spacebar is easy to locate with one hand (your left hand if the mouse is on the right side) while the other hand is on the mouse and your eyes are on the screen. The major exception to the use of the spacebar as an <**Enter**> key is when you are entering text in your drawing. Because a space can be part of a text string, the spacebar must have its usual significance within text commands and some dimension commands.

> **TIP**
>
> Another great convenience provided by the spacebar and <**Enter**> key is that pressing either at the command prompt causes the last command entered to be repeated.

## Right-Click Button and Shortcut Menus

The right button on your mouse can also sometimes be used in place of the <**Enter**> key, but in most cases, there will be an intervening step involving a shortcut menu with options. This, too, is a major heads-up feature, which we explore as we go along. For now, the following steps give you an introduction to shortcut menus.

✔ Press the right button on your mouse. (This action is called *right-clicking* from now on.)
   *This opens a shortcut menu, as shown in Figure 1-23. The top line is a **Repeat LINE** option that can be used to repeat the **LINE** command. (Remember, you can also do this by pressing the spacebar at the command prompt.) You have no use for the other options on this shortcut menu for now.*

✔ Pick any point outside the shortcut menu.
   *The shortcut menu disappears, but AutoCAD takes the picked point as the first point in an object selection window.*

✔ Pick any second point to close the object selection window.
   *In other words, you have to click twice outside the shortcut menu to close it and abort the selection window.*

**Figure 1-23**
Shortcut menu

There are many context-sensitive shortcut menus in AutoCAD. We do not attempt to present all of them but encourage you to explore them along the way. You will find many possibilities simply by right-clicking while in a command or dialog box.

## Relative Coordinates and @

**relative coordinates:** Coordinates given relative to a previously entered point, rather than to the axes of origin of a coordinate system.

Besides typing or picking points on the screen, AutoCAD allows you to enter points by typing coordinates relative to the last point selected. To do this, use the @ symbol and *relative coordinates*. For example, after picking the point (1,1) in the last exercise, you could have specified the point (8,8) by typing **@7,7,** as the second point is over 7 and up 7 from the first point.

## Direct Distance Entry

You can also enter values directly to the dynamic input display. For example, you can pick the first point of a line and then show or type the direction of the line segment you wish to draw, but instead of picking the other endpoint you type in a value for the length of the line. Try this:

✔ Repeat the **LINE** command by pressing **<Enter>** or the spacebar.
  *AutoCAD prompts for a first point.*

> **TIP**
>
> If you press <Enter> or the spacebar at the *Specify first point:* prompt, AutoCAD selects the last point entered, so that you can begin drawing from where you left off.

✔ Press **<Enter>** or the spacebar to select the point (8,8,0), the endpoint of the previously drawn line.
  *AutoCAD prompts for a second point.*

✔ Pull the rubber band diagonally down to the right, as shown in Figure 1-24.
  *Use the dynamic input display to ensure that you are moving along the diagonal at a 45° angle, as shown. The length of the rubber band does not matter, only the direction. Notice that the length is highlighted on the dynamic input display.*

✔ With the rubber band stretched out as shown, type **3.**
  *Notice that the 3 is entered directly on the dynamic input display as the length of the line.*

> **NOTE**
>
> Be aware that in other contexts this angle, which is 45° below the horizon, would be identified as negative 45° to distinguish it from the angle that is 45° above the horizon. This convention is ignored in dynamic input because the visual information removes any ambiguity.

✔ Press **<Enter>** or hit the spacebar.
  *AutoCAD draws a 3.0000 line segment at the angle you have specified. You can also use this method to input an angle. Try this:*

✔ With the length highlighted on the dynamic input display, type **2,** but do not press **<Enter>**.
  *Pressing <Enter> would complete the line segment at whatever angle is showing, as you did in the last step. To move from the length value to the angle value, use the **<Tab>** key on your keyboard before pressing <Enter>.*

**Figure 1-24**
Direct distance entry

✔ Press the **\<Tab\>** key once.

*The value 2.0000 is locked in as the length, as shown in Figure 1-25. You will see a lock icon on the length display and notice that the rubber band no longer stretches, although it can still be rotated. Now you can manually specify an angle.*

**Figure 1-25**
Length locked at 2.0000

✔ Place the rubber band above the horizontal.

✔ Type **45 <Enter>**.

✔ Press **<Enter>** or the spacebar to exit the **LINE** command.
   *Your screen should resemble Figure 1-26.*

**Figure 1-26**
Manually specified angle

## Absolute Coordinates and #

Now, suppose that you wish to draw a line back to the point (8,8). You could easily do this using the snap grid, since that point is on a snap point, but you are not restricted to this method. It is important to know that you can also type the absolute coordinates (8,8) at the *Specify second point:* prompt, but you must first type the number **(#)** sign. The # sign specifies absolute coordinates rather than coordinates relative to the last point. If you do not type #, AutoCAD will assume you are specifying relative coordinates and will draw the line up 8 and over 8 from the current point. Try this:

✔ Press **<Enter>** or the spacebar twice to repeat **LINE** and reconnect to the last point.

✔ Type **#8,8 <Enter>**.
   *AutoCAD interprets these as absolute coordinates and draws the final line segment back to the point (8,8,0).*

✔ Press **<Enter>** or the spacebar to exit the **LINE** command.
*Your screen should resemble Figure 1-27.*

## Undoing Commands with U

✔ To undo the line segment you just drew, type **U <Enter>**, or select the **Undo** tool from the **Quick Access** toolbar, as shown in Figure 1-28.

*U undoes the last command, so if you have done anything else since drawing the line, you need to enter it more than once. In this way, you can walk backward through your drawing session, undoing your commands one by one. As mentioned previously,*

**Figure 1-27**
Absolute coordinates and the # sign

**Figure 1-28**
**Undo** tool

*there is also an **Undo** option within the **LINE** command so that you can undo the last segment drawn without leaving the command.*

---

**NOTE**

Typing **U** actually executes the simple **U** command, which undoes the last command. Selecting the **Undo** tool executes a command called **UNDO**. Although the two commands often have the same effect, **U** is not an alias for **UNDO,** which has more elaborate capabilities, as indicated by the options on the command line. **REDO** can be used to reverse either **U** or **UNDO**. Also note that **R** is not an alias for **REDO**.

✔ Click the **Redo** tool, which is to the right of the **Undo** tool on the **Quick Access** toolbar.

> *This redoes the line you have just undone. AutoCAD keeps track of everything undone in a single drawing session, so you can redo a number of undone actions.*

## Erasing Lines

The **ERASE** command is not explored fully in this chapter, but for now you may want to have access to this important command in its simplest form. Using **ERASE** brings up the techniques of object selection that are common to all editing commands. The simplest form of object selection requires that you point to an object and press the pick button. Try the following:

✔ Select the **Erase** tool from the **Modify** panel of the ribbon, as shown in Figure 1-29.

> *When you enter a modify command, such as **ERASE**, the crosshairs disappear, leaving only the pickbox for selecting objects.*

**Figure 1-29**
**Erase** tool

✔ Move the pickbox so that it is over one of the lines on your screen, as shown in Figure 1-30.

> *When the pickbox touches the line, the line becomes thickened and dashed, as shown in the figure. This is an AutoCAD feature called **rollover highlighting**. As your pickbox rolls over an object, it is highlighted before you select it, so that you can be certain that you are selecting the object you want.*

**rollover highlighting:** A feature that causes geometry on the screen to be highlighted when the pickbox passes over it. This is a visual aid in object selection.

✔ Press the pick button to select the line.

> *The line becomes dotted, indicating that it has been selected.*

✔ Right-click or press **<Enter>** or the spacebar to complete the command.

> *The line disappears.*

✔ Before going on, use **U** or **ERASE** to remove all lines from your drawing, leaving a blank drawing area.

> *Be aware that undoing **ERASE** causes a line to reappear.*

## Ortho Mode

Before completing this section on line drawing, we suggest that you try **Ortho** mode and polar tracking.

✔ Select the **Line** tool from the ribbon.

✔ Pick a starting point. Any point near the middle of the grid will do.

✔ Pick the **Dynamic Input** button to turn off dynamic input.

> *Turning dynamic input off will make it easier to see what is happening with **Ortho** and polar tracking.*

**Figure 1-30**
Rollover highlighting

✔ Pick the **Ortho Mode** button, the fourth from the left on the status bar, to turn **Ortho** mode on.

✔ Move the cursor in slow circles.

*Notice how the rubber band jumps between horizontal and vertical without sweeping through any of the angles between. **Ortho** forces the pointing device to pick up points only along the horizontal and vertical quadrant lines from a given starting point. With **Ortho** on, you can select points at 0°, 90°, 180°, and 270° of rotation from your starting point only (see Figure 1-31).*

**Figure 1-31**
**Ortho** directions

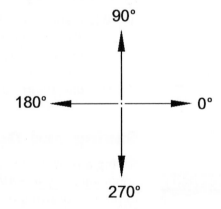

*The advantages of **Ortho** are similar to those of **Snap** mode, except that it limits angular rather than linear increments. It ensures that you get precise and true right angles and perpendiculars easily when that is your intent. **Ortho** becomes more important as drawings grow more complex. In this chapter it is hardly necessary, but it is convenient in Drawings 1-1 and 1-3.*

## Polar Tracking

Polar tracking is an AutoCAD feature that can replace **Ortho** mode in many instances. Try it using the following steps:

✔ Pick the **Polar Tracking** button, the fifth from the left on the status bar, to turn on polar tracking.

*Notice that polar tracking and **Ortho** are mutually exclusive. They cannot both be on at the same time. When you turn polar tracking on, **Ortho** shuts off automatically.*

✔ Move your cursor in a slow circle around the starting point of your line, just as you did with **Ortho** on.

*With polar tracking on, when the rubber band crosses a vertical or horizontal axis (i.e., when the rubber band is at 0°, 90°, 180°, or 270°), a dotted line appears that extends to the edge of the drawing area. This will be more visible on the horizontal than on the vertical. You also see a tooltip label, similar to the dynamic input display, giving a value such as Polar 4.5000<0° (see Figure 1-32). The value is a polar coordinate. By default, polar tracking is set to respond on the orthogonal axes. Polar tracking can be set to track at any angle. In fact, if your polar tracking is picking up angles other than 0°, 90°, 180°, and 270°, it means that someone has changed this setting in your system.*

**Figure 1-32**
Polar tracking

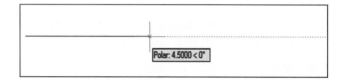

Polar: 4.5000 < 0°

✔ Pick the **Polar Tracking** button to turn polar tracking off.

✔ Move the crosshairs in a circle and observe that polar tracking and **Ortho** are no longer in effect.

## The <Esc> Key

✔ While still in the **LINE** command, press the **<Esc>** (escape) key.

*This aborts the **LINE** command and brings back the command prompt. **<Esc>** is used to cancel a command that has been entered. Sometimes it is necessary to press **<Esc>** twice to exit a command and return to the command prompt.*

## Saving and Opening Your Drawings

Saving a drawing in AutoCAD is just like saving a file in other Windows applications. Use **SAVE** to save an already named drawing. Use **SAVEAS** to name a drawing or to save an already named drawing under a new name. In all cases, a .dwg extension is added automatically to file names to identify them as AutoCAD drawing files.

## The SAVE and SAVEAS Commands

**Figure 1-33**
Save tool

To save your drawing without leaving the drawing window, select the **Save** tool from the **Quick Access** toolbar, as shown in Figure 1-33.

**Figure 1-34**
Save Drawing As dialog box

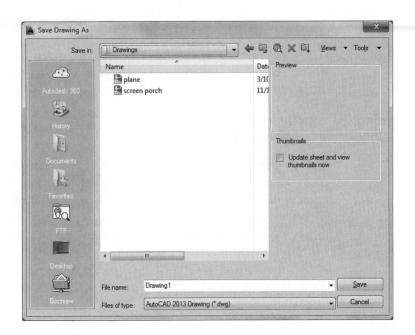

If the current drawing has been previously saved, AutoCAD saves it without an intervening dialog box. If it has not, AutoCAD opens the **Save Drawing As** dialog box, shown in Figure 1-34, and allows you to give the file a new name and location before it is saved. The **Save Drawing As** dialog box is also opened if you select the **Save As . . .** tool, to the right of the **Save** tool.

Enter a name in the **File name:** box. If necessary, you can browse to a different location by clicking on the arrow next to the box at the top labeled **Save in:**. A list of drives and folders opens, and you can select a location from the list.

The **Save Drawing As** dialog box is one of several standard file selection dialog boxes. These boxes all have a very similar format. There is a **File name:** and a **Files of type:** edit box at the bottom, a list of places to look or places to save a file on the left, and a **Look in:** or **Save in:** list at the top. The places list on the left includes standard locations on your own computer. There is an **Autodesk 360** folder, a **History** folder, a **Documents** folder, a **Favorites** folder, your computer's **Desktop,** a folder for **File Transfer Protocol (FTP)** sites for downloading from the Internet, and a link to Autodesk's **Buzzsaw** website. **Buzzsaw** provides project sites where designers can make versions of their drawings available to others on a project team so that collaboration can be facilitated through Internet access.

## Opening Saved Drawings

To open a previously saved drawing, select the **Open** tool from the **Quick Access** toolbar, just to the left of the **Save** tool.

This method brings up the **Select File** dialog box. This is another standard file selection dialog box. It is identical to the **Save Drawing As** dialog box, except that **Save in:** has been replaced by **Look in:**. In this **Select File** dialog box, you can select a file folder or Internet location from the places list on the left or from a directory in the middle. When you select a file, AutoCAD shows a preview image of the selected drawing in the **Preview image** box at the right. This way you can be sure that you are opening the drawing you want.

## Exiting the Drawing Window

To leave AutoCAD click the Windows close button (**X**) at the upper right of the screen. If you have not saved your current drawing, AutoCAD asks you whether you want to save your changes before exiting.

## Getting Started

In this last section we take you through a complete drawing session. We create a new drawing, make some basic changes to the drawing space, draw a simple object, save the drawing, and plot or print it. You will be drawing the image called *Grate* in Figure 1-35. Most of the procedures needed have already been covered in this chapter, but there will be new information, particularly regarding the **PLOT** command. We will provide discussion only where necessary to introduce new information. Here we go.

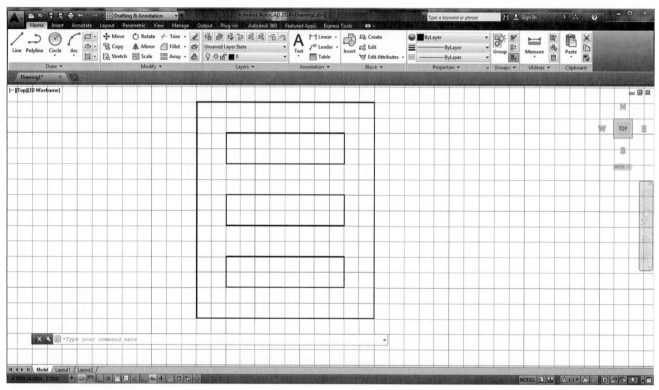

**Figure 1-35**
*Grate* drawing

✔ Type **<Ctrl>+N** or select the **New** tool from the **Quick Access** toolbar.

✔ Press **<Enter>** to accept the default acad.dwt template file.

✔ Pick the **Snap Mode** button so that **Snap** mode is on.

✔ Type **z <Enter>**.

✔ Type **a <Enter>**.

✔ Select the **Line** tool from the ribbon.

✔ Pick the point (3,1).

✔ Pick the point (9,1).

> *You have now drawn the bottom line in the image in Figure 1-35.*

✔ Continuing in the **LINE** command, draw a line from (9,1) to (9,8).

✔ Continuing in the **LINE** command, draw a line from (9,8) to (3,8).

✔ Type **c <Enter>** for the **Close** option, or right-click and pick **Close** from the shortcut menu.

> *The **Close** option draws a line back to the first point (3,1). This completes the outer rectangle in Figure 1-35.*

---

**TIP**

The **Close** option connects the last in a continuous series of lines back to the starting point of the series. In drawing a rectangle, for instance, you simply type **c** in lieu of drawing the last of the four lines. For this to work, the whole rectangle must be drawn without leaving the **LINE** command.

---

✔ Press the spacebar to repeat the **LINE** command.

✔ Pick points (4,2), (8,2), (8,3), and (4,3), and then type **c <Enter>**.
> *This completes the bottom inner rectangle in Figure 1-35.*

✔ Press the spacebar to repeat the **LINE** command.

✔ Pick points (4,4), (8,4), (8,5), and (4,5), and then type **c <Enter>**.
> *This completes the middle rectangle in Figure 1-35.*

✔ Press the spacebar to repeat the **LINE** command.

✔ Pick points (4,6), (8,6), (8,7), and (4,7), and then type **c <Enter>**.
> *This completes the top inner rectangle in Figure 1-35.*

Your first drawing is now complete.

✔ Select the **Grid Display** button to turn off the grid and see your completed drawing.

✔ Select the **Save** tool from the **Quick Access** toolbar.

*At this point you should get specific directions from your instructor regarding where your drawings should be saved. We will use a generic path. Please insert the specific path you are instructed to use, or open the **Save in:** list and navigate to the location where your drawing will be saved.*

✔ In the **File name:** box, type the drawing name *Grate*, preceded by the path designation provided by your instructor, if necessary. For example:

> C:\documents and settings\owner\my documents\autocad drawings\grate

If you have followed the preceding steps correctly, you now have a drawing called *Grate* saved in a folder on your computer or on an attached memory device, and you have the drawing on your screen.

## Plotting or Printing Your Drawing

Here we provide a simple plotting procedure that will allow you to get your drawing out to a printer or plotter. There will be minimal explanation.

✔ Select the **Plot** tool from the **Quick Access** toolbar, as shown in Figure 1-36.

*This opens the **Plot – Model** dialog box shown in Figure 1-37.*
***Model** is added to the dialog box title because we are plotting directly from model space rather than using a paper space layout.*

**Figure 1-36**
**Plot** tool

**Figure 1-37**
**Plot – Model** dialog box

✔ Look at the second panel in the dialog box, labeled **Printer/plotter.** If a printer or plotter is selected you can move on. If the **Name:** box indicates "None", open the list by clicking the arrow at the right and select the name of a plotter or printer connected to your computer or network.

✔ Look at the list under **What to plot:** in the **Plot area** panel.

✔ Click the arrow to open the list.

✔ Select **Limits.**

✔ Now, click the **Preview** button at the bottom of the dialog box.
*You should see a preview similar to the one shown in Figure 1-38. This preview shows what your drawing sheet will look like if you choose to send your drawing to a printer or plotter.*

✔ Press **<Esc>** to return to the dialog box.

✔ Press **OK** to send the drawing to your plotter or **Cancel** if you do not wish to print at this time.
*You are now well prepared to complete, save, and plot any of the drawings at the end of this chapter.*

**Figure 1-38**
Plot preview

# Chapter Summary

In this chapter you became familiar with the basic elements of the AutoCAD drawing window. You know how to use and control some essential features of the **Drafting & Annotation** workspace, including the **Quick Access** toolbar, the coordinate display, the mode buttons, and the ribbon. You can specify drawing points using absolute, polar, and relative coordinates and by pointing using your mouse and the screen crosshairs. You can create a new drawing using a template, switch drawing modes on and off, draw and erase lines, and save your drawing under a new name. You can use the **Plot** dialog box to complete a simple plot based on the limits of your drawing. The drawings at the end of the chapter will put all of these features to work. Completing them will give you a firm foundation in all of these skills, which you will use from now on whenever you enter the AutoCAD drawing space.

# Chapter Test Questions

## Multiple Choice

*Circle the correct answer.*

1. Three modes of the coordinate display are:
   a. Gray, white, invisible
   b. Static, dynamic, polar
   c. Polar, absolute, relative
   d. Accessible, hidden, visible

2. The tool that does **not** appear on the **Quick Access** toolbar is:
   a. **Help**                      c. **New**
   b. **Redo**                      d. **Save As . . .**

3. The numbers on the coordinate display show positions in a:
   a. Matrix coordinate system
   b. Quadratic coordinate system
   c. Graphic coordinate system
   d. Cartesian coordinate system

4. The set of visual aids and command options that move with the crosshairs is called:
   a. Dynamic input display          c. Cursor
   b. Coordinate display             d. Shortcut menu

5. In model space, objects are drawn to:
   a. Scale                          c. Real-world measurements
   b. Fit                            d. CAD standards

## Matching

*Write the number of the correct answer on the line.*

a. Grid display _____          1. 6.5 < 45,0
b. Polar coordinates _____     2. (9.54,6.66)
c. Absolute coordinates _____  3. Limits point selection
d. Relative coordinates _____  4. Visible but not plotted
e. **Snap** mode _____         5. @7,7

## True or False

*Circle the correct answer.*

1. **True or False:** The command line is the best place to enter AutoCAD commands.

2. **True or False:** Snap makes some points impossible to select with the screen cursor.

3. **True or False:** The ribbon gives quick access to all AutoCAD commands.

4. **True or False:** The right mouse button calls up shortcut menus according to context.

5. **True or False:** The # sign indicates that you are going to enter polar coordinates.

## Questions

1. What are the advantages of using the ribbon to enter commands?

2. What are the three different modes of the coordinate display, and how does each mode appear? How do you switch between modes?

3. What is heads-up design? Give three examples of heads-up design features from this chapter.

4. You have just entered the point (1,1,0) and you now wish to enter the point 2 units straight up from this point. How would you identify this point using absolute, relative, and polar coordinates?

5. What is the value and limitation of having **Snap** mode on?

## Drawing Problems

1. Draw a line from (3,2) to (4,8) using the keyboard only.

2. Draw a line from (6,6) to (7,5) using the mouse only.

3. Draw a line from (6,6) to (6,8) using dynamic input.

4. Undo (**U**) all lines on your screen.

5. Draw a square with the corners at (2,2), (7,2), (7,7), and (2,7). Then erase it using the **ERASE** command.

## WWW Exercise (Optional)

AutoCAD is a fully integrated Internet program. If you have Internet access, you can access websites directly from within the AutoCAD program. You must first be connected to your Internet service provider. Once connected, you can move easily in and out of AutoCAD as you access all the resources available on the Web, including **Autodesk 360**, the Autodesk cloud-based file sharing platform. AutoCAD drawings can be published to the Web, transferred as e-mail attachments, uploaded, downloaded, and included as part of websites and home pages. To facilitate your learning, we have a companion website that you are encouraged to access. At this site you will find self-scoring tests, special Web projects related to the material in the chapter, and links to other important and interesting CAD-related websites.

In this chapter we show you how to access Autodesk.com and then take you to our companion website. Once there, take the tests or go to the Web Project page for further instructions.

✔ First, you must be sure that you are connected to an Internet service provider.

> *You may already be connected to the Internet, depending on your system. If you are not, you need to go through a log-in procedure. In most cases, AutoCAD automatically initiates your log-in procedure when you enter a Web command. If this does not happen, do not exit AutoCAD, but use the **Minimize** button (the third button from the right at the top of the screen, with the minus sign) to temporarily leave the AutoCAD drawing window. We cannot give you specific instructions for connecting to the Internet from your system. For these, consult your Internet software documentation, instructor, or system manager.*

✔ If necessary, after connecting to the Internet, click the AutoCAD icon on the Windows taskbar to return to the AutoCAD drawing window.

✔ At the command prompt, type **browser <Enter>**.

> *This is the **BROWSER** command, through which you can access Internet addresses, local network addresses, or locations on your own computer. AutoCAD prompts for an address:*

[Enter Web location (URL)] <http:www.autodesk.com>:

> *The default location is shown within the brackets (< >) and may be different from the one shown here. It can be any valid location on your computer or on the Internet. It is possible to change the default location, but we do not discuss this topic here. As shown, the out-of-the-box default Internet location is Autodesk's own website, http://www.autodesk.com. Pressing **<Enter>** at this prompt takes you directly to this website.*

---

**NOTE**

All descriptions and illustrations of Web pages were current as of the printing of this text. Websites can and should change, so by the time you read this, things may look different.

---

**Figure 1-39**
Autodesk website

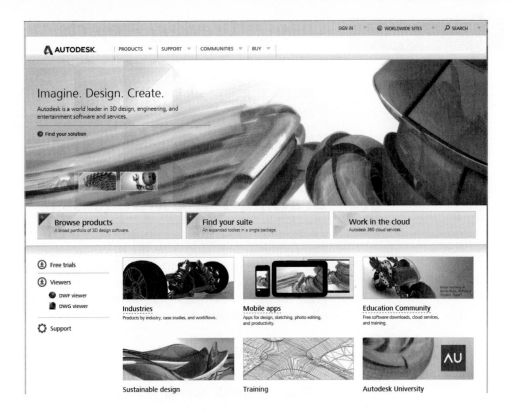

✔ Press **<Enter>** to accept the default website.

> *Wait. . . . If your Internet connection is in order, you will see the Autodesk website home page, as shown in Figure 1-39, or whatever website is the default location on your system.*

## Our Companion Website

On our helpful companion website you will find self-scoring tests, special Web projects, and links to other important and interesting CAD-related websites. To reach any website that is not the current default Web location, type the address at the command line.

✔ Close the Autodesk website.

✔ At the command prompt, type **browser <Enter>,** or press **<Enter>** to repeat the **BROWSER** command.

> *AutoCAD prompts for an address:*

> [Enter Web location (URL)] <http:www.autodesk.com>:

✔ Type www.pearsonhighered.com/dixriley **<Enter>**.

> *If you are properly configured and connected, this opens our companion website home page.*

✔ Select the Companion Website link for *Discovering AutoCAD 2014*, and enjoy your visit!

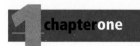
chapter one

# Chapter Drawing Projects

**NOTE**

Units in AutoCAD can represent many different units of measurement. In some cases we use the word *unit* generically when there is no need to refer to specific units such as feet, inches, centimeters, or kilometers.

## **G** Drawing 1-1: *Guide* [BASIC]

Before beginning, look over the drawing page. The first two drawings in this chapter are given without dimensions. Instead, we have drawn them as you will see them on the screen, against the background of a half-unit grid. All these drawings were done using the default half-unit snap, but all points are found on one-unit increments.

### Drawing Suggestions

- If you are beginning a new drawing, type **<Ctrl>+N** or select the **New** tool from the **Quick Access** toolbar.

- Ensure that acad is entered in the **File name:** box of the **Select template** dialog box, and press **<Enter>** to complete the dialog.

- Remember to watch the coordinate display or dynamic input display when searching for a point.

- Be sure that **Snap Mode, Grid Display,** and **Dynamic Input** are all turned on and that **Infer Constraints, Object Snap, 3D Object Snap, Object Snap Tracking, Dynamic UCS, Lineweight,** and **Quick Properties** are turned off. **Ortho Mode** or **Polar Tracking** can be on or off as you wish. **Transparency, Selection Cycling,** and **Annotation Monitor** will have no effect and can also be on or off.

- Draw the outer perimeter first. It is 10 units wide and 7 units high, and its lower left-hand corner is at the point (1.0000,1.0000).

- The **Close** option can be used in all four of the rectangles and squares.

### If You Make a Mistake—U

This is a reminder that you can stay in the **LINE** command as you undo the last line you drew, or the last two or three if you have drawn a series.

- Type **U <Enter>.** The last line you drew will be gone or replaced by the rubber band, awaiting a new endpoint. If you want to go back more than one line, type **U** again, as many times as you need to.

- If you have already left the **LINE** command, the **U** command undoes the last continuous series of lines.

- Remember, if you have mistakenly undone something, you can get it back by using the **Redo** tool. You cannot perform other commands between **U** and **REDO,** but you can redo several **UNDO** commands if they have been done sequentially.

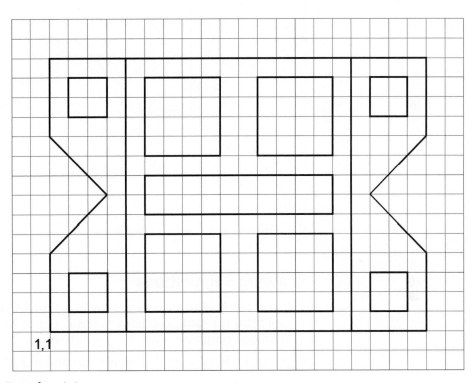

**Drawing 1-1**
Guide

## G Drawing 1-2: *Design #1* [BASIC]

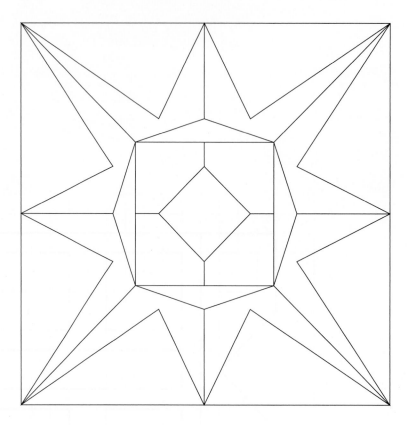

## Drawing Suggestions

- If you are beginning a new drawing, type **<Ctrl>+N** or select the **New** tool from the **Quick Access** toolbar, check to see that you are using the acad.dwt template, and press **<Enter>.**
- Draw the large outside square starting at (2.0000, 1.0000).
- Draw the small inside square.
- Now, connect the lines from the outside square to the inside square.
- Continue connecting lines until the drawing is complete.
- You will need to make sure **Ortho** is off to do this drawing.

## Repeating a Command

Remember, you can repeat a command by pressing **<Enter>** or the space-bar at the command prompt. This is useful in this drawing because you have several sets of lines to draw.

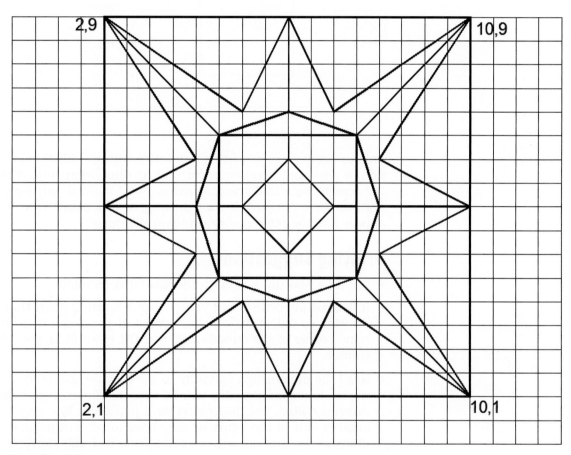

**Drawing 1-2**
Design #1

# Drawing 1-3: *Shim* [INTERMEDIATE]

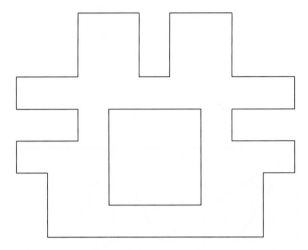

This drawing gives you further practice with the **LINE** command. In addition, it gives you practice in translating dimensions into distances on the screen. Note that the dimensions are included only for your information; they are not part of your drawing at this point. Your drawing should appear like the reference drawing on this page.

## Drawing Suggestions

- Create a new drawing with the acad.dwt template.

- It is most important that you choose a starting point that positions the drawing so that it fits on your screen. If you begin with the bottom left-hand corner of the outside figure at the point (3,1), you should have no trouble.

- Read the dimensions carefully to see how the geometry of the drawing works. It is good practice to look over the dimensions before you begin drawing. Often, the dimension for a particular line may be located on another side of the figure or may have to be extrapolated from other dimensions. It is not uncommon to misread, misinterpret, or miscalculate a dimension, so take your time.

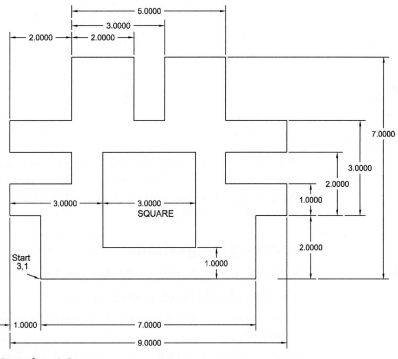

**Drawing 1-3**
Shim

**Drawing 1-4: *Stamp* [INTERMEDIATE]**

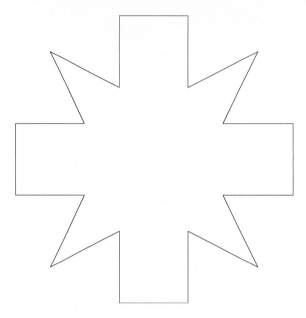

This drawing gives you practice in point selection. You can begin anywhere and use any of the point selection methods introduced in this chapter. We recommend that you try them all, including the use of direct distance entry and the **<Tab>** key.

## Drawing Suggestions

- Create a new drawing with the acad.dwt template.
- **Ortho** should be off to do this drawing.
- The entire drawing can be done without leaving the **LINE** command if you wish.
- If you do leave **LINE,** remember that you can repeat **LINE** by pressing **<Enter>** or the spacebar, and then select the last point as a new start point by pressing **<Enter>** or the spacebar again.
- Plan to use point selection by typing, by pointing, and by direct distance entry. Make use of absolute, relative, and polar coordinates.

**Drawing 1-4**
Stamp

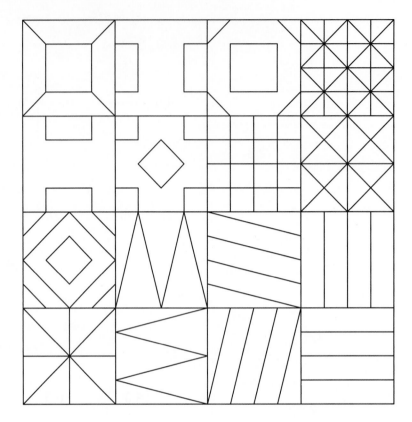

This drawing will give you lots of practice with the **LINE** command. All points are on the 0.50 grid, and the dimensions on the drawing page give all the information you need to complete the drawing.

## Drawing Suggestions

• Begin by drawing an 8 × 8 square.

• Be sure to make frequent use of the spacebar to repeat the **LINE** command.

• Add sixteen 2″-square tile outlines.

• Fill in the geometry in each of the 2″ squares.

**Drawing 1-5**
Tiles

**G** **Drawing 1-6:** *Multi Wrench* [ADVANCED]

This problem is drawn on a square grid. You do not have to draw the grid lines, just the wrench itself. Use your grid display in place of the grid lines to locate points. The grid lines are 0.50 unit apart, so they will match your default grid display setting. The dimensions of the object can be obtained from observing the grid lines.

## Drawing Suggestions

- Because all points are on snap points, it is essential that **Snap Mode** and **Grid Display** be on as you draw.

- Start at (1,2.5) and draw the outline of the wrench first.

- Draw the inner geometry within the wrench.

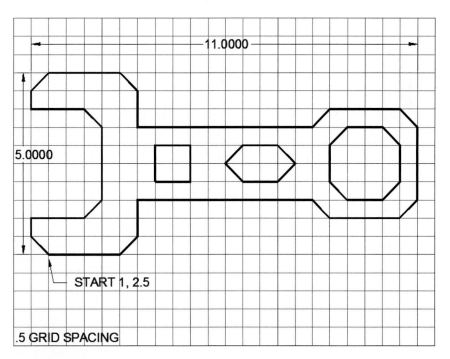

11.0000

5.0000

START 1, 2.5

.5 GRID SPACING

**Drawing 1-6**
Multi Wrench

# 2 chaptertwo

# Circles and Drawing Aids

## CHAPTER OBJECTIVES

- Change the grid setting
- Change the snap setting
- Change units
- Draw circles by specifying a center point and a radius
- Draw circles by specifying a center point and a diameter

- Access AutoCAD online Help features
- Use the **ERASE** command
- Use single-point object snap
- Use the **RECTANG** command
- Customize your workspace
- Plot or print a drawing

### Introduction

In this chapter, you begin to gain control of your drawing environment by changing the spacing of the grid and snap and the units in which coordinates are displayed. You add to your repertoire of objects by drawing circles with the **CIRCLE** command and rectangles with the **RECTANG** command. You explore the many methods of object selection as you continue to learn editing procedures with the **ERASE** command. You gain access to convenient Help features and begin to learn AutoCAD's extensive plotting and printing procedures.

# Changing the Grid Setting

> **TIP**
>
> A general procedure for changing the grid spacing at the command prompt is:
>
> 1. Type **grid <Enter>**.
> 2. Enter a new value.

When you begin a new drawing using the acad.dwt template, the grid and snap are set with a spacing of 0.5000 unit. You can complete drawings without altering the grid and snap settings from the default value. But usually, you will want to change this to a value that reflects your project. You may want a 10-mile snap for a mapping project or a 0.010″ snap for a printed circuit diagram. The grid can match the snap setting or can be set independently.

✔ Create a new drawing by selecting the **New** tool from the **Quick Access** toolbar.

✔ Check to see that acad is in the **File name:** box and press **<Enter>**.
*Once again, this ensures that you begin with the settings we have used in preparing this chapter.*

✔ Turn on **Snap Mode** and **Grid Display.**

✔ Type **z <Enter>** to execute the **ZOOM** command.

## Picking Options from the Command Line

We take this opportunity to demonstrate picking an option from the command line. Notice the blue and gray highlighting on the uppercase letters in each option of this prompt from the **ZOOM** command. In 2014, these letters may be picked just as options on a menu would be. Instead of typing the letter **A** to execute the **All** option, you can pick the word **All** from the command line, as shown in Figure 2-1.

**Figure 2-1**

Picking options from the command line

✔ Pick the highlighted letter **A** for **All** in the command line, as shown.
*The grid is now centered and zoomed to the limits of the drawing. You can pick an option from the command line this way any time you have options showing.*

✔ Type **grid <Enter>**.
*The command line prompt appears like this, with options separated by spaces:*

> Specify grid spacing(X) or [ON OFF Snap Major aDaptive Limits Follow Aspect]<0.5000>:

*If dynamic input is on, you also see part of this prompt next to the crosshairs. You can ignore the options for now. The number 0.5000 shows the current setting.*

✔ In answer to the prompt, type **1 <Enter>** and watch what happens.
   *The screen changes to show a 1-unit grid.*

✔ Try other grid settings. Try **2, 0.25,** and **0.125.**
   *Remember that you can repeat the last command, **GRID,** by pressing **<Enter>** or the spacebar.*

✔ Before going on to the next section, set the grid back to **0.5000.**

## Changing the Snap Setting

> **TIP**
>
> A general procedure for changing the snap setting in the **Drafting Settings** dialog box is:
>
> 1. Right-click the **Grid Display** or **Snap Mode** button and select **Settings.**
> 2. Enter a new snap value.
> 3. Click **OK** to exit the dialog box.

Grid and snap are similar enough to cause confusion. The grid is only a visual reference. It has no effect on selection of points. Snap is invisible, but it dramatically affects point selection. Grid and snap may or may not have the same setting.

## Using the Drafting Settings Dialog Box

Snap can be changed using the **SNAP** command at the prompt, as we did with the **GRID** command in the last section. Both can also be changed in the **Drafting Settings** dialog box, as we do here.

✔ Right-click on the **Snap Mode** or **Grid Display** button and select **Settings** from the shortcut menu, as shown in Figure 2-2.

**Figure 2-2**
Shortcut menu

This opens the **Drafting Settings** dialog box shown in Figure 2-3. **DSETTINGS** is the command that calls up this dialog box, and **ds** is the command alias. Look at the dialog box. It contains some common features, including tabs, check boxes, panels, and edit boxes. When you open from the shortcut menu, the **Snap and Grid** tab should be selected as shown. If not, select it now.

Figure 2-3
**Drafting Settings** dialog
box

✔ If the **Snap and Grid** window is not on top, click its tab to bring it up.

Below the tabs you will see check boxes labeled **Snap On (F9)** and
**Grid On (F7).** You can turn snap and grid on and off by picking the appropriate check box. In your dialog box, check boxes should show that both
snap and grid are on.

> **NOTE**
> • The dialog box has places to set both *x* and *y* spacing. It is unlikely that you want to
> have a grid or snap matrix with different horizontal and vertical increments, but the
> capacity is there if you do.
> • Commands that call dialog boxes, like other commands, can be repeated by pressing
> the spacebar or <Enter>.

The snap and grid settings are shown in edit boxes labeled **Snap X
spacing, Snap Y spacing, Grid X spacing,** and **Grid Y spacing.** You can
double-click in the edit box to highlight the entire text, or point and click
once anywhere inside the box to do partial editing.

To change the snap setting, do the following:

✔ Double-click inside the edit box labeled **Snap X spacing.**
  *The entire number 0.5000 in the **Snap X spacing** box should be
  highlighted.*

✔ Type **1 <Enter>.**

Pressing **<Enter>** at this point is the same as clicking **OK** in the dialog
box. It takes you out of the dialog box and back to the screen.

Snap is now set at 1, and grid is still at 0.5. This makes the snap
setting larger than the grid setting.

✔ Type **L** or select the **Line** tool from the ribbon.
*This enters the **LINE** command. In AutoCAD, you must execute a drawing command before snap affects point selection.*

✔ Move the cursor around the screen.
*You will see that you can access only half the grid line intersections. This type of arrangement is not too useful. Try some other settings.*

✔ Open the dialog box again by right-clicking the **Snap Mode** button on the status bar and then choosing **Settings** from the shortcut menu.

✔ Change the **Snap X spacing** value to **0.25**.
*Move the cursor slowly and observe the coordinate display. This is a more efficient arrangement. With grid set coarser than snap, you can still pick exact points easily, but the grid is not so dense as to be distracting.*

✔ Press **<Enter>** or the spacebar to open the **Drafting Settings** dialog box again.

✔ Set the snap to **0.05**.

✔ Move the cursor and watch the coordinate display.
*Observe how the snap setting is reflected in the available coordinates. How small a snap will AutoCAD accept?*

✔ Try **0.005**.
*Move the cursor and observe the coordinate display.*

✔ Try **0.0005**.
*You could even try 0.0001, but this would be like turning snap off because the coordinate display is registering four decimal places anyway. Unlike the grid, which is limited by the size and resolution of your screen, you can set snap to any value you like. If you try a grid setting that is too small, AutoCAD will default to a larger grid.*

✔ Press **<Esc>** to exit the **LINE** command.

✔ Finally, before you leave this section, set the snap back to **0.25** and leave the grid at 0.5.

---

**TIP**

If you wish to keep snap and grid the same, set the grid to **0** in the **Drafting Settings** dialog box, or enter the **GRID** command and type **s** for the **Snap** option. The grid then changes to match the snap and continues to change whenever you reset the snap. To free the grid, just give it its own value again.

| UNITS | |
|---|---|
| **Command** | Units |
| **Alias** | Un |
| **Menu** | Format |
| **Tool** | [0.0] |

## Changing Units

**TIP**

A general procedure for changing units is:

1. Type **Units <Enter>**.
2. Answer the prompts.

## The Drawing Units Dialog Box

The **Drawing Units** dialog box makes use of drop-down lists, another common dialog box feature.

✔ Type **Units <Enter>.**

> *This opens the **Drawing Units** dialog box shown in Figure 2-4. This dialog box has six drop-down lists for specifying various characteristics of linear and angular drawing units. Drop-down lists show a current setting next to an arrow that is used to open the list of other possibilities. Your dialog box should show that the current **Length Type** in your drawing is decimal units precise to 0.0000 places, and **Angle Type** is decimal degrees with 0 places. Notice also the **Sample Output** area that gives examples of the current units.*

**Figure 2-4**
**Drawing Units** dialog box

✔ Pick the arrow to the right of the word **Decimal**, under **Type** in the **Length** panel of the dialog box.

> *A list drops down with the following options:*

>> Architectural
>> Decimal
>> Engineering
>> Fractional
>> Scientific

> *Architectural units display feet and fractional inches (1'-3 1/2"), engineering units display feet and decimal inches (1'-3.50"), fractional units display units in a mixed-number format (15 1/2), and scientific units use exponential notation for the display of very large*

*or very small numbers (1.55E + 01). With the exception of engineering and architectural formats, these formats can be used with any basic unit of measurement. For example, decimal mode works for metric units as well as English units.*

*In this chapter, we stick to decimal units. If you are designing a house, you are more likely to use architectural units. If you are building a bridge, you might want engineering units. You might want to use scientific units if you are mapping subatomic particles.*

*Whatever your application, once you know how to change units, you can do so at any time. However, as a drawing practice it is best to choose appropriate units when you first begin work on a new drawing.*

✔ Select **Decimal,** or click anywhere outside the list box to close the list without changing the setting.

*Now, we will change the precision setting to two-place decimals.*

✔ Click the down arrow next to 0.0000 in the **Precision** list box in the **Length** panel.

*This opens a list with options ranging from 0 to 0.00000000, as shown in Figure 2-5.*

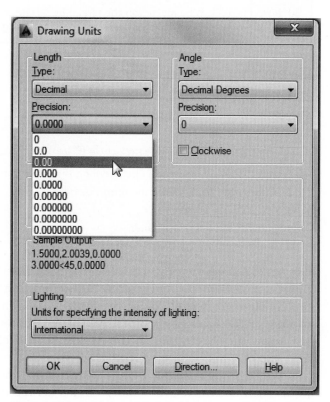

**Figure 2-5**
**Precision** list

*We use two-place decimals because they are more common than any other choice.*

✔ Pick **0.00** from the list, as shown in Figure 2-5.

*The list closes, and 0.00 replaces 0.0000 as the current precision for units of length. Notice that the sample output has also changed to reflect the new setting.*

*The area to the right allows you to change the units in which angular measures, including polar coordinates, are displayed. If you open the* **Angle Type** *list, you see the following options:*

Decimal Degrees
Deg/Min/Sec
Grads
Radians
Surveyor's Unit

*The default system is standard decimal degrees with 0 decimal places, measured counterclockwise, with 0° being straight out to the right (3 o'clock), 90° straight up (12 o'clock), 180° to the left (9 o'clock), and 270° straight down (6 o'clock). We will leave these settings alone.*

✔ Check to see that you have two-place decimal units for length and zero-place decimal degree units for angles.

✔ Pick **OK** to close the dialog box.

---

**TIP**

All dialog boxes can be moved on the screen by picking the blue title area at the top of the dialog box, holding down the pick button, and dragging the box across the screen.

---

## Drawing Circles by Specifying a Center Point and a Radius

| CIRCLE | |
|---|---|
| **Command** | Circle |
| **Alias** | C |
| **Panel** | Draw |
| **Tool** | |

---

**TIP**

A general procedure for drawing a circle is:

1. Pick the arrow below the **Circle** tool on the **Draw** panel of the ribbon.
2. Pick **Center, Radius** from the drop-down list.
3. Pick a center point.
4. Enter or show a radius value.

---

Circles can be drawn by specifying a center point and a radius, a center point and a diameter, two points that determine a diameter, three points on the circle's circumference, two tangent points on other objects and a radius, or three tangent points. All these options appear on a drop-down list below the **Circle** tool on the ribbon. In this chapter, we use only the first two options.

We begin by drawing a circle with radius 3 and center at the point (6,5). Then, we draw two smaller circles centered at the same point. Later we erase them using the **ERASE** command.

---

**NOTE**

The tool that appears on the ribbon changes with the last option selected. If **Center, Radius** was the last **CIRCLE** command option used, the **Center, Radius** tool will be displayed on the ribbon. In this case, **Center, Radius** can be executed without opening the list.

---

✔ Grid should be set to **0.50,** snap to **0.25,** and units to **two-place decimal.**

**Figure 2-6**
**Circle** tool – drop-down list

✔ Pick the arrow below the **Circle** tool on the ribbon, as illustrated in Figure 2-6.

> *This opens the drop-down list shown in the figure. There are many drop-down lists on the ribbon. They allow access to more commands and options without adding to the screen area taken up by the ribbon.* **Center, Radius** *is at the top of the list.*

✔ Select **Center, Radius** from the top of the drop-down list.

> *The command prompt is*

> Specify center point for circle or [3P 2P Ttr (tan tan radius)]:

✔ Pick the center point of the circle you want to draw. In our case, it is the point (6,5).

> *AutoCAD assumes that a radius or diameter will follow and shows the following prompt:*

> Specify radius of circle or [Diameter]:

> *If we type or point to a value now, AutoCAD takes it as a radius because that is the default. Diameter is the only other option still available.*

✔ Move your cursor and observe the rubber band and dragged circle. If your dynamic input display is not on, turn it on by picking the **Dynamic Input** button.

> *Dynamic input is a great feature for drawing circles. It will give you the radius or diameter of the circle you are drawing.*

✔ Watch the dynamic input display and pick a point 3.00 away from the center point.

> *With snap on, you will find that you can move exactly 3.00 only if you are at 0°, 90°, 180°, or 270°.*

> *Your first circle should now be complete.*

---

**TIP**

Another way to create multiple objects of the same type is to use the **Add Selected** option from a shortcut menu. Select an object, right-click to open the shortcut menu, and select **Add Selected** from the menu. This will initiate the command to add an object of the same type you have selected. This method will not enter options. If you don't enter an option, the default option is assumed.

---

✔ Draw two more circles using the same center point, radius method. They should be centered at (6,5) and have radii of 2.50 and 2.00. Use the spacebar to repeat the command or pick the **Center, Radius** tool from the ribbon.

> *The results are illustrated in Figure 2-7.*

## Drawing Circles by Specifying a Center Point and a Diameter

We will draw three more circles centered on (6,5) having diameters of 1, 1.5, and 2. This method of drawing circles is similar to the radius method, except you will see that the rubber band and dynamic input display work differently.

**Figure 2-7**
Circles drawn using **Center, Radius**

✔ Open the **Circle** drop-down list on the ribbon and pick **Center, Diameter.**

✔ Pick the center point at (6,5).

✔ Move the crosshairs away from the center point.

Notice that the crosshairs are now outside the circle you are dragging on the screen (see Figure 2-8). This is because AutoCAD is looking for a diameter, but the last point you gave was a center point. So, the diameter is being measured from the center point out, twice the radius. Also notice that the dynamic input display has responded to the diameter specification and is now measuring the diameter of the circle. Move the cursor around, in and out from the center point, to get a feel for this.

> **NOTE**
> Pressing <Enter> or the spacebar to repeat a command will not repeat the option, unless it is the default option. In this case, the command will default to the **Radius** option, not the **Diameter** option.

✔ Pick a diameter of 1.00.
*You should now have four circles.*

✔ Draw two more circles with diameters of 1.50 and 2.00.
*When you are done, your screen should look like Figure 2-9. Studying Figure 2-10 and using the **HELP** command, as discussed in the next section, will give you a good introduction to the remaining options in the **CIRCLE** command.*

**Figure 2-8**
Dynamic input display

**Figure 2-9**
Six circles

### 3P (Three Points)

Draws a circle based on three points on the circumference.

For example:

### Tan, Tan, Tan

Creates a circle tangent to three objects.

For example:

### 2P (Two Points)

Draws a circle based on two endpoints of the diameter.

For example:

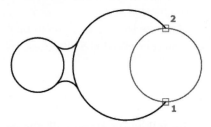

### TTR (Tangent, Tangent, Radius)

Draws a circle with a specified radius tangent to two objects.

Sometimes more than one circle matches the specified criteria. The program draws the circle of the specified radius whose tangent points are closest to the selected points.

For example:

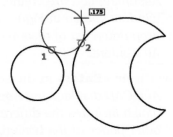

**Figure 2-10**
**Circle** options

# Accessing AutoCAD Online Help Features

The AutoCAD **HELP** command gives you access to an extraordinary amount of information in a comprehensive library of AutoCAD references and information, available both online and in your local software. In this section, we focus on the use of the **AutoCAD 2014 Help** window to gain information about command procedures and capabilities. For a demonstration, we look for further information on the **CIRCLE** command.

The following steps will access AutoCAD's online Help features.

✔ To begin you should be at the command line prompt.

✔ Check to see that you are connected to the Internet. If unable to connect, refer to the information in the Note.

**Figure 2-11**
**Help** tool

✔ Pick the **Help** tool from the title bar, as shown in Figure 2-11.
  *Assuming you are online, this opens the **AutoCAD 2014 Help** window shown in Figure 2-12. Notice the **Search** box and the drop-down list of resources to the left. By default, you search All Content.*

✔ Type **Circle <Enter>** in the search window.
  *AutoCAD displays the **About Circles** page, as shown in Figure 2-13, which includes the different ways of drawing circles, plus links to other pages at the bottom. For more detailed information, you could choose the **CIRCLE (Command)** page, second on the list at the left. Try it.*

✔ Left-click to highlight **CIRCLE (Command).**

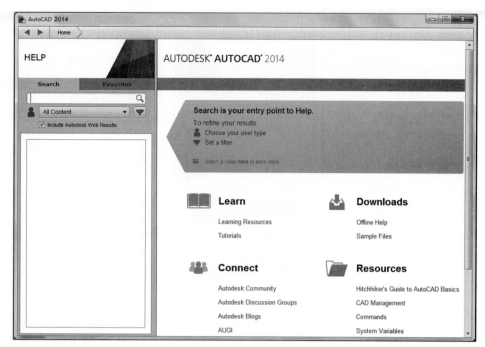

**Figure 2-12**
**AutoCAD Help** window

**Figure 2-13**
**About Circles** page

AutoCAD Help displays the **CIRCLE (Command)** page, as shown in Figure 2-14. If you scroll down the page, you will find information on all of the options in the **CIRCLE** command.

✔ To exit the **AutoCAD Help** window, pick the close button at the top right.

Or, you can minimize it and leave it open in the background.

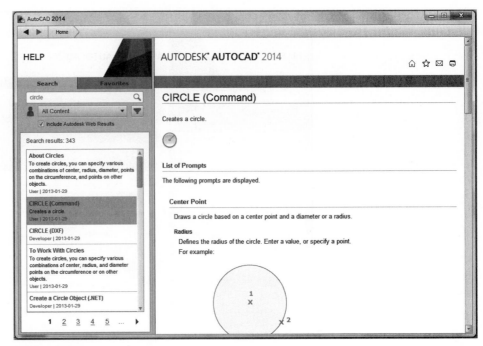

**Figure 2-14**
**CIRCLE (Command)** page

| ERASE | |
|---|---|
| **Command** | Erase |
| **Alias** | E |
| **Panel** | Modify |
| **Tool** | |

**verb/noun:** The selection method in which an edit command is entered prior to objects being selected for editing.

**noun/verb:** The selection method in which an object to be edited is selected prior to entering an edit command.

# Using the ERASE Command

> **TIP**
>
> A general procedure for using the **ERASE** command with verb/noun selection is:
>
> 1. Pick the **Erase** tool from the **Modify** panel of the ribbon.
> 2. Select objects.
> 3. Press <**Enter**> to carry out the command.

AutoCAD allows for many different methods of editing. Fundamentally, there are two different sequences for using most edit commands. These are called the **verb/noun** and the **noun/verb** methods.

In this section, we review the verb/noun sequence and then introduce the noun/verb or "pick first" method along with some of the many methods for selecting objects.

## Verb/Noun Editing

✔ To begin this section you should have the six circles on your screen, as shown previously in Figure 2-9.

*We use verb/noun editing to erase the two outer circles. Here we erase two circles at once.*

✔ Pick the **Erase** tool from the ribbon.

*In the command line and the dynamic input display, you see the prompt*

Select objects:

*This is a very common prompt. You will find it in all edit commands and many other commands as well.*

✔ Pick the outer circle.
*The circle will be highlighted.*

✔ Use the box to pick the second circle moving in toward the center.
*It, too, should now be dotted.*

✔ Press the right button on your mouse to carry out the command.
*This is typical of the verb/noun sequence in most edit commands. Once a command has been entered and a selection set defined, a press of the **<Enter>** key or right button is required to complete the command. At this point the two outer circles should be erased.*

---

**TIP**

In verb/noun edit command procedures where the last step is to press <Enter> to complete the command, it is good heads-up practice to use the right button on your mouse in place of the spacebar or <Enter> key.

---

## Noun/Verb Editing

Now let's try the noun/verb sequence.

✔ Pick the **Undo** tool or type **u** to undo the **ERASE** command and bring back the circles.

✔ Use the pickbox to select the outer circle.
*The circle is highlighted, and your screen should now resemble Figure 2-15. Those little blue boxes are called **grips**. They can be used to edit many AutoCAD objects. For now, you can ignore them.*

**grip:** In AutoCAD, grips are placed at strategic geometric locations on objects in a drawing that have been selected. Several forms of editing can be accomplished by picking, dragging, and manipulating grips.

**Figure 2-15**
Blue grip boxes

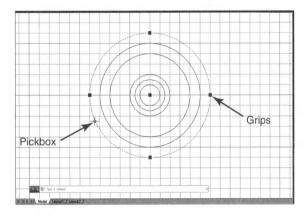

✔ Pick the second circle in the same fashion.
*The second circle also becomes dotted, and more grips appear.*

✔ Pick the **Erase** tool from the ribbon.
*Alternatively, you can type **e** or press the **<Del>** key. Your two outer circles disappear.*

The two outer circles should now be gone. As you can see, there is not much difference between the two sequences. One difference that is not immediately apparent is that there are numerous selection methods available in the verb/noun system that cannot be activated when you pick objects first. We cover other object selection methods momentarily, but first try the **OOPS** command.

## OOPS

✔ Type **oops** and watch the screen.

> *If you have made a mistake in your erasure, you can get your selection set back by typing* **oops**. ***OOPS*** *is to* ***ERASE*** *as* ***REDO*** *is to* ***UNDO***. *You can use* ***OOPS*** *to undo an* ***ERASE*** *command, as long as you have not performed another* ***ERASE*** *in the meantime. In other words, AutoCAD saves only your most recent* ***ERASE*** *selection set.*
>
> *You can also use* ***U*** *to undo an* ***ERASE***, *but notice the difference:* ***U*** *simply undoes the last command, whatever it may be;* ***OOPS*** *works specifically with* ***ERASE*** *to recall the last set of erased objects. If you have drawn other objects in the meantime, you can still use* ***OOPS*** *to recall a previously erased set. However, if you tried to use* ***U***, *you would have to backtrack, undoing any newly drawn objects along the way.*

## Other Object Selection Methods

You can select individual entities on the screen by picking them one by one, but in complex drawings this is often inefficient. AutoCAD offers a variety of other methods. In this exercise, we select circles by the windowing and crossing methods, by indicating **Last** or **L** for the last entity drawn, and by indicating **Previous** or **P** for the previously defined set. There are also options to add or remove objects from the selection set and other variations on windowing and crossing. We suggest that you study Figure 2-16 to learn about other methods. The number of selection options available may seem a bit overwhelming at first, but time learning them is well spent. These same options appear in many AutoCAD editing commands **(MOVE, COPY, ARRAY, ROTATE, MIRROR)** and will become part of your CAD vocabulary in time.

## Selection by Window

Window and crossing selections, like individual object selection, can be initiated without entering a command. In other words, they are available for noun/verb selection. Whether you select objects first or enter a command first, you can force a window or crossing selection simply by picking points on the screen that are not on objects. AutoCAD assumes that you want to select by windowing or crossing and asks for a second point.

Let's try it. We will specify that we want to erase all the inner circles by throwing a temporary selection window around them. The window is defined by two points moving left to right that serve as opposite corners of a rectangular window. Only entities that lie completely within the window are selected (see Figure 2-17).

✔ Pick point 1 at the lower left of the screen, as shown.

> *Any point in the neighborhood of (3.5,1) will do.*
>
> *AutoCAD prompts for another corner:*

Specify opposite corner:

Figure 2-16
Object selection methods
chart

| OBJECT SELECTION METHOD | DESCRIPTION | ITEMS SELECTED |
|---|---|---|
| (W) WINDOW | | The entities within the box. |
| (C) CROSSING | | The entities crossed by or within the box. |
| (P) PREVIOUS | | The entities that were previously picked. |
| (L) LAST | | The entity that was drawn last. |
| (R) REMOVE | | Removes entities from the items selected so they will not be part of the selected group. |
| (A) ADD | | Adds entities that were removed and allows for more selections after the use of remove. |
| ALL | | All the entities currently visible on the drawing. |
| (F) FENCE | | The entities crossed by the fence. |
| (WP) WPOLYGON | | All the entities completely within the window of the polygon. |
| (CP) CPOLYGON | | All the entities crossed by or inside the polygon. |

✔ Pick point 2 at the upper right of the screen, as shown.

*Any point in the neighborhood of (9.5,8.5) will do. To see the effect of the window, be sure that it crosses the outside circle, as shown in Figure 2-17.*

**Figure 2-17**
Window selection

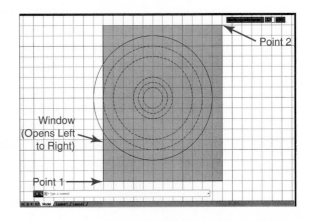

Window
(Opens Left
to Right)

Point 1

Point 2

✔ Pick the **Erase** tool from the ribbon.
*The inner circles should now be erased.*

✔ Type **oops <Enter>** to retrieve the circles once more.
*Because **ERASE** was the last command, typing **u** or selecting the **Undo** tool also works.*

## Selection by Crossing Window

**crossing window:** A selection window that opens from right to left. Everything within the window is selected, along with anything that crosses the window.

Crossing is an alternative to windowing that is useful in many cases where a standard window selection cannot be performed. The selection procedure is similar, but a ***crossing window*** opens to the left instead of to the right, and all objects that cross the window are chosen, not just those that lie completely inside the window.

We use a crossing window to select the inside circles.

✔ Pick point 1 close to (8.0,3.0), as in Figure 2-18.
*AutoCAD prompts:*

Specify opposite corner:

**Figure 2-18**
Crossing window selection

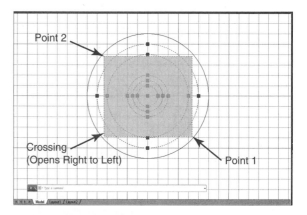

✔ Pick a point near (4.0,7.0).
*This point selection must be done carefully to demonstrate a crossing selection. Notice that the crossing window is shown with dashed lines and a green color, whereas the window box was shown with solid lines and a blue color.*

*Also, notice how the circles are selected: those that cross and those that are completely contained within the crossing window, but not those that lie outside.*

*At this point we could enter the **ERASE** command to erase the circles, but instead we demonstrate how to use the **<Esc>** key to cancel a selection set.*

✔ Press the **<Esc>** key on your keyboard.
*This cancels the selection set. The circles are no longer highlighted, and the grips disappear.*

## Selecting the "Last" Entity

AutoCAD remembers the order in which new objects have been drawn during the course of a single drawing session. As long as you do not close the drawing, you can select the last drawn entity using the **Last** option.

✔ Pick the **Erase** tool.

*Notice that there is no way to specify **Last** before you enter a command. This option is available only as part of a command procedure. In other words, it works only in a verb/noun sequence.*

✔ Type **L <Enter>.**

*One of the smaller circles should be highlighted.*

✔ Right-click to carry out the command.

*The circle should be erased.*

## Selecting the "Previous" Selection Set

The **P** or **Previous** option works with the same procedure, but it selects the previous selection set rather than the last drawn entity.

## Remove and Add

Together, the **Remove** and **Add** options form a switch in the object selection process. Under ordinary circumstances, whatever you select using any of the aforementioned options is added to your selection set. By typing **r** at the *Select objects:* prompt, you can switch to a mode in which everything you pick is deselected or removed from the selection set. Then, by typing **a,** you can return to the usual mode of adding objects to the set.

## Undoing a Selection

The **ERASE** command and other edit commands have an internal undo feature, similar to that found in the **LINE** command. By typing **u** at the *Select objects:* prompt, you can undo your last selection without leaving the edit command you are in and without undoing previous selections. You can also type **u** several times to undo your most recent selections one by one. This allows you to back up one step at a time without canceling the command and starting all over again.

## Select Similar

AutoCAD has a selection option that allows you to quickly select all similar objects in a drawing after only one object has been selected by pointing. Similar objects will be drawn with the same drawing entity, on the same layer, with the same color, and so on. In our drawings all of the circles have the same properties. Try this:

✔ Select the outer circle.

✔ Right-click to open the shortcut menu.

✔ Pick **Select Similar** from the menu.

*All of the circles will be selected. This feature will be most useful when your drawings include a greater variety of objects and properties.*

✔ Press **<Esc>** to deselect the circles.

## Other Options

If you press the **<?>** key at the *Select objects:* prompt, you see the following:

Expects a point or Window Last Crossing BOX ALL Fence WPolygon CPolygon Group Class Add Remove Multiple Previous Undo AUto SIngle SUbobject Object Select objects:

Notice that some options require that you enter two letters, as shown by the uppercase letters. Along with the options already discussed, *All, Fence, WPolygon,* and *CPolygon* are shown in Figure 2-16. *Box, Multiple, AUto,* and *SIngle* are used primarily in programming customized applications. *SUbobject* and *Object* are used in 3D modeling. Look up the **SELECT** command in the AutoCAD **Help** index for additional information on object selection.

## Selection Cycling

When drawings become complex, with many entities overlapping in one area, it can become difficult to select the object you want. The pickbox may touch multiple objects, and selection may become ambiguous. In such cases you can turn on the **Selection Cycling** button, second from the right of the mode buttons on the status bar. With this mode turned on, AutoCAD will display a list of possible objects and let you select the one you want from the list.

## Using Single-Point Object Snap

> **TIP**
>
> A general procedure for using single-point object snap is:
>
> 1. Enter a drawing command, such as **LINE** or **CIRCLE**.
> 2. Right-click while holding down the **<Shift>** or **<Ctrl>** key.
> 3. Select an object snap mode from the shortcut menu.
> 4. Point to a previously drawn object.

**object snap:** A snap mode that locates a geometrically definable point on a previously drawn object, such as the midpoint or endpoint of a line.

We offer this section as a quick introduction to the powerful ***object snap*** feature. Instead of snapping to points defined by the coordinate system, this feature snaps to geometrically specifiable points on objects that you have already drawn. It enables you to select points that you could not locate with the crosshairs or by typing coordinates. In this section we introduce single-point object snaps. You can use them as the opportunity arises, but they are not strictly necessary to complete the drawings in this chapter.

**quadrant:** A point on an object along one of the orthogonal axes, at 0°, 90°, 180°, or 270° from a given point, or the area enclosed between any two adjacent axes.

We use ***quadrant*** and ***tangent*** object snaps to draw a line from one circle tangent to another.

✔ The **Object Snap** and the **Dynamic Input Display** buttons should remain off for this exercise.

✔ Enter the **LINE** command.

**tangent:** A line running perpendicular to the radius of a circle and touching at only one point, or the point where the line and circle touch.

*We are going to draw a line from the quadrant of one circle tangent to another, as shown in Figure 2-19. This will require the use of **Tangent** object snaps. The quadrant point could be easily located without object snap because it is on a grid snap point, but the tangent point could not be located by pointing. When AutoCAD asks for a point, you select an object snap mode from the **Object Snap** shortcut menu.*

✔ At the *Specify first point:* prompt, instead of specifying a point, hold down the **<Shift>** or **<Ctrl>** key and right-click.

*This opens the shortcut menu illustrated in Figure 2-20.*

**Figure 2-19**
Line from quadrant of circle tangent to another

**Figure 2-20**
**Object Snap** shortcut menu

✔ Select **Quadrant** from the shortcut menu.

*This tells AutoCAD that you are going to select the start point of the line by using a **Quadrant** object snap rather than by direct pointing or by entering coordinates.*

✔ Move the crosshairs over the circles in your drawing.

*As you move across the various circles, AutoCAD identifies the many quadrant points and indicates these with a green diamond surrounding each quadrant point. This object snap symbol is called a marker. There are different-shaped markers for each type of object snap. If you let the cursor rest near a marker for a moment, a label appears at the dynamic input display, naming the type of object that has been recognized, as shown in Figure 2-21. This label is called a snap-tip.*

**Figure 2-21**
Object snap quadrant point

✔ Move the crosshairs near the right quadrant of the 2.50 radius circle, point 1 in Figure 2-19.

✔ With the quadrant marker showing, press the pick button.
*The green quadrant marker and the snap-tip disappear, and there is a rubber band stretching from the center of the circle to the cross-hairs position. In the command line, you see the Specify next point: prompt.*
*We use a **Tangent** object snap to select the second point.*

✔ At the *Specify next point or [Undo]:* prompt, open the shortcut menu (**<Shift>** + right-click) and select **Tangent.**

✔ Move the cursor up and to the left, positioning the crosshairs so that they are near the right side of the 2.00 diameter circle.
*When you approach the tangent area, you see the green tangent marker, as shown in Figure 2-22. Here again, if you let the cursor rest, you see a snap-tip.*

**Figure 2-22**
Object snap tangent point

✔ With the tangent marker showing, press the pick button.
*AutoCAD locates the tangent point and draws the line. Notice the power of being able to precisely locate the tangent point in this way.*

✔ Press **<Enter>** to exit the **LINE** command.
*Your screen should now resemble Figure 2-19, shown previously.*

## Using the RECTANG Command

| RECTANG | |
|---|---|
| **Command** | Rectang |
| **Alias** | Rec |
| **Panel** | Draw |
| **Tool** | |

> **TIP**
> A general procedure for using the **RECTANG** command is:
> 1. Select the **Rectangle** tool from the **Draw** panel of the ribbon.
> 2. Pick the first corner point.
> 3. Pick another corner point.

Now that you have created object selection windows, the **RECTANG** command comes naturally. Creating a rectangle in this way is just like creating an object selection window.

✔ To prepare for this exercise, erase all objects from your screen.

✔ Turn on **Snap Mode** and the **Dynamic Input Display**.

**Figure 2-23**
**Rectangle** tool

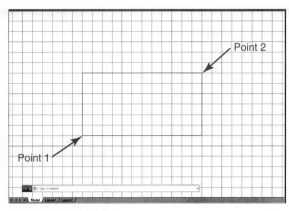

**Figure 2-24**
A 6 × 3 rectangle

✔ Select the **Rectangle** tool from the ribbon, as shown in Figure 2-23.
   *AutoCAD prompts for a corner point:*

   Specify first corner point or [Chamfer Elevation Fillet Thickness Width]:

   *You can ignore the options for now and proceed with the defaults.*

✔ Pick (3.00,3.00) for the first corner point, as shown in Figure 2-24.
   *AutoCAD prompts for another point:*

   Specify other corner point or [Area Dimensions Rotation]:

> **TIP**
> Notice how the coordinate display and dynamic display work differently after you have entered the **RECTANG** command. The coordinate display continues to show absolute coordinates relative to the screen grid. Dynamic input shows polar coordinates relative to the first corner point of the rectangle.

✔ Pick a second point at (9.00,6.00) to create a 6 × 3 rectangle.

   *As soon as you enter the second corner, AutoCAD draws a rectangle between the two corner points and returns you to the command prompt. This is a faster way to draw a rectangle than drawing it line by line. Leave the rectangle on your screen for the plotting demonstration in the "Plotting or Printing a Drawing" section.*

## Customizing Your Workspace

There are many ways you can change your workspace to suit your preferences or the needs of a particular type of drawing. The **Drafting & Annotation** workspace and the **3D Modeling** workspace are usually sufficient, but slight alterations are easy to make and may increase efficiency. Here we make one simple alteration that makes your workspace a little more similar to other software applications you have probably used. We will save the new workspace under a new name, and then you can use it in place of the **Drafting & Annotation** workspace whenever you wish.

   In older versions of AutoCAD, before the appearance of the ribbon and the application menu, menu headings were positioned across the

**menu bar:** A set of drop-down menus that are opened from labels displayed horizontally in a bar that appears below the title bar and above the ribbon. By default the menu bar is not displayed. It can be opened from the **Quick Access** toolbar.

top of the screen and opened pull-down menus, as is common with many other applications. In AutoCAD this interface is called the **menu bar**, and it can be added to your workspace without giving up much space in your drawing area.

✔ Click the arrow at the right end of the **Quick Access** toolbar.
   *This opens the drop-down menu shown in Figure 2-25.*

**Figure 2-25**
Drop-down menu

✔ From the menu, select **Show Menu Bar.**
   *The menu bar is added at the top of the screen between the ribbon and the title bar. Picking any of the headings (**File, Edit, View, Insert,** etc.) will open a pull-down menu. Many commands and procedures are accessible from these menus.*
   *The menu bar can be turned off by reversing this procedure. Here we leave it open and save the current workspace settings under a new name. Because the menu bar is open, we use it to save the workspace.*

✔ From the menu bar, select **Tools > Workspaces > Save Current As. . . .**
   *This sequence is illustrated in Figure 2-26. This executes the **WSSAVE** command, which allows you to save a new workspace. AutoCAD follows with the **Save Workspace** dialog box shown in Figure 2-27.*

✔ Type **Menu Bar <Enter>.**
   *To see that your **Menu Bar** workspace has been saved, select **Tools > Workspaces** again from the menu bar. **Menu Bar** is added to the list of workspaces and is highlighted to show that you are currently in this workspace. At any point you can return to the **Drafting & Annotation** workspace by selecting it from this list or from the list right next to it on the **Quick Access** toolbar. When you do, the menu bar will disappear from your screen.*

**Figure 2-26**
Saving the current workspace

**Figure 2-27**
**Save Workspace** dialog box

# Plotting or Printing a Drawing

AutoCAD's printing and plotting capabilities are extensive and complex.

In this chapter, we perform a very simple type of plot, going directly from your current model space objects to a sheet of drawing paper, changing only one or two plot settings. Different types of plotters and printers work somewhat differently, but the procedure we use here should achieve reasonably uniform results. It assumes that you do not have to change devices or fundamental configuration details. It should work for all plotters and printers and the drawings in this chapter. Here we use a window selection to define a plot area and scale this to fit whatever size paper is in your plotter or printer.

✔ Pick the **Plot** tool from the **Quick Access** toolbar.

> *This opens the **Plot** dialog box illustrated in Figure 2-28. You will become very familiar with it as you continue working in AutoCAD. It is one of the most important dialog boxes you will encounter. It contains many options and can be expanded to allow even more options by clicking the > button at the bottom right. (If your dialog box is already expanded, you can reduce it by clicking the < button.)*

**Figure 2-28**
Plot dialog box

## Specifying a Printer

First, you need to specify a plotter or printer. The second panel from the top is the **Printer/plotter** selection area. Look to see whether the name of a plotting device is showing in the **Name:** list box.

✔ If **None** is displayed in the list box, click the arrow on the right and select a plotter or printer.
*If you are unsure what plotter to use, you can work with AutoCAD's DWF6 ePlot.pc3 utility, which should be present.*

✔ Look at the **Plot scale** panel in the lower right of the dialog box. Locate the **Fit to paper** check box.
*If your plot scale is configured to plot to fit your paper, as it should be by default, then AutoCAD plots your drawing at maximum size based on the paper size and the window you specify.*

✔ If for any reason **Fit to paper** is not checked, click in the box to check it.
*On the **Custom** line below **Plot scale,** you should see edit boxes with numbers like 1 inches = 2.45. Right now the plot area is based on the shape of your display area, and these numbers are inaccessible. When you use a window to create a plot area that is somewhat smaller, these scale numbers change automatically. When you use **Scale** rather than **Fit to paper,** these numbers will be accessible, and you can set them manually or select from a list.*

## Plot Area

Now look at the panel labeled **Plot area** at the lower left. The drop-down list labeled **What to plot** gives you the choice of plotting based on what is on the **Display,** the **Extents** or **Limits** of the drawing, or a **Window** you define. Windowing allows you to plot any portion of a drawing by defining a window in the usual way. AutoCAD bases the size and placement of the plot on the window you define.

✔ Open the **What to plot** list and select **Window.**
> *The **Plot** dialog box disappears temporarily, giving you access to the drawing. AutoCAD prompts for point selection:*

>> Specify window for printing
>> Specify first corner:

✔ Pick the point (1.00,1.00), as shown in Figure 2-29.
> *AutoCAD prompts:*

>> Specify opposite corner:

**Figure 2-29**

Plot window

✔ Select the point (11.00,8.00), as shown in Figure 2-29.
> *As soon as you have picked the second point, AutoCAD displays the **Plot** dialog box again.*

## Plot Preview

**Plot preview** is an essential tool in carrying out efficient plotting and printing. Plot configuration is complex, and the odds are good that you will waste time and paper if you print drawings without first previewing them on the screen. AutoCAD has two types of previews that help you know exactly what to expect when your drawing reaches a sheet of paper.

Without going to a full preview you already have a partial preview on the right side of the **Printer/plotter** panel. It shows you an outline of the effective plotting area in relation to the paper size but does not show an image of the plotted drawing. This preview image will change as you change other plot settings, such as plot area and paper size.

The full preview, accessed from the **Preview** button, gives you a complete image of the drawing on a sheet of drawing paper but does not give you the specific information on the effective drawing area available in the partial preview.

✔ Pick the **Preview** button at the bottom left of the dialog box.
> *You should see a preview image like the one in Figure 2-30. There are more features of the **Plot** dialog box, and you can use full and partial plot previews extensively as you change plot parameters. For*

**Figure 2-30**

Plot preview

> *now, get in the habit of using plot preview. If things are not coming out quite the way you want, you will be able to fix them soon.*

✔ Press **<Esc>** to return to the dialog box.

✔ To save your settings, including your plotter selection, click the **Apply to Layout** button.
> *You are now ready to plot.*

✔ If you want to plot or print the rectangle, prepare your plotter and then click **OK**. Otherwise, click **Cancel.**

---

**NOTE**

Paper sizes are not addressed here. For now, we assume that your plot configuration is correctly matched to the paper in your printer or plotter.

---

Clicking **OK** sends the drawing information to be printed. You can sit back and watch the plotter at work. If you need to cancel for any reason, click **Cancel.**

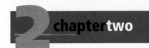

# Chapter Summary

In this chapter you learned to change the settings of the grid and the incremental snap. You learned to change units, to draw circles and rectangles, and to erase objects using many different object selection options. You can now access all of the information available in the AutoCAD Help resources. You were introduced to the powerful object snap feature for specifying points on geometric objects. You also added the menu bar to your customized workspace and began your exploration of AutoCAD's complex plotting and printing features. The drawings at the end of the chapter will provide you opportunities to practice all these new skills.

# Chapter Test Questions

## Multiple Choice

*Circle the correct answer.*

1. Which of these is the least useful snap and grid setting combination?
    a. Snap = **1.0,** grid = **1.0**
    b. Snap = **1.0,** grid = **10.0**
    c. Snap = **1.0,** grid = **2.0**
    d. Snap = **1.0,** grid = **.5**

2. Which of these will **not** open the **Drafting Settings** dialog box?
    a. Type **dsettings <Enter>**
    b. Type **ds <Enter>**
    c. Pick the **Drafting Settings** tool from the ribbon
    d. Right-click the **Snap Mode** button and select **Settings**

3. To switch from decimal to architectural units:
    a. Select **architectural** in the **Drawing Units** dialog box
    b. Type **architectural <Enter>**
    c. Type **drawing units <Enter>**
    d. Pick **architectural** on the status bar

4. When drawing a circle using the **Diameter** option, the rubber band:
    a. Stretches from one side of the circle to the other, twice the radius
    b. Stretches to the circumference of the circle
    c. Stretches from the center point to a point outside the circle
    d. Stretches between two points on the circumference

5. To open a crossing window:
    a. Pick points left to right
    b. Pick points that cross the objects you wish to select
    c. Pick points to create a window around objects you wish to select
    d. Pick points right to left

## Matching

*Write the number of the correct answer on the line.*

a. Decimal units _____          1. 180°

b. Architectural units _____     2. 2.3456, 5.4321

c. Horizontal _____              3. 270°

d. Vertical _____                4. 1'-1/2", 3'-4 3/4"

e. Engineering units _____       5. 1'-0.5", 3'-4.75"

## True or False

*Circle the correct answer.*

1. **True or False:** 3 o'clock = 0°.

2. **True or False:** **C** is an alias for **CIRCLE.**

3. **True or False:** **Last** and **Previous** selections are equivalent.

4. **True or False:** The same selection methods are available in noun/verb and verb/noun editing.

5. **True or False:** In AutoCAD, plot settings are affected by your choice of a plotter.

## Questions

1. Which is likely to have the smaller setting, grid or snap? Why? What happens if the settings are reversed?

2. Where is 0° located in AutoCAD's default units setup? Where is 270°? Where is –45°?

3. How does AutoCAD know when you want a crossing selection instead of a window selection?

4. What is the difference between noun/verb and verb/noun editing?

5. What aspects of a plot are shown in the preview image in the **Printer/plotter** panel of the **Plot** dialog box?

## Drawing Problems

1. Leave the grid at 0.50 and set snap to **0.25.**

2. Use the **3P** option to draw a circle that passes through the points (2.25,4.25), (3.25,5.25), and (4.25,4.25).

3. Use the **2P** option to draw a second circle with a diameter from (3.25,4.25) to (4.25,4.25).

4. Draw a third circle centered at (5.25,4.25) with a radius of 1.00.

5. Draw a fourth circle centered at (4.75,4.25) with a diameter of 1.00.

## WWW Exercise (Optional)

In this voyage to the World Wide Web, we show you how to change the default Uniform Resource Locator (URL) so that you don't have to type a long address every time you go out to the Web.

We show you how to change the default Web location to our companion website. Whether or not you actually want to retain our website as the default, we encourage you to go there now, take the self-scoring review test, and try the Web project.

✔ Type **inetlocation <Enter>.**

*INETLOCATION is a system variable that stores the name of the default URL. AutoCAD prompts:*

Enter new value for INETLOCATION <http:www.autodesk.com>:

*Remember that the address within the arrows is the current default. This value is replaced by the address you enter.*

✔ Type **www.pearsonhighered.com/dixriley <Enter>.**

*The new value is stored, and AutoCAD returns you to the command prompt. Now all you need to do is enter the **BROWSER** command and press **<Enter>** at the prompt.*

✔ Type **browser <Enter>.**

*The AutoCAD prompt shows the new default URL:*

Enter web location (URL) <www.pearsonhighered.com/dixriley>:

✔ Press **<Enter>** to accept the default location.

*Away you go. Good luck on the test.*

## Chapter Drawing Projects

 ## Drawing 2-1: *Aperture Wheel* [BASIC]

This drawing gives you practice creating circles using the center point, radius method. Refer to the table following the drawing for radius sizes. With snap set at 0.25, some of the circles can be drawn by pointing and dragging. Other circles have radii that are not on a snap point. These circles can be drawn by typing in the radius.

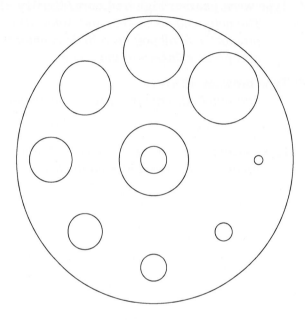

### Drawing Suggestions

GRID = 0.50

SNAP = 0.25

- A good sequence for doing this drawing would be to draw the outer circle first, followed by the two inner circles (H and C) in Drawing 2-1. These are all centered on the point (6.00,4.50). Then begin at circle A and work around clockwise, being sure to center each circle correctly.

- Notice that there are two circles C and two circles H. The two circles having the same letter are the same size.

- Remember, you can type any value you like, and AutoCAD gives you a precise graphic image. However, you cannot always show the exact point you want by pointing. Often it is more efficient to type a few values than to turn snap off or change its setting for a small number of objects.

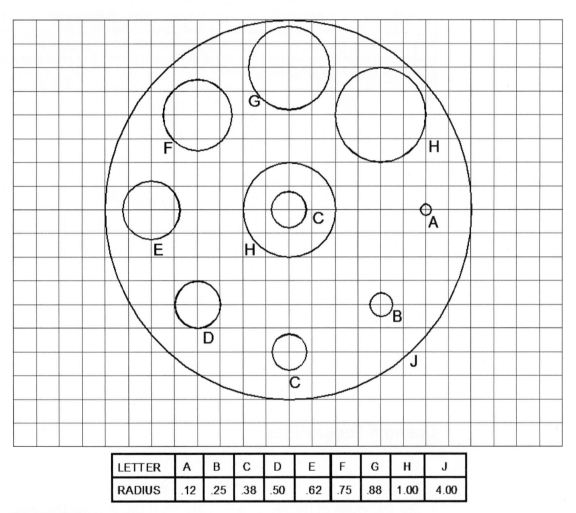

| LETTER | A | B | C | D | E | F | G | H | J |
|--------|-----|-----|-----|-----|-----|-----|-----|------|------|
| RADIUS | .12 | .25 | .38 | .50 | .62 | .75 | .88 | 1.00 | 4.00 |

**Drawing 2-1**
Aperture Wheel

## M Drawing 2-2: *Center Wheel* [BASIC]

This drawing gives you a chance to combine lines and circles and to use the center point, diameter method. It also gives you some experience with smaller objects, a denser grid, and a tighter snap spacing.

> **TIP**
>
> Even though units are set to show only two decimal places, it is important to set the snap using three decimal places (0.125) so that the grid is on a multiple of the snap (0.25 = 2 × 0.125). AutoCAD shows you rounded coordinate values, such as 0.13, but keeps the graphics on target. Try setting snap to either **0.13** or **0.12** instead of 0.125, and you will see the problem for yourself.

## Drawing Suggestions

GRID = 0.25

SNAP = 0.125

- The two views of the center wheel are lined up, making the snap setting essential. Watch the coordinate display as you work and get used to the smaller range of motion.

- Choosing an efficient sequence makes this drawing much easier to complete. Because the two views must line up properly, we suggest that you draw the front view first, with circles of diameter 0.25, 4.00, and 6.00. Then, use these circles to position the lines in the right-side view.

- The circles in the front view should be centered in the neighborhood of (3.50,4.50). This puts the lower left-hand corner of the 1 × 1 square at around (4.50,1.50).

- Note the use of the (Ø) symbol indicating that circles are given diameter dimensions.

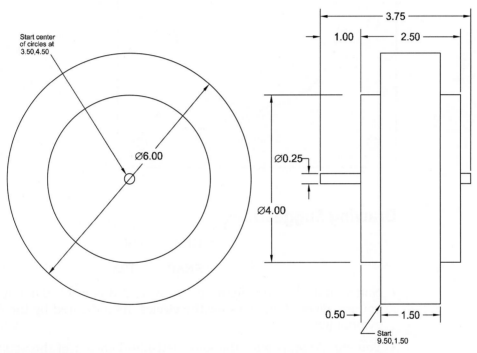

Start center
of circles at
3.50,4.50

Ø6.00

Ø0.25

Ø4.00

3.75

1.00

2.50

0.50

1.50

Start
9.50,1.50

**Drawing 2-2**
Center Wheel

## **M** Drawing 2-3: *Fan Bezel* [INTERMEDIATE]

This drawing should be easy for you at this point. Set grid to **0.50** and snap to **0.125** as suggested, and everything falls into place nicely.

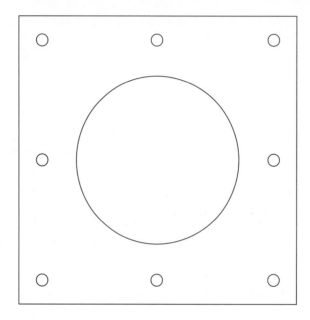

## Drawing Suggestions

GRID = 0.50

SNAP = 0.125

- Notice that the outer figure in Drawing 2-3 is a 6 × 6 square and that you are given diameters for the circles, as indicated by the diameter symbol (Ø).

- You should start with the lower left-hand corner of the square somewhere near the point (3.00,2.00) if you want to keep the drawing centered on your screen.

- Be careful to center the large inner circle within the square.

Ø0.25
6 places

5.00

6.00

2.50

0.50

Ø3.50

0.50

2.50

5.00

6.00

**Drawing 2-3**
Fan Bezel

## M Drawing 2-4: *Switch Plate* [INTERMEDIATE]

This drawing is similar to the last one, but the dimensions are more difficult, and a number of important points do not fall on the grid. The drawing gives you practice using grid and snap points and the coordinate display. Refer to the table that follows Drawing 2-4 for dimensions of the circles, squares, and rectangles inside the 7 × 10 outer rectangle. The placement of these smaller figures is shown by the dimensions on the drawing itself.

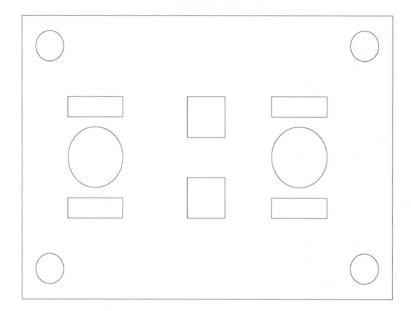

## Drawing Suggestions

GRID = 0.50

SNAP = 0.25

- Turn on **Ortho** or **Polar snap** to do this drawing.

- A starting point in the neighborhood of (1,1) keeps you well positioned on the screen.

| HOLE | SIZE |
|------|------|
| A | Ø.75 |
| B | Ø1.50 |
| C | .50 H x 1.50 W |
| D | 1.00 SQ |

**Drawing 2-4**
Switch Plate

## G Drawing 2-5: *Gasket* [ADVANCED]

Drawing 2-5 gives you practice creating simple lines and circles while utilizing grid and snap. The circles in this drawing have a 0.50 and a 1.00 diameter. With snap set at 0.25, the radii are on a snap point. These circles can be drawn easily by dragging the circle out to show the radius or by typing in the diameter.

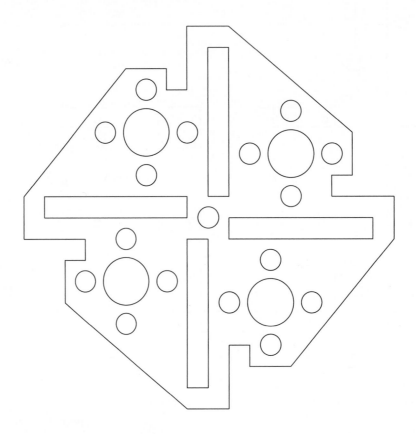

### Drawing Suggestions

GRID = 0.50

SNAP = 0.25

- A good sequence for completing this drawing would be to draw the outer lines first, followed by the inner lines and then the circles.

- Notice that all endpoints of all lines fall on grid points; therefore, they are on a snap point.

**Drawing 2-5**
Gasket

# Drawing 2-6: *Sheet Metal Stamping*
## [ADVANCED]

Drawing 2-6 gives you additional practice creating lines and circles while utilizing grid display and **Snap** mode. The circles in this drawing have a 0.50, a 1.00, and a 3.00 diameter. With snap set at 0.25, the radii are on a snap point but not always on grid line intersections. These circles can be drawn easily by dragging the circle out to show the radius or by typing in the diameter.

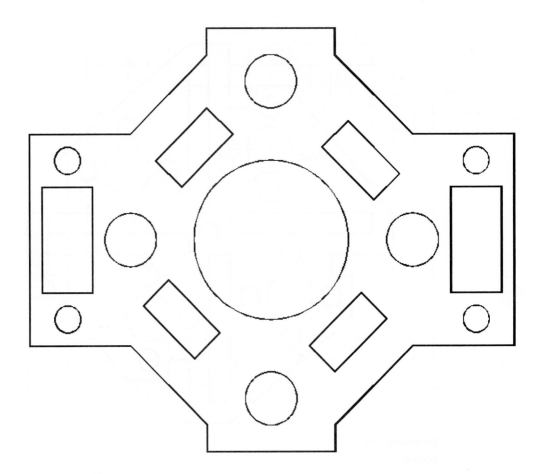

## Drawing Suggestions

GRID = 0.50

SNAP = 0.25

- A good sequence for completing this drawing would be to draw the outer lines first, followed by the inner lines and then the circles.

- Notice that the endpoints of all lines are on snap points but do not always fall on grid line intersections.

- Also, notice that while the placement of most objects in the drawing is symmetrical, the placement of the four smaller rectangles is not.

**Drawing 2-6**
Sheet Metal Stamping

# 3 chapterthree

# Layers, Colors, and Linetypes

# CHAPTER OBJECTIVES

- Create new layers
- Assign colors to layers
- Assign linetypes
- Assign lineweights
- Change the current layer
- Change linetype scale
- Edit corners using **FILLET**
- Edit corners using **CHAMFER**
- Zoom and pan with the scroll wheel
- Use the **ZOOM** command
- Enter single-line text

## Introduction

layer: In CAD practice, a layer is defined with colors, linetypes, and lineweights so that objects of a certain type can be grouped together and treated separately from other types of objects.

CAD is much more than a computerized way to do drafting. CAD programs have many powerful features that have no correlation in manual drawing. Layering is a good example. ***Layers*** are like transparent overlays that can be added to or peeled away from a drawing. Layers are used to separate different aspects of a drawing so that they can be treated independently. Layers exist in the same space and in the same drawing but can be set up and controlled individually, allowing for greater control, precision, and flexibility. In this chapter, you create and use four new layers, each with its own associated color and linetype.

The **ZOOM** command is another bit of CAD magic, allowing your drawings to accurately represent real-world detail at the largest and smallest scales within the same drawing. In this chapter, you also learn to use the **FILLET** and **CHAMFER** commands on the corners of previously drawn objects and to move between adjacent portions of a drawing with the **PAN** command. All these new techniques add considerably to the professionalism of your developing CAD technique.

## Creating New Layers

| LAYER | |
|---|---|
| **Command** | Layer |
| **Alias** | La |
| **Panel** | Layers |
| **Tool** | |

Layers allow you to treat specialized groups of entities in your drawing separately from other groups. For example, you can draw dimensions on a special dimension layer so that you can turn them on and off at will. You can then turn off the dimension layer to prepare drawings that are shown without dimensions. When a layer is turned off, all the objects on that layer become invisible, although they are still part of the drawing database and can be recalled at any time. In this way, layers can be viewed, edited, manipulated, and plotted independently.

> **TIP**
> A general procedure for creating a layer is:
> 1. Select the **Layer Properties** tool from the ribbon.
> 2. Click the **New Layer** icon.
> 3. Type in a layer name.
> 4. Repeat for other new layers.
> 5. Close the **Layer Properties** palette.

It is common practice to put dimensions on a separate layer, but there are many other uses of layers as well. Fundamentally, layers are used to separate colors and linetypes, and these, in turn, take on special significance, depending on the drawing application. It is standard drafting practice, for example, to use small, evenly spaced dashes to represent objects or edges that would, in reality, be hidden from view. On a CAD system, these hidden lines can be put on an independent layer so they can be turned on and off and given their own color to make it easy for the designer to remember what layer he or she is working on.

In this chapter, we present a simple layering system. You should remember that there are countless possibilities. AutoCAD allows a full range of colors and as many layers as you like.

You should also be aware that linetypes and colors are not restricted to being associated with layers. It is possible to mix linetypes and colors on a single layer. Although this might be useful for certain applications, we do not recommend it at this point.

✔ Create a new drawing by selecting the **New** tool from the **Quick Access** toolbar.

✔ Check to see that acad is in the **File name:** box and press **<Enter>**.

✔ If necessary, turn on the **Grid Display.**

✔ Type **z <Enter>** to enter the **ZOOM** command and then **a <Enter>** to zoom all.

## The Layer Properties Manager Palette

The creation and specification of layers and layer properties in AutoCAD is handled through the **Layer Properties Manager** palette. Palettes are like dialog boxes but they are laid out differently and have some different features. The **Layer Properties Manager** palette consists of a table of layers. Clicking the appropriate row and column changes a setting or takes you to another dialog box where a setting can be changed.

**Figure 3-1**
**Layer Properties** tool

✔ Select the **Layer Properties** tool from the ribbon, as shown in Figure 3-1.

*This opens the **Layer Properties Manager** palette illustrated in Figure 3-2. The large open space to the right shows the names and properties of all layers defined in the current drawing. Layering systems can become very complex, and for this reason there is a system to limit or filter the layer names shown on the layer list. This is controlled by the icons at the top left. With no filters specified, the layer list shows all used layers. Currently, **0** is the only defined layer. The icons on the line after the layer name show the current state of various properties of that layer. We get to these shortly.*

*Now, we will create three new layers. AutoCAD makes this easy.*

**Figure 3-2**
*Layer Properties Manager* palette

✔ Pick the **New Layer** icon, as shown in Figure 3-3.

*A newly defined layer, "Layer1," is created immediately and added to the **Layer Name** list box. The new layer is given the characteristics of Layer **0.** We alter these in the "Assigning Colors to Layers" section. First, however, we give this layer a new name and then define three more layers.*

*Layer names can be long or short. We have chosen single-digit numbers as layer names because they are easy to type, and we can match them to AutoCAD's index color numbering sequence.*

**Figure 3-3**
**New Layer** icon

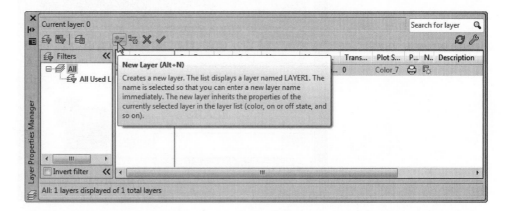

✔ Type **1** for the layer name.
> *Layer1 changes to simply **1**. It is not necessary to press* **<Enter>** *after typing the name.*

✔ Pick the **New Layer** icon again.
> *A second new layer is added to the list. It again has the default name Layer1. Change it to 2.*

✔ Type **2** for the second layer name.

✔ Pick the **New Layer** icon again.

✔ Type **3** for the third layer name and press **<Enter>** to complete the process.
> *At this point, your layer name list should show Layers **0, 1, 2,** and **3,** all with identical properties.*

## Assigning Colors to Layers

We now have four layers, but they are all the same except for their names. We have more changes to make before our new layers have useful identities.

Layer **0** has some unique features, which are not introduced here. Because of these, it is common practice to leave Layer **0** defined the way it is. We begin our changes on Layer **1**.

✔ In the **Layer Properties Manager** palette, pick the white square under **Color** in the **Layer 1** line.
> *Picking the white square in the **Color** column of Layer **1** selects Layer **1** and opens the **Select Color** dialog box illustrated in Figure 3-4. The three tabs in this dialog box show three ways in which colors can be defined in AutoCAD. By default, the **Index Color** tab is probably selected, as shown in Figure 3-4. The Index Color system is a simple numbered selection of 255 colors and shades. The True Color and Color Books systems are standard color systems commonly used by graphic designers. The **True Color** tab can*

**Figure 3-4**
*Select Color* dialog box

*be set to access either the Hue, Saturation, and Luminance (HSL) color model or the Red, Green, Blue (RGB) model. Both of these systems work by mixing colors and color characteristics. The **Color Books** tab gives access to DIC, Pantone, and RAL color books. These standard color sets are also numbered, but they provide many more choices than the AutoCAD index color set. In this chapter we confine ourselves to the **Index Color** tab.*

✔ If necessary, click the **Index Color** tab.

*The **Index Color** tab shows the complete selection of 255 colors. At the top is a full palette of shades 10 through 249. Below that are the nine standard colors, numbered 1 through 9, followed by gray shades, numbered 250 through 255.*

✔ Move your cursor freely inside the dialog box.

*When your cursor is on a color, it is highlighted with a black border.*

✔ Let your cursor rest on any color.

*Notice that the number of the color is registered under the palette next to the words Index color. This is the AutoCAD index color number for the color currently highlighted. Notice also the three numbers on the right following the words Red, Green, Blue. This is the RGB color model equivalent. RGB colors are combinations of red, green, and blue, with 255 shades of each.*

✔ Pick any color in the palette.

*When a color is selected, it is outlined with a black border, and a preview "patch" is displayed on the bottom right of the dialog box against a patch of the current color for comparison. The color is not actually selected in the drawing until you click **OK** to exit the dialog box. For our purposes, we want to select standard red, color number 1 on the strip in the middle of the dialog box.*

✔ Move the white cursor box to the red box, the first of the nine standard colors in the middle of the box.

*Notice that this is index color number 1, and its RGB equivalent is 255,0,0—pure red with no green or blue added.*

✔ Pick the red box.

*You should see the word red and the color red shown in the preview area at the bottom of the dialog box. Note that you can also select colors by typing names or numbers directly in this edit box. Typing **red** or the number **1** is the same as selecting the red color box from the chart.*

✔ Click **OK.**

*Layer **1** is now defined with the color red in the **Layer Name** list box.*

*Next we assign the color yellow to Layer **2**.*

✔ Pick the white square under **Color** in the Layer **2** line, and assign the color yellow, color number 2, to Layer **2** in the **Select Color** dialog box. Click **OK.**

✔ Select Layer **3** and set this layer to green, color number 3.

*Look at the layer list. You should now have Layers **0, 1, 2,** and **3** defined with the colors white, red, yellow, and green.*

## Assigning Linetypes

AutoCAD has a standard library of linetypes that can easily be assigned to layers. There are 46 standard types. In addition to continuous lines, we use hidden lines and centerlines. We put hidden lines in yellow on Layer **2** and centerlines in green on Layer **3**. Layers **1** and **0** retain the continuous linetype.

The procedure for assigning linetypes is almost identical to the procedure for assigning colors, except that you have to load linetypes into the drawing before they can be used.

✔ In the **Layer Properties Manager** palette, pick **Continuous** in the **Linetype** column of the Layer **2** line.

*This selects Layer **2** and opens the **Select Linetype** dialog box illustrated in Figure 3-5. The box containing a list of loaded linetypes currently shows only the continuous linetype. We can fix this by clicking the **Load** button at the bottom of the dialog box.*

✔ Click **Load.**

*This opens the **Load or Reload Linetypes** dialog box illustrated in Figure 3-6. Here you can pick from the list of linetypes available from the standard acad file or from other files containing linetypes, if there are any on your system. You also have the option of loading all linetypes from any given file at once. The linetypes are then defined in your drawing, and you can assign a new linetype to a layer at any time. This makes things easier. It does, however, use up more memory.*

*For our purposes, we load only the hidden and center linetypes we are going to be using.*

**Figure 3-5**
*Select Linetype* dialog box

**Figure 3-6**
*Load or Reload Linetypes* dialog box

✔ Scroll down until you see the linetype labeled **CENTER.**

✔ Click **CENTER** in the **Linetype** column at the left.

✔ Scroll down again until you see the linetype labeled **HIDDEN.**

✔ Hold down the **<Ctrl>** key and click **HIDDEN** in the **Linetype** column.

*The **<Ctrl>** key lets you highlight two separate items in a list.*

✔ Click **OK** to complete the loading process.
*You should now see the center and hidden linetypes added to the list of loaded linetypes. Now that these are loaded, we can assign them to layers.*

> **NOTE**
>
> Make sure that you actually click the word **Continuous**. If you click one of the icons in the Layer **2** line, you might turn the layer off or freeze it so that you cannot draw on it. These properties are discussed at the end of the "Changing the Current Layer" section.

✔ Click **HIDDEN** in the **Linetype** column.

✔ Click **OK** to close the dialog box.
*You should see that Layer **2** now has the hidden linetype. Next, we assign the center linetype to Layer **3**.*

✔ Click **Continuous** in the **Linetype** column of the Layer **3** line.

✔ In the **Select Linetype** dialog box, select the **CENTER** linetype.

✔ Click **OK.**

*Examine your layer list again. It should show Layer **2** with the hidden linetype and Layer **3** with the center linetype. Before exiting the **Layer Properties Manager** palette, we create one additional layer to demonstrate AutoCAD's lineweight feature.*

## Assigning Lineweights

**lineweight:** A value that specifies the width at which a line will be displayed on the screen or in a printed drawing.

*Lineweight* refers to the thickness of lines as they are displayed and plotted. All lines are initially given a default lineweight. Lineweights are assigned by layer and are displayed only if the **Lineweight** button on the status bar is in the on position. In this section, we create a new layer and give it a much larger lineweight for demonstration purposes.

First, we create a new layer because we do not want to change our previous layers from the default lineweight setting.

✔ If Layer **3** is not highlighted, select it now.

✔ Pick the **New Layer** icon in the dialog box.
*Notice that the new layer takes the characteristics of the previously highlighted layer. Our last action was to give Layer **3** the center linetype, so your new layer should have green centerlines and the other characteristics of Layer **3**.*

✔ Type **4** for the new layer name.

✔ Click **Default** (or **Defa ...**) in the **Lineweight** column of Layer **4.**
*This opens the **Lineweight** dialog box, shown in Figure 3-7. We use a rather large lineweight to create a clear demonstration. Be aware that printed lineweights may not exactly match lineweights as shown on the screen.*

✔ Scroll down until you see 0.50 mm on the list.

✔ Pick the 0.50 mm line.
*Below the list you can see that the original specification for this layer was the default and is now being changed to 0.50 mm.*

**Figure 3-7**
*Lineweight* dialog box

✔ Click **OK** to return to the **Layer Properties Manager** palette.

*It is now time to leave the dialog box and see what we can do with our new layers.*

✔ Click the **Close** button at the top left of the palette to exit the **Layer Properties Manager** palette.

*Before proceeding, you should be back in your drawing window with your new layers defined in your drawing. To verify that you have successfully defined new layers, open the **Layer** drop-down list on the ribbon, as shown in Figure 3-8. Notice that this is not the*

**Figure 3-8**
*Layer* drop-down list

*label at the bottom of the **Layer** tab. Clicking that line will open up a tab extension.*

✔ To open the **Layer** list, click the arrow or anywhere in the list box.
   *Your list should resemble the one in Figure 3-8.*

## Changing the Current Layer

In this section, we make each of your new layers current and draw objects on them. You can immediately see how much power you have added to your drawing by the addition of new layers, colors, linetypes, and lineweights.

   To draw new entities on a layer, you must make it the currently active layer. Previously drawn objects on other layers are also visible, but new objects go on the current layer.

   There are two quick methods to establish the current layer. The first works the same as any drop-down list. The second makes use of previously drawn objects. We use the first method to draw the objects in Figure 3-9.

**Figure 3-9**
Objects on different layers

✔ Click anywhere in the **Layer** list box on the ribbon.
   *This opens the list, as shown previously in Figure 3-8.*

✔ Select Layer **1** by clicking to the right of the layer name **1** in the drop-down list.
   *Layer **1** replaces Layer **0** as the current layer on the **Layer** list on the **Layers** panel of the ribbon.*

✔ Using the **RECTANG** command, draw the 6 × 6 square shown in Figure 3-9, with the first corner at (3,2) and the other corner at (9,8).
   *Your square should show the red continuous lines of Layer **1**.*

✔ Click anywhere in the **Layer** list box.

✔ Click to the right of the layer name **2**.
   *Layer **2** becomes the current layer.*

✔ With Layer **2** current, draw the hidden circle in Figure 3-9, centered at (6,5) with radius 2.
   *Your circle should appear in yellow hidden lines.*

✔ Make Layer **3** current and draw a horizontal centerline from (2,5) to (10,5).

*This line should appear as a green centerline.*

✔ Pick the **Show/Hide Lineweight** button on the status bar, as shown in Figure 3-10.

**Figure 3-10**
*Show/Hide Lineweight*
button

✔ Make Layer **4** current and draw a vertical line from (6,1) to (6,9).

*This line should appear as a green centerline with noticeable thickness.*

✔ Pick the **Show/Hide Lineweight** button again to turn off **Lineweight** display.

*With **Lineweight** off, the lineweight of the vertical centerline is not displayed.*

## Making an Object's Layer Current

Finally, we use another method to make Layer **1** current before moving on.

✔ Pick the **Make Object's Layer Current** tool from the **Layers** panel, as shown in Figure 3-11.

*This tool allows us to make a layer current by selecting any object on that layer. AutoCAD shows the prompt:*

Select object whose layer will become current:

**Figure 3-11**
*Make Object's Layer
Current* tool

✔ Select the red square drawn on Layer **1**.

*Layer **1** replaces Layer **4** in the **Layer** list box on the ribbon.*

## Other Properties of Layers

There are several other properties that can be set in the **Layer Properties Manager** palette or, more conveniently, in the **Layer** list box. These settings probably will not be useful to you in this chapter, but we introduce them briefly here for your information.

**On and Off.** Layers can be turned on or off with the lightbulb icon. On and off status affects only the visibility of objects on a layer. Objects on layers that are off are not visible or plotted, but are still in the drawing and are considered when the drawing is regenerated. ***Regeneration*** is the process by which AutoCAD translates the precise numerical data that

**regeneration:** The process through which AutoCAD refreshes the drawing image on the screen by re-creating the image from the numerical database used to store the geometry of the drawing.

make up a drawing file database into the less precise values of screen graphics. Regeneration can be a slow process in large, complex drawings. As a result, it may be useful not to regenerate all layers all the time.

**Freeze and Thaw.**   Frozen layers not only are invisible but also are ignored in regeneration. Thaw reverses this setting. Thawed layers are always regenerated but may not be represented on the screen. Freeze and thaw properties are set using the sun icon, to the right of the lightbulb icon. Layers are thawed by default, as indicated by the yellow sun. When a layer is frozen, the sun icon is replaced with a snowflake.

**Lock and Unlock.**   Next is the lock icon. The **Lock** and **Unlock** settings do not affect visibility but do affect availability of objects for editing. Objects on locked layers are visible, but they cannot be edited. Unlocking reverses this setting.

**Deleting Layers.**   You can delete layers using the **Delete** tool in the **Layer Properties Manager** palette. This is the red **X** just above the word **Name.** However, you cannot delete layers that have objects drawn on them. Also, you cannot delete the current layer or Layer **0.**

## Changing Linetype Scale

> **TIP**
> A general procedure for changing linetype scale is:
> 1. Type **lts <Enter>.**
> 2. Enter a new value.

linetype scale: A value that determines the size and spacing of linetype dashes and the spaces between them.

While you have objects on your screen with hidden lines and centerlines, it is a good time to demonstrate the importance of *linetype scale*. The size of the individual dashes and spaces that make up centerlines, hidden lines, and other linetypes is determined by a global setting called **LTSCALE.** By default, it is set to a factor of 1.00. In smaller drawings, this setting may be too large and cause some of the shorter lines to appear continuous regardless of what layer they are on. Or, in some cases you may want smaller spaces and dashes. To change the linetype scale, use the **LTSCALE** command. Try this:

✔ Type **lts <Enter>.**
*Lts,* of course, is the alias for **LTSCALE.**

✔ Type **.5 <Enter>.**

Notice the change in the size of dashes and spaces in your drawing. The effect of changing linetype scale is illustrated in Figure 3-12.

**Figure 3-12**
Effect of changing linetype scale

| FILLET | |
|---|---|
| **Command** | Fillet |
| **Alias** | F |
| **Panel** | Modify |
| **Tool** | |

**fillet:** In drafting practice, a concave curve at the corner of an object. In AutoCAD, the term *fillet* and the **FILLET** command refer to both concave and convex curves (rounds).

**round:** In drafting practice, a convex curve at the corner of an object.

**chamfer:** An angle cut across the corner of an object.

# Editing Corners Using FILLET

Now that you have a variety of linetypes to use, you can begin to make more realistic mechanical drawings. Often this will require the ability to create filleted, rounded, or chamfered corners. *Fillets* are concave curves on corners and edges, whereas *rounds* are convex. AutoCAD uses the **FILLET** command to refer to both. *Chamfers* are cut on an angle rather than a curve. The **FILLET** and **CHAMFER** commands work similarly.

> **TIP**
>
> A general procedure for creating fillets is:
>
> 1. Pick the **Fillet** tool from the ribbon, or type **f <Enter>.**
> 2. Right-click and select **Radius** from the shortcut menu.
> 3. Enter a radius value.
> 4. Select two lines that meet at a corner.

We modify only the square in this exercise, but instead of erasing the other objects, turn them off, as follows:

✔ If you have not already done so, set Layer **1** as the current layer.

✔ Open the **Layer** list box on the ribbon, and click the lightbulb icons on Layers **2, 3,** and **4** so that they turn from yellow to blue, indicating that they are off.

✔ Click anywhere outside the list box to close it.

> *When you are finished, you should see only the square. The other objects are still in your drawing and can be recalled anytime simply by turning their layers on again.*
>
> *We use the square to practice fillets and chamfers.*

✔ Type **f <Enter>,** or pick the **Fillet** tool from the ribbon, as shown in Figure 3-13.

> *On the command line, you will see options as follows:*
>
> Select first object or [Undo Polyline Radius Trim Multiple]:

**Figure 3-13**
*FILLET* tool

Polylines are not discussed here, but we have something to show you about this option in a moment. **Trim** mode is discussed at the end of this exercise.

The first thing you must do is determine the degree of rounding you want. Because fillets appear as arcs, they can be defined by a radius.

✔ Select **Radius** from the command line options.

> *AutoCAD prompts:*
>
> > Specify fillet radius <0.00>:
>
> *The default is 0.00.*

✔ Type **.75 <Enter>.**

> *You have set 0.75 as the current fillet radius for this drawing. You can change it at any time. Changing the value does not affect previously drawn fillets.*
>
> > *The prompt is the same as before:*
>
> > Select first object or [Undo Polyline Radius Trim Multiple]:
>
> *Notice that you have the pickbox on the screen now without the crosshairs.*

✔ Pick a point on the vertical line on the right near the top corner.

✔ Move the cursor over the horizontal line at the top near the right corner.

> *The top line will be previewed for selection, and a preview image of the fillet will appear in white at the top right corner. This allows you to see what your fillet will look like before you carry out the command.*

✔ Pick the horizontal line at the top near the top right corner.

> *Behold! A fillet! You did not even have to press* ***<Enter>.*** *AutoCAD knows that you are done after selecting two lines.*

## The Multiple Option

We use the **Multiple** option to fillet the remaining three corners of the square. **Multiple** allows you to create multiple fillets without leaving the **FILLET** command.

✔ Press **<Enter>** or the spacebar to repeat **FILLET.**

✔ Select **Multiple** from the command line options.

✔ Select two lines to fillet another corner.

> *You do not have to enter a radius value again because the last value is retained. Also, because you entered the* ***Multiple*** *option, you do not have to reenter the command. Notice again that the preview image of the fillet appeared before you selected the second line.*

✔ Proceed to fillet all four corners.

> *When you are done, your screen should resemble Figure 3-14.*

✔ Press **<Enter>** or the spacebar to exit **FILLET.**

**Figure 3-14**
Multiple fillets on corners

## Trim Mode

**Trim** mode allows you to determine whether you want AutoCAD to remove square corners as it creates fillets and chamfers. Examples of fillets created with **Trim** mode on and off are shown in Figure 3-15. In most cases, you want to leave **Trim** mode on. To turn it off, enter **FILLET** and select **Trim** and then **No Trim** from the command line options.

> **TIP**
>
> **FILLET** may also be used to connect two lines that do not intersect. By setting a fillet radius of 0 and then selecting two lines that do not meet, both lines will be extended to the point where they intersect. Lines do not need to be perpendicular, but they must not be parallel for this to work.

**Figure 3-15**
*Trim* mode on and off

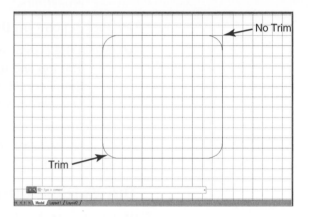

## Editing Corners Using CHAMFER

| CHAMFER | |
|---|---|
| **Command** | Chamfer |
| **Alias** | Cha |
| **Panel** | Modify |
| **Tool** | |

> **TIP**
>
> A general procedure for creating chamfers is:
>
> 1. Pick the **Chamfer** tool from the **Fillet** flyout on the ribbon.
> 2. Right-click and select **Distance** from the shortcut menu.
> 3. Enter a chamfer distance.
> 4. Enter a second chamfer distance or press **<Enter>** for an even chamfer.
> 5. Select two lines that meet at a corner.

The **CHAMFER** command sequence is almost identical to the **FILLET** command, with the exception that chamfers can be uneven. That is, you can cut back farther on one side of a corner than on the other. To do this, you must give AutoCAD two distances instead of one radius value.

In this exercise, we draw even chamfers on the four corners of the square. Using the **Polyline** option, we chamfer all four corners at once.

To access the **Chamfer** tool requires opening a simple drop-down list that has the **Fillet, Chamfer,** and **Blend Curves** tools. We do not address blended curves here.

✔ Open the drop-down list shown in Figure 3-16.

✔ Pick the **Chamfer** tool.

   *Notice that the **Chamfer** tool replaces the **Fillet** tool on the ribbon. AutoCAD prompts:*

   Select first line or [Undo Polyline Distance Angle Trim mEthod Multiple]:

**Figure 3-16**
Drop-down list

**polyline:** A two-dimensional object made of lines and arcs that may have varying widths.

✔ Select **Distance** from the command line options.
*The next prompt is:*

Specify first chamfer distance <0.00>:

✔ Type **1 <Enter>.**
*AutoCAD asks for another distance:*

Specify second chamfer distance <1.00>:

*The first distance has become the default and will give you a chamfer cut evenly on both sides. If you want an asymmetrical chamfer, enter a different value for the second distance.*

✔ Press **<Enter>** to accept the default, making the chamfer distances symmetrical.
*At this point, you could proceed to chamfer each corner of the square independently. However, if you have drawn the square using the* **RECTANG** *command, you have a quicker option. The* **RECTANG** *command draws a* **polyline** *rectangle. Polylines are not discussed here, but for now it is useful to know that a polyline is a single entity comprising multiple lines and arcs. If you have drawn a closed polyline and specify the option in the* **CHAMFER** *or* **FILLET** *command, AutoCAD edits all corners of the object.*

✔ Select **Polyline** from the command line options.
*AutoCAD prompts:*

Select 2D polyline or [Distance Angle Method]:

✔ Run your cursor over any part of the filleted square.
*You see a preview image of the square with chamfers at all four corners.*

✔ Pick any part of the square.
*You should have four neat chamfers on your square, replacing the fillets from the previous section. Your screen should resemble Figure 3-17.*

**Figure 3-17**
*Polyline* chamfer

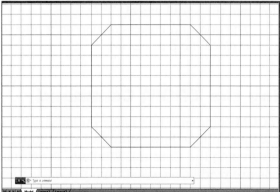

# Zooming and Panning with the Scroll Wheel

The capacity to zoom in and out of a drawing is one of the more impressive benefits of working on a CAD system. When drawings get complex, it often becomes necessary to work in detail on small portions of the drawing space. This is done easily with the **ZOOM** command or with the scroll wheel on your mouse. We begin with the convenient scroll wheel technique and then explore the **ZOOM** command in the next section.

✔ You should have a square with chamfered corners on your screen from the previous section.

Zooming and panning with the scroll wheel is simple and convenient, but less precise than some of the options in the **ZOOM** command. To better control results, position the crosshairs at or near the center of the objects you want to magnify, and do not move the crosshairs between zooms. AutoCAD will zoom in or out centered on the crosshairs' position.

✔ Place the cursor near the center of the chamfered square and turn the scroll wheel forward (away from you) a small amount. If your scroll wheel moves in clicks, one click will do.
*Your screen image will be enlarged.*

✔ Turn the wheel forward again.
*Your screen is further enlarged.*

✔ Turn the wheel back (toward you) to zoom out.

## Panning with the Scroll Wheel

Panning with the mouse is equally simple and does everything the **PAN** command will do.

✔ Place the crosshairs anywhere inside or near the chamfered square.

✔ Press the scroll wheel down gently, so that it clicks, and hold it down.
*As soon as you do this, the crosshairs will be replaced by the pan cursor, which looks like a small hand. With this cursor displayed, you can shift the position of your drawing within the drawing area.*

✔ With the pan cursor displayed, move the mouse slowly in several directions.
*Objects in your drawing, including the screen grid and the X- and Y-axes, move with the motion of your mouse.*

✔ Release the scroll wheel.
*The grid and objects drawn on it have moved, and the crosshairs replace the pan cursor.*

## Using the ZOOM Command

The **ZOOM** command has many options, a few of which we demonstrate here. Other options have more technical functions. Here we demonstrate zooming using the **Extents, Window, Previous,** and **All** options. These options are readily accessed from the navigation bar at the right of the screen.

| ZOOM | |
|---|---|
| **Command** | Zoom |
| **Alias** | Z |
| **Menu** | View |
| **Tool** | |

**Figure 3-18**
*Zoom* tool on drop-down list

## Zoom Extents

Extents refers to the area within a drawing that actually contains complete drawn objects. When you **Zoom** to **Extents,** AutoCAD will display only that area of your drawing where you have actually drawn something. We demonstrate this first because it is the default option on the navigation bar. Since it may have been replaced by another option on your navigation bar, we start by opening the **ZOOM** command drop-down list.

✔ Pick the arrow below the **Zoom** tool on your navigation bar.
   *The **Zoom** tool is the third tool down on the navigation bar. This opens the drop-down tool list shown in Figure 3-18. **Zoom Extents** is at the top of the list.*

✔ Pick the **Zoom Extents** tool from the navigation bar, as shown in Figure 3-18.
   *AutoCAD immediately zooms to display an area containing the complete objects in your drawing.*

> **NOTE**
> • The extents area here is slightly larger than your chamfered square. This is because you have also drawn two lines and a circle on layers that are now turned off. Though these objects are not displayed, they are still part of your drawing and are considered when AutoCAD determines extents.
> • If your navigation bar has been turned off, you can turn it on by typing **navbar** **<Enter>** and then **on <Enter>**.

## Zoom Window

A very common option for zooming is to create a window around the objects you want to magnify. You can select the **Zoom Window** tool from the drop-down list, but you can also force a window selection simply by entering the **ZOOM** command and drawing a window. Try this:

✔ Type **z <Enter>.**
   *This alias executes the **ZOOM** command. The prompt that follows looks like this:*

   [All Center Dynamic Extents Previous Scale Window Object] <realtime>:

   *You can force a window selection by picking two points on the screen.*

✔ Pick a point just below and to the left of the lower left-hand corner of your square (point 1 in Figure 3-19).
   *AutoCAD asks for another point:*

   Specify opposite corner:

   *You are being asked to define a window, just as in the **ERASE** command. This window is the basis for what AutoCAD displays next. Because you are not going to make a window that exactly conforms to the screen size and shape, AutoCAD interprets the window this way: Everything in the window will be shown, plus whatever additional area is needed to fill the screen. The center of the window becomes the center of the new display.*

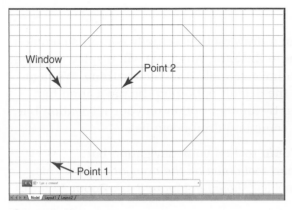

**Figure 3-19**
Selecting window to zoom

**Figure 3-20**
Results of *Zoom Window*

✔ Pick a second point near the center of your square (point 2 in the figure).
*AutoCAD will zoom in dynamically until the lower left corner of the square is enlarged on your screen, as shown in Figure 3-20.*

✔ Using the same method, try zooming up farther on the chamfered corner of the square. If **Snap** mode is on, you might need to turn it off.

*Remember that you can repeat the **ZOOM** command by pressing <**Enter**> or the spacebar. At this point, most people cannot resist seeing how much magnification they can get by zooming repeatedly on the same corner or angle of a chamfer. Go ahead. After a couple of zooms, the angle does not appear to change, though the placement shifts as the center of your window changes. An angle is the same angle no matter how close you get to it, but what happens to the spacing of the grid and snap as you move in?*

*When you are through experimenting with window zooming, try zooming to the previous display, as follows.*

## Zoom Previous

✔ Press <**Enter**> to repeat the **ZOOM** command.

✔ Select **Previous** from the command line options.
*You can also select **Zoom Previous** from the drop-down list on the navigation bar. You should now see your previous display.*
*AutoCAD keeps track of up to 10 previous displays.*

✔ **Zoom Previous** as many times as you can until you get a message that says:

No previous view saved.

## Zoom All

**Zoom All** zooms out to display the limits of the drawing, placing the origin (0,0) at the bottom of the drawing area. It is useful when you have been working in a number of small areas of a drawing and are ready to view the whole scene. It also quickly undoes the effects of zooming or panning repeatedly with the scroll wheel.

To see it work, you should be zoomed in on a portion of your display before executing **Zoom All**.

✔ Use the scroll wheel or the **ZOOM** command to zoom in on a window within your drawing.

✔ Repeat **ZOOM** again.

✔ Select **All** from the command line options, or right-click and select **All** from the shortcut menu.

## Entering Single-Line Text

AutoCAD has many options for drawing text. The simplest allows you to enter single lines of text and displays them as you type. You can backspace through lines to make corrections if you do not exit the command. We provide this brief introduction for those who may wish to label their drawings at this point.

For this exercise we add some simple left-justified text to your drawing. We stay on Layer **1** and add the words "Chamfered Square," as shown in Figure 3-21.

✔ Open the **Text** drop-down list and then pick the **Single Line** text tool from the **Annotation** panel, as shown in Figure 3-22.

**Figure 3-21**
Text added

**Figure 3-22**
**Single Line** text tool

*You see a prompt with three options in the command line:*

Specify start point of text or [Justify Style]:

*Here we use the default method by picking a start point. This gives us standard left-justified text, inserted left to right from the point we pick.*

✔ Pick a start point near the middle left of the square, as shown in Figure 3-21. We chose the point (5,5).

*Study the prompt that follows and be sure that you do not attempt to enter text yet:*

Specify height <0.20>:

*This gives you the opportunity to set the text height. The number you type specifies the height of uppercase letters in the units you have specified for the current drawing. We will specify a slightly larger text height.*

✔ Type **.3 <Enter>**.

*The prompt that follows allows you to place text in a rotated position:*

Specify rotation angle of text <0>:

*The default of 0° orients text in the usual horizontal manner. Other angles can be specified by typing a degree number relative to the polar coordinate system or by showing a point. If you show a point, it is taken as the second point of a baseline along which the text string will be placed. For now, we stick to horizontal text.*

✔ Press **<Enter>** to accept the default angle (0).

*Now it is time to enter the text itself. There is no prompt for text at the command line. Text is entered directly on the screen at the selected start point.*

*Notice that a blinking cursor has appeared at the start point on your screen. This shows where the first letter you type will be placed. Watch the screen as you type, and you can see dynamic text at work.*

✔ Type **Chamfered <Enter>**.

*Remember, you cannot use the spacebar in place of the **<Enter>** key when entering text. Notice that the text cursor jumps down a line when you press **<Enter>**.*

✔ Type **Square <Enter>**.

*The text cursor jumps down again. This is how AutoCAD allows for easy entry of multiple lines of text directly on the screen in a drawing. To exit the command, you need to press **<Enter>** again at the prompt.*

✔ Press **<Enter>** to exit the command.

*This completes the process and returns you to the command prompt. Your screen should resemble Figure 3-21.*

# Chapter Summary

In this chapter you learned how to add layers, colors, linetypes, line-weights, linetype scales, fillets, and chamfers, so now you can create standard mechanical drawings that are more professional and contain more information about the objects represented. You can create layers with distinct qualities and uses to separate different types of information and control these layers independently. These layers can be turned on and off, frozen, thawed, locked, styled for plotting, or ignored in plotting. Additionally you can now zoom in or out of your drawing, pan across the area in which you are working, and add single-line text to your drawings.

# Chapter Test Questions

## Multiple Choice

*Circle the correct answer.*

1. Which linetype is loaded by default?
   a. Solid
   b. Center
   c. Continuous
   d. Diagonal

2. AutoCAD's default color system is:
   a. Pantone
   b. Index
   c. RGB
   d. True Color

3. Which is **not** entered when you create single-line text?
   a. Text height
   b. Rotation angle
   c. Text location
   d. Text color

4. Which of these **cannot** be accomplished using the **Layer** drop-down list?
   a. Create new layers
   b. Set current layer
   c. Turn layers on and off
   d. Freeze and thaw

5. How many layers can you create in AutoCAD?
   a. 255
   b. As many as you like
   c. 256
   d. It depends on your computer

## Matching

*Write the number of the correct answer on the line.*

a. Fillet _____          1. Layer is not visible

b. Off _____            2. Layer cannot be edited

c. Locked _____         3. Always symmetric

d. Layer **0** _____    4. Cannot be deleted

e. Frozen _____         5. Not visible, not regenerated

## True or False

*Circle the correct answer.*

**1. True or False:** You can zoom but not pan with the scroll wheel.

**2. True or False:** Objects on the same layer need not be the same color.

**3. True or False:** It is necessary to match layers and color numbers.

**4. True or False:** Linetypes need to be loaded, but colors do not.

**5. True or False:** You can draw in only one color on one layer.

## Questions

**1.** What linetype is always available when you start a drawing from scratch in AutoCAD? What must you do to access other linetypes?

**2.** Name three ways to change the current layer.

**3.** You have been working in the **Layer Properties Manager** palette, and when you return to your drawing you find that some objects are no longer visible. What happened?

**4.** Describe the use of the scroll wheel for zooming.

**5.** In single-line text, what values must be specified before entering text content?

## Drawing Problems

**1.** Make Layer **3** current and draw a green centerline cross with two perpendicular lines, each 2 units long and intersecting at their midpoints.

**2.** Make Layer **2** current and draw a hidden line circle centered at the intersection of the cross drawn in Step 1, with a diameter of 2 units.

**3.** Make Layer **1** current and draw a red square of 2 units on a side centered on the center of the circle. Its sides run tangent to the circle.

**4.** Use a window to zoom in on the objects drawn in Steps 1, 2, and 3.

**5.** Fillet each corner of the square with a 0.125 radius fillet.

## WWW Exercise (Optional)

The Web project for this chapter takes you deeper into the world of CAD on the Internet. The Web is full of interesting and informative CAD-related websites. There are sites maintained by professional journals and CAD newsgroups, CAD industry sites, sites with drawings that can be viewed or downloaded, sites with tutorials, sites with tips on CAD technique, and sites with information on CAD-related software.

✔ Type **browser <Enter>**.

✔ If you have not made our companion website the default, navigate to it from your default site, using the address www.pearsonhighered.com/dixriley.

*Away you go!*

## Introduction to Autodesk 360 (Optional)

**Autodesk 360** is Autodesk's cloud-based platform for sharing and collaboration using AutoCAD drawings and techniques. Autodesk cloud features allow you to upload, store, share, edit, and comment on drawings. You can allow different levels of access to your **Autodesk 360** drawings so that some contacts may only view the drawing, whereas others can also edit, add comments to, or download the drawing.

For those unfamiliar with cloud-based computing, it is important to understand the difference between common desktop software and the applications that reside in the cloud. The cloud is the name given to applications that function on a remote server rather than on your local computer's hard drive. The full range of AutoCAD techniques you are learning here are made possible by the presence of the AutoCAD 2014 software installed on the computer you are using. A subset of these techniques is now available, free of charge, to anyone who has Internet access. This allows you and others you designate to access your drawings from any computer or device with an Internet connection. All that is required is that you create an **Autodesk 360** account. With this free account, you are allowed up to 3 gigabytes (GB) of server space. Frequent users will be required to have a paid subscription that provides 25 gigabytes of storage, along with other enhanced features.

Here we invite you to explore **Autodesk 360** and to begin to familiarize yourself with its interface and features. We do not provide detailed exercises, but show you how to get started.

> **NOTE**
> Please consult your instructor regarding any restrictions on the use of **Autodesk 360** that may apply to your classroom.

There are a variety of ways to access **Autodesk 360**, both within and outside the AutoCAD software. Within AutoCAD you can begin with the **ONLINEDOCS** command, which takes you directly to the **Autodesk 360** sign-in screen.

✔ From the ribbon, select the **Autodesk 360** tab.
   *You will see the set of panels shown in Figure 3-23.*

✔ Pick the **Launch Website** tool, as shown in Figure 3-23.
   *Notice that this executes the **ONLINEDOCS** command, so the same thing could be accomplished by typing this at the command line. With **AutoComplete**, this command would appear on the list after typing only **on**.*

**Figure 3-23**
**Launch Website** tool

Either method takes you to the **Autodesk 360** sign-in page, as shown in Figure 3-24. If this is your first visit to **Autodesk 360** and you want to continue, you will need to create an account.

✔ If necessary, pick the **Create Account** button.

✔ If you wish to create an account at this time, fill in the information in the window shown in Figure 3-25.

Note that you will have to scroll down to check the **Terms of Service** box. Once you have an account, you will pick the **Sign In** box instead, and then fill in your **Autodesk 360** ID and password.

When you are signed in for the first time, you will see the Welcome screen shown in Figure 3-26.

At this point we leave you to explore on your own. You can watch the video or select one of the other options to learn more about **Autodesk 360.**

✔ When you are done, close the window to disconnect from the website.

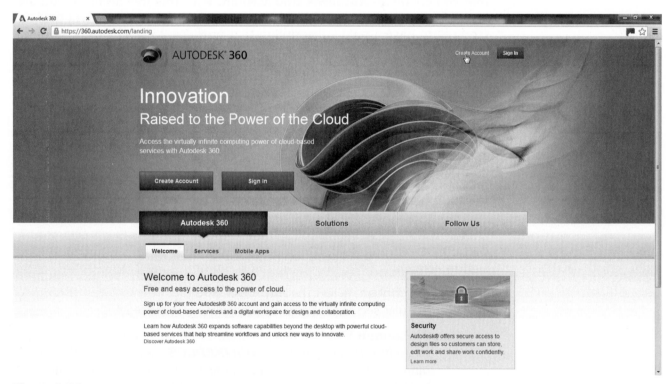

**Figure 3-24**
**Autodesk 360** website

**Figure 3-25**
**Create Account**

**Figure 3-26**
Welcome screen

## Chapter Drawing Projects

 **M**

# Drawing 3-1: *Mounting Plate* [BASIC]

This drawing gives you experience using centerlines, fillets, and chamfers. Because there are no hidden lines, you have no need for Layer **2,** but we continue to use the same numbering system for consistency. Draw the continuous lines in red on Layer **1** and the centerlines in green on Layer **3.**

> **TIP**
>
> Rather than start each drawing as a new drawing, use the **Save Drawing As** dialog box to save drawings under different names so that you don't have to re-create layers in each new drawing.

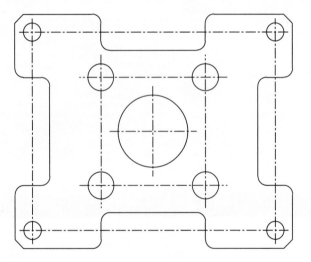

## Drawing Suggestions

$$GRID = 0.5$$
$$SNAP = 0.25$$
$$LTSCALE = 0.5$$

- Change linetype scale along with setting grid and snap.
- Pay attention to the linetypes as you draw, and change the current layer accordingly.
- Draw the Mounting Plate outline with the **LINE** command. Then, chamfer the four corners and fillet all other corners as shown.

**Drawing 3-1**
Mounting Plate

# Drawing 3-2: *Stepped Shaft* [INTERMEDIATE]

This two-view drawing uses continuous lines, centerlines, chamfers, and fillets. You may want to zoom in to enlarge the drawing space you are actually working in, and pan right and left to work on the two views.

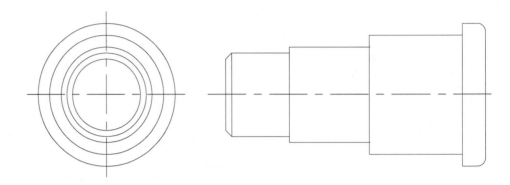

## Drawing Suggestions

GRID = 0.25

SNAP = 0.125

LTSCALE = 0.5

- Center the front view in the neighborhood of (2,5). The right-side view will have a starting point at about (5,4.12), before the chamfer cuts this corner off.

- Draw the circles in the front view first, using the vertical dimensions from the side view for diameters. Save the inner circle until after you have drawn and chamfered the right-side view.

- Draw a series of rectangles for the side view, lining them up with the circles of the front view. Then, chamfer two corners of the leftmost rectangle and fillet two corners of the rightmost rectangle.

- Use the chamfer on the side view to line up the radius of the inner circle.

- Remember to set the current layer to **3** before drawing the centerlines.

## 3D Models of Multiple-View Drawings

If you have any difficulty visualizing objects in the multiple-view drawings in this chapter, you may wish to refer to the images in Drawings 13-5A, B, C, and D. These are 3D solid models derived from 2D drawings.

0.125 X 0.125
CHAMFER

0.125 FILLET

ø1.750

ø2.000

ø2.750

ø3.25

1.375

1.75

2.00

0.50

5.625 REF

**Drawing 3-2**
Stepped Shaft

## M Drawing 3-3: *Base Plate* [INTERMEDIATE]

This drawing uses continuous lines, hidden lines, centerlines, and fillets. The side view should be quite easy once the front view is drawn. Remember to change layers when you want to change linetypes.

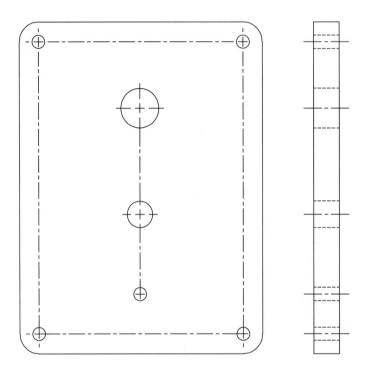

## Drawing Suggestions

GRID = 0.25

SNAP = 0.125

LTSCALE = 0.5

• Study the dimensions carefully and remember that every grid increment is 0.25, and snap points not on the grid are exactly halfway between grid points. The four circles at the corners are 0.38 (actually 0.375 rounded off) over and in from the corner points. This is three snap spaces (0.375 = 3 × 0.125).

• Position the three circles along the centerline of the rectangle carefully. Notice that dimensions are given from the center of the screw holes at top and bottom.

• Use the circle perimeters to line up the hidden lines on the side view, and the centers to line up the centerlines.

**Drawing 3-3**
Base Plate

## M Drawing 3-4: *Template* [ADVANCED]

This drawing gives you practice with fillets, chamfers, layers, and zooming. Notice that because of the smaller dimensions here, we have recommended a smaller **LTSCALE** setting.

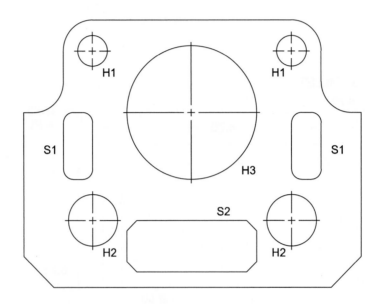

## Drawing Suggestions

GRID = 0.25

SNAP = 0.125

LTSCALE = 0.25

- Start by drawing the outline of the object and then fillet and chamfer as shown.
- Because this drawing appears quite small on your screen, it would be a good idea to zoom in on the actual drawing space you are using and pan if necessary.
- *Typ* is a standard abbreviation for *typical* and indicates that the dimension is used in multiple locations.
- Draw the cutouts labeled S1 and S2 as rectangles and then fillet and chamfer as shown.
- Label all cutouts as shown using the **TEXT** command.

## Regen

When you change a linetype scale setting, you see the message *Regenerating model* in the command line. Regeneration is the process by which AutoCAD translates drawing data into screen images. Regeneration happens automatically when certain operations are performed.

**Drawing 3-4**
Template

## A Drawing 3-5: *Half Block* [INTERMEDIATE]

This cinder block is the first project using architectural units. Set units, grid, and snap as indicated, and everything falls into place nicely.

### Drawing Suggestions

UNITS = Architectural; Precision = 0″ -01/4″

GRID = 1/4″

SNAP = 1/4″

- Start with the lower left corner of the block at the point (0″-01″, 0″-01″) to keep the drawing well placed on the display.

- Set the fillet radius to **1/2″** or **0.5.** Notice that you can use decimal versions of fractions. The advantage is that they are easier to type.

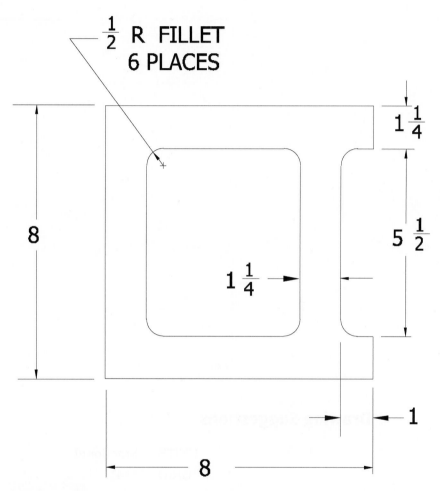

$\frac{1}{2}$ R  FILLET
6 PLACES

**Drawing 3-5**
Half Block

## M Drawing 3-6: *Packing Flange* [ADVANCED]

This drawing uses continuous lines, hidden lines, centerlines, and fillets. The side view should be quite easy once the top view is drawn. Remember to change layers when you want to change linetypes.

## Drawing Suggestions

UNITS = Fractional

GRID = 1/4″

SNAP = 1/16″

LTSCALE = 0.5

- Study the dimensions carefully, and remember that every grid increment is 1/4″, and snap points not on the grid are exactly halfway between grid points. Notice that the units should be set to fractions.

- Begin by drawing the outline and then the three centerlines in the top view. Then, proceed by drawing all circles.

- The circles can be drawn using a center point and a diameter. Position the center of the circle where the centerlines cross, and type in the diameter.

- Use the top view to line up all the lines on the side view.

**1 1/8 DRILL**
**2 HOLES**

$\text{C}_\text{L}$

$5\frac{3}{4}$

$1\frac{1}{2}$ Fillet

$\text{C}_\text{L}$

6

$1\frac{3}{16}$

$8\frac{3}{8}$

$4\frac{1}{8}$ Dia

$2\frac{1}{8}$ Dia

$\frac{1}{4}$ Fillet

$2\frac{5}{8}$

$2\frac{1}{8}$

$1\frac{5}{16}$

3 Dia

**Drawing 3-6**
Packing Flange

# 4 chapterfour

# Templates, Copies, and Arrays

# CHAPTER OBJECTIVES

- Set limits
- Create a template
- Save a template drawing
- Use the **MOVE** command
- Use the **COPY** command
- Use the **ARRAY** command for rectangular arrays
- Create center marks
- Create macros with the **Action Recorder**
- Change plot settings

## Introduction

In this chapter, you learn some real time-savers. If you are tired of defining the same layers, along with units, grid, snap, and ltscale, for each new drawing, read on. You are about to learn how to create your own template drawings. With templates, you can begin each new drawing with setups you have defined and saved in previous AutoCAD sessions, or with a variety of predefined setups included in the software.

In addition, you learn to reshape the grid using the **LIMITS** command and to copy, move, and array objects on the screen so that you do not have to draw the same thing twice. We begin with the **LIMITS** command, because we want to change the limits as part of defining your first template.

## Setting Limits

> **TIP**
>
> A general procedure for changing the limits of your grid is:
>
> 1. Type **Limits <Enter>** or select **Format > Drawing Limits** from the menu bar.
> 2. Enter the coordinates of a lower left corner.
> 3. Enter the coordinates of an upper right corner.
> 4. **Zoom All.**

**limits:** In AutoCAD, two points that define the outer boundaries of the drawing area in a given drawing. The points are defined by ordered pairs in a Cartesian coordinate system, with the first point being the lower left corner and the second being the upper right corner of a rectangular space.

You have changed the density of the screen grid many times, but always within the same space, with $12 \times 9$ **limits.** Now, you will learn how to change the shape by setting new limits to emulate other sheet sizes or any other space you want to represent; but first, a word about model space and paper space.

## Model Space and Paper Space

**layout:** A 2D representation of what a drawing will look like when plotted. Layouts are created in paper space, with viewports in which objects drawn in model space can be positioned and scaled for plotting.

*Model space* is an AutoCAD concept that refers to the imaginary space in which we create and edit objects. In model space, objects are always drawn at full scale (1 screen unit = 1 unit of length in the real world). The alternative to model space is *paper space,* in which screen units represent units of length on a piece of paper. You encounter paper space when you begin to use AutoCAD's **layout** features. A layout is like an overlay on your drawing in which you specify a sheet size, a scale, and other paper-related options. Layouts also allow you to create multiple views of the same model space objects. To avoid confusion and keep your learning curve on track, however, we avoid using layouts for the time being.

In this exercise, we reshape our model space grid to emulate different drawing sheet sizes. This is not necessary in later practice. With AutoCAD, you can scale your drawing to fit any drawing sheet size when it comes time to plot. Ultimately, model space limits should be determined by the overall size and shape of objects in your drawing, not by the paper you are going to use when you plot.

We begin by creating a new drawing and changing its limits from an Architectural A-size sheet ($12 \times 9$) to an Architectural B-size sheet ($18 \times 12$).

✔ Pick the **New** tool from the **Quick Access** toolbar.

> *This brings you to the **Select template** dialog box. At this point we continue to use the acad.dwt template. Once you have created your own template, it will appear in this box along with all the others.*

✔ Press **<Enter>** to select the acad.dwt template.

✔ Type **z <Enter>**.

✔ Type **a <Enter>**.

Thus far we have always worked with the default setting, which displays the grid beyond limits. By changing this so the grid is displayed only to cover the limits, you will get a better sense of what the limits actually are. Later, we will suggest returning to the default setting.

✔ Right-click on the **Snap Mode** or **Grid Display** button on the status bar, and select **Settings** from the shortcut menu.

*This opens the **Drafting Settings** dialog box, with the **Snap and Grid** tab showing. At the bottom right of this tab there is a panel called **Grid Behavior**.*

✔ In the **Grid Behavior** panel, uncheck the box next to **Display grid beyond limits.**

✔ Click **OK.**

*Your grid is now displayed only between the current limits of (0,0) and (12,9), as shown in Figure 4-1.*

**Figure 4-1**
Grid displayed between current limits

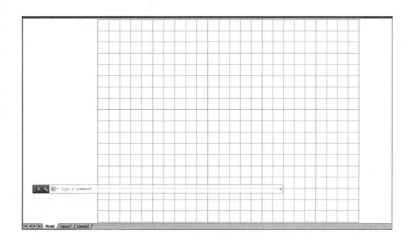

## Setting New Limits

Limits are set using the **LIMITS** command. It will be convenient to locate the **LIMITS** command on the **Format** pull-down menu, so we suggest that you open the menu bar by switching to the **Menu Bar** workspace.

✔ Open the **Workspace** drop-down list on the **Quick Access** toolbar, and switch to the **Menu Bar** workspace, or open the drop-down list to the right of the **Workspace** drop-down list and select **Show Menu Bar.**
*You are now ready to proceed with creating new limits. Leaving your grid where it is gives you visual feedback about what is happening when you change limits.*

*The **LIMITS** command can be typed at the command line prompt or selected from the **Format** menu on the menu bar.*

✔ Type **limits <Enter>,** or select **Format > Drawing Limits** from the menu bar, as shown in Figure 4-2.
*Either way, the **LIMITS** command works in the command area. You see this prompt:*

Reset Model Space limits:

Specify lower left corner or [ON OFF] <0.0000,0.0000>:

*The on and off options control a feature called limits checking. They determine what happens when you attempt to draw outside the drawing limits. With checking off, nothing happens. With checking on, you get a message that displays, "Attempt to draw outside limits", and AutoCAD does not allow you to begin a new entity outside of limits. By default, limits checking is off.*

**Figure 4-2**
Drawing limits

*The default value shows that the current lower left corner of the grid is at (0,0), where we leave it.*

✔ Press **<Enter>** to accept the default lower left corner.
   *AutoCAD prompts:*

   Specify upper right corner <12.0000,9.0000>:

   *Changing these settings changes the size of your grid.*

✔ Type **18,12 <Enter>.**
   *Your grid stretches out to the right to reach the new x limit of 12. The usual **Zoom All** procedure enlarges and centers the grid on your screen.*

✔ Type **z <Enter>** to enter the **ZOOM** command.

✔ Type **a <Enter>** to **Zoom All.**
   *You should have an 18 × 12 grid centered on your screen, as shown in Figure 4-3.*

**Figure 4-3**
18 × 12 grid is centered

✔ Move the cursor to the upper right corner to check its coordinates.
*This is the grid we use for your B-size template drawing.*
*It represents a larger area in model space than the 12 × 9 grid.*

You may want to experiment with setting limits using some of the possibilities shown in Figure 4-4, which is a table of drawing sheet sizes. It shows the two sets of standard sizes. The standard size you use may be determined by your plotter. Some plotters that plot on C-size paper, for example, take a 24 × 18 sheet but do not take a 22 × 17 sheet. This information should be programmed into your plotter driver software and appears in the **Plot Configuration** dialog box in the image preview area. Though we currently work in model space, the same procedures for setting limits will be relevant to setting up your layout in paper space.

**Figure 4-4**
Drawing sheet sizes

| SHEET SIZE | STANDARD | "X" DIM | "Y" DIM |
|---|---|---|---|
| A | ANSI Y14.1 | 11 " | 8.5 " |
| A | ARCHITECTURAL | 12 " | 9 " |
| B | ANSI Y14.1 | 17 " | 11 " |
| B | ARCHITECTURAL | 18 " | 12 " |
| C | ANSI Y14.1 | 22 " | 17 " |
| C | ARCHITECTURAL | 24 " | 18 " |
| D | ANSI Y14.1 | 34 " | 22 " |
| D | ARCHITECTURAL | 36 " | 24 " |
| E | ANSI Y14.1 | 44 " | 34 " |
| E | ARCHITECTURAL | 48 " | 36 " |

SELECT FROM CHART UPPER RIGHT CORNER

SETTING LIMITS FOR PLOTTER CONFIGURATION

"Y" DIM

SHEET SIZE

LOWER LEFT CORNER SETTING STAYS AT 0,0

"X" DIM

After you are finished exploring the **LIMITS** command, you will create the other new settings you want and save this drawing as your B-size template. Once you have saved the new template, you can use it any time you want to create a drawing with 18 × 12 limits.

## Creating a Template

**TIP**

A general procedure for creating a template is:

1. Define layers and change settings (grid, snap, units, limits, ltscale, etc.) as desired.
2. Save the drawing as an **AutoCAD Drawing Template** file.

To make your own *template* so that you can begin new drawings with the settings you want, all you have to do is create a drawing that has those settings and then save it as a template.

✔ Make changes to the current drawing as follows:

| | | | |
|---|---|---|---|
| GRID: | 0.50 ON | COORD: | ON |
| SNAP: | 0.25 ON | LTSCALE: | 0.5 |
| UNITS: | 2-place decimal | LIMITS: | (0,0) (18,12), displayed beyond limits |

✔ Also, ensure that **Snap Mode, Grid Display,** and **Dynamic Input** are on, and that **Infer Constraints, Ortho Mode, Polar Tracking, Object Snap, 3D Object Snap, Object Snap Tracking, Dynamic UCS, Lineweight, Transparency, Quick Properties, Selection Cycling,** and **Annotation Monitor** are off.

> **NOTE**
>
> Do not leave anything drawn on your screen or it will come up as part of the template each time you open a new drawing. For some applications, this is quite useful, but for now, we want a blank template.

✔ Create layers and associated colors, linetypes, and settings to match those in Figure 4-5.

**Figure 4-5**
Creating layers

*Remember that you can make changes to your template at any time. The layers called dim, hatch, and text are not used here, but creating them now saves time and makes your template more complete later.*

At this point, your drawing is ready to be saved as a template, which is the focus of the next task.

## Saving a Template Drawing

> **NOTE**
>
> In situations where several students may be using the same computer at different times during the day or week, changing AutoCAD settings may cause confusion. In this case, your instructor may not want you to save a template file or may want it in a different location or under a different name. Ask your instructor how it is to be done in your class.

A drawing becomes a template when it is saved as a template. Template files are given a .dwt extension and placed in the **Template** file folder.

✔ You should be in the drawing created in the last task. All the drawing changes should be made as described previously.

✔ Pick the **Save** tool from the **Quick Access** toolbar.

*This opens the **Save Drawing As** dialog box shown in Figure 4-6. The **File name:** edit box contains the name of the current drawing. If you have not named the drawing, it is called Drawing1 or Drawing2.*

**Figure 4-6**
**Save Drawing As** dialog box

**NOTE**

The templates included in the AutoCAD software consist of various standard sheet sizes, all with title blocks, borders, and predefined plot styles. These are convenient. At this point, however, they can cause confusion because they are created in paper space and automatically put you into a paper space layout. You have no need for titles and borders in this chapter.

*Below the **File name:** box is the **Files of type:** box, which lists options for saving the drawing.*

✔ Open the **Files of type:** list by clicking the arrow to the right of the list box.

*This opens the list of file-type options. The **AutoCAD Drawing Template** file is eighth on the list in AutoCAD 2014.*

✔ Select **AutoCAD Drawing Template (*.dwt)** file from the list.

*This also opens the **Template** file folder automatically. You see the list of templates commonly seen when creating a new drawing. There are many templates shown that are supplied by AutoCAD. These may be useful to you later. At this point, it is more important to learn how to create your own.*

✔ If necessary, double-click in the **File name:** box.

✔ Type **1B** for the new name. Or, if others also use your computer, you may want to add your initials to identify this as your template.

---

**TIP**

Because template files are listed alphabetically in the file list, it can be convenient to start your template file name with a number so that it appears before the acad and *ANSI standard* templates that come with the AutoCAD software. Numbers precede letters in the alphanumeric sequence, so your numbered template file appears at the top of the list and saves you the trouble of scrolling down to find it.

---

**ANSI standard:** Any one of many guidelines and standards created and promulgated by the American National Standards Institute.

*Once you have typed your drawing name in the **File name:** box and the **Files of type:** box shows the **AutoCAD Drawing Template** file, you are ready to save.*

✔ Click **Save.**

*This opens a **Template Options** dialog box, as illustrated in Figure 4-7. You can ignore it for now.*

**Figure 4-7**
**Template Options** dialog box

---

**NOTE**

If 1B is not at the top of your list after the PTW Templates and Sheet Sets folders, it may be because your list is sorting in descending order. To reverse order, click on **Name.**

---

✔ Click **OK** in the **Template Options** dialog box.

*The task of creating the drawing template is now complete. All that remains is to create a new drawing using the template to see how it works.*

✔ Click the **Close** button **(X)** in the upper right corner of the drawing window.

*Be sure to close the current drawing only and not the AutoCAD application window.*

✔ Pick the **New** tool from the **Quick Access** toolbar.
> *This opens the **Select template** dialog box as usual. However, now 1B is at the top of your list.*

✔ Highlight 1B or the file name you have used on the list of templates.

✔ Press **<Enter>** or click **Open**.
> *A new drawing opens with all the settings from 1B already in place. From now on you can use the 1B template any time you want a drawing with B-size limits along with the layers you have created and the other settings you have specified.*

## Using the MOVE Command

| MOVE | |
|---|---|
| **Command** | Move |
| **Alias** | M |
| **Panel** | Modify |
| **Tool** | |

> **TIP**
>
> A general procedure for using the **MOVE** command is:
>
> 1. Pick the **Move** tool from the **Modify** panel of the ribbon.
> 2. Define a selection set. (If noun/verb selection is enabled, you can reverse Steps 1 and 2.)
> 3. Choose the base point of a displacement.
> 4. Choose a second point.

The ability to copy and move objects on the screen is one of the great advantages of working on a CAD system. It can be said that CAD is to drafting as word processing is to typing. Nowhere is this analogy more appropriate than in the cut-and-paste capacities that the **COPY** and **MOVE** commands give you.

✔ Draw a circle with a radius of **1** near the center of the grid (9,6), as shown in Figure 4-8.

✔ Pick the **Move** tool from the **Modify** panel of the ribbon, as shown in Figure 4-9.
> *You are prompted to select objects to move.*

**Figure 4-8**
Drawing a circle

**Figure 4-9**
**Move** tool

✔ Pick the circle.
> *Your circle becomes dotted.*
> > *In the command line, AutoCAD tells you how many objects have been selected and prompts you to select more.*

✔ Right-click to end object selection.
  *AutoCAD prompts:*

  Specify base point or [Displacement] displacement:

  *Most often, you show the movement by picking two points that give the distance and direction in which you want the object to be moved. The base point does not have to be on or near the object you are moving. Any point will do, as long as you can use it to show how you want your objects moved. This may seem strange at first, but it will soon become natural. Of course, you can choose a point on the object if you wish. With a circle, the center point may be convenient.*

✔ If **Snap Mode** is off, turn it on.

✔ Pick any location not too close to the right edge of the screen.
  *AutoCAD gives you a rubber band from the point you have indicated and asks for a second point:*

  Specify second point or <use first point as displacement>:

  *As soon as you begin to move the cursor, AutoCAD also gives you a circle to drag so you can see the effect of the movement you are indicating. An example of how this might look is shown in Figure 4-10. Let's say you want to move the circle 3.00 to the right.*
  *Watch the dynamic input display, and stretch the rubber band out until the display reads 3.00,0,0.*

**Figure 4-10**
Moving the circle with
**Ortho** on

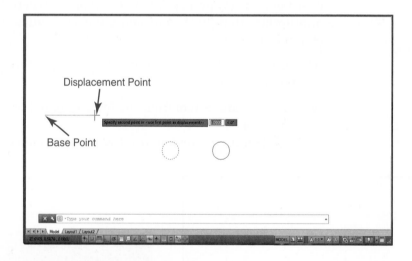

✔ Pick a point 3.00 to the right of your base point.
  *The rubber band and your original circle disappear, leaving you with a circle in the new location.*
  *Now, try a diagonal move.*

✔ If **Ortho Mode** is on, turn it off.

✔ Pick the **Move** tool, or press the spacebar to repeat the command.
  *AutoCAD follows with the Select objects: prompt.*

✔ Select the circle.

✔ Press **<Enter>** or the spacebar to end object selection.
  *AutoCAD prompts for a base point.*

✔ Pick a base point.

✔ Move the circle diagonally in any direction you like.
  *Figure 4-11 is an example of how this might look.*

**Figure 4-11**
Moving the circle diagonally

✔ Try moving the circle back near the center of the screen.
  *It may help to choose the center point of the circle as a base point this time and use the coordinate display to choose a point at or near (9,6) for your second point.*

## Moving with Grips

You can use grips to perform numerous editing procedures. This is probably the simplest of all editing methods. It does have some limitations, however. In particular, you can select only by pointing, windowing, or crossing.

✔ Pick the circle.
  *The circle is highlighted, and grips appear.*
  *Notice that grips for a circle are placed at quadrants and at the center. In more involved editing procedures, the choice of which grip or grips to use for editing is significant. In this exercise, you will do fine with any of the grips.*

✔ Move the pickbox slowly over one of the grips.
  *If you do this carefully, you notice that the pickbox locks onto the grip as it moves over it. When the cursor locks on the grip, the grip turns orange. If you are on one of the quadrant grips, the number 1.00 appears, indicating the diameter of the circle.*

✔ When the crosshairs are locked onto a grip, press the pick button.
  *The color of the selected grip changes again (from orange to red). In the command line, you see*

  Specify stretch point or [Base point Copy Undo eXit]:

  *Stretching is the first of a series of five editing modes that you can activate by selecting grips on objects. The word stretch has many meanings in AutoCAD, and they are not always what you would expect. We do not explore the stretch editing mode and the*

| Repeat MOVE |  |
| Recent Input | ▶ |
| Clipboard | ▶ |
| Isolate | ▶ |
| *✎* Erase |  |
| ✣ Move |  |
| ⚙ Copy Selection |  |
| ⬜ Scale |  |
| ↻ Rotate |  |
| Draw Order | ▶ |
| Group | ▶ |
| ⚙ Add Selected |  |
| ⬚ Select Similar |  |
| ⬚ Deselect All |  |
| Subobject Selection Filter | ▶ |
| ⬚ Quick Select... |  |
| ⬚ QuickCalc |  |
| ⬚ Find... |  |
| ⬚ Properties |  |
| Quick Properties |  |

**Figure 4-12**
Shortcut menu

*STRETCH* command here. For now, we bypass stretch and use the *Move* mode.

AutoCAD has a convenient shortcut menu for use in grip editing.

✔ Right-click.

*This opens the shortcut menu shown in Figure 4-12. It contains all the **Grip Edit** modes plus several other options.*

✔ Select **Move** on the shortcut menu.

*The shortcut menu disappears, and you are in **Move** mode. A preview circle has been added to the cursor. Notice that the prompt has changed to*

Specify move point or [Base point Copy Undo eXit]:

✔ Pick a point anywhere on the screen.

*The circle moves where you have pointed.*

✔ Press **<Esc>** to remove grips.

## Moving by Typing a Displacement

There is one more way to use the **MOVE** command. Instead of showing AutoCAD a distance and direction, you can type a horizontal and vertical displacement. For example, to move the circle 3 units to the right and 2 units up, you would use the following procedure (there is no autoediting equivalent for this procedure):

**1** Pick the circle.

**2** Type **m <Enter>** or pick the **Move** tool.

**3** Type **3,2 <Enter>** in response to the prompt for base point or displacement.

**4** Press **<Enter>** in response to the prompt for a second point.

| COPY | |
| --- | --- |
| Command | Copy |
| Alias | Co |
| Panel | Modify |
| Tool | |

## Using the COPY Command

> **TIP**
>
> A general procedure for using the **COPY** command is:
>
> 1. Pick the **Copy** tool from the **Modify** panel of the ribbon.
> 2. Define a selection set. (Steps 1 and 2 can be reversed if noun/verb selection is enabled.)
> 3. Choose a base point.
> 4. Choose a second point.
> 5. Choose another second point or press **<Enter>** to exit the command.

The **COPY** command works much like the **MOVE** command. First, we make several copies of the circle in various positions on the screen.

✔ Pick the **Copy** tool from the ribbon, as shown in Figure 4-13.

*Note that **c** is not an alias for **COPY** (it is the alias for **CIRCLE**).*

**Figure 4-13**
**Copy** tool

✔ Select the circle.

✔ Right-click to end object selection.
   *AutoCAD prompts for a base point or displacement.*

✔ Pick a base point.
   *As in the **MOVE** command, AutoCAD prompts for a second point.*

✔ Pick a second point.
   *You will see a new copy of the circle. The prompt to specify a second point of displacement has returned in the command line, and another new circle is shown at the end of the rubber band. AutoCAD is waiting for another vector, using the same base point as before.*

✔ Pick another second point.
   *Repeat this process as many times as you wish. If you get into this, you may begin to feel like a magician pulling rings out of thin air and scattering them across the screen. When you finish you should have several copies of the circle on your screen, as shown in Figure 4-14.*

**Figure 4-14**
Copying the circle

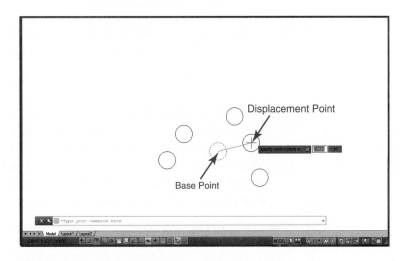

✔ Press **<Enter>** to exit the command.

## Copying with Grips

The grip editing system includes a variety of special techniques for creating multiple copies in all five modes. The function of the **Copy** option differs depending on the **Grip Edit** mode. For now, we use the **Copy** option with the **Move** mode, which provides a shortcut for the same kind of process you just executed with the **COPY** command.

Because you should have several circles on your screen now, we take the opportunity to demonstrate how you can copy or move more than one object at a time.

✔ Pick any two circles.
*The circles you pick should be highlighted, and grips should appear on both, as illustrated in Figure 4-15.*

**Figure 4-15**
Circles highlighted with grips

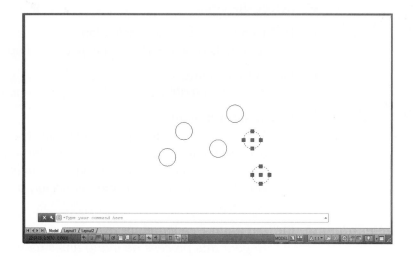

✔ Pick any grip on either of the two highlighted circles.
*The grip should change color.*

✔ Right-click and select **Move** from the shortcut menu.
*This brings you to the **Move** mode prompt:*

Specify move point or [Base point Copy Undo eXit]:

✔ Right-click and select **Copy** to initiate copying.
*AutoCAD prompts for a move point again.*
*You will find that all copying in the grip editing system is multiple copying. Once in this mode, AutoCAD continues to create copies wherever you press the pick button until you exit by typing **x** or pressing the spacebar.*

✔ Move the cursor and observe the two dragged circles.

✔ Pick a point to create copies of the two highlighted circles, as illustrated in Figure 4-16.

✔ Pick another point to create two more copies.

✔ Press **<Enter>** or the spacebar to exit the grip editing system.

✔ Press **<Esc>** to remove grips.

**Figure 4-16**
Copying highlighted circles

Displacement Point

Base Point →

## Using the ARRAY Command—Rectangular Arrays

The **ARRAY** command gives you a powerful alternative to simple copying. An *array* is the repetition of an image in matrix form. This command takes an object or group of objects and copies it a specific number of times in mathematically defined, evenly spaced locations. Once defined, an array becomes an abstract template that can be modified in numerous ways.

There are three types of arrays. *Rectangular* arrays are linear and defined by rows and columns. *Polar* arrays are angular and based on the repetition of objects around the circumference of an arc or circle. *Path* arrays are created by copying objects at evenly spaced intervals along any curve, line, or closed figure. The lines on the grid are an example of a rectangular array; the radial lines on any circular dial are an example of a polar array; path arrays can take many shapes and forms. We explore rectangular arrays in this chapter.

Rectangular arrays are defined by a certain number of rows, a certain number of columns, and the spacing between each. In preparation for this exercise, erase all the circles from your screen. This is a good opportunity to try the **Erase All** option.

✔ Pick the **Erase** tool from the ribbon.

✔ Type **all <Enter>.**

✔ Press **<Enter>** again to complete the command.

✔ Now, draw a single circle, radius 0.5, centered at the point (2,2).

✔ Pick the **Rectangular Array** tool from the **Modify** panel of the ribbon, as shown in Figure 4-17.

> *If the **Polar Array** or **Path Array** tool is showing on the ribbon, open the short list and select the **Rectangular Array** tool. This executes the **ARRAYRECT** command with a **Select objects:** prompt.*

✔ Select the 0.5 radius circle.

✔ Right-click to end object selection.

> *AutoCAD immediately creates an evenly spaced 4 × 3 preview array, as shown in Figure 4-18. Also, you will see the **Rectangular Array** contextual tab, as shown.*

array: A circular or rectangular pattern of objects.

NEW to AutoCAD 2013

Figure 4-17
Rectangular Array tool

Figure 4-18
4 × 3 preview array and
contextual tab

## The Array Contextual Tab

**contextual tab:** A ribbon tab that opens automatically when a certain command is entered. For example, the **Array** tab opens when a previously drawn array is selected.

In certain circumstances AutoCAD will automatically open a ribbon tab that is not otherwise available. This is called a ***contextual tab.*** We have our first example of a contextual tab in the **ARRAY** command. Looking across this tab from left to right, you see the **Type** designation (**Rectangular**) followed by the three panels **Columns, Rows,** and **Levels.** In each of these there are edit boxes for three specifications. If you let your cursor rest in any of these boxes, you will see a tooltip box that identifies the specification. The top is the count, so in our 4 × 3 array there are 4 columns, 3 rows, and 1 level. Levels are the third dimension of arrays and will always have a count of 1 when we are in 2D. The second edit box in the **Columns** panel is the spacing between columns. You can see that the column spacing in our preview array is 1.50. In the **Rows** panel this will be the spacing between rows, which is also 1.50. The level spacing is 1.00, but this has no meaning in our two-dimensional array. The third value is the total distance taken up by the array. It is 4.50 horizontally across the columns and 3.00 vertically along the rows.

To change these values to create an array with our own specifications, we can simply change values in the edit boxes. We will create a 5 × 3 array with 1.0 unit spacing between rows and columns, as shown in Figure 4-19. We do this by adjusting the values in the contextual tab as shown.

> **NOTE**
> If for any reason you have left the **ARRAY** command, you can open the contextual tab again by selecting any item in the array.

**Figure 4-19**
Six grips displayed, 5 × 3 array

✔ Click in the **Columns** edit box and type **5 <Enter>.**

*When you press* ***<Enter>,*** *a column will be added, making a total of 5 columns.*

> **NOTE**
>
> The function symbol that appears at the right of the edit box indicates that you can create arrays based on mathematical relationships and expressions as well as on absolute values.

✔ Click in the **Between** edit box of the **Columns** panel and type **1 <Enter>.**

*The spacing between columns will be reduced to 1.00.*

✔ Click in the **Between** edit box of the **Rows** panel and type **1 <Enter>.**

*The spacing between rows will be reduced to 1.00. At this point, your array should resemble Figure 4-19.*

✔ Press **<Esc>** to exit the **ARRAY** command.

## Using Multifunctional Grips

A more dynamic method for changing array specifications involves the use of multifunctional grips. With the array selected you also have six grips displayed, as shown in Figure 4-20. We can use these grips to alter the values that define the array. Each grip has a specific purpose and can only be used to edit certain values.

✔ Select the array.

✔ Let the cursor hover over the triangular grip at the lower right corner of the array, as shown in Figure 4-20.

*With the cursor resting on the grip you see a box with three options. Selecting among these allows you to use this grip to edit the array in three different ways. This is called a* ***multifunctional grip.*** *With the box showing, you can move the cursor over to select among the three options. The top option,* ***Column Count*** *in this case, is the default option.* ***Column Count*** *allows us to add columns to the array without changing the spacing or the number of rows. The second option,* ***Total Column Spacing,*** *allows us to*

**multifunctional grip:** A grip that can be used to edit objects in multiple ways. When a multifunctional grip is highlighted, AutoCAD displays a list of possible editing modes from which to choose.

Figure 4-20
Multifunctional grips,
contextual tab

change the spacing between columns without changing the number of columns. The third option, **Axis Angle,** allows us to tilt the
columns on an angle.

If you let the cursor hover over other grips you will find that each
has its own set of functions. The exceptions are the two grips immediately above and to the right of the lower left corner. These can only
be used to change the row and column spacing. Therefore, these two
are not multifunctional and will not call up a box of options.

Here we use the lower right corner grip to add five additional
columns.

✔ Pick the triangular grip at the lower right corner.

AutoCAD shows a grid and indicates the number of columns in the
array. Now if you move the cursor to the right, you will see preview
columns added in that direction.

✔ Move the cursor to the right until you have added five additional
columns for a total of ten.

Notice the stretched preview grid and the message that displays,
**Columns = 10,** as shown in Figure 4-21.

Figure 4-21
Preview columns added,
multifunctional grip list

✔ Press the pick button.

*Notice that the right side grips move out to the right side of the array. Now use the top left grip to add three more rows to the top of the array.*

✔ Pick the triangular grip at the top left corner of the array.

✔ Move the cursor upward to add three additional rows, as shown in Figure 4-22.

**Figure 4-22**
Preview ten columns, six rows

✔ Now, examine the changes in the ribbon tab.

*You should see 10 for the number of columns and 6 for the number of rows. We end this section by manipulating array values again to create the 15 column, 9 row array shown in Figure 4-23.*

**Figure 4-23**
Fifteen columns, nine rows

✔ Pick the triangular grip at the lower right corner of the array.

✔ Move the cursor to the right to add five more columns, for a total of 15.

✔ Pick the triangular grip at the top left corner of the array.

✔ Move the cursor up to add three more rows, for a total of 9.

✔ Press **<Esc>** to remove the grips.

*Your screen should resemble Figure 4-23.*

## Array Associativity

By default, AutoCAD arrays are created associatively. This means that all items in the array are defined as members of the array. There are several ways to edit arrays as a whole. Individual items in an array also can be edited separately.

✔ Run the cursor over the array.

*Notice that all items in the array are highlighted when the cursor rests on any item. This shows that the array is being treated as a unit.*

✔ Now hold down the **<Ctrl>** key and run the cursor over the array again.

*With the **<Ctrl>** key down, you can select individual items in the array, which enables you to edit them independently of the entire array. **However, items edited in this way remain associated with the array.** For example, if you move a single circle and then select the whole array, the moved circle will still be selected along with the array. If you want to try this out, a sample procedure would be as follows:*

**1** *Hold the **<Ctrl>** key while selecting a circle from the array.*

**2** *Pick the red grip at the center of the circle.*

**3** *Pick a second point to move the circle.*

**4** *Press **<Esc>** to remove grips.*

**5** *With the selected item in its altered position, run the cursor over the array. Notice that the entire array is previewed for selection, including the item that has been moved.*

## Creating Center Marks

We offer this section as a quick introduction to the powerful dimensioning features of AutoCAD. The **DIM** command leads you to a whole range of dimensioning possibilities. Here we use only the simplest of all dimension objects, the center mark. You will find this technique very useful in completing Drawing 4-4, Test Bracket.

✔ To begin this exercise you should have the array of circles on your screen from the last section, as shown previously in Figure 4-23.

*We begin by adding a simple center mark to one circle, as shown in Figure 4-24.*

**Figure 4-24**
Center mark

✔ Type **dim <Enter>**.

*This enters the **DIMENSION** command, which is really a whole subset of dimensioning commands. There are other ways to enter dimension commands, but at this point we will stick with the* *keyboard. The command line prompt simply gives you another prompt where you indicate the type of dimension you want to add.*

Dim:

✔ Type **cen <Enter>.**

*This specifies a center mark. AutoCAD prompts:*

Select arc or circle:

✔ Pick the circle at the lower left corner of the array, as shown in Figure 4-24.

*AutoCAD adds a center mark as shown in the figure. This is a very simple process. By changing the value of a dimension variable called **DIMCEN,** you can change from a center mark to centerlines, as shown in Figure 4-25. This will be a great help to you in Drawing 4-4.*

**Figure 4-25**
Centerlines

✔ Press **<Esc>** to exit **DIM.**

*Notice this. It is not typical. Pressing **<Enter>** or the spacebar will repeat the Dim: prompt. You must use **<Esc>** to return to the command line prompt.*

✔ Type **dimcen <Enter>.**

*Notice how this differs from what you did before when you typed **dim <Enter>** and then **cen <Enter>.** **DIMCEN** is the name of a system variable. To change a variable at the command line prompt, type the variable name and then enter a new value.*

Enter new value for DIMCEN <0.09>:

*The current value is .09. Values greater than 0 will create center marks. Values less than 0 will create centerlines and a center mark. A value of 0 will create no mark at all. By maintaining the .09 but making it negative, we can create centerlines in a scale similar to the current center mark.*

✔ Type **–.09 <Enter>.**

✔ Type **dim <Enter>.**

✔ Type **cen <Enter>.**

✔ Select the lower left corner circle again.

✔ Press **<Esc>.**

*Your screen should resemble Figure 4-25.*

# Creating Macros with the Action Recorder

Moving, copying, and arraying objects are all great ways to save steps and eliminate repeating steps as you draw. A different but equally important time-saver is the **Action Recorder.** If you have used macro recorders in other programs, the concept and process will be familiar to you. When you identify a keyboard sequence or drawing procedure that you perform repeatedly, it may be a candidate for becoming a recorded action that you can name and then call out by name. The process may be simple, but it takes forethought and often a bit of experimentation. Essentially, you turn on the **Action Recorder,** perform the desired series of actions, turn off the recorder, and then give the recorded sequence a name. Greater utility and flexibility are created by adding pauses for user input.

For this example, we record the action of adding a center mark to one of the circles in your drawing, and then play back the macro so that we can add center marks to other circles just by selecting the circles.

> **Action Recorder:** AutoCAD's program that allows the user to record, save, and name sequences of keystrokes and actions so that frequently repeated actions can be automated. This is similar to macro recording in other programs.

✔ To begin this exercise, you should have the array of circles on your screen, with the center mark on the lower left circle, as shown previously in Figure 4-25.

*We are going to create a macro based on the actions required to add a center mark to a circle. Recall from the last section that this involves typing* **dim <Enter>,** *then typing* **cen <Enter>,** *and then selecting a circle. We will record the first two actions and add a pause for user input so that the playback can be applied to any circle. First, we turn on the* **Action Recorder.** *The* **Action Recorder** *panel is at the left of the* **Manage** *tab.*

✔ Pick the **Manage** tab.

*At the far left on this tab you see the* **Action Recorder** *panel, as shown in Figure 4-26.*

**Figure 4-26**
**Action Recorder** panel

✔ Pick the **Record** button.

*You know when recording has been initiated by the opening of the* **Action Tree** *window, and the replacement of the* **Record** *button with the* **Stop** *button, as shown in Figure 4-27. When you move your cursor into the drawing area, you will also see a small red circle added to the crosshairs, indicating that macro recording is in process. As you perform actions, they will be labeled in the* **Action Tree** *window.*

✔ Type **dim <Enter>.**

*Notice the addition of* **DIM** *to the* **Action Tree,** *under the heading of* *\*ActMacro001\*, which is the default name for this macro.*

**Figure 4-27**
**Stop** button

✔ Type **cen <Enter>**.

> *Cen is added under **DIM.***
>
> We now want to create a pause for user input. For this, notice the three tools just to the right of the **Stop** button. The first allows you to insert a message in your macro, a prompt or a direction for the user. The second is for the insertion of a base point. The third is for user input.

✔ Pick the **Pause for User Input** tool, as shown in Figure 4-28.

> Now when you proceed to pick a circle, the **Action Recorder** will insert a pause, so that any circle may be selected on playback.

**Figure 4-28**
**Pause for User Input** tool

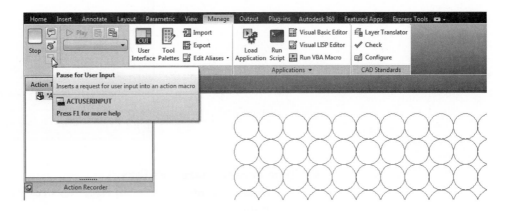

✔ Select the second circle, second row, second column, as shown in Figure 4-29.

✔ Press **<Esc>** to exit the **DIM** command.

> You are now ready to stop recording and give your macro a name.

✔ Pick the **Stop** button.

> Recording is stopped, and the **Action Macro** naming dialog box opens, as shown in Figure 4-30. The default name is entered in the **Action Macro Command Name** box.

**Figure 4-29**
Selecting second circle,
second row, second column

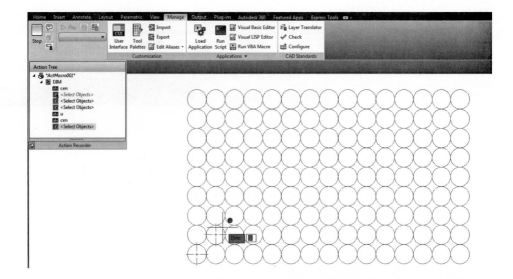

**Figure 4-30**
**Action Macro** naming
dialog box

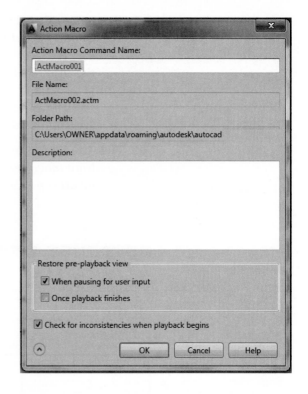

✔ Type **center_mark <Enter>**.

*Notice the underscore. **Action Recorder** does not allow spaces in names.*

✔ Click **OK**.

*Now we can play back the macro any time we want to add a center mark to a circle. In the **Action Recorder** panel there is a drop-down list of recorded macros just below the **Play** button. Your center_ mark macro should be shown as the current macro in this list. If not, open the list and select it.*

✔ With **center_mark** selected in the macro drop-down list, pick the **Play** button.

*Center_mark will be played back. Dim and cen will be entered automatically, and AutoCAD will pause for input, with the Select*

*Arc or Circle: prompt. Notice the **Action Macro** playback icon that has been added to the pickbox.*

✔ Select the third circle, third row, third column to begin building the pattern shown in Figure 4-31.

*When the action macro has run completely, you will see a message box that displays, "The playback of the action macro is complete." You can simply close this box or check the box that displays, "Do not show me this message again."*

**Figure 4-31**
Repeating center_mark macro

✔ Close the **Action Macro - Playback Complete Box.**

*The action macro will make it easy for us to add the center marks as shown. It is important to know that recorded macros work just like commands and can be repeated by pressing **<Enter>** or the spacebar.*

✔ Press **<Enter>** or the spacebar to repeat the center_mark macro, and add a center mark to the fourth circle, fourth row up, fourth column over, as shown in Figure 4-31.

✔ Continue repeating the macro to create the pattern of center marks shown in Figure 4-31.

✔ Press **<Esc>** to return to the command line prompt.

✔ To close the **Action Tree** window, select the **Home** tab or any other tab.

---

**TIP**
Action macros are retained by AutoCAD separate from the drawing in which they are created. Once recorded and named, they can be applied in any drawing.

---

## Changing Plot Settings

In this chapter, we explore various options in the **Plot** dialog box. We have used no specific drawing for illustration. Using plot previews, you can observe the effects of changing plot parameters with any drawing you like and decide at any point whether you actually want to print the results. We remind you to look at a plot preview after making changes. Plot previewing saves you a lot of time and paper and speeds up your learning curve.

✔ To begin this exploration, you should have a drawing or drawn objects on your screen so that you can observe the effects of various changes you make. The drawing you are in should use the 1B template so that limits are set to 18 × 12. The circles drawn in the last task are fine for this demonstration.

✔ Pick the **Plot** tool from the **Quick Access** toolbar.

## The Printer/Plotter Panel

One of the most basic changes you can make to a plot configuration is your selection of a plotter. Different plotters will use different sheet sizes and will have different default settings. We begin by looking into the list of plotting devices and showing you how to add a plotter to the list.

✔ Click the arrow at the right of the **Name:** list in the **Printer/plotter** panel.
*The list you see depends on your system and may include printers, plotters, and any faxing devices you have, along with AutoCAD's DWF6 ePlot.pc3, DWGFx ePlot.pc3, DWG to PD.pc3, Publish to JPG, and PNG utilities, which can be used to send drawing and plotting information to the Internet.*

## The Add-a-Plotter Wizard

For a thorough exploration of AutoCAD plotting, it is important that you have at least one plotter available to select from the **Printer/plotter** list. If you have only a printer, you will probably be somewhat limited in the range of drawing sheets available. You may have only an A-size option, for example. In this chapter you can use the **DWF6 ePlot** utility to simulate a plotter, or you can use the **Add-a-Plotter** wizard to install one of the AutoCAD standard plotter drivers, even if you actually have no such plotter on your system. To add a plotter, follow this procedure:

**1** Close the **Plot** dialog box.

**2** From the ribbon, select **Output > Plotter Manager.**

**3** From the **Plotters** window, select the **Add-a-Plotter** wizard.

**4** Click **Next** on the **Introduction** page.

**5** Check to see that **My Computer** is selected on the **Add Plotter – Begin** page, and then click **Next.**

**6** On the **Plotter Model** page, select a manufacturer and a model, and then click **Next.**

**7** Click **Next** on the **Import Pcp** or **Pc2** page.

**8** Click **Next** on the **Ports** page.

**9** Click **Next** on the **Plotter Name** page.

**10** Click **Finish** on the **Finish** page.

When the wizard is done, the new plotting device is added to your list of plotting devices in the **Plot Configuration** dialog box.

✔ If you have closed the **Plot** dialog box to install a plotter driver, reopen it. Then open the list of plotting devices again.

✔ From the list of plotting devices, select a plotter or the **DWF6 ePlot** utility to simulate a plotter.

## Paper Size

Now that you have a plotter selected, you should have a number of paper size options.

✔ From the **Paper size** list, below the plotter **Name** list, select a B-size drawing sheet.

> *The exact size depends on the plotter you have selected. An ANSI B 17 × 11 sheet is a common choice.*

## Drawing Orientation

Drawing orientation choices are found on the expanded **Plot** dialog box, as shown in Figure 4-32.

**Figure 4-32**
**Plot** dialog box expanded

✔ If your dialog box is not already expanded, click the right arrow button (>) at the bottom right of the dialog box.

> *There are basically two options for drawing orientation: portrait, in which the short edge of the paper is across the bottom, and landscape, in which the long edge is across the bottom. Portrait is typical of a letter or printed sheet of text, and landscape is typical of a drawing sheet. Your plotting device has a default orientation, but you can print either way using the radio buttons. Drawing orientation obviously has a major impact on how the plotting area of the page is used, so be sure to check out the partial preview any time you switch orientations. Try the following:*

✔ Pick the **Preview** button to see how your current drawing orientation is interpreted.

✔ Press **<Esc>** or **<Enter>** to return to the **Plot** dialog box.

✔ Switch from **Landscape** to **Portrait,** or vice versa.

✔ Pick the **Preview** button again to see how drawing orientation changes the plot.

> **TIP**
>
> On some plotters, you have a choice of different paper orientations. You may have an 11 × 17 and a 17 × 11 option, for example. In this case, there should be a correlation between the paper you choose and the drawing orientation. If you are plotting in landscape, select the 17 × 11; in portrait, select the 11 × 17. Otherwise your paper settings will be 90° off from your drawing orientation, and things will get confusing.

✔ For the following task, check to see that your drawing orientation is set to **Landscape.**

*This is the default for most plotters.*

## Plot Area

Look at the **Plot area** panel at the left of the **Plot** dialog box. This is a crucial part of the dialog box that allows you to specify the portion of your drawing to be plotted. Options include **Window, Display, Limits,** and **Extents.** Changes here have a significant impact on the effective plotting area.

The list box shows the options for plotting area. **Display** creates a plot using whatever is actually on the screen. If you used the **ZOOM** command to enlarge a portion of the drawing before entering **PLOT** and then selected this option, AutoCAD would plot whatever was showing in your drawing window. Limits, as you know, are specified using the **LIMITS** command. If you are using our standard Architectural B-size template and select **Limits,** the plot area will be 18 × 12. **Extents** refers to the actual drawing area in which you have drawn objects. It can be larger or smaller than the limits of the drawing.

✔ Try switching among **Limits, Extents, Display,** and **Window** selections, and pick the **Preview** button to see the results.

*Whenever you make a change, also observe the changes in the **Plot scale** boxes showing inches = units. Assuming that **Fit to paper** is checked, you will see significant changes in these scale ratios as AutoCAD adjusts scales according to the area specified.*

## Plot Offset

The **Plot offset** panel is at the bottom left of the **Plot** dialog box. Plot offset determines the way the plot area is positioned on the drawing sheet. Specifically, it determines where the plot origin is placed. The default locates the origin point (0,0) at the lower left of the plotted area and determines other locations from there. If you enter a different offset specification, (2,3), for example, the origin point of the drawing area is positioned at this point instead, and plot locations are determined from there. This has a dramatic effect on the placement of objects on paper.

The other option in **Plot offset** is to **Center the plot.** In this case, AutoCAD positions the drawing so that the center point of the plot area coincides with the center point of the drawing sheet.

✔ Try various plot offset combinations, including **Center the plot,** and pick the **Preview** button to see the results.

# Chapter Summary

The ability to create and save drawing templates is a very significant addition to your set of drawing skills. It allows you to skip many steps in drawing setup and to create your own library of predefined drawing setups for different types of drawings. An essential factor in setting up any drawing or template is the specification of limits that define the size and outer frame of your drawing area in whatever units are appropriate for your application. You have also gained the very significant skill of moving and copying objects you have drawn so that objects do not have to be drawn twice. Or, if many identical objects are to be created in a regular configuration of rows and columns, you can draw one object and multiply it across the desired matrix using the **ARRAY** command. Also, you have learned to add center marks and centerlines to circles and to change various plot settings in the **Plot** dialog box. You have learned to create action macros to record often repeated sequences of keystrokes and selections that can be played back to automate many actions. The drawings at the end of this chapter draw on all these new skills.

# Chapter Test Questions

## Multiple Choice

*Circle the correct answer.*

1. To facilitate creating new drawings from a previous drawing:
   a. Save it in the **Template** folder
   b. Save it in the **Save Drawing As** folder
   c. Save it as a prototype drawing
   d. Save it with all the settings you want, but no objects drawn

2. In the **MOVE** command, after defining a selection set:
   a. Pick a move location
   b. Pick an endpoint
   c. Define a displacement vector
   d. Define a vector location

3. In grip editing, you can select objects by:
   a. Windowing
   b. Typing **L** for **last**
   c. Crossing
   d. Pointing with the pickbox

4. To remove grips:
   a. Press **Cancel**
   b. Pick any point not on an object
   c. Double-click in the drawing area
   d. Press **<Esc>**

5. To access the **Grip Edit** shortcut menu:

    a. Right-click after selecting objects

    b. Pick the **Grip Edit** tool

    c. Right-click the **Grip Edit** button

    d. Right-click on an object you want to edit

## Matching

*Write the number of the correct answer on the line.*

a. Clock face _____          1. Template

b. Grid _____               2. Polar array

c. Macros _____          3. Centerlines

d. .dwt _____             4. **Action Recorder**

e. –.09 _____            5. Rectangular array

## True or False

*Circle the correct answer.*

1. **True or False:** Any drawing may be saved as a template drawing.

2. **True or False:** By default the **COPY** command creates multiple copies of selected objects.

3. **True or False:** Rows are horizontal; columns are vertical.

4. **True or False:** The **Action Recorder** duplicates the function of the **ARRAY** command.

5. **True or False:** It is usually unnecessary to perform a full plot preview.

## Questions

1. Name at least five settings that would typically be included in a template drawing.

2. Where are template drawings stored in a standard AutoCAD file configuration? What extension is given to template file names?

3. What is the value of using a template drawing?

4. How do you access the **Grip Edit** shortcut menu?

5. What is a rectangular array? What is a polar array? What is a path array?

## Drawing Problems

1. Create a C-size drawing template using an ANSI standard sheet size, layers, and other settings as shown in this chapter. Start with your 1B template settings to make this process easier.

2. Open a drawing with your new C-size template and draw a circle with a 2-unit radius centered at (11,8).

3. Using grips, make four copies of the circle, centered at (15,8), (11,12), (7,8), and (11,4).

4. Switch to Layer **2** and draw a 1 × 1 square with its lower left corner at (1,1).

5. Create a rectangular array of the square with 14 rows and 20 columns, 1 unit between rows, and 1 unit between columns.

## WWW Exercise (Optional)

At Chapter 4 of our companion website, you will find a drawing project to complete in addition to the self-scoring chapter test. The drawing project challenges you to use edit commands in place of drawing commands. When you are ready, complete the following steps:

✔ Make sure that you are connected to your Internet service provider.

✔ **Type browser <Enter>.**

✔ If necessary, navigate to our companion website at www.pearsonhigh-ered.com/dixriley.

> *Good luck!*

## Uploading to an Autodesk 360 Account (Optional)

In this section we walk you through the process of uploading a drawing to **Autodesk 360**. In order to complete this exercise, you will need an **Autodesk 360** account with an **Autodesk 360** ID and password. If you have not set these up previously, you can easily do so now. But first, we change one setting from within the AutoCAD software.

✔ In order to prepare for this exercise, you should have a saved drawing to upload to the cloud, and you should know where it is located.

✔ From the ribbon, select the **Autodesk 360** tab.

✔ From the **Autodesk 360** tab, select the **Online Options** tool, as shown in Figure 4-33.

> *This opens the AutoCAD **Options** dialog box, with the **Online** tab open, as shown in Figure 4-34. At the top right there is an **Autodesk 360** button that will take you to the website. On the left is the **Enable automatic sync** selection box, and on the right is the **Sync my settings with the cloud** box. Here we focus on the **Enable** box.*

**Figure 4-33**
**Online Options** tool

**Figure 4-34**
**Autodesk 360 Options**
dialog box

✔ If necessary, deselect the **Enable automatic sync** selection box, as shown in the figure.

> *We suggest that, as a beginning user of **Autodesk 360,** it will be better to control what is saved to the cloud, rather than to have anything you save uploaded there. With the **Enable** box deselected, only those drawings you wish to upload will be sent to the cloud.*
>
> *You are now ready to proceed to your account.*

✔ Pick the **Autodesk 360** button on the upper right of the Online tab.

> *You are now at your **Autodesk 360** account, with a page similar to Figure 4-35. Notice the **Upload Document** button on the upper right, as indicated in the figure.*

**Figure 4-35**
**Autodesk 360** account

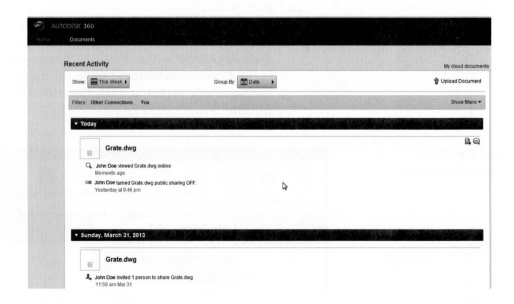

✔ Select the **Upload Document** button.

*This opens a smaller **Upload Documents** dialog box, which asks you to select or drag and drop a drawing file into the box as indicated in Figure 4-36.*

✔ Pick the **Select Documents** button.

*This opens a **File Upload** selection window similar to the one shown in Figure 4-37.*

**Figure 4-36**
**File Upload** selection window

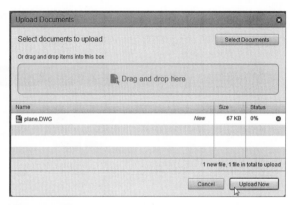

**Figure 4-37**
**Upload Now** button

✔ Browse to the location where your drawing resides, select the drawing, and pick the **Open** button.

*The drawing will be added to your **Upload Documents** dialog box, as shown in Figure 4-37.*

✔ Pick the **Upload Now** button at the lower right of the **Upload Documents** dialog box.

*Notice that a new line, shaded yellow, has been added to your account page, as shown in Figure 4-38. The line displays, "You have 1 new activity that matches the current view".*

**Figure 4-38**
**Recent Activity**

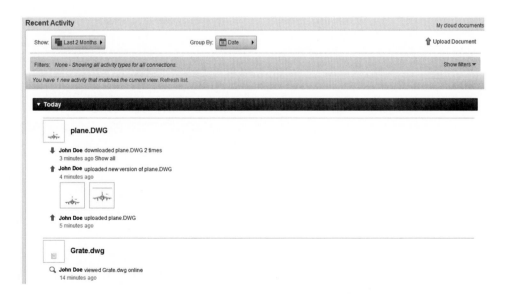

✔ Pick **Refresh list** from the end of the yellow line.
> *Your uploaded drawing is added to your account page under the heading of an activity that took place today. Finally, let's view your drawing in the cloud.*

✔ Pick the thumbnail on the left or the drawing name.
> *Your drawing opens in the **Autodesk 360** viewer, similar to the image in Figure 4-39. Notice the familiar navigation tools on the right. We encourage you to explore while you are here.*

✔ When you are done, close the window to sign out of **Autodesk 360.**

**Figure 4-39**
Refreshed screen

## Chapter Drawing Projects

 ## Drawing 4-1: *7-Pin Trailer Wiring Diagram* [BASIC]

All the drawings in this chapter use your 1B template. Do not expect, however, never to need to change settings. Layers stay the same, but limits change from time to time, and grid and snap change frequently.

This drawing gives you practice using the **COPY** command. There are numerous ways in which the drawing can be done. All locations are approximate except where dimensioned. Set up a layer for each wire color; and draw the wire, box, circle, and text using the color layer that matches.

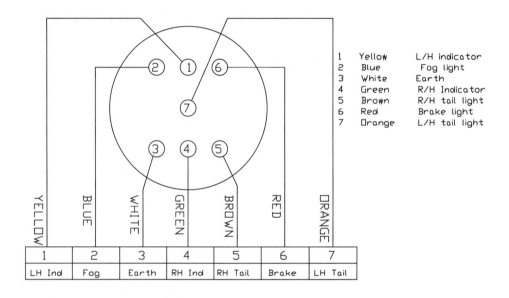

### Drawing Suggestions

GRID = 0.5

SNAP = 0.25

TEXT HEIGHT = .25 for the larger text and .18 for the smaller

- Begin with a 0.25 × 1.50 rectangle starting at (3.00,3.00). Then, array the rectangle to get the 2 × 7 array. Then, draw the circles and connect the wires.

- Use a **Nearest** object snap to get the wire lines to touch the circles.

- Add all text in approximate locations.

ø5.00

ø.50

1.00

1.25

5.25

.50

1.50

Start
3.00,3.00

YELLOW
BLUE
WHITE
GREEN
BROWN
RED
ORANGE

| 1 | 2 | 3 | 4 | 5 | 6 | 7 |
|---|---|---|---|---|---|---|
| LH Ind | Fog | Earth | RH Ind | RH Tail | Brake | LH Tail |

1  Yellow    L/H indicator
2  Blue      Fog light
3  White     Earth
4  Green     R/H Indicator
5  Brown     R/H tail light
6  Red       Brake light
7  Orange    L/H tail light

**Drawing 4-1**
7-Pin Trailer Wiring Diagram

## G Drawing 4-2: *Grill* [BASIC]

This drawing should go very quickly if you use the **ARRAY** command and set the **DIMCEN** system variable to **–.09.**

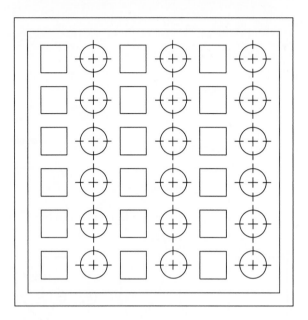

## Drawing Suggestions

GRID = 0.5

SNAP = 0.25

- Begin with a 5.25 × 5.25 square.

- Move in 0.25 all around to create the inside square.

- Draw the small square and the circle with centerlines in the lower left corner first, and then use the **ARRAY** command to create the rest.

- Type **dimcen <Enter>** and change the system variable to **–.09.**

- Then type **dim <Enter>** and **cen <Enter>** to draw the centerlines on the circle. Be sure to do this before arraying the square and the circle.

- Also remember that you can undo a misplaced array using the **U** command.

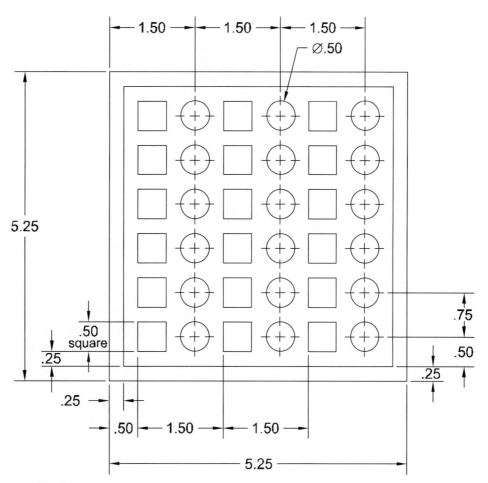

**Drawing 4-2**
Grill

**G** | # Drawing 4-3: *Weave* [INTERMEDIATE]

As you do this drawing, watch AutoCAD work for you and think about how long it would take to do this by hand! The finished drawing looks like the representation shown. For clarity, the drawing shows only one cell of the array and its dimensions.

## Drawing Suggestions

GRID = 0.5

SNAP = 0.125

- Draw the 6 × 6 square; then zoom in on the lower left using a window. This is the area shown in the lower left of the dimensioned drawing.

- Observe the dimensions and draw the line patterns for the lower left corner of the weave. You could use the **COPY** command in several places if you'd like, but the time gained would be minimal. Don't worry if you have to fuss with this a little to get it correct; once you have it right, the rest will be easy.

- Use **ARRAY** to repeat the lower left cell in an 8 × 8 matrix.

- If you get it wrong, use **U** and try again.

**Drawing 4-3**
Weave

## M Drawing 4-4: *Test Bracket* [INTERMEDIATE]

This is a great drawing for practicing much of what you have learned up to this point. Notice the suggested snap, grid, ltscale, and limit settings, and use the **ARRAY** command along with the –.09 centerline dimension to draw the 25 circles on the front view.

## Drawing Suggestions

GRID = 0.25

SNAP = 0.125

LTSCALE = 0.50

LIMITS = (0,0)(24,18)

- Be careful to draw all lines on the correct layers, according to their line-types.

- Draw centerlines through the circles before copying or arraying them; otherwise you will have to go back and draw them on each individual circle or repeat the array process.

- A multiple copy works nicely for the four 0.50-diameter holes. A rectangular array is definitely desirable for the twenty-five 0.75-diameter holes.

- If you have not already done so, change the **DIMCEN** system variable to **–.09.**

- After drawing your first circle and before arraying it, type **dim <Enter>** and then **cen <Enter>** and add centerlines to the circle.

- Create the rectangular array of circles with centerlines as shown.

.375 FILLET
4 PLACES

.25 FILLET
4 PLACES

.125

2.125

9.75

14.00

1.50

11.00

3.00

.25 fillet
12 places

6.50

5.00

8.00

1.50
TYP

.75  TYP

1.50

.75
TYP

1.00

2.00
TYP

Ø.75
25 HOLES

1.00

Ø.50
4 HOLES

**Drawing 4-4**
Test Bracket

# A Drawing 4-5: *Floor Framing* [ADVANCED]

This architectural drawing requires changes in many features of your drawing setup. Pay close attention to the suggested settings.

## Drawing Suggestions

UNITS = Architectural; Precision = 0'-00"

LIMITS = 36', 24'

GRID = 1'

SNAP = 2"

LTSCALE = 12

> **NOTE**
> Be aware that lumber has actual dimensions that are different from the nominal dimensions. A 2 × 10 is actually 1 1/2" × 9 1/4", for example. Here we use nominal dimensions in all drawings.

- Be sure to use foot (') and inch (") symbols when setting limits, grid, and snap (but not ltscale).
- Begin by drawing the 20' × 17'-10" rectangle, with the lower left corner somewhere in the neighborhood of (4',4').
- Complete the left and right 2 × 10 joists by copying the vertical 17'-10" lines 2" in from each side.
- Draw a 19'-8" horizontal line 2" up from the bottom and copy it 2" higher to complete the double joists.
- Array the inner 2 × 10s in a 14-row by 1-column array, with 16" between rows.
- Set to Layer **2,** and draw the three hidden lines down the center.

**Drawing 4-5**
Floor Framing

## A  Drawing 4-6: *Wall Framing* [ADVANCED]

This architectural drawing incorporates rectangular **ARRAY, COPY,** and **MOVE** commands. As in the previous drawing, pay close attention to the drawing setup and remember to use nominal sizes as dimensions indicate.

## Drawing Suggestions

UNITS = Architectural; Precision = 0′-00″

LIMITS = 24′, 18′

GRID = 1′

SNAP = 1″

LTSCALE = 6

- Be sure to use foot (′) and inch (″) symbols when setting limits, grid, and snap (but not ltscale).
- Begin by drawing the 15′-2″ × 9′-4″ rectangle, with the lower left corner at (4′,4′).
- Build the drawing up from the bottom by next drawing the 4″ × 6″ sill.
- Make Layer **2** current and draw a hidden line 2″ × 10″ floor joist on the far left.
- Array the 2″ × 10″ floor joists in a 1-row by 12-column array, with 16″ between rows.
- Continue building the drawing from bottom to top.

**Drawing 4-6**
Wall Framing

## A   Drawing 4-7: *Classroom—Floor Plan*
### [ADVANCED]

This architectural drawing incorporates rectangular **ARRAY, COPY,** and **MOVE** commands. Pay close attention to the drawing setup and remember to use nominal sizes as dimensions indicate.

## Drawing Suggestions

UNITS = Architectural; Precision = 0'-00"

LIMITS = 48', 36'

GRID = 1'

SNAP = 6"

- Be sure to use foot (') and inch (") symbols when setting limits, grid, and snap.

- Begin by drawing the outer walls, with the lower left line at (4',4'). When you get to the wall with the windows, you can draw the windows separately or draw one and array five columns.

- Draw the lower left chair and desk and then array to create the room with 20 desks and chairs.

- Continue by drawing the cabinets, bench, and instructor's desk and chair.

**Drawing 4-7**
Classroom – Floor Plan

chapter**five**

# Arcs and Polar Arrays

# CHAPTER OBJECTIVES

- Create polar arrays
- Draw arcs
- Use the **ROTATE** command
- Use polar tracking at any angle
- Create mirror images of objects on the screen
- Create page setups

## Introduction

Lines and circles are two major components of most drawings. In this chapter, you learn a third major entity, the arc. In addition, you expand your ability to manipulate objects on the screen. You learn to rotate objects and create their mirror images. You learn to save plot settings as named page setups. First, however, we show you how to create polar arrays.

## Creating Polar Arrays

| ARRAY | |
|---|---|
| Command | Array |
| Alias | Ar |
| Panel | Modify |
| Tool | |

Defining a polar array requires more steps than a rectangular array does. There are three qualities that define a polar array, but two are sufficient. A polar array is defined by any combination of two of the following: a certain number of items, an angle that these items span, and an angle between each item and the next. You also have to tell AutoCAD whether to rotate the newly created objects as they are copied.

✔ Create a new drawing with drawing limits set to 18 × 12. You can do this using the 1B template if you have it.

183

**Figure 5-1**
Drawing a vertical line

**Figure 5-2**
**Polar Array** tool

✔ In preparation for this exercise, draw a vertical 1.00 line at the bottom center of the screen, with the lower end at (9.00,2.00), as shown in Figure 5-1.

✔ Select the line.

✔ Open the list of **Array** commands from the **Modify** panel, and select the **Polar Array** tool, as shown in Figure 5-2.

To define a polar array, you need to specify a center point. Polar arrays are built by copying objects around the circumferences of circles or arcs, so we'll need to specify one of these.

✔ Pick a point directly above the line and somewhat below the center of the screen. Ours is (9.00,5.00).

*As soon as you pick the point, AutoCAD shows a preview array with six evenly spaced items in a 360° polar array, as shown in Figure 5-3. Also you see the **Polar Array** contextual tab, as shown. This tab works like the **Rectangular Array** tab, except that the specifications to be made are different. In the first panel of this tab, labeled **Items,** you see the three values required to define a polar array: **Items, Between,** and **Fill.** The second panel is called **Rows,** just as in the **Rectangular Array** tab. We will demonstrate polar array rows momentarily. The third panel is for 3D levels, as also seen in rectangular arrays.*

**Figure 5-3**
Preview array

**Figure 5-4**
Preview array with 12 items

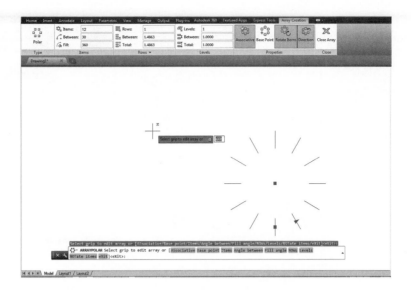

As you see in the drawing area and in the contextual tab, the preview array has 6 items by default, and they are spaced 60° apart to fill a complete circle of 360°. Changing any of these items will generate a new array.

✔ Click in the **Items** edit box and type **12 <Enter>.**

AutoCAD now shows a preview array with 12 items, as shown in Figure 5-4. In the tab edit boxes you see that the 60° spacing has been adjusted to 30°, maintaining a fill angle of 360°.

With this array on your screen we demonstrate polar rows and the **Rotate Items** function. Rows in polar arrays radiate outward from the center point. By changing from the default of one row to three, we create the array shown in Figure 5-5.

✔ Click in the **Rows** edit box, on the top line of the **Rows** panel, and type **3 <Enter>.**

Your screen should resemble Figure 5-5.

**Figure 5-5**
Polar array with row count 3

**Figure 5-6**
**Rotate Items** button

✔ Click the **Rotate Items** button, as shown in Figure 5-6.
  *In the default option, objects are rotated as they are copied to form the array. With* **Rotate Items** *off, they maintain the orientation of the original object.*

✔ Press **<Enter>** to complete the **ARRAY** command.
  *Your screen should resemble Figure 5-6.*

Finally, we use the same center point and source object to define an array that has 20 items placed 15° apart and not rotated when they are copied. This time we will select options from the shortcut menu or the command line rather than using the contextual tab.

✔ Undo the last array, so that you have the single line shown previously in Figure 5-1.

✔ Pick the **Polar Array** tool from the ribbon.

✔ Select the line.

✔ Right-click to end object selection.

✔ Pick (9,5) for the center point.
  *AutoCAD exhibits the preview array with 6 items, filling 360°, shown previously in Figure 5-3.*

✔ Right-click and select **Angle between** from the shortcut menu, or select **Angle between** from the command line.

✔ Type **15 <Enter>** for the angle between items.
  *AutoCAD shows you the preview array with 15° between the six preview items. Using the arrow-shaped grip at the top right, we can add more items while maintaining the 15° between.*

✔ Click on the arrow-shaped grip at the right and drag the rubber band around 270° to the left quadrant at 9 o'clock.
  *This will bring you to a y value on the coordinate display of (5.00), even with the center of the array. Notice that there are now 19 items in the array, spaced 15°, and filling the angle of 270°.*

**Figure 5-7**
Array with 19 items, spaced
15 degrees

✔ Pick the **Rotate Items** button from the contextual tab.

✔ Press **<Enter>** to end the command.
*Your screen should now resemble Figure 5-7.*

This ends our discussion of polar arrays. With the options AutoCAD gives you, there are many possibilities that you can try. As always, we encourage experimentation.

| ARC | |
|---|---|
| **Command** | Arc |
| **Alias** | A |
| **Panel** | Draw |
| **Tool** | |

## Drawing Arcs

> **TIP**
>
> A general procedure for using the **ARC** command is:
>
> 1. Pick an **Arc** tool from the drop-down list on the **Draw** panel of the ribbon.
> 2. Type or show where to start the arc, where to end it, and what circle it is a portion of, using any of the 11 available methods.

**Figure 5-8**
**Arc** drop-down list

Learning AutoCAD's **ARC** command is an exercise in geometry. In this section, we give you a firm foundation for understanding and drawing arcs so that you are not confused by all the available options. The information we give you is more than enough to do the drawings in this chapter and most drawings you encounter elsewhere. Refer to the AutoCAD **Command Reference** and the chart at the end of this section (Figure 5-9) if you need additional information.

AutoCAD gives you eight distinct ways to draw arcs (11 if you count variations in order). With so many choices, some generalizations are helpful.

First, every option requires you to specify three pieces of information: where to begin the arc, where to end it, and what circle it is theoretically a part of. To get a handle on the range of options, look at the list of options on the **Arc** submenu.

✔ Erase any objects left on your screen from the previous section.

✔ Open the **Arc** drop-down list on the ribbon by picking the arrow below the **Arc** tool, as shown in Figure 5-8.

Notice that the options in the fourth panel down (**Center, Start, End,** etc.) are simply reordered versions of those in the second panel (**Start, Center, End,** etc.). This is how we end up with 11 options instead of eight.

More important, **Start** is always included. In every option, a starting point must be specified, although it does not have to be the first point given.

The options arise from the different ways you can specify the end and the circle from which the arc is cut. The end can be shown as an actual point (all **End** options) or inferred from a specified angle or length of chord (all **Angle** and **Length** options).

The circle that the arc is part of can be specified directly by its center point (all **Center** options) or inferred from other information, such as a radius length (**Radius** option), an angle between two given points (**Angle** options), or a tangent direction (the **Start, End, Direction** and **Continue** options).

## The 3P Option

With this framework in mind, we begin by drawing an arc using the simplest method, which is also the default, the three-point option. The geometric key to this method is that any three points not on the same line determine a circle or an arc of a circle. AutoCAD uses this in the **CIRCLE** command (the **3P** option) as well as in the **ARC** command.

✔ Select **3-Point** from the top of the drop-down list.
   *AutoCAD's response is this prompt:*

   Specify start point of arc or [Center]:

   *Accepting the default by specifying a point leaves open all those options in which the start point is specified first.*
   *If you instead type **c** or select **Center** from the shortcut menu, AutoCAD prompts for a center point and follows with those options that begin with a center.*

✔ Pick a starting point near the center of the screen.
   *AutoCAD prompts:*

   Specify second point of arc or [Center End]:

   *We continue to follow the default three-point sequence by specifying a second point. You may want to refer to Figure 5-9 as you draw this arc.*

✔ Select any point 1 or 2 units away from the previous point. Exact coordinates are not important right now.
   *Once AutoCAD has two points, it gives you an arc to drag. By moving the cursor slowly in a circle and in and out, you can see the range of what the third point will produce.*
   *AutoCAD also knows now that you have to provide an endpoint to complete the arc, so the prompt has only one option:*

   Specify end point of arc:

   *Any point you select will do, as long as it produces an arc that fits on the screen.*

✔ Pick an endpoint.

As you can see, three-point arcs are easy to draw. It is much like drawing a line, except that you have to specify three points instead of two. In practice, however, you do not always have three points to use this way.

**Figure 5-9**
**Arc** options

| TYPE | APPEARANCE | DESCRIPTION |
|------|-----------|-------------|
| 3-point | | Clockwise or counterclockwise |
| S, C, E (start, center, end) | | Counterclockwise Radial rubber band indicates angle only, length is insignificant |
| S, C, A (start, center, angle) | | + angle = CCW − angle = CW Rubber band shows angle only, starting from horizontal |
| S, C, L (start, center, length of chord) | | Counterclockwise "Chord" rubber band shows length of chord only, direction is insignificant |
| S, E, A (start, end, angle) | | + angle = CCW − angle = CW Rubber band shows angle only, starting from horizontal |
| S, E, R (start, end, radius) | | Counterclockwise + radius = minor arc − radius = major arc Rubber band shows + radius values only, For − radius (type value) |
| S, E, D (start, end, direction) | | Direction of rubber band is a line tangent to the arc being constructed and runs through the start point |
| CONTIN: (continuous from line) | | Arc begins at end point of previous line or arc and is tangent to it; Rubber band is a chord from start point to end point |

This necessitates the broad range of options in the **ARC** command. The dimensions you are given, and the objects already drawn determine what options are useful to you.

## Start, Center, End

Next, we create an arc using the start, center, end method, the second option illustrated in Figure 5-9.

✔ Type **u <Enter>** or pick the **Undo** tool to undo the three-point arc.

✔ Pick the **Start, Center, End** tool from the drop-down list.

✔ Select a point near the center of the screen as a start point.
   *The prompt that follows is the same as for the three-point option, but the **Center** option has been entered for us.*

   Specify second point of arc or [Center End]: _c
   Specify center point of arc:

✔ Select any point roughly 1 to 3 units away from the start point.
   *The circle from which the arc is to be cut is now clearly determined. All that is left is to specify how much of the circle to take, which can be done in one of three ways, as the following prompt indicates:*

   Specify end point of arc or [Angle chord Length]:

*We pick an endpoint. First, however, try this:*

✔ Move the cursor slowly in a circle and in and out to see how this method works.

*As before, there is an arc to drag, and now there is a radial direction rubber band as well. If you pick a point anywhere along this rubber band, AutoCAD assumes that you want the point where it crosses the circumference of the circle.*

*Notice also that here, as in the polar arrays in this chapter, AutoCAD is building arcs counterclockwise, consistent with its coordinate system. This is the default. In AutoCAD 2014, however, you have the option of switching to the clockwise arc built from the same start point and curving around the circle to the endpoint. This is accomplished by pressing the* **<Ctrl>** *key. Try this:*

✔ Hold down the **<Ctrl>** key and move the crosshairs slightly.

✔ Figure 5-10 shows an example of switching between the counterclockwise and the clockwise arcs.

**Figure 5-10**
Counterclockwise and
clockwise arcs

Arc drags counterclockwise          Hold down control key
                                    and arc drags clockwise

✔ Release the key and the counterclockwise arc will return.

*Whichever arc is showing when you pick an endpoint will be the one retained in your drawing.*

✔ Pick an endpoint to complete the arc.

## Start, Center, Angle

We draw one more arc, using the start, center, angle method, before going on. This method has some peculiarities in the use of the rubber band that are typical of the **ARC** command, and they can be confusing. An example of how the start, center, angle method might look is shown in Figure 5-9.

✔ Undo the last arc.

✔ Pick the **Start, Center, Angle** tool from the drop-down list.

*AutoCAD asks for a start point:*

Specify start point of arc or [Center]:

✔ Pick a start point near the center of the screen.

*AutoCAD prompts:*

Specify second point of arc or [Center End]:_c Specify center point of arc:

✔ Pick a center point 1 to 3 units below the start point.

*AutoCAD prompts with the* **Angle** *option:*

Specify end point of arc or [Angle chord Length]:_a Specify included angle:

You can type an angle specification or show an angle on the screen. Notice that the rubber band now shows an angle only; its length is insignificant. The indicated angle is being measured from the horizontal, but the actual arc begins at the start point and continues counterclockwise, as illustrated in Figure 5-9.

✔ Type **45 <Enter>** or show an angle of 45°.

Now that you have tried three of the basic methods for constructing an arc, we strongly suggest that you study the chart in Figure 5-9 and then try the other options, along with switching to clockwise arcs using the **<Ctrl>** key. The notes in the right-hand column serve as a guide.

The differences in the use of the rubber band from one option to the next are important. You should understand, for instance, that in some cases the linear rubber band is significant only as a distance indicator; its angle is of no importance and is ignored by AutoCAD. In other cases, it is just the reverse: The length of the rubber band is irrelevant, whereas its angle of rotation is important.

> **TIP**
> One additional trick you should try as you experiment with arcs is as follows: If you press **<Enter>** or the spacebar at the *Specify start point [Center]:* prompt, AutoCAD uses the endpoint of the last line or arc you drew as the new starting point and constructs an arc tangent to it. This is the same as the **Continue** option at the bottom of the drop-down list.

This completes the discussion of the **ARC** command. Constructing arcs can be tricky. Another option that is available and often useful is to draw a complete circle and then use the **TRIM** command to cut out the arc you want.

## Using the Rotate Command

**ROTATE** is a fairly straightforward command, and it has some uses that may not be immediately apparent. For example, it frequently is easier to draw an object in a horizontal or vertical position and then rotate it into position rather than to draw it at an angle.

In addition to the **ROTATE** command, there is a **Rotate** mode in the grip edit system, which we introduce later in this section.

✔ In preparation for this exercise, clear your screen and draw a three-point arc using the points (9,6), (11.50,5), and (14,6), as in Figure 5-11.
*We begin by rotating the arc to the position shown in Figure 5-12.*

| ROTATE | |
|---|---|
| Command | Rotate |
| Alias | Ro |
| Panel | Modify |
| Tool | |

**Figure 5-11**
Drawing a three-point arc

**Figure 5-12**
Rotating the arc

**Figure 5-13**
**Rotate** tool

✔ Select the arc.

✔ Pick the **Rotate** tool from the **Modify** panel of the ribbon, as shown in Figure 5-13.

> *You are prompted for a base point:*
>
> Specify base point:
>
> *This is the point around which the object is rotated. The results of the rotation are therefore dramatically affected by your choice of base point.*

✔ Pick the left tip of the arc.

> *The prompt that follows looks like this:*
>
> Specify rotation angle or [Copy Reference] <0>:
>
> *The default method is used to indicate a rotation angle directly. The object is rotated through the angle specified, and the original object is deleted. If you specify the **Copy** option, the original object is retained along with the rotated copy.*
>
> *Move the cursor in a circle, and you will see that you have an arc to drag into place visually. If **Ortho** is on, turn it off to see the complete range of rotation.*

✔ Type **90 <Enter>** or pick a point showing a rotation of 90°.

> *The results should resemble Figure 5-12.*

Notice that when you specify the rotation angle directly like this, the original orientation of the selected object is taken to be 0°. The rotation is figured counterclockwise from there. However, there may be times when you want to refer to the coordinate system in specifying rotation. This is the purpose of the **Reference** option. To use it, you need to specify the present orientation of the object relative to the coordinate system and then tell AutoCAD the orientation you want it to have after rotation. Look at Figure 5-14. To rotate the arc as shown, you can either indicate a rotation of −45° or tell AutoCAD that it is currently oriented to 90° and you want it rotated to 45°. The following steps will rotate the arc using the **Reference** option and retain the original using the **Copy** option.

✔ Repeat the **ROTATE** command.

✔ Select the arc.

✔ Right-click to end object selection.

✔ Pick a base point at the lower tip of the arc.

✔ Type **c <Enter>** or select **Copy** from the command line.

✔ Type **r <Enter>** or select **Reference** from the command line.

> *Notice that both options can be active at once.*

<br>

**Figure 5-14**
Arc rotated 45 degrees

*AutoCAD prompts for a reference angle:*

    Specify the reference angle <0>:

✔ Type **90 <Enter>.**
    *AutoCAD prompts:*

    Specify the new angle or [Points]:

✔ Type **45 <Enter>.**
    *Your screen should now include both arcs shown in Figure 5-14.*

## Rotating with Grips

Rotating with grips is simple, but your choice of object selection methods is limited, as always, to pointing and windowing. Complete the following steps:

✔ Select the two arcs.
    *The arcs are highlighted and grips appear. These grips are espe-cially designed for arcs. If you let the cursor rest on the grips in the middle and the endpoints of each arc, you will see that these grips are multifunctional. The grips at the centers and base point have only one function.*

✔ Pick the grip in the middle of either arc.

✔ Right-click to open the **Grip** shortcut menu.

✔ Select **Rotate.**
    *Move your cursor in a circle, and you will see the arcs rotating around the grip you selected.*

✔ Right-click again and select **Base Point** from the menu, or select **Base Point** from the command line.
    ***Base Point*** *allows you to pick a base point other than the selected grip.*

✔ Pick a base point to the left of the arcs, as shown in Figure 5-15.
    *Move your cursor in circles again. You can see the arcs rotating around the new base point.*

✔ Type **c <Enter>** or select **Copy** from the command line.

Figure 5-15
Arc rotated with grips

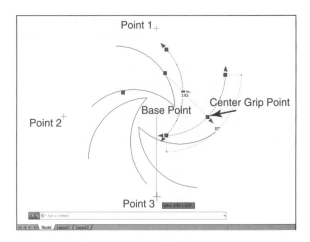

- ✔ Pick a point showing a rotation angle of 90°, as illustrated by the top two arcs in Figure 5-15.

- ✔ Pick a second point showing a rotation angle of 180°, as illustrated by the arcs at the left in the figure.

- ✔ Pick point 3 at 270° to complete the design shown in Figure 5-15.

- ✔ Press **<Enter>** or the spacebar to exit the **Grip Edit** mode.

- ✔ Press **<Esc>** to clear grips.

The capacity to create rotated copies is very useful, as you will find when you do the drawings at the end of this chapter.

## Using Polar Tracking at Any Angle

**polar tracking:** The AutoCAD feature that displays tracking lines at a regular specified angle.

You might have noticed that using **Ortho** or *polar tracking* to force or snap to the 90°, 180°, and 270° angles in the last exercise would make the process more efficient. With polar tracking, you can extend this concept to include angular increments other than the standard 90° orthogonal angles. This feature combined with the rotate copy technique facilitates the creation of rotated copies at regular angles. As an example, we use this process to create Figure 5-16.

To begin this task, erase all but one arc on your screen. This is a good opportunity to use the **Remove** option in the **ERASE** command.

**Figure 5-16**
Using polar tracking with rotate and copy

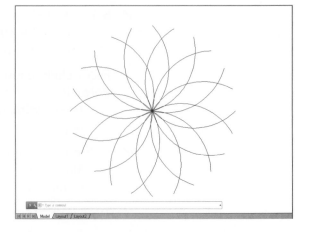

✔ Type **e <Enter>** or pick the **Erase** tool from the ribbon.

✔ Select all the arcs with a window or crossing window.

✔ Type **r <Enter>** to enter the **Remove** option.
*Right-clicking to use the shortcut menu will not work here because the right-click will execute the command and erase the arcs.*

✔ Select the original arc, which is now rotated to 90°.

✔ Press **<Enter>** or right-click to execute the command.
*You are left with one vertically oriented arc.*

✔ If necessary, move the arc near the center of your screen.
*We are going to rotate and copy this arc as before, but first we set polar tracking to track at 30° angles. This is done in the **Drafting Settings** dialog box.*

✔ Turn **Snap Mode** off.

✔ Pick the **Polar Tracking** button on the status bar so that polar tracking is on.

✔ Right-click the same **Polar Tracking** button.
*This opens the list shown in Figure 5-17.*

**Figure 5-17**
**Polar Tracking** shortcut menu

✔ Select **30** from the list.
*Note that 30 replaces 90 as the current increment angle. To specify an angle not shown, select **Settings** and enter the angle value in the **Drafting Settings** dialog box.*

✔ Select the arc.

✔ Click on the grip in the middle of the arc.

✔ Right-click to open the **Grip** shortcut menu.

✔ Select **Rotate.**

✔ Slowly move the cursor in a wide circle around the selected grip.
*Polar tracking now tracks and snaps to every 30° angular increment.*

✔ Select **Copy** from the command line.

✔ Carefully create a copy at every 30° angle until you have created a design similar to Figure 5-16.

✔ Press **<Enter>** to exit **Grip Edit** mode.

✔ Press **<Esc>** to clear grips.

| MIRROR | |
|---|---|
| Command | Mirror |
| Alias | Mi |
| Panel | Modify |
| Tool |  |

# Creating Mirror Images of Objects on the Screen

The **MIRROR** command creates a copy of an original object across an imaginary mirror line, so that every point on the object has a corresponding point on the opposite side of the mirror line at an equal distance from the line.

There is also a **Mirror** mode in the grip edit system, which we explore later in this section.

✔ To begin this exercise, erase all but the horizontal arc on your screen, as shown in Figure 5-18.

> *Here is another opportunity to use the **Remove** option, as described in the previous section.*

✔ Turn **Snap Mode** on.

✔ Keep **Polar Tracking** or **Ortho Mode** on to do this exercise.

✔ Select the arc.

✔ Pick the **Mirror** tool from the ribbon, as shown in Figure 5-19.

> *Now AutoCAD asks you for the first point of a mirror line:*

Specify first point of mirror line:

**Figure 5-18**
Original arc

**Figure 5-19**
**Mirror** tool

> *A mirror line is just what you would expect; the line serves as the mirror, and all points on your original object are reflected across the line at an equal distance and opposite orientation.*
>
> *We show a mirror line along the horizontal between the endpoints of the arc, so that the endpoints of the mirror images are touching.*

✔ Select a point anywhere to the left side of the arc, along the horizontal between the arc endpoints, as in Figure 5-20.

> *You are prompted to show the other endpoint of the mirror line:*

Specify second point of mirror line:

> *The length of the mirror line is not important. All that matters is its orientation. Move the cursor slowly in a circle, and you see an inverted copy of the arc moving with you to show the different mirror images that are possible given the first point you have specified.*

✔ Select a point at 0° from the first point, so that the mirror image is directly above the original arc and touching at the endpoints, as in Figure 5-20.

> *The dragged object disappears until you answer the next prompt, which asks whether you want to delete the original object:*

Erase source objects [Yes No] <N>:

**Figure 5-20**
Mirror line between arc
endpoints

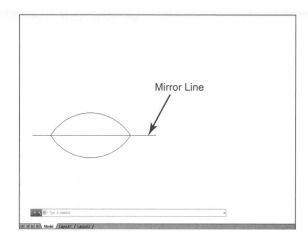

✔ Press **<Enter>** to retain the source object.

> *Your screen should look like Figure 5-20, without the mirror line in the middle.*
>
> *Now let's repeat the process, deleting the original this time and using a different mirror line.*

✔ Repeat the **MIRROR** command.

✔ Select the original (lower) arc.

✔ Right-click to end object selection.

> *Create a mirror image above the last one by choosing a mirror line slightly above the two arcs, as in Figure 5-21.*

✔ Select a first point of the mirror line slightly above and to the left of the figure.

✔ Select a second point at 0° to the right of the first point.

✔ Type **y <Enter>** or select **Yes** from the command line.

> *Your screen should now resemble Figure 5-22.*

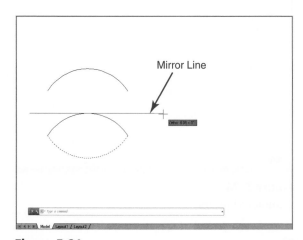

**Figure 5-21**
Mirror line above arc

**Figure 5-22**
Results of mirror

## Mirroring with Grips

In the **Mirror** grip edit mode, the rubber band shows you a mirror line instead of a rotation angle. The option to retain or delete the original is selected through the **Copy** option, just as in the other grip edit modes. Try the following:

✔ Select the two arcs on your screen by pointing or using a crossing window.

*The arcs are highlighted, and the grips are showing.*

✔ If necessary, turn **Ortho Mode** off.

✔ Pick any of the grips.

✔ Right-click and then select **Mirror** from the shortcut menu.

*Move the cursor and observe the dragged mirror images of the arcs. Notice that the rubber band operates as a mirror line, just as in the **MIRROR** command.*

✔ Type **b <Enter>** or select **Base point** from the command line.

*This frees you from the selected grip and allows you to create a mirror line from any point on the screen. Notice the **Specify base point:** prompt on the command line and dynamic input display.*

✔ Pick a base point slightly below the arcs.

✔ Type **c <Enter>** or select **Copy** from the command line.

*As in the **Rotate** mode, this is how you retain the original in a grip edit mirroring sequence.*

✔ Pick a second point at 0° to the right of the first.

*Your screen should resemble Figure 5-23.*

✔ Press **<Enter>** or the spacebar to exit **Grip Edit** mode.

✔ Press **<Esc>** to clear grips.

*We suggest that you complete this exercise by using the **Mirror** grip edit mode with the **Copy** option to create Figure 5-24.*

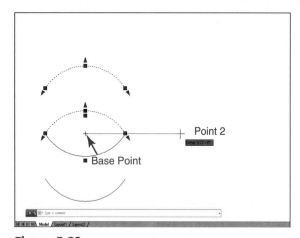

**Figure 5-23**
Mirroring with grips

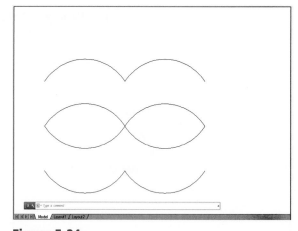

**Figure 5-24**
Completed mirror

## Creating Page Setups

In this chapter, you move to another level in your exploration of AutoCAD plotting. Rather than confine ourselves to plot configurations tied directly to objects visible in your model space drawing area, we continue to plot from model space but introduce the concept and technique of *page setup*. With page setups, you can name and save different plot configurations so that one drawing can produce several different page setups. We define two simple page setups. You do not need to learn any new options, but you do

**page setup:** A group of plot settings applied to a drawing or drawing layout that is named and saved. Page setups can be applied to drawings other than the one in which they are created.

learn to save settings of the options we have covered so far so that you can reuse them as part of a page setup.

✔ To begin this section, you should be in an AutoCAD drawing using 18 × 12 limits.

*We will continue using the objects drawn in the "Creating Mirror Images of Objects on the Screen" section.*

## The Page Setup Dialog Box

A page setup is nothing more than a group of plot settings, like the ones you have previously specified. The only difference is that you give the configuration a name and save it on a list of setups. Once named, the plot settings can be restored by selecting the name, and they can even be exported to other drawings.

You can define a page setup from the **Plot** dialog box or from the **Page Setup** dialog box, accessible through the **Page Setup Manager** on the **Output** tab. There is little difference between the two methods. Here we continue to use the **Plot** dialog box.

✔ Pick the **Plot** tool from the **Quick Access** toolbar.

*You should now be in the **Plot** dialog box. We make a few changes in parameters and then give this page setup a name.*

*We create a portrait setup and a landscape setup. Besides the difference in orientation, the only difference in settings between the two is that the portrait setup is centered, whereas the landscape setup is plotted from the origin.*

✔ Make sure you have a plotter selected in the **Printer/plotter** list.

✔ If necessary, open the **Paper size** list and select an A-size 8.50 × 11.00 sheet (also called Letter).

✔ Select **Limits** in the **Plot area** panel.

✔ Select **Center the plot** in the **Plot offset** panel.

✔ Select the **Portrait** button in the **Drawing orientation** panel.

*Notice how the partial preview image changes. Pause a minute to make sure you understand why the preview looks this way. Assuming you are using the objects drawn in this chapter, or another drawing using 18 × 12 limits, you have model space limits set to 18 × 12. You are plotting to an 8.5 × 11 sheet of paper. The 18 × 12 limits have been positioned in portrait orientation, placed across the effective area of the drawing sheet, scaled to fit, and centered on the paper.*

*Now, you name this page setup.*

✔ Click the **Add** button next to the **Page setup Name** list.

*This opens the **Add Page Setup** dialog box shown in Figure 5-25.*

✔ Type **Portrait** as the page setup name.

**Figure 5-25**
**Add Page Setup** dialog box

✔ Press **<Enter>** or click **OK.**

*This brings you back to the **Plot** dialog box. **Portrait** is now entered in the **Page setup Name** list. That's all there is to it. The portrait page setup information is now part of the current drawing.*

*Next, we define a landscape page setup and put it on the list as well. This setup puts the drawing in landscape orientation and positions it from the origin rather than from the center.*

✔ Select the **Landscape** button in the **Drawing orientation** panel.

*Notice that **Portrait** is no longer in the **Page setup Name** list now that you have changed a parameter.*

✔ Clear the check mark on **Center the plot.**

*Notice that the preview image of the page stays in the portrait position even though the plot will be a landscape plot. This is because the sheet size is 8.5 × 11. If you wanted to rotate this image to the horizontal, you would need to select an 11 × 8.5 sheet. So, now you have the 18 × 12 limits aligned with the left edge of the page, positioned at the origin of the printable area, and scaled to fit. Let's give this setup a name.*

✔ Click **Add** again.

> **NOTE**
>
> Once you have defined page setups, you can access them through the **Page Setup Manager,** opened from the **Output** tab. This dialog box is a simple interface that allows you to select page setups from a list. It will then take you to the **Page Setup** dialog box to modify existing page setups or create new ones. In addition, you can import page setups from other drawings, as described next.

✔ Type **Landscape** in the **Add Page Setup** box.

✔ Press **<Enter>** or click **OK.**

*Back in the **Plot** dialog box, you see that **Landscape** has been entered as the current page setup. You should now restore the portrait settings.*

✔ Open the **Page setup Name** drop-down list and select **Portrait.**

*Your portrait settings, including the **Portrait** radio button and **Center the plot,** are restored.*

✔ Pick the **Preview** button.

*You should see a preview similar to Figure 5-26.*

✔ Press **<Esc>** or **<Enter>** to return to the dialog box.

✔ Open the **Page setup Name** drop-down list again and select **Landscape.**

*Your landscape settings are restored.*

✔ Pick the **Preview** button.

*You should see a preview similar to Figure 5-27. Notice that AutoCAD turns the paper image to landscape orientation in the full preview.*

*This is a simple demonstration, but remember that everything from the sheet size to the plotter you are using and all the settings in the **Plot Configuration** dialog box can be included in a named page setup.*

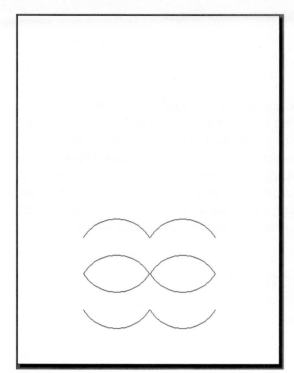

**Figure 5-26**
Plot preview in portrait orientation

**Figure 5-27**
Plot preview in landscape orientation

**NOTE**

Page setups are defined in either model space or paper space as part of a layout. If you create a page setup in model space and then go into a paper space layout, you will not see it on your list. Also, if you define a page setup as part of a paper space layout, you will not see it if you begin a plot from model space.

✔ Press **<Esc>** to return to the **Plot** dialog box.

✔ You can click **OK** to plot or **Cancel** to exit.
   *Either way your page setups will be saved.*

## Importing Page Setups

A powerful feature of page setups is that they can be exchanged among drawings using the **PSETUPIN** command. This allows you to import page setups from a known drawing into the current drawing. The procedure is as follows:

**1** From a drawing into which you would like to import a page setup, open the **Output** tab and select **Page Setup Manager.**

**2** In the **Page Setup Manager,** click the **Import** button.

**3** In the **Select Page Setup From File** dialog box, enter the name and path of the drawing file from which you would like to import a page setup, or open the folder containing the file and select it.

**4** In the **Import Page Setup** box, select the name of the page setup you want to import.

**5** Enter the **Plot** or **Page Setup** dialog box and open the **Page Setup Name** list. The imported page setup should be there.

# Chapter Summary

In this chapter you learned more about drawing and editing objects based on circles and circular frames. You can now create polar arrays of objects copied around an imaginary arc or circle. You learned how to draw arcs, using 11 combinations of three essential types of information. Once drawn, any object may be rotated, or you can create rotated copies and place them at regular angles using polar tracking. You also learned how to create mirror images of drawn objects. Finally, you began to use page setups so that the work you do in defining plot settings can be named and saved and used again for other drawings.

# Chapter Test Questions

## Multiple Choice

*Circle the correct answer.*

1. Which of these is **not** required to define a polar array?

   a. Number of items            c. Angle between items

   b. Start point                d. Angle to fill

2. Which of the following is always specified in defining an arc?

   a. Arc length                c. Center point

   b. Length of chord          d. Start point

3. You are rotating an object from its current position at 45° to a new position at 30° using the **Reference** option. The reference angle will be:

   a. 30°                      c. 15°

   b. 45°                      d. 75°

4. The **Continue** option will begin an arc:

   a. At the endpoint of the last arc drawn

   b. Perpendicular to the last arc drawn

   c. Tangent to the last arc drawn

   d. At the start point of the last arc drawn

5. Polar tracking can be set to track:

   a. At any angle             c. At orthogonal angles only

   b. At 30°                 d. At 90°

## Matching

*Write the number of the correct answer on the line.*

a. Base point _____             1. Plot

b. Mirror line _____            2. **ARC**

c. Angle between items _____      3. **ARRAYPOLAR**

d. Start point _____             4. **ROTATE**

e. Page setup _____            5. **MIRROR**

## True or False

*Circle the correct answer.*

1. **True or False:** It is not possible to plot a landscape-oriented plot on a printer.

2. **True or False:** AutoCAD will not send a plot to a printer or plotter if the drawing limits exceed the sheet size.

3. **True or False:** Polar arrays can be defined around circles or arcs.

4. **True or False:** In order to define an arc, you must first specify a start point.

5. **True or False:** In defining an arc, the rubber band indicates the endpoint.

## Questions

1. What factors define a polar array? How many are needed to define an array?

2. What factors define an arc? How many are needed for any single method?

3. How would you use the **Reference** option to rotate a line from 60° to 90°? How would you accomplish the same rotation without using a reference?

4. What is the purpose of the **Base Point** option in the **Rotate** grip edit mode?

5. What would happen if a drawing created with 18 × 12 limits were printed with a 1:1 scale on an A-size printer? What feature of the **Plot Configuration** dialog box would you use to find out if you weren't sure?

## Drawing Problems

1. Draw an arc starting at (10,6) and passing through (12,6.5) and (14,6).

2. Create a mirrored copy of the arc across the horizontal line passing through (10,6).

3. Rotate the pair of arcs from Step 2 45° around the point (9,6).

4. Create a mirrored copy of the pair of arcs mirrored across a vertical line passing through (9,6).

5. Create mirrored copies of both pairs of arcs mirrored across a horizontal line passing through (9,6).

6. Erase any three of the four pairs of arcs on your screen and re-create them using a polar array.

## WWW Exercise (Optional)

In addition to the self-scoring test, Chapter 5 of our companion website gives you another challenge: to draw an object using a limited number of objects and edit commands. It also gives you links to two new CAD-related websites. When you are ready, complete the following:

✔ Make sure that you are connected to your Internet service provider.

✔ Type **browser <Enter>.**

✔ If necessary, navigate to our companion website at www.pearsonhighered. com/dixriley.

     *Bon voyage!*

## Sharing Drawings in Autodesk 360 (Optional)

In this section we introduce basic options for sharing drawings in **Autodesk 360.** We assume that you have created an **Autodesk 360** account and have uploaded at least one drawing. There are two primary types of sharing we demonstrate here. Private sharing allows you to share your drawing with others who have been designated by you to receive access to a specific drawing. Within the private sharing process, there are four different levels of access. Public sharing can be turned on or off for a particular drawing and provides a link that can be sent to anyone with an e-mail address. When you turn public sharing on for a given drawing, you can further specify whether or not the link allows viewers to download the drawing.

✔ From the ribbon, select the **Autodesk 360** tab.

✔ Pick the **Launch Website** tool.

> *You are now at your **Autodesk 360** account, with a page similar to Figure 5-28. Your uploaded drawing(s) should be listed with thumbnail views, as shown in the figure.*

**Figure 5-28**
**Autodesk 360** account

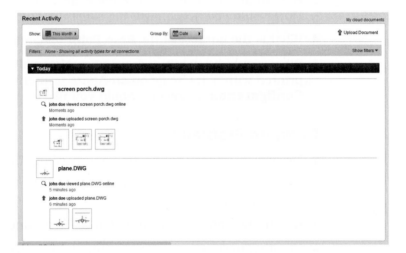

✔ Let your cursor rest anywhere in the section showing the name of the drawing you wish to share.

> *With the cursor in this position, notice the two small icons on the right, shown by the arrow in Figure 5-29. The icon on the right allows you to add comments to your drawing document. The icon on the left opens a menu of action options, including sharing.*

**Figure 5-29**
Add comments or choose action

✔ Pick the **Actions** button to open the menu shown in Figure 5-30.

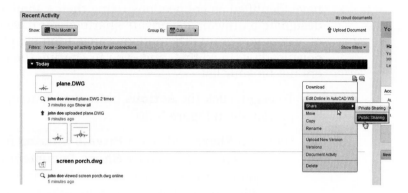

**Figure 5-30**
**Actions** menu

## Public Sharing

✔ Highlight **Share** and pick **Public Sharing,** as shown.

> *This opens the **Public Sharing** dialog box shown in Figure 5-31. Public sharing is simple. There is an **On/Off** button. By default, public sharing is turned off for any drawing. As the text in the box states, turning public sharing on will make the drawing accessible to anyone who has the link to the drawing. The link is provided when you switch from **Off** to **On.***

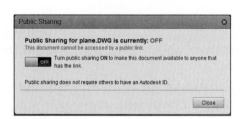

**Figure 5-31**
**Public Sharing** dialog box

**Figure 5-32**
**Public Sharing** button set to **On**

✔ Pick anywhere in the **On/Off** button to turn public sharing on.

> *With the button switched to **On,** you see the dialog box shown in Figure 5-32. The box to the right now contains a link that can be copied into an e-mail. In addition, there are action buttons below the link, and an important check box below, which controls whether those who view the drawing can also download or copy it.*
>
> *As long as the **Public Sharing** button remains **On,** anyone who receives the link will have access. If you switch the button to **Off** again, the link will no longer work to provide access.*

✔ Turn public sharing off before leaving this dialog.

✔ Close the dialog box.

## Private Sharing

Private sharing allows a greater range of access options for people you have identified as connections using their e-mail addresses. When you designate a drawing for private sharing, you have choices about the type of access you grant. The options range from simply viewing the drawing, to downloading, to editing, and even to sharing the drawing further with others not on your list.

✔ To begin, click the **Actions** button again to open the menu shown previously in Figure 5-30.

✔ Highlight **Share** and select **Private Sharing** from the submenu.
   *This opens the smaller **Share Document** dialog box shown in Figure 5-33. As indicated, the drawing is not currently being shared with anyone. In order to share privately you must add at least one e-mail address to your **Connection** list. For purposes of demonstration you may want to add your e-mail address, your instructor's, or some other alternate e-mail address to see how this works. Once you have added a connection, it may be selected from the list that opens when you click on the image button on the right that looks like a person.*

**Figure 5-33**
**Share Document** dialog box

**Figure 5-34**
**Share Document** dialog box expanded

✔ Type an e-mail address in the edit box and click **Add.**
   *The **Share Document** dialog box is expanded, as shown in Figure 5-34. Notice the downward arrow under the word **Access** to the right of the e-mail address. This is where you select options for sharing. The default option is **View and Download.***

✔ Click the down arrow to open the list, as shown in Figure 5-35.
   *Notice that there are four options, with **View document** at the top and **Full Access** at the bottom. When you highlight an option, the*

**Figure 5-35**
**Set Access Level**

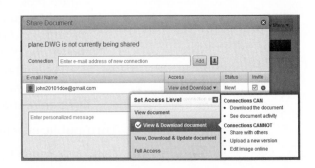

*access level is defined by the lists of what connections can and cannot do. In the figure you see the access definitions for the **View and Download** default option.*

✔ Select other options, and examine the lists of what connections can and cannot do with each level of access.

✔ Select the **View document** option to allow the lowest level of access. *Your dialog box resembles Figure 5-34 again, but **View** has replaced **View and Download**.*

*Now you can decide whether you want to complete the private sharing process by clicking either **Save & Invite** or **Cancel** to abort the process. If you click **Save & Invite,** your connection will receive an e-mail allowing that person to view your drawing in **Autodesk 360.***

✔ When you are done, close the window to sign out of **Autodesk 360.**

chapter**five**

# Chapter Drawing Projects

**A** ## Drawing 5-1: *Hearth* [BASIC]

Once you have completed this architectural drawing as it is shown, you might want to experiment with filling in a pattern of firebrick in the center of the hearth. The drawing itself is not complicated, but little errors become very noticeable when you try to make the row of 4 × 8 bricks across the bottom fit with the arc of bricks across the top, so work carefully.

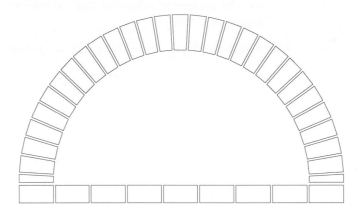

## Drawing Suggestions

UNITS = Architectural
Precision = 0'-01/8″
LIMITS = (0,0)(12',9')
GRID = 1'
SNAP = 1/8″

- Zoom in to draw the wedge-shaped brick indicated by the arrow on the right of the dimensioned drawing. Draw half of the brick only, and mirror it across the centerline as shown. (Notice that the centerline is for reference only.) It is very important that you use **MIRROR** so that you can erase half of the brick later.

- Array the brick in a 29-item, 180° polar array.

- Erase the bottom halves of the end bricks at each end.

- Draw a new horizontal bottom line on each of the two end bricks.

- Draw a 4 × 8 brick directly below the half brick at the left end.

- Array the 4 × 8 brick in a one-row, nine-column array, with 8.5″ between columns.

R3'-2"

R2'-6"

$2\frac{3}{4}$

$3\frac{3}{4}$"

8"

1/2

ERASE BOTTOM HALF OF END
BRICKS AFTER ARRAY

4" x 8" BRICKS
1/2" MORTAR BETWEEN BRICKS

**Drawing 5-1**
Hearth

This drawing makes use of a polar array to draw eight screw holes in a circle. It also reviews the use of layers and linetypes.

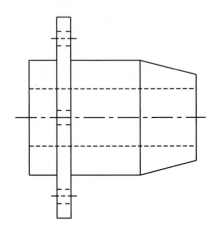

## Drawing Suggestions

GRID = 0.25
SNAP = 0.125
LTSCALE = 0.50
LIMITS = (0,0)(12,9)

- Draw the concentric circles first, using dimensions from both views. Remember to change layers as needed.

- Once you have drawn the 2.75-diameter bolt circle, use it to locate one of the bolt holes. Any of the circles at a quadrant point (0°, 90°, 180°, or 270°) will do.

- Draw a centerline across the bolt hole, and then array the hole and the centerline 360°. Be sure to rotate the objects as they are copied; otherwise, you will get strange results from your centerlines.

Ø,25
8 HOLES EQ SP
ON Ø2.75 B.C.

Ø1.00

.50

.25

3.50

2.00

1.50

1.00

3.25

**Drawing 5-2**
Flanged Bushing

# Drawing 5-3: *Dials* [INTERMEDIATE]

This is a relatively simple drawing that gives you some good practice with polar arrays and the **ROTATE** and **COPY** commands.

Notice that the needle drawn at the top of the next page is for reference only; the actual drawing includes only the plate and the three dials with their needles.

## Drawing Suggestions

$$GRID = 0.25$$
$$SNAP = 0.125$$
$$LTSCALE = 0.50$$
$$LIMITS = (0,0)(18,12)$$

- After drawing the outer rectangle and screw holes, draw the leftmost dial, including the needle. Draw a 0.50 vertical line at the top and array it to the left (counterclockwise—a positive angle) and to the right (negative) to create the 11 larger lines on the dial. How many lines in each of these left and right arrays do you need to end up with 11?

- Draw a 0.25 line on top of the 0.50 line at the top of the dial. Then, use right and left arrays with a **Last** selection to create the 40 small markings. How many lines are in each of these two arrays?

- Complete the first dial, and then use a multiple copy to produce two more dials at the center and right of your screen. Be sure to use a window to select the entire dial.

- Finally, use the **ROTATE** command to rotate the needles as indicated on the new dials.

Detail of pointer

**Drawing 5-3**
Dials

## M Drawing 5-4: *Alignment Wheel* [INTERMEDIATE]

This drawing shows a typical use of the **MIRROR** command. Carefully mirroring sides of the symmetrical front view saves you from duplicating some of your drawing efforts.

## Drawing Suggestions

GRID = 0.25
SNAP = 0.0625
LTSCALE = 0.50
LIMITS = (0,0)(12,9)

- There are numerous ways to use **MIRROR** in drawing the front view. As the reference shows, there is top–bottom symmetry as well as left–right symmetry. The exercise for you is to choose an efficient mirroring sequence.

- Whatever sequence you use, consider the importance of creating the chamfer and the vertical line at the chamfer before mirroring this part of the object.

- Be careful when drawing the vertical line representing the vertical display of the chamfer. Though the chamfer may appear to fall on a snap point, it does not. Zoom in to check this out. Consider using an **Endpoint** object snap to locate the ends of the chamfer.

- Once the front view is drawn, the right-side view is easy. Remember to change layers for center and hidden lines and to line up the small inner circle with the chamfer.

(ORTHO ON)

MIRROR LINES

REFERENCE

0.25

2.875

0.375

0.25

0.06 X 45° CHAMFER
BOTH ENDS

Ø3.00

Ø2.00

Ø0.50

Ø2.75

0.25

1.375

3.00

1.50

6.00

**Drawing 5-4**
Alignment Wheel

There are many arcs in this drawing; we suggest that you use the **3-Point ARC** command to complete this drawing. Look at the overall design of the mallet and find ways to use the **MIRROR** command as well.

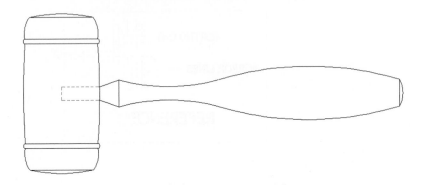

## Drawing Suggestions

$$GRID = 1/4$$
$$SNAP = 1/16$$
$$LTSCALE = 1/2$$
$$LIMITS = (0,0)(18,12)$$

- The arcs that make up the handle are best drawn using **Start, Center, End** or **3-Point Arc.**

- The mallet head can be drawn using **Start, Center, End** and **Start, Center, Radius.**

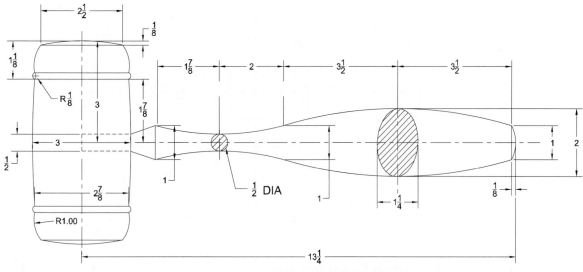

**Drawing 5-5**
Mallet

This drawing will give you additional practice drawing polar arrays and arcs and working with two views of an object.

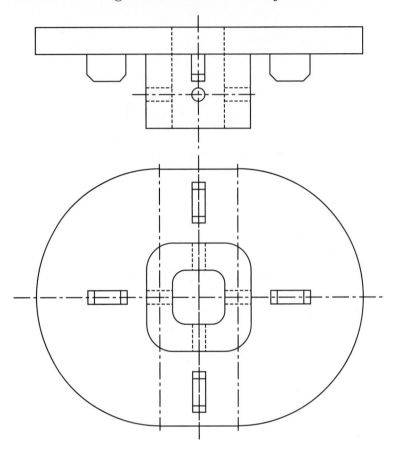

## Drawing Suggestions

GRID = .25
SNAP = .125
LTSCALE = .5
LIMITS = 18,12

- Draw the outline of the front view first.
- Project lines up to draw the top view. Work with both views together, projecting lines as needed to keep the views aligned.
- Draw the arc on the right using **Start, End, Radius.**
- Draw the 1.50 lines. Then draw the arc on the left.
- At the center of the object, draw the inner and outer squares, using the **RECTANG** command. Chamfer using the **Polyline** option.
- Draw the small rectangular tabs in the top view; then chamfer and project lines into the front view.
- After completing the rectangular tabs in the front view, create a polar array.
- Draw all hidden lines as shown. Explore ways to use another polar array.

6.25

.50

.75

1.38

.50

.50

Ø.25 THRU TO CEN
4 HOLES

.12 X .12
CHAMFER
8 PLACES

.38

R.125 FILLET
4 PLACES

2.00
SQ

1.00
SQ

R2.38

.25

.75

R.25 FILLET
4 PLACES

1.50

**Drawing 5-6**
Index Guide

# 6

# chaptersix

# Object Snap

# CHAPTER OBJECTIVES

- Select points with object snap (single-point override)
- Select points with running object snap
- Use object snap tracking
- Use the **OFFSET** command (create parallel objects with **OFFSET**)
- Shorten objects with the **TRIM** command
- Extend objects with the **EXTEND** command
- Use the **STRETCH** command to alter objects connected to other objects
- Create plot layouts

## Introduction

In this chapter, you learn about AutoCAD's very powerful object snap and object tracking features. These take you to a new level of accuracy and efficiency as a CAD operator. You also learn to shorten objects at intersections with other objects using the **TRIM** command or to lengthen them with the **EXTEND** command. You use the **STRETCH** command, which lengthens some objects and shortens others, allowing you, for example, to move windows within walls. Finally, you move into the world of paper space as you begin to use AutoCAD's layout and multiple viewport system.

## Selecting Points with Object Snap (Single-Point Override)

> **TIP**
> A general procedure for using single-point object snap is:
> 1. Enter a drawing command, such as **LINE**, **CIRCLE**, or **ARC**.
> 2. Right-click while holding down the **<Shift>** or the **<Ctrl>** key.
> 3. Select an object snap mode from the shortcut menu.
> 4. Point to a previously drawn object.

In this section we quickly present the single-point override procedure. In the next section we move on to the use of running object snap.

✔ To prepare for this exercise, begin a new drawing using a template with B-size (18 × 12) limits. You can use the 1B template if you have it.

✔ Draw a 6 × 6 square with a 1.50-radius circle centered inside, as in Figure 6-1.

> *To keep the circle centered, draw the square with the **RECTANG** command with corners at (6,3) and (12,9). Then, center the circle at (9,6).*

✔ The **Polar Tracking, Object Snap,** and **Snap Mode** buttons should be off for the rest of this exercise.

✔ Enter the **LINE** command.

We are going to draw a line from the lower left corner of the square to a point on a line tangent to the circle, as shown in Figure 6-2. The corner is easy to locate because you have drawn it on snap, but the tangent will not be.

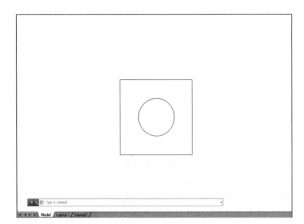

**Figure 6-1**
Square and circle

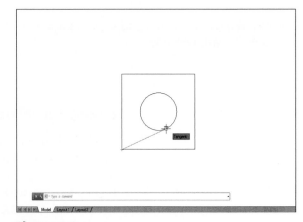

**Figure 6-2**
**Endpoint** and **Tangent** object snaps

We use an **Endpoint** object snap to locate the corner and a **Tangent** object snap to locate the tangent point.

✔ At the *Specify first point:* prompt, instead of specifying a point, hold down the **<Shift>** or the **<Ctrl>** key and right-click.

> *This opens the **Object Snap** shortcut menu.*

✔ Select **Endpoint.**

✔ Move the cursor near the lower left corner of the square.
> *The **Endpoint** object snap marker is a green box surrounding the endpoint.*

✔ With the **Endpoint** object snap marker showing, press the pick button.
> *The green endpoint box and the snap-tip disappear, and there is a rubber band stretching from the lower left corner of the square to the crosshairs position. In the command line, you see the* Specify next point: *prompt.*
>> *We use a **Tangent** object snap to select the second point.*

✔ At the *Specify next point or [Undo]:* prompt, **<Shift>** + right-click and select **Tangent.**

✔ Move the cursor to the right and position the crosshairs so that they are near the lower right side of the circle.
> *When you approach the tangent area, you see the green tangent marker.*

✔ With the tangent marker showing, press the pick button.
> *AutoCAD locates the tangent point and draws the line.*

✔ Press **<Enter>** to exit the **LINE** command.
> *Your screen should now resemble Figure 6-2.*

That's all there is to it. Remember these steps: (1) Enter a command; (2) when AutoCAD asks for a point, **<Shift>** + right-click and select an object snap mode; (3) position the crosshairs near an object to which the mode can be applied and let AutoCAD find the point; and (4) press the pick button.

## Selecting Points with Running Object Snap

> **TIP**
>
> A general procedure for using running object snap is:
>
> 1. Pick the **Object Snap** button on the status bar so that it is on.
> 2. Right-click the **Object Snap** button, and select **Settings** to open the **Drafting Settings** dialog box.
> 3. Select object snap modes from the **Drafting Settings** dialog box.
> 4. Enter drawing commands.
> 5. If there is more than one object snap choice in the area, cycle through using the **<Tab>** key.

So far we have been using object snap one point at a time. Because object snap is not constantly in use for most applications, this single-point method is common. Often, however, you will find that you are going to be using one or a number of object snap types repeatedly and do not need to select many points without them. In this case, you can keep object snap modes on so that they affect all point selection. This is called *running object snap*. We use this method to complete the drawing shown in Figure 6-3. Notice how each line is drawn from a midpoint or corner to a tangent point on the circle. This is easily done with running object snaps.

✔ Pick the **Object Snap** button on the status bar so that it is on.
> *When the button is blue, you are in running object snap. The modes that are in effect depend on the AutoCAD default settings, or*

*whatever settings were last selected. To change settings or to see what settings are on, we open the **Drafting Settings** dialog box.*

**Figure 6-3**
Running object snap mode

**Figure 6-4**
**Object Snap** shortcut menu

✔ Right-click on the status bar **Object Snap** button.

*The shortcut menu shown in Figure 6-4 opens. The blue object snap icons at the top allow you to turn object snap modes on and off without opening the **Drafting Settings** dialog box. However, you can switch only one mode at a time from this list. As soon as you select an icon, the list will close. For this exercise we use the dialog box instead.*

---

**TIP**

Once you have specified object snap modes, you can turn individual object snap modes on or off by right-clicking the **Object Snap** button on the status bar and selecting an object snap mode from the shortcut menu shown in Figure 6-4.

---

✔ Select **Settings.**

*This executes the **OSNAP** command and opens the **Drafting Settings** dialog box with the **Object Snap** tab on top, as shown in Figure 6-5.*

**Figure 6-5**
**Drafting Settings**
dialog box

*You can find a description of all the object snap modes on the chart in Figure 6-6, but for now we use three: **Midpoint, Intersection,** and **Tangent. Midpoint** and **Tangent** you already know. **Intersection** snaps to the point where two entities meet or cross. For practice we use an intersection instead of an endpoint to select the remaining three corners of the square, even though an endpoint could be used instead.*

**Figure 6-6**
**Object Snap** options

| TYPE | APPEARANCE | DESCRIPTION |
| --- | --- | --- |
| CENter | | Snaps to the center of an arc, circle, ellipse, or elliptical arc. |
| ENDpoint | | Snaps to the closest endpoint of an arc, elliptical arc, line, mline, polyline, ray, or to the closest corner of a trace, solid, or 3D face. |
| INSertion | (See Chapter 10) | Snaps to the insertion point of a block, attribute, shape, or text. |
| INTersection | | Snaps to crossing or meeting point of arcs, lines, circles, ellipses, elliptical arcs, mlines, polylines, rays, splines, or xlines. |
| APParent Inter | | Snaps to apparent crossing or meeting point of arcs, lines, circles, ellipses, elliptical arcs, mlines, polylines, rays, splines, or xlines.<br><br>If apparent intersection and intersection are on at the same time, varying results may occur. |
| MIDpoint | | Snaps to the midpoint of an arc, circle, ellipse, elliptical arc, line, mline, polyline, solid, spline, or xline. |
| NEArest | | Snaps to the nearest point on an arc, circle, ellipse, elliptical arc, line, mline point, polyline, spline, or xline. |
| NODe | | Snaps to a point object. |
| PERpendicular | | Snaps to a point on an arc, circle, ellipse, elliptical arc, line, mline, ray, solid, spline, or xline. |
| QUAdrant | | Snaps to nearest quadrant point of an arc, circle, ellipse, or elliptical arc.<br>0, 90, 180, or 270 degrees |
| TANgent | | Snaps to the tangent of an arc, circle, ellipse, or elliptical arc. |
| EXTension | | Snaps to the extension point of an object. Establish an extension path by moving the cursor over the endpoint of an object. A marker is placed on the endpoint. While the endpoint is marked, the cursor snaps to the extension path of the endpoint. |
| PARallel | | Snaps to extension parallel with an object. When the cursor is moved over the endpoint of an object, the endpoint is marked and the cursor snaps to the parallel alignment path to that object. The alignment path is calculated from the current "from point" of the command. |

✔ Select the **Clear All** button.
*This will clear any previous object snap selections that may have been made on your system.*

✔ Select **Midpoint, Intersection,** and **Tangent.**
> *When you are finished, your dialog box should resemble Figure 6-5. Notice that **Object Snap On (F3)** is checked at the top of the box, and **Object Snap Tracking On (F11)** is not checked. We save object snap tracking for the next section.*

✔ Pick the **OK** button.

✔ Enter the **LINE** command.

✔ Position the aperture so that the bottom line is within the box.
> *A green triangle, the midpoint marker, appears.*

✔ With the midpoint marker showing, press the pick button.
> *AutoCAD selects the midpoint of the line and gives you the rubber band and the prompt for the next point.*

✔ Move the crosshairs up and along the lower right side of the circle until the tangent marker appears.

✔ With the tangent marker showing, press the pick button.
> *AutoCAD constructs a new tangent from the midpoint to the circle.*

✔ Press the spacebar to complete the **LINE** command sequence.

✔ Press the spacebar again to repeat **LINE** so you can begin with a new start point.
> *We continue to move counterclockwise around the circle. This should begin to be easy now. There are four steps.*
>
> **1** *Repeat the command.*
>
> **2** *Pick a midpoint or corner intersection on the square.*
>
> **3** *Pick a tangent point on the circle.*
>
> **4** *End the command.*

✔ Position the aperture so that the bottom right corner of the square is within the box.
> *A green X, the intersection marker, appears.*

✔ Press the pick button.
> *AutoCAD snaps to the corner of the square.*

✔ Move up along the right side of the circle so that the tangent marker appears.

✔ Press the pick button.

✔ Press the spacebar to exit **LINE.**

✔ Press the spacebar again to repeat **LINE.**
> *Continue around the circle, drawing tangents from each midpoint and intersection.*

Running object snap should give you both speed and accuracy, so push yourself a little to see how quickly you can complete the figure. Be sure to pay attention to the object snap markers so that you do not select an intersection when you want a tangent, for example.

Your screen should now resemble Figure 6-3. Before going on, study the object snap chart, Figure 6-6. Before you can effectively analyze situations and look for opportunities to use object snap and object snap tracking, you need to have a good acquaintance with all the object snap modes.

**TIP**

Occasionally, you may encounter a situation in which there are several possible object snap points in a tight area. If AutoCAD does not recognize the one you want, you can cycle through all the choices by pressing the <Tab> key repeatedly.

## Object Snap Tracking

**alignment path:** A dotted line used as a visual and snap aid, constructed through an acquired object snap point and extending to the edge of the display horizontally or vertically.

**acquired point:** An object snap point identified and highlighted in object snap tracking mode.

Object snap tracking creates temporary construction lines, called *alignment paths*, from designated object snap points. Alignment paths are constructed through object snap points, called *acquired points*. Once you are in a draw command, such as **LINE**, any object snap point that can be identified in an active object snap mode can be acquired. An acquired point is highlighted with a yellow cross. Once a point is acquired, object snap tracking automatically projects alignment path lines from this point. Alignment paths are dotted lines like those used by polar tracking. They are visual snap aids that extend to the edge of the display horizontally and vertically from the acquired point. They will also pick up specified polar tracking angles. Try the following:

To begin this task, running object snap should be on with **Endpoint** mode in effect; all other modes from the last exercise should be turned off.

Remember the following steps:

**1** Right-click the **Object Snap** button.

**2** Select **Settings.**

**3** Click **Clear All** in the dialog box.

**4** Check **Endpoint.**

**5** Click **OK.**

✔ Pick the **Dynamic Input** button to turn dynamic input off.
   *This is technically not necessary, but you will be able to see other things happening on your screen more easily with the dynamic input display turned off.*

✔ Pick the **Object Snap Tracking** button on the status bar so that it is on.

✔ Enter the **LINE** command.

✔ Select a first point to the left of the square and circle, as shown by point 1 in Figure 6-7.

**Figure 6-7**
Selecting point 1

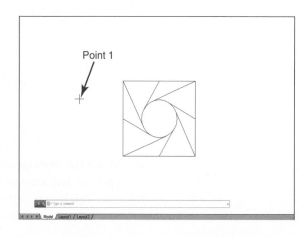

## Point Acquisition

**point acquisition:** The process by which object snap points are acquired for use in object snap tracking. An acquired point is marked by a small green cross.

To take the next step, you need to learn a new technique called ***point acquisition.*** Before a point can be used for object snap tracking, it must be acquired, which is a form of selection. To acquire a point, move the cursor over it so that the object snap marker appears, and pause for about a second without clicking. Try it with the following steps:

✔ Move the cursor over the lower left corner of the square, point 2 in Figure 6-8, so that the endpoint marker appears.

✔ Pause.

✔ Now, move the cursor away from the corner.

> *If you have done this correctly, a small green cross appears at the corner intersection, as shown in Figure 6-9, indicating that this point has been acquired for object snap tracking. (Repeating this procedure over the same point removes the cross.)*

**Figure 6-8**
Endpoint marker

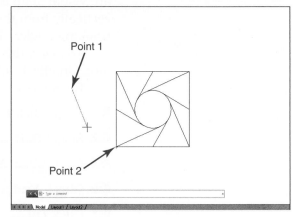

**Figure 6-9**
Acquired point

✔ Move the cursor to a position left of point 2 and even with the horizontal lower side of the square, as shown in Figure 6-10.

> *You see an alignment path and a tracking tip like those shown in Figure 6-10.*

**Figure 6-10**
Alignment path and tracking tip

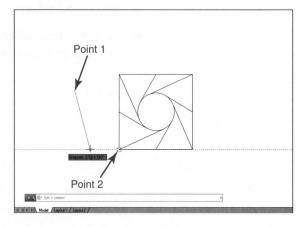

✔ Move the cursor over and down to a position even with and below the vertical left side of the square, as shown in Figure 6-11.

> *You see a different alignment path and tracking tip, like those shown in Figure 6-11.*

*These paths are interesting, but they do not accomplish a great deal because your square is constructed on grid snap points anyway. Let's try something more difficult and a lot more interesting. Here we use two acquired points to locate a point that currently is not specifiable in either object snap or incremental snap.*

✔ Move the cursor up and acquire point 3, as shown in Figure 6-12.
   *Point 3 is the lower endpoint of the line drawn from the midpoint of the top side of the square to a point tangent to the circle. You should now have two acquired points, with two green crosses showing, one at point 2 and one at point 3.*

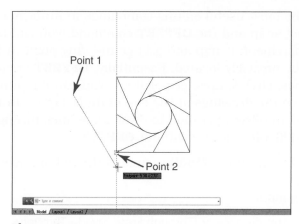

**Figure 6-11**
Vertical alignment path

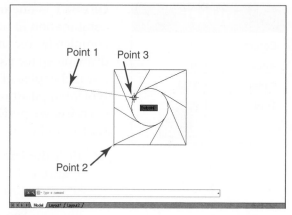

**Figure 6-12**
Acquiring point 3

✔ Move the cursor slowly along the left side of the square.
   *You are looking for point 4, the point where the vertical alignment path from point 2 intersects the horizontal path from point 3. When you near it, your screen should resemble Figure 6-13. Notice the double tracking tip Endpoint: <90, Endpoint: <180.*

**Figure 6-13**
Double tracking tip

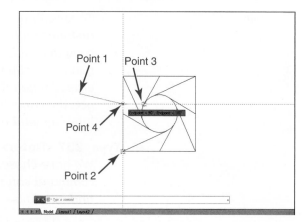

✔ With the double tracking tip and the two alignment paths showing, press the pick button.
   *A line is drawn from point 1 to point 4.*

✔ Press **<Enter>** or the spacebar to exit the **LINE** command.
   *Before going on, we need to turn off the running object snap to* **Endpoint** *mode.*

✔ Pick the **Object Snap** button or press **<F3>** to turn off running object snap.

If you have followed this exercise closely, you have already greatly increased the power of your understanding of CAD technique. You will find many opportunities to use object snap and object snap tracking from now on.

Next, we move on to a very powerful editing command called **OFFSET**. Before leaving object snap, be sure that you have studied the chart in Figure 6-6, which shows examples of all the object snap modes.

## Using the OFFSET Command (Creating Parallel Objects with OFFSET)

| OFFSET | |
|---|---|
| **Command** | Offset |
| **Alias** | O |
| **Panel** | Modify |
| **Tool** | |

**OFFSET** is one of the most useful editing commands in AutoCAD. With the combination of object snap and the **OFFSET** command, you can become completely free of incremental snap and grid points. Any point in the drawing space can be precisely located. Essentially, **OFFSET** creates parallel copies of lines, circles, arcs, or polylines. You can find a number of typical applications in the drawings at the end of this chapter. In this brief exercise, we perform an offset operation to draw some lines through points that would be very difficult to locate without **OFFSET**.

✔ Pick the **Offset** tool from the **Modify** panel of the ribbon, as shown in Figure 6-14.

*AutoCAD prompts:*

Specify offset distance or [Through Erase Layer] <Through>

**Figure 6-14**
**Offset** tool

*To specify an offset distance you can type a number, show a distance with two points, or pick a point that you want the new copy to run through (the **Through** option). The **Erase** option allows you to specify whether the selected object should be retained or erased when the new offset object is drawn. The **Layer** option gives you the capacity to create the new object on the selected object's layer instead of the current layer.*

✔ Type **.257 <Enter>**.

*We have chosen this rather odd number to make the point that this command can help you locate positions that would be difficult to find otherwise. AutoCAD prompts for an object:*

Select object to offset or <exit>:

✔ Select the diagonal line drawn in the last exercise.

*AutoCAD creates a preview offset, but needs to know whether to draw the offset image above or below the line:*

Specify point on side to offset:

✔ Pick a point anywhere below the line.

*Your screen should now resemble Figure 6-15. AutoCAD continues to prompt for objects to offset using the same offset distance. You can continue to create offset objects at the same offset distance by pointing and clicking.*

✔ Pick the line just created.

✔ Pick any point below the line.
   *A second offset line is added, as shown in Figure 6-15. As long as you stay within the **OFFSET** command, you can select any object to offset using the same offset distance.*

✔ Pick the circle in the square.

✔ Pick any point inside the circle.
   *An offset circle is added, as shown in Figure 6-16.*

**Figure 6-15**
Offset line

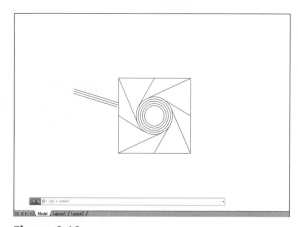

**Figure 6-16**
Offset line and circles

✔ Continue pointing and clicking to create additional offset circles, as shown in Figure 6-16.

✔ Press **<Enter>** to exit the **OFFSET** command.
   *When you exit **OFFSET,** the offset distance is retained as the default, so you can return to the command and continue using the same distance.*

## Shortening Objects with the TRIM Command

| TRIM | |
|---|---|
| **Command** | Trim |
| **Alias** | Tr |
| **Panel** | Modify |
| **Tool** | |

In the next three sections we explore edit commands that allow you to shorten and lengthen objects in your drawing. The **TRIM** command works wonders in many situations where you want to shorten objects at their intersections with other objects. It works with lines, circles, arcs, and polylines. The only limitations are that you must have at least two objects, and they must cross or meet.

✔ In preparation for exploring **TRIM,** clear your screen and then draw two horizontal lines crossing a circle, as in Figure 6-17. Exact locations and sizes are not important.
   *First, we use the **TRIM** command to go from Figure 6-17 to Figure 6-18.*

✔ Open the **Trim/Extend** drop-down list from the **Modify** panel of the ribbon, as shown in Figure 6-19.

**Figure 6-17**
Horizontal lines crossing circle

**Figure 6-18**
Trimming lines at circle

**Figure 6-19**
Pick **Trim** from the **Trim/Extend** drop-down list

✔ From the drop-down list, pick the **Trim** tool, as shown.
   *You begin by specifying at least one cutting edge. A cutting edge is an entity you want to use to trim another entity. That is, you want the trimmed entity to end at its intersection with the cutting edge.*

   Select objects or <select all>:

   *The prompt asks you to select objects to use as cutting edges, or press **<Enter>** for the **Select All** option. The option of selecting all objects is demonstrated shortly.*
   *For now, select the circle as an edge and use it to trim the upper line.*

✔ Pick the circle.
   *The circle becomes dotted and remains so until you leave the **TRIM** command. AutoCAD prompts for more objects until you indicate that you are finished selecting edges.*

✔ Right-click to end the selection of cutting edges.
   *You are prompted for an object to trim:*

   Select object to trim or shift-select to extend or

   [Fence Crossing Project Edge eRase Undo]:

   *This prompt allows you to shift over to the **EXTEND** command by holding down the **<Shift>** key. Otherwise, you select objects to trim using the given options. We follow a simple procedure to trim off the segment of the upper line that lies outside the circle on the left. The important thing is to point to the part of the object that will be removed, as shown in Figure 6-18.*

✔ Point to the upper line to the left of where it crosses the circle.

> *The line is trimmed immediately, but the circle is still dotted, and AutoCAD continues to prompt for more objects to trim.*
>
> *Note that you have an **Undo** option, so that if the trim does not turn out the way you wanted, you can back up without having to leave the command and start over. Also notice the **Erase** option, which allows you to erase objects without leaving the **TRIM** command.*

✔ Point to the lower line to the left of where it crosses the circle.

> *Now you have trimmed both lines.*

✔ Press **<Enter>** or the spacebar to end the **TRIM** operation.

> *Your screen should resemble Figure 6-18.*
>
> *More complex trimming is also easy. The key is that you can select all visible objects or as many edges as you like. An entity can be selected as both an edge and an object to trim, as we demonstrate.*

✔ Repeat the **TRIM** command.

✔ Press **<Enter>** to select all objects.

> *In this case, AutoCAD will not highlight all objects but will proceed as if all objects were selected. There is no need to complete object selection because everything is already selected.*

✔ Point to each of the remaining two line segments that lie outside the circle on the right and to the top and bottom arcs of the circle to produce the bandage-shaped object in Figure 6-20.

✔ Press **<Enter>** to exit the **TRIM** command.

**Figure 6-20**
Trimmed lines and circle

## Extending Objects with the EXTEND Command

| EXTEND | |
|---|---|
| **Command** | Extend |
| **Alias** | Ex |
| **Panel** | Modify |
| **Tool** | |

The procedure for using the **EXTEND** command is the same as for the **TRIM** command, but instead of selecting cutting edges, you select boundaries to which objects are extended. **TRIM** and **EXTEND** are conceptually related, and you can switch from one to the other without leaving the command.

> **TIP**
>
> It is sometimes efficient to draw a temporary cutting edge or boundary on your screen and erase it after using **TRIM** or **EXTEND**.

✔ Leave Figure 6-20, the bandage, on your screen and draw a vertical line to the right of it, as in Figure 6-21.

*We use this line as a boundary to which to extend the two horizontal lines, as in Figure 6-22.*

**Figure 6-21**
Drawing vertical boundary line

**Figure 6-22**
Extending the horizontal lines

✔ From the **Trim/Extend** drop-down list on the ribbon, pick the **Extend** tool, as shown in Figure 6-23.

*You are prompted for objects to serve as boundaries:*

Select objects or <Select All>:

**Figure 6-23**
Pick **Extend** from the **Trim/Extend** drop-down list

*As with the **TRIM** command, any of the usual selection methods work, and there is an option for selecting all objects. For our purposes, simply point to the vertical line.*

✔ Point to the vertical line on the right.

*You are prompted for more boundary objects until you exit object selection.*

✔ Right-click to end the selection of boundaries.

*AutoCAD now asks for objects to extend:*

Select object to extend or shift-select to trim

or [Fence Crossing Project Edge Undo]:

✔ Pick the right half of one of the two horizontal lines.

*You have to point to the line on the side closer to the selected boundary. Otherwise, AutoCAD looks to the left instead of the right and gives you the following message:*

Object does not intersect an Edge

*Arcs and polylines can be extended in the same manner as lines.*

✔ Pick a point on the right half of the other horizontal line. Both lines should be extended to the vertical line.
*Your screen should resemble Figure 6-22.*

✔ Press the spacebar to exit the **EXTEND** command.

## Using STRETCH to Alter Objects Connected to Other Objects

| STRETCH | |
|---|---|
| Command | Stretch |
| Alias | S |
| Panel | Modify |
| Tool | |

The **STRETCH** command is a phenomenal time-saver in special circumstances in which you want to move objects without disrupting their connections to other objects. Often, **STRETCH** can take the place of a whole series of moves, trims, and extends. It is commonly used in such applications as moving doors or windows within walls without having to redraw the walls.

The term *stretch* must be understood to have a special meaning in AutoCAD. When a typical stretch is performed, some objects are lengthened, others are shortened, and others are simply moved.

There is also a **Stretch** mode in the grip edit system, as we have seen previously. It functions very differently from the **STRETCH** command. We look at it later in this section.

First, we do a simple stretch on the objects you have already drawn on your screen.

✔ Pick the **Stretch** tool from the **Modify** panel of the ribbon, as illustrated in Figure 6-24.

**Figure 6-24**
**Stretch** tool

*AutoCAD prompts for objects to stretch.*
*In order for a stretch procedure to be effective, you will want to use at least one crossing-window or crossing-polygon selection in your selection set. Objects crossed by the window will be stretched, while objects within the window or selected individually will simply be moved. If it is not your intent to stretch or shorten some of the objects in your selection set, you probably should be using a different modifying command.*

✔ Point to the first corner of a crossing window, as shown by P1 in Figure 6-25.
*AutoCAD prompts for a second corner:*

    Specify opposite corner:

✔ Point to a second corner, as shown by P2 in Figure 6-25.
*AutoCAD continues to prompt for objects, so we need to show that we are through selecting.*

**Figure 6-25**
Crossing window

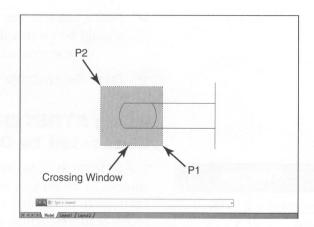

✔ Right-click to end the selection process.

*Now, you need to show the degree and direction of stretch you want. In effect, you show AutoCAD how far to move the objects that are completely within the box. Objects that cross the box are extended or shrunk so that they remain connected to the objects that move.*

*The prompt sequence for this action is the same as the sequence for a move:*

Specify base point or [Displacement]

<Displacement>:

✔ Pick any point near the middle of the screen, leaving room to indicate a horizontal displacement to the right, as illustrated in Figure 6-26.

*AutoCAD prompts:*

Specify second point of displacement

<or use first point as displacement>:

**Figure 6-26**
Horizontal stretch

✔ Pick a second point to the right of the first, as shown in Figure 6-26.

*Having **Ortho** on ensures a horizontal move.*

*The arcs are moved to the right, and the horizontal lines are shrunk as shown. Notice that nothing here is literally being stretched. The arcs are being moved, and the lines are being compressed.*

✔ Try performing another stretch like the one illustrated in Figures 6-27 and 6-28.

*Here the lines are being lengthened while one arc moves and the other stays put, so that the original bandage is indeed stretched.*

**Figure 6-27**
Crossing window

**Figure 6-28**
Stretched object

## Stretching with Grips

Stretching with grips is a simple operation best reserved for simple stretches. Stretches like the ones you just performed with the **STRETCH** command are possible in grip editing, but they require careful selection of multiple grips. The results are not always what you expect, and it takes more time to complete the process. The type of stretch that works best with grips is illustrated in the following exercise:

✔ Pick the lower horizontal line, as shown by the grips in Figure 6-29.
   *The line is highlighted, and grips appear.*

✔ Pick the vertical line.
   *Now, both lines should appear with grips, as in Figure 6-29. We use one grip on the horizontal line and one on the vertical line to create Figure 6-30.*

**Figure 6-29**
Stretching with grips

**Figure 6-30**
Stretching the endpoint of the lower line

✔ Pick the grip at the right end of the horizontal line.
   *As soon as you press the pick button, the grip edit system puts you into **Stretch** mode, and the selected grip changes color.*
   *In the command area, you see the following:*

Specify stretch point or [Base point Copy Undo eXit]:

*We stretch the line to end at the lower endpoint of the vertical line.*

✔ Move the crosshairs slowly downward, and observe the screen.
  *If **Ortho** is off, you see two rubber bands. One represents the line you are stretching, and the other connects the crosshairs to the grip you are manipulating.*

✔ Pick the grip at the bottom of the vertical line.
  *Your screen should resemble Figure 6-30. Notice how the grip on the vertical line works like an object snap point.*

✔ Try one more grip stretch to create Figure 6-31. Stretch the endpoint of the upper line just as you did the lower.

**Figure 6-31**
Stretching the endpoint of the upper line

## Lengthen and Break

Two additional commands related to those introduced in the last three sections are **LENGTHEN** and **BREAK.** They are not required to complete any of the drawings in this chapter, but you should know about them. **LENGTHEN** allows you to lengthen or shorten lines, arcs, and polylines. You will find the **Lengthen** tool on the **Modify** panel extension. The extension is opened by picking the arrow next to the title on the panel title bar. After entering the command, specify a lengthening option and then select objects to modify. There are four lengthening options. **Delta** lengthens by a specified amount (specifying a negative amount will cause shortening). **Percent** lengthens objects by a percentage of their current length. **Total** adjusts selected objects to a new total length, regardless of their current length. **Dynamic** allows you to adjust length dynamically with cursor movement.

   With the **BREAK** command you can break a selected object into separate objects. This can be done without erasing anything, in which case there is no visible difference on your screen, but you will be able to manipulate parts of the broken object independently. Or, you can create a gap between the newly separated objects. To break without creating a gap, use the **Break at Point** tool on the **Modify** panel extension. To break with a gap, use the **Break** tool on the **Modify** panel extension. The **Break** tool can also be used to shorten lines by picking the second point of the "gap" beyond the end of the line. For more information on **BREAK** or **LENGTHEN,** access the AutoCAD Help feature.

## Creating Plot Layouts

Plotting from model space has its uses, particularly in the early stages of a design process. However, when your focus shifts from modeling issues to presentation issues, paper space layouts have much more to offer. The separation of model space and paper space in AutoCAD allows you to focus entirely on modeling and real-world dimensions when you are drawing and then shift your focus to paper output issues when you plot. On the drafting board, all drawings are committed to paper from the start. People doing manual drafting are inevitably conscious of scale, paper size, and rotation from start to finish. When draftspersons first begin using CAD systems, they may still tend to think in terms of the final hard copy their plotter will produce even as they are creating lines on the screen. The AutoCAD plotting system takes full advantage of the powers of a CAD system, allowing us to ignore scale and other drawing paper issues entirely, if we wish, until it is time to plot.

In addition, the paper space world allows us to create multiple views of the same objects without copying or redrawing them and to plot these viewports simultaneously. In this task, we create two layouts of the flanged bushing shown in Figure 6-32. The first layout contains only one viewport. The second is used to demonstrate some basic principles of working with multiple viewports.

**Figure 6-32**
Flanged bushing drawing

## Opening Layout

✔ To begin this exercise, create an approximation of the bushing shown in Figure 6-32, or open this drawing if you have saved it.

*To approximate the drawing, follow these steps:*

**1** *Erase all objects from your screen.*

**2** *Set limits to (0,0) and (12,9). This is critical. If you use different limits, the exercise is difficult to follow.*

**3** *Draw a circle with diameter 3.50 centered at (3.00,4.00).*

**4** *Draw a second circle with diameter 2.50 centered at the same point.*

**5** *Draw a rectangle with first corner at (6.50,2.75) and second corner at (10.00,5.25).*

✔ Before leaving model space, turn off the grid.

*Layouts have their own grid, so if you leave the model space grid on, you see overlapping grids that are confusing.*

✔ Pick the **Layout1** tab on the status bar, as shown in Figure 6-33.

*You see an image similar to the one in Figure 6-34. This is a simple one-viewport layout. AutoCAD has automatically created a single*

**Figure 6-33**
**Layout1** tab

**Figure 6-34**
Paper space viewport

viewport determined by the extents of your drawing. Paper space viewports are sometimes called floating viewports because they can be moved and reshaped. They are like windows from paper space into model space.

Viewports are also AutoCAD objects and are treated and stored as such. You can move them, stretch them, copy them, and erase them. Editing the viewport does not affect the model space objects within the viewport. When a viewport is selected, the border is highlighted, and grips are shown at each corner.

## Switching Between Paper Space and Model Space

✔ Try selecting the viewport border, just as you would select any AutoCAD object.

If you are unable to select the viewport border, you are in still in model space. Whether you have entered Layout 1 in model space or paper space depends on recent AutoCAD activity. If you are still in model space, double-clicking anywhere outside the viewport border will put you into paper space.

✔ If necessary, double-click outside the viewport border to enter paper space.

✔ Try selecting the viewport border again.

*When you are in paper space you will be able to select the viewport border, but not the objects inside.*

✔ Try to select any of the objects within the viewport.

*You cannot. As long as you are in paper space, model space objects are not accessible. To gain access to model space objects while in a layout view, you must double-click inside a viewport.*

✔ Double-click anywhere within the viewport.

*The border of the viewport takes on a bold outline, and the ViewCube and navigation bar appear inside the viewport. The text at the upper left of the viewport indicates that you are in a 2D wireframe top view, seen from the positive Z direction. In 2D modeling this will always be the case.*

*You are now in model space within the viewport. Notice the difference between working within a viewport in a layout and switching into model space by clicking the **Model** tab. If you click the **Model** tab, the layout disappears, and you are back in the familiar model space drawing area.*

✔ Try selecting objects in your viewport again.

*Model space objects are now available for editing or positioning within the viewport. While in the model space of a viewport, you cannot select any objects drawn in paper space, including the viewport border.*

✔ Double-click anywhere outside the viewport border.

*This returns you to paper space.*

✔ Pick the border of the viewport.

✔ Type **e <Enter>** or pick the **Erase** tool from the ribbon.

This eliminates the viewport and leaves you with the image of a blank sheet of paper. Without a viewport, you have no view of model space.

Next, we create a more complex layout by adding our own viewports.

## Modifying a Layout

Layouts can be modified in numerous ways and can be accessed from the **Layout** tabs at the bottom of the drawing area. You are looking at Layout 1, which is based on the 12 × 9 drawing limits of the bushing drawing or the approximation you created at the beginning of this section. We modify the page setup to represent an ANSI D-size drawing sheet and then add three new viewports to the layout.

✔ Select **Output > Page Setup Manager** from the ribbon or **Print > Page Setup** from the application menu.

*This opens **Page Setup Manager** illustrated in Figure 6-35. Layout 1 should be highlighted in the current page setup list.*

✔ Pick the **Modify** button on the right.

*This opens the **Page Setup – Layout1** dialog box shown in Figure 6-36. This is a version of the **Plot** dialog box.*

**Figure 6-35**
**Page Setup Manager** dialog box

**Figure 6-36**
**Page Setup – Layout1** dialog box

In this exercise, we use a D-size drawing sheet for our layout. If you do not have a D-size plotter, we recommend that you use AutoCAD's DWF6 ePlot pc3 driver, which is designed to create electronic plots that can be sent out over the Internet or a local network. If you prefer to use a different-size paper, you have to make adjustments as you go along. If you use A-size, for example, most specifications can be divided by four. We will include A-size specifications at critical points in case you don't have access to a D-size plotter or want to use a printer.

✔ In the **Printer/plotter** panel, select a plotting device that has a D-size sheet option.

✔ In the **Paper size** panel, select an ANSI D (34 × 22) paper size.
*Notice that **Layout** is now the default selection in the **What to plot** list. We have not encountered this selection before because it is not present when you enter the **Plot** dialog box from model space.*

✔ If necessary, check **Landscape** in the **Drawing orientation** panel.

✔ Click **OK.**
*You return to the **Page Setup Manager**. Notice the changes in the panel labeled **Selected page setup details**.*

✔ Pick the **Close** button.
*AutoCAD will adjust the layout image to represent a D-size drawing sheet in landscape.*
*We make a few adjustments to show the drawing sheet with a paper space grid.*

✔ Right-click the **Grid Display** button and select **Settings** from the shortcut menu.

✔ In the **Drafting Settings** dialog box, check the **Snap on** box.

✔ Check the **Grid on** box.

✔ Deselect the **Adaptive grid** button.

✔ Deselect the **Display grid beyond limits** button.

✔ Click **OK.**
*A grid is added to your drawing sheet, giving you a better sense of the structure of your layout.*

✔ Enter the **LINE** command.
*Entering the **LINE** command will allow you to snap to points on the grid.*

✔ Move the cursor over the lower left corner of the paper grid and locate (0,0).
*This is the origin of the plot, indicated by the corner of the dashed border that shows the effective drawing area.*

✔ Move the cursor to the upper right corner of the effective drawing area.
*The exact point depends on your plotter. With the AutoCAD DWF6 ePlot p3 driver and D-size paper, it is (33.50,20.5).*

✔ Press **<Esc>** to cancel the **LINE** command.

Your screen is now truly representative of a drawing sheet. The plot is made 1:1, with 1 paper space screen unit equaling 1 inch on the drawing sheet. There is little reason to do it any other way, because the whole point of paper space is to emulate the drawing sheet on the screen. For the same reason, you will notice there is no ViewCube when you are in paper space. What is being represented is a flat sheet of drawing paper. There are only two dimensions here, even though the objects within the viewport may be presented as 3D views.

Now, we add viewports.

## Creating Viewports

✔ Pick **Layout** tab > **Layout Viewports** panel > **Rectangular** tool from the ribbon, as shown in Figure 6-37.

This enters the **VPORTS** command. AutoCAD prompts:

Specify corner of viewport or

[ON OFF Fit Shadeplot Lock Object Polygonal Restore Layer 2 3 4] <Fit>:

**Figure 6-37**
**Create Rectangle** tool

We deal only with the **Specify corner** option in this exercise. With this option, you create a viewport just as you would a selection window.

✔ Pick point (1.00,1.00) at the lower left of your screen, as shown in Figure 6-38.

If you are not using D-size paper, you can do fine by making your viewports resemble ours in size, shape, and location.

**Figure 6-38**
Creating viewports

✔ Pick an opposite corner, as shown in Figure 6-38. This is (20,13) on a D-size sheet.

> *Your screen is redrawn with the drawing extents at maximum scale centered within the viewport.*
>
> *Now, we create a second viewport to the right of the first.*

✔ Repeat **VPORTS**.

✔ Pick point (24.00,1.00), as shown in Figure 6-38.

✔ Pick point (32.00,13.00), as shown.

## Zooming XP

You have now created a second viewport. Notice that the images in the two viewports are drawn at different scales. Each is drawn to fit within its viewport. This can create problems later when you add dimension and text. You want to maintain control over the scale of objects within viewports and have a clear knowledge of the relationships among scales in different viewports. For this, we use the **Zoom Scale** feature of the **ZOOM** command. We create different zoom magnifications inside the two viewports.

✔ Double-click inside the left viewport.

> *This takes you into model space within the left viewport. We are going to zoom so that the two-view drawing is in a precise and known scale relation to paper space.*

✔ Type **z <Enter>**.

> *Notice the **ZOOM** command prompt:*

> Specify corner of window, enter a scale factor
> (nX or nXP), or [All Center Dynamic Extents Previous Scale Window Object] <real time>:

> *In this task, we use two new options, the paper space scale factor option (**nXP**) and the **Center** option.*

✔ Type **2xp <Enter>** (on A-size paper divide these factors by four, so you will use **.5xp**).

> *This creates only a slight change in the left viewport. XP means times paper. It allows you to zoom relative to paper space units. If you zoom 1xp, then a model space unit takes on the size of a current paper space unit, which in turn equals 1″ of drawing paper. We zoomed 2xp. This means that 1 unit in the viewport equals 2 paper space units, or 2″ on paper. We now have a precise relationship between model space and paper space in this viewport. The change in presentation size is trivial, but the change in terms of understanding and control is great.*

Next, we set an XP zoom factor in the right viewport so that we control not only the model space/paper space scale relations but the scale relations among viewports as well.

✔ Click inside the right viewport to make it active.

> *You are already in model space, so double-clicking is unnecessary.*

✔ Reenter the **ZOOM** command.

> *In the right viewport, we are going to show a close-up image of the right-side view. To accomplish this, we need a larger zoom factor, and we need to be centered on the right-side view.*

✔ Right-click and select **Center** from the shortcut menu, or select **Center** from the command line.

> *AutoCAD asks you to specify a center point.*

✔ Pick a point on the centerline near the center of the flange; that is, the midpoint of the vertical left side of the rectangle.

> *Look at Figure 6-39. The point you select becomes the center point of the right viewport when AutoCAD zooms in.*

>> AutoCAD prompts:
>> Enter magnification or height <13.61>:

**Figure 6-39**
Zooming 4xp

> *Accepting the default would simply center the image in the viewport. We specify an XP value here.*

✔ Type **4xp <Enter>.**

> *Your right viewport is dynamically magnified to resemble the one in Figure 6-39. In this enlarged image, 1 model space unit equals 4″ in the drawing sheet (1 = 1 on A-size).*

Now that you have the technique, we create one more viewport, focusing this time on one of the circle of holes in the flange.

✔ Type **mv <Enter>** to enter the **MVIEW** command.

> *AutoCAD automatically returns you to paper space.*

✔ Pick point (1.00,14.00).

✔ Pick point (9.00,20.00).

✔ Using techniques you used in the previous viewport, enter model space in the new viewport and zoom in, centering on the lower quadrant of the inner circle in the front view, at six times paper (6xp) in the new viewport.

> *This may require the use of a **Center** or **Quadrant** object snap. Remember that you can access a single-point object snap by holding down **<Shift>**, right-clicking, and then selecting from the **Object Snap** shortcut menu.*

> *Your screen should resemble Figure 6-40.*

> *Before proceeding to plot, try a print preview to ensure that you are ready.*

**Figure 6-40**
Three viewports

✔ Double-click outside all viewports to return to paper space.

✔ Pick the **Plot** tool from the **Quick Access** toolbar.

✔ Pick the **Preview** button from the **Plot** dialog box.
  *This full preview should look very much like the layout image. This is the beauty of the AutoCAD plotting system. You have a great deal of control and the ability to assess exactly what your paper output will be before you actually plot the drawing.*

✔ Press **<Esc>** or **<Enter>** to exit the preview.

✔ Close the **Plot** dialog box.

## Maximize Viewport Button

Before going on, we introduce the **Maximize Viewport** button on the status bar. This button not only allows you to switch into model space in any viewport but also maximizes that viewport to fit the display. Once you have maximized a viewport, you can cycle through other viewports and maximize them one at a time. Try this:

✔ Pick the **Maximize Viewport** button on the status bar, illustrated in Figure 6-41.

**Figure 6-41**
**Maximize Viewport** button

*If you entered the model space of a viewport before clicking the button, AutoCAD would maximize that viewport. Otherwise, it will maximize the first viewport you defined. In our case, the lower left viewport is maximized. The maximized image shows you whatever is in the viewport, along with whatever portion of the drawing will*

*fit the display at the magnification defined for that viewport. (If you pause with the selection arrow on the button, you will notice that it is now labeled as the **Minimize Viewport** button, and that small arrows have been added to the left and right of the button.)*

✔ Pick the small arrow to the right or left of the button.
   *The arrows cycle you through other viewports in the order they were defined.*

✔ Pick the arrows to continue cycling through your three viewports.

✔ When you are done, pick the **Minimize Viewport** button again.
   *This will return you to the paper space layout image.*

## Plotting the Multiple-View Drawing

Now we are ready to plot. Plotting a multiple-viewport drawing is no different from plotting from a single view. Just make sure you are in the layout before entering the **PLOT** command.

✔ With Layout 1 on your screen, pick the **Plot** tool from the **Quick Access** toolbar.
   *At this point you should have no need to adjust settings within the **Plot** dialog box because you have already made adjustments to the page setup and the plotting device. Notice the settings that are now included in the layout.*

---

**NOTE**

If you have done this exercise using the DWF6 ePlot p3 driver, you will note that AutoCAD sends your plot to a file rather than to a plotter. Any drawing can be saved to a file to be plotted later. When you use the ePlot utility, your plot will first be saved to a file that can be sent over the Internet.

---

✔ Prepare your plotter. (Make sure you use the right size paper.)

✔ Click **OK.**

**Important:** Be sure to save this drawing with its multiple-viewport three-view layout before leaving this chapter. You may need it later. . . .

# Chapter Summary

You know how to draw basic two-dimensional shapes and to edit them in numerous ways. In this chapter you learned the power of object snap and object snap tracking. You can offset, trim, extend, and stretch previously drawn objects. You also created your first drawing layout with three views, and you controlled the zoom magnification in each view so that you know how objects in the different views are scaled relative to each other and to the scale of the drawing sheet.

# Chapter Test Questions

## Multiple Choice

*Circle the correct answer.*

1. To initiate a single-point object snap:
   a. Enter an object snap mode at the *Select objects:* prompt
   b. Pick the **Object Snap** button from the status bar
   c. Right-click the **Object Snap** button and select **Single Point**
   d. Enter an object snap mode when AutoCAD prompts for point selection

2. To access the **Object Snap** shortcut menu:
   a. Right-click when AutoCAD prompts for point selection
   b. Right-click after entering a draw command
   c. Pick the **Object Snap** button
   d. Pick the **Object Snap Tracking** button

3. An acquired point will be:
   a. Saved in your drawing
   b. An object snap point
   c. Marked with a small green cross
   d. Specified by pressing the pick button

4. In paper space, the typical plot scale is:
   a. Scaled to paper size
   b. Scaled to fit
   c. 1:1
   d. Plot dependent

5. To coordinate layout scales with viewport scales use:
   a. **Viewport Scale**
   b. **Zoom XP**
   c. **Zoom Scale**
   d. **Zoom Viewport**

## Matching

*Write the number of the correct answer on the line.*

a. Cutting edge _____          1. Trim
b. Boundary _____              2. Object snap tracking
c. Intersection _____          3. Stretch
d. Acquired point _____        4. Object snap
e. Crossing window _____       5. Extend

## True or False

*Circle the correct answer.*

1. **True or False:** It is not possible to plot a landscape-oriented plot on a printer.

2. **True or False:** Like incremental snap, object snap will not interfere with ordinary point selection.

3. **True or False:** In using the **TRIM** command, trimmed objects may also serve as cutting edges.

4. **True or False:** In the **Stretch** grip edit mode and the **STRETCH** command, it is necessary to select objects with a crossing window.

5. **True or False:** AutoCAD layouts are always created in paper space.

## Questions

1. How do you access the **Object Snap** shortcut menu?

2. You have selected a line to extend and a boundary to extend it to, but AutoCAD gives you the message "Object does not intersect an edge." What happened?

3. What selection method is always required when you use the **STRETCH** command?

4. Why is it usual practice to plot 1:1 in paper space?

5. Why do we use the **Zoom XP** option when zooming in floating model space viewports?

## Drawing Problems

1. Draw a line from (6,2) to (11,6). Draw a second line perpendicular to the first starting at (6,6).

2. Break the first line at its intersection with the second.

3. There are now three lines on the screen. Draw a circle centered at their intersection and passing through the midpoint of the line going up and to the right of the intersection.

4. Trim all the lines to the circumference of the circle.

5. Erase what is left of the line to the right of the intersection, and trim the portion of the circle to the left, between the two remaining lines.

## WWW Exercise (Optional)

Your exploration of online CAD continues with two more websites that serve as launching pads with links to many other AutoCAD and CAD-related websites. In addition, we offer a challenge to create a design using object snap and a limited number of commands.

- Connect to your Internet service provider.

- Type **browser <Enter>.**

- If necessary, navigate to our companion website at www.pearsonhighered.com/dixriley.
  *Enjoy your visit.*

## Editing Shared Drawings with AutoCAD WS (Optional)

Here we further our exploration of Autodesk cloud features by introducing **AutoCAD WS. AutoCAD WS** is a companion to **Autodesk 360** that allows you to edit drawings in the cloud. Now that you have experience with many of AutoCAD's 2D drawing commands and procedures, you will find much that is familiar in **AutoCAD WS. AutoCAD WS** is a very limited version of AutoCAD itself. It provides a level of functionality appropriate for minor editing and commenting on shared drawings, but would not be very satisfying for the creation of complete drawings. In fact, drawings are not created in the cloud, but only uploaded, shared, and edited there.

Like **Autodesk 360, AutoCAD WS** is free with a 3-GB storage capacity. Subscribers get 25 GB of storage and some enhanced features.

> **NOTE**
>
> Autodesk cloud features change independently of AutoCAD releases, so any of these features may have changed by the time you are reading this.

✔ From the ribbon, select the **Autodesk 360** tab.

✔ Pick the **Launch Website** tool.

✔ If necessary, sign in to your **Autodesk 360** account.

> *Your **Autodesk 360** account should be a somewhat familiar space by now. Your uploaded drawing(s) should be listed with thumbnail views or icons. For this task you will need to choose a drawing you wish to edit. We will not offer specific editing instructions, but will take you to **AutoCAD WS** and help you find your way around.*
>
> *If you do not have a drawing uploaded into **Autodesk 360,** you should upload one now. Then proceed as follows.*

✔ Pick the **Actions** button at the right for any of your uploaded drawings.

> *This will open the menu shown in Figure 6-42.*

✔ Pick the **Edit Online in AutoCAD WS** option as shown.

> *In a short time, **AutoCAD WS** will load along with your drawing, and you will see a page similar to Figure 6-43. The similarity to the AutoCAD interface is obvious, with the simplified ribbon at the top with eight tabs. By default, the **Home** tab is open. This tab has*

**Figure 6-42**
**Action** menu

**Figure 6-43**
**WS Editor**

seven panels, which are not labeled. You see the panel with **Open, Save,** and **Download** tools on the left and the **Design Feed** tool on the far right. The second panel from the left comprises basic draw commands, but there is also a **Draw** tab with additional draw and modify commands.

✔ Open the **Draw** tab to view the options shown in Figure 6-44.
Many of these icons will be familiar to you. If not, there are simple tooltips, like the one for the **Freeline** tool, as shown in Figure 6-45. To the left of the drawing area in Figure 6-43 are three screen options. You are currently in the **Editor** screen. Above this is **Drawings.** If you select **Drawings** you will see a screen that gives access to all the drawings you have uploaded to **Autodesk 360,** with indications as to which have been shared along with options to upload and download more drawings. You can also delete drawings and connect to other online storage services, such as Autodesk's Buzzsaw.

**Figure 6-44**
**Draw** tab

**Figure 6-45**
**Freeline** tool

*Selecting **Messages,** you will see historical information on which drawings have been recently updated, along with messages from Autodesk about any recent changes in website functionality.*

*At the bottom of the drawing area, you see the **AutoCAD WS** command line, and to the right a blue **Share** button, which provides yet another way to make your drawing accessible to others.*

*Finally, at the bottom of the screen is a status bar, with drawing tabs on the left, mode buttons in the middle, and navigation tools on the right.*

*With all you have learned about AutoCAD techniques, you will find your way around with a little exploration and experimentation. One last suggestion before you go.*

**Figure 6-46**
**Design Feed**

✔ Select **Home** tab > **Design Feed** tool.

*This opens a window like the one shown in Figure 6-46 on the right side of your drawing area. Here you can post comments regarding the drawing. The comments become part of the sharing history of the drawing and serve to document the development and collaboration that went into it.*

> **NOTE**
>
> There is also a **Design Feed** tool on the **Autodesk 360** tab in AutoCAD that allows you to post comments on any drawing that has been saved to **Autodesk 360**. In addition, you can add comments while in **Autodesk 360** by selecting the **Comments** tool to the right of the **Actions** tool on the listing for any of your uploaded drawings.

✔ When you are done exploring, close the window to sign out of **Autodesk 360** and **AutoCAD WS,** or close the tabs independently.

## G Drawing 6-1: *Sprocket* [INTERMEDIATE]

This drawing can be done with the tools you now have. It makes use of object snap, **TRIM, OFFSET,** and polar array. Be sure to set the limits large, as suggested.

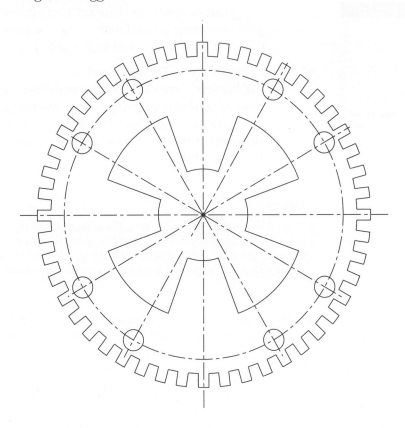

### Drawing Suggestions

GRID = .25

SNAP = 0.0625

LIMITS = (0,0)(24,18)

- Begin by drawing the 12.25- and 11.25-diameter circles centered on the same point near the middle of your display.

- To construct the sprocket teeth, draw a line using the **Quadrant** object snap to locate the point at the top of the 12.25-diameter circle. The second point can be straight down so that the line crosses the 11.25-diameter circle. The exact length is insignificant because you will trim the line back to the inner circle.

- Offset this line .1875 on both sides.

- Trim the first line, and trim and extend the other two lines to the inner and outer circles.

- Create a polar array of these lines and trim them to create the teeth.
- Draw the 10.25 B.C. on the **Centerline** layer.
- Draw a line from the center to the quadrant.
- Use grips to rotate and copy the line to 30° and 60° for the 0.75-diameter circles, and 20° and 70° for the inside cutout.
- Draw two circles where the centerline intersects with the bolt circle.
- Construct a polar array to get the proper hole pattern.
- Draw the 7.44-diameter circle and the 3.25-diameter circle.
- Trim to construct the cutout geometry.

**Drawing 6-1**
Sprocket

## G  Drawing 6-2: *Archimedes Spiral*
### [INTERMEDIATE]

The designs in this drawing are not technical drawings, but they give you valuable experience with important CAD commands. First, you create an accurate Archimedes spiral using a radial grid of circles and lines as a guide. Once the spiral is done, turn off the grid layers and use the spiral to create the designs in the reference drawing.

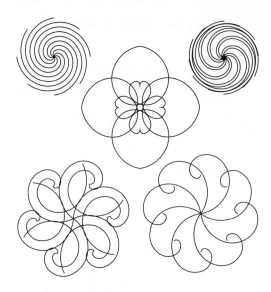

## Drawing Suggestions

GRID = 0.5

SNAP = 0.25

LIMITS = (0,0)(18,12)

LTSCALE = 0.5

- The alternating continuous and hidden lines work as a drawing aid. If you use different colors and layers, they are more helpful. Because all circles are offset 0.50, you can draw one continuous and one hidden circle and then use the **OFFSET** command to create all the others.

- Begin by drawing one of the continuous circles on Layer **0,** centered near the middle of your display; then offset all the other continuous circles.

- Draw the continuous horizontal line across the middle of your six circles, and then array it in a three-item polar array.

- Set to Layer **2,** and draw one of the hidden circles, then the other hidden circles.

- Draw a vertical hidden line and array it as you did the horizontal continuous line.

- Set to Layer **1** for the spiral itself.

- Turn on a running object snap to **Intersection** mode and construct a series of three-point arcs. Be sure to turn off any other modes that might get in your way. Start points and endpoints will be on continuous line intersections; second points always will fall on hidden line intersections.

- When the spiral is complete, turn off Layers **0** and **2.** There should be nothing left on your screen but the spiral itself.

- Once the spiral is complete, use only edit commands to create the designs. For the designs there are no dimensions. Don't be too concerned with precision. Some of your designs may come out slightly different from ours. When this happens, try to analyze the differences. To place all designs on one screen, you will need to increase the limits.

Location of 2nd point of each arc is where hidden lines intersect

DETAIL
Scale 2x1

| SOLID CIRCLE RADII | HIDDEN CIRCLE RADII |
|---|---|
| 0.50 | 0.25 |
| 1.00 | 0.75 |
| 1.50 | 1.25 |
| 2.00 | 1.75 |
| 2.50 | 2.25 |
| 3.00 | 2.75 |

**Drawing 6-2**
Archimedes Spiral

This drawing provides a mental challenge and makes use of many commands and object snap modes with which you are now familiar. As is typical, there are numerous ways to reach the visual result shown. In all methods, you need to think carefully about the geometry of the links and how they are positioned relative to one another. The drawing suggestions here will get you started but will leave you with some puzzles to solve. The letters shown are labels for different styles of links; the numbers in the drawing suggest an order of steps you might take.

## Drawing Suggestions

SNAP = .0625

GRID = .25

LIMITS = (0,0)(24,18)

- Start by drawing the three concentric circles labeled A above the number 1; then use a **Quadrant** object snap to copy these vertically to create the beginning of link B.

- Make another copy of the three circles up .875.

- Draw lines tangent to tangent from the middle and outer circles of the link. The final two vertical lines of link B are offset from a line between the centers of the upper and lower circles.

- Trim lines and circles to complete link B.

- Copy link B up so that the copy is at the upper quadrant point of link B. This will become link C. Stretch the copy to create link C, in which the distance between the lower center and the upper center is 1.25.

- Create a polar array of links B and C with circles A in the center to create a cross pattern.

- The rectangles and squares in Steps 2 and 3 are created by drawing lines from different quadrant points on the links in the array. Fillet the corners of these boxes to the 0.875 radius.

- The diagonal links inside the boxes can be created in a manner similar to links B and C and then copied in polar arrays.

**Drawing 6-3**
Link Design

# Drawing 6-4: *Grooved Hub* [INTERMEDIATE]

This drawing includes another typical application of the rotation techniques just discussed. The hidden lines in the front view must be rotated 120° and a copy retained in the original position. There are also good opportunities to use **MIRROR,** object snap, object snap tracking, and **TRIM.**

## Drawing Suggestions

GRID = 0.5

SNAP = 0.0625

LIMITS = (0,0)(12,9)

LTSCALE = 1

- Draw the circles in the front view, and use these to line up the horizontal lines in the left-side view. This is a good opportunity to use object snap tracking. By acquiring the quadrant of a circle in the front view, you can track along the horizontal construction lines to the left-side view.

- There are several different planes of symmetry in the left-side view, which suggests the use of mirroring. We leave it up to you to choose an efficient sequence.

- A quick method for drawing the horizontal hidden lines in the left-side view is to acquire the upper and lower quadrant points of the 0.625-diameter circle in the front view to track horizontal construction lines. Draw the lines in the left-side view longer than actual length, and then use **TRIM** to erase the excess on both sides of the left-side view.

- The same method can be used to draw the two horizontal hidden lines in the front view. A slightly different method that does not use object tracking is to snap lines directly to the top and bottom quadrants of the 0.25-diameter circle in the left-side view as a guide and draw them all the way through the front view. Then, trim to the 2.25-diameter circle and the 0.62-diameter circle.

- Once these hidden lines are drawn, rotate them, retaining a copy in the original position.

## Creating the Multiple-View Layout

Use this drawing to create the multiple-view layout shown below the dimensioned drawing. This three-view layout is very similar to the one created in the "Creating Plot Layouts" section. Exact dimensions of the viewports are not given. You should create them depending on the paper size you wish to use. What should remain consistent is the scale relationships among the three viewports. On an A sheet, for example, if the largest viewport is zoomed 0.5xp, then the left close-up is 1.0xp, and the top close-up is 1.5xp. These ratios have to be adjusted for other sheet sizes.

**Drawing 6-4**
Grooved Hub

## M Drawing 6-5: *Slotted Flange* [ADVANCED]

This drawing includes a typical application of polar arrays, **ROTATE,** and **TRIM.** The finished drawing should consist of the 2D top view and front view, not the 3D view shown on the drawing page. The centerlines and outline of the large circle in the top view are shown in the reference drawing. Use the 3D view as a reference to draw the 2D top and front views.

Location of Top View

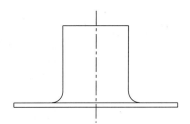

Location of Front View

## Drawing Suggestions

- Begin by drawing the outer 7.50-diameter circle. Then, draw the three circles on the centerline for the center bored hole in the top view.

- Figure out the placement of and draw the bolt circle diameter for the four small circles on the vertical and horizontal centerlines in the top view.

- Draw two complete circles for the slots. These circles should run tangent to the inside and outside of the small circles, or they can be constructed by offsetting the bolt circle centerline.

- You can rotate and copy the circles at the end of the slots into place using grips; then trim what is not needed.

- Complete the front view, making sure to line up the circles and centerlines in the top view with the vertical lines in the front view.

**Ø1.50 thru**
**2.000 C'Bore x .50 deep**

**Ø3.00**

**R2.375**

**R0.50**

**3.58**

**R0.25**
**8 Places**

**Ø0.50 thru**
**4 holes**

**Ø7.50**

**0.20**

**R2.8750**

**50°**

**20°**

**Drawing 6-5**
Slotted Flange

# Drawing 6-6: *Deck Framing* [INTERMEDIATE]

This architectural drawing may take some time, although there is nothing in it you have not done before. Be sure to make the suggested adjustments to your drawing setup before beginning.

## Drawing Suggestions

> UNITS = Architectural; Precision = 0'-00"
>
> LIMITS = (0,0)(48,36)
>
> GRID = 1'
>
> SNAP = 2"

- Whatever order you choose for doing this drawing, we suggest that you make ample use of **COPY, ARRAY, OFFSET,** and **TRIM.**

- Keep **Ortho** on, except to draw the lines across the middle of the squares, representing upright posts.

- With snap set at 2", it is easy to copy lines 2" apart, as you have to do frequently to draw the 2 × 8 studs.

- You may need to turn **Snap Mode** off when you are selecting lines to copy, but be sure to turn it on again to specify displacements.

- Notice that you can use **ARRAY** effectively, but there are three separate arrays. They are all 16" on center, but the double boards in several places make it inadvisable to do a single array of studs all the way across the deck. What you can do, however, is draw, copy, and array all the "vertical" studs at the maximum length first and then go back and trim them to their various actual lengths using the "horizontal" boards as cutting edges.

**Drawing 6-6**
Deck Framing

# Drawing 6-7: *Tool Block* [ADVANCED]

In this drawing, you take information from a 3D drawing and develop it into a three-view drawing. The finished drawing should be composed of the top view, front view, and side view. The reference drawing shows a portion of each view to be developed. You are to complete these views.

Location of
Top View

Location of
Front View

Location of
Side View

## Drawing Suggestions

- Begin by drawing the top view. Use the top view to line up the front view and side view.

- The slot with the angular lines must be drawn in the front view before the other views. These lines can then be lined up with the top and side views and used as guides to draw the hidden lines.

- Be sure to include all the necessary hidden lines and centerlines in each view.

1.000

1.00

6.000

1.250

3.000

Ø.50 Thru
C'Bore .75
x .25 Deep
x 2 Holes

R2.000

Ø.500 Thru
C'Bore
Ø1.000 x .25 Deep
2 Holes

3.750

0.500

4.000

4.000

0.500

2.500

30°

R0.500

7.000

3.000

.625

1.500

6.000

8.000

**Drawing 6-7**
Tool Block

# 7 chapterseven

## Text

# CHAPTER OBJECTIVES

- Enter single-line text with justification options
- Enter text on an angle, and enter text using character codes
- Enter multiline text using **MTEXT**
- Edit text in place with **DDEDIT** and **MTEDIT**
- Modify text with the **Quick Properties** panel

- Use the **SPELL** command
- Change fonts and styles
- Change properties with **MATCHPROP**
- Scale previously drawn entities
- Create tables and fields
- Use AutoCAD templates, borders, and title blocks

## Introduction

| TEXT | |
|---------|------------|
| **Command** | Text |
| **Alias** | (none) |
| **Panel** | Annotation |
| **Tool** | |

Now, it's time for a discussion of adding text to your drawings. In this chapter, you learn to find your way around AutoCAD's **TEXT** and **MTEXT** commands. In addition, you learn many new editing commands that are often used with text but are equally important for editing other objects.

## Entering Single-Line Text with Justification Options

AutoCAD provides two commands for entering text in a drawing. **TEXT** allows you to enter single lines of text and displays them as you type. **MTEXT** allows you to type multiple lines of text in a special text editor and positions them in a windowed area in your drawing. Both commands provide numerous options for placing text and a variety of fonts to use and styles that can be created from them. You probably are already familiar with entering single lines of left-justified text. Here we begin by expanding your technique to include other forms of single-line text.

✔ To prepare for this exercise, create a new drawing using B-size (18 × 12) limits and draw a 4.00-unit horizontal line beginning at (1,1). Then, create five copies of the line 2.00 units apart, as shown in Figure 7-1.

*These lines are for orientation in this exercise only; they are not essential for drawing text. Our first step is a quick review of left-justified text.*

✔ Open the short **Text** drop-down list on the **Annotation** panel and pick the **Single Line** text tool.

✔ Pick a start point at the left end of the upper line.

✔ Press **<Enter>** to accept the default height (0.20).

✔ Press **<Enter>** to accept the default angle (0).

✔ Type **Left <Enter>.**

*Notice that the text cursor jumps below the line when you press <Enter>.*

✔ Type **Justified <Enter>.**

*The text cursor jumps down again, and another Enter text: prompt appears. To exit the command, you need to press <Enter> at the prompt.*

✔ Press **<Enter>** to exit the command.

*This completes the process and returns you to the command line prompt.*
*Figure 7-2 shows the left-justified text you have just drawn.*

**Figure 7-1**
Drawing six lines

**Figure 7-2**
Left-justified text

Before proceeding with other text justification options, we demonstrate one additional feature of **TEXT.**

✔ Press **<Enter>** to repeat the **TEXT** command.

*If you press <Enter> again at this point instead of showing a new start point or selecting a justification option, you go right back to the Enter text: prompt as if you had never left the command. Try it.*

✔ Press **<Enter>** again.

*You see the* Enter text: *prompt in the command line, and the text cursor reappears on the screen just below the word* Justified.

✔ Type **Text <Enter>.**

*Any time you have the* Specify start point: *prompt in the command line, you can also move the text cursor to another point on the screen. Try it.*

✔ Pick a new start point anywhere on the screen.

*The text cursor will move to the new point you have chosen.*

✔ Press **<Enter>** to exit the command.

*Once you have left* **TEXT,** *there are other ways to edit text, which we explore in the "Editing Text in Place with DDEDIT and MTEDIT" and "Modifying Text with the Quick Properties Panel" sections.*

We now proceed to some of the other text placement options, beginning with right-justified text. The options demonstrated in this exercise are all illustrated in Figure 7-3 and in the complete chart of options, Figure 7-4. For the text in this demonstration we also specify a change in height.

**Figure 7-3**
Text options demonstrated

| TEXT JUSTIFICATION | |
|---|---|
| START POINT TYPE ABBREVIATION | TEXT POSITION +INDICATES START POINT OR PICK POINT |
| A | ALIGN |
| F | FIT+ |
| C | CENTER |
| M | MIDDLE |
| R | RIGHT+ |
| TL | +TOP LEFT |
| TC | TOP CENTER |
| TR | TOP RIGHT+ |
| ML | MIDDLE LEFT |
| MC | MIDDLE+CENTER |
| MR | MIDDLE RIGHT+ |
| BL | BOTTOM LEFT |
| BC | BOTTOM+CENTER |
| BR | BOTTOM RIGHT+ |

**Figure 7-4**
Text options

## Right-Justified Text

Right-justified text is constructed from an endpoint backing up, right to left.

✔ Repeat the **TEXT** command.

✔ Right-click and select **Justify** from the shortcut menu shown in Figure 7-5.

*This opens a dynamic input list.*

**Figure 7-5**
Shortcut menu

✔ Select **Right** from the menu.
*Now, AutoCAD prompts for an endpoint instead of a start point:*

Specify right endpoint of text baseline:

✔ Pick the right end of the second line.
*AutoCAD prompts you to specify a text height. This time we change the height to 0.50.*

✔ Type **.5 <Enter>.**

✔ Press **<Enter>** to retain 0° of rotation.
*Notice the larger text cursor at the right end of the second line.*

✔ Type **Right <Enter>.**
*At this point you should have the word "Right" right-justified on the second line.*

✔ Press **<Enter>** to exit the command.
*Your screen should now include the second line of text in right-justified position, as shown in Figure 7-3.*

## Centered Text

Centered text is justified from the bottom center of the text.

✔ Repeat the **TEXT** command.

✔ Select **Justify** from the command line.

✔ Select **Center** from the command line.
*AutoCAD prompts:*

Specify center point of text:

✔ Pick the midpoint of the third line.

✔ Press **<Enter>** to retain the current height, which is now set to 0.50.

✔ Press **<Enter>** to retain 0° of rotation.

✔ Type **Center <Enter>.**

✔ Press **<Enter>** again to complete the command.
*The word "Center" should now be centered, as shown in Figure 7-3.*

## Middle Text

Middle text is justified from the middle of the text both horizontally and vertically, rather than from the bottom center. Previously we have selected from the command line and the shortcut menu; this time we skip these steps by typing in the initial for the option.

✔ Repeat **TEXT.**

✔ Type **m <Enter>.**
*AutoCAD prompts:*

Specify middle point of text:

✔ Pick the midpoint of the fourth line.

✔ Press **<Enter>** to retain the current height of 0.50.

✔ Press **<Enter>** to retain 0° of rotation.

✔ Type **Middle <Enter>**.

✔ Press **<Enter>** again to complete the command.

*Notice the difference between center and middle. Center refers to the midpoint of the baseline below the text. Middle refers to the middle of the text itself, so that the line now runs through the text.*

## Aligned Text

Aligned text is placed between two specified points. The height of the text is calculated proportional to the distance between the two points, and the text is drawn along the line between the two points.

✔ Repeat **TEXT.**

✔ Type **a <Enter>**.

*AutoCAD prompts:*

> Specify first endpoint of text baseline:

✔ Pick the left end of the fifth line.

*AutoCAD prompts for another point:*

> Specify second endpoint of text baseline:

✔ Pick the right end of the fifth line.

*Notice that there is no prompt for height. AutoCAD calculates a height based on the space between the points you chose. There is also no prompt for an angle, because the angle between your two points (in this case 0) is used. You can position text at an angle using this option.*

✔ Type **Align <Enter>**.

*As you type, the text size will be adjusted with the addition of each letter.*

✔ Press **<Enter>** again to complete the command.

*Notice that the text is sized to fill the space between the two points you selected.*

## Text Drawn to Fit Between Two Points

The **Fit** option is similar to the **Align** option, except that the specified text height is retained.

✔ Repeat **TEXT.**

✔ Type **f <Enter>**.

*You are prompted for two points, as in the **Align** option.*

✔ Pick the left end of the sixth line.

✔ Pick the right end of the sixth line.

✔ Press **<Enter>** to retain the current height.

*As with the **Align** option, there is no prompt for an angle of rotation.*

✔ Type **Fit <Enter>**.

*Once again, text size is adjusted as you type, but this time only the width changes.*

✔ Press **<Enter>** again to complete the command.

*This time the text is stretched horizontally to fill the line without a change in height. This is the difference between **Fit** and **Align**. In* the **Align** option, text height is determined by the width you show. With **Fit,** the specified height is retained, and the text is stretched or compressed to fill the given space.

## Other Justification Options

Before proceeding to the next task, take a moment to look at the complete list of justification options. The command line prompt looks like this:

[Align Fit Center Middle Right TL TC TR ML MC MR BL BC BR]:

The same options are on the dynamic input list and are spelled out in the chart shown in Figure 7-4. We have already explored the first five and the default **Left** option. For the others, study the figure. As shown on the chart, *T* is for top, *M* is for middle, and *B* is for bottom. *L, C,* and *R* stand for left, center, and right, respectively. Let's try one:

✔ Repeat **TEXT** and then type **tl <Enter>** for the **Top Left** option, or select **TL** from the dynamic input list or command line.
   *AutoCAD asks you to* Specify top-left point of text:. *As shown in the chart in Figure 7-4, top left refers to the highest potential text point at the left of the word.*

✔ Pick a top left point to place the text, as shown in Figure 7-3.

✔ Press **<Enter>** twice to accept the height and rotation angle settings and arrive at the *Text:* prompt.

✔ Type **top left <Enter>.**
   *The text is entered from the top left position.*

✔ Press **<Enter>** again to complete the command.
   *Your screen should now resemble Figure 7-3.*

## Entering Text on an Angle and Text Using Character Codes

In this section we explore **TEXT** further by entering several lines on an angle, adding special character symbols along the way. We create three lines of left-justified text, one below the other and all rotated 45°, as shown in Figure 7-6.

✔ Repeat the **TEXT** command.
   *You see the familiar prompt:*

   Specify start point of text or [Justify Style]:

**Figure 7-6**
Text on an angle

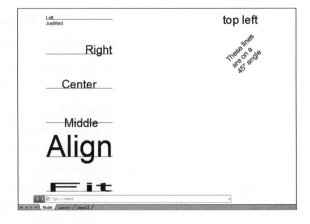

✔ Pick a starting point near (12.00,8.00), as shown in Figure 7-6.

✔ Type **.3 <Enter>** to specify a smaller text size.

✔ Type **45 <Enter>** or show an angle of 45°.
  *Notice that the text cursor is shown at the specified angle.*

✔ Type **These lines <Enter>.**
  *The text is drawn on the screen at a 45° angle, and the cursor moves down to the next line. Notice that the text cursor is still at the specified angle.*

✔ Type **are on a <Enter>.**

## The Degree Symbol and Other Special Characters

The next line contains a degree symbol. Because you do not have this character on your keyboard, AutoCAD provides a special method for drawing it. Type the text with the %% signs just as shown in the following and then study Figure 7-7, which lists other special characters that can be drawn in the same way.

**Figure 7-7**
Control codes and special characters

| Control Codes and Special Characters | |
| --- | --- |
| Type at Text Prompt | Text on Drawing |
| %%O OVERSCORE<br>%%U UNDERSCORE<br>180%%D<br>2.00 %%P.01<br>%%C4.00 | OVERSCORE<br>UNDERSCORE<br>180°<br>2.00 ±.01<br>Ø4.00 |

✔ Type **45%%d**
  ***TEXT*** *initially types the percent symbols directly to the screen, just as you have typed them. When you type the **d,** the character code is translated and redrawn as a degree symbol.*

✔ Add a space and then type **angle <Enter>.**

✔ Press **<Enter>** again to complete the command sequence.
  *Your screen should now resemble Figure 7-6.*

## Entering Multiline Text Using MTEXT

| MTEXT | |
| --- | --- |
| **Command** | MText |
| **Alias** | T |
| **Panel** | Annotation |
| **Tool** | A |

The **MTEXT** command allows you to create multiple lines of text in a text editor and position them within a defined window in your drawing. Like **TEXT, MTEXT** has nine options for text justification and its own set of character codes.

We begin by creating a simple left-justified block of text.

✔ Pick the **Multiline Text** tool from the **Annotation** panel, as shown in Figure 7-8.
  *You see the following prompt in the command line:*

    Specify first corner:

  *Also, notice that a multiline text symbol, "abc", has been added to the crosshairs.*

**Figure 7-8**
**Multiline Text** tool

Fundamentally, **MTEXT** lets you define the width of a group of text lines that you create in a special text editor. As the text is entered, AutoCAD formats it to conform to the specified width and justification method and draws it on your screen. The width can be defined in several ways. The default method for specifying a width is to draw a window on the screen, but this can be misleading. **MTEXT** does not attempt to place the complete text inside the window but only within its width. The first point of the window becomes the insertion point of the text. How AutoCAD uses this insertion point depends on the justification option. The second window point defines the width and the text flow direction (i.e., whether the text lines should be drawn above or below, to the left or right of the insertion point). Exactly how this is interpreted is also dependent on the justification option.

✔ Pick an insertion point near the middle of your drawing area, in the neighborhood of (12.00,5.00).

> *AutoCAD begins a window at the selected point and gives you a new prompt:*

> Specify opposite corner or
> [Height Justify Line spacing Rotation Style Width Columns]:

> *We continue with the default options by picking a second corner. For purposes of demonstration, we show a window 2.00 wide, drawn down and to the right.*

✔ Pick a second point 2.00 to the right and about 1.00 below the first point.

> *As soon as you pick the opposite corner, AutoCAD opens the* **Multiline Text Editor** *at the start point in your drawing. At the same time, the* **Text Editor** *contextual tab on the ribbon replaces other panels on the ribbon, as illustrated in Figure 7-9. The* **Text Editor** *panels give you the capacity to change text styles and fonts (see the "Changing Fonts and Styles" section) and text height, along with many other text features such as bolding and underlining. When you enter text in the editor, it wraps around as it will be displayed in your drawing, according to the width you have specified. This width is represented by the small ruler at the top of the text editing window. Using the two small triangles along the left side of the ruler, you can also set first-line indent and hanging indent tabs for paragraph formatting. If you let the cursor rest along the right side of the ruler, you will see a double arrow that will allow*

**Figure 7-9**
**Multiline Text Editor**

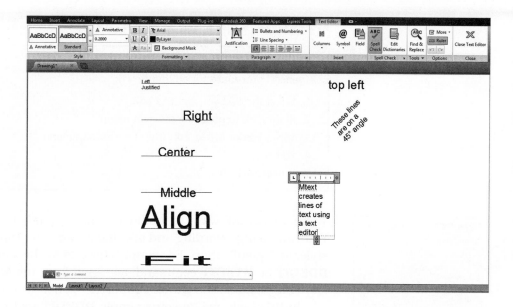

you to expand the width of the window. The two arrows below the ruler allow you to expand the height.

The window is placed at the actual text location, and the text is shown in the window at the same size as it will appear in the drawing, unless this would make it either too large or too small for convenient editing. In such cases, the text size is adjusted to a reasonable size for editing, and the actual size is shown only when the command is completed.

✔ Type **Mtext creates lines of text using a text editor.**

Text appears in the window, as illustrated in Figure 7-9.

✔ Pick a point outside the text editor to leave the editor and complete the command.

You are returned to the drawing window. The **Home** tab of panels returns to the ribbon, and the new text is added, as shown in Figure 7-10. Notice that the text you typed has been wrapped around to fit within the 2.00-width window; the 0.30 height of the text has been retained; and the 1.00 height of the text window you defined has been ignored.

In a moment, we will explore other mtext justification options. First, however, we do some simple text editing with **DDEDIT** and **MTEDIT.**

**Figure 7-10**
**New text added**

# Editing Text in Place with DDEDIT and MTEDIT

**Figure 7-11**
Shortcut menu

**Figure 7-12**
Selecting text on an angle

There are several ways to modify text that already exists in your drawing. You can change wording and spelling as well as properties such as layer, style, and justification. For simple changes in the wording of text, use the **DDEDIT** or **MTEDIT** command, accessed from the **Modify** menu; for property changes, use the **Quick Properties** panel, discussed in the next section.

In this task, we do some simple **DDEDIT** text editing. Then, we use the **MTEDIT** command to show different justification options of mtext paragraphs. In both cases, it is most efficient to select the text first and then use the shortcut menu to enter commands and select options. Start by selecting the first line of the angled text.

✔ Select the words "These lines" by clicking on any of the letters.
*The words "These lines" are highlighted, and a grip appears at the start point of the line, indicating that this single line of text has been selected.*

✔ Right-click to open the shortcut menu shown in Figure 7-11.

✔ Select **Edit** from the shortcut menu, as shown.
*When you make this selection, the shortcut menu disappears, and you see the selected text line highlighted and colored, as shown in Figure 7-12. This is the way **DDEDIT** functions for text created with **TEXT.** If you had selected text created with **MTEXT,** AutoCAD would have put you in the text editor instead.*
*We add the word "three" to the middle of the selected line, as follows.*

✔ Move the screen cursor to the center of the text, between "These" and "lines", and press the pick button.
*A flashing cursor should now be present, indicating where text will be added if you begin typing.*

✔ Type **three** and add a space so that the line reads "These three lines", as shown in Figure 7-13.

✔ Press **<Enter>.**
*The cursor disappears, but you are still in the **DDEDIT** command.*

Now we are going to edit the text you created in **MTEXT.** The first difference you will notice is that because **MTEXT** creates multiple lines of text as a group, you cannot select a single line of text. When you click, the whole set of lines is selected.

**DDEDIT** repeats automatically, so you should have the following prompt in the command line before proceeding:

Select an annotation object or [Undo]:

✔ If not, repeat **DDEDIT**.

✔ Select the text beginning with "Mtext creates".

*DDEDIT recognizes that you have chosen text created with **MTEXT** and opens the **Multiline Text Editor**, with the text window around the chosen paragraph and the **Text Editor** tab of panels appearing on the ribbon.*

✔ Point and click just to the left of the word "lines" in the text editor.

*You should see a white cursor blinking at the beginning of the line.*

✔ Type **multiple** so that the text reads "Mtext creates multiple lines of text using a text editor".

*You may also notice that "Mtext" is underlined in red dashes. This indicates that the text editor does not recognize this word and it may be misspelled. We explore the **SPELL** command in a later section.*

✔ Move the cursor anywhere outside the text editor and press the pick button to exit the **Multiline Text Editor.**

✔ Press **<Enter>** or the spacebar to exit the command.

*You return to the drawing window with the new text added, as shown in Figure 7-14. Next, we explore the **Quick Properties** panel along with the mtext justification options.*

**Figure 7-13**
Adding text

**Figure 7-14**
Multiline text added

## Modifying Text with the Quick Properties Panel

**TIP**

A general procedure for modifying properties is:

1. Select object.
2. Pick the **Quick Properties** button on the status bar.
3. Use the **Quick Properties** panel to specify property changes.
4. Close the **Quick Properties** panel.

**properties:** Characteristics of an object that determine how and where an object is shown in a drawing. Some properties are common to all objects (layer, color, linetype, or lineweight), whereas others apply only to a particular type of object (radius of a circle or endpoint of a line).

All objects in a drawing have characteristics called **properties**. Standard properties for lines include color, layer, linetype, lineweight, and length. Depending on the type of object, there are many additional properties. Properties for text include layer, contents, justification, height, and rotation. There is also a property called annotative, which we do not explore here. In this exercise, you learn how to change the justification property of text with the **MTEXT** command. Other properties can be changed in similar fashion. We use the efficient **Quick Properties** panel, found on the status bar. Begin by drawing a visual reference line, so that changes in justification will be clear.

✔ Draw a 2.00 line just above the mtext paragraph, as shown in Figure 7-15.

*This line will make the placement of different justification options clearer. It should begin at the same snap point that was used as the insertion point for the text. The left end of the line shows the insertion point, and the length shows the width of the paragraph. We have used the point (12.00,5.00) and the 2.00 width.*

✔ Pick the paragraph beginning with "Mtext creates".

*The text will be highlighted, with grips at the top and bottom of the text window.*

✔ Pick the **Quick Properties** button on the status bar, as shown in Figure 7-16.

*With the **Quick Properties** tool on, you see the panel shown in Figure 7-16. It is a floating panel, so it may appear at a different point on your screen. You can move it by clicking and dragging the right or left border of the panel. The panel is in the form of a two-column table, with properties listed on the left and options for change on the right. Some options are changed by typing as you would in an edit box; others open a drop-down list when you select them.*

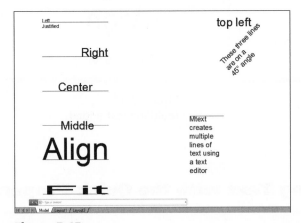

**Figure 7-15**
Draw a 2.00 line

**Figure 7-16**
**Quick Properties** tool

✔ Select **Top left** in the right column opposite **Justify.**

✔ Select the arrow at the right to open the list.

*This opens the drop-down list of justification options shown in Figure 7-17.*

**in-canvas property preview:**
A feature that allows the user to see the effect that changing a property will have prior to actually making the property change.

✔ Highlight **Top center** on the list, as shown.

*When you highlight this selection, the justification property of the mtext in your drawing is immediately adjusted, as shown in Figure 7-18. The paragraph is now previewed in top-centered format. This action, called **in-canvas property preview**, works with many object properties, not just text justification. You may wish to highlight other justification options before moving on. Also study Figure 7-19, which illustrates mtext justification options.*

**Figure 7-17**
Select **Top center**

**Figure 7-18**
Text centered

**Figure 7-19**
Multiline text justification

## MULTILINE TEXT JUSTIFICATION

Mtext controls which part of the text aligns at the intersection point. This is an example of top left text.

top left:
left-justified,
spills down

Mtext controls which part of the text aligns at the intersection point. This is an example of top center text.

top center:
center-justified,
spills down

Mtext controls which part of the text aligns at the intersection point. This is an example of top right text.

top right:
right-justified,
spills down

Mtext controls which part of the text aligns at the intersection point. This is an example of middle left text.

middle left:
left-justified,
spills up and down

Mtext controls which part of the text aligns at the intersection point. This is an example of middle center text.

middle center:
center-justified,
spills up and down

Mtext controls which part of the text aligns at the intersection point. This is an example of middle right text.

middle right:
right-justified,
spills up and down

Mtext controls which part of the text aligns at the intersection point. This is an example of bottom left text.

bottom left:
left-justified,
spills up

Mtext controls which part of the text aligns at the intersection point. This is an example of bottom center text.

bottom center:
center-justified,
spills up

Mtext controls which part of the text aligns at the intersection point. This is an example of bottom right text.

bottom right:
right-justified,
spills up

✔ Select **Top center** to confirm this choice.

✔ To close the panel, pick the **Quick Properties** button on the status bar.
   *This closes the panel and leaves it closed while you continue to edit your drawing.*
      *Before going on, take a look at the **Quick Properties** panel for a line.*

✔ Press **<Esc>** to clear grips.

✔ Select any of the lines in your drawing.

✔ Pick the **Quick Properties** button on the status bar.
   *You see a panel like the one shown in Figure 7-20.*

**Figure 7-20**
Modify line using **Quick Properties**

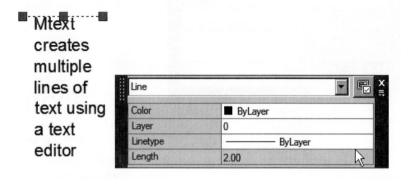

✔ Pick the **Quick Properties** button on the status bar to close the panel.

✔ Press **<Esc>** to clear grips.

---

**TIP**

Ordinarily, you will not want to leave the **Quick Properties** tool on as you work because the panel will open every time you select an object. If you do want to keep it on, so that the panel will open when you select the next object, press **<Esc>** to close the panel instead of turning off the tool.

---

## Using the SPELL Command

| SPELL | |
|---|---|
| **Command** | Spell |
| **Alias** | Sp |
| **Panel** | Tools |
| **Tool** | |

AutoCAD's **SPELL** command is simple to use and will appear familiar to anyone who has used spell-checkers in word processing programs. We use **SPELL** to check the spelling of all the text we have drawn so far.

✔ Type **sp <Enter>** or open the **Annotate** tab of the ribbon and pick the **Check Spelling** tool.
   *You see the **Check Spelling** dialog box shown in Figure 7-21.*
      *At the top left of the box is the **Where to check** list box. The options on the list are **Entire drawing**, **Current space/layout**, and **Selected objects**. For our purposes we use the **Entire drawing** option to check all the spelling in the drawing.*

✔ If necessary, select **Entire drawing** from the **Where to check** list.

✔ Pick the **Start** button.
   *If you have followed the exercise so far and not misspelled any words along the way, you see "MTEXT" in the **Not in dictionary** box and "TEXT" as a suggested correction. Ignore this change; but before you leave **SPELL**, look at what is available: You can ignore a word the checker does not recognize or change it. You can change a single*

**Figure 7-21**
**Check Spelling** dialog box

instance of a word or all instances in the currently selected text. You can add a word to the main dictionary or change to another dictionary.

✔ Click **Ignore.**

If your drawing does not contain other spelling irregularities, you should now see an AutoCAD message that reads:

Spelling check complete.

✔ Click **OK** to close the message box.

✔ Click **Close** to complete the **SPELL** command.

If you have made any corrections in spelling, they are incorporated into your drawing at this point.

## Changing Fonts and Styles

By default, the current text style in any AutoCAD drawing is called Standard. It is a specific form of a font called Arial that comes with the software. All the text you have entered so far has been drawn with the standard style of the Arial font.

Also predefined in all AutoCAD drawings is a style called **Annotative.** The Annotative style is the same as Standard in all ways, except that it includes the annotative property. This property allows you to create text that can be automatically scaled to match the scale of different viewports within the same layout.

*Fonts* are the basic patterns of character and symbol shapes that can be used with the **TEXT** and **MTEXT** commands. *Styles* are variations in the size, orientation, and spacing of the characters in those fonts. It is possible to create your own fonts, but for most of us this is an esoteric activity. In contrast, creating your own styles is easy and practical.

**annotative:** In AutoCAD, text and dimensions with the annotative property can be automatically scaled to match the scale of viewports in a drawing layout.

## Panel Extensions

We begin by creating a variation of the Standard style you have been using. This process will also introduce you to the panel extensions feature of the ribbon. Notice that there is a small triangle facing downward at the right end of the label on each panel of the ribbon. Picking anywhere along the label bar of these panels opens up a panel extension with more tools.

✔ Pick the label of the **Annotation** panel (**Home** tab), as shown in Figure 7-22.

> *This opens the panel extension shown in Figure 7-23. If you move the cursor away from the panel, the extension will close immediately. If you let the cursor rest anywhere on the extension, the extension will stay open. To keep the extension open while moving the cursor elsewhere, you can click on the pushpin at the lower left. To close it, click on the pin icon again.*

**Figure 7-22**
**Annotation** panel label

**Figure 7-23**
**Annotation** panel extension

On the **Annotation** panel extension there are four drop-down lists. Each list gives access to a different form of annotation. Text style, dimension style, and table style will all be introduced in this chapter.

---

**NOTE**

There is also a **Text Style** drop-down list on the **Text** panel of the **Annotate** tab. Make sure that you are clear about the difference between the **Annotate** tab and the **Annotation** panel on the **Home** tab, but either of these locations can be used to access text styles.

---

✔ From the **Annotation** panel extension, pick the **Text Style** tool, as shown in Figure 7-24.

> *You see the **Text Style** dialog box shown in Figure 7-25. You see **Annotative** and **Standard** listed in the **Styles** box. It is possible that other styles are listed. **Standard** should be selected.*
>
> *We will create a new style based on a different font. We call it Vertical because it will be drawn down the display instead of across.*

**Figure 7-24**
**Text Style** tool

**Figure 7-25**
**Text Style** dialog box

✔ Pick the **New** button.

*AutoCAD opens a smaller dialog box that asks for a name for the new text style.*

✔ Type **vertical <Enter>.**

*This returns you to the **Text Style** dialog box, with the new style listed in the **Styles** box. We use the txt.shx font and the vertical text effect to make this style different. The vertical text option is not available with the Standard Arial font and style.*

✔ Open the drop-down list for **Font Name** and scroll down to **txt.shx.**

*A lengthy list of fonts is available.*

✔ Select **txt.shx** to place it in the **Font Name** box.

*The **Vertical** option is now accessible in the **Effects** panel at the lower middle of the dialog box.*

✔ Click the **Vertical** check box in the **Effects** panel.

*Notice the change to vertically oriented text in the **Preview** panel at the lower left of the dialog box.*

*We also give this style a fixed height and a width factor. Notice that the current height is 0.00. This does not mean that your characters will be drawn 0.00 units high. It means that there will be no fixed height, so you can specify a height whenever you use this style. Standard currently has no fixed height, so Vertical has inherited this setting. Try giving our new Vertical style a fixed height.*

✔ Double-click in the **Height** edit box and then type **.5 <Enter>.**

*If you see a message box indicating that you have made changes to the text style, click **OK** to save changes.*

✔ Double-click in the **Width Factor** box and type **2 <Enter>.**

*Vertical should be automatically set as the current text style. If not, you can make it current by highlighting it in the **Styles** list and clicking the **Set Current** button at the right.*

✔ If necessary, click the **Set Current** button to make Vertical the current text style.

✔ Click the **Close** button to exit the **Text Style** dialog box.

*The new Vertical style is now current. To see it in action you need to enter some text.*

✔ Open the **Text** drop-down list and pick the **Single Line** text tool from the **Annotation** panel (on the **Home** tab).

✔ Pick a start point, as shown by the placement of the letter *V* in Figure 7-26.

*Notice that you are not prompted for a height because the current style has height fixed at 0.50. Also notice that the default rotation angle is set at 270. Your vertical text is entered moving down the screen at 270°.*

✔ Press **<Enter>** to retain 270° of rotation.

✔ Type **Vertical <Enter>.**

✔ Press **<Enter>** again to end the **TEXT** command.

*Your screen should resemble Figure 7-26.*

*Next, we create another style using a different font and some of the other style options. Pay attention to the **Preview** panel in the dialog box, which updates automatically to show your changes.*

**Figure 7-26**
Vertical text

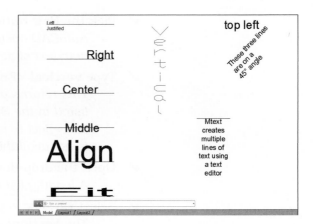

✔ Open the **Annotation Style** drop-down list from the **Annotation** panel extension and pick the **Text Style** tool.

✔ Pick the **New** button.

✔ In the **New Text Style** dialog box, give the style the name **Slanted.**

✔ Click **OK** to close the **New Text Style** box.

✔ Open the **Font Name** list by clicking the arrow.

✔ Scroll to **romand.shx** and stop.
    *Romand stands for Roman Duplex, an AutoCAD font.*

✔ Select **romand.shx.**

✔ Clear the **Vertical** check box.

✔ Set the text **Height** to **0.00.**

✔ Set the **Width Factor** to **1.**

✔ Set **Oblique Angle** to **45.**
    *This causes your text to be slanted 45° to the right. For a left slant, you would type a negative number.*

✔ Click the **Close** button to exit the **Text Style** dialog box.
    *Now, enter some text to see how this slanted Roman Duplex style looks.*

✔ Pick the **Single Line** text tool and answer the prompts to draw the words "Roman Duplex" with a 0.50 height, as shown in Figure 7-27.

**NOTE**
If you change the definition of a text style, all text previously drawn in that style will be regenerated with the new style specifications.

**Figure 7-27**
**Roman Duplex** text

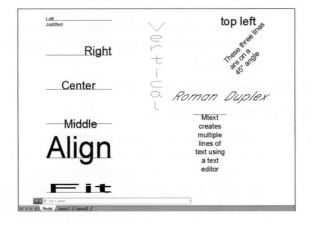

## Switching the Current Style

All new text is created in the current style. The style of previously drawn text can be changed. Once you have a number of styles defined in a drawing, you can switch from one to another by using the **Style** option of the **TEXT** and **MTEXT** commands or by selecting a text style from the **Text Style** drop-down list. Open the **Annotation** panel extension, and then click the arrow at the right of the text style to open the drop-down list. All your currently defined text styles will be available on this list.

## Changing Properties with MATCHPROP

> **TIP**
>
> A general procedure for changing properties with **MATCHPROP** is:
>
> 1. Pick the **Match Properties** tool from the **Clipboard** panel of the ribbon.
> 2. Select a source object with properties you wish to transfer to another object.
> 3. If necessary, specify properties you wish to match.
> 4. Select destination objects.
> 5. Press **<Enter>** to end object selection.

| MATCHPROP | |
|---|---|
| **Command** | Matchprop |
| **Alias** | Ma |
| **Panel** | Modify |
| **Tool** | |

**MATCHPROP** is a very efficient command that lets you match all or some of the properties of an object to those of another object. Properties that can be transferred from one object to another, or to many others, include layer, linetype, color, and linetype scale. These settings are common to all Auto-CAD entities. Other properties that relate to only specific types of entities are thickness, text style, dimension style, and hatch style. In all cases, the procedure is the same.

Here we use **MATCHPROP** to change some previously drawn text to the new Slanted style.

✔ Pick the **Match Properties** tool from the **Clipboard** panel, as shown in Figure 7-28.

> *AutoCAD prompts:*

Select source object:

> *You can have many destination objects, but only one source object.*

✔ Select the text "Roman Duplex", drawn in the last task in the Slanted style.

> *AutoCAD switches to the **Match Properties** cursor, shown in Figure 7-29.*

Select destination object(s) or [Settings]:

**Figure 7-28**
**Match Properties** tool

**Figure 7-29**
**Match Properties** cursor

At this point, you can limit the settings you want to match, or you can select destination objects, in which case all properties are matched.

✔ Select **Settings** from the command line.

*This opens the **Property Settings** dialog box shown in Figure 7-30. The **Basic Properties** panel shows properties that can be changed and the settings that will be used based on the source object you have selected.*

*At the bottom, you see nine other properties in the **Special Properties** panel. These refer to properties and styles that have been defined in your drawing. If any one of these is not selected, **Match Properties** ignores it and matches only the properties selected.*

**Figure 7-30**
**Property Settings** dialog box

✔ Click **OK** to exit the dialog box.

*AutoCAD returns to the screen with the same prompt as before.*

✔ Select the words "Align" and "Vertical" in your drawing.

*These two words are redrawn in the Slanted style, as shown in Figure 7-31. AutoCAD returns the* Select destination objects: *prompt so that you can continue to select objects.*

✔ Press **<Enter>** to exit the command.

**Figure 7-31**
**Align** and **Vertical** text slanted

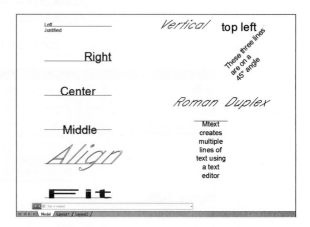

# Scaling Previously Drawn Entities

| SCALE | |
|---------|--------|
| Command | Scale |
| Alias | Sc |
| Panel | Modify |
| Tool |  |

Any object or group of objects can be scaled up or down using the **SCALE** command or the **Scale** grip edit mode. In this exercise, we practice scaling some of the text and lines that you have drawn on your screen. Remember, however, that there is no special relationship between **SCALE** and text and that other types of entities can be scaled just as easily.

✔ Pick the **Scale** tool from the **Modify** panel of the ribbon, as shown in Figure 7-32.

   *AutoCAD prompts you to select objects.*

**Figure 7-32**
**Scale** tool

✔ Use a crossing window (right to left) to select the set of six lines and text drawn in the "Entering Single-Line Text with Justification Options" section.

✔ Right-click to end object selection.

   *You are prompted to pick a base point:*

   Specify base point:

   *The concept of a base point in scaling is critical. Imagine for a moment that you are looking at a square and you want to shrink it using a scale-down procedure. All the sides will be shrunk the same amount, but how do you want this to happen? Should the lower left corner stay in place and the whole square shrink toward it? Or should everything shrink toward the center? Or toward some other point on or off the square? (See Figure 7-33.) This is what you specify when you pick a base point.*

✔ Pick a base point at the left end of the bottom line of the selected set (shown as base point in Figure 7-34).

   *AutoCAD now needs to know how much to shrink or enlarge the objects you have selected:*

   Specify scale factor or [Reference] <1.00>:

**Figure 7-33**
Base point concept

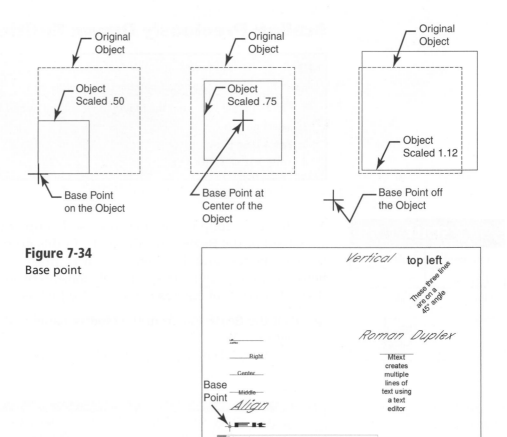

**Figure 7-34**
Base point

We get to the reference method in a moment. When you enter a scale factor, all lengths, heights, and diameters in your set are multiplied by that factor and redrawn accordingly. Scale factors are based on a unit of 1. If you enter 0.5, objects are reduced to half their original size. If you enter 2, objects become twice as large.

✔ Type **.5 <Enter>.**

*Your screen should now resemble Figure 7-34.*

## Scaling by Reference

This option can save you from doing the arithmetic to figure out scale factors. It is useful when you have a given length and you know how large you want that length to become after the scaling is done. For example, we know that the length of the lines we just scaled is now 2.00. Let's say that we want to scale them again so that the length becomes 2.33. This is a scale factor of 1.165 (2.33 divided by 2.00), but who wants to stop and figure that out? This can be done using the following procedure:

**1** Enter the **SCALE** command.

**2** Select the lines.

**3** Pick a base point.

**4** Type **r <Enter>** or right-click and select **Reference** from the shortcut menu.

**5** Type **2 <Enter>** for the reference length.

**6** Type **2.33 <Enter>** for the new length.

## Scaling with Grips

Scaling with grips is very similar to scaling with the **SCALE** command. To illustrate this, try using grips to return the text you just scaled back to its original size.

✔ Use a window or crossing window to select the six lines and the text drawn in the "Entering Single-Line Text with Justification Options" section again.

> *There are several grips on the screen: three on each line and two on most of the text entities. Some of these overlap or duplicate each other.*

✔ Pick the grip at the lower left corner of the word "Fit", the same point used as a base point in the last scaling procedure.

✔ Right-click and select **Scale** from the shortcut menu.

✔ Move the cursor slowly and observe the dragged image.

> *AutoCAD uses the selected grip point as the base point for scaling unless you specify that you want to pick a different base point.*
> *Notice that you also have a **Reference** option as in the **SCALE** command.*
> *As in **SCALE,** the default method is to specify a scale factor by pointing or typing.*

✔ Type **2 <Enter>** or show a length of 2.00. (We reduced the objects by a factor of 0.5, so we need to enlarge them by a factor of 2 to return to the original size.)

> *Your text returns to its original size, and your screen should resemble Figure 7-31 again.*

✔ Press **<Esc>** to clear grips.

## Creating Tables and Fields

| TABLE | |
|---|---|
| Command | Table |
| Alias | (none) |
| Panel | Annotation |
| Tool | |

AutoCAD has many features for creating and managing tables and table data. Table styles can be created and named. Cells can be formatted with text, numerical data, formulas, and fields that update automatically. Data can be extracted from the current drawing into a table or from an external spreadsheet. In this exercise we create a basic table showing three time and date formats and their appearances. The table will include a title, two columns with headers, and three rows of data. We will also take the opportunity to demonstrate the use of fields, which can be inserted and easily updated when the information they hold changes.

✔ To begin this exercise you can be in any AutoCAD drawing.

> *We will continue to use the text demonstration drawing created in this chapter, but will zoom into the area where we insert our table.*

✔ Zoom into an empty window of space in your drawing approximately 5.00 by 5.00.

✔ Pick the **Table** tool from the **Annotation** panel of the ribbon, as shown in Figure 7-35.

**Figure 7-35**
**Table** tool

*This opens the **Insert Table** dialog box, as shown in Figure 7-36. Before inserting the table we specify the size, shape, and style of the table. The Standard table style has a title row, a header row, and any number of rows and columns of data. We will keep the Standard style and specify three rows and two columns.*

**Figure 7-36**
**Insert Table** dialog box

✔ Check to see that **Standard** is selected in the **Table style** panel, **Specify insertion point** is selected in the **Insertion behavior** panel, and **Start from empty table** is selected in the **Insert options** panel.

✔ In the **Column & row settings** panel of the dialog box, use the arrows or the edit box to specify **2** columns.

✔ If necessary, set the column width at **2.50.**

✔ Use the arrows or the edit box to specify **3** rows.

✔ If necessary, set row height at **1** line.

*When you are done, the dialog box should resemble Figure 7-36.*

✔ Click **OK.**

*AutoCAD closes the dialog box and shows a table that moves with your crosshairs as you drag it into place.*

✔ Pick an insertion point.

*You now have an empty table in your drawing. In this table style, you see a title cell on the top row, four additional rows, and two columns of empty data cells. The numbers and letters at the left and top of the table are row and column references only; they are* *not part of the drawing. The text cursor should be blinking in the title cell, awaiting text input. Notice also that the **Text Editor** tab of panels has automatically replaced the **Home** tab of the ribbon.*

*We fill in a title and then two column headers. To ensure consistency, we first specify a text height.*

✔ Double-click in the **Text Height** list box in the **Style** panel at the left of the ribbon, as shown in Figure 7-37, and type **0.2 <Enter>**.
*The text height is now 0.20.*

**Figure 7-37**
Ribbon combo box - **Text Height**

✔ For the title, type **Date and Time Format <Enter>**.
*When you press **<Enter>** the text cursor moves to row 2, column A. The cursor should be blinking in the 2A cell, awaiting input. 2A is a header cell, formatted for text with center justification.*

✔ In the first column, type **Format** and then press **<Tab>**.
*Tabbing takes you to the next header cell.*

✔ Type **Appearance** and press **<Tab>**.
*Once again, tabbing takes you to the next table cell, in this case wrapping around to the next row. You are now in the third row of column A, the first data row. Notice that the column headings are centered in their cells, as shown in Figure 7-38. This center justification for the column headers is part of the definition of this table style.*

---

**TIP**
When entering data in table cells, you can move sequentially through cells using the **<Tab>** key. To reverse direction and move backward, hold down **<Shift>** while pressing **<Tab>**. You can also use the arrow keys on your keyboard to move between table cells.

---

**Figure 7-38**
Entering text

We will be entering time and date format symbols in the **Format** column and actual date and time fields in the **Appearance** column. The text in the **Appearance** column will be inserted as fields that can be updated automatically. We use dates and times because they demonstrate updating very readily.

✔ In the first data row, first column, as shown in Figure 7-38, type **HH:mm <Enter>.**

> *This is the common symbol for time in an hours and minutes format. The uppercase HH indicates that this is 24-hour time (2:00 P.M. will appear as 14:00). Pressing* **<Enter>** *takes you to row 4, column A.*

✔ Type **h:mm:ss tt <Enter>.**

> *This symbolizes time in hours, minutes, and seconds. The tt stands for A.M. or P.M. You will see more of these symbols in a moment.*

✔ In cell 5A type **M/d/yyyy** and press **<Tab>** once.

> *This represents a date in month, day, year format, with a four-place number for the year.*

## Inserting Fields

You are now in cell 5B of the table and instead of typing text here, we will insert a date field, in month, day, year format to match the format column. Then we return to the other rows in this column and enter time fields.

✔ From the **Insert** panel of the ribbon, select the **Field** tool shown in Figure 7-39.

**Figure 7-39**
**Insert Field** tool

> *This will open the* **Field** *dialog box shown in Figure 7-40. There are many types of predefined fields shown in the* **Field names** *box on the left. What appears in the* **Examples** *list in the middle depends on the type of field selected.*

**Figure 7-40**
**Field** dialog box

✔ Select **Date** in the **Field names** list.

*With **Date** selected, you see the example formats for dates and times. There are many options, and you will have to scroll to see them all. Notice that the date format symbols for the selected format are displayed in the **Date format** box above the examples.*

✔ Select the example at the top of the list, which will be the current date in M/d/yyyy format.

✔ With this format selected, click **OK.**

*The date will be entered in the cell as shown in Figure 7-41. It will be displayed in gray, indicating that this is not ordinary text, but a field. If this drawing were to be plotted, the gray would not appear in the plot.*

**Figure 7-41**
Date entered in cell

| Date and Time Format | |
|---|---|
| Format | Appearance |
| HH:mm | |
| h:mm:ss tt | |
| M/d/yyyy | 1/28/2013 |

*At this point we exit the table and return to the drawing.*

**NOTE**

Fields can be inserted anywhere in a drawing. To insert a field without a table, select **Field** from the **Insert** tab, **Data** panel. This will call the **Field** dialog box, and the rest of the process will be the same.

✔ To return to the drawing, press **<Enter>** twice or right-click anywhere in the **Text Editor** tab and select **Close** from the shortcut menu.

*Your table should now resemble Figure 7-41.*

We could have filled out all the table cells without leaving the table, but it is important to know how to enter data after a table has already been created. Different selection sequences will select cells in different ways. For example, if you pick within a cell, you will select the cell, and the **Table** tab of panels will open automatically on the ribbon. Double-clicking within a cell will open the **Text Editor** tab of panels.

✔ Click once inside the first data row, second column, below the **Appearance** header.

*The cell is highlighted with tan borders, and the **Table Cell** tab of panels appears on the ribbon. This tab has a **Field** tool on the **Insert** panel on the right. This is the same tool and serves the same purpose as the **Insert Field** tool on the **Text Editor** tab.*

✔ Pick the **Field** tool from the **Insert** panel on the ribbon.

*The **Field** dialog box opens. We select the **HH:mm** example to match the format we have indicated in the **Format** column. You will find this selection seventh up from the bottom of the **Examples** list. It will have hours and minutes in 24-hour format, with no A.M. or P.M. designation.*

✔ Highlight the **HH:mm** date format example.

*When it is highlighted, **HH:mm** will appear in the **Date format** box.*

✔ Click **OK.**

*Finally, repeat the process to insert a field in the remaining cell.*

✔ Press the down arrow to move down one row.

✔ Pick the **Field** tool from the **Insert** panel on the ribbon.

✔ Select the **h:mm:ss tt** format from the **Examples** list.

*This is just above the HH:mm selection.*

✔ Click **OK.**

✔ Double-click outside the table to end the command.

*Your table should now resemble Figure 7-42 with three fields in the three right-hand data cells. You probably will notice a time difference between cells 3B and 4B.*

**Figure 7-42**
Three fields in data cells

| Date and Time Format | |
|---|---|
| Format | Appearance |
| HH:mm | 11:44 |
| h:mm:ss tt | 11:44:43 AM |
| M/d/yyyy | 1/28/2013 |

## Updating Fields

Fields may be updated manually or automatically, individually or in groups. To update an individual field, double-click the field text and right-click to open the shortcut menu. Select **Update field** from the shortcut menu. This also works with individual fields that are not in a table.

For our demonstration we will update all the fields in our table at once, using the **Insert** tab.

✔ Pick any border of the table.

*This will select the entire table. Grips will be added.*

✔ With the entire table selected, select **Insert** tab > **Data** panel > **Update Fields** from the ribbon, as shown in Figure 7-43.

**Figure 7-43**
**Update Fields** tool

*Notice how the two time fields are updated while the date field remains the same.*

*Fields also update automatically when certain things occur, as controlled by settings in the **User Preferences** dialog box. To reach these settings, right-click on any empty space in the drawing window, and select **Options** from the bottom of the shortcut menu. Select the **User Preferences** tab and then the **Field Update Settings** button in the **Fields** panel. Fields may be automatically* *updated when a file is opened, saved, plotted, regenerated, or transmitted over the Internet. Any combination of these may be selected. By default, all are selected.*

## Using AutoCAD Templates, Borders, and Title Blocks

With knowledge of how to create text and how to use paper space layouts, you can take full advantage of the AutoCAD templates with predrawn borders and title blocks. In this exercise we create a new drawing using an AutoCAD D-size template, add some simple geometry, and add some text to the title block. The work you do here can be saved and used as a start to completing Drawing 7-2, the gauges at the end of the chapter.

✔ Pick the **New** tool from the **Quick Access** toolbar.

✔ In the **Select template** dialog box, select **Tutorial-iMfg.**

✔ With **Tutorial-iMfg** showing in the **File name** box, click **Open.**
    *This opens a new drawing layout with a predrawn border and title block, as illustrated in Figure 7-44. Notice the paper space icon at the lower left of the screen and the **Paper** button on the status bar, which appears on your screen under the drawing window that has replaced the **Model** button. Also notice the window with blue borders that outlines a model space viewport. We enter this viewport and draw a circle to begin the geometry of the drawing.*

**Figure 7-44**
New drawing layout

✔ Double-click inside the blue borders to enter model space in this viewport.
    *The borders will thicken. Turning on the grid gives you a better sense of the drawing space in this viewport.*

✔ Turn on the grid.

✔ If necessary, right-click the **Grid Display** button on the status bar, select **Settings,** and select **Display grid beyond Limits** from the dialog box, so that the grid fills the window.

✔ Enter the **CIRCLE** command.

✔ Create a 2.50-radius circle with center point at (3.00,5.00), as shown in Figure 7-45.

> *As you do this, notice also that having started this drawing with a different template, you have a whole different set of layers and the units are three-place decimal.*

**Figure 7-45**
Creating a circle

✔ Turn off the grid in the viewport.

> *You will not want the model space grid showing when you return to the paper space layout.*

✔ Double-click outside the blue border.

> *The paper space icon returns, and the viewport border is no longer bold. You are now back in paper space. Next, we add two items of text to the title block. To facilitate these entries, we make some changes to the paper space grid and snap.*

✔ Pick the **Grid Display** button to turn on the paper space grid.

✔ Pick the **Snap Mode** button to turn on snap in paper space.

> *Notice that the paper space grid in this template is displaying lines at .500 intervals. Snap is also set to .500, but this is not observable until you enter a drawing command.*

✔ Move the crosshairs to the upper right corner of the "paper."

> *Notice that the layout emulates a 33.000 × 21.000 D-size drawing sheet. We are going to create text in two of the areas of the title block, as shown in Figure 7-46. However, the current snap setting makes this difficult.*

**Figure 7-46**
Adding text

✔ Right-click the **Snap Mode** or **Grid Display** button and select **Settings** to open the **Drafting Settings** dialog box.

*The grid is set to 0.500, but the **Adaptive grid** setting is checked, causing AutoCAD to display the larger 2.500 grid. This effect will change when we zoom in momentarily.*

✔ Change the snap setting to **.250.**

✔ Click **OK** to exit the dialog box.

✔ Type **Z <Enter>** and zoom into a window around the title block, as shown in Figure 7-46.
*You are now ready to add text.*

✔ Pick the **Single Line** text tool from the ribbon, and pick a start point near (28.000,2.500), as shown.

✔ Specify a text height of **.25** and a rotation angle of **0.**

✔ Type **Gauges <Enter>.**

✔ Press **<Enter>** again to exit **TEXT.**

✔ Repeat **TEXT** and type **CSA INC.** at (28.000,1.750), as shown in Figure 7-46.

✔ Press **<Enter>** twice to exit **TEXT.**

✔ **Zoom All** to view the complete layout.
*There you go. You are well on your way to completing Drawing 7-2, complete with title block.*

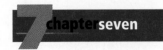

# Chapter Summary

This chapter dramatically increased your skill at working with text in AutoCAD. You have gone from entering simple single-line text to creating paragraph text, text with special characters and symbols, and text in a wide variety of fonts and styles. You learned to alter the properties of text and other objects, to edit text in place in a drawing, to check spelling, and to scale any AutoCAD object. You learned to create tables with any number of cells, rows, and columns and to populate cells with text, numbers, or fields that can be updated automatically or manually. Finally, you created your first layout using an AutoCAD template with title block and border, and added text to that title block.

# Chapter Test Questions

## Multiple Choice

*Circle the correct answer.*

1. To enter single-line text you must first enter all of these **except:**
   a. Alignment
   b. Rotation angle
   c. Start point
   d. Text height

2. To enter multiline text, pick the **Multiline Text** tool and then:
   a. Open the **Multiline Text Editor**
   b. Enter two points
   c. Pick a start point
   d. Pick a justification style

3. **DDEDIT** can be used to change:
   a. Text height
   b. Text location
   c. Text content
   d. Text style

4. AutoCAD borders and title blocks can be found in the:
   a. **Border** folder
   b. **Layout** tab
   c. Acad.dwt template
   d. **Template** folder

5. **MATCHPROP cannot** be used to match:
   a. Text style
   b. Text height
   c. Layer
   d. Transparency

## Matching

*Write the number of the correct answer on the line.*

a. Degree symbol _____

b. Diameter symbol _____

c. **Text Editor** _____

d. tt _____

e. **Scale** _____

1. Contextual tab

2. **Grip Edit** mode

3. %%d

4. %%c

5. A.M.

## True or False

*Circle the correct answer.*

1. **True or False:** Objects can be scaled from different base points with different results.
2. **True or False:** Mtext is drawn within a rectangular box defined by the user.
3. **True or False:** Fields can be updated each time a file is opened.
4. **True or False:** Center-justified text and middle-justified text are two names for the same thing.
5. **True or False:** Fonts are created based on text styles.

## Questions

1. What is the difference between center-justified text and middle-justified text?
2. What is the purpose of %% in text entry?
3. What is the difference between a font and a style?
4. How would you use **SCALE** to change a 3.00 line to 2.75?
5. You wish to use an AutoCAD-provided border and title block for your drawing. Where would you find the one you wish to use?

## Drawing Problems

1. Draw a 6 × 6 square. Draw the word "Top" on top of the square, 0.4 unit high, centered at the midpoint of the top side of the square.
2. Draw the word "Left" 0.4 unit high, centered at the midpoint along the outer left side of the square.
3. Draw the word "Right" 0.4 unit high, centered at the midpoint along the outer right side of the square.
4. Draw the word "Bottom" 0.4 unit high, below the square so that the top of the text is centered on the midpoint of the bottom side of the square.
5. Draw the words "This is the middle" inside the square, 0.4 unit high, so that the complete text wraps around within a 2-unit width and is centered on the center point of the square.

## WWW Exercise (Optional)

In Chapter 7 of our companion website, we ask you to explore the Web and bring back information on an important innovator in the field of architecture. We define your task and give you two links to get you started. We also give you another design challenge and, as always, the self-scoring test for this chapter. So, when you are ready, complete the following:

✔ Make sure that you are connected to your Internet service provider.

✔ **Type browser <Enter>.**

✔ If necessary, navigate to our companion website at www.pearsonhighered.com/dixriley.

*Happy hunting!*

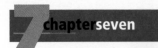

# Chapter Drawing Projects

## G Drawing 7-1: *Title Block* [INTERMEDIATE]

This title block gives you practice in using a variety of text styles and sizes. You may want to save it and use it as a title block for future drawings.

| QTY REQ'D | DESCRIPTION | | PART NO. | ITEM NO. |
|---|---|---|---|---|
| | BILL OF MATERIALS | | | |

| UNLESS OTHERWISE SPECIFIED DIMENSIONS ARE IN INCHES | DRAWN BY: Your Name | DATE | CSA INC. | | |
|---|---|---|---|---|---|
| REMOVE ALL BURRS & BREAK SHARP EDGES | APPROVED BY: | | | | |
| TOLERANCES FRACTIONS ± 1/64 DECIMALS ANGLES ± 0'–15' XX ± .01 XXX ± .005 | ISSUED: | | DRAWING TITLE: | | |
| MATERIAL: | FINISH: | SIZE C | CODE IDENT NO. 38178 | DRAWING NO. | REV. |
| | | SCALE: | DATE: | SHEET | OF |

## Drawing Suggestions

GRID = 1
SNAP = 0.0625

- Make ample use of **TRIM** as you draw the line patterns of the title block. Take your time and make sure that at least the major divisions are in place before you start entering text into the boxes.

- Set to the text layer before entering text.

- Use **TEXT** with all the Standard, 0.09, left-justified text.

- Remember that once you have defined a style, you can make it current in the **TEXT** command. This saves you from restyling more than necessary.

- Use %%D for the degree symbol and %%P for the plus or minus symbol.

ALL TEXT UNLESS OTHERWISE NOTED IS:
Font (SIMPLEX)
Height (0.09)
Left justified

Font (ROMANS)
Height (0.12)
Fit

Font (ROMANT)
Height (0.25)
Fit

Font (GOTHICE)
Height (0.38)
Left justified

Font (STANDARD)
Height 0.25
Left justified

Style (ROMANS)
Height 0.12
Fit

Style (SCRIPTS)
Height (0.12)
Left justified

Font (ROMANT)
Height (0.25)
Middle justified

**Drawing 7-1**
Title Block

## G Drawing 7-2: *Gauges* [INTERMEDIATE]

This drawing teaches you some typical uses of the **SCALE** and **DDEDIT** commands. Some of the techniques used are not obvious, so read the suggestions carefully.

## Drawing Suggestions

GRID = 0.5
SNAP = 0.125

- Draw three concentric circles with diameters of 5.0, 4.5, and 3.0. The bottom of the 3.0 circle can be trimmed later.

- Zoom in to draw the arrow-shaped tick at the top of the 3.0 circle. Then draw the 0.50 vertical line directly below it and the number 40 (middle-justified text) above it.

- These three objects can be arrayed to the left and right around the perimeter of the 3.0 circle using angles of +135° and −135°, as shown.

- Use **DDEDIT** to change the arrayed numbers into 0, 10, 20, 30, and so on. You can do all of these without leaving the command.

- Draw the 0.25 vertical tick directly on top of the 0.50 mark at the top center and array it left and right. There should be 20 marks each way.

- Draw the needle horizontally across the middle of the dial.

- Make two copies of the dial; use **SCALE** to scale them down as shown. Then move them into their correct positions.

- Rotate the three needles into positions as shown.

**Drawing 7-2**
Gauges

This drawing is trickier than it appears. There are many ways that it can be done. The way we have chosen not only works well but also makes use of a number of commands and techniques with which you are probably familiar. Notice that a change in limits is needed to take advantage of some of the suggestions.

## Drawing Suggestions

GRID = 0.50
SNAP = 0.25
LIMITS = (0,0)(24,18)

- Draw two circles, of radius 10.25 and 6.50, centered at about (13,15). These are trimmed later.

- Draw a vertical line down from the center point to the outer circle. We **COPY** and **ROTATE** this line to form the ends of the stamping.

- Use the **Rotate copy** mode of the grip edit system to create copies of the line rotated 45° degrees and −45°. (The coordinate display shows 315°.)

- **TRIM** the lines and the circles to form the outline of the stamping.

- Draw a 1.50-diameter circle in the center of the stamping, 8.50 down from (13,15). Draw middle-justified text, AR, 7.25 down, and AT-1 down from 9.75 (13,15).

- Follow the procedure given in the next subsection to create offset copies of the circle and text; then, use **DDEDIT** to modify all text to agree with the drawing.

## Grip Copy Modes with Offset Snap Locations

Here is a good opportunity to try another grip edit feature. If you hold down the **<Shift>** key while picking multiple copy points, AutoCAD is constrained to place copies only at points offset from each other the same distance as your first two points. For example, try the following steps:

**1** Select the circle and the text.

**2** Select any grip to initiate grip editing.

**3** Select **Rotate** from the shortcut menu.

**4** Type **b** or select **Base point** from the shortcut menu.

**5** Pick the center of the stamping (13,15) as the base point.

**6** Type **c** or select **Copy** from the shortcut menu.

**7** Hold down the **<Shift>** key and move the cursor to rotate a copy 11° from the original.

**8** Keep holding down the **<Shift>** key as you move the cursor to create other copies. All copies are offset 11°.

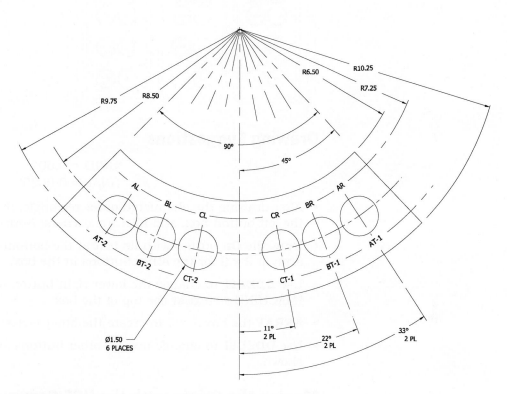

**Drawing 7-3**
Stamping

## G Drawing 7-4: *Control Panel* [INTERMEDIATE]

Done correctly, this drawing gives you a good feel for the power of the commands you now have available to you. Be sure to take advantage of combinations of **ARRAY** and **DDEDIT** as described. Also, read the suggestion on moving the origin before you begin. Moving the origin in this drawing makes it easier to read the dimensions, which are given in ordinate form measured from the (0,0) point at the lower left corner of the object.

### Drawing Suggestions

GRID = 0.50
SNAP = 0.0625

- After drawing the chamfered outer rectangle, draw the double outline of the left button box, and fillet the corners. Notice the different fillet radii.
- Draw the **On** button with its text at the bottom left of the box. Then array it 2 × 3 for the other buttons in the box.
- Use **DDEDIT** to change the lower right button text to **Off** and draw the "MACHINE #" text at the top of the box.
- **ARRAY** the box 1 × 3 to create the other boxes.
- Use **DDEDIT** to change text for other buttons and machine numbers as shown.

### Moving the Origin with the UCS Command

The dimensions of this drawing are shown in ordinate form, measured from a single point of origin in the lower left-hand corner. In effect, this establishes a new coordinate origin. If we move our origin to match this point, then we can read dimension values directly from the coordinate display. This can be done by setting the lower left-hand limits to (−1,−1). However, it can be completed more efficiently using the **UCS** command to establish a user coordinate system with the origin at a point you specify. User coordinate systems are not discussed in depth here. For now, here is a simple procedure:

**1** Type **ucs.**
**2** Type **o** for the **Origin** option.
**3** Point to the new origin.

That's all there is to it. Move your cursor to the new origin, and watch the coordinate display. It should show 0.00,0.00,0.00, and all values are measured from there.

**Drawing 7-4**
Control Panel

# Drawing 7-5: *Angle Bracket* [ADVANCED]

This drawing will give you practice with multiline text and with using an AutoCAD template with border and title block. The drawing is a three-view drawing that will be created in model space, but it will appear in a floating viewport in a paper space layout. The multiline text will be drawn in the layout view in paper space.

## Drawing Suggestions

- Create this drawing using the **Tutorial-iMfg** template.

- In order to create the views in model space and the text in paper space, you will be switching back and forth between model space and the layout view.

- Once you have the drawing open with the borders and title block showing, use **MVIEW** to create a single model space viewport for your three views, as shown in the reference drawing.

- Add the two notes in paper space in the layout view, using **MTEXT.**

- The dimensions in the drawing are for reference only; they are not part of your final drawing.

**Ø1.50**
THRU

2.50

.25 X .25
CHAMFER

R.25
FILLET

3.00

.75

1.25

2.88

.50

R.50 FILLET
2 PLACES

Ø1.00
THRU

1.25

2.00

NOTES:
1. CASTING SHALL BE SMOOTH, WELL
CLEANED, FREE OF HARMFUL POROSITY
CRACKS AND INCLUSIONS, CHILLS,
EXCESS BREE CARBIDES AND ANY OTHER
DEFECTS DETRIMENTAL TO MACHINABILITY,
APPEARANCE OR PERFORMANCE.
2. HEAT TREATMENT:
McQUAID-EHN GRAIN SIZE 5-8 HEAT TO 1550°F
AND QUENCH IN OIL. DRAW TO BRINELL
HARDNESS 241-285. 100% BRINELL REQUIRED

**Drawing 7-5**
Angle Bracket

# Drawing 7-6: *Koch Snowflake* [ADVANCED]

The Koch snowflake design can be done in numerous ways, all involving similar techniques of reference scaling, rotating, and polar arraying. We give you a few suggestions and hints, but you are largely on your own in solving this visual design puzzle.

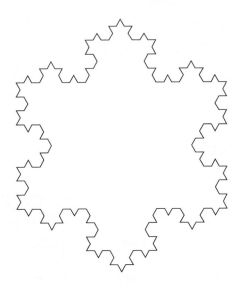

## Drawing Suggestions

- Begin by creating an equilateral triangle. Because it is important to know the center point of this triangle, construct it from a circle, as shown. The radial lines are drawn by arraying a single line from the center point three times in a 360° polar array.

- After drawing the initial equilateral triangle, you make frequent use of reference scaling.

- The number 3 is important throughout this design. Consider how you will use the number 3 in the reference scaling option.

- You will have frequent use for **Center, Intersection,** and **Midpoint** object snaps.

- Do not move the original triangle, so that you can always locate its center point. There are at least two ways to find the center point of other triangles you create. One involves constructing a 3P circle and another involves three construction lines.

- A lot of trimming and erasing is required to create the final design.

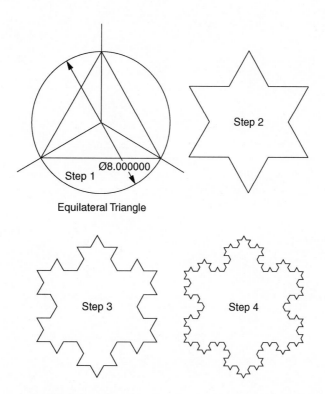

Ø8.000000
Step 1
Equilateral Triangle

Step 2

Step 3

Step 4

**Drawing 7-6**
Koch Snowflake

# 8 chaptereight
## Dimensions

# CHAPTER OBJECTIVES

- Create and save a dimension style
- Draw linear dimensions
- Draw multiple linear dimensions using **QDIM**
- Draw ordinate dimensions
- Draw angular dimensions
- Dimension arcs and circles

- Dimension with multileaders
- Change dimension text
- Use associative dimensions
- Use the **HATCH** command
- Scale dimensions between paper space and model space

## Introduction

The ability to dimension your drawings and add crosshatch patterns greatly enhances the professional appearance and utility of your work. AutoCAD's dimensioning features form a complex system of commands, subcommands, and variables that automatically measure objects and draw dimension text and extension lines. With AutoCAD's dimensioning tools and variables, you can create dimensions in a wide variety of formats, and these formats can be saved as styles. The time saved by not drawing each dimension object line by line is among the most significant advantages of CAD.

## Creating and Saving a Dimension Style

Dimensioning in AutoCAD is highly automated and very easy compared with manual dimensioning. To achieve a high degree of automation while still allowing for the broad range of flexibility required to cover all dimension styles, the AutoCAD dimensioning system is necessarily complex. In the exercises that follow, we guide you through the system, show you some of the options available, and give you a solid foundation for understanding how to get what you want from AutoCAD dimensioning. We create a basic dimension style and use it to draw standard dimensions and tolerances. We leave it to you to explore the many possible variations.

In AutoCAD, it is best to begin by naming and defining a dimension style. A **dimension style** is a set of dimension variable settings that control the text and geometry of all types of AutoCAD dimensions. We recommend that you create the new dimension style in your template drawing and save it so that you do not have to make these changes again when you start new drawings.

dimension style: A set of
dimension variable settings that
control the text and geometry of all
types of AutoCAD dimensions.

✔ To begin this exercise, create a new drawing with 18 × 12 limits (open the 1B template drawing if you have it).

*We make changes in dimension style settings so that all dimensions showing distances are presented with two decimal places, and angular dimensions have no decimals.*

---

**TIP**

If you make changes in the dimension style in a template drawing, these changes become the default dimension settings for any drawing created with that template.

Remember, you find template files in the **Template** folder. Use the **OPEN** command to access the **Select File** dialog box. Select **Drawing Template File (*.dwt)** from the **Files of type:** drop-down list. This automatically opens the **Template** folder. Select the template file you want from the list or thumbnail gallery, and click **Open**.

---

✔ Pick the **Annotate** tab on the ribbon.

*This opens the **Annotate** set of ribbon panels, as shown in Figure 8-1. We will be using the **Annotate** tab frequently throughout this chapter.*

**Figure 8-1**
**Annotate** tab

✔ Pick the **Dimension Style** arrow from the ribbon, as shown in Figure 8-2.

*This is the small diagonal arrow at the right of the **Dimensions** panel title bar. Notice that the **Text, Dimensions, Leaders,** and **Tables** panels all have these style arrows.*

**Figure 8-2**
**Dimension Style** arrow

*This opens the **Dimension Style Manager** shown in Figure 8-3. The current dimension style is called Standard. As with text, the other predefined style is Annotative. The annotative property allows dimensions and other annotative objects to be scaled to show at the correct size in paper layouts. The only difference between the Standard and Annotative styles is the addition of the annotative property to dimensions drawn in that style. We will explore this feature in the "Scaling Dimensions Between Paper Space and Model Space" section.*

**Figure 8-3**
**Dimension Style Manager**
dialog box

To the right of the **Styles** box is a preview that presents a sample image showing many of the settings of the style highlighted in the **Styles** box. The style being previewed is also named at the top of the box. The preview image is updated any time you make a change in a dimension setting.

Below the preview image is a **Description** box. Right now, the description simply indicates that the style is Standard.

✔ Check to see that **Standard** is selected in the **Styles** box.

*Now, we proceed to create a new style based on the Standard style. To the right of the preview is a set of five buttons, the second of which is the **New** button.*

✔ Pick the **New** button.

*This opens the small **Create New Dimension Style** dialog box shown in Figure 8-4.*

*If necessary, double-click in the **New Style Name** edit box to highlight the words **Copy of Standard**.*

**Figure 8-4**
**Create New Dimension**
**Style** dialog box

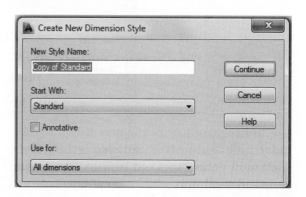

✔ Type a name for the new dimension style. This creates the new dimension style and takes us into the **New Dimension Style** dialog box shown in Figure 8-5. Here there are seven tabs that allow us to make many changes in dimension lines, symbols and arrows, text, fit, primary units, alternate units, and tolerances.

**Figure 8-5**
**New Dimension Style** dialog box

✔ Pick the **Primary Units** tab.

*This brings up the **Primary Units** window, shown in Figure 8-6. There are adjustments available for linear and angular units. The lists under units and angles are similar to the lists used in the*

**Figure 8-6**
**Primary Units** tab

*Drawing Units* dialog box. Notice, however, that dimension units are completely separate from drawing units. They must be set independently and may or may not have the same settings. In the **Linear dimensions** panel, **Unit format** should show **Decimal.** In the **Angular dimensions** panel, **Units format** should show **Decimal Degrees.** If for any reason these are not showing in your box, you should make these changes now. For our purposes, all we need to change is the number of decimal places showing in the **Precision** box. By default, it is 0.0000. We change it to 0.00.

✔ Click the arrow to the right of the **Precision** box in the **Linear dimensions** panel.

*This opens a list of precision settings ranging from 0 to 0.00000000.*

✔ Select **0.00** from the list.

*This closes the list box and shows 0.00 as the selected precision. Notice the change in the preview image, which now shows two-place decimals. At this point, we are ready to complete this part of the procedure by returning to the **Dimension Style Manager.***

*Before leaving the **New Dimension Style** dialog box, open the other tabs and look at the large variety of dimension features that can be adjusted. Each of the many options changes a dimension variable setting. Dimension variables have names and can be changed at the command line by typing in the name and entering a new value; but the dialog box makes the process much easier, and the preview images give you immediate visual feedback.*

*In the **Lines** tab and **Symbols and Arrows** tab you find options for changing the size and positioning of dimension geometry. In the **Text** tab you are able to adjust the look and placement of dimension text. This tab includes the option of selecting different text styles previously defined in the drawing. In the **Fit** tab you can tell AutoCAD how to manage situations in which there is a tight fit that creates some ambiguity about how dimension geometry and text should be arranged. This is also where the annotative property is selected. **Primary Units,** as you know, lets you specify the units in which dimensions are displayed. **Alternate Units** offers the capacity to include a secondary unit specification along with the primary dimension unit. For example, you can use this feature to give dimensions in both inches and centimeters. Tolerances are added to dimension specifications to give the range of acceptable values in, for example, a machining process. The **Tolerances** tab gives several options for how tolerances are displayed.*

✔ Click **OK** to exit the **New Dimension Style** dialog box.

*Back in the **Dimension Style Manager** dialog box you can see that your new dimension style has been added to the list of styles.*

*At this point, you should have at least the new style, Annotative, and Standard dimension styles defined in your drawing. Your new style should be selected and will be the current style. This is indicated by the line at the top of the dialog box where the name of the new style follows the colon after **Current dimension style:**. You can select the other styles in the **Styles** box and see descriptions in the **Description** box relating these styles to the current style. Try it.*

✔ Select **Annotative** in the **Styles** box.

> *The description tells you that Annotative is the same as the new style but with a variable overall scale and different precision for dimensions and tolerances, "+ Overall Scale = 0.0000, Precision = 4, Tol Precision = 4."*
>
> *Conversely, if you set Annotative as the current style, the description of the new style will be relative to Annotative. Try it.*

✔ With **Annotative** selected in the **Styles** box, click the **Set Current** button.

> *"Annotative" now appears in the **Description** box.*

✔ Select your new style in the **Styles** box again.

> *The description now reads, "Annotative + Overall Scale = 1.0000, Precision = 2, Tol Precision = 2." The new style is the same as Annotative but with a fixed scale and two-place decimals.*

✔ Click **Set Current** to set the new style as the current dimension style again.

✔ Click **Close** to exit the **Dimension Style Manager** dialog box.

✔ If you are working in a template drawing, save your changes and close the drawing. Otherwise, move on to the next section.

✔ If you have modified a template, create a new drawing using the modified template.

> *If the new drawing is opened with the modified template, the new dimension style becomes the current dimension style. Its name appears in the **Dimension Style** list box on the **Dimensions** panel of the ribbon.*

## Drawing Linear Dimensions

| DIMLINEAR | |
|---|---|
| **Command** | Dimlinear |
| **Alias** | (none) |
| **Panel** | Annotation |
| **Tool** | |

> **TIP**
>
> A general procedure for drawing linear dimensions is:
>
> 1. Pick the **Linear** tool from the **Dimensions** panel of the ribbon.
> 2. Select an object or show two extension line origins.
> 3. Show the dimension line location.

AutoCAD has many commands and features that aid in the drawing of dimensions. In this exercise, you create some basic linear dimensions in the newly created dimension style.

✔ To prepare for this exercise, draw a (3.00,4.00,5.00) triangle, a 4.00 vertical line, and a 6.00 horizontal line above the middle of the display, as shown in Figure 8-7.

> *We begin by adding dimensions to the triangle.*

✔ If your drawing has a layer for dimensions, open the **Layer** drop-down list on the **Home** tab and make that layer current.

> *The dimensioning commands are streamlined and efficient. Their full names, however, are long. They all begin with dim and are followed by the name of a type of dimension (e.g., **DIMLINEAR**, **DIMALIGNED**, and **DIMANGULAR**). Use the ribbon or the **Dimension** menu to avoid typing these names.*

**Figure 8-7**
Drawing triangle and lines

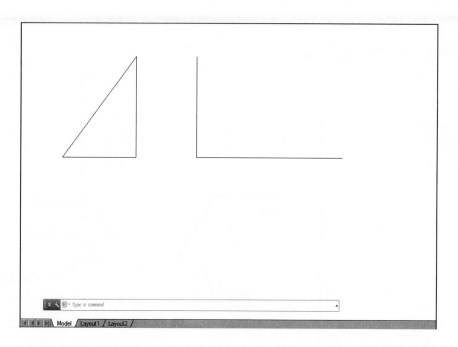

> We begin by placing a linear dimension below the base of the triangle.

✔ Open the **Annotate** tab on the ribbon, and pick the **Linear** tool, as shown in Figure 8-8.

> The ribbon places the last dimension command used at the top of the drop-down list, so it may be necessary to open the drop-down list to access the **Linear** tool.

**Figure 8-8**
**Linear** tool

> This initiates the **DIMLINEAR** command, with the following prompt appearing in the command line:

Specify first extension line origin or <select object>:

> There are two ways to proceed at this point. One is to show where the extension lines should begin, and the other is to select the object you want to dimension and let AutoCAD position the extension lines. In most simple applications, the latter method is faster.

✔ Press **<Enter>** to indicate that you will select an object.

> AutoCAD replaces the crosshairs with a pickbox and prompts for your selection:

Select object to dimension:

✔ Select the horizontal line at the bottom of the triangle, as shown by point 1 in Figure 8-9.

> AutoCAD immediately creates a dimension, including extension lines, dimension line, and text, that you can drag away from the selected line. AutoCAD places the dimension line and text where

**Figure 8-9**

Horizontal linear dimension

you indicate but keeps the text centered between the extension lines. The prompt is as follows:

Specify dimension line location or
[Mtext Text Angle Horizontal Vertical Rotated]:

In the default sequence, you simply show the location of the dimension. If you wish to alter the text content, you can do so using the **Mtext** or **Text** option, or you can change it later with a command called **DIMEDIT. Angle, Horizontal,** and **Vertical** allow you to specify the orientation of the text. Horizontal text is the default for linear dimensions. **Rotated** allows you to rotate the complete dimension so that the extension lines move out at an angle from the object being dimensioned. (Text remains horizontal.)

✔ Pick a location about 0.50 below the triangle, as shown by point 2 in Figure 8-9.

Bravo! You have completed your first dimension. (Notice that our figure and others in this chapter are shown zoomed in on the relevant object for the sake of clarity. You can zoom or not, as you like.)

At this point, take a good look at the dimension you have just drawn to see what it consists of. As in Figure 8-9, you should see the following components: two extension lines, two arrows, a dimension line on each side of the text, and the text itself.

Notice also that AutoCAD has automatically placed the extension line origins a short distance away from the triangle base. (You may need to zoom in to see this.) This distance is controlled by a dimension variable called **DIMEXO,** which can be changed in the **Modify Dimension Style** dialog box.

Next, we place a vertical dimension on the right side of the triangle. You can see that **DIMLINEAR** handles both horizontal and vertical dimensions.

✔ Repeat the **DIMLINEAR** command.

You are prompted for extension line origins as before:

Specify first extension line origin or <select object>:

This time we show the extension line origins manually.

✔ Pick the right-angle corner at the lower right of the triangle, point 1 in Figure 8-10.

   *AutoCAD prompts for a second point:*

   Specify second extension line origin:

**Figure 8-10**
Vertical linear dimension

✔ Pick the top intersection of the triangle, point 2 in Figure 8-10.

   *From here on, the procedure is the same as before. You should have a dimension to drag into place, and the following prompt:*

   Specify dimension line location or
   [Mtext Text Angle Horizontal Vertical Rotated]:

✔ Pick a point 0.50 to the right of the triangle, point 3 in Figure 8-10.

   *Your screen should now include the vertical dimension, as shown in Figure 8-10.*

Now let's place a dimension on the diagonal side of the triangle. For this, we need the **DIMALIGNED** command. The **Aligned** dimension tool is found on the drop-down list opened by the triangle below the **Linear** dimension tool.

✔ Open the **Dimension** tool drop-down list and pick the **Aligned** tool, as shown in Figure 8-11.

**Figure 8-11**
**Aligned Dimension** tool

✔ Press **<Enter>,** indicating that you will select an object.

*AutoCAD gives you the pickbox and prompts you to select an object to dimension.*

✔ Select the hypotenuse of the triangle.

✔ Pick a point approximately 0.50 above and to the left of the line.

*Your screen should resemble Figure 8-12. Notice that AutoCAD retains horizontal text in aligned and vertical dimensions as the default.*

**Figure 8-12**
Aligned dimension

## Drawing Multiple Linear Dimensions Using QDIM

| QDIM | |
|---|---|
| Command | Qdim |
| Alias | (none) |
| Panel | Dimensions |
| Tool | |

**QDIM** automates the creation of certain types of multiple dimension formats. With this command, you can create a whole series of related dimensions with a few mouse clicks. To introduce **QDIM,** we create a continuous dimension series dimensioning the bottom of the triangle, the space between the triangle and the line, and the length of the line itself. Then, we edit the series to show several points along the line. Finally, we change the dimensions on the line from a continuous series to a baseline series. In later tasks, we return to **QDIM** to create other types of multiple dimension sets.

✔ Erase the 3.00 dimension from the bottom of the triangle.

✔ Select the bottom of the triangle and the 6.00 horizontal line to the right of the triangle.

*Noun/verb editing allows you to select objects before entering* **QDIM.** *Your selected lines are highlighted and have grips showing.*

✔ Pick the **Quick Dimension** tool from the ribbon, as shown in Figure 8-13.

*AutoCAD prompts:*

Specify dimension line position, or
[Continuous Staggered Baseline Ordinate Radius Diameter datumPoint Edit seTtings] <Continuous>:

**Figure 8-13**
**Quick Dimension** tool

The options here are various forms of multiple dimensions.
**Continuous, Staggered, Baseline,** and **Ordinate** are all linear
styles. **Radius** and **Diameter** are for dimensioning circles and arcs.
**DatumPoint** is used to change the point from which a set of linear
dimensions is measured. **Edit** has several functions we explore in a
moment. **SeTtings** allows a choice of how associated dimensions
created with **QDIM** work.

Continuous dimensions are positioned end to end, as shown in
Figure 8-14. AutoCAD creates three linear dimensions at once and
positions them end to end.

**Figure 8-14**
Continuous dimensions

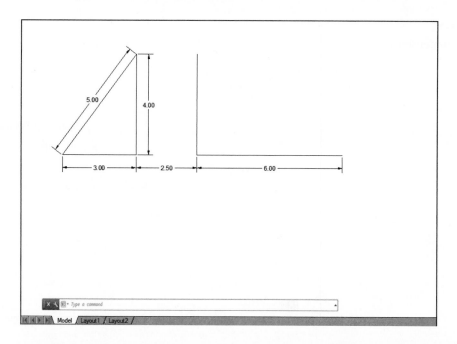

**NOTE**

The objects selected for the **QDIM** command can be dimensions or objects to be
dimensioned. If you select objects, **QDIM** creates new dimensions for these objects; if
you select dimensions, **QDIM** edits or re-creates these dimensions depending on the
options you select.

✔ Pick a point about 0.5 unit below the triangle, as shown in Figure 8-14.
    *Next we edit the dimension on the right, so that the line length is
    measured to several different lengths.*

✔ Repeat **QDIM.**

✔ Select the dimension at the right, below the 6.00 line.
    *Notice that this dimension can be selected independently. The three
    continuous dimensions just created are separate objects, even
    though they were created simultaneously.*

✔ Right-click to end object selection.

> *AutoCAD gives you a single dimension to drag into place. If you pick a point now, the selected 6.00 dimension is re-created at the point you choose. We do something more interesting.*

✔ Select **Edit** from the command line.

> **QDIM** *adds X's at the two endpoints of the dimensioned line and prompts:*

> Indicate dimension point to remove, or [Add eXit] <eXit>:

> *The X's indicate dimension points. We add more dimension points.*

✔ Select **Add** from the command line.

> *The prompt changes slightly, as follows:*

> Indicate dimension point to add, or [Remove eXit] <eXit>:

✔ Pick point 1, as shown in Figure 8-15.

> *This point is 2 units from the left endpoint of the line.* **QDIM** *continues to prompt for points.*

**Figure 8-15**
Baseline dimensions

✔ Pick point 2, as shown in Figure 8-15.

> *This point is 2 units from the right endpoint of the line.*

✔ Press **<Enter>** or the spacebar to end point selection.

> **QDIM** *now divides the single 6.00 dimension into a series of three continuous 2.00 dimensions. We are not done yet. We choose to draw these three dimensions in baseline format.*

✔ Select **Baseline** from the command line.

> **QDIM** *immediately switches the three dragged dimensions to a baseline form.*

> **NOTE**
>
> AutoCAD retains the last option used for drawing dimensions with **QDIM,** so if you were to enter the command now, it would default to **Baseline** rather than **Continuous** dimensions.

✔ Pick a point so that the top, shortest dimension of the three is positioned about 0.5 below the line.

> *Your screen is redrawn with three baseline dimensions, as shown in Figure 8-15. We will have more to say about this powerful command as we go along. In the next task, we use it to create ordinate dimensions.*

## Dimbaseline and Dimcontinue

Baseline and continuous format dimensions can also be created one at a time using individual commands. The following general procedure is used with these commands:

**1** Draw an initial linear dimension.

**2** Pick the **Baseline** or **Continue** tool from the **Dimensions** panel of the ribbon.

**3** Pick a second extension line origin.

**4** Pick another second extension line origin.

**5** Press **<Enter>** to exit the command.

---

**NOTE**

In AutoCAD 2013, baseline and continued dimensions may be drawn either in the current dimension style or in the style of the selected dimension (assuming it is different from the current style). This depends on the setting of the system variable **DIMCONTINUEMODE**. When set to **0**, the default, the current style is used; when set to **1**, the style of the selected dimension is used.

---

## Drawing Ordinate Dimensions

**ordinate dimension:** A dimension given relative to a fixed point of origin rather than through direct measurement of the objects being dimensioned.

*Ordinate dimensions* are another way to specify linear dimensions. They are used to show multiple horizontal and vertical distances from a single point or the corner of an object. Because these fall readily into a coordinate system, it is efficient to show these dimensions as the *x* and *y* displacements from a single point of origin. There are two ways to create ordinate dimensions. AutoCAD ordinarily specifies points based on the point (0,0) on your screen. Using **QDIM,** you can specify a new datum point that serves as the origin for a set of ordinate dimensions. Using **DIMORDINATE,** it is necessary to temporarily move the origin of the coordinate system to the point from which you want dimensions to be specified. In this task, we demonstrate both.

## QDIM and the Datum Point Option

We use ordinate dimensions to specify a series of horizontal and vertical distances from the intersection of the two lines to the right of the triangle. First, we use **QDIM** to add ordinate dimensions along the 4.00 vertical line. Then, we use **DIMORDINATE** to add ordinate dimensions to the 6.00 horizontal line.

✔ Pick the **Quick Dimension** tool from the ribbon.

✔ Select the vertical line.

✔ Right-click to end object selection.

✔ Select **Ordinate** from the command line.

✔ Select a point about 0.5 unit to the left of the line, as shown in Figure 8-16.

> *The two dimensions you see are at the ends of the line and show the y value of each endpoint. Whether in the ordinate option of **QDIM** or in **DIMORDINATE,** AutoCAD automatically chooses the x or y value depending on the object you choose. Because the values you see are measured from the origin at the lower left corner of the grid, they are not particularly useful. A more common use is to measure points from the intersection of the two lines. To complete this set of dimensions, we go back into **QDIM,** select a new datum point, and add and remove dimension points, as shown in Figure 8-17.*

**Figure 8-16**
**Quick Dimension** vertical line

**Figure 8-17**
Datum point

✔ Repeat **QDIM.**

✔ Select the bottom ordinate dimension (7.00 in our illustration).

✔ Select the top ordinate dimension (11.00 in our illustration).
   *Notice that these need to be selected separately.*

✔ Right-click to end geometry selection.

✔ Select **datumPoint** from the command line.
   **Q****DIM** *prompts:*

      Select new datum point:

✔ Select the intersection of the two lines, as shown in Figure 8-17.
   *The new datum point is now established. We add three new dimension points and remove one before leaving **Q****DIM**.*

✔ Select **Edit** from the command line.

✔ Select **Add** from the command line.

✔ Add points 1.00, 2.00, and 3.00 up from the bottom of the vertical line.
   *As you add points, they are marked by X's.*

✔ Select **Remove** from the command line.

✔ Remove the point at the intersection of the two lines.

✔ Press **<Enter>** or the spacebar to end point selection.

✔ Pick a point about 0.5 unit to the left of the vertical line, as before.
   *Your screen should resemble Figure 8-17. Notice that the top dimension is automatically updated to reflect the new datum point. Next, we dimension the horizontal line using the **DIMORDINATE** command.*

## DIMORDINATE and the UCS Command

We use **DIMORDINATE** to create a series of ordinate dimensions above the horizontal 6.00 line. This method requires you to create a new origin for the coordinate system using the **UCS** command. User coordinate systems are most important in 3D drawing and are not explored in depth here. Although **DIMORDINATE** creates only one dimension at a time, it does have some advantages over the **Q****DIM** system. To begin with, you do not have to go back and edit the dimension to add and remove points. Additionally, you can create a variety of leader shapes.

✔ Type **ucs <Enter>**.
   *This executes the **UCS** command. Specifying a new coordinate system by moving the point of origin is the default and is the simplest of many options in the **UCS** command. AutoCAD prompts:*

      Specify origin of UCS or
      [Face NAmed OBject Previous View World X Y Z ZAxis]
      <World>:

✔ Pick the intersection of the two lines.
   *AutoCAD prompts:*

      Specify point on X-axis or <accept>:

✔ Press **<Enter>** to accept the new origin.
   *If you move your cursor to the intersection and watch the coordinate display, you can see that this point is now read as (0.00,0.00,0.00). If your user coordinate system icon is on and set to move to the origin, it moves to the new point. Also, if your grid is on, the origin will move to the new origin point.*

✔ Pick the **Annotate** tab > **Dimensions** panel, and then open the **Dimension** tools drop-down list from the ribbon, as shown in Figure 8-18.

**Figure 8-18**
**Ordinate Dimension** tool

✔ Pick the **Ordinate** dimension tool from the drop-down list, as shown. *AutoCAD prompts:*

Specify feature location:

*In actuality, all you do is show AutoCAD a point and then an endpoint for a leader. Depending on where the endpoint is located relative to the first point, AutoCAD shows dimension text for either an x or a y displacement from the origin of the current coordinate system.*

✔ Pick a point along the 6.00 line, 1.00 to the right of the intersection, as shown in Figure 8-19.

**Figure 8-19**
**Ordinate Dimension** horizontal line

*In the new coordinate system, this point will be (1,0). AutoCAD prompts:*

> Non-associative dimension created
> Specify leader end point or [Xdatum Ydatum Mtext Text Angle]:

*The first line tells you that ordinate dimensions created in this fashion are nonassociative. Associativity is discussed in the "Using Associative Dimensions" section. The second line prompts you to specify a leader endpoint. You can manually indicate whether you want the dimension text to show the x or y coordinate by typing **x** or **y**. However, if you choose the endpoint correctly, AutoCAD picks the right coordinate automatically. You could also provide your own text, but that would defeat the purpose of setting up a coordinate system that automatically gives you the distances from the intersection of the two lines.*

✔ Pick an endpoint 1.00 directly above the line, as shown in Figure 8-19. *Your screen should now include the 1.00 ordinate dimension shown in Figure 8-19.*

✔ Repeat **DIMORDINATE** and add the second ordinate dimension at a point 2.00 from the origin.
    *This will be at the point (2,0).*

✔ Repeat **DIMORDINATE** once more.

✔ Pick a point on the line 3.00 from the origin. The point is (3,0).

✔ Move your cursor left and right to see some of the leader shapes that **DIMORDINATE** creates depending on the endpoint of the leader.

✔ Pick an endpoint slightly to the right of the dimensioned point to create a broken leader similar to the one in Figure 8-19.
    *When you are done, you should return to the world coordinate system. This is the default coordinate system and the one we have been using all along.*

✔ Type **ucs <Enter>**.

✔ Select **World** from the command line.
    *This returns the origin to its original position at the lower left of your screen.*

## Drawing Angular Dimensions

| DIMANGULAR | |
|---|---|
| **Command** | Dimangular |
| **Alias** | (none) |
| **Panel** | Annotation |
| **Tool** | |

> **TIP**
>
> A general procedure for creating angular dimensions is:
>
> 1. Pick the **Annotate** tab > **Dimension** tools drop-down list > **Angular** tool from the **Dimensions** panel of the ribbon.
> 2. Select two lines that form an angle.
> 3. Pick a dimension location.

Angular dimensioning works much like linear dimensioning, except that you are prompted to select objects that form an angle. AutoCAD computes an angle based on the geometry that you select (two lines, an arc, a part of a circle, or a vertex and two points) and constructs extension lines, a dimension arc, and text specifying the angle.

For this exercise, we return to the triangle and add angular dimensions to two of the angles.

✔ Open the **Dimension** tools drop-down list and pick the **Angular** tool, as shown in Figure 8-20.

*The first prompt is:*

Select arc, circle, line, or <specify vertex>:

**Figure 8-20**
**Angular Dimension** tool

*The prompt shows that you can use* **DIMANGULAR** *to dimension angles formed by arcs and portions of circles as well as angles formed by lines. If you press* **<Enter>** *you can specify an angle manually by picking its vertex and a point on each side of the angle. We begin by picking lines.*

✔ Select the base of the triangle.

*You are prompted for another line:*

Select second line:

✔ Select the hypotenuse.

*As in linear dimensioning, AutoCAD now shows you the dimension lines and lets you drag them into place. The prompt asks for a dimension arc location and also allows you the option of changing the text or the text angle:*

Specify dimension arc line location or [Mtext Text Angle Quadrant]:

✔ Move the cursor around to see how the dimension can be placed, and then pick a point between the two selected lines, as shown in Figure 8-21.

*The lower left angle of your triangle should now be dimensioned, as in Figure 8-21. Notice that the degree symbol is added by default in angular dimension text.*

*We dimension the upper angle by specifying its vertex.*

✔ Repeat **DIMANGULAR.**

**Figure 8-21**
Dimension angles

✔ Press **<Enter>**.
   *AutoCAD prompts for an angle vertex.*

✔ If necessary, pick the **Snap Mode** button so that **Snap** mode is turned on.

✔ Point to the vertex of the angle at the top of the triangle.
   *AutoCAD prompts:*

   Specify first angle endpoint:

✔ Pick a point along the hypotenuse.
   *To be precise, this should be a snap point. The most dependable one is the lower left corner of the triangle. AutoCAD prompts:*

   Specify second angle endpoint:

✔ Pick any point along the vertical side of the triangle.
   *All points on the vertical line should be snap points.*

✔ Move the cursor slowly up and down within the triangle.
   *Notice how AutoCAD places the arrows outside the angle when you approach the vertex, and things get crowded. Also notice that if you move outside the angle, AutoCAD switches to the outer angle.*

✔ Pick a location for the dimension arc, as shown in Figure 8-21.

## Angular Dimensions on Arcs and Circles

You can also place angular dimensions on arcs and circles. In both cases, AutoCAD constructs extension lines and a dimension arc. When you dimension an arc with an angular dimension, the center of the arc becomes the vertex of the dimension angle, and the endpoints of the arc become the start points of the extension lines. In a circle, the same format is used, but the dimension line origins are determined by the point used to select the circle and a second point, which AutoCAD prompts you to select. These options are illustrated in Figure 8-22.

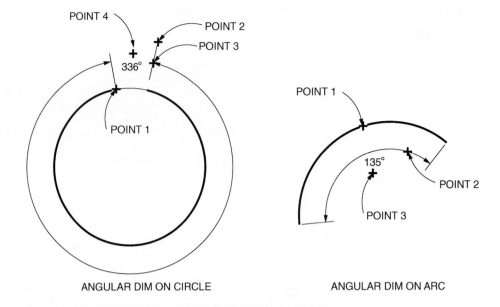

**Figure 8-22**
Angular dimension on arcs and circles

POINT 4
POINT 2
POINT 3
336°
POINT 1
ANGULAR DIM ON CIRCLE

POINT 1
135°
POINT 2
POINT 3
ANGULAR DIM ON ARC

## Dimensioning Arcs and Circles

> **TIP**
> A general procedure for dimensioning arcs and circles is:
>
> 1. Pick the **Annotate** tab > **Dimension** tools drop-down list > **Radius** or **Diameter** tool from the **Dimensions** panel of the ribbon.
> 2. Pick an arc or a circle.
> 3. Pick a leader line endpoint location.

The basic process for dimensioning circles and arcs is as simple as those we have already covered. It can get tricky, however, when AutoCAD does not place the dimension where you want it. Text placement can be controlled by adjusting dimension variables. In this exercise, we create a center mark and some diameter and radius dimensions. Then, we return to the **QDIM** command to see how multiple circles can be dimensioned at once.

✔ To prepare for this exercise, draw two circles, with radii of 2.00 and 1.50, as shown in Figure 8-23. If your drawing has multiple layers, the circles should not be drawn on the dimension layer.

✔ If necessary, return to the dimension layer.

✔ Pick the **Annotate tab** > **Dimensions** panel extension > **Center Mark** tool, as shown in Figure 8-24.
> *Center marks are the simplest of all dimension features to create. They are added automatically as part of some radius and diameter dimensions. AutoCAD prompts:*
>
> Select arc or circle:

✔ Select the smaller circle.
> *A center mark is drawn in the 1.50 circle, as shown in Figure 8-25. The standard center mark is a small cross. The size of the cross can be changed in a small panel at the bottom right of the **Lines** tab and the **Symbols and Arrows** tab of the **Modify Dimension***

**Figure 8-23**
Drawing two circles

**Figure 8-24**
**Center Mark** tool

**Figure 8-25**
Dimensioning diameter and radius

*Style* dialog box. Here you also have a choice of standard continuous lines or broken centerlines to form the mark.

✔ Now, we add the diameter dimension shown on the larger circle in Figure 8-25.

✔ Pick the **Diameter** tool from the **Dimension** tools drop-down list on the **Dimensions** panel.

*AutoCAD prompts:*

Select arc or circle:

✔ Select the larger circle.

*AutoCAD shows a diameter dimension and asks for a dimension line location with the following prompt:*

Specify dimension line location or [Mtext Text Angle]:

*The **Text** and **Angle** options allow you to change the dimension text or put it at an angle. If you move your cursor around, you see that you can position the dimension line anywhere around or inside the circle.*

✔ Pick a dimension position near the top of the 2.00 circle so that your screen resembles Figure 8-25.

*Notice that the diameter symbol prefix and the center mark are added automatically by default.*

## Radius Dimensions

The procedures for radius dimensioning are exactly the same as those for diameter dimensions, and the results look the same. The only differences are the radius value of the text and the use of R for radius in place of the diameter symbol.

We draw a radius dimension on the smaller circle.

✔ Pick the **Radius** tool from the **Dimension** tools drop-down list.

✔ Select the 1.50 (smaller) circle.

✔ Move the cursor around the circle, inside and outside.

✔ Pick a point to complete the dimension, as shown in Figure 8-25.

*The R for radius and the center mark are added automatically.*

## Dimensioning with Multileaders

| MLEADER | |
|---------|---|
| **Command** | Mleader |
| **Alias** | (none) |
| **Panel** | Annotation |
| **Tool** | |

> **TIP**
> A general procedure for dimensioning with multileaders is:
> 1. Pick the **Multileader** tool from the **Leaders** panel of the **Annotate** tab.
> 2. Pick a leader arrowhead location.
> 3. Pick a leader landing location.
> 4. Type dimension text.

**multileader:** In AutoCAD, a multileader is an object with an arrowhead and a leader connecting annotation text or symbols to annotated objects.

Radius and diameter dimensions, along with ordinate dimensions, make use of leaders to connect dimension text to the object being dimensioned. Leaders or *multileaders* can also be created independently to attach annotation to all kinds of objects. Unlike other dimension formats, in which you select an object or show a length, a leader is simply a line or series of lines with an arrow at the end to visually connect an object to its annotation. Thus, when you create a dimension with a leader, AutoCAD does not recognize and measure any selected object or distance. You need to know the dimension text or annotation you want to use before you begin.

We begin by adding a multileader with attached text to annotate the circle at the right. Multileaders appear the same as leaders in other dimension objects, but there are multileader commands and procedures that do not apply to leaders.

✔ Pick the **Annotate** tab > **Leaders** panel > **Multileader** tool, as shown in Figure 8-26.

*AutoCAD prompts for an arrowhead location:*

Specify leader arrowhead location or [leader Landing first Content first Options] <Options>:

**Figure 8-26**
**Multileader** tool

*Leaders consist of an arrowhead, a leader line, and a short landing line connecting the leader to the text or annotation symbol. The options allow you to change the order in which these elements are specified.*
*To attach the arrow to the circle, we use a **Nearest** object snap.*

✔ Hold down **<Shift>** and right-click your mouse to open the **Object Snap** shortcut menu.

✔ Select **Nearest** from the fourth panel of the menu.
*The **Nearest** object snap mode specifies that you want to snap to the nearest point on whatever object you select. If you have not used this object snap mode before, take a moment to get familiar with it. As you move around the screen, you see the **Nearest** snap tool whenever the crosshairs approach an object. If you allow the crosshairs to rest on an object, the Nearest tooltip label appears as well.*

✔ Pick a leader arrowhead location on the upper right side of the larger, 2.00-radius circle.

✔ Pick a point for the leader landing about 45° and 1.50 units up and to the right of the first point.
*The **Text Editor** contextual tab appears on the ribbon. The two arrows just above where your text will be entered allow you to specify a width for the text you will enter.*

✔ Position your cursor within the small gray box with two arrows, as shown in Figure 8-27.

✔ Hold down the pick button, drag the width box out about 2.50 units to the right, and then release the pick button.

✔ Type **This circle is 4.00 inches in diameter <Enter>.**

**Figure 8-27**
**Text Editor** arrows

✔ Click outside the text window to complete the command.

*Your screen should now resemble Figure 8-28. This is a multileader object, and the text is mtext. The entire object, lines, arrow, and text can be selected as a single object.*

*Next, we add a multileader object with an annotation symbol to the smaller circle.*

**Figure 8-28**
Leader and text added

## The Leaders Tool Palette

We add two leaders with simple tag annotations and then use some new tools that allow us to align and gather multileader objects. Here we make our first use of a tool palette. A **tool palette** is simply a collection of tools

**tool palette:** A collection of tools in a tabbed format.

in a tabbed format. You can open tool palettes from several places on the ribbon or the menu bar, but here we demonstrate a quicker method using a keyboard shortcut.

✔ Press **<Ctrl>+3.** This opens the complete tool palettes set, as shown in Figure 8-29.

> *Notice the many tabs along the left side of the palette. At the bottom of these tabs there is a small section that looks like multiple tabs, one on top of another. Picking this section will open a list giving access to additional tool palettes.*

✔ Pick the bottom section of the tool palettes tabs, below the tabs, as shown in Figure 8-30.

> *This opens the list of available tool palettes shown at the left in the figure.*

**Figure 8-29**
Tool palettes - all palettes

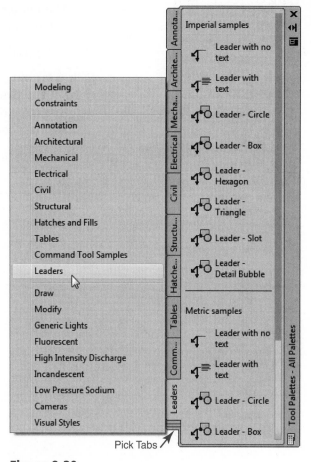

**Figure 8-30**
Tool palettes list

✔ Select **Leaders** from the list.

> *This opens the **Leaders** tool palette, as shown in Figure 8-31.*

This palette contains two sets of leader styles, imperial styles at the top and metric styles at the bottom. There are eight of each, and the lists are identical except for variations in size. We will use the metric **Leader - Circle** style found near the bottom of the palette.

✔ Pick the **Leader - Circle** style from the tool palette, as shown in Figure 8-31.

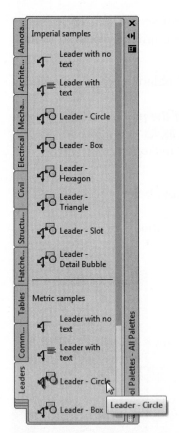

**Figure 8-31**
**Leaders** tool palette

AutoCAD prompts for an arrowhead location or option, as before:

Specify leader arrowhead location or
[leader Landing first Content first Options] <Options>:

*We will use the **Leader - Circle** style to tag the 1.50-radius circle with a number. Nothing is being dimensioned by this leader. It is simply a tag such as might be applied to call out or number an object in a drawing.*

✔ Hold down **<Shift>** and right-click your mouse to open the **Object Snap** shortcut menu.

✔ Select **Nearest** from the fourth panel of the menu.

✔ Position the crosshairs on the upper right side of the 1.50-radius circle and press the pick button.
*The leader is snapped to the circle, and a rubber band appears, extending to the crosshairs. AutoCAD prompts for a second point:*

Specify leader landing location:

✔ Pick a landing location for the leader, at a 45° angle up and to the right of the first point, as shown in Figure 8-32.
*AutoCAD draws a leader, landing line, and circle, as shown, and prompts for a tag number:*

Enter tag number <TAGNUMBER>:

**Figure 8-32**
Leader with text in circle

✔ Type **5 <Enter>.**
*The number 5 has no particular significance here. It is for demonstration only. The number is added to the circle tag, as shown in Figure 8-32. Many of the other leader styles would be identical to this one except for the shape of the tag (box, hexagon, triangle, slot, detail bubble).*

*Next, we add a second multileader from the same annotation tag, connecting to the other circle.*

✔ Click **OK** to close the **Edit Attributes** dialog box.

✔ Close the tool palette.

✔ From the **Leaders** panel, pick the **Add Leader** tool, as shown in Figure 8-33.

  *AutoCAD prompts:*

  Select the multileader:

**Figure 8-33**
**Add Leader** tool

✔ Select the multileader object with the tag "5".

  *AutoCAD connects a rubber-band leader to the original landing line and lets you stretch it out to a new point.*

✔ Using a **Nearest** object snap, connect the added leader to the 2.00 circle.

  *AutoCAD provides another leader so that you can continue to add leaders to this multileader group.*

✔ Press **<Enter>** to end the command.

  *Your screen should resemble Figure 8-34.*

**Figure 8-34**
Leader stretched out

Finally, we use a special multileader alignment command to align the radius dimension on the smaller circle with the multileader annotation tag. This will require replacing the radius dimension with a multileader object.

✔ Erase the **R1.50** dimension from the smaller circle.

✔ Pick the **Multileader** tool from the **Leaders** panel.

✔ **<Shift>** + right-click and select **Nearest** from the **Object Snap** shortcut menu.

✔ Pick a point on the circle near where the previous radius dimension was attached.

✔ Pick a leader landing point so that the leader text will be positioned near where the previous dimension was located.

✔ Type **R1.50 <Enter>.**

✔ Click outside the text window to complete the command.
*If you have done this correctly, your screen will still resemble Figure 8-34.*

✔ Pick the **Align** tool from the **Leaders** panel, as shown in Figure 8-35.
*AutoCAD prompts:*

Select multileaders:

**Figure 8-35**
**Leader Align** tool

✔ Select the multileader with tag 5 and the R1.50 multileader.

✔ Right-click to end object selection.
*AutoCAD prompts:*

Select multileader to align to or [Options]:

*We align the upper tag with the lower text.*

✔ Pick the lower multileader with the R1.50 text.
*You see an alignment line that you can move to align at any angle.*
*To get a perfect vertical alignment, turn on* **Ortho** *mode.*

✔ Pick the **Ortho Mode** button or press **<F8>** to turn on **Ortho** mode.

✔ Pick a point at 90° to create a vertical alignment.
*Your screen should resemble Figure 8-36.*

**Figure 8-36**
Leaders are aligned

# Changing Dimension Text

Dimensions can be edited in many of the same ways that other objects are edited. They can be moved, copied, stretched, rotated, trimmed, extended, and so on. There are numerous ways to change dimension text and placement. Grips can be used effectively to accomplish most changes in placement. Here we demonstrate two ways to change the text.

## The DIMEDIT Command

✔ Type **dimedit <Enter>.**

   *AutoCAD prompts with options:*

   Enter type of dimension editing [Home New Rotate Oblique]
   <Home>:

   *If dynamic input is on, you also see these options on a list.* **Home,
   Rotate,** *and* **Oblique** *are placement and orientation options;* **New**
   *refers to new text content.*

✔ Select **New** from the dynamic input list.

   *AutoCAD opens the* **Text Editor** *contextual tab on the ribbon and
   waits for you to enter text. You see a small blue edit box floating in
   the middle of your drawing area. You can enter text here and then
   indicate which dimensions you want to apply it to.*

   *We change the 5.00 aligned dimension to read 5.00 cm.*

✔ Delete the text inside the edit box.

✔ Type **5.00 cm.**

   *The new text appears in the edit box.*

✔ Click anywhere outside the edit box to close the editor and return to
   the drawing.

   *AutoCAD prompts for objects to receive the new text:*

   Select Objects:

✔ Select the 5.00 aligned dimension on the hypotenuse of the triangle.

✔ Press **<Enter>** or right-click to end object selection.

   *The text is redrawn, as shown in Figure 8-37.*

## The Quick Properties Panel

The **Quick Properties** panel gives you another way to change dimension
text content. Try the following:

✔ Pick the lower baseline dimension on the 6.00 line.

✔ Pick the **Quick Properties** tool on the status bar.

✔ Click in the **Text override** cell.

✔ Type **6.00 cm** in the edit box.

✔ Pick the **Quick Properties** tool again to close the panel.

✔ Press **<Esc>** to clear grips.

   *Your screen is redrawn with the dimension text shown in
   Figure 8-38.*

**Figure 8-37**
Text changed to 5.00 cm

**Figure 8-38**
Text changed to 6.00 cm

## Using Associative Dimensions

By default, most dimensions in AutoCAD are associative with the geometry of the objects they dimension. This means that changes in the dimensioned objects are automatically reflected in the dimensions. If a dimensioned object is moved, the dimensions associated with it move as well. If a dimensioned object is scaled, the position and measurements associated with that object change to reflect the new size of the object. The following exercise illustrates several points about ***associative dimensions.***

**associative dimension:** A dimension that is associated with the object it dimensions, so that if the object moves or changes size, the dimension changes with the object.

✔ Select the 2.00-radius circle.

✔ Pick the center grip and move the circle about 2.00 units to the left, and click again to complete the move.

> *Your screen should resemble Figure 8-39. Notice that the 4.00-diameter dimension moves with the circle, and the leaders from the mtext*

**Figure 8-39**
Results when circle is moved

*dimension text and the multileader tag stretch to maintain connection with the circle, but that the text and tag do not move. We explain this in a moment, but first, try the following steps:*

✔ Select any of the grips.

✔ Right-click to open the **Grip** shortcut menu.

✔ Select **Scale.**

✔ Type **.5 <Enter>** for a scale factor.
   *Your screen is redrawn to resemble Figure 8-40. Notice now that the scale factor is reflected in the diameter dimension (4.00 has changed to 2.00) but not in the leadered text. The diameter dimension is a true associative dimension; it moves and updates to reflect changes in the circle. In the multileadered text, the connection point*

**Figure 8-40**
Results when circle is scaled

*of the leadered dimension is associated with the circle, but the text is not. Therefore, the leader stretches to stay connected to the circle, but the text does not move or change with the circle.*

## Changing Associativity of Dimensions

Nonassociative dimensions can be made associative using the **DIMREAS-SOCIATE** command. Associated dimensions can be disassociated with the **DIMDISASSOCIATE** command. In each case the procedure is a matter of entering the command and selecting dimensions to associate or disassociate. For example, try the following:

✔ Type **dimd** and then select **DIMDISSOCIATE** from the **AutoComplete** list. *Dimdisassociate is not on any toolbar or menu, so this is a great time to take advantage of the **AutoComplete** feature.*
  *AutoCAD prompts:*

  Select dimensions to disassociate . . .
  Select objects:

✔ Select the 2.00-diameter dimension.

✔ Right-click to end object selection.
  *Now, try moving the circle again to observe the changes.*

✔ Select the circle again, select the center grip, and move the circle back to the right.
  *This time the 2.00 diameter does not move with the circle, as shown in Figure 8-41. The multileaders adjust as before to stay attached to the circle, but the diameter dimension is currently not associated to the circle. To reassociate it, use the* **DIMREASSOCIATE** *command, as follows:*

**Figure 8-41**
Results of disassociated dimension

✔ Type **dimr** and select **DIMREASSOCIATE** from the **AutoComplete** list, or select **Annotate** tab > **Dimensions** panel extension > **Reassociate** from the ribbon, as shown in Figure 8-42.

✔ Select the 2.00-diameter dimension.

**Figure 8-42**
**Reassociate** tool

Reassociate
Associates or reassociates selected dimensions to objects or points on objects

DIMREASSOCIATE

Press F1 for more help

✔ Right-click to end object selection.

*AutoCAD recognizes that this is a diameter dimension and prompts for a circle or arc to attach it to. Notice that this means you can associate the dimension to any arc or circle, not just the one to which it was previously attached.*

✔ Select the circle on the left again.

*The diameter dimension moves and attaches to the 2.00-radius circle again, as shown in Figure 8-43.*

**Figure 8-43**
Results of reassociated dimension

## Using the HATCH Command

Automated hatching is another immense time-saver. AutoCAD has two basic methods of hatching. In one method, you select a point within an area to be hatched, and AutoCAD searches for the nearest boundary surrounding the point. In the other method, you specify the boundaries themselves by selecting objects. By default, AutoCAD creates associated hatch patterns. Associated hatching changes when the boundaries around change. Nonassociated hatching is completely independent of the geometry that contains it.

✔ To prepare for this exercise, clear your screen of all previously drawn objects, return to a nondimension layer, and then draw three rectangles, one inside the other, with the word "TEXT" with a height of 1.00 at the center, as shown in Figure 8-44. In order to do this, your inner rectangle should be at least 1.50 high.

| HATCH | |
|---|---|
| **Command** | Hatch |
| **Alias** | H |
| **Panel** | Draw |
| **Tool** | |

**Figure 8-44**
Drawing three rectangles

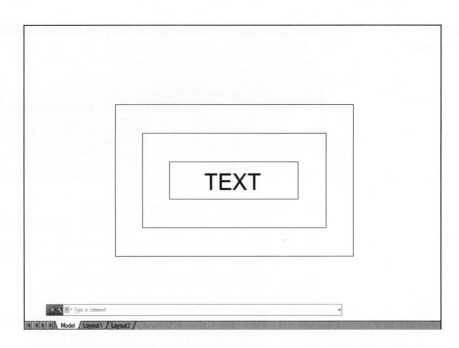

✔ Pick the **Home** tab **> Draw** panel **> Hatch** tool from the ribbon, as shown in Figure 8-45.

> *This initiates the **HATCH** command, which calls the **Hatch Creation** contextual tab, shown in Figure 8-46. The tools in this ribbon tab give you many options for creating hatch and fill patterns, including 50 standard predefined patterns, solid color fills, and gradient fills. The default pattern is ANSI31, a simple pattern of crosshatch lines on a 45° angle. If this pattern is not showing on the **Pattern** panel, you will need to scroll up to find it.*

**Figure 8-45**
Hatch tool

**Figure 8-46**
ANSI31 image

✔ If necessary, scroll to the top of the set of pattern images, using the up arrow at the top right of the panel.

✔ If necessary, pick the ANSI31 image, as shown in Figure 8-46.
> *AutoCAD prompts:*

> Pick internal points or [Select objects Undo seTtings]:

> *This indicates that the default method, picking internal points, is in operation. Typing **S** will switch to the select boundary objects method; typing **T** will take you to the **Hatch and Gradient** dialog box. When you move the cursor into a boundaried area, AutoCAD*

*will show a preview of the area hatched or filled in the current style. In our case that is ANSI31.*

**NOTE**

The **HATCH** command retains the most recent usage. If someone has recently drawn a hatch pattern by selecting objects rather than with internal points, **Select objects** may appear as the default. In this case, simply pick **internal points** from the command line.

✔ Move the crosshairs into the area between the largest and the second largest rectangle and pause.

*You see a preview image similar to Figure 8-47.*

**Figure 8-47**
Preview ANSI31 hatch pattern

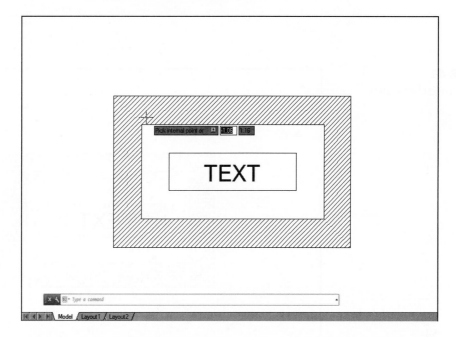

✔ Move the crosshairs into the area between the second largest and the smallest rectangle and pause.

*You see a preview with this area hatched. Notice in each case that AutoCAD recognizes internal and external boundaries.*

✔ Move the crosshairs into the inner rectangle and pause.

*Notice in this preview image that AutoCAD also recognizes text within the boundary and automatically leaves space around the text.*

✔ Now move the crosshairs outside all of the rectangles.

*You are still in the **HATCH** command, but no crosshatching has actually been applied to your drawing yet.*

## Other Predefined Patterns

AutoCAD's standard library of predefined hatch patterns includes 82 patterns that can be accessed from the **Pattern** panel. The arrows at the right of the panel allow you to scroll through the pattern images. The bottom arrow will open a larger window with four rows of images and its own scroll bar on the right. Here, we open the window and scroll down to the Escher pattern.

✔ Click the down arrow at the bottom right of the **Pattern** panel.

*Notice this is the bottom arrow, not the middle arrow, which also points down. You see the window of patterns shown in Figure 8-48.*

**Figure 8-48**
Selecting Escher pattern

**Figure 8-49**
Preview of Escher hatch pattern

✔ Scroll down to the Escher pattern and select it.
   *The window closes, and the row containing the Escher pattern is displayed on the **Pattern** panel, with **Escher** selected. We apply this pattern to the inner, and outer rectangles, as shown in Figure 8-49.*

✔ Move the cursor into the area between the largest and second largest rectangles, and press the pick button.
   *The area is filled with the Escher pattern. To also hatch the inner rectangle, we leave and then reenter the **HATCH** command. This is necessary because the inner rectangle boundaries are within the boundaries of the outer rectangle. To hatch separated areas you can continue without leaving the command.*

✔ Press **<Enter>** to complete the command.

✔ Press **<Enter>** again to reenter **HATCH**.

✔ Move the crosshairs inside the inner rectangle, press the pick button, and press **<Enter>** to complete the command.
   *Your screen resembles Figure 8-49.*

## Gradient Fill

**gradient:** In AutoCAD, a fill pattern in which there is a smooth transition between one color or tint and another color or tint.

To complete this section, we add a ***gradient*** fill pattern to the area between the inner and outer rectangles, as shown in Figure 8-50. This can be done in exactly the same way as entering any predefined hatch pattern, or in a slightly different way, using the drop-down list at the top left of the **Properties** panel of the **Hatch Creation** contextual tab. To use the former method, open the **Pattern** drop-down list and scroll to the gradient fill you want. Using the latter method, opening the drop-down list on the **Properties** panel will automatically take you to the gradient patterns.

**Figure 8-50**
Preview of GR_SPHER gradient fill

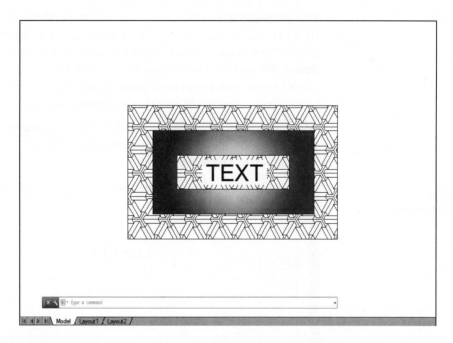

✔  Press **<Enter>** to reenter the **HATCH** command.
*This opens the **Hatch Creation** contextual tab shown in Figure 8-51.*

**Figure 8-51**
Selecting GR_SPHER gradient fill

✔ Open the **Pattern** drop-down list at the top of the **Properties** panel.
*This drop-down list gives access to solid fills of various colors and user-defined hatch patterns and allows you to change the colors in gradient fills.*

✔ Pick **Gradient** from the list.

✔ In the **Pattern** panel, click down using the bottom arrow on the right.

✔ Pick the **GR_SPHER** gradient pattern, first in the row, as shown in Figure 8-51.

✔ Pick a point in the area between the inner and outer rectangles to create the image shown previously in Figure 8-50.

✔ Press **<Enter>** to exit **HATCH.**

## Scaling Dimensions Between Paper Space and Model Space

You probably already know how to create multiple-viewport layouts. Now that you will be adding text and dimensions to your drawings, new questions arise about scale relationships between model space and paper space. The **Zoom XP** feature allows you to create precise scale relationships between model space viewports and paper space units. Now, we will use the annotative property to match dimension and text sizes to those zoom factors.

✔ If you have Drawing 5-2, the Flanged Bushing, as shown in Figure 8-52, open it. Otherwise, create an approximation as described below. Then click the **Layout1** tab.

**Figure 8-52**
Adding text in paper space

**1** Set limits to **(0,0)** and **(12,9).** This is critical. If you use different limits, the exercise is difficult to follow.

**2** Draw a circle with diameter 3.50 centered at (3.00,4.00).

**3** Draw a second circle with diameter 2.50 centered at the same point.

**4** Draw a small 0.25-diameter circle at the lower quadrant of the 2.50 circle.

**5** Draw a rectangle with first corner at (6.50,2.75) and second corner at (10.00,5.25).

**6** Open **Layout1** and create a layout with D-size limits, using the **Page Setup Manager.**

**7** Create three viewports, positioned as shown in Figure 8-52. The coordinates of the corners of the lower left viewport are (1,1) and (20,13). Those of the lower right viewport are (24,1) and (34,13). The upper viewport stretches from (1,14) to (9,20). The zoom factor for the large viewport should be 2xp. The smaller viewport to the right should be at 4xp, centered on the midpoint of the left side of the rectangle, and the smallest viewport at the top should be at 6xp, centered on the small circle at the quadrant of the 2.50 circle.

## Text in Paper Space and Model Space

Text drawn in paper space can be drawn at the 1:1 scale of the layout. Text drawn within viewports will be affected by the viewport scale. Try this:

✔ Double-click anywhere outside the viewports to ensure that you are in paper space.

✔ Pick the **Annotate** tab **> Text** tools drop-down list **> Single Line** text tool from the ribbon.

✔ Pick a start point outside any of the viewports. We chose (15,15).
   *Our text begins about 2.00 units above the right side of the left viewport, as shown in Figure 8-52.*

✔ Type **1 <Enter>** for a text height of 1 unit.

This assumes that you are using the D-size paper space limits. If not, you have to adjust for your own settings. On A-size paper the text height is about 0.25.

✔ Press **<Enter>** for 0° rotation.

✔ Type **Layout 1 <Enter>.**

✔ Press **<Enter>** again to exit.
   *Your screen should have text added, as shown in Figure 8-52.*

✔ Double-click in the lower left, largest viewport to enter model space in this viewport.

✔ Enter the **TEXT** command again.

✔ Pick a start point below the left view in the viewport, as shown in Figure 8-53.

**Figure 8-53**
Adding text in model space

✔ Press **<Enter>** to retain a height of 1.00 unit.

✔ Press **<Enter>** for 0° rotation.

✔ Type **Bushing <Enter>.**

✔ Press **<Enter>** again to exit the command.

*AutoCAD may move objects in the viewport to make room for the text. This should self-correct when you exit the command. Your screen should resemble Figure 8-53.*

What has happened here? Why is "Bushing" drawn twice as big as "Layout 1"? Do you remember the **Zoom XP** scale factor we used in this viewport? This viewport is enlarged by two times paper space, so any text you draw inside it is enlarged by a factor of 2 as well. If you want, try drawing text in either of the other two viewports. You will find that text in the right viewport is magnified four times the paper space size, and text in the uppermost viewport is magnified six times.

You can compensate for these enlargements by dividing text height by factors of 2, 4, and 6, but that can become very cumbersome. Furthermore, if you decided to change the zoom factor at a later date, you would have to re-create any text drawn within the altered viewport. Otherwise, your text sizes in the overall drawing would become inconsistent. The purpose of the annotative property is to add control in situations such as this.

## The Annotative Property

All types of objects used to annotate drawings can be defined as annotative. This annotative property allows you to attach one or more scales to the object. With the property and the correct scale, the scale of the object will match the scale of the viewport, and the annotation will appear at the desired size in paper space. Objects that can have the annotative property include text, dimensions, hatch patterns, tolerances, leaders, symbols, and other types of explanatory symbols, including ones you may define yourself. The property may be applied to individual annotative objects or may be included in a style definition.

We begin by adding the property to create text in the lower viewport at the appropriate scale.

✔ Erase "Bushing" from the lower left viewport.

✔ Pick the **Annotate** tab > **Text** panel > **Text styles** drop-down list > **Annotative** text style, as shown in Figure 8-54.

*Look at the right side of the status bar. If you are in model space in the lower left viewport, you should see a viewport scale indicator, as shown in Figure 8-55. The viewport scale should be 2:1, matching the scale of the current viewport. To the right of the **Viewport Scale** tool is the **Annotation Scale** tool, whose tooltip currently displays, "Annotation scale is not equal to viewport scale: Click to synchronize".*

**Figure 8-54**
**Annotative** text style

**Figure 8-55**
**Annotation Scale** tool

*By synchronizing the annotation scale with the viewport scale, we can cause annotative objects in this viewport to be scaled automatically.*

✔ On the status bar, pick the **Annotation Scale** tool.
*Notice that the viewport scale changes to 1:1. The current scale factor in paper space is 1:1, as usual. To synchronize the viewport scale, AutoCAD changes the viewport scale to match the paper scale. Notice the change in the viewport. We want to return it to 2:1.*

✔ On the status bar, pick the **Viewport Scale** tool and select **2:1** from the long pop-up list.
*The viewport image returns to its previous size. It may seem as though nothing has changed, but now that the annotation and viewport scales are synchronized, annotative text will be adjusted to match paper space units.*

*Now, we draw text in the Annotative style in the left viewport.*

✔ Pick the **Single Line** text tool from the ribbon.

✔ Pick a start point below the objects in the lower left viewport.

✔ Type **1 <Enter>** for a text height.

✔ Press **<Enter>** for 0° rotation.

✔ Type **Bushing <Enter>.**

✔ Press **<Enter>** again to exit the command.
*Your screen should resemble Figure 8-56.*

**Figure 8-56**
Results of **Annotation Scale**

## Controlling Annotation Scale Visibility

Next, we add some dimensions to our viewports and learn more about how scales and viewports can be managed. First, we switch to the Annotative dimension style and override the text of the style. This will be a temporary override; it does not change the default definition of the style.

✔ Pick **Annotate** tab **> Dimensions** panel **> Dimension Style** drop-down list **> Annotative.**

✔ Open the **Dimension Style Manager** by picking the small arrow at the right end of the **Dimensions** panel title bar.

✔ In the **Dimension Style Manager,** pick the **Override** button on the right.

✔ In the **Override Current Style** dialog box, pick the **Text** tab.
*The **Text** tab is shown in Figure 8-57.*

**Figure 8-57**
**Override Current Style** dialog box

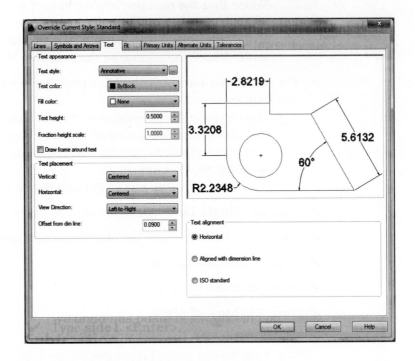

✔ As shown, change **Text height** to **0.5000.**
*When properly scaled, this should make our dimension text half as large as the 1.00 unit text currently showing in paper space and in the lower left viewport.*

✔ Click **OK** to exit the **Override Current Style** dialog box.

✔ Close the **Dimension Style Manager.**

✔ Open the **Dimension** tools drop-down list and pick the **Radius** tool.

✔ Pick the small bolt hole circle at the bottom quadrant of the bushing, as shown in Figure 8-58.

**Figure 8-58**
Picking the small bolt hole circle

✔ Pick a dimension location as shown.

*Your screen should resemble Figure 8-58. Notice that the dimension just added does not appear in the top viewport, even though the bolt hole being dimensioned is clearly visible in that viewport. The annotative property has also made this possible.*

*Look at the right side of the status bar again. To the right of the* **Annotation Scale** *tool, you see the tool illustrated in Figure 8-59. This is the AutoCAD annotation symbol with a tiny blue lightbulb image behind it. The tooltip for this tool will display, "Annotation Visibility: Show annotative objects for current scale only".*

**Figure 8-59**
**Annotation Visibility** tool

✔ Pick the **Annotation Visibility** tool.

*The tool changes to show a yellow (on) lightbulb. The tooltip now displays, "Annotation Visibility: Show annotative objects for all scales". Look closely at the upper left viewport. A large dimension leader has been added. If you were to pan to see the dimension text, you would see that it is 1.50 units high, three times the 0.50 unit height of the text in the lower left viewport. This, once again, is the result of the viewport scales, with the lower viewport at 2:1 and the upper viewport at 6:1.*

## Annotative Objects with Multiple Scales

But what if we want a dimension or other annotative object to appear in two different viewports and still retain the correct size in relation to paper space? This can be handled by assigning more than one scale to an annotative object or group of annotative objects. To complete this exploration we will add a linear dimension to the lower left viewport and assign it two scales, so that it will appear at the same height in the right viewport.

✔ You should be in the lower left viewport to begin this exercise.

✔ Pick the **Linear** tool from the **Dimension** tools drop-down list.

✔ Right-click to select an object to dimension.

✔ Pick the vertical side of the right view of the bushing, as shown in Figure 8-60.

✔ Pick a dimension line location, as shown.

*Your screen should resemble Figure 8-61. We have the familiar problem that the dimension text appears twice as large in the right viewport, where the viewport scale is 4:1 instead of 2:1, as it is in the lower left viewport. Our goal is to display this dimension in both viewports at the same size. This will require two changes. First we match the annotation scale to the viewport scale in this viewport. Second, we add a second scale to the dimension object so that it can be displayed at both scales.*

✔ Double-click in the right viewport.

*Notice here that the* **Viewport Scale** *tool on the status bar shows 4:1.*

**Figure 8-60**
Dimensioning right view of bushing

**Figure 8-61**
Text appears twice as large

✔ Pick the **Annotation Scale Synchronization** tool, to the right of the **Viewport Scale** indicator.

*The viewport scale changes to 1:1 to synchronize with the annotation scale, shrinking the objects in the viewport.*

✔ Open the **Viewport Scale** list and select **4:1.**

*Though it appears we have not accomplished anything, we now have a match between the viewport scale and the annotation scale in this viewport, but the dimension is still twice as large as in the left viewport.*

✔ Select the dimension.

*You may need to turn off snap to do this effectively. When the dimension is selected, you will see grips in both viewports.*

✔ Right-click to open the shortcut menu shown in Figure 8-62.

✔ Highlight **Annotative Object Scale** and then select **Add/Delete Scales,** as shown in the figure.

*This opens the **Annotation Object Scale** dialog box shown in Figure 8-63. Notice that **2:1** is the only scale showing in the **Object Scale List.***

✔ Pick the **Add** button.

*You see the **Add Scales to Object** dialog box shown in Figure 8-64.*

**Figure 8-62**
**Add/Delete Scales**

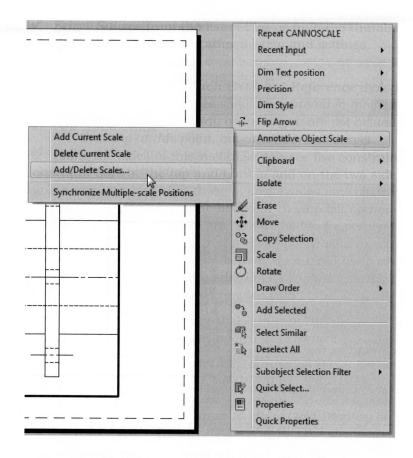

| | |
|---|---|
| Add Current Scale | |
| Delete Current Scale | |
| Add/Delete Scales... | |
| Synchronize Multiple-scale Positions | |

Repeat CANNOSCALE
Recent Input ▶

Dim Text position ▶
Precision ▶
Dim Style ▶
Flip Arrow

Annotative Object Scale ▶

Clipboard ▶

Isolate ▶

Erase
Move
Copy Selection
Scale
Rotate
Draw Order ▶

Add Selected

Select Similar
Deselect All

Subobject Selection Filter ▶
Quick Select...
Properties
Quick Properties

**Figure 8-63**
**Annotation Object Scale** dialog box

**Figure 8-64**
**Add Scales to Object** dialog box

    ✔ Select **4:1,** as shown.

    ✔ Click **OK.**
        *4:1 is added to the **Object Scale List** below 2:1.*

    ✔ Click **OK** to return to the drawing.
        *The dimension in the right viewport is adjusted to the 4:1 scale in*
        *the right viewport.*

✔ Finally, pick the **Annotation Visibility** tool again.

*The oversized dimension in the upper viewport vanishes, but the scaled dimension in the right viewport remains. Your screen resembles Figure 8-65.*

**Figure 8-65**
Scale is adjusted in right viewport

## Turning Viewport Borders Off

We have used the borders of our viewports as part of our plotted drawings in this drawing layout. Frequently, you want to turn them off. In a typical three-view drawing, for example, you do not draw borders around the three views.

In multiple-viewport paper space layouts, the visibility of viewport borders is easily controlled by putting the viewports on a separate layer and then turning the layer off before plotting. You can make a "border" layer, for example, and make it current while you create viewports. You can also use the **Quick Properties** panel to move viewports to the border layer later.

# Chapter Summary

You now have solid knowledge of AutoCAD's extensive dimensioning capabilities. You can create and save dimension styles much as you previously created text styles. You can create dimensions in numerous common formats including linear and aligned dimensions, radius and diameter dimensions, baseline or continued dimensions, and dimensions using leaders and multileaders. You can apply several dimensions at once using **QDIM;** and you can edit dimension placement, dimension text content, and dimension properties. To further enhance your drawings, you also know how to add hatch and gradient patterns to your drawings. Finally, you learned the uses of associative dimensions and of the annotative property, which allows you to control the scaling of text so that it is consistent among viewports and in paper space.

# Chapter Test Questions

## Multiple Choice

*Circle the correct answer.*

1. To move the origin point of a drawing use the:
   a. **MOVE** command
   b. **ORIGIN** command
   c. **UCS** command
   d. **UCSICON** command

2. Which of the following does **not** adjust when an object with associative dimensions is moved?
   a. Start point of a leader
   b. Text of a radius dimension
   c. Text of a linear dimension
   d. Multileader text

3. Which of the following **cannot** be hatched using the **HATCH** command?
   a. A 355° arc
   b. A rectangle
   c. A circle
   d. An irregular quadrilateral

4. Dimension units are set in the:
   a. **Units** dialog box
   b. **Dimension Style** dialog box
   c. **Dimension Units** dialog box
   d. **Annotation** dialog box

**5.** The default dimension style is called:

 a. Annotative

 b. Linear

 c. Standard

 d. Dimstyle

## Matching

*Write the number of the correct answer on the line.*

a. Multiple dimension _____    1. Viewport scale

b. Datum point _____    2. Baseline

c. UCS origin _____    3. **DIMORDINATE**

d. Vertex _____    4. **DIMANGULAR**

e. Annotative dimension _____    5. **QDIM**

## True or False

*Circle the correct answer.*

**1. True or False:** By default, dimension style units are the same as drawing units.

**2. True or False:** Mtext is drawn within a rectangular box defined by the user.

**3. True or False:** The default dimension style is Annotative.

**4. True or False:** Center-justified text and middle-justified text are two names for the same thing.

**5. True or False:** Fonts are created based on text styles.

## Questions

**1.** You are working in a drawing with units set to architectural, but when you begin dimensioning, AutoCAD provides four-place decimal units. What is the problem? What do you need to do so that your dimensioning units match your drawing units?

**2.** What is a **Nearest** object snap, and why is it important when dimensioning with leaders?

**3.** Why is it useful to move the origin of the coordinate system to make good use of ordinate dimensioning? What option to do this is available in the **QDIM** command?

**4.** What is associative dimensioning? What command makes a nonassociative dimension associative?

**5.** Paper space is at a 1:1 plotting scale; two viewports in a layout are at 8:1 and 2:1 viewport scales. What do you have to do so that a single annotation object will appear at the same scale in both viewports?

## Drawing Problems

1. Create a new dimension style called Dim-2. Dim-2 uses architectural units with 1/2″ precision for all units except angles, which use two-place decimals. Text in Dim-2 is 0.5 unit high.

2. Draw an isosceles triangle with vertexes at (4,3), (14,3), and (9,11). Draw a 2-unit circle centered at the center of the triangle.

3. Dimension the base and one side of the triangle using the Dim-2 dimension style.

4. Add a diameter dimension to the circle, and change a dimension variable so that the circle is dimensioned with a diameter line drawn inside the circle.

5. Add an angle dimension to one of the base angles of the triangle. Make sure that the dimension is placed outside the triangle.

6. Hatch the area inside the triangle and outside the circle using any predefined crosshatch pattern.

## WWW Exercise (Optional)

In Chapter 8 of our companion website, we challenge you to find information on a great innovator in the field of graphic arts whose name has come up in this chapter. We give you links to get you started and then send you on your way. We also offer you another design challenge and, as always, the self-scoring test for this chapter. So, when you are ready, complete the following:

✔ Make sure that you are connected to your Internet service provider.

✔ Type **browser <Enter>.**

✔ If necessary, navigate to our companion website at www.pearsonhighered.com/dixriley.
    *Happy hunting!*

## Chapter Drawing Projects

## Drawing 8-1: *Tool Block* [INTERMEDIATE]

In this drawing, the dimensions should work well without editing. The hatch is a simple user-defined pattern used to indicate that the front and right views are sectioned views.

### Drawing Suggestions

GRID = 1.0

SNAP = 0.125

HATCH line spacing = 0.125

- As a general rule, complete the drawing first, including all crosshatching, and then add dimensions and text at the end.

- Place all hatching on the **hatch** layer. When hatching is complete, set to the **dim** layer and turn the **hatch** layer off so that hatch lines do not interfere when you select lines for dimensioning.

- The section lines in this drawing can be easily drawn as leaders. Set the dimension arrow size to **0.38** first. Check to see that **Ortho** is on; then begin the leader at the tip of the arrow and make a right angle as shown. After picking the other endpoint of the leader, press **<Enter>** to bring up the first line of annotation prompt. Type a space and press **<Enter>** so you have no text. Press **<Enter>** again to exit.

- You need to set the **DIMTIX** variable to **On** to place the 3.25-diameter dimension at the center of the circle in the top view and **Off** to create the leader style diameter dimension in the front section.

**Drawing 8-1**
Tool Block

## Drawing 8-2: *Flanged Wheel* [INTERMEDIATE]

Most of the objects in this drawing are straightforward. The keyway is easily done using the **TRIM** command. If necessary, use the **Edit** shortcut menu or grips to move the diameter dimension, as shown in the reference.

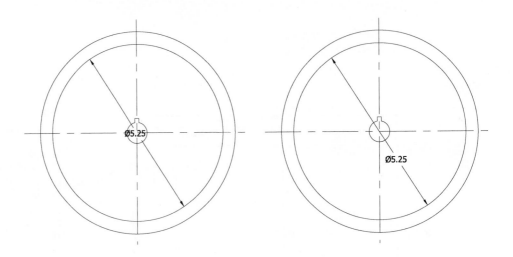

### Drawing Suggestions

GRID = 0.25

SNAP = 0.0625

HATCH line spacing = 0.50

- You need a 0.0625 snap to draw the keyway. Draw a $0.125 \times 0.125$ square at the top of the 0.63-diameter circle. Drop the vertical lines down into the circle so they can be used to trim the circle. **TRIM** the circle and the vertical lines, using a window to select both as cutting edges.

- Remember to set to layer **hatch** before hatching, layer **text** before adding text, and layer **dim** before dimensioning.

**Drawing 8-2**
Flanged Wheel

KEYWAY
0.12 W × 0.12 H

Ø6.00

R1.00

Ø5.25

Ø0.62

1.00

2.00

5.00

**Drawing 8-3: *Knob* [INTERMEDIATE]**

This drawing makes use of the procedures for hatching and dimensioning you learned in the last two drawings. In addition, it uses an angular dimension, leaders, and %%c for the diameter symbol.

## Drawing Suggestions

GRID = 0.125

SNAP = 0.0625

HATCH lines pacing = 0.25

- You can save some time on this drawing by using **MIRROR** to create half of the right-side view. Notice, however, that you cannot hatch before mirroring because the **MIRROR** command reverses the angle of the hatch lines.

- Create a polar array with a 0.625-diameter circle to get the indentations in the knob on the circular views. Trim as necessary.

- Add the notes to the hole dimensions by using the **DIMEDIT** command.

- Notice that the diameter symbols in the vertical dimensions on the right-side view are not automatic. Use %%c to add the diameter symbol to the text.

**Drawing 8-3**
Knob

# Drawing 8-4: *Nose Adapter* [INTERMEDIATE]

Make ample use of **ZOOM** to work on the details of this drawing. Notice that the limits are set larger than usual, and the snap is rather fine by comparison.

## Drawing Suggestions

LIMITS = (0,0) (36,24)

GRID = 0.25

SNAP = 0.125

HATCH line spacing = 0.25

- You need a 0.125 snap to draw the thread representation shown in the reference. Understand that this is nothing more than a standard representation for screw threads; it does not show actual dimensions. Zoom in close to draw it, and you should have no trouble.

- This drawing includes two examples of simplified drafting practice. The thread representation is one, and the other is the way in which the counterbores are drawn in the front view. A precise rendering of these holes would show an ellipse because the slant of the object dictates that they break through on an angle. However, to show these ellipses in the front view would make the drawing more confusing and less useful. Simplified representation is preferable in such cases.

(thread representation)

30° TYP

0.125

Reference

0.25 DIA THRU
C'BORE 0.50 DIA 2 0.625 DEEP
4 HOLES EQ SP AS SHOWN

2.75

1.625

0.50

30°

Ø6.00
REF

Ø11.00

6.00 PITCH DIA
12 THREADS PER INCH

(SEE REFERENCE)

Ø8.00

**Drawing 8-4**
Nose Adapter

**A** Drawing 8-5: *Plot Plan* [INTERMEDIATE]

This architectural drawing makes use of three hatch patterns and several dimension variable changes. Be sure to make these settings as shown.

## Drawing Suggestions

GRID = 10′

SNAP = 1′

LIMITS = (0′,0′)(180′,120′)

LTSCALE = 2′

- The "trees" shown here are symbols for oaks, willows, and evergreens.
- **HATCH** opens a space around text inside a defined boundary; however, sometimes you want more white space than **HATCH** leaves. A simple solution is to draw a rectangle around the text area as an inner boundary. Later you can erase the box, leaving an island of white space around the text.

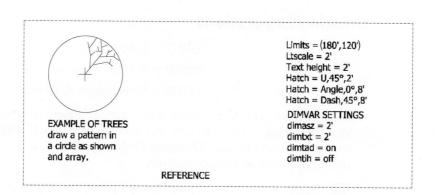

EXAMPLE OF TREES
draw a pattern in
a circle as shown
and array.

REFERENCE

Limits = (180',120')
Ltscale = 2'
Text height = 2'
Hatch = U,45°,2'
Hatch = Angle,0°,8'
Hatch = Dash,45°,8'

DIMVAR SETTINGS
dimasz = 2'
dimtxt = 2'
dimtad = on
dimtih = off

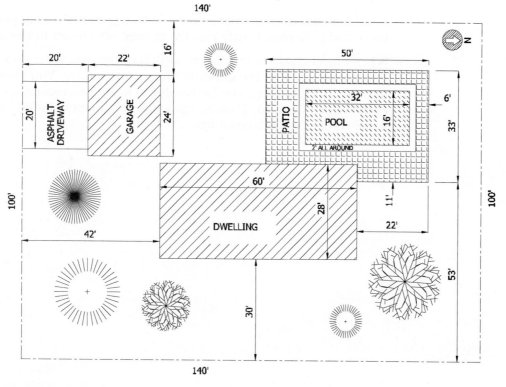

**Drawing 8-5**
Plot Plan

# Drawing 8-6: *Panel* [ADVANCED]

This drawing is primarily an exercise in using ordinate dimensions. Both the drawing of the objects and the adding of dimensions are facilitated dramatically by this powerful feature.

## Drawing Suggestions

GRID = 0.50

SNAP = 0.125

UNITS = three-place decimal

- After setting grid, snap, and units, create a new user coordinate system with the origin moved in and up about 1 unit each way. This technique was introduced in the "Drawing Ordinate Dimensions" section. For reference, here is the procedure:

  **1** Select **View** tab > **Coordinates** panel > **Origin** tool from the ribbon.

  **2** Pick a new origin point.

- From here on, all the objects in the drawing can be easily placed using the $x$ and $y$ displacements exactly as they are shown in the drawing.

- When objects have been placed, switch to the **dim** layer and begin dimensioning using the ordinate dimension feature. You should be able to move along quickly, but be careful to keep dimensions on each side of the panel lined up. That is, the leader endpoints should end along the same vertical or horizontal line.

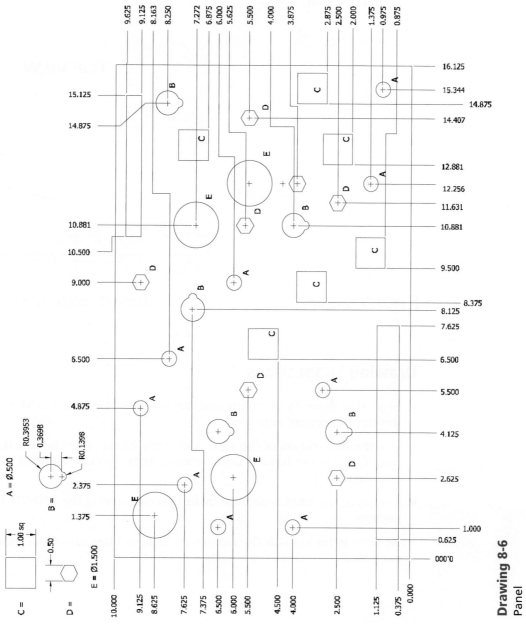

**Drawing 8-6**
Panel

# Drawing 8-7: *Angle Support* [ADVANCED]

In this drawing, you are expected to use the 3D view to create three orthographic views. Draw a front view, top view, and side view. The front and top views are drawn showing all necessary hidden lines, and the right-side view is drawn in full section. The finished multiview drawing should be fully dimensioned.

TOP VIEW

FRONT VIEW                    RIGHT SIDE VIEW

## Drawing Suggestions

- Start this drawing by laying out the top view. Use the top view to line up the front view and side view.

- Use the illustration of the right-side view when planning out the full section. Convert the hidden lines to solid lines and use **HATCH** to create crosshatching.

- Complete the right-side view in full section, using the ANSI31 hatch pattern.

- Be sure to include all the necessary hidden lines and centerlines in each view.

Right Side View

**Drawing 8-7**
Angle Support

**Drawing 8-8:** *Mirror Mounting Plate*
**[ADVANCED]**

This drawing introduces AutoCAD's geometric tolerancing capability, an additional feature of the dimension system. Geometric tolerancing symbols and values are added using a simple dialog box interface. For example, to add the tolerance values and symbols below the leadered dimension text on the 0.128-diameter hole at the top middle of the drawing, follow these steps. All other tolerances in the drawing are created in the same manner.

- After creating the objects in the drawing, create the leadered dimension text beginning with .128 DIA THRU . . . as shown.

- Select **Tolerance** from the **Dimension** menu, or pick the **Tolerance** tool from the **Dimensions** panel extension, as illustrated in Figure 8-66.

- Fill in the values and symbols as shown in Figure 8-67. To fill in the first black symbol box, click the box and select a symbol. To fill in the diameter symbol, click the second black box, and the symbol is filled in automatically. To fill in any of the **Material Condition** boxes, click the box and select a symbol.

- Click **OK**.

- Drag the **Tolerance** boxes into place below the dimension text, as shown in the drawing.

**Figure 8-66**
**Tolerance** tool

**Figure 8-67**
**Geometric Tolerance** dialog box

# 9 chapternine
## Polylines

# CHAPTER OBJECTIVES

- Draw polygons
- Draw donuts
- Use the **FILL** command
- Draw straight polyline segments
- Draw polyline arc segments
- Edit polylines with **PEDIT**

- Draw splines
- Create path arrays
- Draw revision clouds
- Draw points
- Use constraint parameters
- Use AutoConstrain and inferred constraints

## Introduction

This chapter should be fun, because you will be learning a large number of new commands. You will see new things happening on your screen with each command. The commands in this chapter are used to create special entities, some of which cannot be drawn any other way. All of them are complex objects made up of lines, circles, and arcs, but they are stored and treated as singular entities. Some of them, such as polygons and donuts, are familiar geometric figures, whereas others, such as polylines, are peculiar to CAD. We will also return to the **ARRAY** command to create path arrays built along curved paths. In addition to these new entities you will learn a new drawing method by applying geometric and dimensional constraints to previously drawn objects to achieve design objectives.

| POLYGON | |
|---|---|
| **Command** | Polygon |
| **Alias** | Pol |
| **Panel** | Draw |
| **Tool** | 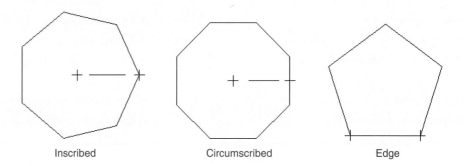 |

# Drawing Polygons

> **TIP**
>
> A general procedure for drawing polygons is:
>
> 1. Pick the **Polygon** tool from the **Draw** panel extension of the ribbon.
> 2. Type the number of sides.
> 3. Pick a center point.
> 4. Indicate inscribed or circumscribed.
> 5. Show the radius of the circle.

Among the most interesting and flexible of the entities you can create in AutoCAD is the *polyline*, a two-dimensional object made of lines and arcs that may have varying widths. In this chapter, we begin with two regularly shaped polyline entities, polygons and donuts. These entities have their own special commands, separate from the general **PLINE** command ("Drawing Straight Polyline Segments" and "Drawing Polyline Arc Segments" sections), but are created as polylines and can be edited just as any other polyline would be.

Polygons with any number of sides can be drawn using the **POLYGON** command. In the default sequence, AutoCAD constructs a polygon based on the number of sides, the center point, and a radius. Optionally, the **Edge** option allows you to specify the number of sides and the length and position of one side (see Figure 9-1).

**Figure 9-1**
Polygon drawing methods

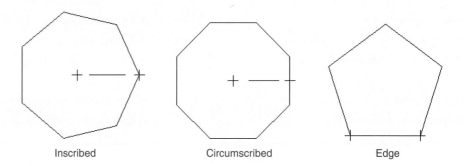

Inscribed          Circumscribed          Edge

✔ Create a new drawing with 18 × 12 limits.

✔ Pick the **Polygon** tool from the list under the **Rectangle** tool on the **Draw** panel, as shown in Figure 9-2.

*AutoCAD's first prompt is for the number of sides:*

Enter number of sides <4>:

**Figure 9-2**
**Polygon** tool

✔ Type **8 <Enter>.**
*Next, you are prompted to show either a center point or the first point of one edge:*

Specify center of polygon or [Edge]:

✔ Pick a center point, as shown by the center mark on the left in Figure 9-3.
*From here the size of the polygon can be specified in one of two ways, as shown in Figure 9-1. The radius of a circle is given, and the polygon is drawn either inside or outside the imaginary circle. In the case of the inscribed polygon this means that the radius is measured from the center to a vertex of the polygon. In the circumscribed polygon the radius is measured from the center to the midpoint of a side. You indicate which option you want by typing*
***i*** *or* ***c,*** *or by selecting from the dynamic input menu. The prompt is:*

Enter an option [Inscribed in circle Circumscribed about circle] :

**Inscribed** *is the default. We use the* **Circumscribed** *option instead.*

**Figure 9-3**
Polygon **Circumscribed** and **Edge** options

✔ Select **Circumscribed about circle** from the dynamic input menu or the command line.
*Now, you are prompted to show a radius of this imaginary circle (i.e., a line from the center to the midpoint of a side):*

Specify radius of circle:

✔ Pick a radius similar to the one in Figure 9-3.
*We leave it to you to try the* **Inscribed** *option. We draw one more polygon, using the* **Edge** *option.*

✔ Press **<Enter>** or the spacebar to repeat the **POLYGON** command.

✔ Type **5 <Enter>** for the number of sides.

✔ Type **e <Enter>** or select **Edge** from the command line.
*AutoCAD issues a different series of prompts:*

Specify first endpoint of edge:

✔ Pick point 1, as shown on the right in Figure 9-3.
*AutoCAD prompts:*

Specify second endpoint of edge:

✔ Pick a second point as shown.
*Your screen should resemble Figure 9-3.*

| DONUT | |
|---|---|
| **Command** | Donut |
| **Alias** | Do |
| **Panel** | Draw |
| **Tool** | |

# Drawing Donuts

A donut in AutoCAD is a polyline object represented by two concentric circles. The donut is the space between the circles.

The **DONUT** command is logical and easy to use. You show a center point and inside and outside diameters and then draw as many donut-shaped objects of the specified size as you like.

✔ Clear your display of polygons before continuing.

✔ Pick the **Donut** tool from the **Draw** panel extension of the ribbon, as shown in Figure 9-4.

> *AutoCAD prompts:*
>
> Specify inside diameter of donut <0.50>:
>
> *We change the inside diameter to 1.00.*

**Figure 9-4**
**Donut** tool

✔ Type **1 <Enter>**.

> *AutoCAD prompts:*
>
> Specify outside diameter of donut <1.00>:
>
> *We change the outside diameter to 2.00.*

✔ Type **2 <Enter>**.

> *AutoCAD prompts:*
>
> Specify center of donut or [exit]:

✔ Pick any point.

> *A donut is drawn around the point you chose, as shown by the "fat" donuts in Figure 9-5. (If your donut is not filled, see the next section, "Using the FILL Command.")*
>
> *AutoCAD stays in the* **DONUT** *command, allowing you to continue drawing donuts.*

**Figure 9-5**
Donuts drawn with **FILL** on

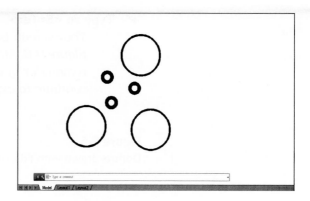

✔ Pick a second center point.

✔ Pick a third center point.
*You should now have three "fat" donuts on your screen as shown.*

✔ Press **<Enter>** or right-click to exit the **DONUT** command.
*Now draw the "thin" donuts in the figure.*

✔ Repeat **DONUT.**

✔ Change the inside diameter to **3.00** and the outside diameter to **3.25.**

✔ Draw three or four "thin" donuts, as shown in Figure 9-5.
*When you are done, leave the donuts on the screen so that you can see how they are affected by the **FILL** command.*

## Using the FILL Command

> **TIP**
> A general procedure for turning **FILL** on and off is:
> 1. Type **fill <Enter>**.
> 2. Select **on** or **off.**
> 3. Type **re <Enter>** or select **Regen** from the **View** menu.

Donuts and wide polylines (in the "Drawing Straight Polyline Segments" and "Drawing Polyline Arc Segments" sections) are all affected by **FILL.** With **FILL** on, these entities are displayed and plotted as solid filled objects. With **FILL** off, only the outer boundaries are displayed. (Donuts are shown with radial lines between the inner and outer circles.)

✔ For this exercise, you should have at least one donut on your screen from the "Drawing Donuts" section.

✔ Type **fill <Enter>.**
*AutoCAD prompts:*

Enter Mode [ON OFF] <ON>:

*These options are also shown on the dynamic input menu.*

✔ Select **off** from the dynamic input menu.
*You do not see any immediate change in your display when you do this. To see the effect, you have to regenerate your drawing.*

✔ Type **re <Enter>.**

*Your screen is regenerated with **FILL** off and should resemble Figure 9-6. Many of the special entities that we discuss in the remainder of this chapter can be filled, so we encourage you to continue to experiment with **FILL** as you go along.*

**Figure 9-6**
Donuts drawn with **FILL** off

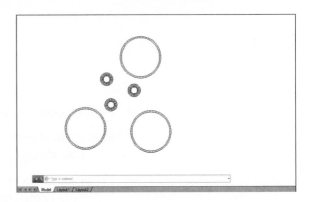

| PLINE | |
|---|---|
| **Command** | Pline |
| **Alias** | Pl |
| **Panel** | Draw |
| **Tool** | |

## Drawing Straight Polyline Segments

> **TIP**
> A general procedure for drawing straight polylines is:
> 1. Pick the **Polyline** tool from the **Draw** panel of the ribbon.
> 2. Pick a start point.
> 3. Type or select **Width, Halfwidth,** or other options.
> 4. Pick other points.

Text, dimensions, and hatch patterns are all created as complex entities that can be selected and treated as single objects. In this chapter, we are focusing on the polyline. You have already drawn several polylines without going through the **PLINE** command. Donuts and polygons both are drawn as polylines and therefore can be edited using the same edit commands that work on other polylines. You can, for instance, fillet all the corners of a polygon at once, using the **Pline** option in the **FILLET** command. Using the **PLINE** command itself, you can draw anything from a simple line to a series of lines and arcs with varying widths. Most important, you can edit polylines using many of the ordinary edit commands as well as a set of specialized editing procedures found in the **PEDIT** command.

We begin by creating a simple polyline rectangle. The process is much like drawing a rectangular outline with the **LINE** command, but the result is a single object rather than four distinct line segments.

✔ Clear your display of donuts before continuing.

✔ Pick the **Polyline** tool from the **Draw** panel of the ribbon, as shown in Figure 9-7.

*AutoCAD begins with a prompt for a starting point, as in the **LINE** command:*

Specify start point:

✔ Pick a start point, similar to P1 in Figure 9-8.

*From here the **PLINE** prompt sequence becomes more complicated:*

Current line width is 0.00
Specify next point or [Arc Halfwidth Length Undo Width]:

**Figure 9-7**
**Polyline** tool

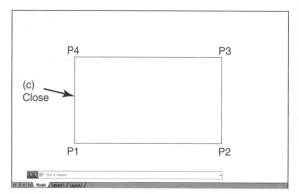

**Figure 9-8**
Drawing a closed polyline rectangle

*The prompt begins by giving you the current line width, left from any previous use of the **PLINE** command.*

*Then, the prompt offers options in the usual format. The **Arc** option leads you into another set of options that deals with drawing polyline arcs. We save polyline arcs for the next section. We get to the other options momentarily.*

*Here we draw a series of 0-width segments, just as we would in the **LINE** command.*

> **NOTE**
>
> • The **Close** option is very important in drawing closed polylines. AutoCAD recognizes the polyline as a closed object only if you use the **Close** option.
>
> • The **Halfwidth** option differs from the **Width** option only in that the width of the line to be drawn is measured from the center out. With either option, you can specify by showing a width rather than typing a value.

✔ Pick an endpoint, similar to P2 in Figure 9-8.

*AutoCAD draws the segment and repeats the prompt. Notice that after you have picked two points, AutoCAD adds a **Close** option to the command line prompt.*

✔ Pick another endpoint, P3 in Figure 9-8.

✔ Pick another endpoint, P4 in Figure 9-8.

✔ Type **c <Enter>** or right-click and select **Close** from the shortcut menu to complete the rectangle, as shown in Figure 9-8.

✔ Now, run the cursor over any part of the polyline rectangle.

*You can see that the entire rectangle is previewed, rather than just the side you pointed to. This means, for example, that you can fillet or chamfer all four corners of the rectangle at once.*

Now, let's create a rectangle with wider lines.

✔ Enter the **PLINE** command.

✔ Pick a starting point, as shown by P1 in Figure 9-9.
*AutoCAD prompts:*

> Specify next point or [Arc Close Halfwidth Length Undo Width]:

*This time we need to make use of the* **Width** *option.*

**Figure 9-9**
Drawing an outer closed
polyline rectangle

✔ Type **w <Enter>** or select **Width** from the command line.
*AutoCAD responds with:*

> Specify starting width <0.00>:

*You are prompted for two widths, a starting width and an ending width. This makes it possible to draw tapered lines. For this exercise, our lines have the same starting and ending width.*

✔ Type **.25 <Enter>.**
*AutoCAD prompts:*

> Specify ending width <0.25>:

*Notice that the starting width has become the default for the ending width. To draw a polyline of uniform width, we accept this default.*

✔ Press **<Enter>** or the spacebar to keep the starting width and ending width the same.
*AutoCAD returns to the previous prompt and gives you a .25-wide rubber band to drag on the screen.*

✔ Pick an endpoint, as shown by P2 in Figure 9-9.

✔ Continue picking points P3 and P4 to draw a second rectangle, as shown in Figure 9-9. Use the **Close** option to draw the last side.
*When the object is complete, AutoCAD creates joined corners. If you do not close the last side, the lower left corner overlaps rather than joins. Be aware also that once a polyline has been given a width, it is affected by the* **FILL** *setting.*

The only options we have not discussed in this exercise are **Length** and **Undo. Length** allows you to type or show a value and then draws a segment of that length starting from the endpoint of the previous segment and continuing in the same direction. (If the last segment was an arc, the length is drawn tangent to the arc.) **Undo** undoes the last segment, just as in **LINE.**

In the next task, we draw polyline arc segments.

# Drawing Polyline Arc Segments

> **TIP**
>
> A general procedure for drawing polyline arcs is:
>
> 1. Enter the **PLINE** command.
> 2. Pick a start point.
> 3. Specify a width.
> 4. Type a **<Enter>** or select **Arc** from the command line.
> 5. Type or select options or pick an endpoint.

A word of caution: Because of the flexibility and power of the **PLINE** command, it is tempting to think of polylines as always having weird shapes, tapered lines, and strange sequences of lines and arcs. Remember, **PLINE** may also be used to create simple sets of lines, polygons, or arcs.

Having said that, we proceed to construct our own weird shape to show what can be done. We draw a polyline with three arc segments and one tapered line segment, as shown in Figure 9-10. We call this thing a goose-necked funnel. You may have seen something like it at your local garage.

**Figure 9-10**
Drawing a goosenecked funnel

- ✔ Enter the **PLINE** command.

- ✔ Pick a new start point, as shown by P1 in Figure 9-10.

- ✔ Type **w <Enter>** or select **Width** from the command line to set new widths.

- ✔ Type **0 <Enter>** for the starting width.

- ✔ Type **.5 <Enter>** for the ending width.

- ✔ Type **a <Enter>** or select **Arc** from the command line.
  *This opens the arc prompt, which looks like this:*

  > Specify endpoint of arc or
  > [Angle CEnter Direction Halfwidth Line Radius Secondpt Undo Width]:

  *Let's look at this prompt for a moment. To begin with, there are four options that are familiar from the previous prompt. **Halfwidth, Undo,** and **Width** all function exactly as they would in drawing straight polyline segments. The **Line** option returns you to the previous prompt so that you can continue drawing straight line segments after drawing arc segments.*

  *The other options, **Angle, CEnter, Direction, Radius, Secondpt,** and **Endpoint of arc,** allow you to specify arcs in ways* similar to those in the **ARC** command. AutoCAD assumes that the arc you are constructing will be tangent to the last polyline segment entered. You can override this assumption with the **CEnter** and **Direction** options, which allow you to establish different directions.

✔ Pick an endpoint to the right, as shown by P2 in Figure 9-10, to complete the first arc segment.

---
**TIP**

If you did not follow the order shown in the figures and drew your previous rectangle clockwise, or if you drew other polylines in the meantime, you may find that the arc does not curve below the horizontal, as shown in Figure 9-10. This is because AutoCAD starts arcs tangent to the last polyline segment drawn. Fix this by using the **Direction** option. Type **d <Enter>** and then pick a point straight down. Now, you can pick an endpoint to the right, as shown.

---

*AutoCAD prompts again:*

> Specify endpoint of arc or
>
> [Angle CEnter CLose Direction Halfwidth Line Radius Secondpt Undo Width]:

*For the remaining two arc segments, retain a uniform width of 0.50.*

✔ Enter points P3 and P4 to draw the remaining two arc segments as shown.
*Now, we draw two straight segments to complete the polyline.*

✔ Right-click and select **Line** from the shortcut menu.
*This takes you back to the original prompt.*

✔ Pick P5 straight up about 1.00 unit, as shown.

✔ Right-click and select **Width** from the shortcut menu.

✔ Press **<Enter>** to retain 0.50 as the starting width.

✔ Type **3 <Enter>** for the ending width.

✔ Pick an endpoint up about 2.00 units, as shown by P6.

✔ Press **<Enter>** or the spacebar to exit the command.
*Your screen should resemble Figure 9-10.*

## Editing Polylines with PEDIT

| PEDIT | |
|---|---|
| **Command** | Pedit |
| **Alias** | Pe |
| **Panel** | Modify |
| **Tool** | |

The **PEDIT** command provides a subsystem of special editing capabilities that work only on polylines. We do not attempt to have you use all of them. Most important is that you be aware of the possibilities so that when you find yourself in a situation calling for a **PEDIT** procedure, you know what to look for. After executing the following steps, study Figure 9-14, the **PEDIT** chart.

We perform two edits on the polylines already drawn.

✔ Pick the **Edit Polyline** tool from the **Modify** panel extension, as shown in Figure 9-11.
*This executes the **PEDIT** command. You are prompted to select a polyline:*

> Select polyline or [Multiple]:

**Figure 9-11**
**Edit Polyline** tool

✔ Select the outer 0-width polyline rectangle drawn in the "Drawing Straight Polyline Segments" section.

*Notice that **PEDIT** works on only one object at a time. You are prompted as follows:*

> Enter an option [Open Join Width Edit
> vertex Fit Spline Decurve Ltype gen Reverse Undo]:

*These same options are displayed in a drop-down menu on the dynamic input display. **Open** is replaced by **Close** if your polyline has not been closed. **Undo** is self-explanatory. Other options are illustrated in Figure 9-14. **Edit vertex** brings up the subset of options shown on the right side of the chart. When you do vertex editing, AutoCAD marks one vertex at a time with an X. You can move the X to other vertices by pressing **<Enter>** or typing **n.***

*Now, we edit the selected polyline by changing its width.*

✔ Type **w <Enter>** or select **Width** from the dynamic input display menu or the command line.

*This option allows you to set a new uniform width for an entire polyline. All tapering and variation are removed when this edit is performed.*

*AutoCAD prompts:*

> Specify new width for all segments:

✔ Type **.25 <Enter>.**

*Your screen is redrawn to resemble Figure 9-12.*

*The prompt is returned and the polyline is still selected so that you can continue shaping it with other **PEDIT** options.*

**Figure 9-12**
Changed polyline width

✔ Press **<Enter>** or the spacebar to exit **PEDIT.** This exiting and reentering is necessary to select another polyline to edit, using a different type of edit. This time we illustrate another way to enter the **PEDIT** command.

✔ Select the goosenecked funnel polyline.

✔ Right-click to open the shortcut menu.

✔ Highlight **Polyline** and select **Edit Polyline** from the submenu.

*This time we try the **Decurve** option, which straightens all curves within the selected polyline.*

✔ Type **d <Enter>** or select **Decurve** from the dynamic input display menu or the command line.

✔ Press **<Enter>** or the spacebar to exit **PEDIT**.

*Your screen should resemble Figure 9-13.*

To complete this exercise, we suggest that you try some of the other editing options. In particular, you can get interesting results from **Fit** and **Spline.** Be sure to study the **PEDIT** chart (Figure 9-14) before going on to the next task.

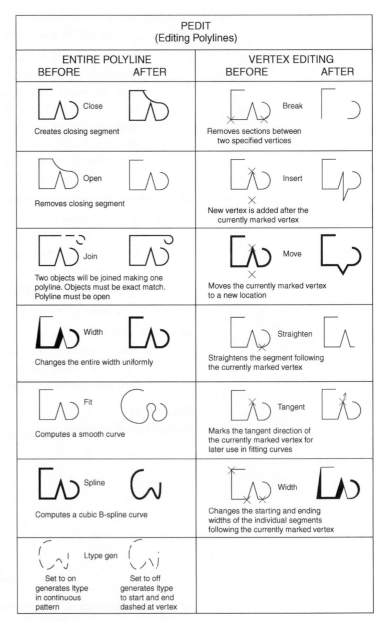

**Figure 9-14**
Polyline editing chart

**Figure 9-13**
Decurved polyline

| SPLINE | |
|---|---|
| **Command** | Spline |
| **Alias** | Spl |
| **Panel** | Draw |
| **Tool** |  |

**spline:** A smooth curve passing through or near a specified set of points according to a mathematical formula.

# Drawing Splines

> **TIP**
>
> A general procedure for drawing spline curves is:
>
> 1. Pick the **Spline Fit** tool from the **Draw** panel extension of the ribbon.
> 2. Pick points.
> 3. Close or specify start and end tangent directions.

A **spline** is a smooth curve passing through or near a specified set of points. In AutoCAD, splines are created in a precise mathematical form called *nonuniform rational B-spline* (NURBS). Splines can be drawn to fit the specified points, or to be controlled by a framework of vertices. In either case, splines can be drawn with varying degrees of tolerance, meaning the degree to which the curve is constrained by the defining points. In addition to tolerance and the set of points needed to define a spline, tangent directions can be specified for the starting and ending portions of the curve. Splines can be used to create any smooth curve that can be defined by a set of control points. In this task, we use a simple fit point **SPLINE** to draw a curve surrounding the polylines drawn in previous sections.

✔ Pick the **Spline Fit** tool from the **Draw** panel extension, as shown in Figure 9-15.

　　*AutoCAD prompts:*

　　　Specify first point or [Method Knots Object]:

　　*We will specify a point. The **Method** option allows you to switch from the fit point method to a control vertices method. **Knots** gives you a choice among three ways in which the spline curve may fit the specified points. Based on distinct mathematical formulae, each will yield a slightly different curve. **Object** converts polylines to equivalent splines.*

✔ Pick a point roughly 1.00 unit to the left of the top element of the horizontal polyline, P1, as shown in Figure 9-16.

　　*AutoCAD prompts:*

　　　Enter next point or [start Tangency toLerance Undo]:

　　*You can continue to enter fit points, specify a tangent direction for the beginning of the curve, or specify a tolerance value.*

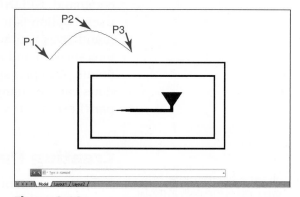

**Figure 9-15**
**Spline Fit** tool

**Figure 9-16**
Pick points P1, P2, P3 then <Enter>

✔ Pick a second point about 1.00 unit above the left side of the horizontal polyline, P2, as shown in Figure 9-16.

*As soon as you have two points, AutoCAD shows a spline that drags with your cursor as you select a third point. The prompt also changes:*

Enter next point or [end Tangency toLerance Undo]:

***End Tangency*** *has replaced* ***start Tangency, toLerance*** *is still available for change, and you can undo your last segment.*

✔ Pick a third point, P3, as shown in Figure 9-16.

*Now that you have three points, a* ***Close*** *option is added. From here on, you are on your own as you continue entering points to surround the polylines. We have made no attempt to specify precise points. We used 12 points to go all the way around without crossing the polylines, as shown in Figure 9-17. The exact number of points you choose is not important for this task.*

**Figure 9-17**
Pick points P1 to P12 then press <Enter>

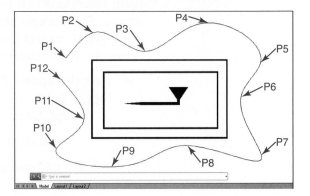

✔ Continue selecting points to surround the polylines without touching them.

✔ After you reach and pick a point similar to P12 in Figure 9-17, press **<Enter>** or the spacebar.

*This indicates that you are finished specifying points.*
*Your screen resembles Figure 9-17.*

## Editing Splines

Splines can be edited in the usual ways, but they also have their own edit command, **SPLINEDIT.** Because splines are defined by sets of points, one useful option is to use grips to move grip points. The **SPLINEDIT** command gives you additional options, including the option to change the tolerance, to add fit points for greater definition, or to delete unnecessary points. An open spline can be closed, or the start and end tangent directions can be changed. To access **SPLINEDIT,** select **Home** tab > **Modify** panel extension > **Edit Spline** tool from the ribbon.

## Creating Path Arrays

**path array:** An array created by copying objects repeatedly at regular intervals along a selected linear or curved path.

Spline curves and polylines present good opportunities to create ***path arrays***. You already know how to draw rectangular and polar arrays. Path arrays are very similar, but are drawn along a path rather than in a rectangular or circular matrix. For this quick demonstration, we will add a circle to your drawing and array it along the spline curve you have just drawn. Much of what you know about arrays will apply equally to path arrays.

✔ To begin, draw a circle with a **0.50** radius at the lower end of the spline curve, as shown in Figure 9-18.

*We use the **Path Array** tool to create the array of circles shown in Figure 9-19*

✔ Select **Home** tab > **Modify** panel > **Array** drop-down list> **Path Array** tool from the ribbon.

*AutoCAD prompts for object selection.*

✔ Select the circle.

✔ Press **<Enter>** to end object selection.

*AutoCAD prompts for selection of a path curve.*

✔ Select the spline curve.

*AutoCAD creates a preview array similar to the one shown in Figure 9-19. Notice the **Array** contextual tab. Here you can modify your array just as you would do with rectangular and polar arrays. The numbers in your array will depend on the size and shape of your curve. You can also manipulate the array count using the arrow-shaped grip.*

**Figure 9-18**
Drawing a circle

**Figure 9-19**
**Path Array** preview

✔ Try using the numbers in the contextual tab or the arrow-shaped grip to create a path array with ten items, similar to Figure 9-20.

**Figure 9-20**
**Path Array** with ten items

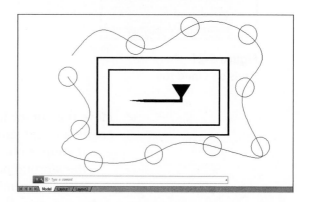

| REVCLOUD | |
|---|---|
| Command | Revcloud |
| Alias | (none) |
| Panel | Draw |
| Tool | |

# Drawing Revision Clouds

> **TIP**
> A general procedure for drawing a revision cloud is:
> 1. Pick the **Revision Cloud** tool from the **Draw** panel extension.
> 2. Pick a start point and draw a rough circle around the desired area.
> 3. Bring the cloud outline back to the start point, and let AutoCAD close the cloud automatically.

**revision cloud:** A closed object made of many small arcs typically used to surround an area in a drawing to indicate that it has been edited.

*Revision clouds* are a simple graphic means of highlighting areas in a drawing that have been edited. They are primarily used in large projects where a number of people are working on a drawing or a set of drawings. Revision clouds can be very quickly created to highlight an error or a place where changes have been made. They have a shape that is very unlikely to be confused with any actual geometry in your drawing. Try this:

✔ Pick the **Revision Cloud** tool from the **Draw** panel extension, as shown in Figure 9-21.

 *AutoCAD prompts:*

   Minimum arc length: 0.50 Maximum arc length: 0.50
   Specify start point or [Arc length Object Style] <Object>:

 *Drawing a revision cloud is a simple matter of moving the cross-hairs in a circle around an area, as if you were circling it with a pencil in a paper drawing. We draw a cloud around the open end of the spline curve.*

✔ Pick any point about 1.00 away from the open left end of the spline curve, as shown in Figure 9-22.

 *AutoCAD prompts:*

   Guide crosshairs along cloud path . . .

**Figure 9-21**
**Revision Cloud** tool

**Figure 9-22**
Creating a revision cloud

✔ Move the cursor in a rough circle around the open ends of the curve to create a cloud similar to the one shown in Figure 9-22.

 *If snap is on, AutoCAD temporarily turns it off. When you come near the starting point, the cloud closes automatically. Your screen should resemble Figure 9-22.*

## Creating Revision Clouds from Drawn Objects

Our revision cloud is adequate, but what if you wanted to create a neater, more precise-looking revision cloud? Revision clouds can also be created from circles, rectangles, or other closed objects. These can be drawn in the usual manner and then converted to clouds using the **Object** option. The **Arc length** option allows you to change the size of the individual arcs that make up the cloud. As you might expect, a completed revision cloud is a polyline. Good practice may require that you create revision clouds on a special layer. We complete this section by creating a revision cloud from a true circle and then reversing the small arcs that make up the cloud.

✔ **Erase** or **Undo** the revision cloud around the open end of the spline curve.

✔ Enter the **CIRCLE** command, and draw a circle centered between the two endpoints of the curve.

✔ Pick the **Revision Cloud** tool from the **Draw** panel extension.

✔ Press **<Enter>** or the spacebar for the **Object** option.

✔ Select the circle.

AutoCAD converts the circle to a revision cloud and offers you the option of reversing the direction of the arcs.

✔ Type **<Enter>,** or select **Yes** from the dynamic input display menu.
*Your screen resembles Figure 9-23.*

Finally, you can create a revision cloud from previously drawn polylines, as long as they are closed.

✔ Pick the **Revision Cloud** tool from the **Draw** panel extension.

✔ Press **<Enter>** or the spacebar for the **Object** option.

✔ Pick the outer rectangle, created previously in the "Drawing Straight Polyline Segments" section.

✔ Press **<Enter>** to complete the command without reversing the arcs.
*Your screen resembles Figure 9-24.*

**Figure 9-23**
Converting a circle to a revision cloud

**Figure 9-24**
Converting a polyline to a revision cloud

| POINT | |
|---|---|
| **Command** | Point |
| **Alias** | Po |
| **Panel** | Draw |
| **Tool** | |
| | |

# Drawing Points

**TIP**

A general procedure for drawing point objects is:

1. Pick the **Multiple Points** tool from the **Draw** panel extension of the ribbon.
2. Pick a point.

On the surface, this is the simplest draw command in AutoCAD. However, if you look at Figure 9-25, you can see figures that were drawn with the **POINT** command that do not look like ordinary points. This capability adds a bit of complexity to the otherwise simple **POINT** command.

✔ Erase objects from previous exercises.

✔ Turn off the grid.

✔ Pick the **Multiple Points** tool from the **Draw** panel extension, as shown in Figure 9-26.

**Figure 9-25**
Drawing points

**Figure 9-26**
**Multiple Points** tool

✔ Pick a point anywhere on the screen.

*AutoCAD places a point at the specified location and prompts for more points. Look closely, and you can see the point you have drawn. Besides those odd instances in which you may need to draw tiny dots like this, points can also serve as object snap nodes and can be used to divide and measure lines.*

*What about those circles and crosses in Figure 9-25? AutoCAD has 18 other simple forms that can be drawn as points. Before we change the point form, we need to see our options.*

✔ Pick **Home** tab > **Utilities** panel extension > **Point Style** from the ribbon, as shown in Figure 9-27.

*AutoCAD displays a **Point Style** dialog box with an icon menu, as shown in Figure 9-28. It shows you graphic images of your choices. You can pick any of the point styles shown by pointing. You can also change the size of points using the **Point Size** edit box.*

**Figure 9-27**
**Point Style** tool

**Figure 9-28**
**Point Style** dialog box

✔ Pick the style in the middle of the second row.

✔ Click **OK** to exit the dialog box.

*When you close the dialog box, any points previously drawn are updated to the new point style. Notice that this means you can have only one point style in your drawing at a time. New points are also drawn with this style.*

✔ Pick the **Multiple Points** tool from the **Draw** panel extension.

✔ Pick a point anywhere on your screen.

*AutoCAD draws a point in the chosen style, as shown previously in Figure 9-25.*

*If you have selected the **Multiple Points** tool from the ribbon, AutoCAD continues to draw points wherever you pick them until you press **<Esc>** to exit the command. If you have entered **POINT** from the command line or selected **Single Point** from the **Draw** menu, you have to repeat it to draw more points.*

✔ Pick another point.

*Draw a few more points, or return to the dialog box to try another style.*

✔ Press **<Esc>** to exit the **POINT** command.

*Notice that you cannot exit **POINT** by pressing **<Enter>** or the spacebar.*

## Using Constraint Parameters

**parametric design:** The set of processes involved in creating design drawings based on defined relationships and related dimensional values among aspects of a design. Typically, drawings created in this manner can be altered and adjusted when parameter values change.

We are about to explore an entirely new way to draw in AutoCAD. ***Parametric design***, using geometric and dimensional constraints, provides you with a new set of drawing tools and a different way to approach the drawing area. Typically, drawing objects involves specifying points, distances, and angles within a two- or three-dimensional coordinate system. In parametric design instead of beginning with specifiable values, you specify a set of geometric ideas and relationships that define the shape you want to draw. The shape is constrained by these values and relationships, but shapes drawn in this way can be updated to show the effect of changing one or more values. When values change, the object will update while maintaining the defined relationships. In essence, this is the approach taken by a designer who wants to create an object fulfilling certain numeric requirements.

In this exercise we draw a parallelogram with two sides double the length of the other two, using geometric and dimensional constraints and parameters. We do not start with distances and angles, but just with these geometric and numeric concepts.

✔ To begin, clear your screen of all objects.

✔ Turn off all the mode buttons on the status bar.
   *You should have a blank screen with none of the usual landmarks and drawing aids active.*

✔ Enter the **PLINE** command, and draw a rough parallelogram like the one shown in Figure 9-29. It may be any size and any angle, but be sure to **Close** it.

**Figure 9-29**
Drawing a rough parallelogram

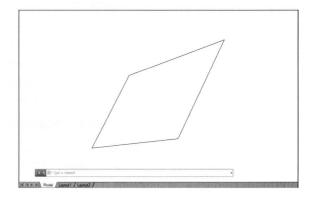

## Geometric Constraints

We've made our figure very rough on purpose. No doubt you can draw one that looks a lot more like a parallelogram. However, without snap or other aids, your lines may look parallel but probably are not. Now that we have the outline of our shape, we can specify geometric relationships, or constraints, to turn our sketch into a clearly defined and precise object. For this we need new tools accessible on the **Parametric** tab. On this tab there are 12 *geometric constraints*. They are used to set relationships between drawing objects.

**geometric constraint:** A property that limits the placement and size of an object in a drawing through specification of its relationship to other objects or to its geometric environment.

✔ Open the **Parametric** tab and pick the **Parallel** tool from the **Geometric** panel, as shown in Figure 9-30.

**Figure 9-30**
**Parallel** tool

*Observe the **Parametric** tab. There are three panels, covering geometric constraints, dimensional constraints, and constraint management. We use the parallel constraint to make our figure into a true parallelogram. In the command line prompt you see:*

GcParallel
Select first object:

✔ Select line 1, as shown in Figure 9-31.
*AutoCAD prompts for a second object:*

Select second object:

*Notice the importance of the order of selection. The second object will be adjusted to be parallel to the first.*

✔ Select line 2, as shown in Figure 9-31.
*Line 2 is adjusted to bring it parallel to line 1.*

✔ Pick the **Parallel** tool again and make line 3 parallel to line 4.
*When you are done, your drawing should resemble Figure 9-32. Notice the colored squares near each of the lines. These are called **constraint bars**. In our case they are just single boxes, but often you will have more than one constraint applied, and then the boxes will be displayed together and will look more like bars. If you let your cursor rest on any of these, a tooltip will appear, giving the label for this constraint.*

*Each of the geometric constraint tools has its own icon that appears in constraint bars as an indication that these constraints have been applied. Geometric constraints can be shown or hidden in a drawing. If yours are not visible, pick the **Show All** tool on the **Geometric** panel.*

**constraint bar:** A small square or set of squares that AutoCAD places next to an object to which a constraint has been applied. Each type of constraint has its own icon that is displayed in the square.

**Figure 9-31**
Line 1 adjusts parallel to line 2

**Figure 9-32**
Parallel constraint markers

✔ Let your cursor rest on one of the parallel constraint markers.
*The constraint is highlighted, along with the marker on the opposite, parallel side, and the two parallel lines, as shown in Figure 9-33. When you rest the cursor on any constraint marker, the related constraint markers are also highlighted, so that you can see how the geometry is defined. The small x to the right of the bar can be used to hide the constraint bar.*

**Figure 9-33**
Constraint is highlighted

✔ Select any side of the parallelogram.

✔ Pick any of the grips and move the cursor around.
    *Notice how the angles and lengths of the sides are now constrained always to be parallel, even though there are still a great many possible shapes stretching from the point you selected.*

✔ Press **<Esc>** twice to clear grips.

## Dimensional Constraints

**dimensional constraint:** A value or expression that limits the length and position of an object in a drawing. Dimensional constraints appear in the drawing area similar to standard dimensions but are not plotted.

Next, we add a ***dimensional constraint*** to one of the sides. Once defined, a dimensional constraint can be changed at any time, and all related geometry will be adjusted to maintain relationships defined by the constraints.

✔ Pick the **Aligned** tool from the **Dimensional** panel of the **Parametric** tab, as shown in Figure 9-34.
    *Creating dimensional constraints is nearly the same as creating regular dimensions. In fact, regular associative dimensions can be converted to dimensional constraints.*
    *AutoCAD prompts:*

    DcAligned
    Specify first constraint point or [Object Point & line 2Lines]
    <Object>:

**Figure 9-34**
DIMCONSTRAINT Aligned tool

✔ Press **<Enter>** to indicate that an object will be selected.

✔ Select line 1, as shown in Figure 9-35.
    *AutoCAD prompts for a dimension line location.*

✔ Pull the dimensional constraint down below line 1, as shown, and press the pick button.
    *Notice that the text for the dimension is highlighted as shown, and that unlike a regular dimension, this constraint has a name (d1).*

**Figure 9-35**
Dimensional constraint

*Ours shows d1 = 10.9647. Yours should be different, but we will fix that. Often, you want to change this value, because the ability to manipulate the dimension is the purpose of the dimensional constraint. You can change it now or come back to it later. We change it.*

**NOTE**

Dimensional constraints, like geometric constraints, can be shown or hidden in your drawing. If your constraint disappears when you press **<Enter>,** pick the **Show Dynamic Constraints** tool on the **Dimensional** panel.

✔ Type **10 <Enter>.**
*Your screen should resemble Figure 9-36.*

**Figure 9-36**
Changing dimensional
constraint to 10

Your drawing now has three different constraints. The two pairs of sides are constrained to be parallel, and the lower side, line 1, is constrained to be 10 units long, until we choose to change that value. One way to change the value is to select the dimensional constraint, right-click to open a shortcut menu, and then select **Edit Constraint** from the menu. When we do this, the dimension text will again be highlighted just as if we had never left the command.

## The Parameters Manager

parameter: A value that can be varied from one representation of an object to another.

Here we change the value another way, using the **Parameters Manager.** This will also give us the opportunity to create a new *parameter* that we will apply to the adjacent sides of the parallelogram.

✔ Pick the **Parameters Manager** tool from the **Manage** panel, as shown in Figure 9-37.

Figure 9-37
Parameters Manager tool

This opens the **Parameters Manager** palette, shown in Figure 9-38. It is a simple table of parameters. For each parameter there is a name followed by an expression or a value. If the value is a constant, then the expression and the value are the same. We change the name to something more useful and then create a second dimensional constraint defined by an expression.

✔ Double-click the name **d1.**
   *"d1" should be highlighted in blue.*

✔ Type **side1 <Enter>.**
   *The name in the table is changed from d1 to side1. It is also changed in the drawing.*

   *Next, we create a dimensional constraint so that the sides adjacent to side1 will be half as long as side1.*

✔ Pick the **Creates a new user parameter** button on the **Parameters Manager** palette, as shown in Figure 9-39.

Figure 9-38
Parameters Manager palette

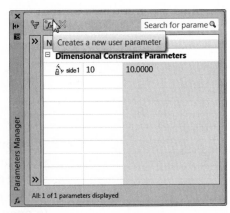

Figure 9-39
Creates a new user parameter button

*New data are added to the table, setting up a new section for user-defined parameters, meaning that they are defined in the **Parameters Manager** but not necessarily in the drawing. We call this parameter side2.*

✔ Double-click on the name **user1** and change it to **side2**.

✔ Click in the **Expression** column of side2 and type **side1/2 <Enter>**.

*Side2 is now 5, or half the length of side1, as shown in the* ***Parameters Manager*** *in Figure 9-40. However, this does not affect the drawing because side2 has not been applied to any geometry in the drawing yet.*

**Figure 9-40**
Dimensional constraints
side1

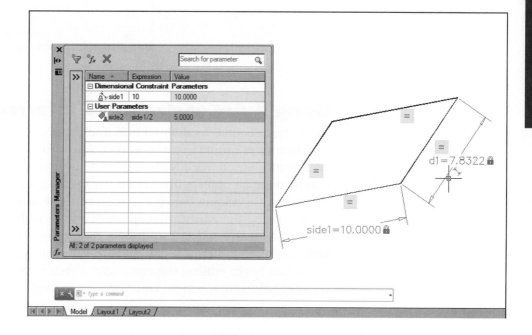

✔ Pick the **Aligned** tool from the **Dimensional** panel.

✔ Press **<Enter>**.

✔ Select line 3.

✔ Pull the dimensional constraint away from line 3 and press the pick button, as shown in Figure 9-40.

*Notice the dimension text. Ours shows d1 = 7.8322.*

✔ Type **side2 <Enter>**.

*The line at side2 is now evaluated with the expression that defines the variable side2. The dimension reads* ***fx:d1=side2,*** *and your drawing resembles Figure 9-41. Before we leave the* ***Parameters Manager,*** *we change the value of side1 and see how it is interpreted in the drawing.*

✔ Double-click the number **10** in the **Expression** column.

✔ Type **20 <Enter>**.

*In the* ***Parameters Manager,*** *side1 is now 20, and side2 is now 10. This is reflected in the size of the parallelogram. Before leaving this section you may want to try selecting any of the grips and stretching the object to see that there are still many possible forms for this object that are consistent with the constraints. In all cases, the opposite sides will be parallel, and the lower side will be twice as long as its adjacent sides.*

✔ Close the **Parameters Manager.**

**Figure 9-41**
d1 = side2

## Using AutoConstrain and Inferred Constraints

In the last section we defined and applied geometric and dimensional constraints manually, one at a time. AutoCAD can also apply geometric constraints automatically, based on its analysis of selected geometry. This can be done as objects are drawn, by turning on the **Infer Constraints** button on the status bar. It can also be done after objects have been drawn, using the **AutoConstrain** tool on the ribbon. As an example of what this means, when you draw a rectangle, you assume that adjacent sides are perpendicular and opposite sides are equal. But what happens when you begin editing the rectangle? Stretching a rectangle will ignore these relationships unless constraints are applied.

✔ To begin this exercise, erase all objects from your screen.

✔ Using the **RECTANG** command, draw a single rectangle, as shown by the rectangle on the left in Figure 9-42. Exact size and location are not critical.

> *This is a normal, unconstrained rectangle. Next we draw the rect-angle on the right with inferred constraints.*

**Figure 9-42**
Drawing two rectangles

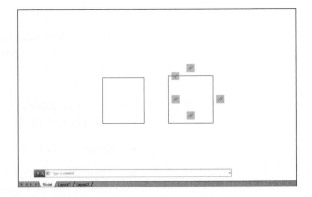

✔ Pick the **Infer Constraints** button from the left end of the status bar, as shown in Figure 9-43.

> *Infer Constraints should now be on.*

✔ Using the **RECTANG** command, draw a second rectangle, as shown in Figure 9-42.

**Figure 9-43**
Infer Constraints button

Along the sides of this rectangle you see five constraint bars. The constraint bars at the top and bottom and on the two sides are parallel constraints, showing that these opposite sides are constrained to be parallel. The constraint bar on the line near the top left corner shows that the lines meeting at this corner are constrained to be perpendicular. A little geometry will convince you that if the opposite sides are parallel and the lines at this corner are perpendicular, then the other corners are perpendicular intersections also, so additional constraint bars would be redundant. Next we stretch both rectangles using grips.

✔ Select both rectangles so that grips appear.
*The grips on both rectangles are identical.*

✔ Pick the upper left corner grip on the left rectangle, and stretch the vertex up and to the left, as shown in Figure 9-44.

**Figure 9-44**
Stretching the rectangles

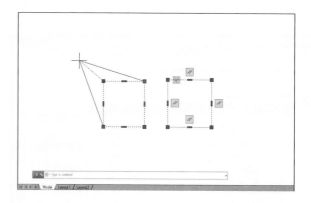

✔ Pick the upper right corner grip on the right rectangle, and stretch the rectangle up and to the right, as shown.
*Notice the difference. The unconstrained rectangle is stretched to form an irregular quadrilateral. The constrained rectangle retains its rectangular shape.*

✔ Undo the two stretches.
*Your screen resembles Figure 9-42 again.*

## Using AutoConstrain

We now use the **AutoConstrain** tool to add geometric constraints to the rectangle on the left.

✔ Pick **Parametric** tab > **Geometric** panel > **AutoConstrain** tool from the ribbon, as shown in Figure 9-45.
*AutoCAD prompts:*

Select objects or [Settings]:

**Figure 9-45**
**AutoConstrain** tool

✔ Select the rectangle on the left.

*AutoCAD prompts for more objects. Instead we will look at the* ***Settings*** *dialog box.*

✔ Right-click and select **Settings** from the shortcut menu.

*This calls the* ***Constraint Settings*** *dialog box shown in Figure 9-46. Here you can limit the constraints that AutoCAD will apply. Otherwise, AutoCAD will apply any constraint shown by its analysis of the selected geometry.*

✔ Click **OK**.

*Your screen resembles Figure 9-47. Six constraints are added. The left rectangle is constrained just as the right one, with the addition of a horizontal constraint.*

**Figure 9-46**
**Constraint Settings** dialog box

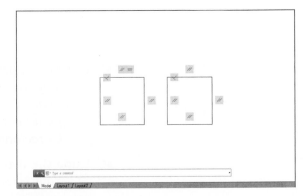

**Figure 9-47**
Six constraints are added

# Chapter Summary

You now have at your disposal a large number of new commands for drawing and editing complex objects consisting of various shapes made of lines and arcs. Polygons, donuts, and polylines drawn with the **PLINE** command all create polyline objects that you can edit with the **PEDIT** command. You can also create splines, which have their own editing features; path arrays, which can be drawn along spline or polyline paths; points, which can be created in 19 different styles; and revision clouds, which are primarily used in marking up designs but may be creatively applied as part of a drawing as well. At this point you know how to draw most of AutoCAD's two-dimensional entities, and you have had your first experience using geometric and dimensional constraints, along with AutoConstrain and inferred constraints, to draw objects consistent with specific design objectives.

# Chapter Test Questions

## Multiple Choice

*Circle the correct answer.*

1. Which of these **cannot** be given width using **PEDIT?**
   a. Rectangle
   b. Circle
   c. Polygon
   d. Polyline

2. A polygon can be drawn around the outside of a circle using which option?
   a. **Radius**
   b. **Inscribed**
   c. **Circumscribed**
   d. **Edge**

3. Polyline arcs are drawn:
   a. Tangent to the rubber band
   b. Tangent to the last polyline selected
   c. Tangent to the last polyline arc segment
   d. Tangent to the last polyline drawn

4. Geometric constraints cannot be added:
   a. Using **PEDIT**
   b. Using AutoConstrain
   c. Using inferred constraints
   d. By selecting objects

5. Dimensional constraints cannot be added:
   a. Using inferred constraints
   b. By selecting an object
   c. Using AutoConstrain
   d. By selecting constraint points

## Matching

*Write the number of the correct answer on the line.*

a. **Circumscribed** _____
b. Outer radius _____
c. **Halfwidth** _____
d. **Direction** _____
e. **Fit tolerance** _____

1. Polyline
2. Polygon
3. Polyline arc
4. Spline
5. Donut

## True or False

*Circle the correct answer.*

1. **True or False:** When drawing a polyline, using the **Close** option will have the same effect as using an **Endpoint** object snap to snap back to the first point.

2. **True or False:** Polylines, donuts, splines, and polygons can all be edited with **PEDIT**.

3. **True or False:** Revision clouds can be drawn freehand or created from previously drawn objects.

4. **True or False:** Spline curves touch each point you pick.

5. **True or False:** Geometric and dimensional constraints are maintained when an object is edited.

## Questions

1. Why does **PLINE** prompt for two different widths?

2. Why is it important to use the **Close** option when drawing closed polygons using the **PLINE** command?

3. How does AutoCAD decide in which direction to draw a polyline arc?

4. What is the difference between a spline curve constructed with a 0 tolerance and one with a 0.5 tolerance?

5. What is the difference between a geometric constraint and a dimensional constraint? Which can be applied using the **AutoConstrain** tool?

## Drawing Problems

1. Draw a regular six-sided polygon centered at (9,6) with a circumscribed radius of 3.0 units. The top and bottom sides should be horizontal.

2. Fillet all corners of the hexagon with a single execution of the **FILLET** command, giving a radius of 0.25 unit.

3. Give the sides of the hexagon a uniform width of 0.25 unit.

4. Draw a 0.50-width polyline from the midpoint of one angled side of the hexagon to the midpoint of the diagonally opposite side.

5. Draw a second 0.50-width polyline, using the other two angled sides so that the two polylines cross in the middle.

6. Draw a 1.50 radius circle centered at (9,6).

7. Convert this circle to a revision cloud.

## WWW Exercise (Optional)

In Chapter 9 of our companion website, we challenge you to find information on one of the twentieth century's greatest architects. We give you two links to get you started, and then you are on your own. We also offer you another design challenge and the self-scoring test for this chapter. When you are ready, complete the following:

✔ Make sure that you are connected to your Internet service provider.

✔ Type **browser <Enter>.**

✔ If necessary, navigate to our companion website at www.pearsonhighered.com/dixriley.

# Chapter Drawing Projects

## G Drawing 9-1: [*Backgammon Board*]
### [INTERMEDIATE]

This drawing should go very quickly. It is a good warm-up that gives you practice with **PLINE.** Remember that the dimensions are always part of your drawing now, unless otherwise indicated.

### Drawing Suggestions

GRID = 1.00

SNAP = 0.125

- First, create the 15.50 × 17.50 polyline frame as shown.

- Draw a 0-width 15.50 × 13.50 polyline rectangle and then **OFFSET** it 0.125 to the inside. The inner polyline is actually 0.25 wide, but it is drawn on center, so the offset must be half the width.

- Enter the **PEDIT** command and change the width of the inner polyline to 0.25. This gives you your wide filled border.

- Draw the four triangles at the left of the board and then array them across. The filled triangles are drawn with the **PLINE** command (starting width 0 and ending width 1.00); the others are just outlines drawn with **LINE** or **PLINE.** (Notice that you cannot draw some polylines filled and others not filled.)

- The dimensions in this drawing are straightforward and should give you no trouble. Remember to set to layer **dim** before dimensioning.

**Drawing 9-1**
Backgammon Board

## **G** Drawing 9-2: *Dartboard* [INTERMEDIATE]

Although this drawing may seem to resemble the previous one, it is quite a bit more complex and is drawn in an entirely different way. We suggest you use donuts and trim them along the radial lines. Using **PLINE** to create the filled areas here would be less efficient.

### Drawing Suggestions

$$\text{LIMITS} = (0,0)(24,18)$$
$$\text{GRID} = 1.00$$
$$\text{SNAP} = 0.125$$

- The filled inner circle is a donut with 0 inner diameter and 0.62 outer diameter.

- The second circle is a simple 1.50-diameter circle. From here, draw a series of donuts. The outside diameter of one becomes the inside diameter of the next. The 13.00- and 17.00-diameter outer circles must be drawn as circles rather than donuts so they are not filled.

- Draw a radius line from the center to one of the quadrants of the outer circle and array it around the circle.

- You may find it easier and quicker to turn **FILL** off before trimming the donuts. Also, use layers to keep the donuts separated visually by color.

- To trim the donuts, select the radial lines as cutting edges. This is easily done using a very small crossing window around the center point of the board. Otherwise, you have to pick each line individually in the area between the 13.00 and 17.00 circles.

- Draw the number 5 at the top of the board using a middle text position and a rotation of 2°. Array it around the circle, and then use the **DDEDIT** command to change the copied 5s to the other numbers shown.

**Drawing 9-2**
Dartboard

DIAMETERS
Ø.62
Ø1.50
Ø7.50
Ø8.25
Ø13.00
Ø17.00

# Drawing 9-3: *Printed Circuit Board*
## [ADVANCED]

This drawing uses donuts and polylines. Also notice the ordinate dimensions.

## Drawing Suggestions

UNITS = 4-place decimal

LIMITS = (0,0)(18,12)

GRID = 0.5000

SNAP = 0.1250

- Because this drawing uses ordinate dimensions, moving the 0 point of the grid using the **UCS** command makes the placement of figures very easy.

- The 26 rectangular tabs at the bottom can be drawn as polylines.

- After placing the donuts according to the dimensions, draw the connections to them using polyline arcs and line segments. These are simple polylines of uniform 0.03125 half width. The triangular tabs are added later.

- Remember, AutoCAD begins all polyline arcs tangent to the last segment drawn. Often, this is not what you want. One way to correct this is to begin with a line segment that establishes the direction for the arc. The line segment can be extremely short and still accomplish your purpose. Thus, many of these polylines consist of a line segment, followed by an arc, followed by another line segment.

- There are two sizes of the triangular tabs, one on top of the rectangular tabs and one at each donut. Draw one of each size in place and then use multiple **COPY, MOVE,** and **ROTATE** commands to create all the others.

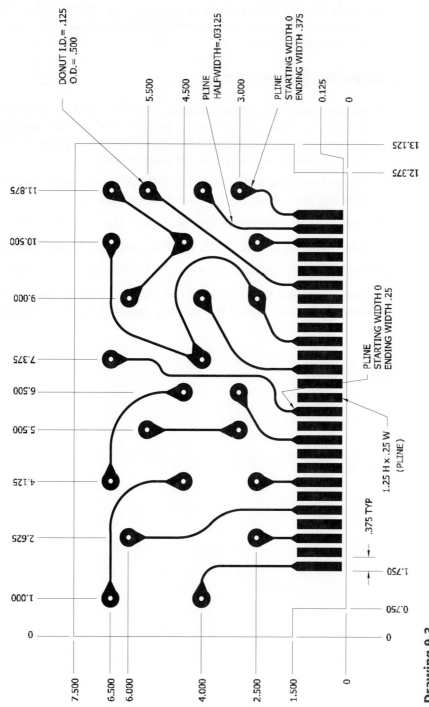

**Drawing 9-3**
Printed Circuit Board

417

## G Drawing 9-4: *Race Car* [ADVANCED]

This is an attractive drawing that requires the creation of shapes using donuts and polylines, along with text in different styles and a gradient hatch to fill and form details of the race car. The drawing does not have to be exact in all details, but you should try to make it a close approximation of the race car shown.

### Drawing Suggestions

- Measure and scale this drawing using the grid of squares as a guide. Determine what size you want to draw the race car on your screen, and set your grid accordingly. The corner of each square on the page will be represented by a grid point on your screen.

- Draw the two wheels using the **DONUT** command; this will determine how big your drawing will be when completed.

- Enter the **PLINE** command, and draw the outline of the race car.

- Add detail using the **LINE, PLINE,** and **TEXT** commands.

- Set your text styles to best match the text shown on this drawing.

- Use a gradient hatch to give the finished look to the car. Be sure your boundaries are closed so that the gradient hatch works properly.

Drawn by: Samantha Chipman

**Drawing 9-4**
Race Car

This architectural drawing makes extensive use of both the **POLYGON** command and the **OFFSET** command.

## Drawing Suggestions

UNITS = Architectural

GRID = 1′

SNAP = 2″

LIMITS = (0′,0′)(48′,36′)

- All radii except the 6″ polygon are given from the center point to the midpoint of a side. In other words, the 6″ polygon is inscribed, whereas all the others are circumscribed.

- Notice that all polygon radii dimensions are given to the outside of the 2″ × 4″. Offset to the inside to create the parallel polygon for the inside of the board.

- Create radial studs by drawing a line from the midpoint of one side of a polygon to the midpoint of the side of another, or the midpoint of one to the vertex of another as shown; then, offset 1″ each side and erase the original. Array around the center point.

- Trim lines and polygons at vertices.

- You can make effective use of **MIRROR** in the elevation.

Polygon radii 6"

Polygon radii 2'-0"

Polygon radii 6'-0"

Polygon radii 6'-4"

ROOF FRAMING

4'

4"

4"
(TYP)

1'-2"

8"
(TYP)

6"

2'-4"

4"
(TYP)

8'

2'-6"

4"

4"

4" THK CONCRETE SLAB

All lumber 2" x 4" unless otherwise noted

FRONT ELEVATION

**Drawing 9-5**
Gazebo

This drawing of a plot plan for a proposed office building is drawn in model space in a single viewport on a standard AutoCAD architectural layout. It will give you practice working with a layout as well as using polylines and a revision cloud as introduced in this chapter.

## Drawing Suggestions

UNITS = Architectural

GRID = 10'

SNAP = 6'

LIMITS = (0',0') (500',400')

LTSCALE = 200

- Create this drawing by selecting **Tutorial-Arch.dwt** as the template. This puts you in the drawing layout with the title block shown in the reference drawing.

- Switch to model space and make the changes to the drawing setup listed here.

- Use polylines for the walkways and road lines and for the direction arrows and building outlines.

- Use **REVCLOUD** to draw the outline around future parking.

- Return to the paper space layout to plot with the title block.

**Drawing 9-6**
Office Building

## G Drawing 9-7: *Clock Face* [ADVANCED]

This drawing gives you practice using different filled polyline forms. All procedures for creating the clock face, ticks, hands, and numbers should be familiar from this chapter and from other drawings you may have done.

## Drawing Suggestions

- Notice the architectural units used in the drawing. Observe the dimensions and select appropriate limits, grid, and snap settings.
- All three hands can be drawn as filled polylines.
- Clock ticks are also filled polylines.
- The font is Impact.

**Drawing 9-7**
Clock Face

# 10 chapter ten

# Blocks, Attributes, and External References

## CHAPTER OBJECTIVES

- Create groups
- Create blocks
- Insert blocks into the current drawing
- Create dynamic blocks
- Add constraints to dynamic blocks
- Access data in a block table
- Use the Windows Clipboard

- Insert blocks and external references into other drawings
- Use the AutoCAD **DesignCenter**
- Define attributes
- Work with external references
- Extract data from attributes
- Create tool palettes
- Explode blocks

### Introduction

Working effectively in a professional design environment requires more than proficiency in drafting techniques. Most design work is done in collaboration with other designers, engineers, managers, and customers. This chapter begins to introduce you to some of the techniques and features that allow you to communicate and share the powers of AutoCAD with others.

To begin, you learn to create groups and blocks. A **group** is a set of objects defined as a single entity that can be selected, named, and manipulated collectively. A **block** is a set of objects defined as a single entity and saved so that it can be scaled and inserted repeatedly and potentially passed on to other drawings. Blocks become part of the content of a drawing that can be browsed, viewed, and manipulated within and between drawings using the AutoCAD **DesignCenter** or the **Content Explorer.** The **DesignCenter** and other functions, including the Windows

**group:** A set of objects defined as a single entity that can be selected, named, and manipulated collectively.

**block:** A set of objects defined as a single entity and saved so that it can be scaled and inserted repeatedly and potentially passed on to other drawings.

427

xref: Short for external reference.

attribute: In AutoCAD, a value that can be attached to a block definition to give textual or numeric information about an individual block reference.

Clipboard and externally referenced drawings (*xrefs*), allow AutoCAD objects and drawings to be shared with other drawings and applications and with CAD operators at other workstations on a local network or on the Internet. In this chapter, we also introduce you to block attributes. An *attribute* is an item of information attached to a block, such as a part number or price, that is stored along with the block definition. All the information stored in attributes can be extracted from a drawing into a spreadsheet or database program and used to produce itemized reports. Like text and dimensions, attributes and blocks can be given the annotative property and scaled automatically to match a viewport scale.

The procedures introduced in this chapter are among the most complex you will encounter. Particularly in the exercises where you are working with two drawings, it is very important to follow the text and instructions closely and to save your work if you do not complete the exercise in one session.

## Creating Groups

> **TIP**
> A general procedure for creating groups is:
> 1. Pick **Home** tab > **Group** panel > **Group** from the ribbon.
> 2. Select objects to be included in the group definition.
> 3. Right-click to end object selection.
> 4. Type a name or description for the group, if desired.
> 5. Press **<Enter>** or the spacebar to complete and exit the command.

The simplest way to create a collective entity from previously drawn entities is to group them into a unit with the **GROUP** command. Groups can be given names and can be selected for all editing processes.

In this exercise, we form groups from objects that also are used later to define blocks. In this way, you get a feel for the different functions of these two methods of creating collections of objects. You begin by creating simple symbols for a computer, monitor, digitizer, and keyboard. Take your time getting these right because once created, they can also be inserted when you complete Drawing 10-1 at the end of the chapter.

**1** Create a new drawing and make the following changes, if necessary, in the drawing setup:

**2** Set to Layer **0** (the reason for doing this is discussed in the note accompanying this list).

**3** Change to architectural units, with precision = 0′–0″. Using architectural units will facilitate moving on to Drawing 10-1, which is an architectural layout of a CAD room.

**4** Set GRID = **1′**.

**5** Set SNAP = **1″**.

**6** Set LIMITS = **(0′,0′) (12′,9′)**. Be sure to include the feet symbol.

**7** **Zoom All.**

**NOTE**

Blocks created on Layer **0** are inserted on the current layer. Blocks created on any other layer stay on the layer on which they are created. Inserting blocks is discussed in the "Inserting Blocks into the Current Drawing" section.

✔ Draw the four objects shown in Figure 10-1.

*Draw the geometry only; the text and dimensions in the figure are for your reference only and should not be on your screen. Notice that the computer is a simple rectangular representation of an old-style computer CPU that sits horizontally under the monitor. Later we will modify the definition of this block so that it has the flexibility to also represent a typical tower-style computer.*

**Figure 10-1**
Draw objects

✔ Save this drawing as *Source*.

*We will be working with two drawings later in this chapter and call them* Source *and* Target *for clarity.* Source *will have 12′ × 9′, A-size architectural limits, and* Target *will have 18 × 12 decimal units. This will give you experience in some important issues about working with multiple drawings. For now you continue working in* Source *and do not need to create* Target *until later on.*

*We define the keyboard as a group.*

✔ Pick the **Group** tool from the ribbon, as shown in Figure 10-2.

*AutoCAD prompts:*

Select Objects or [Name Description]

**Figure 10-2**
**Group** tool

*Groups can be named and saved. Descriptions may be added to help in retrieving previously defined groups. We simply use the* **GROUP** *command to create a group that can be selected as one object.*

✔ Select the keyboard outer rectangles and small rectangles using a window.

✔ Select **Name** from the command line.

✔ Type **Keyboard <Enter>** to give this group a name.
*The keyboard is now defined in the drawing as a selectable group. To see that this is so, try selecting it.*

✔ Position the crosshairs anywhere on the keyboard, and observe the rollover selection preview.

You see from the highlights that the complete group is previewed. That is all you need to do with groups at this point. Groups are useful for copying and manipulating sets of objects that tend to stay together. Groups resemble blocks, which we explore in the next section. Groups are easier to define, and you can edit individual objects in groups more easily than you can edit them in blocks. Blocks have other advantages, however, including the capacity to be shared with other drawings.

Before going on, notice the three tools to the right of the **Group** tool in the **Group** panel. The top tool allows you to reverse the process so that objects are no longer treated as a group. The second tool allows you to add and remove objects from a group without undoing the group definition. The third tool allows you to select and edit objects within a group while the group is still defined.

## Creating Blocks

| BLOCK | |
|---|---|
| **Command** | Block |
| **Alias** | B |
| **Panel** | Draw |
| **Tool** | |

**TIP**

A general procedure for creating blocks is:

1. Pick the **Create** tool from the **Block** panel on the **Home** tab of the ribbon.
2. Type a name.
3. Pick an insertion point.
4. Select objects to be included in the block definition.

Blocks can be stored as part of an individual drawing or as separate drawings. They can be inserted into the drawing in which they were created or into other drawings and can be scaled as they are inserted. In AutoCAD, blocks can also be defined as *dynamic*, meaning that they are flexible and can be altered in specific ways to represent variations of the basic geometry of the block. In general, the most useful blocks are those that can be used repeatedly in many drawings and therefore can become part of a library of predrawn objects used by you and others. In mechanical drawing, for instance, you might want a set of screws drawn to standard sizes that can be used at any time. If you are doing architectural drawing, you might find a library of doors and windows useful. You will see examples of predefined symbol libraries later in this chapter when you explore the AutoCAD **DesignCenter** and tool palettes.

**NOTE**

Blocks created on Layer **0** are inserted on the current layer. Blocks created on any other layer stay on the layer on which they were created. Inserting blocks is discussed in the "Inserting Blocks into the Current Drawing" section.

We create our first block from the "computer" in your drawing.

✔ Pick the **Create** tool from the **Block** panel on the **Home** tab of the ribbon, as shown in Figure 10-3.

**Figure 10-3**
**Create Block** tool

*This executes the **BLOCK** command and opens the **Block Definition** dialog box shown in Figure 10-4.*

**Figure 10-4**
**Block Definition** dialog box

✔ Type **computer** in the **Name** box.
*Next, we select an object to define as a block.*

✔ Pick the **Select objects** button in the middle of the dialog box.
*It may be necessary to clear the check mark from the **Specify On-screen** box before you can do this. If this box is checked, the **Select objects** button will not be accessible, and you will be returned to the command line prompt for object selection.*
*The dialog box disappears, giving you access to objects in the drawing.*

✔ Select the computer rectangle.
*AutoCAD continues to prompt for object selection.*

**NOTE**

Be sure to use the **Select objects** button, not the **Quick Select** button. **Quick Select** executes the **QSELECT** command and opens the **Quick Select** dialog box. The purpose of this dialog box is to establish filtering criteria so that defined types of objects can be selected more quickly in a complex drawing, filtering out objects that do not meet the selection criteria.

✔ Right-click to end object selection.
*This brings you back to the dialog box.*
*Blocks are intended to be inserted into drawings, so any block definition needs to include an insertion base point. Insertion points and insertion base points are critical in using blocks. The insertion*

base point is the point on the block that is at the intersection of the crosshairs when you insert the block. Therefore, when defining a block, try to anticipate the point on the block you will most likely use to position the block on the screen. If you do not define an insertion base point, AutoCAD uses the origin of the coordinate system, which may be quite inconvenient.

✔ Pick the **Pick point** button at the left side of the dialog box.
*Here again, you may need to clear the check mark from the **Specify On-screen** box first.*

✔ Hold down **<Shift>** and right-click to open the **Object Snap** shortcut menu.

✔ Use a **Midpoint** object snap to pick the middle of the bottom line of the computer as the insertion point, as shown in Figure 10-5.
*When creating blocks, you have three choices regarding what happens to objects included in the block definition, shown by the three buttons in the **Objects** panel, just below the **Select objects** button. Objects can be retained in the drawing separate from the block definition, converted to an instance of the new block, or deleted from the screen. In all instances, the object data are retained in the drawing database as the block definition.*

**Figure 10-5**
Define objects as blocks

*A common practice is to create a number of blocks, one after the other, and then assemble them at the end. To facilitate this method, select the **Delete** button. With this setting, newly defined blocks are erased from the screen automatically. They can be retrieved using **OOPS** if necessary (but not **U**, as this would undo the block definition). In our case, deleting blocks as we define them also helps make a clearer distinction between block references and block definitions.*

✔ Select the **Delete** button.
*The block definition is complete.*

✔ Click **OK** to exit the dialog box.
*You have created a "computer" block definition. The computer has vanished from your screen but is in the drawing database and can*

*be inserted using the **INSERT** command, which we turn to momentarily. Now, repeat the **BLOCK** process to make a keyboard block.*

✔ Repeat **BLOCK.**

✔ Type **keyboard** in the block **Name** box.

✔ Pick the **Select objects** button.

✔ Pick the keyboard group defined in the previous section.

✔ Right-click to end object selection.

✔ Pick the **Pick point** button.

✔ Pick the midpoint of the bottom line of the keyboard as the insertion base point, using a **Midpoint** object snap, if necessary.

✔ Click **OK.**

✔ Repeat the blocking process two more times to create monitor and mouse blocks, with insertion base points, as shown in Figure 10-5.
  *When you are finished, your screen should be blank. At this point, your four block definitions are stored in your drawing base. In the next section, we insert them into your current drawing to create a computer workstation assembly. Before going on, take a look at these other commands that are useful in working with blocks.*

| Command | Usage |
|---|---|
| BASE | Allows you to specify a base insertion point for an entire drawing. The base point is used when the drawing is inserted into other drawings. |
| DBLIST | Displays information for all entities in the current drawing database. Information includes type of entity and layer. Additional information depends on the type of entity. For blocks, it includes insertion point, *x* scale, *y* scale, rotation, and attribute values. |
| EXPLODE | Reverses an instance of a block so that objects that have been combined in the block definition are redrawn as individual objects. Exploding a block reference has no effect on the block definition. |
| LIST | Lists information about a single block or entity. Information listed is the same as that in **DBLIST,** but for the selected entity only. |
| PURGE | Deletes unused blocks, layers, linetypes, shapes, or text styles from a drawing. |
| WBLOCK | Saves a block to a separate file so that it can be inserted in other drawings. Does not save unused blocks or layers and therefore can be used to reduce drawing file size. |

## Inserting Blocks into the Current Drawing

| INSERT | |
|---|---|
| Command | Insert |
| Alias | I |
| Panel | Block |
| Tool | |

**TIP**

A general procedure for inserting blocks is:

1. Pick the **Insert** tool from the ribbon.
2. Type or select a block name.
3. Pick an insertion point.
4. Answer prompts for horizontal and vertical scale and for rotation angle.

The **INSERT** command is used to position block references in a drawing. Here you begin to distinguish between block definitions, which are not visible and reside in the database of a drawing, and block references, which are instances of a block inserted into a drawing. The four block definitions you created in the "Creating Blocks" section are now part of the drawing database and can be inserted into this drawing or any other drawing. In this section, we focus on inserting into the current drawing. In the next section, we explore sharing blocks between drawings.

Among other things, these procedures are useful in creating assembly drawings. Assembling blocks can be done efficiently using appropriate object snap modes to place objects in precise relation to one another. Assembly drawing is the focus of the drawings at the end of this chapter.

In this section, we insert the computer, monitor, keyboard, and mouse back into the drawing to create the workstation assembly shown in Figure 10-6.

✔ If you are still on Layer **0,** you may wish to switch to another layer.

**Figure 10-6**
Inserted blocks

## The Insert Tab

There is an **Insert** tool just to the left of the **Create** tool on the **Block** panel on the **Home** tab of the ribbon. But there is a more complete set of tools related to blocks and external references available on the **Insert** tab. We'll switch to that tab now.

✔ Pick the **Insert** tab from the ribbon.
> *This opens a new set of tools, as shown in Figure 10-7. Notice the* **Insert** *tool on the* **Block** *panel at the far left, and the* **Create Block** *and* **Block Editor** *tools on the* **Block Definition** *panel.*

**Figure 10-7**
Insert tool

✔ Pick the **Insert** tool from the ribbon, as shown in Figure 10-7.
> *This executes the* **INSERT** *command and opens the* **Insert** *dialog box shown in Figure 10-8. In addition to the block* **Name** *list box at the top of the dialog box, there are several scaling options that allow you to scale and rotate the block as you insert it. This vastly increases the flexibility and power of the blocking system. The issue*

**Figure 10-8**
**Insert** dialog box

*of scaling becomes particularly important when you move between drawings. What would happen if you inserted a 20′ object into a drawing that has 12′ ×9′ limits? We shall see in the "Creating Dynamic Blocks" section.*

*Unlike the **SCALE** command, which automatically scales both horizontally and vertically, blocks can be stretched or shrunk in either direction independently as you insert them. You can type an x scale factor or specify both an x and a y scale factor. Use of z is reserved for 3D applications. The **Uniform Scale** option scales x, y, and z uniformly.*

*Now is a good time to see that your block definitions are still in your database.*

✔ Click the down arrow in the **Name** list box.
   *You should see a list like this:*

      Computer

      Keyboard

      Monitor

      Mouse

✔ Select **Computer** from the list.

✔ Click **OK** to exit the dialog box and begin inserting the block.
   *From here on, you follow prompts from the command line or dynamic input display. AutoCAD now needs to know where to insert the computer, and you see this prompt:*

      Specify insertion point or [Basepoint Scale X Y Z Rotate]:

   *AutoCAD gives you a block to drag into place. Notice that it is positioned with the block's insertion base point at the intersection of the crosshairs.*

✔ Pick a point near the middle of the screen, as shown previously in Figure 10-6.
   *If your current layer is other than Layer **0,** you will notice that the block is inserted on the current layer even though it was created on Layer **0.** Remember that this works only with blocks drawn on Layer **0.** Blocks drawn on other layers stay on the layer on which*

*they were drawn when they are inserted. This not only creates some inflexibility but also may add unwanted layers if the block was drawn on a layer that does not exist in the new drawing.*
*Now, let's add a monitor.*

✔ Repeat the **INSERT** command.

*Notice that the last block inserted is retained as the default block name in the block **Name** box. This facilitates procedures in which you insert the same block in several different places in a drawing.*

✔ Select **Monitor** from the **Name** list.

✔ Click **OK**.

✔ Pick an insertion point 2 or 3 inches above the insertion point of the computer, as shown in Figure 10-6.

*You should have the monitor sitting on top of the computer and be back at the command line prompt. We next insert the keyboard, as shown in Figure 10-6.*

✔ Repeat **INSERT**.

✔ Select **Keyboard** from the **Name** list.

✔ Click **OK**.

*Pick an insertion point 1 or 2 inches below the computer, as shown in Figure 10-6.*
*You should now have the keyboard in place.*

✔ Repeat **INSERT** once more and place a mouse block reference to the right of the other block references, as shown in Figure 10-6.

*Congratulations! You have completed your first assembly. Next we modify the definition of the computer block so that it becomes dynamic and may be used to represent different styles and sizes of computer.*

## Creating Dynamic Blocks

> **TIP**
> A general procedure for creating a dynamic block is:
> 1. Pick the **Block Editor** tool from the **Insert** tab of the ribbon.
> 2. Select a block. (Steps 1 and 2 can be reversed.)
> 3. From the **Block Authoring Palettes**, select a parameter.
> 4. Specify the parameter location.
> 5. From the **Block Authoring Palettes**, select an action.
> 6. Specify the action location.

**dynamic block:** In AutoCAD, a block defined with variable parameters that can be specified in any individual block reference.

***Dynamic blocks*** are blocks that can be altered without redefining the block. They are created using the **Block Editor.** The editor is a whole subsystem of screens, symbols, and commands that allows you to add dynamic parameters to newly defined or previously defined blocks. A *parameter* here is an aspect of the geometry of a block definition that may be designated as a variable. Parameters are always associated with *actions*. When a dynamic block is inserted, it takes the standard form of its original definition. Unlike other blocks, however, once a dynamic block is inserted it can be selected and altered in specific ways. The ways in which a dynamic block can be altered depend on the parameters and actions that have been added to the definition. Parameters and actions are effective for creating blocks that may be adjusted through various simple editing procedures. When the goal is to define more complex relationships among different geometric and dimensional features of a block object, dynamic blocks can be defined with geometric and dimensional constraints (constraint parameters), which can be manipulated like other constraints.

In this exercise we will demonstrate dynamic capabilities by adding a linear parameter and a stretch action to the computer block. This will allow us to adjust the shape of the computer so that it may represent a tower-style computer as well as one placed horizontally under the monitor. In the next section we apply constraint parameters to make the monitor block dynamic, while ensuring that certain relationships are maintained.

✔ To begin this task, you should be in our *Source* drawing with the four blocks inserted in the last section, shown in Figure 10-6.

✔ Select the computer block.

✔ Pick the **Block Editor** tool from the **Block Definition** panel on the **Insert** tab of the ribbon, as shown in Figure 10-9.

> *This executes the **BEDIT** command and opens the **Edit Block Definition** dialog box shown in Figure 10-10. Because you selected the computer block before entering the dialog box, the computer block should be selected in the block list, and an image of the block should be displayed in the **Preview** box. Once inside the **Block Editor,** you have access to a set of commands and procedures that cannot be accessed anywhere else. All these commands begin with the letter B and work on blocks that have been selected for editing.*

**Figure 10-9**
**Block Editor** tool

**Figure 10-10**
**Edit Block Definition** dialog box

✔ Click **OK.**

> *This brings you to the **Block Authoring Palettes** window, shown in Figure 10-11, and the **Block Editor** contextual tab of panels. On the right is the block itself in a special editing window where you can work directly on the block geometry. The light gray hue*

*distinguishes this screen from the regular drawing area. The **Block Authoring Palettes** on the left has four tabs. The first is for defining parameters, the second is for actions, the third is for sets of parameters and actions that are frequently paired, and the fourth is for geometric constraints. Here we add a linear parameter so that the width of the block can be altered; then, we add a stretch action to show how the parameter can be edited after it is inserted.*

**Figure 10-11**
**Block Authoring Palettes**

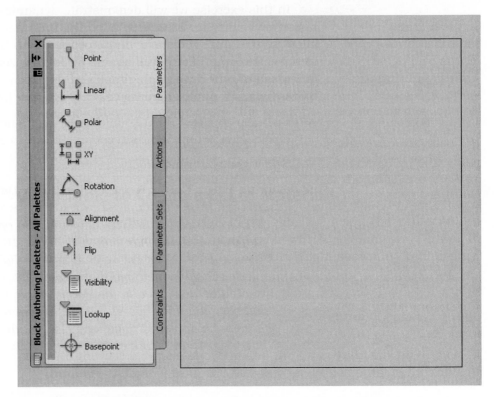

✔ From the **Parameters** tab of the palettes, select **Linear.**
    *This executes the **BPARAMETER** command with the **Linear** option. Other options are shown on the palette. AutoCAD prompts:*

    Specify start point or
    [Name Label Chain Description Base Palette Value set]:

    *We specify a parameter indicating that the width of the computer may be altered.*

✔ Use an **Intersection** or **Endpoint** object snap to pick the upper left corner of the computer block.
    *AutoCAD displays a Distance label, a line, and two arrows.*

✔ Use an **Intersection** or **Endpoint** object snap to pick the upper right corner of the computer block, as shown by the triangular grip in Figure 10-12.
    *The length of the parameter is now established. AutoCAD prompts you to specify a label location.*

✔ Pick a location point for the **Distance1** parameter label, as shown in Figure 10-12.
    *The parameter is now defined, but it is incomplete because there is no action defined for altering the parameter. The yellow box with the exclamation point is an alert to remind you of this.*

**Figure 10-12**
Distance label

✔ Click the **Actions** tab on the **Block Authoring Palettes.**
  *The **Actions** tab is shown in Figure 10-13.*

**Figure 10-13**
**Actions** tab

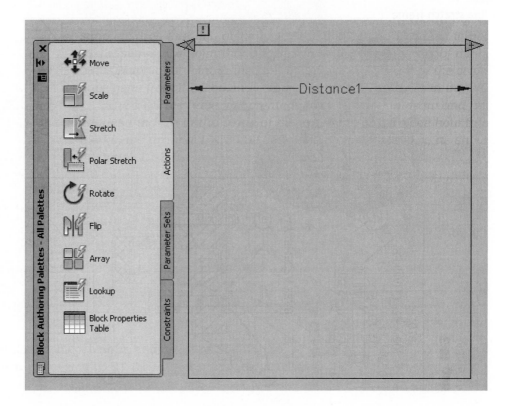

✔ Select **Stretch.**
  *This executes the **BACTION** command with the **Stretch** option.*
  *AutoCAD prompts:*

  Select Parameter:

✔ Select any part of the parameter or its label.
*AutoCAD prompts:*

> Specify parameter point to associate with action
>
> or enter [sTart point Second point] <Start>:

*The points you can select are the two triangles at the top corners of the block. These are the start point and the endpoint of the linear parameter. The behavior of the geometry is dependent on the point you select.*

✔ Pick the right endpoint.
*With this point selected we will be able to alter the width of the rectangle from the right side. AutoCAD now asks you to specify a stretch frame, just as you would do in the* **STRETCH** *command.*

> Specify first corner of stretch frame or [CPolygon]:

*This window will frame the portion of the rectangle to be stretched.*

✔ Pick two points to define a stretch frame around the right side of the rectangle, as shown in Figure 10-14.
*AutoCAD now asks you to select objects.*

✔ Select the computer rectangle.

✔ Right-click or press **<Enter>** to end object selection.

**Figure 10-14**
Define stretch frame

A stretch action symbol is added to the block in the area of the stretch, as shown in Figure 10-15. If you let your cursor rest on the symbol, you will see that it is named *Stretch*.

## The Test Block Window

The block now has a linear parameter with a stretch action. We can use the **Test Block** window to see how this is working before we leave the **Block Editor.**

**Figure 10-15**
Stretch action symbol

✔ Pick the **Test Block** tool from the **Open/Save** panel on the **Block Editor** contextual tab of the ribbon, as shown in Figure 10-16.

*This opens a simple window with the same light gray background, but only the block is showing. It is more efficient to test the block here than to leave the **Block Editor** and return to the drawing.*

✔ Select the block.

*The block is highlighted with an arrow at the point associated with the stretch action, as shown in Figure 10-17. The grip at the bottom shows the insertion point of the block.*

✔ Pick the arrow point at the upper right corner of the block.

**Figure 10-16**
**Test Block** tool

**Figure 10-17**
Stretch action arrow

✔ Stretch the block right and left to see how the block can be stretched.
*You can stretch the block horizontally to any length. This is just a test, however; nothing you do here will be saved.*

✔ Pick any point to complete the stretch.
*Now, we exit the **Test Block** window and return to the **Block Editor.***

✔ Pick the **Close Test Block Window** tool, as shown in Figure 10-18.
*This returns you to the **Block Editor.** We are ready to return to the drawing. Like the **Close Test Block Window** button, the **Close Block Editor** button is at the right of the ribbon.*

**Figure 10-18**
**Close Test Block Window**
tool

✔ Click the **Close Block Editor** button to exit the block editing system.
*AutoCAD displays a message asking whether you want to save changes to the block.*

✔ Click **Save the Changes** to save the new block definition.
*This brings us back to the drawing editor. The four block references are assembled there as before. The computer block has been updated, but there is no visible change until we select it. To complete this exercise we select the computer and implement the stretch action.*

✔ Select the computer.
*The computer is highlighted, and the new dynamic block grip has been added to indicate the linear parameter, just as it was in the **Test Block** window, as shown in Figure 10-19.*

**Figure 10-19**
Dynamic block grip is added

✔ Select the dynamic block grip on the upper right corner of the computer block.

✔ Move your cursor to the left to shrink the computer block to a 6″ width.
*We now have a narrowed version of the computer block, which will represent a tower-style computer. All we need to do is to move it over to the left.*

✔ Using the square grip, move the computer 6″ to the left, as shown in Figure 10-20.

**Figure 10-20**
Computer shape has changed

✔ Press **<Esc>** to remove grips.

> *Your screen should resemble Figure 10-20.*
>
> *This has been a brief introduction to the capabilities of dynamic blocks of the **Block Editor**. In the next section we add geometric and dimensional constraints to the monitor block, so that it can represent different-sized monitors.*

## Adding Constraints to Dynamic Blocks

> **TIP**
>
> A general procedure for creating a dynamic block with constraints is:
>
> 1. Pick the **Block Editor** tool from the **Insert** tab of the ribbon.
> 2. Select a block. (Steps 1 and 2 can be reversed.)
> 3. In the **Block Editor,** add geometric and dimensional constraints.
> 4. Test the block.
> 5. Close the **Block Editor.**

Constraint parameters provide the capability to create dynamic blocks in which geometric and dimensional relationships among different aspects of the block are carefully controlled. Once defined in this way, it also becomes possible to insert blocks with numeric data that exactly define the object, while adhering to general design specifications. In this section we add constraints to the monitor block so that it becomes dynamic and may be used to represent different-sized monitors without losing its overall shape. We begin by entering the **Block Editor** with the monitor block selected.

✔ Select the monitor block.

✔ Pick the **Block Editor** tool from the **Insert** tab of the ribbon.

✔ Press **<Enter>** in the **Edit Block Definition** dialog box.

You are now in the **Block Editor** with the monitor block showing in the edit area. We apply two geometric and two dimensional constraints. Notice that the **Block Editor** contextual tab has geometric and dimensional constraint panels exactly like those on the **Parametric** tab. Our design specifications for the monitors represented by this dynamic block will include the following constraints: The front and back will be parallel, the front and the two sides will have equal lengths, and the current proportion in the widths of the front and back (11:7) will be maintained. First, we use AutoConstrain to add parallel and equal constraints.

✔ Pick the **AutoConstrain** tool from the **Geometric** panel.

✔ Select the monitor.

✔ Press **<Enter>** to end object selection.

The front and back sides are constrained to be parallel, and the sides are constrained to be equal. Notice also that a horizontal constraint has been added, as shown in Figure 10-21. Since we might want the freedom to insert a monitor that is not horizontal, we eliminate this constraint.

**Figure 10-21**
Geometric constraints

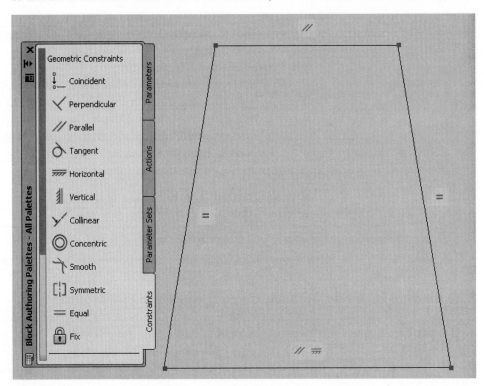

**NOTE**

If you have not drawn the sides of the monitor equal, you can remedy this by selecting the **Equal** constraint tool and picking the two sides.

✔ Right-click on the horizontal constraint and select **Delete** from the shortcut menu.

*The horizontal constraint disappears, leaving the other constraints in place.*

Next, we add a constraint to make the front and the two sides equal. Since the two sides are already equal, we need to select only one side.

✔ Pick the **Equal** constraint tool from the **Geometric** panel.

✔ Select the 11″ front edge of the monitor for the first object.

*AutoCAD prompts:*

Select second object:

✔ Select either of the two sides.

*An equal constraint marker will be added to the front, and the length of the two sides will adjust to be equal to the front edge, as shown in Figure 10-21. Notice that there are now two constraints applied to the front edge.*

*Next, we add dimensional constraints to the front and back.*

✔ Pick the **Linear** tool from the **Dimensional** panel.

✔ Press **<Enter>** so that you can select an object.

✔ Select the 11″ front edge.

✔ Pick a dimension line location below the monitor, as shown in Figure 10-22.

**Figure 10-22**
Dimensional constraints

✔ Press **<Enter>** to accept the name and value of the constraint.

*The constraint is added, as shown in Figure 10-22.*

✔ Pick the **Linear** tool from the **Dimensional** panel again.

✔ Press **<Enter>**.

✔ Pick the 7″ back edge.

✔ Pick a dimension line location above the monitor, as shown in Figure 10-22.

✔ Press **<Enter>** to accept the name and value.

*Finally, we open the **Parameters Manager** and specify a proportional relationship between the front and back.*

✔ Pick the **Parameters Manager** tool from the **Manage** panel on the **Block Editor** contextual tab of the ribbon.

*The position of the **Parameters Manager** will depend on its most recent use. It may be located at the left, covering part of the ribbon. It* *may be floating within the drawing area. It may also be collapsed if the* **Auto-hide** *feature has been activated. In any case, when you open it you will see a table with d1 and d2 defined as shown in Figure 10-23. We create the proportion directly in the constraint entry for d2.*

**Figure 10-23**
**Parameters Manager**

✔ Double-click in the **Expression** column of the row for d2.

✔ Type **d1*7/11 <Enter>.**
   *This expression ensures that the current proportion between front and back edges will be maintained at all sizes. The label on the constraint changes to "d2 = d1*7/11".*

   *Our block now has all the constraints required by our design specifications. We move to the* **Test Block** *window to try it out before leaving the* **Block Editor.**

✔ Close the **Parameters Manager.**

✔ Pick the **Test Block** tool from the **Open/Save** panel.

✔ Select the monitor.

✔ Pick the arrow-shaped grip at the front right of the monitor.

✔ Stretch the monitor larger and smaller.
   *You see that all of the constraints are maintained at all sizes of the monitor.*

✔ Pick any point to complete the stretch.

✔ Close the **Test Block** window.

✔ Close the **Block Editor.**
   *AutoCAD warns you that the edited block is not fully constrained.*

✔ Select **Save changes.**
   *The monitor block reference is updated and adjusted slightly.*

✔ Select the monitor block and use the grip to see that you can vary the size of the monitor, just as you did in the **Test Block** window.

## Accessing Data in a Block Table

The addition of constraints to dynamic blocks adds the capacity to specify variable block dimensions in a block table. Once a table of block variations is defined, all you have to do is pick a grip on the block to open a shortcut menu where you can select from the list of block variations. To demonstrate, we open the monitor block in the **Block Editor** again, add a block table, and define three more size variations. Then we return to the drawing and select one of these new block sizes from the **Block Table** shortcut menu.

✔ To begin, you should be in the *Source* drawing.

*There are four blocks on your screen. Two of them—the computer and the monitor—are dynamic blocks.*

✔ Select the monitor block.

✔ Pick **Insert** tab > **Block Definition** panel > **Block Editor.**

✔ Press **<Enter>** or click **OK** to open the monitor block.

You are in the **Block Editor** contextual tab with the **Block Authoring Palettes** and the monitor block showing in the editing area. The two dimensional parameters are shown. Block tables hold parameter information for the selected block. First, you must attach a table to the block and then add data to it.

✔ Pick the **Block Table** tool from the **Dimensional** panel, as shown in Figure 10-24.

*AutoCAD prompts:*

Specify parameter location or [Palette]:

*Before you can create a block table, you need to designate a point from which the table and associated shortcut menu can be opened.*

**Figure 10-24**
**Block Table** tool

✔ Pick a point in the middle of the block, as shown in Figure 10-25.

*The prompt gives you the opportunity to have either no grip or one grip added to the block.*

**Figure 10-25**
Pick point

✔ Press **<Enter>** to accept one grip.

> *This opens the **Block Properties Table** dialog box, shown in Figure 10-26. It is blank until you take steps to add properties to it.*

✔ Pick the **Add Properties** tool, as shown.

> *You see the **Add Parameter Properties** dialog box, shown in Figure 10-27. It shows the two distance parameters defined in the last section.*

**Figure 10-26**
**Block Properties Table**

**Figure 10-27**
**Add Parameter Properties** dialog box

✔ Hold down the **<Shift>** key and highlight **d1** and **d2**.

✔ Click **OK.**

> *You are now back in the **Block Properties Table,** with d1 and d2 showing as column headers. Each row will represent a different configuration of the block constraints, by varying the values under d1 and d2. Try this:*

✔ Click once in the cell below **d1.**

✔ Type **12 <Enter>.**

Two things happen. The value in column d2 is calculated from the expression = d1*7/11. Our units are set to 0 decimal places precision, so the result is rounded to 8″. Also, a second row is added. We add a second configuration.

✔ Type **16 <Enter>.**

Along with converting the 16″ to 1′-4″, the table calculates d2, rounded off to 10″, and adds a third row. We will add one more configuration.

✔ Type **20 <Enter>.**

The rounded value for d2 is 1′-1″. You now have a table of three variations of the block parameters for the monitor block. Ignoring the issue of rounded values, the dimensional constraints are maintained in each version.

✔ Click **OK** to leave the **Block Properties Table** dialog box.

Notice the grip and the block table icon. We complete this exercise by returning to the drawing to see how it works.

**NOTE**

As in the **Parameters Manager,** the **Block Properties Table** allows you to create new parameters that are not yet defined in the drawing. You would do this by picking the **New User Parameter** tool to the right of the **Add Properties** tool, that is, the middle of the three tools at the top of the dialog box.

✔ Pick the **Close Block Editor** button.

✔ Select **Save changes.**

You are in the drawing again. Nothing has changed visually, except that the monitor is slightly larger.

✔ Select the monitor.

*There is a new block properties table grip.*

✔ Pick the new triangular grip, as shown in Figure 10-28.

**Figure 10-28**
Triangular grip opens shortcut menu

This opens the shortcut menu, as shown. The menu shows the three values of d1 we entered in the table. The complete table, as shown previously, can be accessed from the bottom of the menu.

✔ Pick **1′-8″.**

The monitor is resized, as shown in Figure 10-29. You may need to use the grips to adjust its position and that of the mouse and keyboard.

✔ Press **<Esc>** to remove grips.

**Figure 10-29**
Resizing monitor

In the next two sections, we explore moving drawn objects between applications using the Windows Clipboard and moving blocks between drawings.

## Using the Windows Clipboard

In this section we begin our exploration of sharing blocks and other data among drawings. The Windows Clipboard makes it very easy to copy objects from one AutoCAD drawing to another or into other Windows applications. **CUTCLIP** removes the selected objects from your AutoCAD drawing, whereas **COPYCLIP** leaves them in place. When you send blocks to another AutoCAD drawing via the Clipboard, they are defined as blocks in the new drawing as well. Block names and definitions are maintained, but there is no option to scale, as there is when you **INSERT** blocks.

In this section, we create a new drawing called *Target* and copy the assembled workstation into it. The steps would be the same to copy the objects into another Windows application. The procedure is very simple and works with any Windows application that supports Windows object linking and embedding (OLE).

✔ To begin this task you should be in the *Source* drawing with the assembled blocks on your screen, resembling Figure 10-30.
   *To access **COPYCLIP** and **CUTCLIP** commands, we will return to the **Home** tab of the ribbon.*

✔ Pick the **Home** tab of the ribbon.

✔ Pick the **Copy Clip** tool from the **Clipboard** panel at the right end of the ribbon, as shown in Figure 10-31.
   *This executes the **COPYCLIP** command. AutoCAD prompts for object selection.*

**Figure 10-30**
*Source* drawing

**Figure 10-31**
Copy Clip tool

✔ Using a window selection, select all the objects in the computer work-station assembled in the "Inserting Blocks into the Current Drawing" section.

✔ Right-click to end object selection.

*AutoCAD saves the selected objects to the Clipboard. Nothing happens on your screen, but the selected objects are stored and can be pasted back into this drawing, another AutoCAD drawing, or another Windows application. Next, we create a new drawing.*

✔ Create a new drawing with 18 × 12 limits and decimal units.

*We call this drawing Target. Notice that you can have multiple drawings open in a single AutoCAD session.*

✔ Save the new drawing, giving it the name *Target*.

*Target should now be open in the drawing area with Source also open in the background. To demonstrate, we will use the drawing file tabs, which become useful whenever you have more than one drawing open.*

✔ Let your cursor rest on the **Source** drawing file tab, as shown in Figure 10-32.

*This opens a thumbnail image representing the Source drawing and two drawing layouts, which we have not created, so they are represented with a standard layout icon. For now these thumbnails are hardly necessary. You can switch between the two open drawings simply by clicking the **Source** tab or the **Target** tab to bring whichever drawing you want to the foreground.*

*We will stay with the current drawing, Target.*

**Figure 10-32**
Source drawing file tab

**Figure 10-33**
Paste tool

✔ Move your cursor away from the drawing file tabs to keep *Target* in the foreground.

✔ In *Target*, pick the **Paste** tool from the **Clipboard** panel, as shown in Figure 10-33.

*AutoCAD prompts for an insertion point and gives you an image to drag into place. You see a very large image of the keyboard, as shown in Figure 10-34. Actually, the whole workstation is there, but the computer, monitor, and mouse are off the screen. They are so large because the scale of this drawing is very different from the one the objects were drawn in. The original drawing has been set up with architectural units and limits so that its block definitions can be used in Drawing 10-1, CAD Room, at the end of the chapter.*

*In the new drawing, the 18 × 12 limits and decimal units are being interpreted as inches, so the keyboard is coming in at 17", covering most of the screen. Without the scaling capacity of the **INSERT** command, you have no control over this interpretation.*

**Figure 10-34**
Pick insertion point

✔ Pick an insertion point at the lower left of your screen, as shown in Figure 10-34.

*That's all there is to it. It is equally simple to paste text and images from other compatible Windows applications into AutoCAD. Just reverse the process, cutting or copying from the other application and pasting into AutoCAD.*

*We undo this paste before moving on.*

✔ Press **U** until everything has been undone in *Target*.

*The issue of scaling is handled differently when you paste AutoCAD objects into other applications. In those cases, objects are automatically scaled to fit in the document that receives them. Most applications have their own sizing feature, which allows you to adjust the size of the objects after they have been pasted.*

## Inserting Blocks and External References into Other Drawings

> **TIP**
>
> A general procedure for inserting a block into another drawing is:
>
> 1. Prepare a drawing or block to be inserted into another drawing.
> 2. Open a second drawing.
> 3. Enter the **INSERT** or **XATTACH** command.
> 4. Enter the name and path of the drawing to be inserted or referenced, or browse to find the file.
> 5. Answer prompts for scale and rotation.

Any drawing can be inserted as a block or external reference into another drawing. The process is much like inserting a block within a drawing, but you need to specify the drawing location. In this task, we attach *Source* as an external reference in *Target*. The process for inserting blocks into other drawings is identical to attaching an external reference, but the result is different.

# External References

> **NOTE**
>
> The use of external references requires careful project and file management. Creating dependency of one drawing on another opens up possibilities for confusion. If a file is moved or renamed, for example, the path to the external reference could be lost.

**external reference:** In AutoCAD, a reference that points to a drawing or block that is not in the database of the current drawing, so that information from the external reference is available within the current drawing but is maintained in the external drawing database.

An ***external reference*** is a bit of information within one drawing that provides a link to another drawing. If the path to the external drawing is clear and accessible, objects from the referenced drawing appear in the current drawing just as if they had been created there.

Externally referencing a drawing is a powerful alternative to inserting it as a block. Because attaching a reference loads only enough information to point to and access data from the externally referenced drawing, it does not increase the size of the current drawing file as significantly as **INSERT** does. Most important, if the referenced drawing is changed, the changes are reflected in the current drawing the next time it is loaded or when the **Reload** option of the **XREF Manager** is selected. This allows designers at remote locations to work on different aspects of a single master drawing, which can be updated as changes are made in the various referenced drawings.

✔ You should be in *Target* to begin this task, with everything undone.

> *At this point we return to the* Source *drawing. To switch back, use the drawing file tab.*

✔ Pick the **Source** drawing file tab to bring this drawing back into the foreground.drawing file tab to bring this drawing back into the foreground.

> *Now, you are back in your original drawing with the computer workstation objects displayed as shown previously in Figure 10-30. You could use this drawing as a block or external reference without further adjustment, but using the **BASE** command to add an insertion base point for the drawing is convenient. **BASE** works for either blocking or referencing.*

✔ Pick the **Set Base Point** tool from the **Block** panel extension of the ribbon, as shown in Figure 10-35.

> *This tool is also available on the **Block** panel extension of the **Insert** tab.*
>
> *AutoCAD prompts:*
>
> Enter base point, <0'-0", 0'-0", 0'-0">:
>
> *This indicates that the current base point is at the origin of the grid. We move it to the lower left corner of the keyboard.*

**Figure 10-35**
**Set Base Point** tool

✔ Pick the lower left corner of the keyboard.

*The new base point is registered, but there is no change in the drawing. To see what we have accomplished, we have to save* Source *and return to* Target.

> **NOTE**
>
> Be sure to pay attention to where you are saving the *Source* drawing so that you can easily find it again. If you are uncertain, open the application menu.

✔ Save **Source.**

*If you don't save the drawing after changing the base point, the base point is not used when the drawing is referenced.*

✔ Click the **Target** drawing file tab.

*This returns you to your* Target *drawing. There should be no objects in this drawing. We use the* **XATTACH** *command here to attach* Source *as an external reference in* Target.

✔ To access attachment tools, pick the **Insert** tab.

✔ Pick **Insert** tab > **Reference** panel > **Attach** tool, as shown in Figure 10-36.

*This will open the* **Select Reference File** *dialog box, as shown in Figure 10-37. This is basically the same dialog box you see when you enter any command in which you select a file.*

**Figure 10-36**
**Attach** tool

**Figure 10-37**
**Select Reference File** dialog box

✔ Make sure that **Drawing (*.dwg)** is selected in the **Files of type** list.

*This will facilitate finding your drawing.*

✔ Navigate to the folder that contains *Source*, using the **Up One Level** button, the location buttons on the left, or the **Find** feature under **Tools**, if necessary, to locate *Source*.

✔ Select **Source** from the list of files or from the thumbnail gallery, depending on your operating system and settings.

✔ Click **Open.**

> *This opens the **Attach External Reference** dialog box, shown in Figure 10-38. **Source** should be entered in the **Name** box. Notice that* Source *is already open, so you are not actually opening the drawing at this point, but attaching it to* Target.

**Figure 10-38**
**Attach External Reference**
dialog box

✔ Click **OK** to exit the dialog box.

> *You are now back to the* Target *drawing window. As in the last task, you have a very large image of the keyboard, but this time there is a prompt for scale factors in the command line.*

✔ Select **Scale** from the command line.

> *This option takes a uniform scale factor for the complete inserted drawing.*

✔ Type **1/8 <Enter>.**

> *You could also type **.125,** but it is worth noting that the **INSERT** and **XATTACH** commands take fractions or scale ratios at the scale factor prompt.*

✔ Pick an insertion point near the middle of the screen.

> *At this scale, the workstation appears on your screen much as it does in the* Source *drawing. The slightly transparent image reminds you that this is an external reference.*

Stop for a moment to consider your two drawings. *Source* is closed but has been attached as an external reference. *Source* has the architectural units and 12 × 9 limits established at the beginning of the chapter. It has four separate blocks currently assembled into a workstation. *Target* has decimal units and 18 × 12 limits and has one instance of *Source* attached as an external reference, scaled down to 1/8. In the tasks that follow, we continue to make changes to these drawings. Later, you will see that changes in *Source* are reflected in *Target*. In the next task, we introduce another powerful tool for managing drawing data, the AutoCAD **DesignCenter**.

## Using the AutoCAD DesignCenter

**DesignCenter:** In AutoCAD, a palette that provides access to content in open or closed drawings at local or remote locations.

The AutoCAD **DesignCenter** enables you to manipulate drawing content similar to the way Windows Explorer handles files and folders. The interface is familiar, with a tree view on the left and a list of contents on the right. The difference is the types of data you see. With the **DesignCenter** you can look into the contents of open or closed drawing files and easily copy or insert content into other open drawings. Blocks, external references, layers, linetypes, dimension styles, text styles, table styles, and page layouts are all examples of content defined in a drawing that can be copied into another drawing to reduce duplicated effort.

In this task, we begin by opening the **DesignCenter** and examining some of the available content.

✔ To begin this task you should have *Target* open on your screen.

✔ Type **<Ctrl>+2** or pick **Insert** tab > **Content** panel > **DesignCenter** tool from the ribbon, as shown in Figure 10-39.

**Figure 10-39**
**DesignCenter** tool

*This executes the **ADCENTER** command and opens the **DesignCenter** palette shown in Figure 10-40. If you or someone else has used **DesignCenter** on your computer, you are likely to see something slightly different from our illustration, because the **DesignCenter** stores changes and resizing adjustments. In particular, if you do not see the tree view on the left as shown, you have to use the **Tree View Toggle** button to restore the tree view to your palette before going on.*

✔ If necessary, pick the **Tree View Toggle** button, as shown in Figure 10-41.
*Your **DesignCenter** should now have a tree view on the left and a content area on the right.*

The **DesignCenter** is a complex palette that gives you access to a vast array of resources. There is a toolbar-like set of buttons at the top of the palette, including the **Tree View Toggle** button. Below these are three tabs and below these is the main work area of the palette. The tree view area shows a hierarchically arranged list of files, folders, and locations. The content area shows icons representing drawings and drawing contents of the folders or files currently selected in the tree view. What appears in the tree view depends on which tab is selected. The **Folders** tab shows the

**Figure 10-40**
DesignCenter palette

**Figure 10-41**
Tree View Toggle button

complete desktop hierarchy of your computer. The **Open Drawings** tab lists only open AutoCAD drawings. **History** shows a history of drawing files that have been specifically opened in the **DesignCenter.** We begin by selecting the **Open Drawings** tab and seeing what the **DesignCenter** shows us regarding our current drawing.

✔ Click the **Open Drawings** tab.

*Now, you have a very simple window with the open drawings and content types in the tree view and the content area, as shown in Figure 10-42.*

**Figure 10-42**
Open Drawings tab

You see icons representing standard content types: **Blocks, DetailViewStyles, Dimstyles, Layers, Layouts, Linetypes, Multileaderstyles, SectionViewStyles, Tablestyles, Textstyles, Visualstyles,** and **Xrefs** (external references). All drawings show the same list, although not all drawings have content defined in each category.

In the tree view, the list of types is as far as you can go. In the palette, however, there is another level.

✔ If necessary, highlight **Target.dwg** in the tree view.

✔ Double-click **Xrefs** in the tree view at the end of the list.

*You see an icon representing the attached* Source *drawing in the content area, as shown in Figure 10-43. If you'd like, check out the other contents as well. Double-click on* **Dimstyles,** *for example, and you find the Standard, Annotative, and any other style defined in this drawing.*

*Now try looking into* Source. *It is still open, but notice that its contents would still be accessible in the* **DesignCenter** *if it were closed. You would just have to browse to it in the* **Folders** *tab.*

**Figure 10-43**
Attached *Source* drawing icon

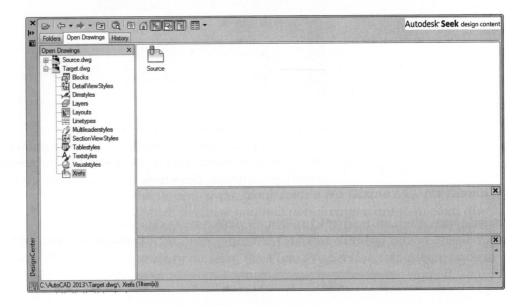

✔ Highlight **Source** in the **Open Drawings** tab.

*It is not necessary to open the list of contents under* **Source** *in the tree view. As long as* **Source** *is selected, you can open contents in the content area. You will notice no difference in the content area because* Source *and* Target *have the same content elements.*

✔ With **Source** selected in the tree view, double-click the **Blocks** icon in the content area.

*You see the familiar set of four blocks shown in Figure 10-44. At this point you could drag any of these blocks right off the palette into* Target. *Instead, we insert a symbol from the* **DesignCenter**'s *predrawn sample blocks. These are easily located using the* **Favorites** *button.*

✔ Click the **Home** button at the top of the **DesignCenter** palette, as shown in Figure 10-45.

**Figure 10-44**
Four blocks shown

**Figure 10-45**
**Home** button

✔ Double click the **en-us** icon in the content area, as shown in Figure 10-46.

**Figure 10-46**
en-us icon

✔ Double click the **DesignCenter** icon in the content area.

> *This takes you to the **DesignCenter** folder, which contains sample drawings and blocks, as illustrated in Figure 10-47. In the content area, you see a set of sample drawing thumbnails.*

✔ Double-click **Home - Space Planner.dwg.**

> *As soon as you select this drawing, you again see the familiar set of icons for standard drawing content.*

**Figure 10-47**
Sample drawings and blocks

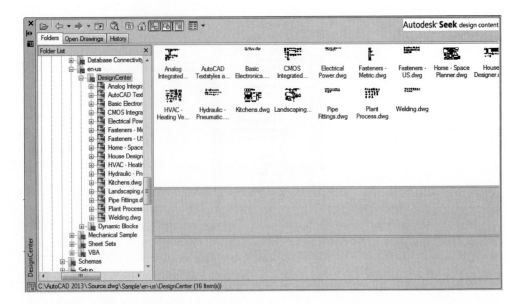

**Figure 10-48**
Select the computer terminal

✔ Double-click the **Blocks** icon in the content area.

> *Now, you see a set of blocks representing household furniture, as shown in Figure 10-48. Look for the computer terminal. We insert this symbol, which is similar to our own workstation symbol, into Target.*
>
> *Blocks can be inserted from the **DesignCenter** by dragging, but there are some limitations, as you will see.*

✔ Select the **Computer Terminal** block in the palette.

✔ Pick the computer terminal and drag the block slowly into the Target drawing area.

> *As soon as you are in the drawing area, you see a very large image of the computer block. This is a now-familiar scaling problem.*

✔ Return your cursor to the palette without releasing the pick button until your cursor is back in the palette.

> *There is a more precise and dependable method for inserting blocks from the **DesignCenter**. This second method allows you to scale the block as you insert it. First, however, it is convenient to put the **DesignCenter** palette in **Auto-hide** mode.*

## Auto-hide

**Auto-hide:** A feature of AutoCAD palettes that allows them to collapse so that only the title bar appears when the palette is open but not in use.

The *Auto-hide* feature allows you to keep a palette open without cluttering your screen. When the cursor is in the drawing area, the palette will collapse to show just the title bar. When you roll the cursor over the title bar, the palette will expand and all its features will be accessible.

✔ Click the **Auto-hide** button, the two arrows just below the **Close** button at the top of the palette title bar.
   *The palette collapses to hide everything but the title bar.*

✔ Move the cursor over the palette title bar so that the palette opens again.
   *As long as the cursor remains inside the palette, it remains open. When the cursor remains outside the palette, it will collapse again.*

✔ Right-click on the computer block.
   *This opens a shortcut menu.*

✔ Select **Insert Block.**
   *You see the **Insert** dialog box with **Computer Terminal** in the **Name** edit box. From here on, the procedure is just like inserting a block within its original drawing.*

✔ If necessary, select the **Uniform Scale** check box and clear the check mark for the **Specify On-screen** box.

✔ Enter **1/8** or **.125** in the **X Scale** box in the middle of the dialog box.

✔ Click **OK.**
   *As the dialog box closes, the **Auto-hide** feature activates, and the **DesignCenter** collapses so that only the title bar remains. This makes it easy to pick an insertion point in the drawing area.*

✔ Select an insertion point above or below the workstation Xref, as shown in Figure 10-49.

**Figure 10-49**
Specify the insertion point

✔ Move the cursor back into the **DesignCenter** title bar.
   *The palette opens again.*

✔ Click the **Open Drawings** tab.

✔ Highlight **Target.dwg.**

✔ Double-click the **Blocks** icon in the palette.
   *You see that the **Computer Terminal** block definition from the Home - Space Planner drawing is now in the database of Target.*

## Other Features of the DesignCenter

Before we leave the **DesignCenter,** here are a few more features, controlled by the buttons at the top. Across the toolbar, the **Load** button opens a standard file selection dialog box where you can load any folder or drawing file into the **DesignCenter.** The **Back** and **Forward** buttons take you to previous tree view and content area displays. The **Up** button takes you up one level in whatever folder hierarchy you are exploring. The **Search** button opens a **Search** dialog box, allowing you to search for files, folders, and text in a variety of ways familiar in Windows applications. The **Favorites** button takes you to a set of defined favorite locations. By default, this includes the **DesignCenter** folder and the AutoCAD predefined hatch pattern sets. The **Home** button, as we have seen, takes you directly to the **DesignCenter** folder. The **Tree View Toggle** button opens and closes the tree view panel. With the panel closed, there is more room to view contents. The **Preview** button opens and closes a panel below the content area that shows preview images of selected contents. The **Description** button opens and closes a panel below the **Preview** panel that displays text describing a selected block. Finally, the **Views** button allows choice over the style in which content is displayed in the content area. Before moving on, close the **DesignCenter.**

✔ Click the **Close** button at the top of the **DesignCenter** title bar.

## The Content Explorer

Content Explorer: In AutoCAD, a feature that allows users to search for drawing content in local folders, on a network, or on the Internet.

In AutoCAD there is another tool available that in many ways duplicates the functions of the **DesignCenter.** The *Content Explorer* gives access to content in other drawings on your computer, on a network, or on the Internet. It is in many ways easier to use than the **DesignCenter,** but requires that you first tell it where to look for content. You do this by loading folders that you want to explore into a list. These are called *watched folders.* Watched folders are indexed, and content in files in these folders becomes accessible, just as in the **DesignCenter.** The **Content Explorer** also has an easy-to-use search function that searches for content based on text strings, similar to the way Internet search engines work. There are basically two ways to use **Content Explorer.** By using the **Autodesk Seek** window, you can search through content available online directly from Autodesk. Using the **Watched Folder** window, you select folders on your own computer or network to explore. An example of how **Content Explorer** works with watched folders is as follows:

**1** From the ribbon, select **Plugs-Ins** tab > **Content Explorer.**

**2** If you see **Search Autodesk Seek** in the search window at the top of the **Content Explorer,** pick the down arrow next the large **S,** and select **Home** from the drop-down list.

**3** From the **Home** palette, pick **Add Watched Folder . . . ,** as shown in Figure 10-50.

**4** From the **Select Watched Folder** window, browse to a folder you want to access, select it, and click **OK.**

**Figure 10-50**
**Content Explorer - Add**
**Watched Folder . . .**

**5** To search for content through all drawings in all watched folders, enter a text string in the search box. Content containing the text string as part of a name will appear in the window.

**6** To explore content in an individual drawing, open the folder and double-click on the drawing file. Here you will see content similar to that shown in the content area of the **DesignCenter.**

## Defining Attributes

> **TIP**
>
> A general procedure for defining attributes is:
>
> 1. Open the **Insert** tab and pick the **Define Attributes** tool from the **Block Definition** panel.
> 2. Specify attribute modes.
> 3. Type an attribute tag.
> 4. Type an attribute prompt.
> 5. If desired, type a default attribute value.
> 6. Include the attribute in a block definition.

We have introduced many new concepts in this chapter. We have gone from creating and inserting blocks in a single drawing to sharing drawing content between drawings. Now, we add variable information to block definitions using AutoCAD's attribute feature. When you add attributes to a block definition, you create the ability to pass drawing data between drawings and non-graphic applications, typically database and spreadsheet programs. Attributes hold information about blocks in a drawing in a form that can be read out to other programs and organized into reports or bills of materials. Whereas dynamic block features allow you to vary the size and geometrical relationships in a block reference, attributes hold specific labels, descriptions, part numbers, and other data that are independent of the mathematical form of the object. For example, without changing the visual aspect of our workstation assembly, we can define it as a block and use it to represent different

| | Repeat ACDCINSERTBLOCK |
|---|---|
| | Recent Input ▸ |
| | Edit Xref In-place |
| | Open Xref |
| | Clip Xref |
| | External References... |
| | Clipboard ▸ |
| | Isolate ▸ |
| | Erase |
| | Move |
| | Copy Selection |
| | Scale |
| | Rotate |
| | Draw Order ▸ |
| | Add Selected |
| | Select Similar |
| | Deselect All |
| | Subobject Selection Filter ▸ |
| | Quick Select... |
| | Properties |
| | Quick Properties |

**Figure 10-51**
Xref shortcut menu

hardware configurations. One instance of the workstation block could represent a computer with a Core 2 processor and a 20″ CRT monitor, whereas another instance of the same block could represent a computer with a Quad Core processor and a 24″ LCD monitor. Those descriptive labels—Core 2, Quad Core, 20″ CRT, 24″ LCD—can all be handled as attributes. If you wish, you can look ahead to Figure 10-54 to get an idea of what this looks like.

In this task we will create variable and visible attribute tags for computer processors and monitors, along with a constant and invisible tag to label the mouse in each workstation. When we have defined these attributes, we create a block called *workstation* that includes the whole computer workstation assembly and its attributes. To accomplish this, we return to *Source* and add attributes to our workstation assembly there. Because *Source* is now attached to *Target* as an external reference, we can later return to *Target* and update it with the new information from *Source*.

Assuming you are still in *Target* from the previous section, we begin this task by demonstrating AutoCAD's **XOPEN** command, which allows you to quickly open an Xref from within a drawing without searching through a file hierarchy to locate the referenced drawing.

✔ Select the computer workstation in *Target* that you originally drew in *Source* and attached to *Target* as an external reference.
   *The workstation is highlighted, and a grip is placed at the previously defined insertion base point.*

✔ With the external reference highlighted, right-click.
   *This opens the lengthy shortcut menu shown in Figure 10-51.*

✔ Select **Open Xref.**
   *This is a convenient way to open an externally referenced drawing from within the drawing where it is attached. Source opens in the drawing area. You should see the original workstation assembly on Layer **1** in this drawing, just as you created it in the "Creating Blocks" section. Source is open just as if you had opened it using the **OPEN** command. You now have the two drawings open again. Source is current, with Target open in the background.*

   *We are going to add attributes to these blocks in Source and then define the whole assembly and its attributes as a single block called* workstation. *First, we define an attribute that allows us to specify the type of processor in any individual reference to the workstation block.*

✔ Open the **Insert** tab and pick the **Define Attributes** tool from the **Block Definition** panel, as shown in Figure 10-52.
   *This executes the **ATTDEF** command and opens the **Attribute Definition** dialog box shown in Figure 10-53.*

**Figure 10-52**
**Define Attributes** tool

**Figure 10-53**
**Attribute Definition** dialog box

Look first at the check boxes at the top left in the **Mode** panel. For our purposes only **Lock position** should be checked. These are the default settings, which we will use in this first attribute definition. When our workstation block is inserted, the processor attribute value will be visible in the drawing (because **Invisible** is not selected), variable with each insertion of the block (because **Constant** is not selected), not verified (**Verify** is not selected), and not preset to a value (**Preset** is not selected). We will not be able to reposition the text within the block, because **Lock position** is selected by default, and we will use single-line text, because **Multiple lines** is not selected.

Next, look at the **Attribute** panel to the right. The cursor should be blinking in the **Tag** edit box. Like a field name in a database file, a tag identifies the kind of information this particular attribute is meant to hold. The tag appears in the block definition as a field name. In occurrences of the block in a drawing, the tag is replaced by a specific value. Processor, for example, could be replaced by Core 2.

✔ Type **Processor** in the **Tag** edit box.

✔ Move the cursor to the **Prompt** edit box.

As with the tag, the key to understanding the attribute prompt is to be clear about the difference between block definitions and block references. Right now, we are defining an attribute. The attribute definition becomes part of the definition of the workstation block and is used whenever workstation is inserted. With the definition we are creating, there is a prompt whenever we insert a workstation block that asks us to enter information about the processor in a given configuration.

✔ Type **Specify processor type.**

We also have the opportunity to specify a default attribute value, if we wish, by typing in the **Default** value edit box. Here, we leave this field blank, specifying no default value in our attribute definition.

The panel labeled **Text Settings** allows you to specify text parameters as you would in **TEXT**. Visible attributes appear as text on the screen. Therefore, the appearance of the text needs to be specified. We will specify a height and also add the annotative property so that the text can be scaled to appear at a scaled height within a layout viewport.

✔ Click the check box next to **Annotative.**

✔ Double-click in the edit box to the right of **Text height** and then type **4.**
   If you click the **Text height** button to the right, the dialog box disappears so that you can indicate a height by picking points on the screen.
   Finally, AutoCAD needs to know where to place the visible attribute information in the drawing. You can type in x, y, and z coordinate values, but you are more likely to pick a point.

✔ Check to see that **Specify on-screen** is checked in the **Insertion Point** panel.

✔ Click **OK.**
   The dialog box disappears to allow access to the screen. You also see a Start point: prompt in the command line.
   We place our attributes 3″ below the keyboard.

> **NOTE**
> The button to the right of the **Default** value edit box allows you to insert a field as the attribute value. In that case the attribute would automatically update when the field data changed.

✔ Pick a start point 3″ below the left side of the keyboard (see Figure 10-54).
   The dialog box disappears and the attribute tag PROCESSOR is drawn as shown. Remember, this is an attribute definition, not an occurrence of the attribute. PROCESSOR is our attribute tag. After we define the workstation as a block and the block is inserted, answer the Specify processor type: prompt with the name of a processor type, and the name itself will be shown in the drawing rather than this tag.
   We proceed to define two more attributes using some different options.

**Figure 10-54**
Attribute tags

✔ Repeat **ATTDEF.**

> *We use all the default modes, but we provide a default monitor value in this attribute definition.*

✔ Type **MONITOR** for the attribute tag.

✔ Type **Specify monitor type** for the attribute prompt.

✔ Type **20″ CRT** for the default attribute value.

> *Now, when AutoCAD shows the prompt for a monitor type, it also shows 20″ CRT as the default, as you will see.*
>
> *You can align a series of attributes by selecting the **Align below previous attribute definition** check box at the lower left of the dialog box.*

✔ Select the **Align below previous attribute definition** check box.

✔ Click **OK** to complete the dialog.

> *The attribute tag MONITOR should be added to the workstation below the PROCESSOR tag, as shown in Figure 10-54.*
>
> *Next, we add an invisible preset attribute for the mouse. Invisible means that the attribute text is not visible when the block is inserted, although the information is in the database and can be extracted. Preset means that the attribute has a default value and does not issue a prompt to change it.*

✔ Repeat **ATTDEF.**

✔ Select the **Invisible** check box.

✔ Select the **Preset** check box.

✔ Type **MOUSE** for the attribute tag.

> *You do not need a prompt, because the preset attribute is automatically set to the default value. There is no need to add the annotative property because the attribute is not visible when the drawing is plotted.*

✔ Type **MS Mouse** in the **Default** value edit box.

✔ Select the **Align below previous attribute definition** check box to position the attribute below MONITOR in the drawing.

✔ Click **OK** to complete the dialog.

> *The MOUSE attribute tag should be added to your screen, as shown in Figure 10-54. When a workstation block is inserted, the attribute value MS Mouse is written into the database, but nothing appears on the screen because the attribute is defined as invisible.*
>
> *Finally comes the most important step of all: We must define the workstation as a block that includes all our attribute definitions.*

✔ Pick the **Create Block** tool from the **Block Definition** panel.

✔ Type **workstation** for the block name.

✔ Pick the **Select objects** button.

✔ Window the workstation assembly and all three attribute tags.

✔ Right-click to end object selection.

✔ Pick the **Pick point** button.

✔ Pick an insertion base point at the midpoint of the bottom of the keyboard.

✔ If necessary, select the **Delete** button.

✔ Click **OK** to close the dialog box.
*The newly defined block disappears from the screen.*

The workstation block with its three attribute definitions is now present in the *Source* drawing database. Before moving on, we insert three instances of the block and provide some notes on editing attributes and attribute values.

## Inserting Blocks with Attributes

Inserting blocks with attributes is no different from inserting any block, except that you will be prompted for attribute values.

✔ To complete this task, insert three workstations, using the following procedure (note the attribute prompts):

**1** Type **I <Enter>** or pick the **Insert** tool from the **Block** panel of the ribbon.

**2** Select **workstation** from the **Name** list.

**3** Click **OK** to exit the dialog box.

**4** Pick an insertion point.

**5** Answer the attribute prompts for monitors and processors.

*We specified two different configurations for this exercise, as shown in Figure 10-55. The first two are Core 2 processors with the default 20" CRT monitor. The third is a Quad Core processor with a 24" LCD monitor. This exercise will be easier to follow if you use the same attribute values. Notice that you are not prompted for mouse specifications because that attribute is preset.*

*When you are done, your screen should resemble Figure 10-55.*

**Figure 10-55**
Blocks with attributes

## Editing Attribute Values and Definitions

Once you begin to work with defined attributes, you may have occasion to edit them. The first thing to consider whenever you edit attributes is whether you wish to edit attribute values in a block reference or whether you want to edit the actual attribute definition. Editing an attribute value merely replaces an attribute value in one instance of the block that has been inserted into your drawing. Editing the attribute definition changes the block definition itself, so that all instances of the block currently inserted or inserted in the future will be changed. There are four major commands used to edit attributes. **ATTDISP, ATTEDIT,** and **EATTEDIT** work on attribute values in blocks that have been inserted, whereas **BATTMAN** works directly on attribute definitions. The following chart explains their uses.

| Command | Usage |
|---------|-------|
| ATTDISP | Allows control of the visibility of all attribute values in inserted blocks, regardless of their defined visibility mode. There are three options. **Normal** means that visible attributes are visible and invisible attributes are invisible. **On** makes all attributes visible. **Off** makes all attributes invisible. |
| ATTEDIT | Allows single or global editing of attribute values from the command line. Global editing allows editing text strings in all attribute values that fit criteria you define. |
| EATTEDIT | Opens the **Enhanced Attribute Editor** dialog box for editing individual attribute values in inserted blocks. It allows you to change individual attribute values, text position, height, angle, style, layer, and color of attribute values. |
| BATTMAN | Opens the **Block Attribute Manager** and allows editing of attribute definitions. In this dialog box you can edit tags, prompts, default values, and modes for all blocks defined in a drawing. Changes are made directly to the block definition and reflected in blocks subsequently inserted. |

# Working with External References

You have made numerous changes to the drawing called *Source.* Attributes have been added, a workstation block has been created, and three references to the new block have been inserted into the drawing, with attached attribute information. This provides us a good opportunity to turn our attention back to *Target* and look at the *Source* external reference there to see how Xrefs work in action.

✔ Before leaving *Source,* pick the **Save** tool on the **Quick Access** toolbar to save your changes.

> *This is not just to safeguard changes. It is necessary to save changes to an Xref before the changes can be read into another drawing.*

✔ Select the **Target** drawing file tab.

> *You should be back in* Target *with a single workstation Xref and a computer terminal block on your screen, as shown previously in Figure 10-49. You should also see a notification balloon in the lower right corner of your screen, as shown in Figure 10-56, indicating that an externally referenced drawing has been changed and giving you the name of the Xref. To clearly appreciate the use of this notification, imagine for a moment that you are working with a team of designers. The focus of the project is a master drawing that contains references to several external drawings, and these drawings are being created or edited by designers at various locations*

**Figure 10-56**
External reference notification balloon

connected by a network or the Internet. The external reference update notification instantly informs anyone looking at the master drawing that one or more of the external references have changed and should be reloaded to keep things up to date. Be aware that this notification would not appear if the changes made to Source had not been saved.

The first thing we need to do is reload the Source Xref to bring our changes into Target.

✔ Click the blue underlined link to *Source* in the notification balloon.
This updates the external reference to Source, which now includes all three references to the workstation block. Target is updated to reflect the changes in Source, as shown in Figure 10-57. Following are a few notes on working with external references.

**Figure 10-57**
Updated *Target* drawing

## Reloading Attached References

If you need to update an attached reference when the notification balloon is not showing, follow these steps:

**1** Type **ext** and select **EXTERNALREFERENCES** from the **AutoComplete menu.**

**2** In the **External references** palette, highlight the external reference you wish to reload.

**3** Right-click and select **Reload** from the shortcut menu.

## Editing External References in Place

External references can be edited within the current drawing and even used to update the original referenced drawing. This should be done sparingly and for simple edits only; otherwise the current drawing will expand to take up more memory, and the point of using an external reference instead of a block reference will be lost. To edit a block or external reference in place, select the reference, then right-click and select **Edit Xref In-place** from the shortcut menu.

## Clipping External References

External references can also be clipped so that only a portion of the referenced drawing is actually displayed in the current drawing. This allows different users on the same network to share portions of their drawings without altering the original drawings. Clipping boundaries can be defined by a rectangular window, a polygon window, or an existing polyline. Clipping is performed with the **XCLIP** command and can be used on block references as well as external references. To clip a reference, select it, right-click, and select **Clip Xref** from the shortcut menu.

For example, you could clip the attributes in *Target* so that only the workstations remained visible. The process would be:

**1** In *Target,* select the three workstation references to *Source.*

**2** Right-click to open the shortcut menu.

**3** Select **Clip Xref.**

**4** Press **<Enter>** to accept the default, rectangular boundary.

**5** Pick two points to define a window around the workstations, but not around the attributes.

Clipping an instance of an Xref does not alter the Xref definition; it only suppresses the display of the objects outside the clipping boundary.

In the next section, we return to our attribute information.

## Extracting Data from Attributes

Many types of data can be extracted from a drawing and quickly formatted into tables or linked to external applications. Extracted data can be transferred to spreadsheet or database programs for use in the preparation of parts lists, bills of material, and other documentation. For example, with a well-managed system of parts and attributes, you can do a drawing of a construction project and get a complete price breakdown and supply list directly from the drawing database, all processed by computer. To accomplish this, you need carefully defined attributes and a program such as Microsoft Excel that is capable of receiving the extracted information and formatting it into a useful report.

In this demonstration, you extract attribute information from blocks in *Source* and place it in an AutoCAD table, which you insert back into the drawing. The steps are the same as if you were exporting the information to a spreadsheet or database program but can be completed successfully without leaving AutoCAD. If you are in *Target* from the previous task, you start by switching back to *Source.*

✔ Select the **Source** drawing file tab to bring *Source* back into the foreground.

> *The three workstation blocks and their attribute values should be on your screen.*

Figure 10-58
Extract Data tool

✔ Pick the **Extract Data** tool from the **Linking & Extraction** panel on the **Insert** tab, as shown in Figure 10-58.

> You see the **Data Extraction** wizard, as shown in Figure 10-59. This wizard takes you through eight steps of selecting data to extract and creating a table that can be exported or inserted.
>
> The first step in this wizard is to select a template file or to create a file from scratch. The template can be a previous extraction laid out to receive the information from your attributes.

Figure 10-59
Data Extraction wizard

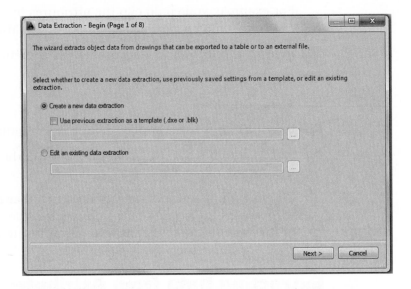

✔ If necessary, select the **Create a new data extraction** button.

✔ Click **Next.**

> This brings you to the **Save Data Extraction As** dialog box. This is a standard file-saving dialog box. The extracted data must first be saved to a file with a .dxe extension. This is true even if you are going to insert it back into your current drawing.

✔ Type **workstation data <Enter>** in the **File name** box.

> This takes you to the **Data Extraction - Define Data Source** dialog box shown in Figure 10-60. In the **Data source** panel of this dialog box you can choose to extract data from the current drawing and/or drawing sheet set or from selected objects only. The panel below that gives the path of the current drawing. **Drawings/Sheet set** and **Include current drawing** should be selected in this box.

✔ Click **Next.**

> This brings you to the **Data Extraction - Select Objects** dialog box shown in Figure 10-61. Here we begin to narrow down the type of data we want to extract. Currently all objects in the drawing are displayed. Our goal is to extract just the attribute data from the three workstation blocks in the drawing.

**Figure 10-60**
**Data Extraction - Define Data Source** dialog box

**Figure 10-61**
**Data Extraction - Select Objects** dialog box

✔ Deselect the **Display all object types** box.

> *This gives you access to the two buttons below. **Display blocks only** should be selected by default. On the right are two other options: **Display blocks with attributes only** and **Display objects currently in-use only**.*

✔ Select **Display blocks with attributes only.**

> *At this point the only thing displayed in the **Objects** list should be the workstation block.*

✔ Click **Next.**

> *Now you see the **Data Extraction - Select Properties** dialog box shown in Figure 10-62. The **Category filter** on the right allows us to narrow down to attributes only.*

✔ Deselect all the categories except **Attribute,** as shown in the figure.

> *You should see only the monitor, mouse, and processor attributes in the **Properties** list, as shown.*

✔ Click **Next.**

> *In the **Data Extraction - Refine Data** dialog box shown in Figure 10-63, the data are displayed and grouped according to the*

**Figure 10-62**
**Data Extraction - Select Properties** dialog box

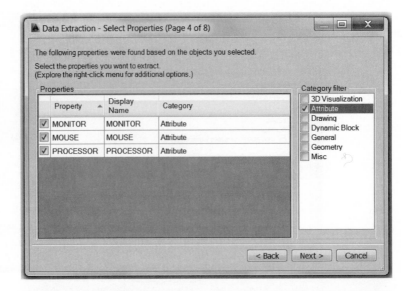

**Figure 10-63**
**Data Extraction - Refine Data** dialog box

selections made in the three boxes at the bottom: **Combine identical rows, Show count column,** and **Show name column.** They should all be selected by default.

✔ Click **Next.**

The next box gives you the choice of extracting to an external file or to an AutoCAD table.

✔ Select the first choice, **Insert data extraction table into drawing.**

✔ Click **Next.**

You are now in a **Table Style** dialog box. We will stick with the Standard table style but will add a title.

✔ Double-click in the edit box below **Enter a title for your table.**

✔ Type **Workstation Data.**

✔ Click **Next.**

✔ Click **Finish.**

You have completed the attribute extraction process; all that remains is to insert the table into your drawing. You see a very small table connected to the crosshairs.

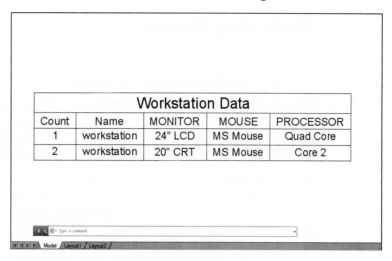

✔ Pick a point on your screen below the middle block reference.

✔ Zoom into a window around the inserted table.

*Your screen should resemble Figure 10-64.*

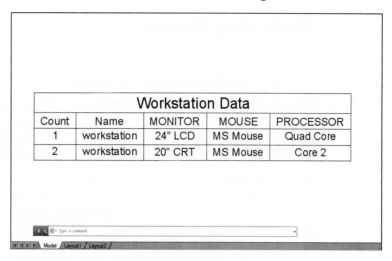

**Figure 10-64**
Inserted table

| Workstation Data | | | | |
|---|---|---|---|---|
| Count | Name | MONITOR | MOUSE | PROCESSOR |
| 1 | workstation | 24" LCD | MS Mouse | Quad Core |
| 2 | workstation | 20" CRT | MS Mouse | Core 2 |

## Creating Tool Palettes

Given your knowledge of blocks, Xrefs, and the **DesignCenter,** at this point you also have use for another AutoCAD feature. *Tool palettes* are simply collections of blocks placed very accessibly in a format that is much simpler than the **DesignCenter** palette.

The real power of tool palettes comes from the ease with which you can populate them with your own content. Try this:

✔ Pick the **DesignCenter** tool from the **Content** panel on the **Insert** tab.

✔ If necessary, click the **Open Drawings** tab.

✔ If necessary, highlight *Source.dwg* and open the **Source** list.

✔ Double-click the **Blocks** icon.

*You can see the set of blocks in* Source, *including the workstation, computer, keyboard, monitor, and mouse blocks.*

✔ Right-click anywhere in the content area.

✔ From the shortcut menu, select **Create Tool Palette** at the bottom of the menu.

*A tool palette is opened with a new tab, labeled* **Source,** *from the name of the drawing. This palette tab has the five blocks from* Source, *as shown in Figure 10-65. It's that simple. You now have your own tool palette to work with. The blocks on this tab can be dragged into the drawing.*

*Keep in mind that the tools on a tool palette are accessible only as long as the reference is clear. If they originate from an externally referenced drawing, the reference path must be clear and accessible. If the referenced drawing is moved or deleted, the tool will no longer be available.*

**Figure 10-65**
**Source** tool palette created

> **TIP**
>
> If your **Source** tool palette does not open automatically, select **View** tab > **Palettes** panel > **Tool Palettes** tool. This opens the whole set of tool palettes, with the **Source** tab open at the top.

✔ Close the **Source** tool palette and the **DesignCenter**.

*In the next and final section of this chapter you learn how to reverse the block definition process.*

## Exploding Blocks

> **TIP**
>
> A general procedure for exploding blocks is:
>
> 1. Type **x \<Enter\>,** or pick the **Explode** tool from the **Modify** panel of the ribbon.
> 2. Select objects.
> 3. Right-click to end object selection and carry out the command.

The **EXPLODE** command undoes the work of the **BLOCK** command. It takes a set of objects that have been defined as a block and re-creates them as independent entities. **EXPLODE** works on dimensions, hatch patterns, and associative arrays as well as on blocks created in the **BLOCK** command or tools inserted from a tool palette. It does not work on externally referenced drawings until they have been attached permanently through the **Bind** option of the **XREF** command.

| EXPLODE | |
|---|---|
| Command | Explode |
| Alias | X |
| Panel | Modify |
| Tool | |

> **NOTE**
>
> Exploding removes only one layer of block definition. If a block is made up of other blocks, these "nested" blocks remain as independent blocks after exploding. Attribute value information is removed by exploding, leaving the attribute tag instead.

✔ To begin this task, you should have *Source* open on your screen.

*Let's try exploding a workstation.*

✔ If necessary, **Zoom All** to see the complete drawing.

✔ Pick **Home** tab > **Modify** panel > **Explode** tool from the ribbon, as shown in Figure 10-66.

*You are prompted to select objects.*

**Figure 10-66**
**Explode** tool

✔ Select the center workstation.

✔ Right-click to end object selection and carry out the command.

*You should notice immediately that the attribute values are replaced by attribute tags. Run your cursor over any part of the workstation and observe the preview highlighting.*

*All the component parts of the previously blocked workstation can now be selected separately, including the attribute tags. If you select the computer rectangle, you see that the parameter and action are once again accessible. If you select the monitor, you see the constraint parameter and block table markers.*

# Chapter Summary

Congratulations! This has been a tough chapter with a lot of new information and procedures to learn. You have gained a greater sense of the tools available for using AutoCAD in collaborative work environments. You have learned to create groups and blocks from previously drawn objects and to explode blocks and other collective entities back into independent objects. You have learned to insert blocks into the current drawing and to insert one drawing into another. Through the dynamic block feature, you can create blocks with flexible parameters, and geometric and dimensional constraints, so that a single block definition can be used to represent different variations of the same basic object. Using block tables, you can create a set of these variations by entering numeric data and letting AutoCAD extrapolate the impact on block parameters. As an important alternative to using blocks, you have seen how one drawing can be attached to another as an external reference that can be updated in the current drawing when the referenced drawing changes. The AutoCAD **DesignCenter** and the **Content Explorer** are additional tools that allow you to share blocks, layers, text styles, layouts, and other types of content between drawings. You have learned to attach information to objects in your drawing in the form of attributes that can be extracted and manipulated in spreadsheet and database programs. Finally, you have seen how easy it can be to create a tool palette with blocks accessible from your current drawing. For simpler applications, objects can be saved to the Windows Clipboard and then inserted into other AutoCAD drawings or other types of documents. Through these new techniques, you should appreciate that AutoCAD has powerful features that go well beyond the one-person, one-workstation arena to include collaboration among individuals, companies, and work sites around the globe.

# Chapter Test Questions

## Multiple Choice

*Circle the correct answer.*

1. Which of these **cannot** be found in the AutoCAD **DesignCenter**?
   a. Layers
   b. Blocks
   c. External references
   d. Block tables

2. If a base point is **not** defined in an inserted drawing, the base will be the:
   a. Midpoint of the block
   b. Insertion point
   c. Origin point
   d. Datum point

3. While blocks are inserted, xrefs are:
   a. Linked
   b. Attached
   c. Referenced
   d. Hyperlinked

4. Every parameter in a dynamic block must have:
   a. An action
   b. A constraint
   c. A base point
   d. A block table

5. The name that identifies an attribute in an attribute definition is called a(n):
   a. **ATTDEF**
   b. Field
   c. Tag
   d. Attribute prompt

## Matching

*Write the number of the correct answer on the line.*

a. Insert _____          1. Attribute

b. Attach _____          2. Block

c. Tag _____             3. Block table

d. Parameter _____       4. **DesignCenter**

e. Tree view _____       5. Xref

## True or False

*Circle the correct answer.*

1. **True or False:** Base points are included in block definitions, insertion points in block references.

2. **True or False:** External references are updated automatically when the referenced drawing changes.

3. **True or False:** Parameters, actions, constraints, and block tables are added to dynamic blocks in the **Block Editor** contextual tab.

4. **True or False:** To redefine a block as separate entities you must return to the block definition.

5. **True or False:** A block table has attribute fields that can be updated.

## Questions

1. Why is it usually a good idea to create blocks on Layer **0**?

2. What would you have to do to create blocks with geometry that could be edited after they were inserted?

3. What is the purpose of the yellow exclamation point that appears whenever you add a parameter to a block?

4. What other complex entities can be exploded besides blocks?

5. What happens to attribute values when a block is exploded?

## Drawing Problems

1. Open a new drawing with 18 × 12 limits and create a hexagon circumscribed around a circle with a 1.0-unit radius.

2. Define an attribute to go with the hexagon and circle. The tag should identify the two as a hex bolt; the prompt should ask for a hex bolt diameter. The attribute should be visible in the drawing, center justified 0.5 unit below the block, with text 0.3 unit high.

3. Create a block with the bolt and its attribute. Leave a clear screen when you are done.

4. Draw a rectangle with lower left corner at (0,4) and upper right corner at (18,8).

5. Insert 0.5-diameter hex bolts centered at (2,6) and (16,6). Insert a 1.0-unit hex bolt centered at (9,6). The size of each hex bolt should appear beneath the bolt.

## WWW Exercise (Optional)

The new material in this chapter opens the door to several new Internet access procedures. In this exercise, we show you how to insert hyperlinks into drawings so that anyone using your drawing can jump from an object directly to a specified Internet address. All you have to do is insert a hyperlink and make sure that whoever wants to use that hyperlink is connected to the Internet at the time. Hyperlinks can also be used to connect to other drawing files, views, or layouts. For demonstration, we insert a hyperlink into *Source*, attached to a workstation block. The hyperlink is defined to link to our companion website. Then, we go through the procedure for connecting to the website through the hyperlink. Here we go.

✔ To begin this task, you should be in **Source.dwg.**
   *If for any reason this drawing is not readily available, any drawing will do, but the illustrations will not match.*

✔ If you have not already done so, connect to your Internet service provider.

✔ Select **Insert** tab > **Data** panel > **Hyperlink** tool from the ribbon, as shown in Figure 10-67.
   *Hyperlinks are connected to objects, so AutoCAD prompts you to select objects. The prompt is plural, indicating that you can select more than one object to connect to the same hyperlink.*

✔ Select the workstation on the left.

✔ Select the workstation on the right.

**Figure 10-67**
**Hyperlink** tool

✔ Right-click to end object selection.
*This brings you to the **Insert Hyperlink** dialog box shown in Figure 10-68. Look over the box to see the array of options you have for linking through this feature.*

**Figure 10-68**
**Insert Hyperlink** dialog box

✔ Type www.pearsonhighered.com/dixriley in the **Type the file or Web page name** edit box.

✔ Click **OK** to exit the dialog box.
*The dialog box disappears. The links have been inserted, but nothing happens until you select a hyperlink.*

✔ Move your cursor over either of the selected workstations. (We chose the one on the left.) When you see the hyperlink cursor, as shown in Figure 10-69, let the cursor rest.
*You see the hyperlink symbol and below it the hyperlink specification, as shown in Figure 10-69.*

✔ With the hyperlink symbol displayed, press the pick button.
*The workstation is selected but nothing else happens.*

✔ Right-click anywhere in the drawing area.
*A shortcut menu appears with **Hyperlink** on the bottom.*

**Figure 10-69**
Hyperlink symbol

✔ Highlight **Hyperlink** at the bottom of the shortcut menu.
*This opens a submenu, as shown in Figure 10-70.*

**Figure 10-70**
Shortcut menu

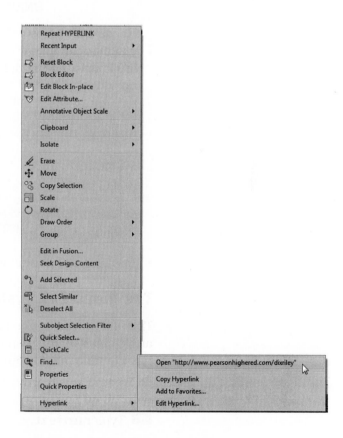

✔ Select **Open "http://www.pearsonhighered.com/dixriley"**.
*See you at the website!*

# Chapter Drawing Projects

## A Drawing 10-1: *CAD Room* [INTERMEDIATE]

This architectural drawing is primarily an exercise in using blocks and attributes. Use your workstation block and its attributes to fill in the workstations and text after you draw the walls and countertop. New blocks should be created for the plotters and printers, as described subsequently. The drawing setup is consistent with *Source* from the chapter so that blocks can be easily inserted without scaling. When you have completed this drawing, you might want to try extracting the attribute information to a word processor or Excel file.

### Drawing Suggestions

UNITS = Architectural; Precision = 0'-0'

GRID = 1'

SNAP = 1'

LIMITS = (0',0')(48',36')

- The "plotter" block is a 1 × 3 rectangle, with two visible, variable attributes (all the default attribute modes). The first attribute is for a manufacturer, and the second is for a model. The "printer" is 2 × 2.5 with the same type of attributes. Draw the rectangles, define their attributes 8" below them, create the block definitions, and then insert plotter and printer as shown.

> **NOTE**
>
> Do not include the labels "plotter" and "laser printer" in the block, because text in a block is rotated with the block. This would give you inverted text on the front counter-top. Insert the blocks and add the text afterward. The attribute text can be handled differently, using the **MIRRTEXT** system variable.

- The largest "plotter" was inserted with a *y* scale factor of 1.25.

### The MIRRTEXT System Variable

The four workstations on the front counter could be inserted with a rotation angle of 180°, but then the attribute text would be inverted also and would have to be turned around using **EATTEDIT.** Instead, we have reset the **MIRRTEXT** system variable so that we could mirror blocks without inverting attribute text:

**1** Type **mirrtext.**

**2** Type **0.**

Now, you can mirror objects on the back counter to create those on the front. With the **MIRRTEXT** system variable set to **0,** text included in a **MIRROR** procedure is not inverted, as it would be with **MIRRTEXT** set to **1.** This applies to attribute text as well as ordinary text. However, it does not apply to ordinary text included in a block definition.

**Drawing 10-1**
CAD Room

**A**

# Drawing 10-2: *Office Plan* [INTERMEDIATE]

This drawing is primarily an exercise in the use of predrawn blocks and symbols. With a few exceptions, everything in the drawing can be inserted from the AutoCAD **DesignCenter.**

## Drawing Suggestions

- Observe the overall 62′ × 33′ dimensions of the office space and choose appropriate architectural limits, snap settings, and grid settings for the drawing.

- We have not provided dimensions for the interior spaces, so you are free to choose dimensions as you wish.

- All walls can be drawn as 6″-wide filled polylines.

- All doors and furniture can be inserted from the **DesignCenter.**

- The large meeting room table is not predrawn. Create a simple filleted rectangle with dimensions as shown. It might be defined and saved as a block for future use.

33 ft.

Sink

Toilet

File Cabinet
Lamp
Computer
Desk
Phone
Chair

Copy Machine

Sink

Toilet

Sofa

Table

Lamp
File Cabinet
Computer
Desk
Phone
Chair

Chair
Phone
Desk
Computer
File Cabinet
Lamp

Copy Machine

Copy Machine

Sofa

62 ft.

Copy Machine

Lamp
File Cabinet
Computer
Desk
Phone
Chair

Sofa

Chair

Plant

Sofa

Table

Chair

Chair

Desk
10' × 5'

Chair

Chair

Chair

Office Area = 2050 sq ft

**Drawing 10-2**
Office Plan

# Drawing 10-3: *Base Assembly* [INTERMEDIATE]

This is a good exercise in assembly drawing procedures. You draw each of the numbered part details and then assemble them into the base assembly.

## Drawing Suggestions

We no longer provide you with units, grid, snap, and limit settings. You can determine what you need by looking over the drawing and its dimensions. Remember that you can always change a setting later if necessary.

- You can either create your own title block from scratch or develop one from a previous drawing. Once created and saved or wblocked, a title block can be inserted and scaled to fit any drawing. AutoCAD also comes with drawing templates that have borders and title blocks.

## Using Table to Create a Bill of Materials

**1** To create the bill of materials in this drawing, select the **Table** tool from the ribbon and insert a Standard table with 4 columns and 5 rows. Row height should be specified to match the height shown in the drawing.

**2** Once the table is inserted, click outside the table to complete the command.

**3** Click once in the title row to open the **Table** group of panels on the ribbon.

**4** With the **Table** panels showing and the title row highlighted, pick the **Unmerge Cells** tool from the **Merge** panel. Click outside the table again to complete the command. This will eliminate the title row and leave you with 7 data rows.

**5** Adjust column width by first selecting the entire table, then clicking and dragging a grip at the top of a column. Press **<Esc>** to remove grips.

## Managing Parts Blocks for Multiple Use

You draw each of the numbered parts (B101-1, B101-2, etc.) and then assemble them. In an industrial application, the individual part details would be sent to different manufacturers or manufacturing departments, so they must exist as separate, completely dimensioned drawings as well as blocks that can be used in creating the assembly. An efficient method is to create three separate blocks for each part detail: one for dimensions and one for each view in the assembly. The dimensioned part drawings include both views. The blocks of the two views have dimensions, hidden lines, and centerlines erased.

Think carefully about the way you name blocks. You may want to adopt a naming system such as the following: B101-1D for the dimensioned drawing, B101-IT for a top view without dimensions, and B101-1F for a front view without dimensions. Such a system makes it easy to call out all the top view parts for the top view assembly, for example.

- Notice that the assembly requires you to do a considerable amount of trimming away of lines from the blocks you insert. This can be easily completed, but you must remember to explode the inserted blocks first.

**Drawing 10-3**
Base Assembly

# Drawing 10-4: Double Bearing Assembly [ADVANCED]

ASSEMBLY DRAWING

BUSHING

HEX HEAD BOLT

1/2-13 × 2 1/4 UNC-2A

NOTE: FILLETS AND ROUNDS 1/8 RADIUS
EXCEPT AS NOTED

DRAWING COMPLIMENTS OF DAVID SUMMER

33/64 DRILL (6) HOLES

CAP

R1.25

R0.75

29/64 DRILL × 1 1/2 DEEP
1/2 13 UNC × 1 1/8 DEEP
(6) HOLES

BASE

R0.75 R1.25

45°

R0.25

| ITEM NO. | DESCRIPTION | | PART NO. | QTY |
|---|---|---|---|---|
| 4 | HEX HEAD BOLT | 1/2-13 UNC × 2.25 LG | DB1-4 | 6 |
| 3 | BUSHING | | DB1-3 | 2 |
| 2 | CAP | | DB1-2 | 1 |
| 1 | BASE | | DB1-1 | 1 |

DRAWN BY: | DATE

DRAWING TITLE
Double Bearing

DRAWING NO.
Drawing 10-4

SIZE | SCALE: | DATE: | REV
| | SHEET OF

Drawing 10-4

# Drawing 10-5: *Scooter Assembly* [ADVANCED]

WHEEL DETAIL

| ITEM NO. | DESCRIPTION | | PART NO. | QTY |
|---|---|---|---|---|
| 13 | HEX NUT | 1/4-20 UNC | S100-13 | 8 |
| 12 | TRUSS HEAD SCREW | 1/4-20 UNC × 1.50 LG | S100-12 | 8 |
| 11 | HEX NUT | 3/8-16 UNC | S100-11 | 4 |
| 10 | HEX HEAD BOLT | 3/8-16 UNC × 5.00 LG | S100-10 | 1 |
| 9 | HEX HEAD BOLT | 3/8-16 UNC × 4.00 LG | S100-9 | 1 |
| 8 | HEX HEAD BOLT | 3/8-16 UNC × 3.25 LG | S100-8 | 2 |
| 7 | BRACE | | S100-7 | 1 |
| 6 | SPACER | | S100-6 | 3 |
| 5 | KICK STAND | | S100-5 | 1 |
| 4 | FOOT REST | | S100-4 | 1 |
| 3 | FRAME | | S100-3 | 1 |
| 2 | HANDLE BAR | | S100-2 | 2 |
| 1 | WHEEL | | S100-1 | 2 |

DRAWN BY: DATE:

CAD Support Associates

DRAWING TITLE:
SCOOTER ASSEMBLY

DRAWING NO.
Drawing 10-5

SIZE | REV.

SCALE: | DATE: | SHEET OF

**Drawing 10-5**
Sheet 1 of 2 (assembly drawing)

**Drawing 10-5**
Sheet 2 of 2 (details drawings)

# 11

# Isometric Drawing

## CHAPTER OBJECTIVES

- Use isometric snap
- Switch isometric planes
- Use **COPY** and other edit commands
- Draw isometric circles with **ELLIPSE**

- Draw text aligned with isometric planes
- Draw ellipses in orthographic views
- Save and restore displays with **VIEW**

### Introduction

Learning to use AutoCAD's isometric drawing features should be a pleasure at this point. There are very few new commands to learn, and anything you know about manual isometric drawing is easier on the computer. Once you know how to get into the isometric mode and change from plane to plane, you can rely on previously learned skills and techniques. Many of the commands you have learned will work readily, and you will find that using the isometric drawing planes is an excellent warm-up for 3D wireframe and solid modeling.

### Using Isometric Snap

> **TIP**
>
> A general procedure for entering isometric snap mode is:
>
> 1. Right-click the **Snap Mode** or **Grid Display** button on the status bar.
> 2. Select **Settings**.
> 3. In the **Drafting Settings** dialog box, select the **Isometric snap** radio button.
> 4. Click **OK**.

To begin drawing isometrically, you need to switch to the isometric snap style and the 2D model space grid. You find the grid and crosshairs behaving in ways that might seem odd at first, but you quickly get used to them.

✔ Begin a new drawing using decimal units and 18 × 12 limits.

✔ Right-click the **Snap Mode** or **Grid Display** button on the status bar.

✔ Select **Settings** from the shortcut menu.
   *You see the **Drafting Settings** dialog box.*

✔ Click the **Isometric snap** radio button in the **Snap type** panel at the lower left.
   *The **Grid snap** button must be selected also, but it should be on by default.*

> **NOTE**
> Because AutoCAD retains the isoplane setting from the most recent drawing session, it is possible that your crosshairs may be turned to the right or left isoplane instead of the top, as shown. It is not necessary to change the setting in this task.

✔ In the **Grid style** area at the upper right, check the **2D model space** box.
   *With this setting your grid will be a matrix of dots instead of lines. The grid of dots will turn along the isometric angles; the lined grid will not.*

✔ Remove the check from the **Adaptive** check box in the **Grid behavior** panel at the lower right.

✔ Click **OK**.
   *At this point, your grid and crosshairs are reoriented and presented as dots instead of lines, resembling Figure 11-1. This is the 2D model space grid in isometric mode. Grid points are placed at 30°, 90°, and 150° angles from the horizontal. The crosshairs are initially turned to define the left isometric plane. The three **isoplanes** are discussed in the "Switching Isometric Planes" section.*

**isoplane:** One of three planes used for isometric drawing. In AutoCAD these planes are called left, right, and top.

✔ To get a feeling for how this snap style works, enter the **LINE** command and draw some boxes, as shown in Figure 11-2.
   *Make sure that **Ortho** is off and **Snap** is on, or you will be unable to draw the lines shown.*

**Figure 11-1**
Isometric grid

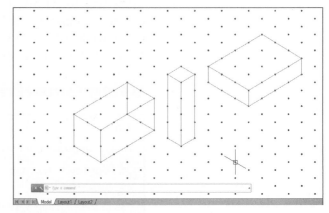

**Figure 11-2**
Isometric boxes

# Switching Isometric Planes

If you tried to draw the boxes in the preceding section with **Ortho** on, you discovered that it is impossible. Without changing the orientation of the crosshairs, you can draw in only two of the three isometric planes. We need to be able to switch planes so that we can leave **Ortho** on for accuracy and speed. There are several ways to do this, but the simplest, quickest, and most convenient way is to use the <**F5**> key (or <**Ctrl**>+**E**).

Before beginning, take a look at Figure 11-3. It shows the three planes of a standard isometric drawing. These planes are often referred to as top, front, and right. However, AutoCAD's terminology is top, left, and right. We stick with AutoCAD's labels in this chapter.

**Figure 11-3**
Isometric planes

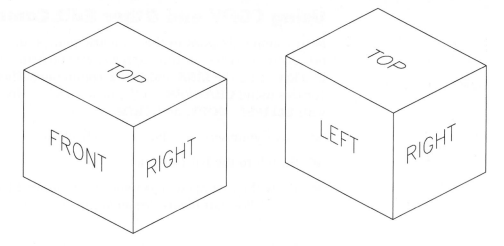

Now look at Figure 11-4, and you can see how the isometric crosshairs are oriented to draw in each of the planes.

**Figure 11-4**
Isometric crosshairs

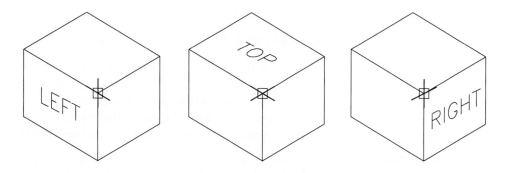

✔ Press <**F5**> (or <**Ctrl**>+**E**) to switch from left to top.

✔ Press <**F5**> again to switch from top to right.

✔ Press <**F5**> once more to switch back to left.

✔ Now turn **Ortho** on and draw a box outline like the one in Figure 11-5. *You need to switch planes several times to accomplish this. Notice that you can switch planes using <**F5**> without interrupting the **LINE** command. If you find that you are in the wrong plane to construct a line, switch planes. Because every plane allows movement in two of the three directions, you can always move in the direction you want with one switch. However, you may not be able to hit the snap point you want. If you cannot, switch planes again.*

**Figure 11-5**
Isometric box outline

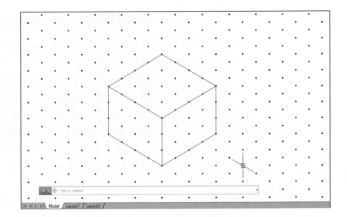

## Using COPY and Other Edit Commands

Most commands work in the isometric planes just as they do in standard orthographic views. In this exercise, we construct an isometric view of a bracket using the **LINE** and **COPY** commands. Then, we draw angled corners using **CHAMFER**. In the next task, we draw a hole in the bracket with **ELLIPSE, COPY,** and **TRIM.**

✔ Clear your screen of boxes and check to see that **Ortho** mode is on.

✔ Switch to the left isoplane.

✔ Draw the L-shaped object shown in Figure 11-6.
   *Notice that this is drawn in the left isoplane and that it is 1.00 unit wide.*

✔ Next, we copy this object 4.00 units back to the right to create the back surface of the bracket.

✔ Pick the **Copy** tool from the ribbon.

✔ Select all the lines in the L.

✔ Right-click to end object selection.

✔ Pick a base point at the inside corner of the L.
   *It is a good exercise to keep **Ortho** on, switch planes, and move the object around in each plane. You can move in two directions in each isoplane. To move the object back to the right, as shown in Figure 11-7, you must be in either the top or the right isoplane.*

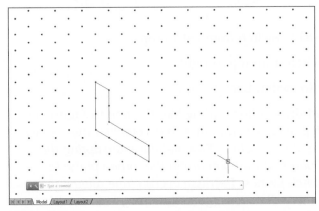

**Figure 11-6**
Drawing an L shape

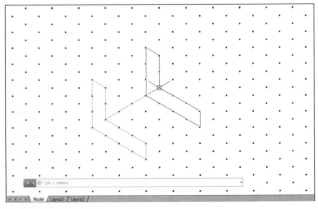

**Figure 11-7**
Copying the L shape

✔ Switch to the top or right isoplane and pick a second point of displacement 4.00 units back to the right, as shown in Figure 11-7.

✔ Press **<Enter>** to exit **COPY.**

✔ Enter the **LINE** command and draw the connecting lines in the right plane, as shown in Figure 11-8.

**Figure 11-8**
Drawing connecting lines

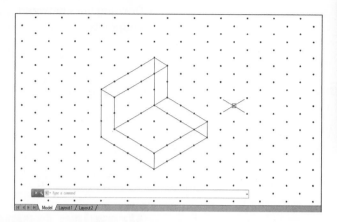

## Creating Chamfers in an Isometric View

Keep in mind that inclined edges in an isometric view do not show true lengths. Edges of inclined planes must be drawn between endpoints located along paths that are vertical or horizontal in one of the three drawing planes. In our exercise, we create inclined edges by using the **CHAMFER** command to cut the corners of the bracket. This is no different from using **CHAMFER** in orthographic views.

✔ Pick the **Chamfer** tool from the **Fillet** drop-down list on the ribbon.

✔ Right-click and select **Distance** from the shortcut menu.
 *AutoCAD prompts for a first chamfer distance.*

✔ Type **1<Enter>.**

✔ Press **<Enter>** to accept 1.00 as the second chamfer distance.

✔ Pick two edges of the bracket to create a chamfer, as shown in Figure 11-9.

✔ Repeat **CHAMFER.**

✔ Chamfer the other three corners so that your drawing resembles Figure 11-9.

**Figure 11-9**
Chamfering corners

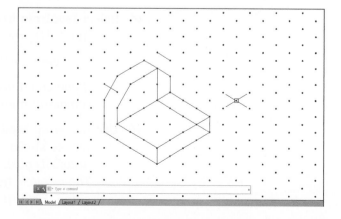

✔ To complete the bracket, enter the **LINE** command and draw lines between the new chamfer endpoints.

✔ Finally, erase the two unseen lines on the back surface to produce Figure 11-10.

**Figure 11-10**
Drawing lines between endpoints

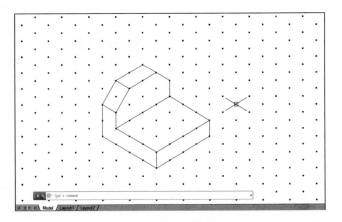

## Drawing Isometric Circles with ELLIPSE

| ELLIPSE | |
|---|---|
| **Command** | Ellipse |
| **Alias** | El |
| **Panel** | Draw |
| **Tool** | |

isocircle: The elliptical representation of a circle in an isometric drawing.

The **ELLIPSE** command can be used to draw true ellipses in orthographic views or ellipses that appear to be circles in isometric views (called *isocircles* in AutoCAD). In this task, we use the latter capability to construct a hole in the bracket.

✔ To begin this task you should have the bracket shown in Figure 11-10 on your screen.

*To draw an isocircle you need a center point. Often, it is necessary to locate this point carefully using temporary lines, object snap tracking, or point filters. You must be sure that you can locate the center point before entering the **ELLIPSE** command.*

*In our case, it is easy because the center point is on a snap point.*

✔ Type **el <Enter>**.

*There is an **Ellipse** tool on the ribbon and an **Ellipse** selection on the **Draw** menu, but these automate an initial option and do not give you access to the **Isocircle** option.*

*AutoCAD prompts:*

Specify axis endpoint of ellipse or [Arc Center Isocircle]:

*The option we want is **Isocircle**. Ignore the others for the time being.*

✔ Select **Isocircle** from the command line.

*AutoCAD prompts:*

Specify center of isocircle:

*If you could not locate the center point, you would have to exit the command now and start over.*

✔ Use the **Snap Mode** and **Grid Display** tools to pick the center of the surface, as shown in Figure 11-11.

*AutoCAD gives you an isocircle to drag, as in the **CIRCLE** command. The isocircle you see depends on the isoplane you are in. To understand this, try switching planes to see how the image changes.*

**Figure 11-11**
Ellipse isocircle

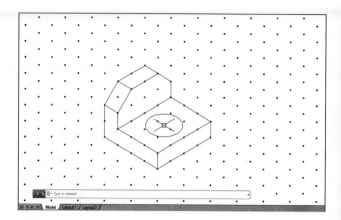

✔ Stretch the isocircle image out and then press **<F5>** to switch iso-planes. Observe the isocircle. Try this two or three times.

✔ Switch to the top isoplane before moving on.
*AutoCAD prompts for a radius or diameter:*

Specify radius of isocircle or [Diameter]:

*A radius specification is the default here, as it is in the **CIRCLE** command.*

✔ Pick a point so that your isocircle resembles the one in Figure 11-11.
*Next, we use the **COPY** and **TRIM** commands to create the bottom of the hole.*

✔ Enter the **COPY** command.

✔ Select the isocircle.

✔ Right-click to end object selection.

✔ Pick the top front corner of the bracket.
*Any point can be used as the base point. By picking the top front corner, the bottom front corner gives you the exact thickness of the bracket.*

✔ Pick the bottom front corner. Make sure that you are in an isoplane that allows movement from top to bottom.
*Your screen should now resemble Figure 11-12. The last thing we must do is trim the hidden portion of the bottom of the hole.*

**Figure 11-12**
Copy isocircle

✔ Press <**Enter**> to exit **COPY.**

✔ Enter the **TRIM** command.

✔ Pick the first isocircle as a cutting edge.
   *It may help to turn off snap to make these selections.*

✔ Right-click to end cutting edge selection.

✔ Select the hidden section of the lower isocircle.

✔ Press <**Enter**> to exit **TRIM.**
   *The bracket is now complete, and your screen should resemble Figure 11-13.*

**Figure 11-13**
Trimming lower isocircle

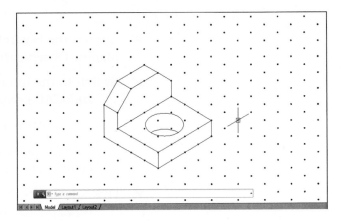

## Drawing Text Aligned with Isometric Planes

Adding text to isometric drawings has some challenges you may not have encountered previously. To create the appearance that text aligns with an isometric plane, it needs to be altered in two ways. First, the whole line of text needs to be rotated to align with one side of the plane. Second, the obliquing angle of individual characters needs to be adjusted to match the tilt of the plane. Rotation angle, you recall, is handled through the command sequence of the **TEXT** command. Obliquing angle is set as a text style characteristic using the **STYLE** command.

Typically text in an isometric drawing will align with one of the three isometric planes. In order to demonstrate how this works, we add single-line text to each of the planes in the bracket, as shown in Figure 11-14. Though we will be drawing in three planes, we can accomplish this with

**Figure 11-14**
Drawing text in isometric view

only two new text styles. These will be simple variations of the Standard text style, with the oblique angles we need for isometric alignment. The right isoplane will use a 30° oblique angle, while the top and left planes will use a –30° angle.

✔ To begin, you should be in the bracket drawing created in the last section. You should be in isometric snap and grid mode.

✔ Open the **Annotation** panel extension and pick the **Text Style** tool at the top left, next to the name of the current style (**Standard**).

*This opens the **Text Style** dialog box. Our first new text style will be used for drawing text in the right isoplane. If you look at Figure 11-14, you can easily see that this text (the word Right) is rotated along the 30° X-axis of the isoplane. What may be less obvious is that the individual characters are also drawn at a 30° oblique angle. We enter the rotation angle when we draw the text. Here we set the oblique angle for this plane.*

✔ Pick the **New . . .** button.

✔ In the **New Text Style** dialog box, type **isotext30.**

✔ Click **OK.**

✔ Change the **Oblique Angle** to **30.**

✔ Click **Apply**.

*We repeat these steps to create a style with –30° obliquing angle.*

✔ Pick the **New . . .** button.

✔ In the **New Text Style** dialog box, type **isotext-30.**

✔ Click **OK.**

✔ Change the **Oblique Angle** to **-30.**

✔ Click **Apply**.

✔ Highlight **isotext30** in the **Styles** list and pick the **Set Current** button.

✔ Click **Close.**

✔ If you see a message saying the current text style has been modified, click **Yes.**

*You should now be back in the drawing with **isotext30** as the current text style. We are now ready to add our text.*

✔ Pick the **Single Line** text tool from the **Annotation** panel.

✔ Pick a start point on the right front side of the bracket, as shown by the placement of the word *Right* in Figure 11-14.

✔ Specify a text height of .**30.**

✔ Type **30 <Enter>** for the rotation angle.

✔ Type **Right <Enter>.**

✔ Press **<Enter>.**

*The word* Right *should be drawn on the bracket, as shown in Figure 11-14. Now draw the word* Left *on the left isoplane, as shown. This will use the **isotext-30** style and a rotation angle of –30°.*

✔ Open the **Annotation** panel extension and pick **isotext-30** from the **Text Style** drop-down list.

✔ Pick the **Single Line** text tool from the **Annotation** panel.

✔ Pick a start point on the left side of the bracket, as shown by the placement of the word *Left* in Figure 11-14.

✔ Press <**Enter**> for a text height of .**30.**

✔ Type –**30** <**Enter**> for the rotation angle.

✔ Type **Left** <**Enter**>.

✔ Press <**Enter**>.

Finally, for text in the top isoplane, use **isotext-30** with a rotation angle of +30°.

✔ Pick the **Single Line** text tool from the **Annotation** panel.

✔ Pick a start point on the top of the bracket, as shown by the placement of the word *Top* in Figure 11-14.

✔ Press <**Enter**> for a text height of .**30.**

✔ Type **30** <**Enter**> for the rotation angle.

✔ Type **Top**<**Enter**>.

✔ Press <**Enter**>.
*Your screen should resemble Figure 11-14.*

This completes the present discussion of isometric drawing. You can find more in the drawing suggestions at the end of this chapter.

Now, we go on to explore the nonisometric use of the **ELLIPSE** command and then introduce the **VIEW** command for saving named views in a drawing.

## Drawing Ellipses in Orthographic Views

**orthographic view:** One of six standard views in which the observer's point of view is normal to the front, back, left, right, top, or bottom plane of the drawing.

The **ELLIPSE** command is important not only for drawing isocircles but also for drawing true ellipses in *orthographic views*. There is also an option to create elliptical arcs.

An ellipse is determined by a center point and two perpendicular axes of differing lengths. In AutoCAD, these specifications can be shown in two nearly identical ways, each requiring you to show three points (see Figure 11-15). In the default method, you show two endpoints of an axis and then show half the length of the other axis, from the midpoint of the first axis out. (The midpoint of an axis is also the center of the ellipse.) The other method allows you to pick the center point of the ellipse first, then the endpoint of one axis, followed by half the length of the other axis.

> **NOTE**
> If your grid does not return to its original shape, it may be because isometric snap values have been retained in the **Snap X** and **Grid X** spacing boxes. To fix this, reenter the **Drafting Settings** dialog box and manually return **Snap X spacing** to **0.25** and **Grid X spacing** to **0.50.**

**Figure 11-15**
Ellipse axis and center

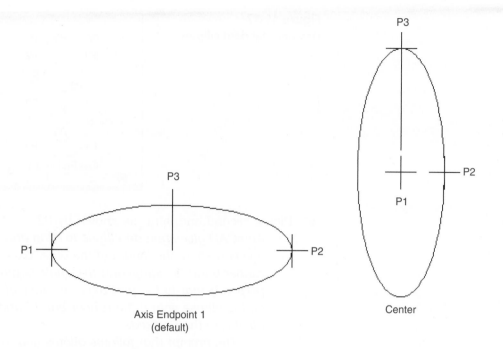

Axis Endpoint 1
(default)

Center

✔ In preparation for this exercise, return to the standard **Snap** mode and **Grid** mode using the following procedure:

**1** *Right-click on the **Snap Mode** or **Grid Display** button, and open the **Drafting Settings** dialog box from the shortcut menu.*

**2** *Click the **Rectangular snap** radio button.*

**3** *Remove the check from the **2D model space** grid box.*

**4** *Click **OK.***

*Your grid is returned to the standard pattern of lines, and the crosshairs are horizontal and vertical again. Notice that this does not affect the isometric bracket you have just drawn.*

*We briefly explore the **ELLIPSE** command and draw some standard ellipses.*

✔ Pick the **Axis, End** tool from the **Ellipse** drop-down list on the **Draw** panel, as shown in Figure 11-16.
*AutoCAD prompts:*

Specify axis endpoint of ellipse or [Arc Center]:

**Figure 11-16**
**Ellipse Axis, End tool**

✔ Pick an axis endpoint, as shown by P1 on the ellipse at the lower left in Figure 11-17.
*AutoCAD prompts for the other endpoint:*

Specify other endpoint of axis:

**Figure 11-17**
Drawing standard ellipses

✔ Pick a second endpoint, as shown by P2.

*AutoCAD gives you an ellipse to drag and a rubber band so that you can show the length of the other axis. Only the length of the rubber band is significant; the angle is already determined to be perpendicular to the first axis. Because of this, the third point falls on the ellipse only if the rubber band happens to be exactly perpendicular to the first axis.*

*The prompt that follows allows you to show the second axis distance as before, or a rotation around the first axis:*

Specify distance to other axis or [Rotation]:

*The **Rotation** option is awkward to use, and we do not explore it here; see the **AutoCAD Command Reference** for more information.*

✔ Pick P3 as shown.

*This point shows half the length of the other axis.*

The first ellipse should now be complete. Now, we draw one showing the center point first, using the **Center** ellipse tool from the ribbon.

✔ Pick the **Center** tool from the **Ellipse** drop-down list on the **Draw** panel of the ribbon.

*This automates the entry of the **Center** option.*

*AutoCAD gives you a prompt for a center point:*

Specify center of ellipse:

✔ Pick a center point, as shown by P1 at the middle left in Figure 11-17.

*Now, you have a rubber band stretching from the center to the end of an axis and the following prompt:*

Specify endpoint of axis:

✔ Pick an endpoint, as shown by P2 in Figure 11-17.

*The prompt that follows allows you to show the second axis distance as before, or a rotation around the first axis:*

Specify distance to other axis or [Rotation]:

✔ Pick an axis distance, as shown by P3.

*Here again the rubber band is significant for distance only. The point you pick falls on the ellipse only if the rubber band is stretched perpendicular to the first axis. Notice that it is not so in Figure 11-17.*

## Drawing Elliptical Arcs

Elliptical arcs can be drawn by trimming complete ellipses or by using the **Arc** option of the **ELLIPSE** command. Using the **Arc** option, you first construct an ellipse in one of the two methods shown previously and then show the arc of the ellipse that you want to keep.

✔ Pick the **Elliptical Arc** tool from the **Ellipse** drop-down list on the **Draw** panel of the ribbon.

✔ Pick a first axis endpoint, as shown by P1 at the upper left in Figure 11-17.

✔ Pick a second endpoint, P2 in the figure.

✔ Pick P3 to show the second axis distance.

> *AutoCAD draws an ellipse as you have specified, but the image is only temporary. Now, you need to show the arc you want drawn. The two options are **Parameter** and **Included angle**. **Parameter** takes you into more options that allow you to specify your arc in different ways, similar to the options of the **ARC** command. We'll stick with the default option.*

✔ Pick P4 to show the angle at which the elliptical arc begins.

> *Move the cursor slowly now and you can see all the arcs that are possible starting from this angle.*

✔ Pick P5 to indicate the end angle and complete the command.

## Saving and Restoring Displays with VIEW

| VIEW | |
|---|---|
| Command | View |
| Alias | V |
| Panel | Views |
| Tool | |

The word *view* in connection with the **VIEW** command has a special significance in AutoCAD. It refers to any set of display boundaries that have been named and saved using the **VIEW** command. It also refers to a defined 3D viewpoint that has been saved with a name. Views that have been saved can be restored rapidly and by direct reference rather than by redefining the location, size, or viewpoint of the area to be displayed. **VIEW** can be useful in creating drawing layouts and any time you know that you will be returning frequently to a certain area of a large drawing. It saves you from having to zoom out to look at the complete drawing and then zoom back in again on the area you want. It can also save the time required in creating a 3D viewpoint. In this chapter, we use 2D views only.

Imagine that we have to complete some detail work on the area around the hole in the bracket and also on the top corner. We can define each of these as a view and jump back and forth at will.

✔ To begin this exercise, you should have the bracket on your screen, as shown in Figure 11-18.

✔ Pick the **View** tab **> Views** panel **> View Manager** tool from the ribbon, as shown in Figure 11-19.

> *This opens the **View Manager** dialog box shown in Figure 11-20. At the left is a list of views, including **Current, Model Views, Layout Views,** and **Preset Views.** In this chapter we have use for only the **Current** view, which we will define and label with a name.*

**Figure 11-18**
Defining views

**Figure 11-19**
**View Manager** tool

**Figure 11-20**
**View Manager** dialog box

✔ Pick the **New . . .** button.
> *This takes you to the **New View/Shot Properties** dialog box shown in Figure 11-21. Notice that the **Current display** button is selected in the **Boundary** panel of the **View Properties** tab. All we have to do is give the current display a name to save it as a named view.*

✔ Type **bracket** in the **View name** edit box.

✔ Click **OK**.
> *The **View Manager** dialog box reappears, with **bracket** now showing under the heading **Model Views.** All views defined in model space will be listed as **Model Views.** Views defined in paper space will be listed as **Layout Views.** Next, we use a window to define a smaller model space view.*

✔ Pick the **New . . .** button to return to the **New View/Shot Properties** dialog box.

✔ Type **hole** in the **View name** edit box.
> *This view zooms in on the hole.*

✔ Pick the **Define window** button in the **Boundary** panel.
> *The dialog box closes, giving you access to the screen. The current view is outlined within the drawing area. The rest of the drawing is grayed out.*

**Figure 11-21**
New View/Shot Properties
dialog box

✔ Pick first and second corners to define a window around the hole in the bracket, as shown previously in Figure 11-18.
   *A window outline of the new view is shown, with the rest of the drawing grayed out.*

✔ Press <**Enter**> to return to the **New View/Shot Properties** dialog box.

✔ Click **OK** to complete the definition.
   *You are now back in the **View Manager** dialog box with **bracket** and **hole** on the list of **Model Views**. Define one more view to show the upper left corner of the bracket, as shown in Figure 11-18.*

✔ Pick the **New . . .** button.

✔ Type **corner** for the view name.

✔ Pick the **Define window** button.

✔ Define a window, as shown in Figure 11-18.

✔ Press <**Enter**> to return to the dialog box.

✔ Click **OK** to close the **New View/Shot Properties** dialog box.
   *You have now defined three model views. To see the views in action we must set them as current. Notice that the new view names are now displayed in a list on the **Views** panel, as shown in Figure 11-22.*

**Figure 11-22**
New view list on the **Views** panel

✔ Double-click on **hole** in the **Views** list.

✔ Click **OK.**

> *Your screen should resemble Figure 11-23.*
> *Now, switch to the corner view.*

✔ Press **<Enter>** to reopen the **View Manager.**

✔ Double-click on **corner** in the **Views** list.

✔ Click **OK.**

> *Your screen should resemble Figure 11-24.*

**Figure 11-23**
Hole view

**Figure 11-24**
Corner view

# Chapter Summary

In this chapter you were introduced to how the grid display and **Snap** mode can be used to facilitate drawing in geometry other than the standard orthographic 2D representation. Specifically you learned the use of the isometric grid to draw isometric images. In this mode grid points are shown at 30°, 90°, and 150° angles, and the crosshairs can be oriented to the top, left, and right isoplanes. You used the **<F5>** key to switch among these planes, and the **LINE, COPY,** and **TRIM** commands to draw simple objects in isometric orientation. You also drew single-line text aligned with each of the three isoplanes. You learned the use of the **ELLIPSE** command to create circles that appear as ellipses in isometric planes and also drew ellipses in standard orthographic views. Finally, you were introduced to the **VIEW** command, which allows you to define any screen display as a named view that can be restored at any time.

# Chapter Test Questions

## Multiple Choice

*Circle the correct answer.*

1. Change to this in order to align the grid with isometric planes:
   a. Change grid to polar
   b. Change grid to isometric
   c. Change grid to 2D model space
   d. Change snap to 2D model space

2. Which of these does **not** name an isoplane in AutoCAD?
   a. Right
   b. Left
   c. Front
   d. Top

3. The command used to draw circles in isometric views is:
   a. **ISOCIRCLE**
   b. **ELLIPSE**
   c. **ISOPLANE**
   d. **CIRCLE**

4. To align text with isometric planes, make changes to:
   a. Rotation and oblique angle
   b. Text style and alignment
   c. Alignment style and rotation
   d. Rotation angle and text style

5. The minimum number of points required to define an elliptical arc are:

a. 2

b. 3

c. 4

d. 5

## Matching

*Write the number of the correct answer on the line.*

a. Isoplane switch _____          1. Ellipse

b. Isocircle _____          2. 30°, 30°

c. Right isoplane text _____          3. 30°, –30°

d. Top isoplane text _____          4. **<F5>**

e. Default view _____          5. Current display

## True or False

*Circle the correct answer.*

1. **True or False:** Isometric drawings are two-dimensional.

2. **True or False:** Isometric drawings show no true distances.

3. **True or False:** To draw an isometric circle it is necessary to specify a center point.

4. **True or False:** In order to switch isoplanes you must open the **Drafting Settings** dialog box.

5. **True or False:** Drawing isocircles is the same as drawing ellipses in orthographic views.

## Questions

1. What are the angles of the crosshairs and grid points in an isometric grid?

2. What are the names for the isometric planes in AutoCAD?

3. What is an isocircle? Why are isocircles drawn in the **ELLIPSE** command?

4. How many different isocircles can you draw that have the same radius and the same center point?

5. What rotation angle and oblique angle are used to align text with each of the three isoplanes?

## Drawing Problems

1. Using the isometric grid, draw a 4 × 4 square in the right isoplane.

2. Copy the square back 4.00 units along the left isoplane.

3. Connect the corners of the two squares to form an isometric cube. Erase any lines that would be hidden in this object.

4. Use text rotation and obliquing to draw the word *Top* in the top plane of the cube so that the text is centered on the face and aligned with its edges. The text should be 0.5 unit high.

5. In a similar manner, draw the word *Left* at the center of the left side and the word *Right* at the center of the right side. All text should align with the face on which it is located.

## WWW Exercise (Optional)

You are now ready for Chapter 11 of the companion website. Complete the following steps:

✔ Make sure that you are connected to your Internet service provider.

✔ Type **browser<Enter>.**

✔ If necessary, navigate to our companion website at www.pearsonhighered.com/dixriley.

*Good luck on the test!*

# Chapter Drawing Projects

## Drawing 11-1: *Isometric Projects*
[INTERMEDIATE]

This drawing is a direct extension of the exercises in the chapter. It gives you practice in basic AutoCAD isometrics and in transferring dimensions from orthographic to isometric views.

### Drawing Suggestions

- Set your grid to .**50** and your snap to .**25** to create all the objects in this project. Your grid should match the grid of this drawing. Notice that some lines do not fall on grid points, but halfway between.

- There is no **Arc** option when you use **ELLIPSE** to draw isocircles, so semicircles such as those at the back of the holes must be constructed by first drawing isocircles and then trimming or erasing unwanted portions.

- To draw the portion of the isocircle that shows the depth of a circle, copy the isocircle down or back, snapping from endpoint to endpoint of other lines in the view that show the depth.

- Often, when you try to select a group of objects to copy, there are many crossing lines that you do not want to include in the copy. This is an ideal time to use the **Remove** option in object selection. First, window the objects you want along with those nearby that are unavoidable, and then remove the unwanted objects one by one.

- Sometimes, you may get unexpected results when you try to trim an object in an isometric view. AutoCAD divides an ellipse into a series of arcs, for example, and trims only a portion. If you do not get the results you want, use a **Nearest** object snap to control how the object is trimmed.

**Drawing 11-1**
Isometric Projects

**Drawing 11-2: *MP3 Player* [ADVANCED]**

This drawing introduces text and combines a complete set of 2D views with an isometric representation of the object. Placing objects on different layers so they can be turned on and off during **TRIM** and **ERASE** procedures makes things considerably less messy.

## Drawing Suggestions

- Use the box method to create the isometric view in this drawing. That is, begin with an isometric box according to the overall outside dimensions of the MP3 player. Then, trim and add the details.

- The dial is made from isocircles with copies to show thickness. You can use **Tangent** object snaps to draw the front-to-back connecting lines.

- Use a gradient hatch for the video window area.

- Use the **isotext30** and **isotext-30** text styles created in the chapter for drawing the text in the left and right isoplanes, as shown.

DETAIL- A
SCALE: 10:1

TYP
R.50

This drawing courtesy of:
Steve Curtin

SEE DETAIL - A

**Drawing 11-2**
MP3 Player

**Drawing 11-3:** *Fixture Assembly* [ADVANCED]

This is a difficult drawing. It takes time and patience but teaches you a great deal about isometric drawing in AutoCAD.

## Drawing Suggestions

- This drawing can be completed either by drawing everything in place as you see it or by drawing the parts and moving them into place along the common centerline that runs through the middle of all the items. If you use the former method, draw the centerline first and use it to locate the center points of isocircles and as base points for other measures.

- As you go, look for pieces of objects that can be copied from other objects. Avoid duplicating efforts by editing before copying. In particular, when one object covers part of another, be sure to copy it before you trim or erase the covered sections.

- To create the chamfered end of Item 4, begin by drawing the 1.00-diameter cylinder 3.00 long with no chamfer. Then, copy the isocircle at the end forward 0.125. The smaller isocircle is 0.875 (7/8), because 0.0625 (1/16) is cut away from the 1.00 circle all around. Draw this smaller isocircle and trim away everything that is hidden. Then, draw the slanted chamfer lines using **LINE,** not **CHAMFER.** Use the same method for Item 5.

- In both the screw and the nut, you need to create hexes around isocircles. Use the dimensions from a standard bolt chart.

- Use three-point arcs to approximate the curves on the screw bolt and the nut. Your goal is a representation that looks correct. It is impractical and unnecessary to achieve exact measures on these objects in the isometric view.

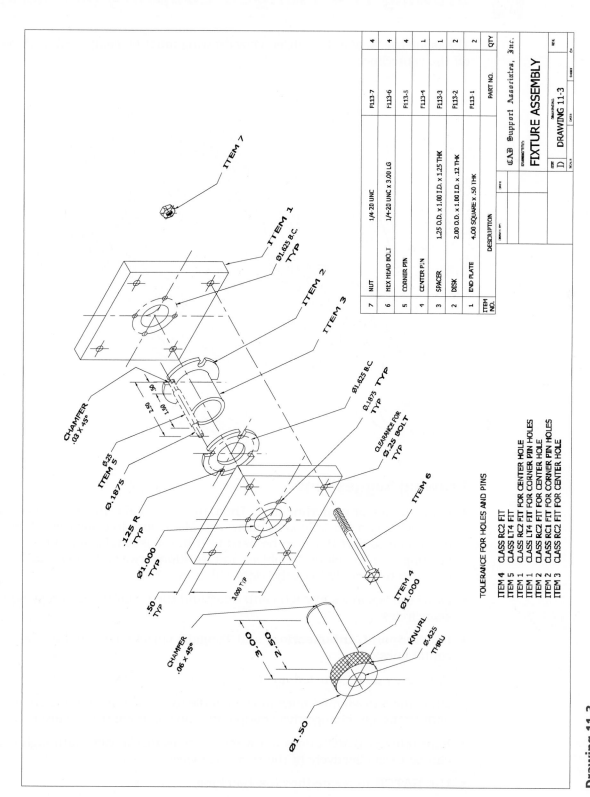

| 7 | NUT | | 1/4-20 UNC | F1137 | 4 |
| 6 | HEX HEAD BOLT | | 1/4-20 UNC x 3.00 LG | F113-6 | 4 |
| 5 | CORNER PIN | | | F113-5 | 4 |
| 4 | CENTER PIN | | | F113-4 | 1 |
| 3 | SPACER | | 1.25 O.D. x 1.00 I.D. x 1.25 THK | F113-3 | 1 |
| 2 | DISK | | 2.00 O.D. x 1.00 I.D. x .12 THK | F113-2 | 2 |
| 1 | END PLATE | | 4.00 SQUARE x .50 THK | F113-1 | 2 |
| ITEM NO. | DESCRIPTION | | | PART NO. | QTY |

**CAB Support Associates, Inc.**

DRAWN BY:

**FIXTURE ASSEMBLY**

| SIZE | DRAWING NO. | REV. |
|---|---|---|
| D | DRAWING 11-3 | |
| SCALE | DATE | SHEET |

TOLERANCE FOR HOLES AND PINS

ITEM 4   CLASS RC2 FIT
ITEM 5   CLASS LT4 FIT
ITEM 1   CLASS RC2 FIT FOR CENTER HOLE
ITEM 1   CLASS LT4 FIT FOR CORNER PIN HOLES
ITEM 2   CLASS RC2 FIT FOR CENTER HOLE
ITEM 2   CLASS RC1 FIT FOR CORNER PIN HOLES
ITEM 3   CLASS RC2 FIT FOR CENTER HOLE

**Drawing 11-3**
Fixture Assembly

## M Drawing 11-4: *Flanged Coupling* [ADVANCED]

The isometric view in this three-view drawing must be completed working off the centerline.

## Drawing Suggestions

- Draw the major centerline first. Then, draw vertical centerlines at every point where an isocircle is to be drawn. Make sure to draw these lines extra long so that they can be used to trim the isocircles in half. By starting at the back of the object and working forward, you can take dimensions directly from the right-side view.

- Draw the isocircles at each centerline, and then trim them to represent semicircles.

- Use **Endpoint, Intersection,** and **Tangent** object snaps to draw horizontal lines.

- Trim away all obstructed lines and parts of isocircles.

- Draw the four slanted lines in the middle as vertical lines first. Then, with **Ortho** off, change their endpoints, moving them 0.125 closer.

- Remember, **MIRROR** does not work in the isometric view, although it can be used effectively in the right-side view.

- Use **HATCH** to create the crosshatching.

- If you have made a mistake in measuring along the major centerline, **STRETCH** can be used to correct it. Make sure that **Ortho** is on and that you are in an isoplane that lets you move the way you want.

**Ø.375**
**4 HOLES EQ SP**
**ON 5.125 DIA B.C.**

Ø1.250

Ø6.00

.125X45°
CHAMFER

8.00
3.25
2.13
1.88
1.13

Ø4.25
Ø2.00
Ø1.50
Ø3.00

.13 TYP
.63 TYP
.13 TYP
2.00
2.50

**Drawing 11-4**
Flanged Coupling

# Drawing 11-5: *Garage Framing* [ADVANCED]

This is a fairly complex drawing that takes lots of trimming and careful work. Changing the **SNAPANG** (snap angle) variable so that you can draw slanted arrays is a method that can be used frequently in isometric drawing.

## Drawing Suggestions

- You will find yourself using **COPY, ZOOM,** and **TRIM** a great deal. **OFFSET** also works well.

- You may want to create some new layers with different colors. Keeping different parts of the construction walls, rafters, and joists on different layers allows you to have more control over them and adds a lot of clarity to what you see on the screen. Turning layers on and off can considerably simplify trimming operations.

- You can cut down on repetition in this drawing by using arrays on various angles. For example, if the **SNAPANG** variable is set to 150°, the 22' wall in the left isoplane can be created as a rectangular array of studs with 1 row and 17 columns set 16″ apart. To do so, follow this procedure:

  **1** Type **snapang.**

  **2** Enter a new value so that rectangular arrays are built on isometric angles (30° or 150°).

  **3** Enter the **ARRAY** command and create the array. Use negative values where necessary.

  **4** Trim the opening for the window.

- One alternative to this array method is to set your snap to **16″** temporarily and use **COPY** to create the columns of studs, rafters, and joists. Another alternative is to use the grip edit offset snap method beginning with an offset snap of 16″ (i.e., press <**Shift**> when you show the first copy displacement and continue to hold down <**Shift**> as you make other copies).

- The cutaway in the roof that shows the joists and the back door is drawn using the standard nonisometric **ELLIPSE** command. Then, the rafters are trimmed to the ellipse, and the ellipse is erased. Do this procedure before you draw the joists and the back wall. Otherwise, you will trim these as well.

- Use **CHAMFER** to create the chamfered corners on the joists.

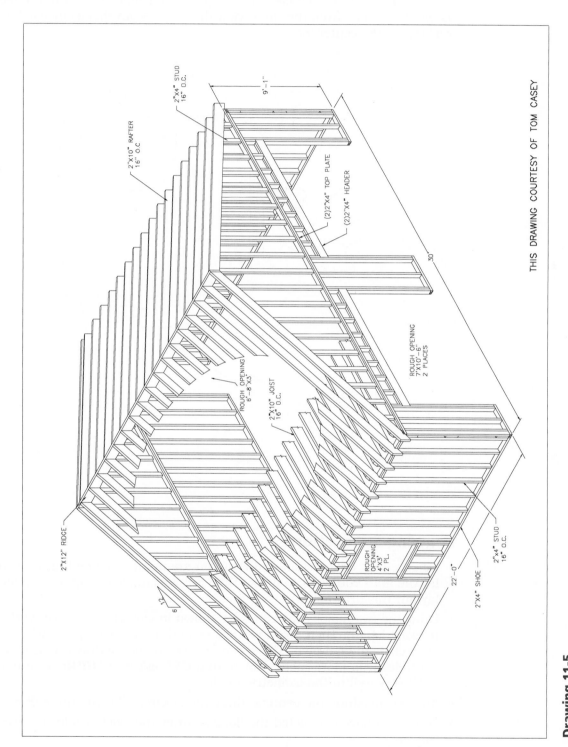

THIS DRAWING COURTESY OF TOM CASEY

**Drawing 11-5**
Garage Framing

521

# Drawing 11-6: *Cast Iron Tee* [ADVANCED]

The objective of this exercise is to complete the isometric view of the tee using dimensions from the three-view drawing. Begin this isometric by working off the centerline.

## Drawing Suggestions

- Be sure that **Ortho** is on and that you are in an isoplane that is correct for the lines you want to draw. Take full advantage of object snap as you lay out this drawing.
- Draw the two major centerlines as shown in isometric first. Draw them to exact length. Then, draw vertical centerlines at every point where an isocircle is to be drawn. These centerlines should be drawn longer so the isocircles trim more easily. Notice that **OFFSET** and **MIRROR** do not work very well in the isometric mode.
- After establishing the centers, draw the isocircles for the three flanges.
- When you have completed the flanges, draw the isocircles for the wall of the tee.
- Draw all horizontal and vertical lines and trim away all nonvisible lines and parts of isocircles. Fillet the required intersections.
- After completing the outline of the tee, use **HATCH** to create the crosshatching.

$\emptyset\frac{9}{16}$ THRU
4 HOLES
EQ SPACED
ON $\emptyset 5\frac{3}{4}$
BOLT CIRCLE
TYP 3 FLANGES

ALL FILLETS &
ROUNDS 1/8R

$\emptyset 3$

11

$5\frac{1}{2}$

$\frac{3}{4}$
TYP

$\frac{1}{2}$
TYP

$\emptyset 7\frac{1}{2}$

$5\frac{1}{2}$

TYP

**Drawing 11-6**
Cast Iron Tee

# Drawing 11-7: *Valve* [ADVANCED]

For the purposes of this chapter, the isometric view is most important. The three detail views, the title block, and the border can be included or not, as assigned.

| DRAWN BY: | DATE | CAD Support Associates, Inc. | | |
|---|---|---|---|---|
| | | DRAWING TITLE: <br> **ISOMETRIC SECTION** <br> **NUMBER 6 VALVE** | | |
| | | SIZE <br> **B** | DRAWING NO. <br> **6-11-6** | REV. <br> **0** |
| | | SCALE: | DATE: | SHEET     OF |

## Drawing Suggestions

- Use the box method to create the isometric view in this drawing. Begin with an isometric box according to the overall outside dimensions of the valve. Then, go back and cut away the excess so the drawing becomes half the valve, exposing the interior details of the object.

- As in all section drawings, no hidden lines are shown.

- In addition to flat surfaces indicated by hatching, the interior is made up of isocircles of different sizes on different planes.

- Keep all construction lines and centerlines until drawing is complete (draw them on a separate layer, and you can turn off that layer when you don't need them).

- The tapped holes are drawn with a series of isocircles that can be arrayed. This is only a representation of a screw thread, so it is not drawn to precise dimensions. Draw one thread, and copy it to the other side.

Ø1 1/8

A          A

4 13/16

7/16 - 14 UNC-3B THD
3/4 DEEP MAX
4 HOLES EQ SP ON Ø3 5/8 B.C.

1/16          3 3/8

5 9/16

1/16

Ø3 5/8          Ø2 1/16

3/4

R 1/4 TYP

3/16          Ø2 1/2          1/16 TYP

4 13/16          Ø3 1/4          1 3/4

Ø1.00          1 1/8          Ø1 3/4          2 1/4

64°          9/16          2 3/8          2 9/16

7/16          Ø1 3/8          1/16

Ø4 1/8          1/16          Ø1/2

45°          45°

SECTION A-A

**Drawing 11-7**
Valve

# 12 chapter twelve
# 3D Modeling

# CHAPTER OBJECTIVES

- Create and view a 3D wireframe box
- Define user coordinate systems
- Explore the **3D Basics** workspace
- Create solid boxes and wedges
- Access different visual styles
- Create the union of two solids
- Work with DUCS

- Create composite solids with **SUBTRACT**
- Create chamfers and fillets on solid objects
- Practice 3D gizmo editing
- Render solid models
- Change viewpoints with the ViewCube
- Create layouts with multiple views

## Introduction

In this chapter we will take a step-by-step journey into 3D AutoCAD space. We begin in the familiar territory of the **Drafting & Annotation** workspace. Then we bring the Z-axis into play and move your viewpoint so that your drawing begins to represent objects in 3D space that you can present from any angle. Once oriented in three dimensions, we create a wireframe box and then define new user coordinate systems that allow us to draw and edit in any plane in this 3D space. From there, we switch to the **3D Basics** workspace to create and edit a true solid model. To complete the trip, we render the model with lighting and texture to give it a realistic appearance and then use the model to create a layout with multiple views.

## Creating and Viewing a 3D Wireframe Box

It is now time to begin thinking in three dimensions. In the first two sections you will bridge the gap between 2D and 3D by creating a very simple **wireframe model.** In the "Exploring the 3D Basics Workspace" section, you will move on to solid modeling. Like 2D and isometric drawings, wireframe models represent objects by outlining their edges and boundaries. Wireframe models are drawn line by line, edge by edge. Whereas wireframe modeling is the logical extension of 2D drafting into three dimensions, solid modeling uses a completely different logic, as you will see.

**wireframe model:** A three-dimensional model that represents only the edges and boundaries of objects.

In this section we continue to use the **Drafting & Annotation** workspace. As we work our way into 3D space, your UCS icon becomes important, so first check to see that it is visible (see Figure 12-1). If not, follow this procedure to turn it on:

**1** Type **ucsicon <Enter>.**

**2** Select **On** from the dynamic input list.

**Figure 12-1**
UCS icon

For now, simply observe the icon as you go through the process of creating a three-dimensional box, and be aware that you are currently working in the same coordinate system that you have always used in AutoCAD. It is called the **world coordinate system** (WCS), to distinguish it from others you create yourself beginning in the "Defining User Coordinate Systems" section.

**world coordinate system:** In AutoCAD, the default coordinate system in which the point of origin is at the intersection of the default X-, Y-, and Z-axes. All user coordinate systems are defined relative to the world coordinate system.

Currently, the origin of the WCS is at the lower left of your grid. This is the point (0,0,0) when you are thinking 3D, or simply (0,0) when you are in 2D. The x coordinates increase to the right horizontally across the screen, and the y coordinates increase vertically up the screen, as usual. The Z-axis, which we have ignored until now, currently extends out of the screen toward you and perpendicular to the X- and Y-axes and the plane of the screen. This orientation of the three planes is called a *plan view.* Soon we will switch to a front right top, or southeast, isometric view.

Let's begin.

✔ Create a new drawing with decimal units and 18 × 12 limits (use the 1B template if you have it).

✔ **Zoom All.**

✔ Draw a 4.00 × 2.00 rectangle with the lower left corner at (4,2,0), as shown in Figure 12-1.

## Changing Viewpoints

**viewpoint:** The point in space from which a three-dimensional object is viewed.

To move immediately into a 3D mode of drawing and thinking, our first step is to change our *viewpoint* on this object. There are several methods for defining 3D points of view. Of these the simplest and most efficient method is the **View Manager** dialog box. For now, this is the only method you need.

✔ Select the **View** tab > **Views** panel > **View Manager** tool from the ribbon.
*This opens the **View Manager** dialog box, which is used to create named views. In this chapter, we use the **Preset Views** option.*

✔ Click the + sign next to **Preset Views** in the **Views** list.
*This opens the list of simple cube images shown in Figure 12-2. These represent 10 standard preset views. Imagine your point of view to be perpendicular to the dark blue face of the cube in each case. In the six orthographic views (top, bottom, left, etc.), objects are presented from points of view along each of the six axis directions. You see objects in the drawing from directly above (top, positive Z) or directly below (bottom, negative Z), or by looking in along the positive or negative X-axis (left and right) or the positive or negative Y-axis (front and back).*

**Figure 12-2**
**View Manager** dialog box

*The four isometric views present objects at 45° angles from the X- and Y-axes and take you up 30° degrees out of the XY plane. We use a southeast isometric view. It is simple if you imagine a compass. The lower right quadrant is the southeast. In a southeast isometric view, you are looking in from 45° in this quadrant and down at a 30° angle. Try it.*

✔ Select **SE Isometric** from the list of views.

✔ Pick the **Set Current** button.

✔ Click **OK.**

The dialog box closes, and the screen is redrawn to the view shown in Figure 12-3. Notice how the grid and the coordinate system icon have changed to show our current orientation. These visual aids are extremely helpful in viewing 3D objects on the flat screen and imagining them as if they were positioned in space.

**Figure 12-3**
Southeast isometric view

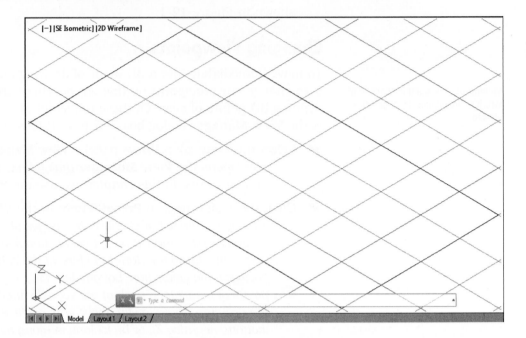

At this point you may want to experiment with the other views in the **View Manager** dialog box. You will probably find the isometric views most interesting. Pay attention to the grid and the icon as you switch views. Variations of the icon you may encounter here and later on are shown in Figure 12-4. With some views, you have to think carefully and watch the icon to understand which way the object is being presented. It is helpful to remember that the X-axis is always shown in red, the Y-axis in green, and the Z-axis in blue.

**Figure 12-4**
Variations of UCS icons

When you have finished experimenting, be sure to return to the southeast isometric view shown in Figure 12-3. We use this view frequently throughout this chapter.

## Entering 3D Coordinates

Next, we create a copy of the rectangle placed 1.50 above the original. This brings up a basic 3D problem: AutoCAD interprets point selections as being in the XY plane, so how does one indicate a point or a displacement in the Z direction? In wireframe modeling there are three possibilities: typed 3D coordinates, X/Y/Z point filters, and object snaps. Object snap is useful only if an object has already been drawn above or below the XY plane, so it is no help right now. We use typed coordinates first and then discuss how point filters can be used as an alternative.

3D coordinates can be entered from the keyboard in the same manner as 2D coordinates. Often, this is an impractical way to enter individual points in a drawing. However, within **COPY** or **MOVE,** entering from the keyboard provides a simple method for specifying a displacement in the Z direction.

✔ Pick the **Home** tab **> Modify** panel **> Copy** tool from the ribbon.
*AutoCAD prompts for object selection.*

✔ Select the complete rectangle.

✔ Right-click to end object selection.
*AutoCAD now prompts for the base point of a vector or a displacement value:*

> Specify base point or displacement or [Displacement mOde]
> <Displacement>:

*Typically, you would respond to this prompt and the next by showing the two endpoints of a displacement vector. However, we cannot show a displacement in the Z direction by pointing. This is important for understanding AutoCAD coordinate systems. Unless an object snap is used, all points picked on the screen with the pointing device are interpreted as being in the XY plane of the current UCS. In wireframe modeling, without an entity outside the XY plane to use in an object snap, there is no way to point to a displacement in the Z direction.*

✔ Type **0,0,1.5 <Enter>.**
*AutoCAD now prompts:*

> Specify second point of displacement, or [Array] <use first point as
> displacement>:

*You can type the coordinates of another point, or press **<Enter>** to tell AutoCAD to use the first entry as a displacement from (0,0,0). In this case, pressing **<Enter>** indicates a displacement of 1.50 in the Z direction and no change in X or Y.*

✔ Press **<Enter>.**

*AutoCAD creates a copy of the rectangle 1.50 directly above the original. Your screen should resemble Figure 12-5.*

**Figure 12-5**
Copy of rectangle

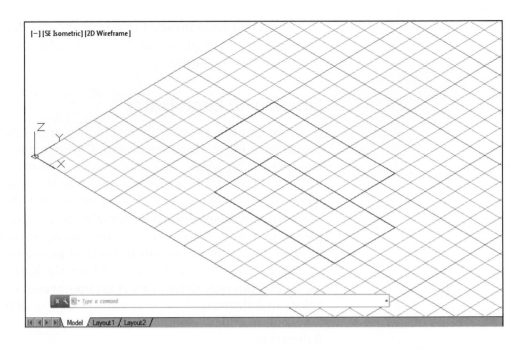

## X/Y/Z Point Filters

point filter: A system for specifying
a point by first filtering one or two
coordinate values from a given point
and then specifying the other
value(s) independently.

***Point filters*** are very useful in 3D. In a point filter, we filter some of the
coordinate values from one point and change others to specify a new point.
To see how this works, notice that in the displacement we just entered, the
only thing that changes is the $z$ value. Note also that we could specify that
same displacement using any point in the XY plane as a base point. For
example, (3,6,0) to (3,6,1.50) would show the same displacement as (0,0,0)
to (0,0,1.50). In fact, we don't even need to know what the $x$ and $y$ values
are as long as we know that they don't change and that the $z$ value does.

That is how an .XY point filter works. We borrow, or "filter," the $x$ and
$y$ values from a point, without needing to know what the values actually
are, and then specify a new $z$ value. Other types of filters are possible, of
course, such as .Z, in which $z$ is constant while $x$ and $y$ change, or .YZ,
where $y$ and $z$ are constant and $x$ changes.

You can use a point filter, like an object snap, any time AutoCAD asks
for a point. After a point filter is specified, AutoCAD always prompts with
*of*. In an .XY filter, you are being asked, "You want the $x$ and $y$ values of
what point?" In response, you pick a point, and then AutoCAD asks you to
fill in $z$. We demonstrate the use of point filters in the "Rendering Solid
Models" section, where we use them to position lights in a model to be
rendered.

## Using Object Snap

We now have two rectangles floating in space. Our next job is to connect
the corners to form a wireframe box. This is easily managed using **Endpoint** object snaps, and it is a good example of how object snaps allow us
to construct entities not in the XY plane of the current coordinate system.

✔ Right-click the **Object Snap** button on the status bar.
*For now, this is the regular **Object Snap** button, not the **3D Object
Snap** button.*

✔ Select **Settings** from the shortcut menu.

✔ Make sure that **Object Snap On** is checked at the top left of the dialog box.

✔ Pick the **Clear All** button.

✔ Pick the **Endpoint** check box.

✔ Click **OK.**

> *The running **Endpoint** object snap is now on and affects all point selections.*

Now, we draw some lines:

✔ Turn **Snap Mode** off.

✔ Enter the **LINE** command and connect the upper and lower corners of the two rectangles, as shown in Figure 12-6.

**Figure 12-6**
Connecting corners

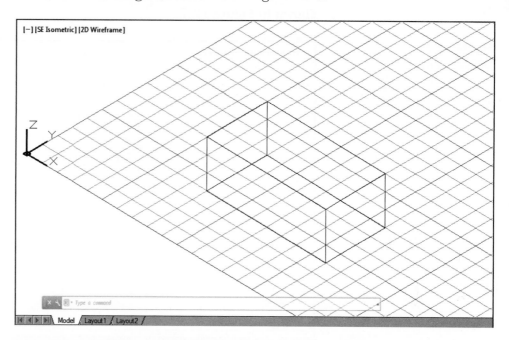

Before going on, pause to take note of what you have drawn. The box on your screen is a true 3D model. Unlike an isometric drawing, it can be turned, viewed, and plotted from any point in space. It is not, however, a solid model or a surface model. It is only a set of lines in 3D space. Removing hidden lines or shading would have no effect on this model, because no surfaces are represented.

In the next section, you begin to define your own coordinate systems that allow you to perform drawing and editing functions in any plane you choose.

| UCS | |
|---|---|
| **Command** | Ucs |
| **Alias** | uc |
| **Panel** | Coordinates |
| **Tool** | |

# Defining User Coordinate Systems

In this task, you begin to develop new vocabulary and techniques for working with objects in 3D space. The primary tool is the UCS icon, which can be moved and rotated to create new user-defined coordinate systems.

Until now, we have had only one coordinate system to work with. All coordinates and displacements have been defined relative to a single point of origin. Keep in mind that *viewpoint* and *coordinate system* are not the same, although they use similar vocabulary. In the previous section, we changed our point of view, but the UCS icon changed along with it, so that the orientations of the X-, Y-, and Z-axes relative to the object were retained. With the **UCS** command or by direct manipulation of the UCS icon, you can free the coordinate system from the viewpoint and define new coordinate systems at any point and any angle in space. When you do, you can use the coordinate system icon and the grid to help you visualize the planes you are working in, and all commands and drawing aids function relative to the new system.

The coordinate system we are currently using, WCS (world coordinate system), is unique. It is the one we always begin with. The square at the base of the coordinate system icon indicates that we are working in the WCS. A UCS is nothing more than a new point of origin and a new orientation for the X-, Y-, and Z-axes.

We begin by defining a UCS in the plane of the top of the box, as shown in Figure 12-7.

**Figure 12-7**
UCS top view

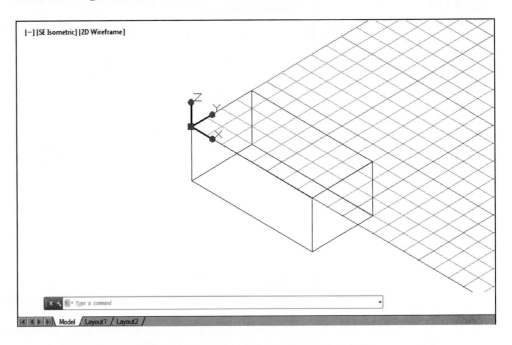

✔ Leave the **Endpoint** object snap on as you begin this exercise.

*In AutoCAD you can select and manipulate the UCS icon like other objects. When you do, grips will appear, which can be used to change the position and orientation of the icon, which in turn changes the orientation and origin of the coordinate system.*

✔ Move the cursor over the UCS icon. When it is highlighted in yellow, press the pick button.

*Grips appear at the origin and along each of the three axes, as shown in Figure 12-8. The square grip at the origin is used to move the icon to a new origin point. The circular grips on each axis are used to rotate the icon.*

*We use the square grip to move the icon to the top left corner of the box and define a new UCS in the plane of the top of the box.*

✔ Pick the square grip at the base of the UCS icon.

*As you move the cursor away from the world coordinate system origin, the icon moves with you, and a rubber band is added. Also,*

**Figure 12-8**
Grips appear on UCS icon

*if you let the cursor rest, a multifunctional grip message appears, as shown in Figure 12-9. This shows that you can use the grip to move the icon in different ways, with or without changing the alignment of the icon. You can also move the icon back to the WCS origin.*

**Figure 12-9**
Multifunctional grip message appears

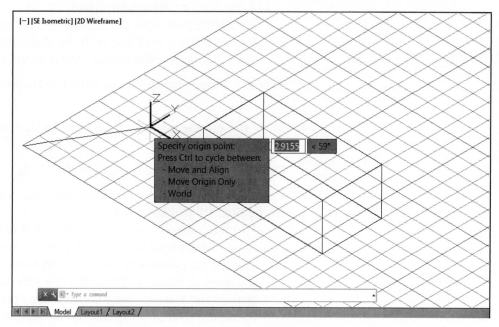

✔ Use the **Endpoint** object snap to select the top left corner of the box, as shown by the location of the icon in Figure 12-7.

*The grid origin moves to the corner of the box. The **Endpoint** object snap ensures that you actually select the top corner. Without it, you can easily pick a point that appears to be the upper corner of the box, but is actually a point in the current XY plane. Notice that the colors have gone from the icon, indicating that we are no longer in the WCS.*

*The UCS we have just created makes it easy to draw and edit entities that are in the plane of the top of the box. To see how this works, we draw a 1 × 3 unit rectangle on top of the box, as shown in Figure 12-10.*

**Figure 12-10**
Drawing a rectangle on top of the box

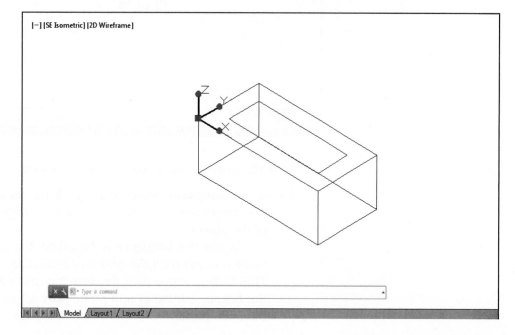

✔ Pick the **Object Snap** tool to turn the running object snap off.

✔ Pick the **Snap Mode** tool to turn on grid snap.

✔ Enter the **LINE** or **RECTANG** command and draw a 1 × 3 rectangle on top of the box, as shown in Figure 12-10.

> We define two more UCSs, one that aligns the XY plane with the left face of the box and one with the right. For these we will need to move the origin and change the rotation of the icon.

✔ Pick the **Object Snap** tool to turn the running **Endpoint** object snap on.

✔ Move the cursor over the UCS icon so that it is highlighted again, and press the pick button.

✔ Pick the box grip at the origin of the UCS.

✔ Using the **Endpoint** object snap, pick the lower front left of the wireframe box, P1 in Figure 12-11.

> You have moved the origin of the UCS to P1, but we now need to rotate the icon so that the left front of the box is in the XY plane. The X-axis is already aligned with the bottom edge of the box, but we need to rotate Y. The grips are still displayed. Using the circular grip on the Y-axis, along with the **Endpoint** object snap, we can rotate the icon and the coordinate system as desired.

**Figure 12-11**
UCS origin moved to P1

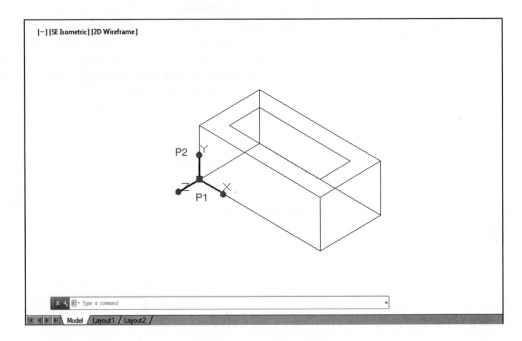

✔ Pick the grip on the Y-axis of the UCS icon.

✔ Using the **Endpoint** object snap, pick P2, as shown in Figure 12-11.

> The object snap ensures that the new axis aligns with the left side of the object.
>
> When this sequence is complete, the coordinate system icon has rotated along with the grid and moved to the new origin, as shown. This UCS is convenient for drawing and editing in the left plane of the box, or editing in any plane parallel to the front plane, such as the back plane.

✔ Turn off running object snap, enter the **LINE** or **RECTANG** command, and draw a 0.5 × 3 unit rectangle in the left plane of the box, as shown in Figure 12-12.

> *Finally, we use the same procedure to create a UCS in the plane of the right side of the wireframe box.*

**Figure 12-12**
Drawing a rectangle in the left plane

✔ Highlight and select the UCS icon.

✔ Pick the square grip at the origin of the icon.

✔ Pick the lower front right corner of the box for the origin, as shown in Figure 12-13.

> *There is no need to use an object snap here because this point is in the current XY plane. The UCS icon moves to the selected point. Now we rotate the icon to align with the right side of the box.*

**Figure 12-13**
Moving and rotating UCS

✔ Pick the **Object Snap** tool to turn the running **Endpoint** object snap on again.

✔ If necessary, select the UCS icon again.

✔ Pick the circular grip on the *X*-axis.

✔ Pick the back right corner of the box.
   *You should now have the XY plane of your UCS aligned with the right side of the box, as shown in Figure 12-13.*

✔ Pick the **Object Snap** tool to turn the running object snap off.

✔ Enter the **LINE** or **RECTANG** command and draw a 0.5 × 1.0 unit rectangle in the right plane of the box, as shown in Figure 12-14.

> **NOTE**
>
> To switch between *perspective projection* and *parallel projection*, right-click on the **ViewCube** and select **Parallel** or **Perspective** from the shortcut menu.

**perspective projection:** Three-dimensional representation of objects along lines that converge at a distant vanishing point.

**parallel projection:** Three-dimensional representation of objects along parallel lines so that distance values are maintained regardless of the viewer's perspective.

**Figure 12-14**
Drawing a rectangle in the right plane

## Exploring the 3D Basics Workspace

***Solid modeling*** is in many ways easier than wireframe modeling. You can draw a complete solid object in a fraction of the time it would take to draw it line by line. Furthermore, once the object is drawn, it contains more information than a wireframe model and can be manipulated in numerous ways. As we move on to solid modeling in this section, we create a new drawing and switch to the acad3D template and the **3D Basics** workspace.

✔ Pick the **New** tool from the **Quick Access** toolbar.

✔ In the **Template** list, select the **acad3D** template.
   *This will be just below the acad template in the **Select template** dialog box. With the acad3D template you will still be in the **Drafting & Annotation** workspace, but there will be a change in*

**solid modeling:** A system of creating 3D objects from combinations of 3D solid primitive objects.

*visual style, as shown in Figure 12-15. Notice the 3D coordinate system icon in the middle of the grid with a solid blue arrow for the Z-axis, a solid red arrow for the X-axis, and a solid green arrow for the Y-axis and the 3D cursor with three narrow lines in colors similar to the UCS icon colors.*

*Next we switch to the* **3D Basics** *workspace.*

**Figure 12-15**
acad3D template

✔ Pick the **Workspace** drop-down list from the **Quick Access** toolbar to open the **Workspace** list.

✔ Select **3D Basics** from the list.

> *Your screen should resemble Figure 12-16. This is the* **3D Basics** *workspace. The drawing area has not changed, but you have a new set of tool panels on the ribbon. These are tools devoted to 3D solid modeling and rendering procedures. Notice that there is a new set of tabs and that the* **Home** *tab in this workspace is different from the one in* **Drafting & Annotation.***
>
> *In the sections that follow you create a solid model using several of the tools on the* **3D Basics** *workspace ribbon.*

**Figure 12-16**
**3D Basics** workspace

## Creating Solid Boxes and Wedges

Solid modeling requires a type of thinking different from any of the drawings you have completed so far. Instead of focusing on lines and arcs, edges and surfaces, you need to imagine how 3D objects may be pieced together by combining or subtracting basic solid shapes. This building block process is called *constructive solid geometry* and includes joining, subtracting, and intersecting operations. A simple washer, for example, can be made by cutting a small cylinder out of the middle of a larger cylinder. In AutoCAD solid modeling, you can begin with a flat outer cylinder, then draw an inner cylinder with a smaller radius centered at the same point, and then subtract the inner cylinder from the outer, as illustrated in Figure 12-17.

**constructive solid geometry:** A system of three-dimensional modeling that represents solid objects as composites made by combining simple shapes, called primitives.

**Figure 12-17**
Constructive solid geometry

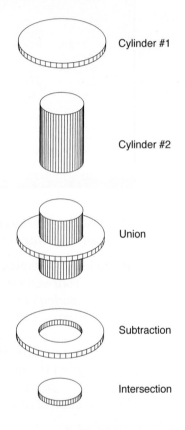

Cylinder #1

Cylinder #2

Union

Subtraction

Intersection

This operation, which uses the **SUBTRACT** command, is the equivalent of cutting a hole and is one of three *Boolean operations* (after the mathematician George Boole) used to create composite solids. **UNION** joins two solids to make a new solid, and **INTERSECT** creates a composite solid in the space where two solids overlap (see Figure 12-17).

In this chapter, you create a composite solid from the union and subtraction of several solid primitives. Primitives are 3D solid building blocks—boxes, cones, cylinders, spheres, wedges, and torus. They all are regularly shaped and can be defined by specifying a few points and distances. Most are found on the drop-down list at the left of the **Create** panel.

To begin drawing, we make two adjustments to your grid.

**Boolean operations:** Logical operations, such as union, subtraction, and intersection, based on the mathematical ideas of George Boole, that delineate how simple solid shapes can be combined to construct composite solid objects.

✔ Type **Z <Enter>** and then **A <Enter>** to zoom to the limits of this drawing.

*The acad3D template drawing has 12 × 9 limits, but the grid is initially drawn larger to give a fuller perspective. Zooming all will take you closer to the actual limits.*

✔ Turn **Snap Mode** on.

✔ Right-click the **Grid Display** button and select settings from the shortcut menu.

✔ Deselect the **Adaptive grid** check box in the **Grid behavior** panel.

✔ Click **OK**.

> *You should now have a grid line at each 0.5000 interval and a bolder grid line at each 2.5000 interval. Snap, like grid, is set at 0.5000. Your screen resembles Figure 12-18.*

**Figure 12-18**
Grid lines

## The BOX Command

✔ Zoom in slightly to a window on the area around the 3D UCS icon.

✔ Pick the **Box** tool from the **Create** panel on the ribbon, as shown in Figure 12-19.

> *Boxes can be drawn from the base up, or they can be drawn from the center out. In either case you specify a length and width, or two corners and then a height. AutoCAD prompts:*

> Specify first corner or [Center]:

> *We start with the default method, showing two corners of the base, and then typing the height.*

✔ Pick a first corner point at (1.0000,1.0000), P1 in Figure 12-20.

> *AutoCAD prompts for a second corner:*

> Specify second corner or [Cube Length]:

| BOX | |
| --- | --- |
| **Command** | Box |
| **Alias** | - |
| **Panel** | Modeling |
| **Tool** | |

**Figure 12-19**
**Box** tool

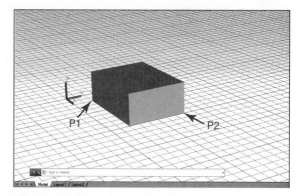

**Figure 12-20**
Drawing a box, points P1, P2

With the **Cube** option, length, width, and height will all be equal. With the **Length** option, you show length and width, rather than corners. We draw a box with a length of 4, width of 3, and height of 1.5.

✔ Pick a point 4.00 over in the X direction and 3.00 back in the Y direction, as shown by P2 in Figure 12-20.
*This will be the point (5.0000,4.0000) on the coordinate display. The dynamic input display will show the x and y distances. AutoCAD will give you a box shape that can be stretched up or down in the Z direction and prompts for a height:*

Specify height or [2Point]:

> **NOTE**
>
> Be careful not to rest the cursor on any of the faces of the box so that an outline is highlighted. If this happens, AutoCAD will begin drawing the wedge in the plane of that face. This is a very powerful capability we explore later in this exercise, but it will not be helpful right now.

✔ Move the cursor up and down and observe the box. Also observe the height specification shown on the dynamic input display.
*We are drawing a box of height 1.5000, but incremental snap must be used carefully in the Z direction. There is also no object above the XY plane for object snap. So, as in our wireframe example, typing is the most reliable option for specifying height.*

✔ Make sure the box is stretched in the positive Z direction before you enter the height; otherwise, AutoCAD will take the height as a negative and will draw the box below the XY plane.

✔ Type **1.5 <Enter>.**
*Your box is complete and should resemble Figure 12-20.*

## The WEDGE Command

| WEDGE | |
|---|---|
| Command | Wedge |
| Alias | We |
| Panel | Modeling |
| Tool | |

Next, we create a solid wedge. The process is exactly the same. Again, we use the default option of showing length and width by picking two corner points.

✔ Pick the **Wedge** tool from the **Solid Primitives** drop-down list (under **Box**) on the **Create** panel.
*AutoCAD prompts:*

Specify first corner of wedge or [Center]:

✔ Pick the front corner point of the box, P1 in Figure 12-21.
*As in the **BOX** command, AutoCAD prompts for a cube, length, or the other corner:*

Specify corner or [Cube Length]:

✔ Pick a point 4.00 over in the X direction and 3.00 back in the Y direction, as shown by P2 in Figure 12-21.
*This point should be easy to find because the back corner lines up with the back of the box already drawn.*
*After you pick the second corner, AutoCAD shows the wedge and prompts for a height.*

**Figure 12-21**
Drawing a wedge, points
P1, P2

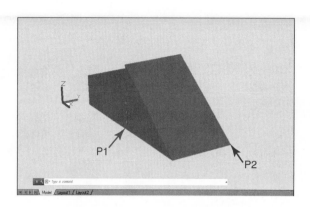

✔ Move the cursor up and down and watch the wedge stretch. Make sure that you have the wedge stretched in the positive Z direction before you enter the height.

✔ Type **3 <Enter>.**

*AutoCAD draws the wedge you have specified. Notice that a wedge is simply half a box, cut along a diagonal plane.*

*Your screen should resemble Figure 12-21. The box and wedge on your screen are true solids and are different from anything you have drawn previously. In the "Creating the Union of Two Solids" section, we join them to form a new composite solid.*

## Accessing Different Visual Styles

Visual styles are simple, default styles for presenting 3D images of the objects in your drawing. You are familiar with the 2D wireframe visual style. In this chapter you have used the Realistic style, the default in the acad3D template. Before moving on, it will be useful to switch to a style that more readily displays the borders between objects. Take a minute to view your box and wedge presented in the other predefined styles. At the right end of the **Home** tab of the ribbon, on the **Layers** panel there is a drop-down list of visual styles, with **Realistic** showing as the current style.

✔ Click the drop-down list arrow to the right of the word **Realistic** on the **Layers** panel.

*This opens the set of images shown in Figure 12-22. There are 10 preset styles. Styles vary in how they show edges and how they treat solid objects. To get a feel for them, select each style, and observe the effects.*

✔ One by one, try each of the 10 visual styles.

*You will find some of these styles to be very different from what you are used to seeing. The 10 styles show a great variety in how objects are presented and outlined. In our case it will be useful to show the edges around and between objects as we go through this exercise, so we will switch to the **Shades of Gray** style.*

✔ Select **Shades of Gray** before moving on.

*Your screen should resemble Figure 12-23.*

**Figure 12-22**
**Layers** panel

**Figure 12-23**
Shades of gray

## Creating the Union of Two Solids

**Figure 12-24**
**Union** tool

| UNION | |
|---|---|
| **Command** | Union |
| **Alias** | Uni |
| **Panel** | Edit |
| **Tool** | |

Unions are simple to create and usually easy to visualize. The union of two objects is an object that includes all points that are on either of the objects. Unions can be performed just as easily on more than two objects. The union of objects can be created even if the objects have no points in common (i.e., they do not touch or overlap).

Right now we have two distinct solids on the screen; with **UNION** we can join them.

✔ Pick the **Union** tool from the **Edit** panel, as shown in Figure 12-24.
*AutoCAD prompts you to select objects.*

✔ Use a crossing window to select both objects.

✔ Right-click to end object selection.
*If you run your cursor over the model now, you see that there is no border between the box and the wedge. They have become one object. Your screen should resemble Figure 12-25.*

**Figure 12-25**
Union of wedge and box

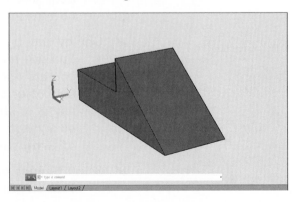

# Working with DUCS

In this task, we draw another solid box while demonstrating the use of the ***dynamic user coordinate system (DUCS).*** This feature allows you to establish coordinate systems "on-the-fly" aligned with the faces of previously drawn solids. In this exercise we draw a thin box on top of the box from the last section and then move it to the middle of the composite object. In the next section we move it, stretch it, and subtract it to form a groove.

**dynamic user coordinate system (DUCS):** In AutoCAD, the 3D system that creates a temporary user coordinate system aligned with the face of a 3D object.

✔ To begin this task you should have the union of a wedge and a box on your screen, as shown in Figure 12-25.

> *We begin by drawing a second box positioned on top of the first box.*

✔ If necessary, pick the **Allow/Disallow Dynamic UCS** button on your status bar so that it is on.

✔ Pick the **Box** tool from the drop-down list on the **Create** panel.

✔ Run the cursor slowly over the faces of the composite object on your screen.

> *As you do this, notice that the faces are highlighted with a black dashed border as you cross them. Also notice the 3D cursor. The 3D cursor will turn to align with each face as the face is highlighted. This includes the diagonal face, which turns the cursor on an angle.*

✔ Move the cursor over the diagonal face on the right side of the wedge and observe the orientation of the 3D cursor.

✔ Let the cursor rest on the top of the box so that it is highlighted, as shown in Figure 12-26.

> *With this face highlighted, AutoCAD will create a temporary coordinate system aligned with the top of the box.*

**Figure 12-26**
Face highlights

✔ With the top face highlighted, carefully move the cursor to the front left corner of the top of the box and press the pick button.

> *This creates a coordinate system aligned with the top face and its origin at the selected point, as shown in Figure 12-27. This is*

**Figure 12-27**
Cursor aligns with top face

*similar to the first user coordinate system you created in the "Defining User Coordinate Systems" section. As you move the cursor now, the base plane of the new box you are drawing will be in the plane of the top of the box.*

✔ Select **Length** from the command line.
   *With the **Length** option, you show the length and the width of the base separately, rather than by showing the opposite corner. AutoCAD prompts for a length.*

✔ Move your cursor along the front edge of the box 4.0000 units to the point where the box and the wedge meet.

✔ Pick this point to show the length.
   *AutoCAD prompts for the width.*

✔ Move the cursor over 0.5000 toward the back of the box and pick a point to indicate the width.
   *AutoCAD prompts for a height.*

✔ Make sure that the cursor stretches the box in the positive Z direction and type **2 <Enter>.**
   *Your screen should resemble Figure 12-28.*
   *Next, we move the new box so that the midpoint of its top front edge is at the midpoint of the top of the wedge.*

**Figure 12-28**
Drawing a new box

# Creating Composite Solids with SUBTRACT

| SUBTRACT | |
|---|---|
| Command | Subtract |
| Alias | Su |
| Panel | Edit |
| Tool |  |

**SUBTRACT** is the logical opposite of **UNION.** In a union operation, all the points contained in one solid are added to the points contained in other solids to form a new composite solid. In a subtraction, all points in the solids to be subtracted are removed from the source solid. A new composite solid is defined by what is left.

In this exercise, we use the objects already on your screen to create a slotted wedge. First, we need to move the thin upper box into place, then we copy it to create a longer slot, and finally we subtract these narrow boxes from the union of the box and the wedge.

✔ To begin this task, you should have the composite box and wedge solid and the thin box on your screen, as shown in Figure 12-28.
   *Before subtracting, we move the box to the position shown in Figure 12-29.*

✔ Pick the **Move** tool from the **Modify** panel of the ribbon, as shown in Figure 12-30.

**Figure 12-29**
Moving box to midpoint of wedge

**Figure 12-30**
**Move** tool

✔ Select the narrow box drawn in the last task.

✔ Right-click to end object selection.

✔ At the *Specify base point or displacement:* prompt, use a **Midpoint** object snap to pick the midpoint of the top right edge of the narrow box.

✔ At the next *Specify second point or displacement:* prompt, use another **Midpoint** object snap to pick the top edge of the wedge.
   *This moves the narrow box over and down. If you were to perform the subtraction now, you would create a slot, but it would run only through the box, not the wedge. We can create a longer slot by creating a second copy of the narrow box over to the right.*

✔ Pick the **Copy** tool from the **Modify** panel, as shown in Figure 12-31.

**Figure 12-31**
**Copy** tool

✔ Select the narrow box.

✔ Right-click to end object selection.

*We want to create a copy to the right in a line parallel to the X-axis. This can be easily done by picking the origin for the first point and then picking a point along the X-axis.*

✔ Pick the origin of the WCS for the displacement base point.

✔ Pick (3,0,0) for the second point.

✔ Press **<Enter>** to exit the command.

*Your screen should resemble Figure 12-32.*

**Figure 12-32**
Copying box

## Subtraction

The rest is easy. **SUBTRACT** works just like **UNION,** but the results are quite different.

✔ Pick the **Subtract** tool from the **Edit** panel, as shown in Figure 12-33.

*AutoCAD asks you to select objects to subtract from first:*

Select solids and regions to subtract from . . .
Select objects:

**Figure 12-33**
**Subtract** tool

✔ Pick the composite of the box and the wedge.

✔ Right-click to end selection of source objects.

*AutoCAD prompts for objects to be subtracted:*

Select solids and regions to subtract . . .
Select objects:

✔ Pick the two narrow boxes.

✔ Right-click to end selection.

*Your screen should resemble Figure 12-34.*

**Figure 12-34**
Subtracting the two narrow boxes

To complete this object, we draw a solid cylinder aligned with the diagonal face of the wedge and subtract it to form a hole on the right side below the slot.

✔ Pick the **Cylinder** tool from the **Solid Primitives** drop-down list, as shown in Figure 12-35.
> *AutoCAD prompts:*

> Specify center point for base of cylinder or [3P 2P Ttr Elliptical] <0,0,0>:

*We use the default method of picking a center point and then specifying a base radius and a height. Be sure to move your cursor slowly and carefully so that you can observe the dynamic user coordinate system in action.*

✔ Move the cursor over the lower front corner of the diagonal face, as shown in Figure 12-36.

*The face will be highlighted, and AutoCAD will create a temporary coordinate system aligned with the face and with the lower front corner as the origin. If you moved onto the face from another corner, that would become the temporary origin. Notice in the illustration*

**Figure 12-35**
**Cylinder** tool

**Figure 12-36**
Move cursor over diagonal face

*how the point where the cursor rests has become (0.0000,0.0000,0.0000) in the new coordinate system. We use this coordinate system to locate the center point of the cylinder.*

✔ Move the cursor over and up to the point (1.5000,1.0000,0.0000) in the new coordinate system and press the pick button.

*The point is selected, and the 3D cursor moves to this point, aligned with the angle of the face, as shown in Figure 12-37. This point has been selected as the center point of the base of the cylinder and has also become the origin of another temporary coordinate system. AutoCAD prompts:*

Specify base radius [Diameter]:

**Figure 12-37**
Cursor aligns with angle of face

✔ Type **.25 <Enter>.**

*AutoCAD prompts for a height:*

Specify height [2Pt Axis endpoint]:

✔ Stretch the cylinder in the negative Z direction.

✔ Type **3 <Enter>.**

Your screen should resemble Figure 12-38. The exact height of the cylinder is not significant because it will be subtracted from the composite object. Note that the same results could be achieved by stretching the cylinder in the positive Z direction and typing **−3.**

**Figure 12-38**
Stretching the cylinder

Now it's time to subtract.

✔ Pick the **Subtract** tool from the ribbon.

✔ Select the composite object.

✔ Right-click to end object selection.

✔ Select the cylinder.

✔ Right-click to end object selection.
*Your screen should resemble Figure 12-39.*

**Figure 12-39**
Subtracting the cylinder

## Creating Chamfers and Fillets on Solid Objects

Constructing chamfers and fillets on solids is simple, but the language of the prompts can cause confusion due to some ambiguity in the designation of edges and surfaces to be modified. We begin by putting a chamfer on the back left edge of the model.

✔ To begin this task, you should have the solid model shown in Figure 12-39 on your screen.
*In the **3D Basics** workspace you will find the **Chamfer** and **Fillet** tools on a **Modify** panel extension.*

✔ Open the **Modify** panel extension and pick the **Chamfer** tool.
*The first chamfer prompt is the same as always:*

Select first line or [Undo Polyline Distance Angle Trim mEthod Multiple]:

✔ Select point 1, as shown in Figure 12-40.

**Figure 12-40**
Pick edge P1 and P2

*The selection preview will highlight the whole solid, but when you pick point 1, AutoCAD highlights the back left surface, displays the geometry from which the object is constructed, and prompts:*

```
Base surface selection . . .
Enter surface selection option [Next OK (current)] <OK>:
```

*We are constructing a chamfer that will cut across the front left surface of the object. However, chamfers and fillets happen along edges that are common to two surfaces. What is a base surface in relation to a chamfered edge? Actually, it refers to either of the two faces that meet at the edge where the chamfer will be. As long as you pick this edge, you are bound to select one of these two surfaces, and either will do. Which of the two surfaces is the base surface and which is the adjacent surface does not matter until you enter the chamfer distances, and then only if the distances are unequal. However, AutoCAD allows you to switch to the other surface that shares this edge, by typing **n** for the **Next** option or selecting **Next** from the dynamic input display or the command line.*

✔ Press **<Enter>**.

*AutoCAD prompts:*

```
Specify base surface chamfer distance or [Expression]:
```

*The **Expression** option allows you to specify chamfer distances with a mathematical expression instead of an actual value.*

✔ Type **.5 <Enter>** for the base surface distance.

*Now, AutoCAD prompts:*

```
Specify other surface chamfer distance or [Expression] <0.5000>:
```

*Now, you can see the significance of the base surface. The chamfer is created with the first distance on the base surface side and the second distance on the other surface side.*

✔ Type **.75 <Enter>** for the other base surface distance.

*This will construct a chamfer that cuts 0.5 down into the left side and 0.75 forward along the top side.*

*Now, AutoCAD prompts for the edge or edges to be chamfered:*

```
Select an edge or [Loop]:
```

The **Loop** option constructs chamfers on all edges of the chosen base surface. Selecting edges allows you to place them only on the selected edges. You have no difficulty selecting edges if you pick the edge you wish to chamfer again. The only difference is that you need to pick twice, once on each side of the slot.

✔ Pick the top left edge of the model, to one side of the slot (point 1 in Figure 12-40 again).

✔ Pick the same edge again, but on the other side of the slot (point 2 in Figure 12-40).

✔ Press **<Enter>** to end edge selection (right-clicking opens a shortcut menu).

*Your screen should resemble Figure 12-41.*

**Figure 12-41**
Chamfering edges

## Creating Fillets

The procedure for creating solid fillets is simpler. There is one step fewer because there is no need to differentiate between base and other surfaces in a fillet.

✔ Pick the **Fillet** tool from the **Modify** panel extension.
*AutoCAD gives you current settings and prompts:*

Select first object or [Undo Polyline Radius Trim Multiple]:

✔ Pick the front edge of the angled wedge face, as shown in Figure 12-42.
*AutoCAD prompts:*

Enter fillet radius:

**Figure 12-42**
Pick front edge of wedge

✔ Type **.25 <Enter>.**
*The next prompt looks like this:*

Select an edge or [Chain Loop Radius]:

***Chain*** *allows you to fillet around all the edges of one side of a solid object at once. For our purposes, we do not want a chain. Instead, we want to select the front and back edges of the diagonal face.*

✔ Pick the back edge of the angled wedge face.
*You see this prompt again:*

Select an edge or [Chain Loop Radius]:

*The prompt repeats to allow you to select more edges to fillet.*

✔ Press **<Enter>** to end selection of edges.
*Your screen should resemble Figure 12-43.*

**Figure 12-43**
Filleting edges of wedge

## Practicing 3D Gizmo Editing

gizmo: In AutoCAD 3D modeling, one of three coordinate system icons that facilitate editing of solid models. The three gizmos are for moving, rotating, and scaling models.

*Gizmos* are 3D icons that facilitate editing in strict relation to the current coordinate system. Using the **Move** gizmo, you can easily move objects along lines parallel to the *X*-, *Y*-, or *Z*-axis. Using the **Rotate** gizmo, you can rotate objects around these same lines. Using the **Scale** gizmo, you can scale along any of the axes, through the plane of any two axes, or uniformly in all directions. Here we demonstrate moving and rotating.

✔ Open the **Gizmo** drop-down list from the **Selection** panel, as shown in Figure 12-44.
*You see the three gizmos, along with a **No Gizmo** tool. **No Gizmo** is a useful option, because you will not always want the visual distraction of gizmos appearing each time you select an object. We begin with the **Move** gizmo.*

**Figure 12-44**
**Gizmo** drop-down list

✔ Pick the **Move Gizmo** tool.
*This ensures that the **Move** gizmo is active and at the top of the list, which it may be by default.*

✔ Select the model.
*The model is highlighted with the **Move** gizmo at the center, as shown in Figure 12-45.*

✔ Run your cursor over the gizmo slowly.

As you slowly cross over an axis, a construction line is displayed with the color of that axis. Also, the axis is highlighted in gold. In Figure 12-45

**Figure 12-45**
Move gizmo icon

you see the *X*-axis highlighted with a red construction line extending in both directions. If you move into the quadrant between two axes, the square between those two axes will be highlighted in gold, indicating you are in the plane of those two axes.

✔ Move your cursor so that the *X*-axis is highlighted.

✔ Press the pick button.

✔ Move the model back and forth along the *X*-axis.
   *Next, we try rotation.*

✔ With the object still highlighted and the **Move** gizmo showing, pick the **Rotate Gizmo** tool from the **Selection** panel.

The **Rotate** gizmo replaces the **Move** gizmo, as shown in Figure 12-46. The elliptical red, green, and blue circles represent the three planes of rotation. We demonstrate rotation in the XY plane, around the *Z*-axis.

**Figure 12-46**
Rotate gizmo icon

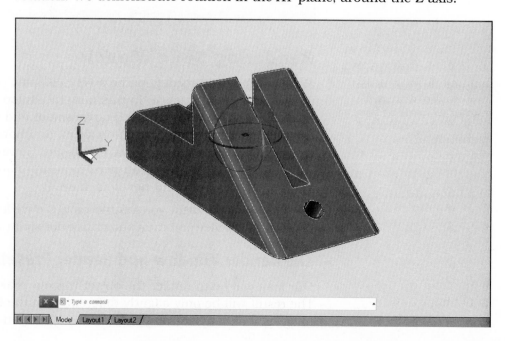

- ✔ Move your cursor over the blue ellipse so that it turns gold, as shown. *When the blue ellipse is highlighted gold, a blue Z-axis is displayed.*
- ✔ Press the pick button.
- ✔ Drag the model to perform rotation around the Z-axis.
- ✔ Drag the model back to a position similar to its original rotation.
- ✔ Press the pick button to complete the procedure.

The **Scale** gizmo is a bit more complex, and we will not demonstrate it here. As shown in Figure 12-47, the **Scale** gizmo is similar to the **Move** gizmo, except that it has gold triangulating lines drawn between each pair of axes and boxes at the end. By highlighting an individual axis, you can create scaling along that axis. By highlighting a bar in the plane between any two axes, you can scale in both of these directions. By highlighting the complete pattern of gold lines and gold boxes all at once, you can create uniform scaling in all directions.

**Figure 12-47**
Scale gizmo icon

## Rendering Solid Models

*Rendering* a solid model can be a very complex process requiring a great deal of time and expertise. In this task we explore simple visual style changes and then move on to the placement and setting of lights. Knowing the various lights, how to position them, and how to understand their respective settings is a good place to begin. However, this knowledge alone will not take you very far. You need to accumulate hours of experience to know what you want and how to achieve it.

**rendering:** The process by which the mathematical data used to describe a solid model are translated into pixels and represented on a computer screen.

- ✔ To begin this task, you should have the wedge on your screen in a southeast viewpoint, as shown previously in Figure 12-43.

### The Render Window and Render Presets

Our task will be to render the object without making any lighting changes. The result will be only slightly different from the **Shades of Gray** style image you already see on your screen. When you render an object, it can be shown in a special render window or within a viewport. The render window is used by default. Also, you have a choice of five different render settings that control the degree of precision in the rendering. There is a **Draft** setting, for example, that you may wish to use in a complex drawing where you want a quick rendering. At the other end of the spectrum is a **Presentation** setting, which contains more detail and is therefore drawn more slowly. The default setting is **Medium.**

We begin by changing from **Medium** to **Presentation. Render** and many related tools are found on the **Render** tab on the ribbon.

✔ Pick the **Render** tab.

*The **Render** tab is shown in Figure 12-48. Toward the right end of the **Render** tab is the **Render** panel. At the top of the **Render** panel is the **Presentation** style list, with **Medium** showing as the current setting.*

**Figure 12-48**
**Render** tab

---

**NOTE**

You can also send rendered images directly to a viewport instead of the render window. To render to a viewport, pick the **Advanced Render Settings** button to the right of the title bar on the **Render** panel. This opens a tool palette. On the **Render Context** list, the second line is **Destination.** Change **Destination** from **Window** to **Viewport.** Make the viewport you want current and then pick the **Render** tool.

---

✔ Open the list and select **Presentation.**

*We are now ready for our first rendering.*

✔ Pick the **Render** tool, as shown in Figure 12-49.

*AutoCAD opens the render window and draws the rendered image shown in Figure 12-50. Like other windows the render window can be minimized and maximized. The render window also retains all renderings that are done in this drawing session so that you can switch back and forth and keep a record of where you have been. Rendering requires a lot of trial and error, so this history is useful. On the right are various numerical values describing your rendering.*

**Figure 12-49**
**Render** tool

---

**NOTE**

Depending on previous usage of your computer, you may see the message **Autodesk Materials Library - Medium Image library is not installed.** In this case you have a choice of either downloading and installing the library, or continuing to work without using the library. Either way, you can check the **Do not show this dialog again** box to avoid seeing this dialog box each time you go to render an image.

---

✔ Close the render window, or click the AutoCAD drawing name label on the Windows taskbar to return to the drawing window.

*Next, we add a background to the viewport.*

**Figure 12-50**
Render window

Render: 100.0%

## Changing the Background and Naming Views

You may find that certain rendered images are too light against the Auto-CAD background screen color. You can remedy this by changing to a different background through the **View Manager** dialog box. When the background is changed in a viewport, it is retained in the rendering of that viewport. Here we change to a gradient background for dramatic effect. Using the default settings the gradient will be in shades of gray.

✔ Type **View <Enter>.**

✔ In the **View Manager** dialog box, pick the **New . . .** button.

✔ In the **New View/Shot Properties** dialog box, open the list in the **Background** panel at the bottom.

✔ From the drop-down list, select **Gradient.**

This opens the **Background** dialog box shown in Figure 12-51. You see a **Preview** panel with a gradient pattern from darker to lighter gray. At the bottom is a **Gradient options** panel that allows you to change the gradient colors and to rotate the middle border.

> **NOTE**
> The technique of saving named views can also be used to save more complex configurations of lights, materials, and light settings. When you have achieved a scene you wish to keep, it is a good idea to save it as a named view.

✔ Click **OK** to accept the default gradient scheme.
   *This takes you back to the **New View/Shot Properties** dialog box, where you must name the background view before you can apply it.*

✔ In the **View name** box, type **Gradient.**

**Figure 12-51**
**Background** dialog box

✔ Click **OK.**

> *Back in the **View Manager** dialog box, notice the preview image at the bottom right. To change your viewport to this view, you must set it as current.*

✔ Pick the **Set Current** button at the upper right.

✔ Click **OK.**

> *You should now see your shaded model with a gradient background.*

✔ If your grid is on, turn it off.

✔ Pick the **Render** tab.

> *The gradient background is retained in the render window.*

## Spotlight

Although you have done nothing to add lights to the current model, there is light present. It is the default viewport lighting and is added automatically. It provides light from two sources and produces the effect you see. When you add your own lighting, you will have the option of turning off default lighting. We begin by adding a spotlight.

Three types of light are accessible from the **Create Light** drop-down list shown in Figure 12-52. We are going to add a spotlight on the right side of the object, aimed in along the slot. Light placement is probably the most important consideration in rendering. Lights can be placed using point filters or typed coordinates. Keep in mind that lights are usually positioned above the XY plane and are often alone in space. Point filters can be very helpful in this situation because there is nothing to snap the lights onto.

✔ Pick the **Spot** tool from the **Create Light** drop-down list on the **Lights** panel, as shown in Figure 12-52.

**Figure 12-52**
Spot light tool

At this point, AutoCAD may present a **Lighting – Viewport Lighting mode** message that asks whether you want to turn off default lighting.

✔ If necessary, pick the **Turn off the default lighting** option.

AutoCAD adds a spot light icon to the crosshairs and prompts:

> Specify source location <0,0,0>:

Spotlights have a target and a source position. As is the case with real spotlights, AutoCAD-rendered spotlights are carefully placed and aimed at a particular point in the drawing. The light falls in a cone shape and diminishes from the center of the cone. The area of the focal beam is called the hotspot. The surrounding area where the light fades is called the falloff area.

For this exercise, we place a light above and to the right of the wedge, aimed directly into the front of the slot. We use object snap and an .XY filter to place the target and the light source where we want them.

✔ At the prompt for a light source, type **.xy <Enter>** or open the **Object Snap** shortcut menu, highlight **Point Filters**, and select **.XY.**

AutoCAD prompts **.xy of** and waits for you to choose a point in the XY plane.

✔ Pick a point 1.0 unit to the right of the composite wedge, the point (10,2.5,0).

AutoCAD now prompts for a z value:

> (need Z):

✔ Type **4 <Enter>.**

This will place the source location to the right and above the wedge. Now, AutoCAD prompts for the target location:

> Specify target location <0,0,–10>:

We use a **Midpoint** object snap to place the target at the right end of the slot.

✔ **<Shift>** + right-click, and select **Midpoint** from the **Object Snap** menu.

✔ Use the **Midpoint** object snap to select the midpoint of the right end of the slot.

The target point is now specified, and AutoCAD offers further options to adjust the spotlight. AutoCAD prompts:

> Enter option to change
> [Name Intensity factor Status Photometry Hotspot Falloff shadoW Attenuation filter Color eXit] <eXit>:

These same options are shown on the dynamic input display. We will not change any options at this point.

✔ Press **\<Enter\>** to exit the command.

*The wedge will be shaded, showing the effect of the spotlight shining on the end of the slot. The shading is rather dark. We add some sunlight.*

✔ Pick the **Sun Status** tool, as shown in Figure 12-53, to turn it on.

*The shaded image brightens. Your shaded wedge should resemble Figure 12-54. Sunlight can be edited to represent different locations, times of day, and dates. The default sunlight specification is 3:00 P.M. in your current city, current date. We explore these settings later. Before adding another light, try rendering the object.*

**Figure 12-53**
Sun Status tool

**Figure 12-54**
Shaded wedge

✔ Pick the **Render** tool.

**NOTE**

Notice the small flashlight image that has been added to the drawing. It indicates the placement of lights. This is called a *glyph* and can be turned on and off using the **Light glyphs** tool. It is on the **Lights** panel extension of the **Render** tab.

*In a few moments, the image in your render window should resemble Figure 12-55. Notice how the spotlight is treated more precisely in the rendered model. There are numerous ways to adjust this cone of light. We adjust two settings to achieve the softer lighting effect shown in Figure 12-56.*

**Figure 12-55**
Rendered spotlight

**Figure 12-56**
Softer lighting effects

## The Lights in Model Palette

The **Lights in Model** tool opens a palette in which you can easily make changes to light characteristics. We open it to change the hotspot and intensity settings.

✔ Close the render window and return to the drawing window.

✔ Pick the arrow at the right of the **Lights** panel title bar, as shown in Figure 12-57.

**Figure 12-57**
**Lights in Model** tool

✔ Double-click the name **Spotlight1** in the **Lights in Model** palette.
*This opens the light **Properties** palette, shown in Figure 12-58. It also adds a display of the hotspot and falloff cones in the drawing area. With the display, you can change the light cones by dragging on the grips. We will instead make the changes numerically in the palette. The first line of the palette gives you the opportunity to change the name. Here we leave it alone. The settings we change are on lines five and seven. The default spotlight cone has a large beam with a quick falloff. We shrink the hotspot and leave the falloff where it is. We also lessen the light intensity.*

**Figure 12-58**
**Properties** palette

✔ Click once in the **Hotspot angle** edit box.

✔ Change the **Hotspot specification** to **20** and press **<Enter>**.
*Observe carefully when you make this change, and you can see the cone display adjust.*

✔ Click once in the **Intensity factor** edit box.

✔ Change the **Intensity setting** to **0.5** and press **<Enter>.**

✔ Close the **Properties** palette.

✔ Close the **Lights in Model** palette.

✔ Pick the **Render** tool.

> *In a few moments, your screen should resemble Figure 12-56, shown previously. Next, we add a point light.*

✔ Press **<Esc>,** or click the AutoCAD drawing button on the Windows taskbar to return to the drawing.

## Point Light

Point light works like a lightbulb with no shade. It radiates outward equally in all directions. The light from a point light is attenuated over distance.

In this exercise, we place a point light right inside the slot of the wedge. This clearly shows the lightbulb effect of a small point of light radiating outward.

✔ Pick the **Point** tool from the **Create Light** drop-down list on the **Lights** panel.

> *For a point light, you need to specify only a source location because point light has no direction other than outward from the source. AutoCAD gives you a light glyph to drag into place. The prompt is:*

> Specify source location <0,0,0>:

> *We use typed coordinates to locate this light.*

✔ At the prompt, type **4,2.5,1.5 <Enter>.**

> *Because the slot is at 1.00 from the XY plane, this puts the point light just above the bottom of the slot. This time around we use the dynamic input display to change the intensity. With point light there is no hotspot or falloff.*

✔ Select **Intensity factor** from the dynamic input display.

✔ Type **3 <Enter>** for the intensity level.

✔ Press **<Enter>** to complete the light specification.

> *The effect of the point light appears immediately.*

✔ Pick the **Render** tool.

> *Your rendered object should resemble Figure 12-59. In this image, you can clearly see the effect of the point light within the slot along with the spotlight falling on the right side of the object.*

**Figure 12-59**
The effect of the point light

## Sunlight Editing

Sunlight editing is easy and produces dramatic changes. The arrow at the right of the title bar on the **Sun & Location** panel opens a **Sun Properties** palette, which allows you direct access to many sunlight settings. But even more accessible are the two sliders for date and time on the **Sun & Location** panel, as shown in Figure 12-60. We begin by adjusting the time of day using the second slider.

**Figure 12-60**
**Sun & Location** panel

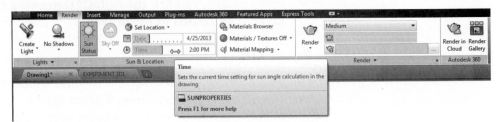

✔ Move your cursor into the **Time** box in the **Sun & Location** panel, so that the two-way arrow, labeled **SUNPROPERTIES,** appears.

✔ Drag the slider slowly left and right. Observe the effect.
*As you drag the slider, let it rest here and there and observe the changes in lighting in your model. As you would expect, nighttime hours will produce darkened results, whereas daylight hours will produce a wide range of sunlit effects.*

✔ Move the slider to the left to specify a time approximately. Let the slider rest inside the **Time** box and use the arrow keys on your keyboard to take your slider to exactly 2:00 P.M.

✔ Pick the **Render** tool.
*This is only a one-hour difference, but the effect is significant, as shown in Figure 12-61.*
*In addition to the **Time** slider there is a **Date** slider, which will adjust your lighting to replicate different dates in the year.*

**Figure 12-61**
One-hour difference

## Geographic Location

Time and date will affect lighting differently at different points on the planet, so geographic information will also affect the interpretation of lighting data. Picking the **Set Location** tool, the globe at the top of the **Sun & Location** panel, allows you to specify a geographic location. The tool opens a box with three choices. First, you can access information from a KML (Keyhole

Markup Language) or KMZ (KML zipped) file. These are file formats used by Google Earth to display geographic data. Second, you can import current data directly from a location in Google Earth. Third, you can open the **Geographic Location** dialog box and enter location values manually.

## Attaching Materials

The last rendering technique we explore is the addition of materials and textures to a solid model. Materials can be created or selected from AutoCAD's materials library. Each material definition has its own characteristic color, texture, and response to light. Materials can also be created or modified. Changing an object's material dramatically affects the way it is rendered, so it usually makes sense to attach materials before adjusting light intensity and color. In this exercise, we take you through the procedure of loading materials from the AutoCAD library and attaching them to an object. When you experiment on your own, you will see color effects that we cannot show here.

To the right of the **Sun & Location** panel is the **Materials** panel. Picking the arrow at the right of the **Materials** panel title bar will open a tool palette for editing qualities of materials in your drawing. Here you can even create your own materials. For our purposes we will follow a simpler path of applying a material from Autodesk's **Materials Library** directly to your wedge. These materials are found in the **Materials Browser.**

✔ Pick the **Materials Browser** tool from the top of the **Materials** panel of the ribbon.

> *This opens the **Materials Browser** palette, shown in Figure 12-62. Your palette may look different from ours if others have opened it*

**Figure 12-62**
**Materials Browser** palette

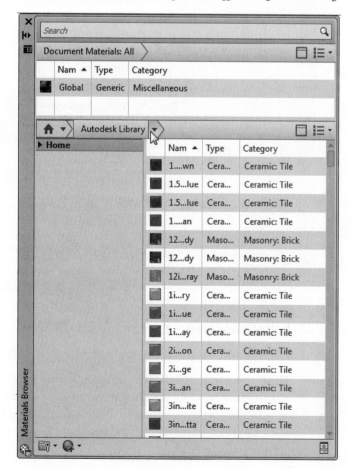

*and used it. In the browsing window on the left you have the option of browsing through materials of your own creation or through Autodesk's library.*

**NOTE**

If the attached material does not appear on your model, try clicking the **Materials and Textures** drop-down list on the **Materials** panel. There are three settings: **Materials on/ Textures on, Materials on/Textures off,** and **Materials off/Textures off.** You need materials and textures on to produce the results shown here.

✔ Pick **Autodesk Library.**

*This opens a list of material types, beginning with Ceramic. Each of these list items will open a set of material varieties, represented by the images on the left. We will add an anodized bronzed aluminum to our model.*

✔ Scroll down and select **Metal** from the list, as shown in Figure 12-63.

**Figure 12-63**
Select **Metal**

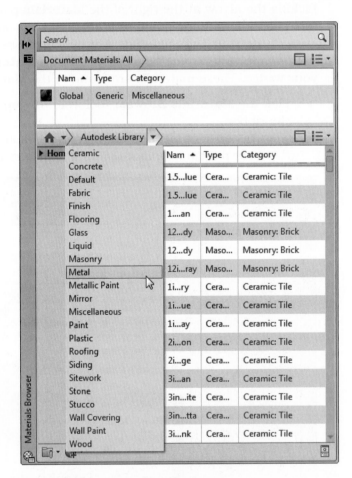

✔ Select **Anodized – Bronze,** as shown.

✔ Click on the **Anodized – Bronze** image and drag it into the drawing area.

✔ Drag the image over the composite wedge.

*Assuming your render destination is the render window, a vertical black line to one side of the model will appear to indicate that material has been added, but you will not see the material until you render.*

✔ Close the **Materials Browser.**

✔ Pick the **Render** tool to complete the rendering.
    *The material and texture shown in Figure 12-64 will be added to your model in the render window.*

✔ If necessary, close the render window.

**Figure 12-64**
Rendering with material texture

## Changing Viewpoints with the ViewCube

**Figure 12-65**
ViewCube

**ViewCube:** In AutoCAD, an icon representing standard orthographic and isometric viewpoints, used to change viewpoints in a 3D drawing or viewport.

You've probably been wondering what that cube up in the right corner of your drawing screen is for. We've mentioned it before, but it is much more useful now that you know something about 3D viewpoints. This is the **ViewCube,** shown in Figure 12-65. It is a very easy and logical way to change viewpoints in a 3D drawing. Once you understand what the cube represents, all you need do is pick the cube position that represents the viewpoint you want to specify. In essence, this is the same cube represented in the named **Preset Views** we encountered at the beginning of the chapter. The front of the cube corresponds to the front point of view, where you are looking in along the north–south Y-axis of your coordinate system. From this perspective, the X-axis is running left to right, east to west in front of you, and the Z-axis is running vertically, top to bottom. Relative to this position, the viewpoint we have been using throughout this chapter is up and to the right. With the front of the **ViewCube** facing us, it is represented by the upper right corner.

✔ Run your cursor over the **ViewCube** without pressing the pick button.

When you run your cursor over the **ViewCube,** you see that the different positions on the cube are highlighted as you go. On each face there are nine selectable positions. In the middle is the face-on position, labeled right, for example. It is at some point along the axis normal to that face and at 0 on the other two axes. There are two other types of positions, side and corner, that are not labeled but can be selected. There are four sides, representing the view from 45° angles between each pair of axes, and 0° from the third axis. So, for example, the front right view is the side between the front and right faces of the cube, and represents a viewpoint between the X- and Y-axes but within the XY plane (Z = 0). The corners represent the isometric views, which are 45° off from all three axes. Our front right top view is an example. The small image of a house above and to the left represents the home view, which AutoCAD defines as top left front in the current drawing. This puts your point of view in the area of the origin of the coordinate system. Once you know how the cube represents coordinate space, all you need do is pick a corner, side, or face of the **ViewCube** to switch to that view. Try it.

✔ Pick the right face of the **ViewCube,** labeled with the word RIGHT.
> *Objects on your screen move to put you at the "right" viewpoint, as shown in Figure 12-66.*

**Figure 12-66**
Right viewpoint

✔ Pick the arrow at the left side of the right face of the **ViewCube.**
> *Your viewpoint moves to the front right view shown in Figure 12-67.*

**Figure 12-67**
Front right viewpoint

✔ Pick the front right top corner of the cube to return to a front right top view.

## Creating Layouts with Multiple Views

NEW to AutoCAD 2013

We close this chapter on 3D modeling by creating a paper space layout with orthographic projections of our model. This is an impressive and easy-to-use feature, demonstrating once again the power of solid modeling and the flexibility we have now that our model is drawn.

✔ To begin, you should have the solid wedge model on your screen, as shown previously in Figure 12-61 (**Materials off**) or Figure 12-64 (**Materials on**).

We create a layout with two orthographic projections, one 3D image, and one detail, as shown in Figure 12-68. This will be most easily accomplished by first switching to the **3D Modeling** workspace.

✔ Pick the down arrow at the right of the **Workspace** drop-down list on the **Quick Access** toolbar, and select **3D Modeling** from the list.
> *The ribbon switches to the **3D Modeling** workspace ribbon shown in Figure 12-69.*

**Figure 12-68**
Creating a layout

DETAIL A
SCALE 1:1

**Figure 12-69**
**3D Modeling** workspace

✔ Pick **Layout** tab > **Base** tool > **From Model Space,** as shown in Figure 12-70.

*This initiates the **VIEWBASE** command and indicates that you will create the base view in the layout from the objects currently in model space. The other option is to create views from objects in Inventor, Autodesk's specialized software for three-dimensional mechanical design. AutoCAD prompts:*

Select objects or [Entire model] <Entire model>:

**Figure 12-70**
**Base View from Model Space**

✔ Press **<Enter>** to select the entire model.
*AutoCAD prompts for a layout name.*

Enter new or existing layout name to make current or [?] <Layout1>:

*For our purposes we can accept the default name, **Layout1**.*

✔ Press **<Enter>** to accept the default name for the new layout.
*AutoCAD opens a paper space layout and gives you an image of the model to drag into place. We position our first projection at the bottom left, as shown in Figure 12-71. Our model is placed at (2.50,2.00).*

✔ Move the cursor to position the view in the lower left corner of the layout, as shown. Press the pick button to complete the placement. Ours is placed at (2.50,2.00).
*AutoCAD gives you a prompt with many options for manipulating your projection:*

Select option [sElect Orientation Hidden lines Scale Visibility Move eXit] <eXit>:

*We exit and move on.*

**Chapter 12** | 3D Modeling  **569**

**Figure 12-71**
Shaded figures

✔ Press **<Enter>** to exit this prompt.

*Now AutoCAD gives you a second projection to drag into place. If we stick to orthogonal directions, we will get orthogonal projections. AutoCAD prompts:*

Specify location of projected view or <exit>:

✔ Move the cursor directly upward to create the top view placement shown in Figure 12-71. Ours is placed at (2.50,6.00).

*AutoCAD continues to prompt for view locations.*

✔ Move the cursor to a position diagonally opposite the first view, as shown by the 3D view in Figure 12-71. Ours is at (8.00,6.00)

*Notice that this diagonal placement creates a 3D image. At this point you could create another orthogonal projection to the right, but instead we will place a detail view in this area. To do this we leave the **VIEWBASE** command.*

✔ Press **<Enter>** to exit the command.

*The projections are adjusted to 2D wireframe images, as shown in Figure 12-72. Our final step is to create the detail at the right, as shown previously in Figure 12-68.*

**Figure 12-72**
Wireframe figures

## View Details

✔ Pick the **Circular Detail** tool from the **Create View** panel, as shown in Figure 12-73.

*AutoCAD prompts for a parent view. This is the view the detail will be drawn from.*

> Select parent view:

**Figure 12-73**
**Circular Detail** tool

✔ Select the 3D wireframe view at the top right.

*Since we are creating a detail with a circular border, AutoCAD prompts for a center point.*

✔ Make sure that object snap mode is off for the remainder of this exercise.

✔ **<Shift>** + right-click and select **Midpoint** from the shortcut menu.

✔ Carefully select the midpoint of the edge at the bottom front of the slot.

*AutoCAD prompts for the size of the boundary.*

> Specify boundary size:

*This will be the radius of the circle surrounding the detail. There are other options here that may be specified before or after you size the boundary. You can drag out the circle or enter a radius value.*

✔ Type **.5 <Enter>** for the circular boundary radius.

*AutoCAD prompts for a location:*

> Specify location of detail.

*Here again the prompt includes many of the same options included in the previous prompt.*

✔ Pick a location point. We chose (6.00,3.00).

*At this point we could exit the command, and AutoCAD would draw our detail at the location and size we have specified, using the same wireframe presentation as the parent view. Instead, we will specify a shaded presentation.*

✔ Select **Hidden lines** from the dynamic input display or the command line.

*This calls up a further set of options:*

> Select style [Visible lines vIsible and hidden lines Shaded with visible lines sHaded with visible and hidden lines From parent]
> <From parent>:

✔ Select **Shaded with visible lines** from the dynamic input display or the command line.

> *AutoCAD returns the same set of options so that we can continue to modify our detail. We will exit the command.*

✔ Press **<Enter>** to exit the command.

Your screen should resemble Figure 12-68, as shown previously, with the three views and the detail and callout.

# Chapter Summary

In this chapter you learned a whole new way of creating design images with AutoCAD. You learned to manipulate coordinate systems so that you can create a new system at any point and any orientation in space. You learned to use your cursor in conjunction with these coordinate systems, along with other dynamic coordinate systems AutoCAD creates automatically, to draw 3D wireframe and solid models, and to draw and edit in the different planes of these models. You saw how you can easily switch among 10 different visual styles for representing 3D objects on your screen. You learned a whole new set of constructive geometry concepts and techniques for creating objects by combining solid primitives in union, subtraction, and intersection procedures. You learned to modify solid objects using familiar editing tools, 3D variations of these tools, and other tools, such as 3D gizmos, that have no counterpart in two dimensions. You used powerful lighting and rendering commands to produce realistic 3D shaded models. You learned the ViewCube method of changing points of view in a 3D drawing and used the **VIEWBASE** command to create multiple view layouts from a single 3D model.

# Chapter Test Questions

## Multiple Choice

*Circle the correct answer.*

1. In a southwest isometric viewpoint, objects are viewed from a point where:
   a. *x* is positive, *y* is positive, *z* is positive
   b. *x* is negative, *y* is negative, *z* is positive
   c. *x* is negative, *y* is positive, *z* is negative
   d. *x* is positive, *y* is negative, *z* is positive

2. The point (3,3,3) **cannot** be specified by:
   a. Typing
   b. Point filters
   c. Pointing
   d. Object snap

3. 3D gizmos are **not** used to:
   a. Move solids
   b. Rotate solids
   c. Scale solids
   d. Stretch solids

4. Attaching materials to solids is accomplished through the:
   a. **ATTACH** command
   b. **Materials Browser**
   c. Materials Manager
   d. **Materials** dialog box

5. The west face of the **ViewCube** is labeled:

    a. Left

    b. West

    c. Front

    d. Back

## Matching

*Write the number of the correct answer on the line.*

a. Conceptual _____              1. Gizmo

b. UCS _____                     2. World

c. Solid modeling _____      3. Constructive solid geometry

d. Rotate intersection _____   4. Boolean operation

e. Intersection _____           5. Visual style

## True or False

*Circle the correct answer.*

1. **True or False:** The world coordinate system can be rotated.

2. **True or False:** In the standard 3D UCS icon the *Z*-axis is red.

3. **True or False:** In the acad3D template the grid is presented in perspective projection.

4. **True or False:** 3D fillets can be created with the same command as 2D fillets.

5. **True or False:** In order to create the union of two solid objects, the objects must overlap.

## Questions

1. What 3D solid objects and commands would you use to create a square nut with a bolt hole in the middle?

2. Describe the effects of union, subtraction, and intersection.

3. When is it important to use an object snap to rotate the UCS icon to establish a new coordinate system?

4. How would you use a point filter to place a spotlight 5.0 units above the point (3,5,0)?

5. What are the shapes and qualities of spotlights and point lights?

## Drawing Problems

1. Open a new drawing with the acad3D template and change the snap setting to **0.25.** Zoom in as needed.

2. Draw a solid wedge, with a 5.0 × 5.0 unit base and a height of 2.5.

3. Draw a 3.0 × 3.0 box with a height of 2.0, normal to the angled face of the wedge, with the front left corner in 1.0 and over 1.0 from the two edges of the face of the wedge.

4. Draw a 0.75-radius cylinder with its base aligned and centered at the center of the right front face of the box drawn in Step 3. This cylinder should have a height of 7.0 extending back through the box in the negative Z direction of the DUCS aligned with the right front face of the box.

5. Draw a 0.50-radius cylinder with the same alignment and center point. This cylinder should have a height of 10.0 units extending in the same direction as the first cylinder.

6. Draw a 0.25-radius cylinder with height 13.0. Align and center it with the previous two cylinders.

## WWW Exercise (Optional)

Complete the following:

✔ Make sure that you are connected to your Internet service provider.

✔ Type **browser <Enter>.**

✔ If necessary, navigate to our companion website at www.pearsonhighered.com/dixriley.

*See you there.*

## Chapter Drawing Projects

 ## Drawing 12-1: *Flange* [INTERMEDIATE]

We begin with three 3D models for this chapter. They will give you a feel for this whole new way of putting objects together on the screen. Look the objects over, and consider what primitive shapes and Boolean processes will be required to complete the models. In each case, the finished drawing is the 3D model itself. The orthographic views are presented to give the information you need to draw the solid models correctly. They may be included as part of your completed drawing, or your instructor may prefer that you just complete the model.

### Drawing Suggestions

- You can complete this drawing with two commands.
- Begin with the bottom of the flange in the XY plane, and draw three cylinders, all with the same center point and different heights.
- Draw four 0.500-diameter holes on the quadrants of a 3.5 circle around the same center point.
- Subtract the middle cylinder and the four small cylinders to create the completed model.

Ø.500
4 holes
EQ SPACED
ON Ø3.500 B.C.

Ø1.500
THRU

Ø2.375

.25 CHAMFER

1.875

.250

Ø4.750

**Drawing 12-1**
Flange

# Drawing 12-2: *Link Mount* [ADVANCED]

This drawing is very manageable with the techniques you learned in this chapter. When you have finished drawing this model, you may wish to experiment with adding materials, lights, and changing point of view.

## Drawing Suggestions

- You will need a 0.25 snap for this drawing.

- Before you begin, notice what the model consists of, and think ahead to how it will be constructed. You have a filleted 8 × 8 box at the base, with four cylindrical holes. A flat cylinder sits on top of this at the center. On top of the cylinder you have two upright boxes, filleted across the top and pierced through with 1.50-diameter cylindrical holes.

- Beginning the base box at (0,0,0) will make the coordinates easy to read in the WCS.

- After drawing the flat cylinder on top of the base, draw one upright box on the centerline of the cylinder. Move it 0.5 left, and then make a copy 1.00 to the right. You will make frequent use of DUCS throughout the modeling process.

- After drawing the base, the flat cylinder, and the upright boxes, add the four cylinders to the base and a single cylinder through the middle of the two upright boxes.

- Leave the subtracting of the cylinders until last. In particular, fillet the base and the upright boxes before you do any subtraction.

- All subtraction can be done in one step. When you do this, you will also create unions at the same time. Select the base, the flat cylinder, and the upright boxes as objects to subtract from. Select the other cylinders as objects to subtract. When you are done, the remaining object will be a single object.

**Drawing 12-2**
Link Mount

## M Drawing 12-3: *Bushing Mount* [ADVANCED]

This drawing gives you more practice in the techniques used in Drawing 12-2. The addition of the bushing is a primary difference. Although the geometry of the bushing can be used to create the hole in the mount, the mount and the bushing should be created and retained as separate objects.

Use an efficient sequence in the construction of all composite solids. In general, this means saving union, subtraction, and intersection operations until most of the solid objects have been drawn and positioned. This approach also allows you to continue to use the geometry of the parts for snap points as you position other parts.

### Drawing Suggestions

- Begin with the bottom of the mount in the XY plane. This means drawing a 6.00 × 4.00 × 0.50 solid box sitting on the XY plane.

- Draw a second box, 1.50 × 4.00 × 0.50, in the XY plane. This becomes the upright section at the middle of the mount. Move it so that its own midpoint is at the midpoint of the base.

- Draw a third box, 1.75 × 0.75 × 0.50, in the XY plane. This is copied and becomes one of the two slots in the base. Move it so that the midpoint of its long side is at the midpoint of the short side of the base. Then, move it over 1.125 along the *X*-axis.

- Create 0.375-radius fillets at each corner of the slot.

- Copy the filleted box 3.75 to the other side of the base to form the other slot.

- Create a 1.25-diameter cylinder in the center of the mount, where it can be subtracted to create the hole in the mount upright. Using DUCS at the center point of the upright mount, you can draw this cylinder with a height of 1.5 so that it can also be used to form the bushing.

- Copy the cylinder out to the right of the mount directly along the centerline of the mount.

- Draw a second cylinder to form the top of the bushing.

- Draw a 0.375 cylinder through the center of the bushing.

- Subtract the 0.375 cylinder from the bushing to create the hole in the center.

- Subtract the boxes and cylinders to form the slots in the base and the bushing-sized cylinder to form the hole in the mount.

Mount

**Drawing 12-3**
Bushing Mount

Bushing

# Drawing 12-4: *Picnic Table* [ADVANCED]

This drawing is quite different from the previous three. It can be a challenge getting the legs correctly angled and in place. Still, you will find that everything here can be done with techniques learned in this chapter.

## Drawing Suggestions

- We recommend that you start with the XY plane at the bottom of the table legs and move everything up into the Z direction. First, draw nine 2″ × 6″ boards, 8′ long. You can draw one board and array the rest 1″ apart.

- The five middle boards that become the tabletop can be copied up 2′-4″ in the Z direction. The four outer boards that become the bench seats move up 1′-4″.

- Draw a 2″ × 4″ brace even with the front edge of the table and the same width as the tabletop. Also draw the 2″ × 6″ board even with the front of the bench seats and stretching from the outer edge of one seat to the outer edge of the other. Copy these two braces to the other end of the table and then move each copy in 1′.

- Draw the center brace across the middle of the five tabletop boards.

- Draw a single 2″ × 6″ board extending down perpendicular to the tabletop. Draw it at the front edge of the table. This will later be moved to the middle of the table and become one of four legs. It will be trimmed, so draw it long: 3′ or more will do.

- Rotate the leg 30° and use temporary 2″ × 6″ blocks as shown in the reference figure to trim the legs. These will be drawn overlapping the top and bottom of the leg and then subtracted to create the correctly angled leg.

- **MIRROR, COPY,** and **MOVE** this leg to create the four table legs.

**Drawing 12-4**
Picnic Table

# chapterthirteen

## More Modeling Techniques and Commands

# CHAPTER OBJECTIVES

- Draw polysolids
- Draw cones
- Draw pyramids
- Draw torus
- Slice and section solids

- Perform mesh modeling
- Adjust viewpoints with **3DORBIT**
- Create 3D solids from 2D outlines
- Walk through a 3D landscape
- Create an animated walk-through

## Introduction

In addition to the primary methods involved in 3D solid modeling, AutoCAD has numerous other commands and techniques that facilitate the creation of particular 3D shapes. These include commands that produce regular 3D solid primitives, such as cones and spheres, commands that allow you to create 3D objects by revolving or extruding 2D outlines of 3D objects, and commands that create mesh models that can be shaped in ways that solids cannot. The addition of these techniques will make it possible for you to create all kinds of 3D models you cannot create with solid primitives. As we explore these new possibilities, we will also use the **3D Modeling** workspace.

## Drawing Polysolids

Most of this chapter is devoted to introducing commands for drawing shapes other than boxes, wedges, and cylinders. Some are created as simple solid primitives; others are derived from previously drawn meshes, lines, and

| POLYSOLID | |
|---|---|
| Command | Polysolid |
| Alias | - |
| Panel | Modeling |
| Tool | |

**polysolid:** A 3D entity similar to a 2D polyline, but with the dimension of height added along with width and length.

curves. In this first section we draw a ***polysolid.*** Polysolids are drawn just like 2D polylines, but they have a height as well as a width. Like polylines, they can have both straight line and arc segments. Ours will include both.

✔ Create a new drawing using the acad3d template.

✔ Open the **Workspace** drop-down list from the **Quick Access** toolbar, and select **3D Modeling** workspace from the list.

## Drawing in Multiple Tiled Viewports

A major feature needed to draw effectively in 3D is the ability to view an object from several different points of view simultaneously as you work on it. Here we introduce a three-viewport configuration so that you can see what is happening from different viewpoints simultaneously. If you do not continually examine 3D objects from different points of view, it is easy to create entities that appear correct in the current view but are clearly incorrect from other points of view. As you work, remember that these viewports are simple model space ***tiled viewports.*** Tiled viewports cover the complete drawing area, do not overlap, and cannot be plotted simultaneously. Plotting multiple viewports is accomplished in paper space layouts with floating viewports.

**tiled viewports:** Viewports that cover the drawing area and do not overlap. Tiled viewports may show objects from different points of view, but are not plotted.

✔ Pick the **View** tab > **Model Viewports** panel > **Named Viewports** tool from the ribbon, as shown in Figure 13-1.

*Notice that this selection is not available on the **3D Basics** workspace ribbon. This opens the **Viewports** dialog box shown in Figure 13-2.*

**Figure 13-1**
**Named Viewports**

**Figure 13-2**
**Viewports** dialog box

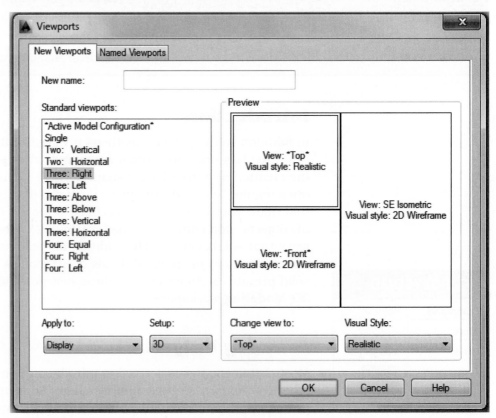

✔ If necessary pick the **New Viewports** tab.

✔ Highlight **Three: Right.**

✔ Open the **Setup** list and select **3D.**

✔ Click **OK** to exit the dialog box.

You now see three viewports, as shown in Figure 13-3. The view on the right is a southeast isometric view. The top left viewport is a plan view, and the bottom viewport shows a front view. These viewpoints are labeled in the upper left corner of each viewport. The front view has a different UCS than the views in the other two viewports. The coordinate system has been rotated so that the Z-axis still points out of the screen. If the UCS in this viewport were the same as the others, the Y-axis would be pointing out of the screen, and the Z-axis would be vertical in the plane of the screen. Since you would be looking in along the XY plane, you would have no ability to use the cursor in this viewport. Still, the change in color in this viewport shows the horizon in the world coordinate system even though the axes are rotated 90°.

**Figure 13-3**
Three viewports

✔ Click in the right viewport to make it active.

✔ Turn on the grid in the right viewport.

✔ Turn on **Snap Mode** and **Ortho Mode.**

*We are now ready to begin drawing in this viewport configuration. Once you have defined viewports, any drawing or editing in the active viewport appears in all the viewports. As you draw, watch what happens in all viewports. You may need to zoom out or pan to get full views in each viewport.*

✔ Pick the **Home** tab > **Modeling** panel > **Polysolid** tool from the ribbon, as shown in Figure 13-4.

*AutoCAD prompts:*

POLYSOLID specify start point or [Object Height Width Justify] <Object>:

*To ensure that your polysolid looks like ours, we will specify a height.*

**Figure 13-4**
**Polysolid** tool

✔ Right-click and select **Height** from the shortcut menu.

✔ Type **4 <Enter>** for the height.
   *AutoCAD returns the original prompt.*

✔ Pick point (2.5,2.5,0) for a start point.
   *AutoCAD shows you a polysolid to drag. It will appear like a wall in the 3D viewport and can be stretched out, like drawing a line segment. With **Ortho** on it will stretch only orthogonally. AutoCAD prompts for the next point.*

✔ Pick the point (10,2.5,0) for the next point.
   *Notice that this makes this segment 7.5 units long. From here, you could continue to draw straight segments, but we switch to an arc.*

✔ Right-click and select **Arc** from the shortcut menu.
   *AutoCAD shows an arc segment and prompts for an endpoint. With **Ortho** on you can stretch in only two directions.*

✔ Pick the point (10,8,0) for the arc endpoint.
   *Now, we switch back to a line segment.*

✔ Right-click and select **Line** from the shortcut menu.
   *AutoCAD shows a straight segment beginning at the endpoint of the arc and prompts for a next point.*

✔ Pick the point (2.5,8,0) for the next point. Again this is a length of 7.5 units.
   *Finally, we will switch to arc again and then use the **Close** option to complete the polysolid.*

✔ Right-click and select **Arc** from the shortcut menu.

✔ Type **c <Enter>** to close.
   *Your screen should resemble Figure 13-5.*

**Figure 13-5**
Polysolid

| CONE | |
|---|---|
| Command | Cone |
| Alias | - |
| Panel | Modeling |
| Tool |  |

**frustum cone:** A cone that does not rise to a point. It has a bottom radius and a top radius and is therefore flat-topped.

# Drawing Cones

## Solid Cone Primitives

Cones are easily drawn by specifying a base and a height. The **CONE** command can also be used to draw flat-topped cones, called *frustum cones,* as we do in a moment.

✔ Erase the polysolid from the "Drawing Polysolids" section.

✔ Pick the **Cone** tool from the **Solid Primitives** drop-down list on the **Modeling** panel, as shown in Figure 13-6.

**Figure 13-6**
**Cone** tool

*Notice that this is the same drop-down list as in the **3D Basics** workspace. AutoCAD prompts:*

> Specify center point of base or [3P 2P Ttr Elliptical]:

*Notice the other options, including the option to create cones with elliptical bases.*

*You can specify the base in either the top viewport or the right viewport. Using the top viewport will give you a better view of the base and its coordinates.*

✔ Click in the top left viewport to make it active.

✔ Turn on **Snap Mode** in this viewport.

✔ Pick point (5,5,0) for the center of the cone base.
*AutoCAD prompts:*

> Specify base radius or [Diameter] <0.0000>:

✔ In the top left viewport show a radius of 2.
*AutoCAD draws a cone in each viewport and prompts for a height:*

> Specify height or [2P Axis endpoint] <0.0000>:

✔ Move the cursor and observe the cones in each viewport.
*If you look carefully, you will notice that the cone in the top viewport appears to tilt slightly to the left. This viewport is drawn in*

*perspective projection. The tilt effect is a result of the perspective projection. The other viewports show that there is no actual tilt. The perspective projection can cause some problems in plan views such as the upper left viewport. We will fix this later in the "Drawing Torus" section.*

✔ Pick a point to indicate a height of 4.
   *The cone is complete, and your screen will resemble Figure 13-7.*

**Figure 13-7**
Cone

## Frustum Cones

Next, we create a cone with a negative z height and a different top radius.

✔ Pick the **Cone** tool from the **Modeling** panel.

✔ In the top left viewport, pick the point (10,5,0) for the base center.

✔ As before, show a radius of 2.
   *Move the cursor, and observe the cones in each viewport. We want to create a cone that drops down below the XY plane. Notice that we cannot do this in the active top view.*

✔ Click in the right viewport to make it active.
   *Drag the cone downward, and notice the effects in the right and bottom left viewports. There will be no change in the top viewport because the negative direction is away from you on the other side of the XY plane of the screen.*
   *We also want this cone to have a flat top, so we need to specify this before specifying the height.*

✔ Right-click and select **Top Radius** from the shortcut menu.
   *AutoCAD prompts:*

      Specify top radius <0.0000>:

   *Move the cursor again to see the range of possibilities. You can create anything, from a very large, wide, flat cone to a long, narrow one. The top radius can be larger or smaller than the base radius. Also, the top can be below the base.*

✔ Type **5 <Enter>** for a top radius.
   *AutoCAD prompts again for a height.*

✔ Make sure the right viewport is showing the cone in the negative direction, and type **8 <Enter>** for a height.

*Your screen should resemble Figure 13-8.*

**Figure 13-8**
Cone with negative *z* height

## Drawing Pyramids

| PYRAMID | |
|---|---|
| **Command** | Pyramid |
| **Alias** | Pyr |
| **Panel** | Modeling |
| **Tool** | |

Drawing pyramids is much like drawing cones. Instead of a circular base, pyramids will have polygons at the base and possibly at the top. The process for drawing the base polygon is similar to using the **POLYGON** command.

✔ Pick the **Pyramid** tool from the **Solid Primitives** drop-down list on the **Modeling** panel.

*AutoCAD prompts:*

Specify center point of base or [Edge Sides]:

*The default is a four-sided base. We will opt for six sides.*

✔ Right-click and select **Sides** from the shortcut menu, or select **Sides** from the command line.

*AutoCAD prompts for the number of sides.*

✔ Type **6 <Enter>**.

*AutoCAD takes this information and repeats the initial prompt. If you pick a center point, it will then prompt for the inscribed or circumscribed polygon. Recall that for a circumscribed polygon the radius will be drawn out to a vertex; for an inscribed polygon it will be drawn to the midpoint of a side. We proceed with the **Inscribed** option.*

✔ Pick (15,5,0) for the center point.

✔ Right-click and select **Inscribed** from the shortcut menu.

*AutoCAD prompts for the first point of an edge.*

✔ Pick the point (17,5,0) to show a radius of 2.

*AutoCAD draws the base and prompts for height:*

✔ Make sure your screen shows the pyramid in the positive direction, and type **4 <Enter>**.

*Your screen should resemble Figure 13-9.*

**Figure 13-9**
Pyramid

## Drawing Torus

| TORUS | |
|---|---|
| Command | Torus |
| Alias | Tor |
| Panel | Modeling |
| Tool | |

*Torus* is another solid primitive shape that is easily drawn. It is like drawing a donut in 2D and requires an outer radius as well as a tube radius. Try this:

✔ Pick the **Torus** tool from the bottom of the **Solid Primitives** dropdown list on the **Modeling** panel.

> *AutoCAD prompts:*
>
> Specify center point or [3P 2P Ttr]:
>
> *The **Three-point, Two-point,** and **Tangent Tangent Radius** options work just as they do in the **CIRCLE** command. We will place a torus behind and above the frustum cone.*

✔ Type **10,10,4 <Enter>** for a center point.

> *Notice the z coordinate of 4, which places the torus above the XY plane.*
>
> *AutoCAD prompts for a radius or diameter.*

✔ Type **2 <Enter>.**

> *Now, AutoCAD prompts for a second radius, the radius of the torus tube.*

✔ Type **.5 <Enter>.**

## Switching to Parallel Projection

Notice how the torus appears off center in the upper and lower left viewports. As mentioned previously, this is caused by the perspective projection. Having a perspective projection in a plan view is counterproductive. Here we switch to parallel projection in both of these viewports.

✔ Make sure that the upper left viewport is active.

✔ Right-click the **ViewCube** in the upper left viewport.

✔ Select **Parallel.**

Your upper left viewport should resemble the one in Figure 13-10. This figure also shows the lower left viewport in parallel projection. The same procedure will accomplish this.

**Figure 13-10**
Upper left viewport in parallel projection

✔ Make sure that the lower left viewport is active.

✔ Right-click the **ViewCube** in the lower left viewport.

✔ Select **Parallel.**
*As shown, the lower left viewport is now in parallel perspective, and the horizon is no longer represented.*

## Slicing and Sectioning Solids

In addition to Boolean operations, there are other methods that create solid shapes by modifying previously drawn objects. In this section we explore slicing and sectioning.

## Slice

| SLICE | |
|---|---|
| **Command** | Slice |
| **Alias** | SI |
| **Panel** | Solid Editing |
| **Tool** |  |

The **SLICE** command allows easy creation of objects by cutting away portions of drawn solids on one side of a slicing plane. In this exercise we slice off the tops of a pyramid and a cone. For this purpose we will work in the front view in the lower left viewport.

✔ You should have the objects and viewports on your screen as shown in Figure 13-10 to begin this exercise.

✔ Click in the lower left viewport to make it active.

✔ Check to see that **Snap Mode** and **Ortho Mode** are on in this viewport.

✔ Pick the **Slice** tool from the **Solid Editing** panel, as shown in Figure 13-11.
*AutoCAD prompts for objects to slice.*

✔ Select the cone on the left and the pyramid on the right of the viewport.

**Figure 13-11**
**Slice** tool

✔ Right-click to end object selection.

*AutoCAD prompts:*

> Specify start point of slicing plane or [planar
> Object/Surface/Zaxis/View/XY/YZ/ZX/3points] <3points>:

*This prompt allows you to define a plane by pointing, by selecting a
planar object or surface of an object, or by using one of the planes
of the current coordinate system. We can specify a plane with two
points in the front view.*

✔ Pick point (2.5,2,0) to the left of the cone.

✔ Pick point (17.5,2,0) to the right of the pyramid.

*AutoCAD now has the plane defined but needs to know which side
of the plane to cut.*

✔ Pick a point below the specified plane.

*The tops of the cone and pyramid will be sliced off, as shown in
Figure 13-12.*

**Figure 13-12**
Tops of pyramid and cone
sliced off

## Section

Sectioning is accomplished by creating a section plane and then picking
options from a shortcut menu. Here we create a section plane through
three of the objects on your screen and then create 3D section images.

✔ Click once in the top left viewport to make it active.

✔ If necessary, zoom out in this viewport so that all objects are completely visible within the viewport.

✔ Turn off **Ortho Mode** and **Object Snap** in this viewport.

✔ Pick the **Section Plane** tool from the **Section** panel, as shown in
Figure 13-13.

**Figure 13-13**
**Section Plane** tool

*AutoCAD prompts:*

Select face or any point to locate section line or [Draw section/ Orthographic]:

*We begin by using point selection.*

✔ Pick point (2.5,2.5,0).
*AutoCAD shows a plane and prompts for a through point.*

✔ Pick point (12.5,12.5,0).
*The section plane is drawn. Your screen should resemble Figure 13-14. At this point there is no image of the sectioning that this plane will create. To create section images, we select from a shortcut menu.*

**Figure 13-14**
Section plane

✔ Select the section plane in any of the viewports.
*A set of 3D grips and a gizmo will be added. The line used to create the plane will be highlighted.*

✔ With the plane selected, right-click to open the shortcut menu shown in Figure 13-15.
*Note the many options, including **Rotate, Copy Selection, Activate live sectioning** (you can view section images as you move the section plane), and the option to create a jogged section. We use the option to generate a 3D section.*

✔ Select the **Generate 2D/3D section** option, as shown.
*This opens the small dialog box shown in Figure 13-16.*

✔ Pick the **3D Section** button.

**Figure 13-15**
**Section Plane** shortcut menu

**Figure 13-16**
**Generate Section/Elevation** dialog box

✔ Pick the **Create** button.
> *Three section images are created and can be dragged around in your viewports. Sections are like blocks and require a base point, scale factors, and a rotation.*

✔ Click once in the right viewport to make it active.

✔ Pick an insertion point behind the original objects, as shown by the placement of objects in Figure 13-17.
> *AutoCAD prompts for an x scale factor.*

**Figure 13-17**
Three section images created

✔ Press **<Enter>** to specify the default scale factor of 1.
> *AutoCAD prompts for a y scale factor.*

✔ Press **<Enter>** again to specify a y scale factor of 1.
> *AutoCAD prompts for a rotation.*

✔ Press **<Enter>** to retain the default 0 rotation.
> *Your right viewport will resemble Figure 13-17. The section images may not be visible in the other two viewports. Notice that the three section objects are treated as a single object even though they are disconnected. The **EXPLODE** command can be used to separate them. Once exploded, each part can be moved and edited like any other solid object on your screen.*

## Mesh Modeling

**mesh modeling:** A 3D modeling system in which 3D mesh objects are created with faces that can be split, creased, refined, moved, and smoothed to create realistic free-form models.

***Mesh modeling*** is a system that allows you to create free-form mesh solids with adjustable levels of smoothness to better represent real objects. This exercise takes you through a complete mesh modeling project, introducing many of the concepts, features, and procedures available in this system of 3D drawing.

✔ To begin, erase all objects from your screen, or begin a new drawing using the acad3D template.

✔ **Zoom All.**

✔ For this section, also return to a single viewport by making the right viewport active, and then selecting **View** tab > **Viewports** panel extension > **Viewport Configuration** drop-down list > **Single** from the ribbon, as shown in Figure 13-18.

✔ Pick **View** tab > **Views** panel > **View Manager** > **SE Isometric** > **Set Current** > **OK.**

*This will take you to a higher angle necessary for some of the steps that follow.*

✔ Pick the **Mesh** tab from the ribbon.

*We begin by drawing a mesh cylinder. Mesh primitives are created just like solid primitives, but they can be edited very differently. Knowing what works with meshes and what works with solids is an important aspect of this type of drawing, as you will see.*

✔ Turn on **Snap Mode, Grid Display,** and **Ortho Mode.**

✔ Pick the **Mesh Cylinder** tool from the **Mesh Primitives** drop-down list, as shown in Figure 13-19.

**Figure 13-18**
**Viewport Configuration - Single**

**Figure 13-19**
**Mesh Cylinder** tool

✔ Pick (5,5,0) for the center point of the base.

✔ Stretch the cylinder out to show a radius of 2.5.

✔ Make sure that the cylinder is stretched in the positive Z direction and type **5 <Enter>.**

You have a complete mesh cylinder, as shown in Figure 13-20. Notice that the cylinder has distinct faces on all sides and that the presentation is

**Figure 13-20**
Mesh cylinder

faceted, instead of smooth and rounded, as a solid cylinder would be. The faces give us opportunities to shape and mold the object. Smoothness will be added later. In mesh modeling, we begin with faceted images that serve as an outline for the smooth object we wish to create. It will also be useful to use a visual style with edges visible.

✔ Pick **View** tab > **Visual Styles** drop-down list (not the **Visual Styles** panel extension) > **Shaded with Edges.**

In this exercise we manipulate this cylinder to form the semblance of a stylized coffee mug. The first step is to pull an edge out away from the center to form the outline of a handle.

## Subobject Filters

Looking at the mesh cylinder, you see that it is divided into faces. The faces meet at common edges, and at each corner of a face there is a vertex. These three elements, faces, vertices, and edges, are common to all meshes and are called *subobjects.* The importance of subobjects is that they can be selected individually or in groups for editing. When a subobject is moved, for example, its connections to other subobjects in the mesh are maintained, and the image is adjusted to accommodate the move.

To facilitate the selection of subobjects, the **Mesh** tab has a **Filters** drop-down list on the **Selection** panel. This list has tools for selecting only faces, only edges, or only vertices.

✔ Pick **Home** tab > **Selection** panel > **Filters** drop-down list > **Edge,** as shown in Figure 13-21.

**subobject:** In AutoCAD mesh modeling, a face, edge, or vertex that can be independently selected for editing.

**Figure 13-21**
**Edge** tool

To begin molding this cylinder into the shape of a mug, we select a single edge and move it outward.

✔ Move your cursor over the cylinder.

As you do this, each edge you cross will be highlighted. Some of the edges will not be in the front of the cylinder as it is now positioned, so look carefully to see that the edge you want is selected.

For this exercise, it is important that you select the edge shown. This edge lies in the plane that is parallel to the YZ plane, and this ensures that we can use **Ortho** mode to get a clean and symmetrical result.

✔ With the middle front left edge selected, as shown, press the pick button.

✔ If necessary, pick the **Move Gizmo** tool from the **Selection** panel.
> *Your screen should resemble Figure 13-22.*
>> *Gizmos can be used to move, rotate, or scale subobjects as well as complete objects. In this case we will move the edge 1.5 in its plane parallel to the Y-axis.*

✔ Rest your cursor on the Y-axis of the gizmo so that the green construction line is showing.

✔ With the Y-axis construction line showing, press and hold the pick button.

✔ Without releasing the pick button, stretch the edge out to the left, as shown in Figure 13-23.

**Figure 13-22**
Gizmo aligns with selected edge

**Figure 13-23**
Stretch edge out to left

✔ Still without releasing the pick button, type **1.5 <Enter>.**

✔ Press **<Esc>** to remove the gizmo.
> *Your screen should resemble Figure 13-24.*
>> *Next, we select all the middle two rings of faces on the top of the cylinder and move them down 4.75 to create the inside of the mug.*

✔ Pick the **Face** tool from the **Filters** drop-down list on the **Selection** panel.
> *Now as you move the cursor over the cylinder, faces will be highlighted instead of edges.*

✔ Select each of the 16 inner faces on the top of the cylinder, as shown in Figure 13-25.
> *As each face is selected with the pick button, a red dot appears, as shown.*

**Figure 13-24**
Stretched edge

**Figure 13-25**
Sixteen faces selected

✔ With the 16 faces selected, move your cursor so that the vertical blue line on the **Move** gizmo appears and the blue arrow turns gold.

✔ Press and hold the pick button.

✔ Without releasing the pick button, stretch the faces downward.

✔ Make sure that **Ortho Mode** is on; if it is not, press **<F8>.**

✔ With **Ortho** on and the faces stretched downward, type **4.75 <Enter>.**

*Notice how the outer faces stretch along their edges with the inner faces to maintain the connections.*

*Your screen should resemble Figure 13-26.*

**Figure 13-26**
Inside faces stretched down

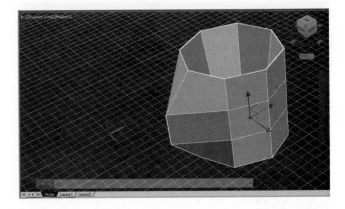

*To complete this object we smooth the mesh, convert it to a solid, and then subtract a cylinder to form a hole in the handle. The order in which we do things is important because of the limitations of both solids and meshes. Only mesh primitives can be smoothed, and only solids can be combined using Boolean operations. In a task like this one, we do all our subobject manipulation on the mesh primitive first; then we smooth the mesh. Finally, we convert the mesh to a solid so that we can do a subtraction. Although it is possible to convert either way, a solid converted to a mesh will not have the same clearly organized structure of meshes found in a mesh primitive.*

*Having completed the structure of our mesh, we can now add smoothness.*

## Smoothing Meshes

Meshes can be presented with varying levels of smoothness. At each level, the overall outline is maintained, but the number of faces increases until all the faces blend into a smooth surface. Each added level multiplies the number of mesh faces by four. Adding smoothness is simple.

✔ Pick the **Smooth More** tool from the **Mesh** panel, as shown in Figure 13-27.

**Figure 13-27**
**Smooth More** tool

*Your screen resembles Figure 13-28. Faces have been multiplied and diminished in size. Edges have been softened, and the object has a more rounded look. The dark lines show the original faces, but each original face is divided into four faces.*

✔ If necessary, select the complete object.

✔ Right-click to end object selection.

✔ Pick the **Smooth More** tool again.

✔ If necessary, select the complete object.

✔ Right-click to end object selection.

*Your screen resembles Figure 13-29. The mesh is smoothed further. The number of faces has increased dramatically. Each original face is now divided into 16 faces. The appearance is much smoother, but the new divisions are still clearly visible on the faceted surfaces. We can smooth the mesh even more.*

**Figure 13-28**
Faces divided and smoothed

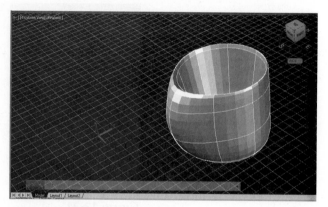

**Figure 13-29**
Mesh smoothed further

✔ Pick the **Smooth More** tool.

✔ If necessary, select the complete object again.

✔ Right-click to end object selection.

*Your screen resembles Figure 13-30. It is still smoother, with still more faces. If you look closely you can see 8 × 8 patterns on each original face, 64 faces each. But these faces are still distinct and visible. We can go one more level.*

✔ Pick the **Smooth More** tool.

**Figure 13-30**
Faces still distinct and visible

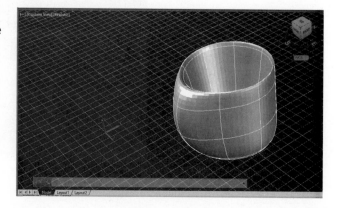

✔ If necessary, select the complete object.

✔ Right-click to end object selection.

Your screen resembles Figure 13-31. You can no longer see or count the divided faces. The edge lines still show the original faces, but we have reached the fourth and final level of smoothness. If we attempt to go further, we get a message that says: "One or more meshes in the current selection cannot be smoothed again."

Next, we draw a solid cylinder and subtract it from the mesh to create a hole in the handle. Although we could do this in the current view, procedures will be much clearer and more reliable if we temporarily change to a plan view. We use the ViewCube and move in two steps. First we move our viewpoint over to the southwest isometric. This view is also called the "home" view because it puts us directly over the origin of the world coordinate system.

✔ Move your cursor over the **ViewCube** so that the small house icon appears above the cube, as shown in Figure 13-32.

**Figure 13-31**
Final level of smoothness

**Figure 13-32**
House icon appears above **ViewCube**

✔ Pick the house icon.

*This moves your viewpoint so that your screen resembles Figure 13-33. Notice the red X-axis and the green Y-axis that converge off the screen in the direction from which you are looking, putting you roughly at the origin.*

*The second step is to move to a top, or plan, viewpoint.*

✔ Move your cursor over the Top face of the **ViewCube,** and press the pick button, as shown in Figure 13-34.

**Figure 13-33**
Viewpoint moved

**Figure 13-34**
Top face of **ViewCube**

*Your screen resembles Figure 13-35. This is a standard plan view in the WCS, with the X- and Y-axes aligned with the sides of the display. We draw a 1.0-diameter solid cylinder at (0,2.5), move it into the handle, rotate it, and subtract it to complete our drawing. So far in this exercise we have been working with a mesh object. From here on we will work with solids.*

✔ Pick the **Home** tab on the ribbon.
   *Remember that the **Home** tab has solid modeling tools, whereas the **Mesh** tab has mesh modeling tools.*

✔ Pick the **Cylinder** tool from the **Solid Primitives** drop-down list on the **Modeling** panel.

✔ Pick (0,2.5,0) for the center of the base, as shown in Figure 13-36.

**Figure 13-35**
Standard plan view

**Figure 13-36**
Drawing a cylinder

✔ Pick a radius point 0.50 from the center of the cylinder.

✔ Type **5 <Enter>** for the cylinder height.
   *Next, we move the cylinder 5 units to the right to center it within the stretched portion of the mesh.*

✔ Pick the **Move** gizmo from the **Selection** panel.

✔ Pick **No Filter** from the **Filter** drop-down list.

✔ Select the solid cylinder.

✔ Move the cursor to highlight the red *X*-axis on the **Move** gizmo.

✔ Press and hold the pick button.

✔ Drag the cylinder to the right.

✔ Without releasing the pick button, type **5 <Enter>**.

✔ Press **<Esc>** to remove the gizmo.
   *Your screen resembles Figure 13-37. For the next step, we return to the southeast isometric view.*

✔ Pick the southeast corner of the **ViewCube,** as shown in Figure 13-38.
   *Your screen resembles Figure 13-39. To rotate the cylinder 90°, we switch to the **Rotate** gizmo.*

✔ Open the **Gizmo** drop-down list on the **Selection** panel and pick the **Rotate Gizmo** tool.

**Figure 13-37**
Cylinder moved

**Figure 13-38**
Pick southeast corner of
**ViewCube**

✔ Select the solid cylinder.

✔ Move the cursor to highlight rotation in the green XZ plane, around
the *Y*-axis, as shown in Figure 13-40.

**Figure 13-39**
Southeast viewpoint

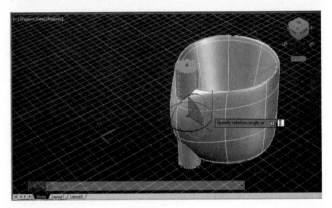

**Figure 13-40**
**Rotate** gizmo

✔ Type **90 <Enter>.**

✔ Press **<Esc>** to remove the gizmo.
*Your screen resembles Figure 13-41.*

**Figure 13-41**
Cylinder rotated

## Converting Meshes to Solids

Only meshes can be smoothed; only solids can be combined. Before we can
subtract the solid cylinder from the smoothed mesh, we have to convert

the mesh to a solid. This process is simplified by initiating the subtraction first. Before AutoCAD performs the subtraction, it will give us the option of converting the mesh to a solid. Conversion is simple, but you should not convert until you are sure that you are satisfied with the shaping of the mesh. If you attempt to convert back to a mesh, the mesh created will not be well organized and will be difficult to shape.

✔ Pick the **Home** tab **> Solid Editing** panel **> Subtract** tool from the ribbon.

✔ Select the mesh object.

✔ Right-click to end object selection.

> *AutoCAD presents the message shown in Figure 13-42. You have three choices of what to do with the mesh objects in your selection set.*

✔ Select the middle option, **Convert selected objects to smooth 3D solids or surfaces.**

> *AutoCAD prompts for objects to subtract.*

✔ Select the solid cylinder.

✔ Right-click to end object selection.

> *Your screen should resemble Figure 13-43. This is a simple but effective model. To achieve more realism and more definition, consider that faces can be split and creases added before editing. Creased edges retain their positions when adjacent faces are moved. By adding creases and additional faces to the edges on both sides of the handle, for example, you could create a narrower, more finely shaped handle.*

**Figure 13-42**
Converting to 3D solid

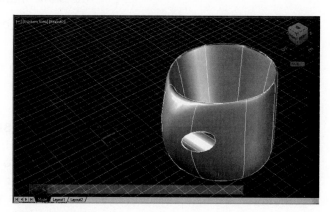

**Figure 13-43**
Cylinder subtracted

| 3DORBIT | |
|---|---|
| **Command** | 3Dorbit |
| **Alias** | 3do |
| **Panel** | Navigate |
| **Tool** | |

## Adjusting Viewpoints with 3DORBIT

## Orbit

The **3DORBIT** command is a dramatic method for adjusting 3D viewpoints and images. **3DORBIT** has many options and works in three distinct modes. We begin with **Orbit** and then explore **Free Orbit** and **Continuous Orbit.** The standard views such as the top, front, and isometric views found on the ViewCube are generally all you need for the creation and editing of objects, and sticking with these views keeps you well grounded and clear about your position in relation to objects on the screen. However, when you move from drawing and editing into presentation, you find **3DORBIT** vastly more satisfying and freeing than the static viewpoint options.

The model created in the last section will work well for a demonstration of **3DORBIT.**

✔ Pick the **View** tab > **Navigate** panel > **Orbit** drop-down list > **Orbit** tool from the ribbon, as shown in Figure 13-44.
*Notice the orbit cursor that replaces the crosshairs.*

**Figure 13-44**
**Orbit** tool

✔ Press the pick button and slowly move the cursor in any direction.
*The model moves along with the cursor movement.*

✔ Move the cursor left and right, using mostly horizontal motion.
*Horizontal motion creates movement parallel to the XY plane of the world coordinate system.*

✔ Move the cursor up and down, using mostly vertical motion.
*Vertical motion creates movement parallel to the Z-axis of the world coordinate system. You can create any viewpoint on the model using these simple motions. Notice also that the ViewCube moves in the same manner as the model.*

✔ Move the cursor back to create a point of view similar to the one we started with.

✔ Press **<Enter>** to exit **3DORBIT.**

## Free Orbit

In **Free Orbit** mode, **3DORBIT** makes use of a tool called an *arcball,* as shown in Figure 13-45. The center of the arcball is the center of the current viewport. Therefore, to place your objects near the center of the arcball, you must place them near the center of the viewport; or, more precisely, you must place the center point of the objects at the center of the display.

**Figure 13-45**
Arcball

✔ If necessary, use **Pan,** or pan with the scroll wheel, to adjust the model so that it is roughly centered on the center of the viewport.

✔ Turn off the grid display.

> *Before entering **3DORBIT** you can select viewing objects. **3DORBIT** performance is improved by limiting the number of objects used in viewing. Whatever adjustments are made to the viewpoint on the selected objects are applied to the viewpoint on the entire drawing when the command is exited. In our case, we have just one object to view, so we can use the whole drawing.*

✔ Pick **Free Orbit** from the **Orbit** drop-down list.

> *Your screen is redrawn with the arcball surrounding your model, as shown in Figure 13-45.*

## The Arcball and Rotation Cursors

The arcball is a somewhat complex image, but it is very easy to use once you get the hang of it. It also gives you a more precise handle on what is happening than the **Orbit** mode does. We already know that the center of the arcball is the center of the viewport, or the center of the drawing area in this case, since we are working in a single viewport. AutoCAD uses a camera–target analogy to explain viewpoint adjustment. Your viewpoint on the drawing is called the *camera position.* The point at which the camera is aimed is called the *target.* In **3DORBIT,** the target point is fixed at the center of the arcball. As you change viewpoints you are moving your viewpoint around in relation to this fixed target point.

There are four modes of adjustment, which we take up one at a time. Each mode has its own cursor image, and the mode you are in depends on where you start in relation to the arcball. Try the following steps:

✔ Carefully move the cursor into the small circle at the left quadrant of the arcball, as shown in Figure 13-45.

> *When the cursor is placed within either the right or the left quadrant circle, the horizontal rotation cursor appears. This cursor consists of a horizontal elliptical arrow surrounding a small sphere, with a vertical axis running through the sphere. Using this cursor creates horizontal motion around the vertical axis of the arcball. This cursor and the others are shown in Figure 13-46.*

✔ With the cursor in the left quadrant circle and the horizontal cursor displayed, press the pick button and hold it down.

✔ Slowly drag the cursor from the left quadrant circle to the right quadrant circle, observing the model and the 3D UCS icon as you go.

> *As long as you keep the pick button depressed, the horizontal cursor is displayed.*

✔ With the cursor in the right quadrant circle, release the pick button.

> *You have created a 180° rotation. Your screen should resemble Figure 13-47.*

✔ With the cursor in the right quadrant circle and the horizontal cursor displayed, press the pick button again and then move the cursor slowly back to the left quadrant circle.

**Figure 13-46**
**3DORBIT** cursor chart

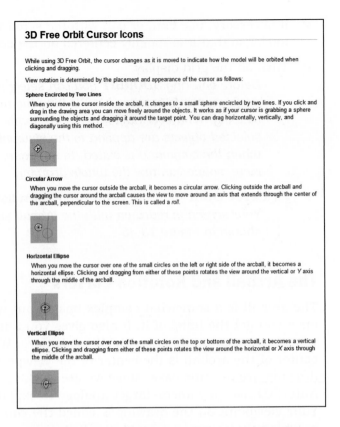

**3D Free Orbit Cursor Icons**

While using 3D Free Orbit, the cursor changes as it is moved to indicate how the model will be orbited when clicking and dragging.

View rotation is determined by the placement and appearance of the cursor as follows:

**Sphere Encircled by Two Lines**
When you move the cursor inside the arcball, it changes to a small sphere encircled by two lines. If you click and drag in the drawing area you can move freely around the objects. It works as if your cursor is grabbing a sphere surrounding the objects and dragging it around the target point. You can drag horizontally, vertically, and diagonally using this method.

**Circular Arrow**
When you move the cursor outside the arcball, it becomes a circular arrow. Clicking outside the arcball and dragging the cursor around the arcball causes the view to move around an axis that extends through the center of the arcball, perpendicular to the screen. This is called a *roll*.

**Horizontal Ellipse**
When you move the cursor over one of the small circles on the left or right side of the arcball, it becomes a horizontal ellipse. Clicking and dragging from either of these points rotates the view around the vertical or *Y* axis through the middle of the arcball.

**Vertical Ellipse**
When you move the cursor over one of the small circles on the top or bottom of the arcball, it becomes a vertical ellipse. Clicking and dragging from either of these points rotates the view around the horizontal or *X* axis through the middle of the arcball.

**Figure 13-47**
180-degree rotation

*You have moved the image roughly back to its original position. Now, try a vertical rotation.*

✔ Move the cursor into the small circle at the top of the arcball.
*The vertical rotation cursor appears. When this cursor is visible, rotation is around the horizontal axis, as shown in the chart in Figure 13-46.*

✔ With the vertical rotation cursor displayed, press the pick button and drag down toward the circle at the lower quadrant.

✔ This time, do not release the pick button but continue moving down to the bottom of the screen.
*The viewpoint continues to adjust, and the vertical cursor is displayed as long as you hold down the pick button. Notice that* **3DORBIT** *uses the entire screen, not just the drawing area. You*

*can drag all the way down through the command line, the status bar, and the Windows taskbar.*

✔ Spend some time experimenting with vertical and horizontal rotation.

*Note that you always have to start in a quadrant to achieve horizontal or vertical rotation. What happens when you move horizontally with the vertical cursor displayed or vice versa? How much rotation can you achieve in one pick-and-drag sequence vertically? What about horizontally? Are they the same amount? Why is there a difference?*

✔ When you have finished experimenting, try to rotate the image back to its original position, shown previously in Figure 13-45.

*If you are unable to get back to this position, don't worry. We show you how to do this easily in a moment. Now let's try the other two modes.*

✔ Move the cursor anywhere outside the arcball.

*With the cursor outside the arcball you can see the roll icon, the third icon in the chart in Figure 13-46. Rolling creates rotation around an imaginary axis pointing directly toward you out of the center of the arcball.*

✔ With the roll icon displayed, press the pick button and drag the cursor in a wide circle well outside the circumference of the arcball.

*Notice again that you can use the entire screen, outside of the arcball.*

✔ Try rolling both counterclockwise and clockwise.

✔ Release the pick button and then start again.

*Note that you must be in the drawing area with the roll icon displayed to initiate a roll and that you must stay outside the arcball.*

*Finally, try the free rotation cursor. This is the most powerful, and therefore the trickiest, form of rotation. It is also the same as the **Orbit** mode. The free cursor appears when you start inside the arcball or when you cross into the arcball while rolling. It allows rotation horizontally, vertically, and diagonally, depending on the movement of your pointing device.*

✔ Move the cursor inside the arcball and watch for the free rotation icon.

✔ With the free rotation icon displayed, press the pick button and drag the cursor within the arcball.

*Make small movements vertically, horizontally, and diagonally. What happens if you move outside the arcball?*

*The free rotation icon gives you a less restricted type of rotation. Making small adjustments seems to work best. Imagine that you are grabbing the model and turning it a little at a time. Release the pick button and grab again. You may need to do this several times to reach a desired position.*

✔ Try returning the image to approximate the southeast isometric view before proceeding.

## Other 3DORBIT Features

**3DORBIT** is more than an enhanced viewpoint command. While you work within the command you can adjust visual styles, projections, and even create a continuous-motion effect. **3DORBIT** options are accessed through the shortcut menu shown in Figure 13-48. We explore these from the bottom up, looking at the lower two panels and one option from the second panel.

✔ Right-click anywhere in the drawing area to open the shortcut menu.

**Figure 13-48**
**Orbit** shortcut menu

| | |
|---|---|
| | Exit |
| | Current Mode: Constrained Orbit |
| | Other Navigation Modes ▶ |
| ✓ | Enable Orbit Auto Target |
| | Animation Settings ... |
| | Zoom Window |
| | Zoom Extents |
| | Zoom Previous |
| ✓ | Parallel |
| | Perspective |
| | Reset View |
| | Preset Views ▶ |
| | Named Views |
| | Visual Styles ▶ |
| | Visual Aids ▶ |

## Preset and Reset Views

In the second from the bottom panel, there is a **Preset Views** option that provides convenient access to the standard 10 orthographic and isometric viewpoints, so that these views can be accessed without leaving the command. Above this is a **Reset View** option. This option quickly returns you to the view that was current before you entered **3DORBIT.** This is a great convenience, because you can get pretty far out of adjustment and have a difficult time finding your way back.

✔ Select **Reset View** from the shortcut menu.
   *Regardless of where you have been within the **3DORBIT** command, your viewpoint is immediately returned to the view shown previously in Figure 13-45. If you have not left **3DORBIT,** the view is reset to whatever view was current before you reentered the command. If you have attempted to return to this view manually using the cursors, you can see that there is still a slight adjustment to return your viewpoint to the precise view.*

## Visual Aids and Visual Styles

✔ Right-click to open the shortcut menu again.
   *On the bottom panel, you can see **Visual Styles** and **Visual Aids** selections. Highlighting **Visual Aids** opens a submenu with three options: **Compass, Grid,** and **UCS icon.** The **Grid** option is useful for turning the grid on and off without leaving the command. The **Compass** adds an adjustable gyroscope-style image to the arcball.*

*There are three rings of dashed ellipses showing the planes of the X-, Y-, and Z-axes of the current UCS. Try this if you like. We do not find it particularly helpful.*

*The third option on the submenu turns the 3D UCS icon on and off.*

*Highlighting* **Visual Styles** *opens a submenu with the ten 3D visual styles. We have been working in the* **Shaded with Edges** *style. This allows you to change styles without leaving the command. Switching to* **Realistic,** *for example, would remove the edges that are left from the original face borders. Try it.*

✔ Highlight **Visual Styles** and then select **Realistic** from the submenu.
*Your model is redrawn without edges.*

## Continuous Orbit

Continuous orbit may not be the most useful feature of AutoCAD, but it is probably the most dramatic and the most fun. With continuous orbit you can set objects in motion that continues when you release the pick button.

✔ Right-click to open the shortcut menu again.

✔ Highlight **Other Navigation Modes** in the second panel.
*This opens a submenu shown in Figure 13-49. We explore some of the* **Camera** *and* **Walk** *and* **Fly** *options in the "Walking Through a 3D Landscape" section.* **Continuous Orbit,** *like* **Free Orbit** *and* **Orbit** *(called* **Constrained Orbit** *on this menu), can also be initiated directly from the navigation bar. It actually executes a different command called* **3DCORBIT.**

✔ Select **Continuous Orbit** from the submenu.
*The arcball disappears, and the continuous orbit icon is displayed, consisting of a sphere surrounded by two ellipses, as shown in Figure 13-50. The concept is simple: Dragging the cursor creates a motion vector. The direction and speed of the vector are applied to the model to set it in rotated motion around the target point. Motion continues until you press the pick button again.*

**Figure 13-49**
**Navigation** submenu

**Figure 13-50**
Continuous orbit icon

**Chapter 13** | More Modeling Techniques and Commands    **611**

✔ With the continuous orbit cursor displayed, press and hold the pick button, then drag the cursor at a moderate speed in any direction.
*We cannot illustrate the effect, but if you have done this correctly, your model should now be in continuous rotation. Try it again.*

✔ Press the pick button at any time to stop rotation.

✔ Press and hold the pick button again and drag the cursor in a different direction, at a different speed.

✔ Press the pick button to stop rotation.

✔ Press the pick button, drag, and release again.
*Now, try changing directions without stopping.*

✔ While the model is spinning, press and hold the pick button and drag in another direction.
*Have a ball. Experiment. Play. Try to create gentle, controlled motions in different directions. Try to create fast spins in different directions. Try to create diagonal, horizontal, and vertical spins.*

---

**TIP**

The best way to achieve control over continuous orbit is to pick a point actually on the model and imagine that you are grabbing it and spinning it. It is much easier to communicate the desired speed and direction in this way. Note the similarity between the action of continuous orbit and the free rotation or constrained orbit icon. The grabbing and turning are the same, but continuous orbit keeps moving when you release the pick button, whereas free rotation stops. Also notice that however complex your dragging motion is, continuous orbit registers only one vector, the speed and direction of your last motion before releasing the pick button.

---

*One more trick before we move on:*

✔ Set your model into a moderate spin in any direction.

✔ With your model spinning, right-click to open the shortcut menu.
*The model keeps spinning. Many of the shortcut menu options can be accessed without disrupting continuous orbit.*

✔ Select **Reset View** from the shortcut menu.
*The model makes an immediate adjustment to the original view and continues to spin without interruption.*

✔ Open the shortcut menu again.

✔ Highlight **Visual Styles** and select **Conceptual.**
*The style is changed and the model keeps spinning—pretty impressive.*

✔ To stop continuous orbit, press the pick button once without dragging.

✔ Press **<Enter>, <Esc>,** or the spacebar to exit **3DCORBIT.**
*You return to the command prompt, but any changes you have made in point of view and visual style are retained.*

## Creating 3D Solids from 2D Outlines

**extruding:** A method of creating a three-dimensional object by projecting a two-dimensional object along a straight path in the third dimension.

In this chapter you have created several 3D solid primitives and one mesh model. In this section, we look at three commands that create 3D objects from 2D outlines. We explore *extruding*, revolving, and sweeping 2D shapes to create complex 3D objects.

| EXTRUDE | |
|---|---|
| Command | Extrude |
| Alias | Ext |
| Panel | Modeling |
| Tool | |

## Extrude

✔ To begin, erase all objects from your screen, or begin a new drawing using the acad3d template.

✔ **Zoom All.**

*We begin by drawing a square and extruding it.*

✔ Turn **Snap** mode on.

✔ Pick the **Home** tab > **Draw** panel > **Rectangle** tool from the ribbon.

✔ Pick the point (5.0,5.0,0) for the first corner.

✔ Pick the point (10.0,10.0,0) for the second corner.

✔ Pick the **Extrude** tool from the **Modeling** panel, as shown in Figure 13-51.

*AutoCAD prompts for objects to extrude.*

**Figure 13-51**
**Extrude** tool

✔ Select the square.

✔ Press **<Enter>** to end object selection.

*The **EXTRUDE** command will automatically convert the 2D square to a solid and give you an image to stretch in the positive or negative Z direction. The prompts also allow you to extrude in a direction other than along the Z-axis by drawing a directional line or using a preexisting line as a path.*

*We will use the **Direction** option to create a slanted solid.*

✔ Select **Direction** from the command line.

*AutoCAD prompts for the first point of a direction vector. The vector can be drawn anywhere.*

✔ Pick the point (10,10,0) for the start point.

*To place the endpoint above the XY plane, we use a point filter.*

✔ At the prompt for an endpoint, type **.xy <Enter>** for an .XY point filter.

✔ At the *of* prompt, pick the point (10,12.5,0).

✔ At the *need z* prompt, type **2 <Enter>.**

*Your screen will resemble Figure 13-52. Before moving on to revolving, we demonstrate the technique of pressing and pulling solid objects.*

**Figure 13-52**
Extruded rectangle

## Presspull

The **PRESSPULL** command allows you to extend a solid object in a direction perpendicular to any of its faces.

✔ Pick the **Presspull** tool from the **Modeling** panel, as shown in Figure 13-53.

> *AutoCAD prompts you to select a face. The prompt is:*

> Select object or bounded area:

✔ Pick the front face.

> *AutoCAD gives you an image to drag and a dynamic UCS with Z normal to the face.*

✔ Pull in the positive and negative directions, perpendicular to the selected face.

✔ With the object pulled in the positive direction, type **3 <Enter>.**

> *Your screen should resemble Figure 13-54.*

**Figure 13-53**
**Presspull** tool

**Figure 13-54**
Front face pulled

## Revolve

| REVOLVE | |
|---------|---|
| **Command** | Revolve |
| **Alias** | Rev |
| **Panel** | Modeling |
| **Tool** | |

The **REVOLVE** command creates a 3D solid by continuous repetition of a 2D shape along the path of a circle or arc around a specified axis. Here we draw a rectangle and revolve it 180° to create an arc-shaped model. Along the way we also demonstrate how a 2D object can be converted to a 3D planar surface.

> **NOTE**
> Coordinate systems can sometimes get out of order after a DUCS has been in use. To correct this, simply pick the **World** tool at the upper right corner of the **Coordinates** panel. This will return you to the world coordinate system.

✔ Pick the **Rectangle** tool from the **Draw** panel.

✔ Pick the point (15,5,0) for the first corner point.

✔ Pick the point (17.5,10,0) to create a 2.5 × 5.0 rectangle.

> *Next, we use the **Convert to Surface** tool to make this a rectangular surface rather than a wireframe outline. Note that this is for demonstration only. As in the **EXTRUDE** command, you can create a 3D solid directly from a 2D outline with the **REVOLVE** command.*

✔ Pick the **Home** tab > **Solid Editing** panel extension > **Convert to Surface** tool from the ribbon, as shown in Figure 13-55.

> *Notice that there is also a **Convert to Solid** tool, which will convert a model made of 3D surfaces to a solid model. AutoCAD prompts for object selection.*

✔ Select the rectangle.

✔ Right-click to end object selection.

> *The rectangle will become a 3D surface, and your screen will resemble Figure 13-56.*

**Figure 13-55**
**Convert to Surface** tool

**Figure 13-56**
Rectangle becomes a 3D surface

✔ Pick the **Home** tab > **Modeling** panel > **Extrude** drop-down list > **Revolve** tool from the ribbon, as shown in Figure 13-57.

> *AutoCAD prompts for objects to revolve.*

**Figure 13-57**
**Revolve** tool

✔ Select the rectangular surface.

✔ Press **<Enter>** to end object selection.

> *AutoCAD gives several options for defining an axis of rotation:*

> Specify axis start point or define axis by [Object/X/Y/Z] <Object>:

> *You can give start points and endpoints, select a line or polyline that has been previously drawn, or use one of the axes of the current UCS.*

✔ Pick the point (20,0,0) for a start point.

✔ Pick the point (20,12.5,0) for an endpoint.

> *Next, AutoCAD needs to know how much revolution you want. The default is a full 360° circle.*

> Specify angle of revolution or [STart angle/Reverse/EXpression] <360>:

Here we start at the horizon, 0°, and revolve through 180°, placing both ends of the arc on the XY plane.

✔ Select **STart angle** from the command line.
*AutoCAD prompts for an angle.*

✔ Press **<Enter>** to accept the default start angle, or type **0** if your angle has been changed.
*AutoCAD now prompts for an angle of revolution.*

✔ Type **180 <Enter>.**
*The revolved solid will be created and your screen will resemble Figure 13-58.*

**Figure 13-58**
Revolved solid

## Helix

| HELIX | |
|---|---|
| **Command** | Helix |
| **Alias** | (none) |
| **Panel** | Draw |
| **Tool** | |

We have two more techniques to demonstrate before moving on. First, we use the **HELIX** command to create a 3D spiral outline. Then, we use the **SWEEP** command to convert the helix to a solid coil.

✔ Pick the **Helix** tool from the **Draw** panel extension, as shown in Figure 13-59.
*Helix characteristics can be changed using the **Properties Manager.** Among the default specifications are two shown in the prompt area. Number of turns will be the number of times the spiral shape goes around within the height you specify. The twist will be either counterclockwise or clockwise.*

**Figure 13-59**
Helix tool

✔ Pick the point (12.5,–5.0,0) for the center point of the helix base.
*AutoCAD prompts for a base radius:*

Specify base radius or [Diameter] <1.0000>:

*The default will be retained from any previous use of the command in the current drawing session.*

✔ Pick a second point to show a radius of 2.5000.

*AutoCAD now prompts for a top radius, showing that you can taper the helix to a different top height, similar to the options with the **CONE** and **PYRAMID** commands. We specify a smaller top radius.*

✔ Type **1 <Enter>** or pick a point to show a radius of 1.0000.

*AutoCAD prompts for a height.*

✔ Make sure the helix is stretched in the positive direction, and type **4 <Enter>.**

*The helix is drawn, as shown in Figure 13-60.*

| SWEEP | |
|---|---|
| **Command** | Sweep |
| **Alias** | (none) |
| **Panel** | Modeling |
| **Tool** | |

## The SWEEP Command

Finally we sweep a circle through the helix path to create a solid coil.

✔ Pick the **Circle Center, Radius** tool from the **Draw** panel.

✔ Anywhere on your screen, create a circle of radius 0.5.

✔ Pick the **Sweep** tool from the **Extrude** drop-down list on the **Modeling** panel, as shown in Figure 13-61.

*AutoCAD prompts for objects to sweep.*

**Figure 13-60**
Helix

**Figure 13-61**
**Sweep** tool

✔ Select the circle.

✔ Press **<Enter>** to end object selection.

*AutoCAD prompts:*

Select sweep path or [Alignment/Base point/Scale/Twist]:

*The default is to select a path, such as the helix. By default the object being swept will be aligned perpendicular to the sweep path. The **Alignment** option can be used to alter this. **Base point** allows you to start the sweep at a point other than the beginning of the sweep path. **Scale** allows you to change the scale of the objects being swept. By default the object being swept will remain perpendicular to the path at every point. To vary this and create a more complex sweep, use the **Twist** option. Here we use the default sweep path.*

✔ Select the helix.

*Your screen should resemble Figure 13-62.*

Figure 13-62
Swept helix

That completes this section on modeling techniques. In the final two sections we demonstrate the use of **CAMERA** and **WALK** commands to move your point of view through the 3D landscape, and **ANIPATH** to create an animated walk-through.

## Walking Through a 3D Landscape

AutoCAD has features that allow you to move your point of view through the 3D space of a drawing. This is particularly useful in architectural drawings in which you can create a simulated walk-through of a model. In this section we demonstrate the use of the **WALK** command to navigate through the objects on your screen. The process involves creating a camera and a target and then using arrow keys to move the camera. Our goal will be to make it possible to navigate under the cylinder, as if we were walking under an arch.

### Camera and Target

The first step will involve creating camera and target locations.

✔ To begin, you should be in a view similar to that shown previously in Figure 13-62.

✔ If necessary, turn on the grid.

> *You may want to have the menu bar showing for this section because the commands we will be using are more easily located there. Remember to turn on the menu bar, select the down arrow at the right end of the **Quick Access** toolbar, and select **Show Menu Bar** from the bottom of the list.*

✔ Type **cam <Enter>** or pick **View > Create Camera** from the menu bar.
> *AutoCAD prompts for a camera location. We will start with a location on the axis of the cylinder.*

✔ Pick the point (20,–10), as shown by the camera icon in Figure 13-63.
> *AutoCAD now prompts for a target location. In our case we want to point the camera along the axis of the cylinder. The distance to the*

Figure 13-63
Camera location

**Figure 13-64**
**Dynamic Input**
menu

*target is not significant. AutoCAD shows the target with an image representing an expanding field of vision in the direction specified.*

✔ Pick the point (20,–5), as shown by the field of vision symbols in Figure 13-63.

*AutoCAD shows you a set of options on the **Dynamic Input** menu in Figure 13-64. We choose the **View** option, which will change our display to align with the camera's point of view on the target.*

✔ Select **View** from the command line or the **Dynamic Input** menu.

*With another small menu, AutoCAD asks us to verify that we wish to switch to the camera view.*

✔ Select **Yes** from the menu.

This completes the command and switches your view to the camera view shown in Figure 13-65. We are now ready to proceed with our walk.

**Figure 13-65**
Camera view

## The 3DWALK and 3DFLY Commands

The **3DWALK** and **3DFLY** commands use identical procedures, but **3DWALK** keeps you in the XY plane, whereas **3DFLY** allows you to move above or below the plane. Here we enter **3DWALK,** walk through the arch, turn left to view the other objects, then turn around and walk back between the objects.

✔ Type **3dw** or pick **View > Walk and Fly > Walk** from the menu bar.

*You see the **Position Locator** palette in Figure 13-66. This palette shows a plan view of the objects in the drawing with a red circle representing the camera position and a green triangle representing the target and field of vision. Before we begin to move through the view, it may be helpful to zoom out in the **Position Locator** to give us a little more room to work with.*

**Figure 13-66**
**Position Locator** palette

✔ If necessary, click once on the **Zoom out** tool at the top of the **Position Locator.**

*Your objects should appear smaller in the **Position Locator,** as shown in Figure 13-66. We use the forward arrow to move through the arch. Notice that AutoCAD also positions a green cross on the screen, indicating the target position.*

✔ Press the up arrow key on your keyboard once to move forward.

*You move a "step" closer to the arch. Notice also that the camera and target image move forward on the **Position Locator** palette.*

✔ Continue pressing the up arrow and observing the screen image as well as the **Position Locator.**

**Figure 13-67**
Camera location image is
beyond arch

✔ Walk through the arch until you reach the other side. Watch the
**Position Locator** to ensure that you move the camera location
completely through the arch.

> *At this point the camera location image on the **Position Locator**
> should be completely beyond the arch, as shown in Figure 13-67.*

✔ Press the left arrow once and observe the **Position Locator** palette.

> *The camera and target image will shift to the left on the palette, and
> your viewpoint will shift in the drawing, but you will see no change
> because there is nothing but the horizon in this direction.*

✔ Press the left arrow again.

> *Notice that the camera image continues to move to the left, but the
> target is still straight ahead.*

✔ Continue moving to the left until the camera and target image is
between the cylinder and the boxes to the left.

✔ Move the cursor over the green triangle representing the field of vision
in the **Position Locator.**

> *When the cursor is in this position, it will appear with a hand icon,
> as used in the **PAN** command. With the hand icon showing, you can
> move and expand the field of vision.*

✔ With the hand icon showing and resting on the field of vision triangle,
press and hold the pick button, and drag the triangle around 180°.

> *Your camera is now pointing toward the coil. Your screen should
> resemble Figure 13-68.*

**Figure 13-68**
Camera pointing toward coil

✔ Continue using the arrow keys and the mouse along with the pan
cursor to move through the objects on your screen.

> *There is one other trick you should try. In addition to changing your
> field of vision in the **Position Locator**, you can change it directly in
> the drawing by dragging your mouse. Whereas moving the field of
> vision triangle will only create movement within the XY plane, the
> mouse can be moved up, down, sideways, and diagonally to view
> whatever objects are accessible from your current camera location.
> Try it.*

✔ Press and hold the pick button, and drag the mouse right and left, up and down to view the objects in your drawing. As you do this, observe the changes in the field of vision triangle in the **Position Locator** palette.

✔ When you are done, press **<Enter>** to exit the command.
*The objects will remain in whatever view you have created. Of course, you can return to your previous view using the **U** command.*

## Creating an Animated Walk-Through

The ability to walk through a landscape is impressive, but for presentation purposes it may be more important to have the walk-through animated so that any potential client can see the view without having to interact with AutoCAD in the ways you have just learned. Here we use the **ANIPATH** command to create a simple animation of a walk-through that is slightly different from the one we did manually in the last section. We begin by switching to a plan view.

✔ Select the **View** tab and then pick the **Top** view from the **Views** panel.
*Regardless of what was in your view previously, you should now be in the plan view shown in Figure 13-69.*

Animations follow paths specified by lines, polylines, or 3D polylines. For our purposes we will draw the simple polyline path shown in Figure 13-70. First, we will draw it with right angles and then fillet one corner, as shown.

**Figure 13-69**
Plan view

**Figure 13-70**
Polyline animation path

✔ Pick the **Home** tab > **Draw** panel > **Polyline** tool from the ribbon.

✔ Pick the point (20,–5) for a start point.

✔ Pick the point (20,3.5) for the next point.

✔ Pick the point (12.5,3.5) for the next point.

✔ Pick the point (12.5,1.0) for the final point.

✔ Press **<Enter>** to complete the polyline and exit the command.
*Now, we fillet the right corner to complete the path. The fillet will have a significant impact on the animation.*

✔ Type **F <Enter>** or pick the **Fillet** tool from the **Modify** panel.

✔ Select **Radius** from the command line.

✔ Type **2 <Enter>** for a radius specification.

✔ At the prompt for a first object, select the vertical line segment on the right.

✔ At the prompt for a second object, select the horizontal segment.
   *Your screen should resemble Figure 13-70.*
   *We are now ready to create an animation.*

✔ Type **ani <Enter>** or select **View > Motion Path Animations . . .** from the menu bar.
   *This executes **ANIPATH** and opens the **Motion Path Animation** dialog box shown in Figure 13-71.*

**Figure 13-71**
**Motion Path Animation** dialog box

✔ In the dialog box, pick the **Path** button in the middle of the **Camera** panel, and then pick the **Select** button to its right.
   *The dialog box disappears, giving you access to the drawing area.*

✔ Select the polyline.
   *The polyline is selected and AutoCAD asks for a **Path Name,** as shown in Figure 13-72.*

**Figure 13-72**
**Path Name** dialog box

✔ Click **OK** to accept the default name (Path1).
   *This brings you back to the dialog box. We make one more critical adjustment.*

✔ In the **Animation settings** panel on the right, change the **Duration** setting to **10.**

*If we did not change this setting, the animation would move very quickly, and it would be difficult to see what was happening.*

✔ Make sure the **When previewing show camera preview** box is checked.

✔ Pick the **Preview** button at the bottom left of the dialog box.
    *AutoCAD shows you an animation preview. Watch closely. What you see will be an animation based on moving a camera along the specified path. Notice the difference between the gentle turn along the fillet path and the abrupt turn at the final right angle. When the animation is done, your **Animation Preview** box should resemble Figure 13-73. Closing the **Preview** takes you back to the dialog box, where you can continue to modify and preview the animation, or save it to a WMV file.*

**Figure 13-73**
Animation preview

✔ Click the **X** in the upper right corner to close the **Animation Preview.**
    *This brings you back to the **Motion Path Animation** dialog box.*
        *At this point you can cancel the animation and return to your drawing, or click **OK** to save it. If you click **OK,** AutoCAD will initiate a process of creating a video. It will be saved as a WMV file that can be played back by other programs such as Windows Media Player. Once created, you can run the video by opening the file and following the Windows Media Player procedure.*
        *There you have it. Congratulations on your first video.*

# Chapter Summary

In this chapter you have learned to draw polysolids, cones, pyramids, torus, and mesh models, and to extrude 2D objects to form 3D solids. You can slice and section solids and convert 2D outlines into 3D solids and surfaces. You learned to use powerful tools for creating and adjusting 3D points of view and can present objects in continuous orbit. You learned to create a controlled walk-through of a 3D model and can record an animated walk-through for playback in AutoCAD or other media software.

# Chapter Test Questions

## Multiple Choice

*Circle the correct answer.*

1. Which of these **cannot** be extruded?

   a. Line                    c. Circle

   b. Polysolid               d. Rectangle

2. Which of these is **not** a solid?

   a. Extruded circle         c. Torus

   b. Swept rectangle         d. Helix

3. In **3DWALK,** the _____ is always in the XY plane.

   a. camera location         c. field of vision

   b. target location         d. viewpoint

4. Unlike **3DWALK** and **3DFLY,** an animated walk-through requires a:

   a. Camera                  c. Path

   b. Target                  d. Gizmo

5. Mesh **models** should be converted to solid models:

   a. Before editing

   b. After changing visual styles

   c. Before rendering

   d. After smoothing

## Matching

*Write the number of the correct answer on the line.*

a. Floating viewport _____        1. Solid primitive

b. Tiled viewport _____           2. Not plotted

c. Torus _____                    3. Plotted

d. Face _____                     4. Subobject

e. Arcball _____                  5. **3DORBIT**

# True or False

*Circle the correct answer.*

1. **True or False:** Tiled viewports are required for editing 3D models.

2. **True or False:** In a **Three: Right** viewport configuration, all three viewports are in parallel projection by default.

3. **True or False:** In a **Three: Right** viewport configuration, all three viewports use the same coordinate system.

4. **True or False:** You can select the face of a solid box without a filter, but the filter makes it easier.

5. **True or False:** Only meshes can be smoothed; only solids can be combined.

# Questions

1. Name at least three commands that create 3D models from 2D objects.

2. While still in the **3DORBIT** command, what is the quickest way to return to the view you started with before entering **3DORBIT?** How do you access this feature without leaving the **3DORBIT** command?

3. How many direction vectors are specified by the motion of your mouse in the **Continuous Orbit** mode?

4. What elements must be present in your drawing before you can use the **3DWALK** and **3DFLY** commands?

5. What additional element must be present before you can create an animated walk-through?

# Drawing Problems

1. Beginning with a blank drawing using the acad3D template, draw a 0.5-radius circle anywhere on your screen.

2. Draw a helix with center point at (0,0,0), base radius 5.0, top radius 1.0, and height 5.0.

3. Sweep the circle through the helix path to create a solid coil. Erase the helix.

4. Draw a cone with base center at (0,0,0), radius 5.0, and height 6.5.

5. Subtract the coil from the cone.

6. Create a section view of the object; cut along the YZ plane.

# WWW Exercise (Optional)

Whenever you are ready, complete the following:

✔ Make sure that you are connected to your Internet service provider.

✔ Type **browser <Enter>.**

✔ If necessary, navigate to our companion website at www.pearsonhighered.com/dixriley.

# Chapter Drawing Projects

# G Drawing 13-1: *REVOLVE Designs* [ADVANCED]

The **REVOLVE** command is fascinating and powerful. As you become familiar with it, you might find yourself identifying objects in the world that can be conceived as surfaces of revolution. To encourage this process, we have provided this page of 12 revolved objects and designs. The next drawing is also an application of the **REVOLVE** procedure.

To complete the exercise, you need only the **PLINE** and **REVOLVE** commands. In the first six designs, we have shown the path curves and axes of rotation used to create the design. In the other six, you are on your own.

Exact shapes and dimensions are not important in this exercise, but imagination is. When you have completed our designs, we encourage you to invent your own. Also, consider adding materials and lights to any of your designs and viewing them from different viewpoints using **3DORBIT.**

**Drawing 13-1**
REVOLVE Designs

## Drawing 13-2: *Tapered Bushing* [ADVANCED]

This is a more technical application of the **REVOLVE** command. By carefully following the dimensions in the side view, you can create the complete drawing using **PLINE** and **REVOLVE** only.

### Drawing Suggestions

- Use at least two viewports with the dimensioned side view in one viewport and the 3D isometric view in another.

- Create the 2D outline as shown and then **REVOLVE** it 270° around a centerline running down the middle of the bushing.

- When the model is complete, consider how you might present it in different views on a paper space layout.

**Drawing 13-2**
Tapered Bushing

## G  Drawing 13-3: *Globe* [ADVANCED]

This drawing uses a new command. The **SPHERE** command creates a 3D sphere, and you should have no trouble learning to use it at this point. You will find it on the **Solid Primitives** drop-down list on the **Modeling** panel. Like a circle, it requires only a center point and a radius or diameter.

## Drawing Suggestions

- Use a three-viewport configuration with top and front views on the left and an isometric 3D view on the right.

- Use 12-sided pyramids to create the base and the top part of the base.

- Draw the 12.25 cylindrical shaft in vertical position, and then rotate it around what will become the center point of the sphere, using the angle shown.

- The arc-shaped shaft holder can be drawn by sweeping or revolving a rectangle through 226°. Considering how you would do it both ways is a good exercise. Then, choose one method, or try both.

- As additional practice, trying adding a light and rendering the globe as shown in the reference drawing.

**Drawing 13-3**
Globe

# Drawing 13-4: *Pivot Mount* [ADVANCED]

This drawing gives you a workout in constructive geometry. We suggest you do this drawing with completely dimensioned orthographic views and the 3D model as shown. Also, create a sliced view of the model as shown in the reference figure.

## Drawing Suggestions

- Begin by analyzing the geometry of the figure. Notice that it can be created entirely with boxes, cylinders, and wedges, or you can create some objects as solid primitives and others as extruded or revolved figures. As an exercise, consider how you would create the entire model without using any solid primitive commands (no boxes, wedges, or cylinders). What commands from this chapter would be required?

- When the model is complete, create the sliced view as shown.

- Create the orthographic views and place them in paper space viewports.

- Add dimensions in paper space.

**Drawing 13-4**
Pivot Mount

# Drawings 13-5 [ADVANCED]

The drawings that follow are 3D solid models derived from 2D drawings. You can start from scratch or begin with the 2D drawing and use some of the geometry as a guide to your 3D model.

**Drawing 13-5a**
Flanged Bushing, Stepped Shaft, Base Plate

**Drawing 13-5b**
Test Bracket, Packing Flange

**Drawing 13-5c**
Alignment Wheel, Grooved Hub

**Drawing 13-5d**
Slotted Flange, Tool Block

**Drawing 13-5e**
Flanged Wheel, Nose Adapter

**Drawing 13-5f**
Angle Support, Mirror Mounting Plate

33/64 DRILL (6) HOLES

7.00
6.00
3.50
4.00
3.00
1.50

R.75    R1.25    1.25

CAP

29/64 DRILL X 1 1/2 DEEP
1/2 13 UNC X 1 1/8 DEEP
(6) HOLES

6.00
3.00    1.50    4.00

R0.25    3.50    7.00

R.75    R1.25
1.00
1.50
45°    .50    1.50
4.50
9.50

BASE

④
③
②
①    ASSEMBLY DRAWING

Ø1.50    Ø2.00
Ø1.12    .50
4.50

BUSHING

1/2-13 X 2 1/4 UNC-2A

HEX HEAD BOLT

NOTE: FILLETS AND ROUNDS 1/8 RADIUS
EXCEPT AS NOTED

| 4 | HEX HEAD BOLT 1/2-13 UNC x 2.25 LG | DB1-4 | 6 |
| 3 | BUSHING | DB1-3 | 2 |
| 2 | CAP | DB1-2 | 1 |
| 1 | BASE | DB1-1 | 1 |
| ITEM NO. | DESCRIPTION | PART NO. | QTY |

DRAWING TITLE:

Double Bearing

**Drawing 13-5g**
Double Bearing

**Drawing 13-5h**
Base Assembly

# A
## appendix
## Drawing Projects

The drawings on the following pages are offered as additional challenges and are presented without suggestions. They may be drawn in two or three dimensions and may be presented as multiple-view drawings, hidden-line drawings, or rendered drawings. In short, you are on your own to explore and master everything you have learned.

**26'-6"**
**8'-0"**　　**18'-6"**　　**7'-0"**　　　**22'-6"**

**9'-0"**

**24'-0"**

**24'-0"**

12'-0" x 16'-6"
Living Room

Living Room

18'-6" x 6'-0"
Kitchen

Kitchen

4'

12'-0" x 12'0"
Bedroom

Bedroom

closet
8' x 2'-6"

5'-6" x 6'
Bath

Bath

closet

Bedroom

closet

Bath

Bath

closet

Bedroom

Living Room

Kitchen

Kitchen

Living Room

| DRAWN | | DATE | ⬆ ➡ CAD Support Associates |
|---|---|---|---|
| | | | ⬅ ⬇ P.O. Box 317, Needham, MA 02192 |
| CHECKED | | | (817) 455-8570 |
| APPROVED | | | **4 UNIT APARTMENT** |

| SIZE E | DRAWING NO. | CSA-1 | | REV. A |
|---|---|---|---|---|
| SCALE: 1/4=1' | | | SHEET 1 OF 1 | |

FLOW UNIT
No. 1

FLOW UNIT
No. 2

CAD Support Associates
P.O. Box 317, Needham, MA 02192
(617) 455-8570

FLUID SAMPLER
SCHEMATIC

SIZE
C

DRAWING NO.
CSA3

REV.
A

SHEET 1 OF 1

SCALE:

DRAWN

DATE

CHECKED

APPROVED

E

646

E

InLine Reagent

Diluting Reagent(s)

Flushing Reagent

Waste

Analysis Module 1

Analysis Module 2

Analysis Module 3

Flush Pump

M

FLUSH PUMP ASSY

Sample Loop

Rotary Slide Valve

Sample Loop

Rotary Slide Valve

Sample Loop

Rotary Slide Valve

(Probe Wash Functions)

Sip Pump

M

Mixer Pump

M

Mixer Magnet

30 psi air

Mixer Pump

M

Mixer Magnet

30 psi air

Mixer Pump

M

Mixer Magnet

30 psi air

Sample Probe

SIP PUMP ASSY.

VALVE MIXER ASSY. 3

VALVE MIXER ASSY. 2

VALVE MIXER ASSY. 1

SIP TOWER ASSY.

EXPANSION MODULE

DILUTER

| DRAWN | DATE | ⬆️ ➡️ CAD Support Associates |
|---|---|---|
| | | ⬅️ ⬇️ P.O. Box 317, Needham, MA 02192 (617) 455-8570 |
| CHECKED | | |
| APPROVED | | DILUTER |

| | SIZE C | DRAWING NO. CSA4 | REV. A |
|---|---|---|---|
| | SCALE: | | SHEET 1 OF 1 |

| ITEM NO. | DESCRIPTION | | | PART NO. | QTY. |
|---|---|---|---|---|---|
| 20 | FLAT HD SCREW  #8-32 UNC X .25 LG | | | D400 F7 | 1 |
| 19 | PAN HD SCREW  5/16-18 UNC X .18 LG | | | D400 F6 | 1 |
| 18 | THREADED STUD  1/4-24 UNF X 1.25 LG | | | D400 F5 | 1 |
| 17 | BINDER HD SCREW  #10-24 UNC X 3.75 LG | | | D400 F4 | 1 |
| 16 | BINDER HD SCREW  #10-24 UNC X 1.62 LG | | | D400 F3 | 1 |
| 15 | TRUSS HD SCREW  1/4-20 UNC X .88 LG | | | D400 F2 | 1 |
| 14 | PAN HD SCREW  #10-24 UNC X .38 LG | | | D400 F1 | 2 |
| 13 | PIN   .12 DIA (CUT LENGTH TO SUIT) | | | D400 C2 | 3 |
| 12 | ANGLE ADJUSTOR | | | D400 I | 1 |
| 11 | PIVOT | | | D400 H | 1 |
| 10 | THUMB KNOB | | | D400 G | 1 |
| 9 | BLADE | | | D400 E | 1 |
| 8 | CAP IRON | | | D400 D | 1 |
| 7 | WEDGE SPRING | | | D400 C1 | 1 |
| 6 | WEDGE LEVER | | | D400 C | 1 |
| 5 | WEDGE IRON | | | D400 B | 1 |
| 4 | GRIP | | | D400 A | 1 |
| 3 | KNOB | | | D400F | 1 |
| 2 | MOUNTING PLATE | | | D400 K | 1 |
| 1 | BASE | | | D400 L | 1 |

DRAWN
P. RILEY

DATE
5-22-87

CHECKED

APPROVED

CAD Support Associates
P.O. Box 317, Needham, MA  02192
(617) 456-8570

JACK PLANE

SIZE
C

DRAWING NO.   D400

REV.
A

SCALE: 1/1

SHEET  1  OF  1

ITEM (7)

WEDGE SPRING

D400C1

MAT'L: .03 SPRING STEEL

ITEM (5)

WEDGE IRON

D400C

MAT'L: STEEL

ITEM (3)

KNOB

D400F

MAT'L: WOOD

ITEM (4)

GRIP

D400A

MAT'L: WOOD

ITEM (1)

BASE

D400L

MAT'L: C.I.

DETAILS-JACK PLANE
CSA5B

.56 R
4 PLACES

.62

.25

.06  .25        .157 DIA

.50                     .25

.44 R
2 PLACES

.56        .18 R

.88R

ITEM (6)

WEDGE LEVER

D400C

MAT'L: STEEL

.38 DIA

3.12

.32

.06

.10 DIA

.19 R

0.13        .06

2.59 R

ITEM (12)

ANGLE ADJUSTOR

D400I

MAT'L: STEEL

ITEM (11)

PIVOT

D400H

MAT'L: STEEL

.68        .38 R

.25

.25
2 PL

1.00

.12 DIA

.44

.12

.56 R
2 PL

.18

.25 DIA

.88        45°

5.00

5/16-18 UNC

2.75

2.00

.75        1.25

.18

1.75        .50        .50        1.00

.38

.38 R
2 PL        .75        1.00

.06        ITEM (8)

.54        D400D

.58        CAP IRON

MAT'L: STEEL

DETAILS-JACK PLANE
CSA5C

ITEM ②
MOUNTING PLATE
D400K

MAT'L: STEEL

ITEM ⑨
BLADE
D400E

MAT'L: STEEL

SECTION A-A

AUXILIARY VIEW

.12 DIA

.25 R

45°

.18

.31

1.12

.31

.34 .25

.25

.88

.88

.58

.12 RAD
4 PLACES

.44

.31

.75

1/4-24 UNF X .25 DP

.88

1/4-24 UNF
X .25 DEEP

.75 .50 .25

.12

4.50

2.18

1.44

.68

.88

.12 DIA

2.12

.75 .50

A

A

2.12

2.06

.38

1/4-20 UNC THRU

.12 R

7.25

.68 DIA

.22 R

1.00

.88

.38

1.00 1.75

4.06

.98

75°

.06

DETAILS-JACK PLANE
CSA5D

ITEM (14)
D400F1
#10-24 UNC X .38 LG
PAN HD SCREW

ITEM (19)
D400F6
5/6-18 UNC X .18 LG
PAN HD SCREW

ITEM (15)
D400F2
#1/4-20 UNC X .88 LG
TRUSS HD SCREW

CUT TO FIT

.128 DIA

ITEM (13)
D400C2
PIN
MAT'L: STEEL

ITEM (16)
D400F3
#10-24 UNC X 1.62 LG
BINDER HD SCREW

ITEM (17)
D400F4
#10-24 UNC X 3.75 LG
BINDER HD SCREW

ITEM (18)
D400F3
#1/4-24 UNF X 1.25 LG
STUD

ITEM (20)
D400F7
#8-32 UNC X .25 LG
FLAT HD SCREW

.03 X 45° CHAMFER

.19
.38
.12
Ø.62
Ø.38
.32
1.00

MEDIUM KNURL

Ø1.00

ITEM (10)
THUMB KNOB
D400G
MAT'L: BRASS

Ø.88
X .12 DEEP C'BORE

#1/4-24 UNF THRU

DETAILS-JACK PLANE
CSA5E

PULLEY

CAD Support Associates
P.O. Box 917, Needham, MA 02116
(617) 455-8970

DRAWN | DATE
CHECKED
APPROVED

SIZE C | DRAWING NO. CSA6 | REV. A
SCALE 1/1 | SHEET 1 OF 1

Ø4.25
0.25
0.13
2.13
1.75
0.50
0.75
0.75
6.50
R.25 TYP
Ø2.50
R .12 TYP
2.38
1.50
Ø2.75
Ø3.38
Ø5.00
Ø1.50

M

FIRST FLOOR PLAN
1/4" = 1'

FRONT ELEVATION
RIGHT SIDE ELEVATION

SHEET NO. A—4

HPA
DESIGN
Building Designers

14-DB Providence Highway
Norwood, MA 02062
(617) 769-8001
(508) 520-3256
FAX (617) 769-7881

| JOB NO. | 95246 |
| DATE | DECEMBER 13, 1995 |
| DRAWN BY | ATK |
| CHECKED BY | HPA |
| REVISION | DATE |
| PATH: | MICHON\14 |
| SCALE | 1/4" = 1'-0" |

A  FRONT ELEVATION
   1/4" = 1'

RIGHT SIDE ELEVATION

1/4" = 1'-0"

ROOF RAFTER

CEILING JOIST

NOTE:
SEE SECTION C/A-10
FOR CEILING JOIST
HEIGHT & LOCATION
@ MASTER BEDROOM

C  TRAY CEILING
    SECTION
    3/4" = 1'-0"

STAIR DETAIL
B  1/4" = 1'

5'-0 3/4"
3'-4 7/8"
1'-7 7/8"
1'-0 3/4"
1'-2 1/8"
2 TRDS
@ 9" EA
2'-2 3/4"
1'-2 1/8"
3'-4 7/8"
6'-3 3/4"
1'-7 7/8"
3'-0"
4 TRDS
@ 9" EA
3'-4 7/8"
2'-2 3/4"
1'-2 1/8"
3 TRDS
@ 9" EA
1'-2 1/8"
1'-0 3/4"
3'-4 7/8"
5'-0 3/4"
3'-8"
1'-4 3/4"
3'-0"
13'-1 1/2"
4'-0"
1'-0 3/4"
1'-7 7/8"

SEE PLAN

LINE OF HOUSE

1ST FLR
DECK
FINISHED GRADE
(ELEV. VARIES)

STEPS TO GRADE
AS REQUIRED

12" DEEP CONC
LANDING @
BOTTOM OF STAIR

SIDE

SEE PLAN FOR LIMIT OF DECK

2x4 RAILS
2X2 BALUSTERS
@ 6" O.C. MAX
4x4 P.T. POST

1ST FLR
DECK
FINISHED GRADE

RAILING
HEIGHT

12" CONCRETE
SONOTUBE @ 4'-0"
BELOW GRADE MIN.

REAR

B  TYPICAL DECK
    ELEVATIONS
    1/4" = 1'

SECTION THRU
RAKE BOARD

1/2" CDX PLY @ ROOF
BLOCKING
1X2 RAKE TRIM
BROSCO CROWN
MOULDING #8009
(3-5/8" TALL)
1X8 RAKE BOARD
BLOCKING
EXTERIOR STUD WALL
CEDAR CLAPBOARDS
4" TO THE WEATHER

RAKE RETURN
AT EAVE

LEAD FLASHING
OVER PINE BOARD
1X2 RAKE TRIM
BLOCKING
BROSCO CROWN
MOULDING #8009
1X8 BAND BOARD
BLOCKING

C  DETAIL @
    RAKE RETURN
    1-1/2" = 1'

**A**

SCHOOL BUS

SIZE | DRAWING NO. CSA12 | REV. A
SCALE: | | SHEET 1 OF 1

| | DATE |
|---|---|
| DRAWN | |
| CHECKED | |
| APPROVED | |

K2

CO. NAME

7'-6'

21'-8'

1'-10"

2'-5"

2'-7"

9'-7"

1'-6"

4'-6"

3'

26'-3"

3'-5"

2'-7"

5'-10"

6'-6'

2'-8"

7'-9"

3'-2"

6'-2"

8'

7'-8"

G

PASSENGER LOCOMOTIVE

Scale

0 1 2 3 4 5

CAD Support Associates
P.O. Box 317, Needham, MA 02192
(617) 465-8570

PASSENGER
LOCOMOTIVE

SIZE | DRAWING NO. | REV.
A

SCALE: NONE | SHEET _ OF _

DRAWN
P.RILEY
CHECKED
APPROVED
DATE

G

Drawing Courtesy of: Brian Tufts

3D MODEL

Ø3.250⁺·⁰⁰⁵ ⟂ A .005

30°  30°

Ø.1770 THRU
5 HOLES SP AS SHOWN
ON Ø2.875 B.C.

R1.68

Ø.180 THRU
8 HOLES EQ SP
ON Ø4.500 B.C.

45°
TYP

22½°
TYP

Ø3.478⁺·⁰²⁵ ⟂ A .005

Ø2.500⁺·⁰⁰⁵

Ø.1251 DOWEL PIN HOLE
2 HOLES 180° APART
ON Ø4.500 B.C.

1.88

1.00

Ø5.00

.03 x 45°
CHAMFER

.38

1.140

.967

0.569

-A-

Ø3.50

A .005

⫽ A .005

SECTION  A - A

THIS DRAWING COURTESY OF BRANDIN ANDREWS

| UNLESS OTHERWISE SPECIFIED DIMENSIONS ARE IN INCHES | DRAWN BY: BRANDIN ANDREWS | DATE: | | CSA | | |
|---|---|---|---|---|---|---|
| REMOVE ALL BURRS & BREAK SHARP EDGES | APPROVED BY: | | | | | |
| TOLERANCES | ISSUED | | DRAWING TITLE: | | | |
| FRACTIONS ±1/64  DECIMALS .X ±.005  .XX ±.010  .XXX ±.005  ANGLES ±0° 15' | | | MOUNTING PLATE | | | |
| MATERIAL: MAGNESIUM AZ31B | FINISH: DO THIS DRAWING ANODIZE TO BLACK TO MIL-S-3171C, TYPE 4 | | CODE IDENT NO. 26785 | B | DRAWING NO. CSA15 | REV. |
| | | | SCALE: | | DATE: | SHEET: | OF |

M

Drawing Courtesy of:
Jason Webber

Ø 7/16 x 3/4" DEEP MAX
4 HOLES EQ SP ON Ø3⅝ B.C.

Section A-A

M

| QTY REQD | DESCRIPTION | PART NO. | ITEM NO. |
|---|---|---|---|
| | BILL OF MATERIALS | | |

DRAWN BY: Jason Webber    DATE:
APPROVED BY:
ISSUED:

UNLESS OTHERWISE SPECIFIED DIMENSIONS ARE IN INCHES
REMOVE ALL BURRS & BREAK SHARP EDGES

TOLERANCES
FRACTIONS ±1/64
ANGLES ±0°-15'
DECIMALS
.X ± .020
.XX ± .010
.XXX ± .005

MATERIAL
MAGNESIUM
AZ31B

FINISH
DOW49 GALVANIC ANODIZE TO
BLACK; TO MIL-8-317C; TYPE 4

PART NO. CSA

DRAWING TITLE
VALVE NO. 6

CODE IDENT NO  B  21351    DRAWING NO  CSA16

SCALE         DATE         SHEET    OF

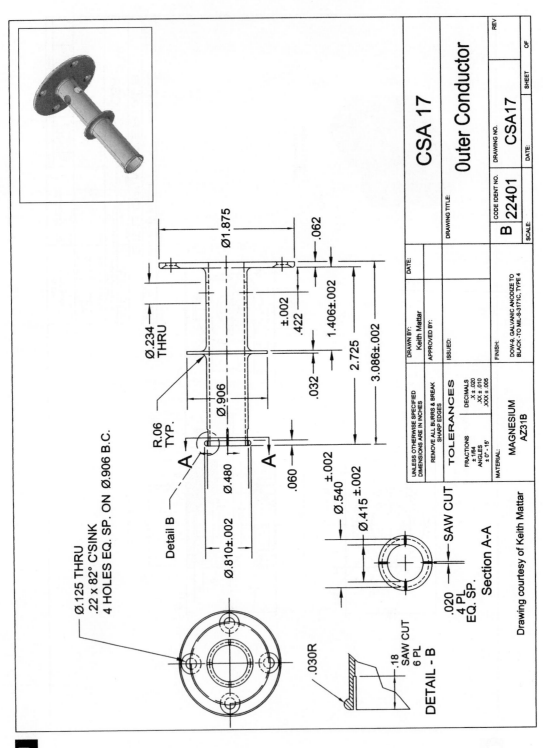

Ø1.875

.062

Ø.234
THRU

±.002

.422

1.406±.002

2.725

3.086±.002

Ø.906

.032

R.06
TYP.

A

Detail B

Ø.480

A

.060

Ø.810±.002

Ø.540

Ø.415 ±.002

SAW CUT

.020
4 PL
EQ. SP.

Section A-A

Ø.125 THRU
.22 x 82° C'SINK
4 HOLES EQ. SP. ON Ø.906 B.C.

.030R

.18
SAW CUT
6 PL

DETAIL - B

Drawing courtesy of Keith Mattar

| UNLESS OTHERWISE SPECIFIED DIMENSIONS ARE IN INCHES | | DRAWN BY: Keith Mattar | DATE: | | | |
|---|---|---|---|---|---|---|
| REMOVE ALL BURRS & BREAK SHARP EDGES | | APPROVED BY: | | | CSA 17 | REV |
| TOLERANCES | | ISSUED: | | DRAWING TITLE: | | |
| FRACTIONS ± 1/64 ANGLES ± 0° - 15° | DECIMALS .X ± .020 .XX ± .010 .XXX ± .005 | | | | Outer Conductor | |
| MATERIAL: MAGNESIUM AZ31B | | FINISH: DOW-9, GALVANIC ANODIZE TO BLACK -TO MIL-S-317IC, TYPE 4 | | CODE IDENT NO. B 22401 | DRAWING NO. CSA17 | |
| | | | | SCALE: | DATE: | SHEET OF |

M

# Creating
# Customized Panels

This appendix provides a partial introduction to some of the many ways in which AutoCAD can be customized to fit the needs of a particular industry, company, or individual user. At this point you probably know how to create customized tool palettes. Tool palettes give you easy access to libraries of frequently used blocks, symbols, and commands. You can also create customized toolbars and ribbon panels to store sets of frequently used commands or commands that you modify to suit your preferences. Creating your own panels is a simple and powerful feature that also gives you some idea of the more complex customization options available.

You will learn about AutoCAD's **Customize User Interface (CUI)** dialog box, where you can customize many elements of the AutoCAD interface. This appendix takes you through the procedure of creating your own panel and modifying the behavior of some basic commands. On completing this exercise, you will have added a simple panel to your **Home** tab and have the necessary knowledge to create other panels of your own design. The techniques you learn will also be applicable to customizing other elements in the **CUI** dialog box.

> **NOTE**
> The ability to create and customize AutoCAD elements is a powerful feature. We strongly discourage you from making changes in the standard AutoCAD set of panels. Adding, removing, or otherwise changing standard commands can lead to confusion and to the need to reload the AutoCAD menu. You create less confusion if you customize only new elements that you create yourself. You can modify or remove these without disturbing AutoCAD configurations.

There are two levels to creating a customized panel. At the first level, you simply create the panel, give it a name, and add whatever commands you wish to put there. This can be very handy for putting together sets of tools that would otherwise be located on different panels and menus. At the second level, you actually modify the function of a command and then alter its name and the look of its toolbar button image so that it functions differently from the standard AutoCAD command. In this exercise, we begin by creating a new panel and then add standard and customized command tools to the panel.

## Creating a Customized Panel

**TIP**

A general procedure for creating a ribbon panel is:

1. Open the **Manage** tab and pick the **User Interface** tool from the **Customization** panel.
2. Open the **Ribbon** folder.
3. Right-click **Panels.**
4. Select **New Panel** from the shortcut menu.
5. Give the new panel a name by overtyping in the **Customizations in All Files** window.
6. Select a **Category** from the **Command List.**
7. Find tools on the **Command List,** and drag them up to **Row 1** of the new panel in the **Customizations in All Files** window.
8. Click **OK** to exit the dialog box.

You can begin this exercise in any AutoCAD drawing and in any workspace with a ribbon.

✔ Open the **Manage** tab and pick the **User Interface** tool from the **Customization** panel, as shown in Figure B-1.

*This opens the **Customize User Interface (CUI)** dialog box, shown in Figure B-2. This is a centralized location for customizing various elements of the AutoCAD interface. Elements that can be customized are listed in the **Customizations in All Files** window on the upper left.*

**Figure B-1**
**User Interface** tool

✔ Open the **Ribbon** folder in the **Customizations in All Files** window on the left.

✔ Right-click **Panels.**

✔ Select **New Panel** from the shortcut menu.

*This opens the **Ribbon** panels folder on the left and the **Panel Preview** and **Properties** windows on the right side of the **CUI** dialog box. A new panel is added to the bottom of the list of panels. The default name is **Panel1** (or **Panel2** if someone has already created a **Panel1** on your system). This name will do fine for our purposes. Next, we add a command to the new panel.*

**Figure B-2**
**Custom User Interface**
dialog box

*The procedure for adding commands to a panel is simple. You select a command from the **Command List** and then drag it up to the name of the panel. For our purposes, we bring together three very common commands. The first we add without any customization. In the next section we add two customized commands. The **Command List** window at the bottom left of the **CUI** dialog box has a drop-down list that allows you to limit the commands in the list at the bottom. We begin by adding the standard **LINE** command.*

✔ Click the arrow to open the drop-down list in the **Command List** window at the bottom left of the dialog box.

✔ Open the **All Commands Only** list.
   *You see a list beginning with **All Commands Only** and ending with **Legacy.***

✔ In the list of command categories, select **Draw**.
   *This opens a list of **Draw** commands in the **Command List** below.*

✔ Scroll down the list until you see the **LINE** command and tool button image.
   *From here, it is a simple matter of dragging the tool up to **Row 1** of **Panel1**.*

✔ Pick the **Line** tool, hold down the pick button, and drag the tool up to **Row 1**, under **Panel1**.

*When you are in the correct position, there will be a blue arrow to the right of **Row 1**.*

✔ With the blue arrow showing, drop the command by releasing the pick button.

*You see a **Button Image** and a **Properties** window for this command on the right. The **Line** tool is added to the **Panel Preview**, and **Line** is added to **Panel1, Row 1** in the **Customizations in All Files** window, as shown in Figure B-3. Your new panel currently has one tool and the title bar, showing **Panel1** in the **Panel Preview**.*

**Figure B-3**
**Line** tool in **Panel1** Preview

*Before we can see the panel in our drawing interface, we need to assign it to a ribbon tab. We could drag the panel up to a tab, but the lists are long, so copying and pasting will work better.*

✔ Right-click **Panel1** and select **Copy** from the shortcut menu.

✔ Scroll up in the **Customizations in All Files** window until you see the **Tabs** folder under the **Ribbon** folder (it's a long way up).

✔ Pick the + sign next to **Tabs** to open the folder.
*We add Panel1 to the Home 2D tab.*

✔ Right-click **Home 2D** and select **Paste** from the shortcut menu.
*You see Panel1 at the bottom of the list of panels in the Tools tab, just below Home – Clipboard.*

✔ Click **OK** to close the **CUI** dialog box.

✔ If necessary, switch to the **Drafting & Annotation** workspace and pick the **Home** tab on the ribbon.
*You see Panel1 at the right of the ribbon, as shown in Figure B-4.*

**Figure B-4**
Panel1 added to end of ribbon

## Creating Customized Tools

**TIP**

A general procedure for creating a customized tool is:

1. With the **Customize User Interface** dialog box open, pick the **Create a new command** tool in the **Command List** window.
2. In the **Properties** window, give the command a new name.
3. Edit the command macro associated with the tool button.
4. In the **Button Image** window, click **Edit**, then edit the button image in the **Button Editor**.
5. Save the edited button image.
6. Check to see that the tool works the way you want it to.

In this section, we offer a simple introduction to the possibilities of customization through the use of customized commands. In the "Creating a Customized Panel" section, you created a new panel with one tool. In this section, we show you how to customize tools. These new tools will function differently from standard AutoCAD commands.

✔ You should be in an AutoCAD drawing with the new panel created in the "Creating a Customized Panel" section.

✔ Pick **Manage** tab > **Customization** panel > **User Interface** tool to open the **Customize User Interface** dialog box.
*In the Command List window, you see two buttons that look like stars to the right of the drop-down list. The one to the right is the Create a new command tool.*

✔ Pick the **Create a new command** tool, as shown in Figure B-5.
*This opens the Properties window shown in Figure B-6. This is a very powerful and interesting place in the AutoCAD system. Here you can change the command name associated with a tool, change the appearance of a tool button, and edit the macro that determines, to an extent, how the command functions. You do not actually create*

new commands but have the ability to determine default options
that are entered automatically as part of the command procedure.
For example, it might be useful to have a version of the **LINE** command that draws only one line segment and then returns you to
the command line prompt. This is easily accomplished with a little
knowledge of AutoCAD macro language. **Macros** are automated key
sequences. By automatically entering an extra press of the **<Enter>**
key after drawing a single line segment, we can complete the command sequence as desired.

First, though, let's give this tool button a name to differentiate it
from the standard **Line** tool.

✔ Double-click in the **Name** edit box and type **Line1 <Enter>.**
This is a good descriptive name, and it also associates it with
**Panel1.** Notice that **Line1** is also added to the **Command List.**

Next, we modify the macro so that the command is complete after one
line segment is drawn. For the purposes of this exercise, you need to know
only two items of AutoCAD macro language. The semicolon (;) is the macro
language equivalent to pressing **<Enter>.** When AutoCAD sees a semicolon
in a macro, it acts as though the user has pressed **<Enter>** or the spacebar. The backslash character (\\) is the pause for user input character.

When AutoCAD reads a backslash in a macro, it waits for something to be entered through the keyboard or the pointing device.

✔ Click in the box next to **Macro** and add **_line;\\;** to the macro, so that the complete macro reads **^C^C_line;\\;**

*It is very important that this be entered exactly as shown, without extra spaces. Macro language, like any programming language, is very fussy.*

*Let's analyze what these characters do.*

| ^C^C | The macro equivalent of typing **<Ctrl>+C** (or the **<Esc>** key) twice, which cancels any command in progress before entering the **LINE** command |
|---|---|
| Line | Types **Line** at the command line prompt |
| ; | Like pressing **<Enter>** after typing the command |
| \ | Waits for user to specify the first point |
| \ | Waits for user to specify a second point |
| ; | Like pressing **<Enter>** or the spacebar, ends the command sequence |

In a moment, we will try executing this new command, but first let's change the button image to show that the command sequence for this customized tool is different from the standard **LINE** command. So that we do not have to start from scratch, we first locate the **Line** button image in the **Button Image** window. Unfortunately, the selection of images is quite long. The **Line** button image is in the 37th row, third column.

✔ Open the **Button Image** window and scroll down until you see the **Line** button image, in the fourth column.

   *When you let your cursor rest on the image, the label will be*
   ***RCDATA_16_LINE.***

✔ Select the **Line** button image.

✔ Click **Edit** in the **Button Image** window.

   *This opens the **Button Editor** dialog box illustrated in Figure B-7. This box provides simple graphics tools for creating or editing button images. The four tools include a drawing "pencil" for drawing individual grid cells, a **Line** tool, a **Circle** tool, and an **Erase** tool. In addition, there is a grid and a color palette. We simply shorten the **Line** button image to differentiate it from the regular **Line** tool.*

✔ Click and drag the **Erase** tool from the top right and use it to erase the lower left half of the **Line** button image, as shown in Figure B-8.

**Figure B-7**
**Button Editor**

**Figure B-8**
Create new **Line** button image

✔ Click **Save.**

   *This opens a **Save Image** dialog box.*

✔ Type **Line1** for the name of the tool button.

   *Notice that there will now be two aspects of this modified **LINE** command in the CUI file: the **Line1** command, which is the **LINE** command modified by the additional macro characters, and the tool button image stored as a .bmp file. We refer to both of them as **Line1.***

✔ Click **OK** in the **Save Image** box.

✔ Close the **Button Editor** box to return to the **Customize User Interface** dialog box.

✔ Finally, we need to add **Line1** to **Panel1** before we leave the **CUI** dialog box. Open the **Ribbon** folder in the **Customizations in All Files** window.

✔ Open the **Panels** folder.

✔ Scroll to the bottom of the list and open **Panel1.**

✔ In the **Command List** window, make sure **All Commands Only** is showing in the drop-down list.

> *This is necessary. You will not find the new command **Line1** in the list of **Draw** commands.*

✔ If necessary, scroll down to find **Line1.**

✔ Pick the **Line1** tool and drag it up to **Row 1** under **Panel 1.**

✔ With the blue arrow showing, drop **Line1** in **Row 1.**
> *The **Line1** tool is added to your **Panel Preview.***

✔ Click **Apply** to execute the changes to your customized tool button.
> *Now, let's close the **CUI** dialog box and try our new tool.*

✔ Click **OK.**
> *The dialog box closes, leaving you in the drawing area.*

✔ If necessary, open the **Home** tab on the ribbon.
> ***Panel1** should be at the far right with the standard **Line** tool and the new **Line1** tool.*

✔ Pick the **Line1** tool from **Panel1.**

✔ Select a first point anywhere in your drawing area.

✔ Select a second point.
> *You should be back to the command line prompt. If this did not happen, check the syntax on the macro for your **Line1** tool.*

Next, we return to the **CUI** dialog box and add one more new command to **Panel1.** We create a command based on **ERASE** that erases a single object and then exits the command.

✔ Pick the **Manage** tab > **Customization** panel > **User Interface** tool from the ribbon.

✔ Pick the **Create a new command** tool in the **Command List** window.

✔ Double-click in the **Name** edit box and type **Erase1 <Enter>.**

✔ In the **Macro** edit box, add **_erase;\;**
> *The macro should read*

```
^C^C_erase;\;
```

> *Consider how this macro works. After canceling any other command, it types **erase,** and then the first semicolon enters the **ERASE** command. The \ tells AutoCAD to wait for input. After the user points to one object, the second semicolon completes the command and returns to the command line prompt.*

✔ If necessary, open the **Button Image** window.

✔ Scroll down to find the **Erase** button image in the first column, as of this writing.

✔ Select the **Erase** button image.

✔ Click **Edit** in the **Button Image** window to open the **Button Editor.**

✔ Use the **Erase** tool and the **Line** tool to create the button image shown in Figure B-9.
*This image shows the eraser head over a single object.*

**Figure B-9**
Create new **Erase** button image

✔ Save the modified image as **Erase1.**

✔ Close the **Button Editor.**

✔ Open the **Ribbon** folder in the **Customizations in All Files** window.

✔ Open the **Panels** folder.

✔ Scroll down to **Panel1.**

✔ Open **Panel1.**

✔ Open **Row 1.**

✔ If necessary, scroll to the **Erase1** command in the **Command List** window.

✔ Drag **Erase1** up to **Row1.**

✔ Click **Apply** to apply changes to the **Erase1** tool.
*The **Erase1** tool is added to your **Panel Preview.***

✔ Click **OK** to close the **CUI** dialog box.
*The **Erase1** tool has been added to **Panel1**. Finally, try your new tools to see that they are working.*

✔ Use the **Line1** tool to draw a single line segment.

✔ Use the **Erase1** tool to erase the line.

Be aware that pressing the spacebar to repeat one of these commands repeats the regular AutoCAD command, not the macro you created for your customized panel.

# C appendix

# Menus, Macros, and the CUI Dialog Box

When you begin to look below the surface of AutoCAD as it is configured straight out of the box, you find a whole world of customization possibilities. This open architecture, which allows you to create your own menus, commands, toolbars, tool palettes, ribbon panels, and automated routines, is one of the reasons for AutoCAD's success. It is characteristic of all AutoCAD releases and has allowed a vast network of third-party developers to create custom software products tailoring AutoCAD to the particular needs of various industries and tasks.

The **Customize User Interface** dialog box is the largest single resource for customizing elements of the AutoCAD menu system. In this appendix we briefly explore the vocabulary of AutoCAD macro language and show how it is used with the elements in the **CUI** dialog box. The intention of this discussion is not to make you an AutoCAD developer but to give you a taste of what is going on in the CUI system. After reading this, you should have a sense of what elements are readily available for customization.

## The CUI Dialog Box

In the **CUI** dialog box all elements are customized in the same way. All elements are represented by starred entries in the tree view on the left and **Properties** windows on the right. Some elements also have **Button Image** windows.

Following is a list of the elements in the tree view with a brief discussion of each. The "Characters Used in AutoCAD Macros" section further discusses AutoCAD macro language characters.

✔ To view the **CUI** dialog box, open the **Manage** tab and pick the **User Interface** tool from the **Customization** panel.

The tree view is in the top left window and includes workspaces, quick access toolbars, the ribbon, toolbars, menus, shortcut menus,

675

keyboard shortcuts, double-click actions, mouse buttons, LISP files, legacy, and partial customization files. Click any of these to see a description in the **Information** window on the right. Following is a brief description of each.

**Workspaces.**   Workspaces are a simple form of customization. Workspaces consist of ribbon tabs and panels, menus, palettes, and toolbars. By selecting elements to add to or remove from the drawing area, you can create unique and customized configurations. These can be saved as workspaces and then opened together as a named workspace. The AutoCAD default workspace includes all the elements you are used to seeing. A simple example of customizing a workspace is to open the menu bar and then save this configuration as a **Menu Bar** workspace. Then, whenever you want to be in this workspace, you pick the **Workspace** drop-down list on the **Quick Access** toolbar and switch to the **Menu Bar** workspace.

**Quick Access Toolbars.**   A quick access toolbar is displayed on the AutoCAD application window title bar. The standard quick access toolbar is called **Quick Access Toolbar1** and is displayed in all default workspaces. This toolbar can be customized by picking the arrow at the right and selecting tools from the drop-down list. Other quick access toolbars can be created and added to the **CUI** dialog box using the same procedures used to create other elements.

**Ribbon.**   The ribbon is the interface most frequently used for locating and executing AutoCAD commands. Additional ribbon panels and tabs can be created and modified. We do not recommend modifying the standard AutoCAD ribbon tabs or panels.

**Toolbars.**   Toolbars can be created and added to the tree view list of toolbars. You probably will not use toolbars as much as in the past because the ribbon interface is more efficient. The procedures used for creating panels work the same for creating toolbars. You can also modify existing toolbars using the same techniques used to create new ones. We do not recommend modifying the AutoCAD toolbars.

**Menus.**   These are the standard menus you see on the menu bar. If you open the **Menus** folder in the **CUI** dialog box, you see the list, from **File** to **Help.** If you open **File,** you see the list of commands on the **File** menu, from **New** to **Exit.** Most entries on menus refer to commands, and they work exactly like the tool button entries on toolbars and ribbon panels. For example, click **New** on the **Menu** list, and you will see the **Button Image** for the **New** command on the top right and the **Properties** window below that. The macro for this line on the menu is **^C^C_new.**

**Shortcut Menus.**   Here you will find a list of standard shortcut menus. Under **Grips Cursor Menu,** for example, you will see familiar grip modes and options that appear when you right-click while in the grip editing system.

**Keyboard Shortcuts.** This list is a good place to explore the complete keyboard shortcuts available. For example, open the tree view, then the **Keyboard Shortcuts** list, and look under **New.** You will find that this is the place where **<Ctrl>+N** is established as the keyboard shortcut for entering the **New** command. There are 39 keyboard shortcuts defined here, including many you've probably never noticed. The **Temporary Overrides** list shows key combinations that will temporarily override a setting without changing it. Most of these use the **<Shift>** key in combination with another key.

**Double-Click Actions.** This list determines what action is taken when you double-click with the cursor resting on an object in a drawing. The action taken depends on the type of object present and is a customizable feature. By default, many objects call the **Quick Properties** panel. The following are some other examples: double-clicking on a polyline will execute the **PEDIT** command, on a multiline will execute **MLEDIT,** or on an attribute definition will execute **ATTEDIT.**

**Mouse Buttons.** The options with a standard two-button mouse are pretty limited, but this list gives you a place for customizing pointing devices with more than the two buttons.

**LISP Files.** AutoCAD allows you to create customized routines in other languages in addition to the macro language presented here. AutoLISP is a programming language based on LISP, which is a standard list processing language. You see AutoLISP statements in place of some macros in the **Properties** window. LISP statements are enclosed in parentheses.

**Legacy.** *Legacy* refers to elements of the drawing area that are no longer in common use but are still supported for those who like to use them. This includes screen menus, tablet menus, and image tile menus. You do not need to know about these unless you are working on a system that uses legacy features.

**Partial Customization Files.** The way to create customized user interface files is to add partial files to the standard file. Thus, you do not lose the original and can go back to it at any time. If you open this entry, you will see that there are currently four partial customization files, including one called **CUSTOM.** It contains all the elements of the standard file, but there are no entries under the main element headings. To create your own partial customization file, you can start with **CUSTOM** and add commands and macros to any of the elements.

This completes the tour of the **CUI** dialog box. In the next section you will find additional macro characters and their meanings.

## Characters Used in AutoCAD Macros

The following table lists some menu and macro characters you find in many elements of the CUI file.

## Most Common AutoCAD Macro Characters

| | |
|---|---|
| & | Placed before a letter that can be used as an alias; the letter will be underlined on the menu. |
| ; | Same as pressing **<Enter>** while typing. |
| ^ | **<Ctrl>.** |
| ^C | **<Ctrl>+C;** same as pressing **<Esc>.** |
| ^C^C | Double cancel; cancels any command and ensures a return to the command prompt before a new command is issued. |
| POPn | Section header, where *n* is a number between 1 and 16, identifying one of the 16 possible menu areas; POP0 refers to the cursor menu. |
| [ ] | Brackets enclose text to be written directly to the screen or menu area. Eight characters are printed on the screen menu. The size of menu items on the menu varies. |
| [–] | Writes a blank line on a menu. |
| – | English-language flag. |
| , | Transparent command modifier. |
| ( ) | Parentheses enclose AutoLISP and DIESEL expressions. |
| \ | Pause for user input; allows for keyboard entry, point selection, and object selection; terminated by pressing **<Enter>** or the pick button. |
| ~ | Begins a menu label that is unavailable; can be used to indicate a function not currently in use. |
| *^C^C | Causes the menu item to repeat. |

# D

# Additional Tools for Collaboration

In addition to the programming and customizing tools that are used by a single user at a computer workstation, there are numerous tools that are encountered only in collaborative environments, where the workspace extends beyond the individual and the individual computer. You may be familiar with some of these tools. In this appendix, we briefly introduce more of these tools, so that readers may enter a collaborative environment with some understanding of these processes. These tools are not necessary for the completion of any independent drawing, but they belong in your repertoire of techniques.

## CAD Standards

The CAD Standards feature is important in work environments where drawings from one organization may be used in other organizations or departments. Using CAD Standards files allows quick checking and modifying of drawings to ensure that externally created or outsourced drawings use standards compatible with standards in place for drawings created in-house. AutoCAD's CAD Standards feature requires the use of a drawing standards file. This can be any drawing that uses the desired standards, including layer definitions and properties, dimension styles, text styles, and linetypes. To understand the issues involved, imagine that in Your Company, Inc. all drawings have a standard layer (we'll call it Layer1) that is red. To support this practice, a certain Drawing A has been defined as a CAD Standards file (saved with a .dws extension). Your Company receives Drawing B from Their Company. Drawing B and Drawing A both have a layer called Layer1, but in Their Company, Layer1 is yellow. As Your Company's CAD expert, you must ensure that Drawing B complies with Your Company's standards. You proceed as follows:

✔ Open **Drawing B.**

✔ Select the **Manage** tab > **CAD Standards** panel > **Configure** tool from the ribbon.
   *This opens the **Configure Standards** dialog box.*

✔ Click the <+> button to add a Standards file.

✔ From the **Select Standards file** dialog box, select **Drawing A.dws** as the CAD Standards file.

✔ In the **Configure Standards** dialog box, click the **Check Standards** button.

> *This opens a dialog box that shows you any discrepancies between Drawing A.dws and Drawing B.*

✔ Pick the **Fix** button to alter Layer1 in Drawing B to match the standard of Drawing A.

Now that Drawing A is defined as a Standards file for Drawing B, whenever you try to change a property in Drawing B and it does not match a standard, you will get a *Standards Violation* notification in the lower right corner of your screen. You can use the blue link to run a standards check and fix the problem, or you can ignore and close the message.

## Layer Translation

Layer translation is closely related to CAD Standards checking. It works similarly but addresses only layers and allows you to adjust the layers in any drawing to match layers in another drawing. You are not restricted to using drawings that have been defined as Standards files but can use any drawing to shape any other drawing. Properties that can be matched are all the properties that define layers. To translate Layer1 properties in Drawing A to Layer1 properties in Drawing B:

✔ Open *Drawing B.*

✔ Select the **Manage** tab > **CAD Standards** panel > **Layer Translator** tool from the ribbon.

> *This opens the **Layer Translator**. Layers in the current drawing are shown in the **Translate From** panel. There is nothing in the **Translate To** panel until we load a drawing.*

✔ Click **Load.**

> *This opens a **Select Drawing File** dialog box. You can select a drawing, a template drawing, or a CAD Standards drawing file.*

✔ Navigate to the folder where Drawing A is located.

✔ Select **Drawing A.**

> *Notice that this can be any drawing. It does not have to be a .dws drawing.*

✔ Click **Open.**

> *Layers from Drawing A are now listed in the **Translate To** panel.*

✔ Highlight **Layer1** in both panels.

✔ Click **Map.**

> *The proposed translation shows in the **Layer Translations Mapping** panel.*

✔ Click **Translate.**

✔ Click **Yes** to save or **No** to eliminate the old layer information in Drawing B.

# Management of Named Objects

When managing multiple drawings from different sources, you are likely to encounter the problem of duplicate definitions. For example, what happens when a drawing that is externally referenced or block-inserted has layers, linetypes, text styles, dimension styles, blocks, or views with names that are the same as those in the current drawing? Good question. In the case of blocked drawings, name definitions in the current drawing override those in the inserted block, regardless of its origin. In the case of Xrefed drawings, named objects are given special designations that eliminate the duplication. For example, if Drawing B is attached to Drawing A and both have a layer called FLOOR, a new layer called B|FLOOR is created in A.

# Sheet Set Management

Most industrial design projects involve not one drawing but a set of drawings detailing different views or different aspects of a single design. When a design project is to be communicated to a client or a consultant, it is likely to be represented by a whole set of related drawings. Sets of drawings like these, called *sheet sets,* may be created manually by saving particular layouts from individual drawings and then assembling all the relevant layouts and views in a single location. This process can become quite complex, especially when the individual drawings are on different computers and rely on external references, font files, plot files, and so on that may reside in different locations. To facilitate the creation of sheet sets, AutoCAD includes a system called the **Sheet Set Manager.** Through this interface, layouts from individual drawings are collected into a new drawing. Here, layouts can easily be organized into categories and subsets so that the sheet set presents a coherent design concept. One sheet of the set may be designated as the title sheet, and this may display a table showing the organizational hierarchy of the complete sheet set. Sheets in the sheet set are given numbers and designations shown in standard symbol blocks that update automatically if the number and organization of the sheet set changes. Consider the following workflow:

- Create drawings in model space.

- In each drawing, create layouts with a design presentation image.

- Using the **Sheet Set Manager,** collect layouts from all relevant drawings into a single set.

- Create a title sheet listing all layouts (sheets) and showing how they are organized.

- Create a sheet set package that contains the sheet set and all files required to view the set, all organized through the **Sheet Set Manager.**

- Archive the sheet set.

- eTransmit the sheet set to a client or consultant.